MW00340011

Among the several systematic theologies that have recently been released, Doug Kelly's three-volume work deserves special attention. It is comprehensive in its coverage of the doctrinal issues, and it combines exegesis with careful analysis of the historical and present-day theological literature. Volume Two, *The Beauty of Christ: a Trinitarian Vision*, is now available, and its approach to Christology is striking indeed. Quite remarkably, and delightfully, it organizes the biblical teaching under the category of "beauty" – the beauty of three divine persons united to one another in love. Here, Kelly reminds us of Jonathan Edwards, Augustine, and many other great writers of the church who have not only taught us accurately, but have motivated us to *love* the Lord who has so loved us.

JOHN FRAME
Professor of Systematic Theology and Philosophy,
Reformed Theological Seminary, Orlando, Florida

It is no overstatement to say that *The Beauty of Christ* is one of the most remarkable treatments of Christology in recent history. Douglas Kelly's viewpoints consistently acknowledge the supreme authority of Scripture. Yet, he masterfully interacts with a wide range of philosophers and Christian theologians from the patristic period to our current post-critical setting. His treatments of the person and work of Christ, as well as the states of his humiliation and exaltation, reflect scholarship second to none. His focus on Christ's beauty reflects his own deeply personal devotion to Christ and inspires the same in his readers. I am confident that this is one of those rare books that will shape both scholarly and pastoral theology for generations to come.

RICHARD L. PRATT, JR.
Adjunct Professor of Old Testament, Reformed Theological Seminary

The second volume of Douglas Kelly's *Systematic Theology* is a tour de force of Christological discussion. Beginning with the thesis that Christ is an object of beauty both to God and to the believer, Professor Kelly explores the many dimensions of that beauty in Scripture and in theology. Engaging with all the relevant material, ancient and modern, but constantly rooted in the biblical testimony, this is one of the most comprehensive treatments of the Person and Work of Jesus Christ available. It grounds the doctrine of the Saviour in the self-disclosure of the Triune God, and raises our vision above the mundane to the heavenly. It is a feast for the mind and for the heart.

IAIN D. CAMPBELL
Pastor, Point Free Church of Scotland, Isle of Lewis, Scotland

The present volume is nothing less than remarkable. Writing a comprehensive systematic theology today is challenging enough. So many fine studies are available to us that we might wonder, how can anyone add significantly new material to such a body? And yet this text does so, and with astonishing depth. Professor Kelly brings to this second volume of the projected three-volume systematic theology a unique combination of specialties. Based on solid biblical exegesis, the work interacts with many church fathers, including notable ones from the orthodox (Greek) tradition and such rarities as the French protestants, such as Pierre Courthial. Perhaps the most moving section in this volume is on the seven last words of Christ on the cross. After investigating these pages, though, the reader will be moved, not to admire Douglas Kelly's great learning, but to bow the knee, lost in wonder, love and praise for our beautiful savior.

WILLIAM EDGAR
Professor of Apologetics,
Westminster Theological Seminary, Philadelphia, Pennsyvlania

As a longstanding beneficiary of Professor Kelly's writings, I have been eagerly waiting for the second volume of his systematic theology. It does not disappoint. This is Professor Kelly at the height of his powers and Reformed theology at its classical best, involving a constructive dialogue between exegesis, historical theology and the contemporary world. Kelly's knowledge of theology is breathtaking; his willingness to interact in a critically appreciative manner with everyone from Athanasius to T. F. Torrance and beyond is a joy to witness; and the manner in which he grounds his thinking in the life and witness of the church – the church through all the ages – is a model to which others should aspire.

CARL R. TRUEMAN
Paul Woolley Professor of Church History,
Westminster Theological Seminary, Philadelphia, Pennsylvania

Those who enjoyed Dr Kelly's first volume *The God Who Is* will not be disappointed by the second. In the forest of recent and not-so recent systematic theologies (including some dead wood) this tree stands out, for four reasons. Kelly writes beautifully and negociates the most difficult subjects, of which there are a few in this volume, with consummate ease and pastoral warmth. Secondly, he draws on an extensive knowledge of the Christian tradition and puts it to good use. Furthermore, Kelly understands that orthodox Christology is best understood as functionning in a trinitarian context, so no-one can entertain the idea that a penal and substitutionary atonement, for example, conflicts with trinitarian unity. Finally, Kelly speaks to different situations and enters into dialogue with recent christological thought. More power to Kelly's pen for the next volume we say!

PAUL WELLS
Emeritus Professor at the Faculté Jean Calvin, Aix-en-Provence, France

This second volume in Dogmatics by Douglas Kelly is as impressive and invaluable as his previous one. It is most impressive because of its comprehensiveness, covering in a detailed manner every aspect of the great mystery of Christ from a sound and orthodox point of view. At the same time it is most invaluable because of its broad theological range, drawing from what is best in the Reformed theological tradition, but also from the great Fathers of the early Church and Orthodox and Roman Catholic theologians. It certainly brings out the "Beauty of Christ" by gathering the authentic witness of prophets, apostles, fathers and theologians to the person and work of the Lord Jesus Christ, the Creator and Savior of the world. There is an amazing rich content to this volume, which brings out "the riches of assured understanding and the knowledge of God's mystery in Christ, in whom are hid all the treasures of wisdom and knowledge." For its rich and coherent content, as well as for its discussions of critical questions raised by contemporary academics, this volume will prove most valuable to all students of theology, theologians and believing Christians.

GEORGE DION DRAGAS
Professor of Patrology and Patristics,
Holy Cross Greek Orthodox School of Theology, Brookline, Massachusetts

The second volume of Systematic Theology by Douglas Kelly is indeed an echo of the voice in the wilderness of the greatest prophet John the Baptist that introduces our Lord Jesus Christ in His fullness. In the midst of the already many other writings on this topic, this volume proves invaluable because it effectively incorporates the author's personal experiences with God's saving grace in our Lord Jesus Christ. One can feel the passion of the author to reveal several other mysteries that are "not yet" written from an integrated perspective. The author puts himself as both an object and subject to interact with the thinkings of the Old Testament prophets, New Testament apostles, Church fathers, theologians, and even contemporary scholars.

As an Asian Reformed theologian, I strongly recommend this volume to all theology students and theologians as one of the best textbooks in systematic theology of this century.

YAKUB B. SUSABDA
President, Reformed Theological Seminary, Jakarta, Indonesia

Dr. Kelly was able to produce a work about Christ that combines sound exegesis, knowledge of the history of Christian doctrine, pastoral concerns and relevance – for instance, the issue of translation for Muslim language communities. As a Brazilian theologian, I do appreciate these features which make his book relevant and necessary also in the Latin American context.

AUGUSTUS NICODEMUS LOPES
Vice-President, Andrew Jumper Graduate Center,
Presbyterian Church of Brazil, Sao Paulo, Brazil

Professor Kelly, a long-time professor at Reformed Theological Seminary, is one of the best wordsmiths of our time. My comments are inadequate to convey to you the value of the volume, which is virtually a masterpiece of theology.

Decades ago, the Lord had granted me a unique opportunity to study under Professor Kelly at Reformed Theological Seminary in Jackson, Mississippi. As a former student of Dr. Kelly, I must admit that I am heavily indebted to him as I surely profited immeasurably from knowing him, even to the point of my experiencing a spiritual conversion during his lectures in Systematic Theology, Calvin's Institutes in particular. That experience resulted in my work of translating and publishing the Calvin's Institutes into the Chinese language many years later. Professor Kelly has the heart of a pastor, as can be seen in his introduction to the second edition of the Calvin's Institutes (Chinese edition), and he has been very well received by many Chinese people and has touched their hearts.

Professor Kelly is a great scholar, both as a writer and as a theologian. His keen judgment is shown throughout his writing, in which he sticks closely to Scripture, examining almost every verse in its context. This work will prove to be of inestimable value to all those who wish to study the multifaceted doctrine of Christ. It will prove to be a safe guide through the labyrinth of some critical discussions. By far, Professor Kelly's outstanding work was the Christology of the entire Bible; to which he brought not only a profound understanding of biblical languages, but also a deep reverence for the Word of God and an unusual gift for expression. Nothing has been written that compares with this work in the breadth of erudition and the firmness with which Professor Kelly sets forth his own convictions on the many disputed points of Messianic interpretation.

The beauty of Christ as displayed in the Trinitarian context is a unique feature of this book. It is with great pleasure that I recommend this volume of Systematic Theology. I have personally derived much profit and pleasure from it. There is no other book of this magnitude, or of such value, to be found.

JOSEPH CHIEN
Director/Publisher, Calvin Publications, Taiwan
Pastor, Chinese Reformed Congregation of Taipei

The author persuasively, cogently and masterfully defends, expounds and argues the doctrine of Christ not simply in the light of history of the doctrine but also in the light of the Scripture itself. He is unique and innovative in developing the doctrine in terms of thorough, exhaustive and well-balanced exegetical works on the relevant biblical references, in presenting a holistic, profound, and clear Reformed doctrine from the Trinitarian perspective, and in opening a new horizon of methodology in systematic theology. He is very much successful in portraying realistically and elevating sublimely the beauty of Christ to the wide spectrum of his contemporary readers. This book deserves to be called as one of the best in its kind.

IN WHAN KIM
Professor Emeritus and Former President,
Chongshin University and Seminary, Seoul, Korea

This second volume of Professor Douglas Kelly's Systematic Theology must be given a prominent place in personal and Seminary libraries. And it needs to be read and referred to regularly by pastors, ministerial students, academics and church members . It is a treasure we can ill afford to neglect and leave unused.

I found this volume extremely satisfying, absorbing and so stimulating that I found it difficult to stop reading and re-reading it ! The title of the volume provides the clue to its contents: *The Beauty of Christ: A Trinitarian Vision*.

Professor Kelly's methodology assumes that the Triune God is 'supremely personal' and that it is rewarding for us to use God's Word extensively for there we see *most clearly* His beauty. For that reason Douglas Kelly majors on collating, exegeting and applying a broad range of key biblical passages, doctrines and words. This biblical approach is enriched by valuable insights from the Easrly and Medieaval Church Fathers, Reformers, Post-Reformation theologians along with considerable contemporary interaction with theologians, including Orthodox and Roman Catholic scholars.

The work is comprehensive, competent, Confessional, scholarly and pastoral but the pervading note of worship towards the Triune God in these pages evoked adoration, love and amazement on the part of this reader.

The entire book is to be commended, although I have by now my favourite sections and chapters. And I love the way the author introduces Part Three on the Exaltation of Christ – *It is the most glorious event that ever happened* (p. 445) while two pages later he affirms: '*Never did the power of the Triune God shine forth more beautifully with such glory and power than in the bodily resurrection of Jesus Christ*' (p. 447).

I appeal to all preachers to read this volume as a matter of urgency. Why? One major reason is that it will help you to show your congregation even more clearly and helpfully the beauty of Christ.

D. ERYL DAVIES
Research Supervisor, Wales Evangelical School of Theology, Bridgend, Wales

The title of this volume makes it stand out immediately. It, like that of Thomas Schreiner's recent book, *The King in His Beauty: A Biblical Theology of the Old and New Testaments*, draws attention to the glory of God as central to the biblical faith. For me, two things most characterise this volume. First, there is the emphasis on exposition of the biblical text. This is often where Douglas Kelly is at his best, which is what should be true of any book on systematic theology. Secondly, the vast knowledge that he has of historical theology, and his ability to garner references from patristic writers, those in the medieval period, and to later scholars, makes it a wonderful resource in tracing the development of Christian concepts. The use of so much excellent patristic material in particular distinguishes this book from other modern evangelical systematic theologies.

ALLAN HARMAN
Research Professor of Old Testament,
Presbyterian Theological College, Melbourne, Australia

Over the centuries, Christian theologians have often associated three things: goodness, truth and beauty. It is surely even harder to convey the beauty than the goodness and truth of Jesus Christ in the theological writing. Doug Kelly has succeeded. This is dogmatics as it should be done: a dogmatics of the warm heart. The author has put at our disposal his wide range of knowledge in historical theology from the Church Fathers onwards, so that we become conscious not of the independent theologian spinning out his own ideas but of the chorus of praise to Christ that unites the cloud of witnesses from biblical times until today. Can we ask more of dogmatics than this?

STEPHEN WILLIAMS
Professor of Systematic Theology, Union Theological College, Belfast, Northern Ireland

I love a good Systematic theology – and this is a good systematic theology. Volume 2 of Doug Kelly's Systematic Theology is about my favourite subject, the person and work of Christ. Its opening section is wonderful speaking about the beauty of Christ. Kelly uses sources as varied as Edwards, Aquinas, the early Church Fathers and Kant to interact with the Biblical text and show us what the Scripture says about Christ. Some think such systematic theologies are dry and scholastic. Not this one. It is scholarly, biblical and does what the introduction says – shows us the beauty of Christ in the context of the Trinity, his humiliation and his exaltation. If you are going to proclaim the Good News of Jesus- you need a good grasp of who he is. This book will really help.

DAVID ROBERTSON
Pastor, St Peter's Free Church, Dundee, Scotland

This book is a must read for those who serve in a cross cultural ministry context and are committed to contextualization. This book offers very specific and sharp guidelines in order to communicate Christ cross culturally in an appropriate manner and to steer away from proclaiming a Christ other than the true Christ. Dr. Kelly has established the validity of the need to contextualize alongside the sober reminder that contextualization should not come at the expense of the truth of the Son of God.

RAHMIATI TANUDJAJA
Academic Dean, Southeast Asia Bible Seminary, East Java, Indonesia

SYSTEMATIC THEOLOGY

VOLUME TWO

Grounded in Holy Scripture and
understood in the light of the Church

DOUGLAS F. KELLY

THE BEAUTY OF CHRIST: A TRINITARIAN VISION

ⅢENTOR

Douglas F. Kelly is the Richard Jordan Professor of Theology, Reformed Theological Seminary, Charlotte, North Carolina.

Scripture quotations are taken, unless otherwise stated, from the Authorised Version/King James Version, 1611.

hardback ISBN 978-1-78191-293-5
ePub ISBN 978-1-78191-375-8
Mobi ISBN 978-1-78191-376-5

10 9 8 7 6 5 4 3 2 1

Published in 2014
in the
Mentor Imprint
by
Christian Focus Publications Ltd.,
Geanies House, Fearn, Ross-shire,
IV20 1TW, Scotland, Great Britain

www.christianfocus.com

Cover design by Daniel van Straaten
Printed in the United States of America

CONTENTS

PART THREE
The Exaltation of Christ

This volume is dedicated to my grandchildren,
those present and those to come:

Katherine H. Kelly
Douglas F. Kelly, III
Mary Martha Kelly
Malcolm G. Kelly
Duncan W. B. Kelly

My prayer for them is that God will have them in the communion of saints, where in union with Christ, He makes real what He says through the Apostle Paul: 'But we all, with open face beholding as in a glass the glory of the Lord, are changed into the same image from glory to glory, even as by the Spirit of the Lord' (II Cor. 3:18).

THANKS AND ACKNOWLEDGEMENTS

First, I offer profound thanks to so many who have lifted up the writing of this second volume of my Systematic Theology in frequent prayer: both at home and in prayer meetings in many churches in America and Scotland. I have often sensed the help of the Holy Spirit throughout this project, and know that it has been in answer to many a prayer to the Father in Jesus' Name.

I am grateful to Reformed Theological Seminary for a sabbatical leave for the year 2010/2011, where we lived in Edinburgh, and did most of this work. I thank my alma mater, New College (University of Edinburgh), for allowing me to be a visiting fellow, with access to the library and to friends who teach there. The Free Church of Scotland College in Edinburgh also generously let me use their library. The Banner of Truth Trust once again allowed me to live in their property, and to have an office with them: special thanks are due to Rev. Iain Murray, Rev. Jonathan Watson, and Margaret MacLeod of the Banner. Also, thanks are due to the faithful staff of the Banner, particularly Colin Roworth and Mark Sutherland, who have been very helpful.

We were constantly lifted up by the Church we have long attended in Edinburgh: Holyrood Abbey Church of Scotland, and its minister, Rev. Phil Hair. Some of its members and elders, such as Ken and Fiona Colville, Murdo and Emma MacLeod, and others, were of encouragement to us during that time. I am grateful to some of the good Christian women of Edinburgh, who are able scholars, for going through the manuscript of volume 2 with suggestions: Anne Sydserff, Morellen Thompson, and Heather Johnson (now back in North Carolina). Jean-Marc Berthoud of Lausanne, Rev. Matt Miller of Greenville Associate Reformed Presbyterian Church (Greenville, SC), and my wife, Caroline, then read over the manuscript, and felt that it needed revisions, which I have now carried out as best I could.

My student assistants (present and former) have been of constant help: Alex Mark of RTS – Charlotte, NC, Rev. Johnathan Keenan of Memphis, TN, Rev. Paul Mulner of Winston-Salem, NC, Rev. Mark Miller of Lancaster, SC, Taylor Ince of New College, Edinburgh, and Jay Crout of RTS – Charlotte, Rev. Ken McMullen of RTS – Charlotte Library has faithfully helped me, as has my longtime secretary, Tari Williamson. In particular, Paul Mulner and Tari Williamson assisted with Hebrew and Greek fonts, and Tari also proofread the manuscript. My cousin, Dr. Sandy Stewart of NC State University in Raleigh, NC, read over part of the manuscript. Dr. John T. Slotemaker of Fairfield University, Connecticut, and Bertrand Rickenbacher of Lausanne sent me valuable material. Jean-Marc Berthoud was in frequent contact with me, and interacted with the manuscript with insight. I am grateful to my colleagues, Dr. J. Ligon Duncan of Jackson, MS, and Dr. W. Duncan Rankin of Houston, TX, for help with one of the appendices. Many thanks to my publisher, William Mackenzie of Christian Focus Publications, and also to Willie Mackenzie, as well as to my editor, Rev. Malcolm Maclean, and Martin MacLean, all of Inverness, for all they have done to make this second volume appear.

My thanks also to Dr. Randy Randall of Flint, Texas, for a generous grant to help with the indexing of this second volume, as he did with the first volume.

The assistance of several friends enabled us to take a longer than usual Sabbatical: Thomas Peaster, of Yazoo City, MS, Dr. Michael Brown, Jim Atkins, and Coble Adams of Dillon, SC, the session of Reedy Creek Presbyterian Church, Minturn, SC, Rev. William F. Fulton of Austin, TX, and a friend in Jackson, MS. Jacques Sandoz of Paris has sent me information on some details in the French culture, and Blake and Julia Schwarz have helped me. Thanks to Mairead Macdonald of the Gaelic College in Skye for help with a reference. Todd Whiting and Jason Garvey of the Global Campus of Reformed Theological Seminary have assisted me with computer problems, as has my teaching assistant, Josh Grimm.

I pray for all of them, as well as for myself, and for the readers of this volume, this prayer of Moses: 'And let the beauty of the Lord our God be upon us; and establish thou the work of our hands upon us; yea, the work of our hands establish thou it' (Ps. 90:17).

INTRODUCTION

THE BEAUTY OF CHRIST:
THE TRINITARIAN CONTEXT OF CHRISTOLOGY

In the announcement by the Archangel Gabriel of the miraculous conception of the Son of God to the Virgin Mary, the evangelist Matthew immediately recognized the fulfillment of the prophecy of Isaiah: 'Behold, a virgin shall be with child, and shall bring forth a son, and they shall call his name Emmanuel, which being interpreted is, God with us' (Matt. 1:23, quoting Isaiah 7:14). In this second volume of our series, we are to consider the beauty of Christ with God, and the beauty of Christ with us, for he is Immanuel, 'God with us,' that is: (1) From all eternity, he is God, and (2) within the space/time series which he created, he has come down to be 'God with us'. It is particularly his coming down to us that accomplishes the ultimate restoration of purity and beauty to humanity and the cosmos and which constitutes the great theme of this second volume of Systematic Theology.

I. The Beauty of Christ with God

The eternal beauty of the One true God is most wonderfully concentrated in the Son of his love, in whose face we see the heart of the Father revealed (John 14:5-13). Christ comes as God made man, in order to show us who God is, and in so doing to save us and to renew the entire cosmos, which was his creation to begin with (John 1:3). God the eternal Son, who was made flesh by miraculous divine action in the womb of the chosen Jewish maiden, the Virgin Mary, finds his essential identity precisely as eternal God. He is *God the Son*; He has a Father, the Lord God Almighty, with whom and in whom, in the ineffable bond of charity of the Holy Spirit, he mutually indwells and coinheres, one of three coequal, undivided and yet distinct divine persons within the one Being of God.

Methodology

Since the Triune God is supremely personal: three Persons in one Being, it is worthy of the best efforts of our lives to seek to grasp something of the true character and beautiful qualities of the divine personhood. This is a most demanding task, for there is always mystery in personal being, even of a single human child, much more of the sovereign God, who is eternally three in one! But this generous God, who chooses not to be without us, has created us so that we may know him in supremely happy fellowship with him (John 17:3). It is in his written Word that we find the character and personal qualities of the God who chooses to reveal himself most clearly and authoritatively expressed. Hence, all that is to be said in this volume about the divine beauty, and especially that of the incarnate Son, in whose face we most clearly see the heart of the Father revealed, will be based on a reverent reading of the Holy Scriptures.

But I must add something more here to clarify the theological approach (or 'methodology') of this volume. While this volume is always seeking to open the relevant scriptural texts, to point out their 'scope' and to follow their 'scope,' as the basis of wholesome doctrine of 'the faith once delivered to the saints' (Jude 3), I have found it impossible to do so apart from 'the communion of saints' across many centuries, and from various traditions both East and West. That was also the case in the first volume of this series, which was for that purpose entitled: *Systematic Theology: Grounded in Holy Scripture and Understood in Light of the Church.*

Christ, in one of his parables, speaks of a householder bringing forth out of his treasure 'things that are new and old' (Matt. 13:52). That is what I have felt impelled to do with the veritable treasury of the theological writings of Church Fathers, Scholastics, Reformers, Puritans and Moderns. It is in a certain sort of communion with their minds that I have learned so much, and I am often quoting them both (1) to illuminate the scriptural truths I wish to express in this volume, and also (2) to expose others to the uplifting qualities of what these partially buried treasures still have to say.

As far as my own Protestant Reformed Tradition is concerned, it does seem that for some reason (perhaps the Enlightenment with its anti-Medieval spirit?), the eyes of many good theologians were functionally turned away from Medieval saints and earlier Church Fathers in the eighteenth and nineteenth centuries. Yet not long before, such mighty Reformed thinkers as John Calvin, John Owen, Thomas Goodwin and Samuel Rutherford, in the sixteenth and seventeenth centuries, had mined gold and silver out of Patristic and Scholastic mines (although not without frequently severe criticism of these sources, where they failed to match up to Holy Scripture). It will take many years to tell, but it is my hope and prayer that these volumes may alert many Christian scholars to such beneficent sources, where they may – to change the figure – winnow afresh grain from chaff. That then is why I so frequently quote from others, and I trust that it will not be distracting from the main thrust of the text.

Guidance from Jonathan Edwards and Richard of Saint Victor on God and Beauty

Jonathan Edwards ascribes the origin of all beauty to God: '...the foundation and fountain of all being and all beauty ... of whom, and through whom, and to whom is all being and all perfection; and whose being and beauty are, as it were, the sum and comprehension of all existence and excellence.'[1] Roland A. Delattre shows that Edwards' understanding of beauty requires the love within the Trinity: ''Tis peculiar to God that he has beauty within Himself.'[2] Edwards goes on to note that there needs to be a plurality of persons in God for beauty to exist, for it requires 'consent' (or pleasure in the other). Here his reasoning is much like that of Richard of St. Victor, who saw that for love to exist, God had to be more than one Person at the same time.[3] In Edwards' words: 'One alone cannot be excellent' or beautiful 'inasmuch as in such case there can be no consent... Therefore, if God is excellent, there must be a plurality in God; otherwise there can be no consent in Him.'[4]

It is quite impossible even to begin speaking of Christ, the eternal Son of God, without bowing before the entire Godhead: Father, Son, and Holy Spirit. As Gregory of Nazianzus said: 'No sooner do I conceive of the one than I am illumined by the splendour of the three; no sooner do I distinguish them than I am carried back to the one. When I think of any one of the three, I think of Him as the whole, and my eyes are filled, and the greater part of what I am thinking escapes me.'[5] Elsewhere he said: 'When I say God, I mean Father, Son and Holy Spirit.'[6]

Perichoresis and Love

This *perichoretic* relationship[7] of the three Persons within the one Godhead, in which each of the three distinct persons coinheres, or mutually dwells within the other, in a delightful, fully satisfying, and eternal interchange of life, light, and love, could rightly be said to constitute the fundamental beauty and all-sufficiency of God. That is, much of the beauty of God lies in the happy difference between the three distinct persons: Father, Son, and Holy Spirit – loving, loved, and love itself, or giving, receiving, and gift.

Gregory of Nyssa speaks of this beauty as love of that which is infinitely good: 'The Deity is in very substance beautiful; and to the Deity the soul will in its state of purity have affinity, and will embrace it as like itself. Whenever this happens, then, there will be no longer need of the impulse of desire to lead the way to the beautiful...'[8] He adds:

---

1. Jonathan Edwards, *The Nature of True Virtue* (University of Michigan Press: Ann Arbor Paperback, 1960), 15.

2. Jonathan Edwards, 'Notes on the Mind' in Harvey G. Townsend, ed., *The Philosophy of Jonathan Edwards From His Private Notebooks* (University of Oregon Press: Eugene, Oregon, 1955), 45, quoted in Roland A. Delattre, *Beauty and Sensibility in the Thought of Jonathan Edwards: An Essay in Aesthetics and Theoogical Ethics* (Wipf & Stock Publishers: Eugene, Oregon, 2006), 18.

3. See D. F. Kelly, *Systematic Theology*, vol. one, 274-276.

4. Jonathan Edwards, *Miscellanies* (Yale University Collection of Edwards Manuscripts: Yale University Library), 117. Delattre adds: 'On this platform Edwards erects his ontological doctrine of the Trinity,' op. cit., 18.

5. Gregory Nazianzus, *Oration* 40,41.

6. *Oration* 45,4.

7. See volume 1 of this series, pp. 489-493.

8. Gregory of Nyssa, *On the Soul and the Resurrection*, (Nicene and Post-Nicene Fathers, Eerdmans: Grand Rapids, 1956), 449. I owe many of these references to Gregory of Nyssa, as well as a number of the concepts behind them, and their bearings, to David Bentley Hart, *The Beauty*

For the life of the Supreme Being is love, seeing that the beautiful is necessarily lovable to those who recognize it, and the Deity does recognize it, and so this recognition becomes love, that which He recognizes being essentially beautiful...no satiety interrupting this continuous capacity to love the beautiful, God's life will have its activity in love; which life is thus in itself beautiful, and is essentially of a loving disposition towards the beautiful, and receives no check to this activity of love...when you have a good, as here, which is in its essence incapable of a change for the worse, then that good will go on unchecked into infinity.[9]

It is as though the face of each of the three divine persons shines with serene beauty and profoundest delight as they look upon one another, according to the suggestion of Saint Augustine:

Therefore that unspeakable conjunction of the Father and His image is not without fruition, without love, without joy. Therefore that love, delight, felicity, or blessedness, if indeed it can be worthily expressed by any human word, is called by him, in short Use; and it is the Holy Spirit in the Trinity, not begotten, but the sweetness of the begetter, and of the begotten, filling all creatures according to their capacity...[10]

Augustine views the wonders of creation as having their source in the perfect beauty of the Creator: '...For in that Trinity is the supreme source of all things, and the most perfect beauty, and the most blessed delight. Those three, therefore, both seem to be mutually determined to each other, and are in themselves infinite...'[11]

This beauty of loving and giving, receiving and sharing the gift within the three persons of the Holy Trinity lies behind God's original giving of himself to reveal himself to his image-bearers (Gen. 1:27,28), and then to redeem them from sin once they had fallen away from him (John 3:16; Rom. 8:32; I John 4:7-14). Such action means that in some true sense God has made a place for us within the beauty of the divine circumincession (or *perichoresis*). And so our High Priest prays to the Father: 'Father, I will that they also, whom thou hast given me, be with me where I am; that they behold my glory, which thou hast given me: for thou lovedst me before the foundation of the world' (John 17:24).

Both 'ontological' inner Trinitarian relationships of beauty and 'economical' movements both in the very act of creation and into redemptive history to save a lost humanity are joined in many places, not least in John 1:14: 'And the word was made flesh and dwelt among us, (and we beheld his glory, the glory as of the only begotten of the Father,) full of grace and truth.'[12] It was the Word (or Logos), the Father's eternal

---

of the Infinite: The Aesthetics of Christian Truth (William B. Eerdmans Publishing Company: Grand Rapids, Michigan, 2003).

9. Gregory of Nyssa, op. cit., 450.

10. Augustine, *On the Trinity*, VI, X, 10 (Nicene and Post-Nicene Fathers, Eerdmans: Grand Rapids, 1956), 103.

11. Ibid., VI, X, 12.

12. This passage is exegeted in detail in chapter 3 of this volume.

Son (as John 1:18 makes clear), who became incarnate for our salvation. Or, in the words of Isaiah 7:14, 'God with us' is none less than the eternal God within himself.

His coming down to us in the flesh is an aspect of the internal beauty of God; each person of the Trinity giving himself to the others, and receiving the returns of love from each one. We have some grasp of this in the Father giving himself to the Son and Spirit, the Son giving himself back to the Father and the Spirit, and the Spirit proceeding from both, and uniting both in ineffable ties of love, as he continually returns to them within the undivided oneness of the perichoretic Being.

Andrew Murray in *The Holiest of All: An Exposition of the Epistle to the Hebrews* commenting on the contrast in Hebrews 1:5 ('Unto which of the angels said he at any time, Thou art my Son...') between the Son of God and the angels, takes us into the beauty of the love within the Trinity, and then outward to ourselves:

> ... God has a Son. This is the mystery of divine love; and that in a double sense. Because God is love He begets a Son, to whom He gives all He is and has Himself, in whose fellowship He finds His life and delight, through whom He can reveal Himself, with whom He shares the worship of all His creatures. And because God is love, this Son of God becomes the Son of Man, and the Son of Man, having been perfected for evermore, enters through death and resurrection into all the glory that belonged to the Son of God. And now this Son of God is to us the revelation, the bearer, of the love of the divine Being. In Him the love of God dwells in us; in Him we enter and rest in it. When God speaks to us in this His Son, it is the infinite love imparting itself to us, becoming the inward life of our life.[13]

Saint Thomas Aquinas defines Beauty

Long before Murray (nineteenth century) and Edwards (eighteenth century), it was also in the context of Trinitarian theology that Saint Thomas Aquinas had developed his definition of beauty (in the thirteenth century). In so doing, he was following Saint Augustine (fifth century),[14] who followed Saint Hilary (fourth century).[15] In *Summa Theologiae* (I. 39), Thomas expounds major issues in Trinitarian theology: I. 27-38: the divine processions; I. 28 – the divine relations, and I. 29-38 – the divine persons. Then, as John T. Slotemaker points out: 'In question 39 Thomas analyzes how specific attributes or properties can be appropriated to the

---

13. Andrew Murray, *The Holiest of All: An Exposition of the Epistle to the Hebrews* (Oliphants Ltd.: London, 1965), 52, 53.

14. Augustine quotes (with one change) Hilary's 'triad' for beauty within the Trinitarian relations: *infinitas, species,* and *usus in munere.* The change made by Augustine (*De Trinitate* VI.10.11) is in the adjective for God. While Hilary says 'infinity', Augustine says 'eternal in Fatherhood', as discussed by John T. Slotemaker, 'Pulchritudo Christi: The Sources of Thomas Aquinas's Understanding of the Beauty of Christ,' in *Archa Verbi: Yearbook for the Study of Medieval Theology,* Vol. 8/2011 (Aschendoff Verlag: Munster, 2011), 119.

15. In *De Trinitate,* Book II, Hilary ascribes *infinitas* to the Father, *species in imagine* to the Son, and *usus in munere* to the Holy Spirit; that is, infinity to the Father, 'beauty in image' to the Son, and service (or application or making fruitful) in ministry to the Holy Spirit.

divine persons.'[16] Here is where St. Thomas sets forth the beauty of God. Dr. Slotemaker adds: '...Thomas argues that when one examines God absolutely according to His being...the appropriations of Hilary apply: eternity to the Father, species to the Son, and use to the Holy Spirit.'[17] These three terms, taken together, constitute the beauty of the Lord.

Hence, in ST I. 39. a. 8 co., Thomas attributes *species* to the Son, by which, following Augustine, he means 'beauty'.[18] While Hilary describes the Son as *species* (which could be rendered 'form'), Augustine stated that *species* actually should be taken as meaning 'beauty' in the harmony between the divine persons. Then Thomas goes on to list (in ST I. 39. a. 8) three properties of the beauty of the Son: *integritas sive perfectio, proportio sive consonantia,* and *claritas* (i.e. integrity or completeness, right proportion or harmony, and brightness).

The first quality of beauty is integrity or perfection, and 'is understood to be in the Son because the Son is of the same nature as the Father'.[19] Integrity means that the Son lacks nothing, for as Thomas stated, 'things that lack something are thereby ugly'.[20] Or, as Dr. Caponi writes: 'Integrity is a divine attribute: God lacks nothing proper to divinity or the achieving of his ends.'[21] Thomas emphasizes 'the correlation between the being (nature) of the Son and the being of the Father'.[22]

The second quality of beauty in the analysis of Saint Thomas is proportion or harmony. That is, the Son is the express image of the Father. 'Beauty, for Augustine and Thomas, is the perfect *imago* of the perfect being – The Son of God, as the *imago Dei*, is the perfect image of the perfect being, the Father.'[23] Concerning this primary relationship between the Father and the Son, Thomas states: 'Right proportion (*debita proportio*) is consonant with what is proper to the Son inasmuch as he is the express image of the Father.'[24] Caponi adds: 'Wherever there is right relationship – whether the rectitude flows from the will of God or from canons of human creativity – there is beauty.'[25]

The third quality of beauty, according to Saint Thomas, is *claritas*. That is, 'the Son as Word, is the light and splendor of the intellect.' According to Holy Scripture, 'God is light,' and his Son is light. Christ is 'the true light' (John 1:9), and thus can proclaim: 'I am the light of the world' (8:12). Or as the Nicene Creed affirms, Christ is 'light of light.' Hebrews 1:3 says that

---

16. Slotemaker, art. cit., 133.

17. Ibid.

18. Dr. Slotemaker shows that Thomas is following 'Augustine's analysis in *De Trinitate* VI.10.11, and his reading of Hilary's attribution of *species* to the Son, which substantively informs Thomas's analysis of the Son as beauty' (art. cit., 135).

19. Slotemaker, art. cit., 135.

20. ST, I. 39. 8, resp., discussed in Francis J. Caponi, 'Beauty, Justice, and Damnation in Thomas Aquinas,' in *Pro Ecclesia*, Vol. XIX, No. 4, 392.

21. Ibid., 393.

22. Slotemaker, art. cit., 135.

23. Ibid.

24. ST, I, 39, 8, resp.

25. Caponi, art. cit., 392.

'He is the radiance of the glory of God, and the express image of his nature (or *character* in Greek).'

Thomas' doctrine of beauty is heavily indebted to Augustine, who interpreted the beauty of God '... as the beauty (*pulchritudo*) that accompanies the harmony (*congruentia*) and equality (*aequalitas*) between the persons.'[26] This Augustinian (Thomist) concept of the centrality of harmony for the existence of beauty is rather differently approached in Jonathan Edwards. As Delattre wrote: '...the primary model of beauty for Edwards is being's consent to being, rather than proportion or harmony.'[27] But what Edwards says about 'the consent of being to being' as concerns God himself, although not the same, is not really contradictory to Augustine's (and Thomas') emphasis on 'congruence'. Edwards speaks of this willing harmony (or congruence) between Father and Son as 'consent': 'One alone cannot be excellent' or beautiful 'inasmuch as in such case there can be no consent.'[28] So what does Edwards mean by 'consent to being'?

Jonathan Edwards defines beauty

Edwards considers communion to be the primary beauty of cordial consent among beings.[29] As concerns the Holy Trinity, Edwards states that 'God exerts Himself towards Himself no other way than in infinitely loving and delighting in Himself, in the mutual love of the Father and the Son. This makes the third – the personal Holy Spirit, or the holiness of God – which is His infinite beauty. And this is God's infinite consent to being in general [*Mind* 45, Part 9].'[30]

He says it in a slightly different way elsewhere: 'The Holy Ghost is Himself the delight and joyfulness of the Father in that idea [of Himself which He has in the Son], and of the idea in the Father...So that, if we turn in all the ways in the world, we shall never be able to make more than these three, God, the idea of God, and delight in God [*Misc.* 94].'[31]

The ancient doctrine of *perichoresis* enables us to think together congruence and cordial consent to being. As Hilary said: 'They [i.e. the three divine persons] reciprocally contain one another, so that one should permanently envelope, and also be permanently enveloped by the Other, whom yet he envelopes.'[32] This means that the three persons of the blessed Trinity are eternally one in being (thus, *congruent*), and at the same time, delight in the personal distinction of each other, taking delight in neither being dissolved into an amorphous mass, nor in being personally separated (thus, joyful *consent* to the personal and distinct being of the others). The oneness in being, and triune distinctiveness of the three

---

26. Slotemaker, art. cit., 121.

27. Delattre, op. cit., 23.

28. Edwards, *Misc.* 117, quoted in Delattre, op. cit., 18.

29. Delattre, op. cit., 108.

30. Quoted in Ibid., 152.

31. Ibid., 154.

32. Hilary, *De Trinitate*, III. 1.

divine persons, with their joyful interchange of light, life, and love, is the origin and fountain of all beauty of whatever sort.

Beauty and peace

This beauty of the Lord can also be approached through the concept of the serene peace that reigns within the blessed Trinity. David Bentley Hart has set it forth extensively (in his *The Beauty of the Infinite*), in contrast to the bitterness and violence found in so much of Post-modern deconstructionism, with its competing power claims of discordant communities of 'interpretation'.

Some fifty years earlier, the Scottish Presbyterian Pastor, William Still of Aberdeen (1911-1997), grasped the beauty of the Triune Persons in terms of the peace that flows through the Being of God:

> God is the God of peace. He is at peace, in and with himself. A fundamental implication of the Holy Scriptures is that the triune God was, is and ever shall be in perfect accord with himself, person with person, office with office, and that he is satisfied with himself in the fulness and perfection of his wisdom, love and power. When infinite intelligence finds infinite perfections in itself, infinite stability and integrity of character are assured. This integrity is simply another name for God's righteousness, or rightness.... He rejoices in it so much that he desires it for his creatures, and that, not only for its own sake as a seed, but for its fruit which is peace (Isa. 32:17; Heb. 12:11).[33]

Although it has been our intention to deal first with (1) God in himself, and only then, with (2) God with us, it is finally impossible to separate conceptually, with any strictness, these two aspects of the Trinity (*ontological* and *economical*), as we see in the quotation immediately above. That is because we time-bound, space-bound humans can only enter into a certain understanding (true, but limited) of these eternal, ontological Trinitarian realities through *the economy* (as the Church Fathers called it) of the history of creation, of providence, and of the redemption of the lost creation, as Father, Son, and Holy Spirit create the cosmos out of nothing, plan for its future, and enter into its sinful brokenness through covenantal relationships, in order to restore it, as testified to by patriarchs, prophets, and apostles in Holy Scripture, as Karl Rahner brings out in *The Trinity*,[34] in which he shows that the economic Trinity is the ontological Trinity, and the ontological Trinity is the economic Trinity. In my understanding, however, this important fundamental identity does not have to abolish the traditional Orthodox distinction (but *not* separation) between the essence of the ontological Trinity and the energies manifested in the outward actions of the Triune God.[35]

---

33. William Still, *Towards Spiritual Maturity: Overcoming all evil in the Christian Life*, Revised Edition (Christian Focus: Geannies House, Fearn, Ross-shire, Scotland, 2010), 12, 13.

34. Karl Rahner, *The Trinity*, 24-33.

35. *A total abolition* of this traditional distinction would lead to a sort of univocal (rather than analogical) affirmation of distinctions within our understanding of the Being of God, and of the language we employ about him. Jean-Marc Berthoud has explored the direction one strand of this univocal identity has taken in some of the scholastic theories of 'created grace' in *Le règne terrestre*

II. The Beauty of Christ with us

Isaiah tells us that Christ is 'Immanuel: God with us,' and the evangelist Matthew puts Gabriel's annunciation of Christ's conception and Virgin Birth into this context. The triune God spoke worlds into existence, and placed the Adamic race in it, so that the Father could prepare for his Son an immaculate bride, and it is in terms of this relationship of love that all cosmic and human history unfolds. The Father's love to the Son overflows into his preparation of a massive people, who will share forever in that divine love, which will be celebrated with boundless joy at 'the marriage supper of the Lamb' (Rev. 19:7-9; 21:2). The spotless bride, though called when marred by sin and its ugliness, has now been washed in the blood of the Son whiter than the snow from all her unsightly blotches, and perfected in holy beauty by the indwelling of the Holy Spirit. And the world in which this bride is born, grows up, and is sanctified is one that still reflects the divine beauty of the heavenly Bridegroom.

Beauties of Creation point to God

The God whose own inner-trinitarian relations are beautiful has created beauty outside himself, and such created beauty says something significant about who God is in his own Being. The Psalms frequently praise him for such created beauty that reflects his own inherent loveliness.

From the very beginning of creation, the triune God displayed much of his beauty in the realm of nature, calling what he had made 'very good' [טוֹב מְאֹד] as in Genesis 1:31. This beauty is frequently pointed out in the Psalms: 'O Lord our Lord, how excellent is thy name in all the earth! Who hast set thy glory above the heavens' (Ps. 8:1); 'The heavens declare the glory of God; and the firmament sheweth his handywork...' (Ps. 19:1); 'Thou crownest the year with thy goodness; and thy paths drop fatness' (Ps. 65:11); 'The Lord is good to all: and his tender mercies are over all his works. All thy works shall praise thee, O Lord; and thy saints shall bless thee'; 'Praise ye the Lord. Praise ye the Lord from the heavens: praise him in the heights...Let them praise the name of the Lord: for his name alone is excellent; his glory is above the earth and heaven' (Ps. 148:1, 13).

Gregory of Nyssa in almost poetic fashion sings high praises to God for how he shows his own beauty in the wonders of the created order. Gregory describes the beauties both of (1) the natural realm and also (2) those of the human person, all of which reflect the splendor of the triune God.

First, he describes the loveliness of nature, as he meditates upon Genesis 2:1 ('The heaven and the earth were finished'): '...the particular things were adorned with their appropriate beauty; the heaven with the rays of the stars, the sea and air with the living creatures that swim and fly, and the earth with all varieties of plants and animals...the earth was full, too, of her produce, bringing forth fruits at the same time with flowers; the meadows were full of all that grows therein, and all the mountain

---

de Dieu (L'Age d'Homme: Lausanne, 2011).

ridges...were crowned with young grass, and with the varied produce of the trees, just risen from the ground, yet shot up at once into their perfect beauty; and all the beasts that had come into life at God's command were rejoicing, we may suppose, and skipping about, running to and fro in the thickets in herds according to their kind, while every sheltered and shady spot was ringing with the chants of the song-birds...'[36]

Pierre Viret on Beauty in the birds and the natural environment

The sixteenth-century Swiss Reformer, Pierre Viret (1511-1571), pastor of the Church in Lausanne, and colleague of John Calvin, also drew attention to the birds as a way of grasping attributes of God, their Creator. In a meditation on 'The Admirable Instinct of the Birds,' he speaks of such things as their architectural ability in building nests (describing them as 'masons'), and using a beak, which is effective in breaking hard seeds and cracking open thick shelled nuts, thereby feeding their young. Then he comments on God's words to Job about his need to consider the ways of the beasts whom God created, and thereby to perceive great attributes of God himself: 'It should come as no surprise when the Lord proposes the example and nature of the animals and birds he created, in order to teach him to recognize through these creatures God's own great power, wisdom, goodness and foresight.'[37]

A world and millennium and a half away from Gregory, and two centuries away from Viret, Jonathan Edwards, in early eighteenth-century New England, grasped with equal enthusiasm how the beauties of nature lead us up to the beauties of God (especially of Christ):

> When we are delighted with flowery meadows and gentle breezes of wind, we may consider that we only see the emanations of the sweet benevolence of Jesus Christ; when we behold the fragrant rose and lily, we see his love and purity. So the green trees and fields, and singing of birds, are the emanations of his infinite joy and benignity; the easiness and naturalness of trees and vines [are] shadows of his infinite beauty and loveliness; the crystal rivers and murmuring streams have the footsteps of his sweet grace and bounty.... That beauteous light with which the world is filled in a clear day is a lively shadow of his spotless holiness and happiness, and delight in communicating himself.[38]

Pierre Viret also traced out the loveliness of God's generous Being by arguing that God gave to mankind through the excellencies of the created order, not only what was necessary for survival, but also what was

---

36. Gregory of Nyssa, *On the Making of Man*, in *Nicene and Post-Nicene Fathers, Volume V* (I.5), p. 389.

37. Originally published in *Dialogues du désordre qui est a present au monde* (1545), Third Dialogue: *La métamorphose*, 300-302. I have taken this section from a collection of extracts from Viret (and have translated it into English): C. Schnetzler, et al., *Pierre Viret d'Àpres Lui-Meme* (Lausanne: Georges Bridel & Cie, 1911), 272. A brief and useful biography of Pierre Viret appeared in 2010 by Jean-Marc Berthoud: *Pierre Viret: A Forgotten Giant of the Reformation: The Apologetics, Ethics, and Economics of the Bible* (Zurich Publishing: Tallahassee, Florida, 2010).

38. Jonathan Edwards, Miscellany No. 108, *Works*, 13: 278-80.

beautiful to see, and what excited our desires. That is, our Creator goes far above strict necessity, and provides a diversity of things that are lovely to behold and melodious to hear:

> God not only provided these things [e.g. rivers, trees, animal inhabitants, waters, and birds...] to take care of the basic needs of mankind, but also to minister to their desires and pleasures, and to do so, he joined an excellent beauty to things that are profitable and useful. For how lovely it is to see beautiful islands in the sea, and [on the land] beautiful and clear fountains and running streams...flowing down the mountains...and then the beautiful little birds moving about, flying and singing among the trees with great melody and natural music![39]

Cecil F. Alexander expressed the natural beauty and the divine goodness in a hymn:

The purple-headed mountain,
    The river running by,
The sunset, and the morning
    That brightens up the sky,
The cold wind in the winter,
    The pleasant summer sun,
The ripe fruits in the garden, -
    He made them every one.

The tall trees in the greenwood,
    The meadows where we play,
The rushes by the water,
    We gather every day, -
He gave us eyes to see them,
    And lips that we might tell
How great is God Almighty,
    Who has made all things well.[40]

Beauty in humankind

Gregory of Nyssa, after praising the Lord's loveliness in nature, then goes on to trace how much of his own beauty God placed within mankind:

> ...So human nature also, as it was made to rule the rest, was, by its likeness to the King of all, made as it were a living image, partaking with the archetype both in rank and in name, not vested in purple, nor giving indication of its rank by sceptre and diadem (for the archetype itself is not arrayed with these), but in stead of the purple robe, clothed in virtue, which is in truth the most royal of all raiment, and in place of the sceptre, leaning on the bliss of immortality, and instead of the royal diadem, decked with the crown of righteousness; so that it is shown to be perfectly like to the beauty of its archetype in all that belongs to the dignity of royalty.[41]

---

39. Viret in Schnetzler, et al., op. cit., 269.

40. "All things bright and beautiful' by Cecil Frances Alexander (1823-1895).

41. Gregory of Nyssa, *On the Making of Man*, (IV.1), p. 391.

Jonathan Edwards taught that both bodily beauty and beauty of soul within humanity reflected something of the perfections of Christ. He wrote:

> ...when we behold the beauty of man's body in its perfection we still see like emanations of Christ's divine perfections, although they do not always flow from the mental excellencies of the person that has them. But we see far the most proper image of the beauty of Christ when we see beauty in the human soul.[42]

In other words, he means that a person who is notably handsome or beautiful in his or her face and bodily build may or may not be indwelt by the Spirit of Christ. (One can think of the many human specimens over the millennia of the mythological Aphrodite or Adonis). Even so, their physical comeliness, in some way, comes from the beauty of the Lord. Yet Edwards holds that there is no beauty to compare with the beauty of 'Christ in you, the hope of glory' (Col. 1:27); that is, nothing on earth can be more beautiful than the personality of a believing man or woman, who is being sanctified by the Spirit of God into an ever fuller measure of likeness to Christ. Paul makes this point when he describes some of 'the messengers of the churches' as being 'the glory of Christ' (II Cor. 8:23).

In a remarkable meditation, Gregory interconnects the divine beauty within the human frame with the love that reigns within the Trinity:

> And if you were to examine the other points also by which the divine beauty is expressed, you will find that to them too the likeness in the image which we present is perfectly preserved. The Godhead is mind and word: for 'in the beginning was the Word' (John 1:1), and the followers of Paul 'have the mind of Christ' which speaks in them: humanity too is not far removed from these: you see in yourself word and understanding, an imitation of the very Mind and Word. Again, God is love, and the fount of love: for this the great John declares that 'love is of God' and 'God is love' (I John 4:8): the Fashioner of our nature has made this to be our feature too: for 'hereby' (John 13:35). He says, 'shall all men know that ye are my disciples, if ye love one another' – thus, if this be absent, the whole stamp of the likeness is transformed.[43]

That is to say, Gregory relates the beauty in creation, and especially in humanity, to the relationships within the Holy Trinity, such as (in his words immediately above) 'the Godhead,' 'Word,' and 'mind.' Those relationships are distinctive aspects (or actually, persons) of the love that God is. And we are invited into that love, for God and for one another, thereby showing the divine image.

We shall outlast the Beauties of Nature

C. S. Lewis with insight says that we shall outlast the beauties of nature, and that we are defined by the splendour *they represent*, rather than by themselves:

---

42. J. Edwards, *Misc.* 108, quoted in Delattre, op. cit, 181-82.

43. Gregory of Nyssa, op. cit., (V.2).

Nature is mortal; we shall outlive her. When all the suns and nebulae have passed away, each one of you will still be alive. Nature is only the image, the symbol; but it is the symbol Scripture invited me to use. We are summoned to pass in through Nature, beyond her, into the splendour which she fitfully reflects.[44]

When Adam, head of the human race, rebelled, and by his sin brought death into the world (cf. Gen. 3 and Rom. 5:12-21), it caused a disastrous marring of his original beauty and integrity. God's just judgment upon Satan, the woman, the man, and the cosmos manifested the beauty of his pure righteousness, in which he, consistent with his holy character, punished the ugly cancer of sin, and provided a way for the restoration of mankind and the entire created order. This grace is seen in the first promise of the Gospel in Genesis 3:15,16 (expounded elsewhere). The malign ugliness of the disintegration of the beautiful order brought about by sin and death would not have the last word. Beauty would be restored, as is reflected in Romans 8:18-22, when it promises that 'the creature itself also shall be delivered from the bondage of corruption into the glorious liberty of the children of God' (v. 21).

The history of the Biblical covenants relates this long story of God's grace preserving a people through righteous Noah, and calling out Abraham to be 'father of the faithful.' As we saw elsewhere (vol. 1, chapter 6), the seed of Eve, the seed of Noah, the seed of Abraham would appear in the womb of the Virgin Mary to carry out the total fulness of the restoration of righteousness, life and beauty that his earthly forerunners had pointed towards in their own divinely ordained, but necessarily limited, ways.

The final consummation wrought by the manifestation of the Person and atoning work of Christ will be the out-raying of the glory of the triune God throughout the entire universe, when the resurrected one returns, and takes his people up to that realm that needs no temple, sun, nor moon: 'And the twelve gates were twelve pearls; every several gate was of one pearl: and the street of the city was pure gold, as it were transparent glass. And I saw no temple therein: for the Lord God Almighty and the Lamb are the temple of it. And the city had no need of the sun, neither of the moon, to shine in it: for the glory of God did lighten it, and the Lamb is the light thereof' (Rev. 21:21-23).

Scriptural longings for and expressions that indicate beauty

This triune God, three in one, and one in three, whom we see most clearly in Christ, is at times mentioned in his own inspired revelation in terms of the most exquisite beauty. Psalm 90:17 is a concluding prayer by Moses (for the ancient Hebrew tradition ascribes this Psalm to him), who had sought to see the personal glory of God in the closest possible way (cf. Exod. 33:18).[45] Moses cries out for 'the beauty of the Lord our God' as chief object of his intercession on behalf of the people of God. In response to Moses' request in Exodus 33:18 to see the glory

---

44. C. S. Lewis, *The Weight of Glory and Other Addresses* (HarperOne: New York, 1980), 44.

45. 'And he said, I beseech thee, shew me thy glory.'

of God, the Lord says (in verse 19), 'I will make all my goodness (or beauty) pass before thee, and I will proclaim the name of the LORD before thee.'

Insofar as all faithful theology is finally an opening of the clear teaching of the Holy Scriptures on any particular subject, in order to lay hold of the beauty that Moses longed to see and that Christ so fully exemplified and reflected, it is necessary to look at some of the specific Hebrew and Greek words that are used in Scripture to convey the sense of 'beauty.'

Shekinah glory (or beauty)

A major manifestation of this divine beauty was the glory cloud (spoken of by the *post-Biblical* rabbis as *shekinah*), which, according to the Hebrew signification, indicated a bright outshining of supernatural light.[46] Jonathan Edwards takes us to the point:

> ...God's glory [is] often represented by an effulgence, or emanation, or communication of light, from a luminary or fountain of light. What can so naturally and aptly represent the emanation of the internal glory of God; or the flowing forth and abundant communication of that infinite fulness of good that is in God? Light is very often in Scripture put for comfort, joy happiness, and for good in general.[47]

Another Hebrew word, closely related to the outshining of the cloud of glory, was *kabod*, which actually implies that this divine beauty has *weight*. Jonathan Edwards also writes of this aspect of something so beautiful that it is 'heavy'. He correctly points out that 'glory' is often the translation in the English Bible of the original Hebrew word *kabod*. He adds:

> The root it comes from, is either the verb, (כבד) which signifies *to be heavy*, or make heavy, or from the adjective (כָּבֵד) which signifies heavy or weighty.... The Hebrew word (כָּבוֹד) ... commonly translated as glory.... Sometimes it is used to signify what is *internal, inherent,* or in the *possesion* of the person: and sometimes for *emanation, exhibition,* or *communication* of this internal glory...[48]

Closely related to *kabod* [כבד] is doxa [δοξα]. Kittel notes that in the New Testament, *doxa* (which he relates to the Old Testament word, *kabod*) '... denotes "divine and heavenly radiance," the "loftiness and majesty" of God, and even the "being of God" and his world.'[49]

The weighty glory was lovely, radiant and protective to the covenant people (as it stood behind them as a block to the hostile army of Pharaoh).

---

46. The precise word *shekinah* is not found in the Old Testament. W. Van Gemeren states: 'Although the word "Shekinah" does not occur in the Bible, the root *skn* occurs not only in the verb ("dwell"), but also in the noun *miskan* ("dwelling place," "tabernacle") and the name Shecaniah ("Yahweh dwells"; e.g. I Chron. 3:21f.)... The Aramaic Tg. Onkelos renders this verse: "He will cause his Shekinah to dwell in the dwelling-place of Shem."' W. A. VanGemeren, 'Shekinah,' *International Standard Bible Encyclopedia*, vol. 4, G. Bromiley, ed. (Eerdmans: Grand Rapids, MI, 1988), 466.

47. Jonathan Edwards, *Works* (Banner of Truth: Edinburgh, 1974 reprint), vol. 1, 117-18.

48. Ibid., 116.

49. Kittel, *Theological Dictionary of the New Testament*, translated by G.. Bromiley (Eerdmans: Grand Rapids, MI, 1965), vol. III, 237.

At the same time, it was terrifying and confounding to their enemies (e.g. see Exodus 14:19-25). The Old Testament at times ascribes this glory directly to the Lord.

According to some verses in the Old Testament, the glory of the Lord can, in a certain sense, be seen in lightning. Kittel's *Theological Dictionary of the New Testament* finds in *kabod yhvh* [כבד יהוה] '...traits which point strongly to the phenomenon of a thunderstorm.' He mentions Psalm 97:1 with clouds, lightning, and hills melting like wax, the vision in the call of Ezekiel, with storm, cloud, fire, lightning and the noise of rushing water, as well as the overhanging thunder clouds during the revelation at Sinai (Exod. 19:16), with the Lord descending in the fire (v. 18). But *kabod* also is employed for the personal beauty of the Lord in Exodus 33:18, where Moses desires to see the *kabod* of the Lord. After hiding Moses in a cleft of the rock, and covering him with his hand, the Lord makes his *kol tobhi* [כָּל-טוּבִי] to pass by.[50]

In Exodus 40:34f., the cloud covers the tent and the *kabod yhvh* fills it on the inside. Kittel concludes: 'The nature of the *kabod* itself is to be conceived as a radiant, fiery substance... The *kabod* is a manifestation of the glory of God.'[51] Much later in the history of Israel, David prayed that he might behold 'the power and the glory [כְּבוֹדֶךָ] of the Lord in the sanctuary' (Ps. 63:2).

Why look at so many terms for beauty?

In English and most of the modern European languages, there is a main word for beauty, and several more terms express substantially the same concept (such as 'lovely,' 'comely,' or 'handsome' etc. in English). There seem to be even more words to convey something like 'beauty' in Hebrew than in our Indo-European tongues, so far as I know (as a non-expert in that subject). Hence, a careful survey of the many words somehow related to the idea of 'beauty' throughout the Old Testament would involve many pages. It is not appropriate to attempt that here, but nevertheless, since God is so central to the Old Testament, and since 'beauty' is so frequently found on its pages (sometimes directly describing God, and sometimes not), we must look at a few more of the main words for beauty in the Torah, as a pointer to how the inspired text would have its readers think of God's own beauty.

A major Old Testament (Hebrew) word related to beauty is *yph* [יָפֶה]: something like 'fair or very beautiful.'[52] In the Song of Solomon it is often applied to the beautiful bride, and the beauty of Jerusalem, although it is not directly ascribed to God, yet it is understood that such beauty ultimately comes from him. The Hebrew word related to *'wh* [יָפִי] can describe 'the desire of the eyes' or 'pleasing to the eyes.' This desire is

---

50. Kittel, op. cit., vol. II, 239.

51. Ibid., 240.

52. Van Gemeren et al., 3636. *Dictionary of Old Testament Theolgoy and Exegesis*, 5 Vols (Paternoster Press, Carlisl, 1997).

closely related to the longing for God, and to a husband's longing for his bride (as in Psalm 45:11 [יָפְיֵךְ], which the Church Fathers saw as a messianic prophecy of Christ's pleasure in his church).[53]

Another word for beautiful is *n'h* [נָוֶה], and it means something like lovely or appropriate.[54] In Exodus 15:2 and Psalm 93:5 forms of it are directly attributed either to God or to his house, and it is also used in many other connections in the Old Testament. The Hebrew word *p'r* [פָּאַר] can refer to God beautifying his people with salvation, and other forms of it speak of ascribing glory to the Lord (I Chron. 22:5).[55] A form of it is used in Isaiah 63:12 to speak of God's arm of glory that went at Moses' right hand to make for himself an everlasting name. The Hebrew word *tob* [טוֹב] (frequently used during the six days of creation – declaring them 'good') is also directly used to speak of the goodness (or beauty) of God himself, as in Exodus 33:18-19, where Moses asks God to show him his glory.[56]

The word *r'h* [רָאָה] (generally to have visions, or a manifestation of the Lord in a particular place – as in Genesis 12:7), appears in various forms in many Old Testament texts, and for example, in Psalm 34:8, the Psalmist is told 'to taste and see that the Lord is good (or beautiful to be seen or experienced)'.[57] It is used to describe the physical beauty of Sarah, Rebecca, and Rachel (cf. Gen. 12:11; 26:7; 29:17).

No beauty

On the contrary, Isaiah 53:2 says that there was 'no beauty' in him to make us desire the suffering servant, who was physically abused for our sakes so terribly that we 'hid our faces from him,' and yet it is the good news of all time that, 'with his stripes we are healed.' All the beauty we believers shall ever have comes from the ugly disfigurement and grief of 'the servant of the LORD.'

It is precisely in this place of 'no beauty' that the people of God have traced the supreme beauty. That is what the seventeenth-century English poet, George Herbert saw as he expressed it in a poem on 'Dulness'. He speaks of Christ in his 'bloody death and undeserved,' and adds: 'Thou art my loveliness, my life, my light, Beauty alone to me...'[58]

John Wesley (1703-1791) in his translation of a hymn of N. von Zinzendorf (1700-1760), sings of how the sight of this strange beauty of the cross transforms those who see it:

---

53. Ibid., 203.

54. Ibid., 5533.

55. Ibid., 6995.

56. Ibid., 3201.

57. Ibid., 8011.

58. George Herbert, 'Dulness' in *George Herbert and the Seventeenth Century Religious Poets*, selected and edited by Mario A. Di Cesare, (W.W. Norton & Company: New York ,1978). A daily devotional guide to Herbert's poetic appreciation of the beauty of Christ in all of his graces and ways is found in Gerrit Scott Dawson *Love Bade Me Welcome: Daily Readings with George Herbert* (Glen Lorien Books: Lenoir, North Carolina, 1997).

Jesus thy blood and righteousness
My beauty are, my glorious dress;
Midst flaming worlds, in these arrayed,
With joy shall I lift up my head.

There are various Hebrew words that directly indicate what all can understand as beauty, such as *shepher* [שֶׁפֶר], which speaks of having 'a beautiful inheritance' in Psalm 16:6,[59] while *tipheret* [תִּפְאֶרֶת] refers to the beauty and majesty of God, as in Psalm 96:6.[60] *noam* [נֹעַם] is ascribed directly to God, as in Psalm 27:4, expressing the desire to behold the beauty of the Lord.[61]

Probably though, *kabod* and *shekinah* come most closely to what the New Testament speaks of as God's glory and brightness (or beauty) - as in John 1:14, Hebrews 1:3, and Revelation 21:23 and 22:5, among many other references in the Apocalypse. And these two concepts, scattered throughout several Old Testament passages, generally lie behind the Greek words employed in crucial texts on beauty or glory in the New Testament, as in John, Hebrews, Revelation, and elsewhere.

New Testament words for beauty usually come through the LXX Translation of the Hebrew Old Testament

Of course, most of the Greek words used in the New Testament come through the LXX, in which the third century B. C. Jewish scholars rendered the Hebrew Torah into Greek. The crucial word in the New Testament for the divine beauty is *doxa* (or 'glory'), although *kalos* [καλος] is also important (to be discussed below). Kittel shows that *doxa* was used some 280 times in the LXX, and that of those renderings, *kabod* lies behind 180 of them.[62] Hence, 'since *kabod* can have the sense of "power," "splendour," "human glory," *doxa* takes on the same meaning.... The *doxa theou* is the "divine glory" which reveals the nature of God in creation and in His acts, which fill both heaven and earth.'[63]

In addition to *doxa*, the Greek word *kalos* is widely used. 'It is most often the [LXX] rendering of *yafeh* [יָפֶה], e.g. Gn. 12:14; 29:17; 39:6; 41:2, etc., often with the addition τῷ εἴδει (יְפַת מַרְאֶה), and thus denoting 'beautiful in respect of outward appearance...'[64] It often means 'morally good' and can be used synonymously with *agathos*.[65] In the Gospels, at times it refers to a 'beautiful' work, such as the woman anointing Jesus in Mark 14:3ff. In John, it is used of Christ as 'the good Shepherd' (or 'beautiful Shepherd').

Beautiful outward appearance is manifest in the glory cloud. This same *shekinah* glory often rested upon the wilderness Tabernacle, and in later days

---

59. Van Gemeren, op cit., 8231.

60. Ibid., 6286.

61. Ibid., 5276.

62. Kittel, op. cit., vol. II, 242.

63. Ibid., 243, 244.

64. Ibid., vol. III, 543.

65. Ibid., 544.

filled Solomon's Temple at its dedication with such holy brightness that the priests had to go running outside it (cf. I Kings 8). The *kabod* and the *shekinah* are partial descriptions of God's own beauty, especially as it radiates from his Triune personal relations into the created order, especially to his chosen people, as Edwards suggested when he spoke of *kabod* as 'communication of this internal glory' (immediately above). The essay 'The Weight of Glory' by C. S. Lewis, which I have already quoted, addressed this topic as well. Whether in terms of glory or weight or lovely form, God's beauty consists in the inner relationships of light, life and love within the Trinity (i.e. known as 'the ontological Trinity'), and then, consequently into the saving economy for the human race within creation (known as 'the economical Trinity').

Inner-trinitarian beauty and creational beauty are often joined

The beauty of the inner Trinitarian relations and the beauty of its shining outwards into the space/time universe through Christ are joined together in various passages, such as Hebrews 1:1-2: '[God] hath in these last days spoken unto us by his Son, whom he hath appointed heir of all things, by whom also he made the worlds; who being the brightness of his glory, and the express image of his person, and upholding all things by the word of his power, when he had by himself purged our sins, sat down on the right hand of the Majesty on high...'[66] The Apostle Paul speaks of this connection between the beautiful within the Trinity and the beautiful derived from him within his created image bearers in the process of redemption: 'For God, who commanded the light to shine out of darkness, hath shined in our hearts, to give the light of the knowledge of the glory of God in the face of Jesus Christ' (II Cor. 4:6), and also, in the immediately preceding chapter: 'But we all with open face, beholding as in a glass the glory of the Lord, are changed unto the same image from glory to glory, even as by the Spirit of the Lord' (II Cor. 3:18).

Varied illustrations of creational beauty in nature and in human creativity

Beauty can be defined not only by heavy significance and outshining radiance, but also by 'comely' or well-proportioned form: perhaps like a very beautiful human face, or the symmetry of an eighteenth-century Georgian manor house in England, constructed, let us say, according to the designs of Palladio or Inigo Jones, or a Low-country South Carolina, Greek-revival plantation mansion with high white columns, supporting an imposing veranda at the end of a long avenue of ancient oak trees,[67] or the master painting of a gorgeous landscape by Constable, or the rendition of a beautiful city (such as Venice) by Canalleto, or a marble statue carved by Michelangelo in Rome or Florence. Such admirably proportioned beauty is seen in the elegant structure of the Chateau of Chenonceaux that with rare loveliness spans its white stone arches over the Loire River in France.

---

66. See Chapter 3 of this volume for detailed exegesis of Hebrews 1.

67. Saint Thomas speaks of the beauty (or 'limited integrity') of a well-constructed building that realizes the architect's ideal (cf. ST I.73.1).

In a new (2013) book on classical art by Scottish artist Charles Harris, *Trust Your Eye* , he suggests that in the more than six hundred years of classical art (i.e. from Giotto – 1267 to 1337, to the nineteenth century French Impressionists), the basis of their beauty is rooted in: "...three essential characteristics: the organic unity of the individual forms, the unity of the whole through mathematical proportions and through the balance and harmony of opposing tensions; beauty with economy; and a description of Life that eliminated the incidental or irrelevant."[68] He adds: "A motivation to become part of the natural world also led to a tradition of unity and composition where everything is seen in relationship to this same harmony, and to represent it in terms of space and light."[69] Harris believes that beautiful painting comes from a certain discovery of 'rightness' "...which conveys itself immediately to the eye and shows where everything is."[70]

Harris asks: "So... why is this great art beautiful?" He answers: "In great Art we do both see and literally experience God's own Light: 'The Light that lighteth every man who cometh into the world. It is the light of honest human intellect or faith; which, when combined with craft skills, makes classical traditional art all the more meaningful to the human eye; without any need for words, its content reaches us naturally and self-evidently. This is not subjective as the beautiful exists everywhere for us all to see."[71]

Or beauty could be traced in a different mode in the gorgeous blue colors in the 'petals' of the circular rose window of the Cathedral of Notre Dame in Paris, ending their great and delicate length with roseate tones, or the stunning bluish hues in some of the splendid long and high windows of Chartres. To change the figure, beautiful and stately proportions could also be seen in the flight of Canadian geese in V-formation across a snow-covered North Carolina upland meadow, or the rising up of a large covey of quail from a cut-over corn field, when frightened by a bird-dog. Or one can see this elegant beauty of movement as a herd of deer splash through a shallow stream in the early twilight, in response to the noise of a farm-truck rattling down the dirt road.

Or in yet a different way, beauty can be traced in the sound of a bird song, the water flowing over Niagara Falls, or a Medieval Plain Song, a Fugue of J. S. Bach, or his 'Saint Matthew Passion,' Handel's 'Messiah,' a Sonata of Mozart, a Symphony of Beethoven, Rachmaninov's 'Vespers' sung by a choir in Saint Sophia Cathedral in Kiev, a melodious rendition of some of the grand African-American 'spirituals' by the Mississippi Mass Choir, or some of the Welsh hymns of William Williams or Titus Lewis, or the pointed Psalms sung by boys' choirs in English Cathedrals and University Chapels, or unaccompanied Scottish Gaelic Psalmody in some of the heavily attended churches in the Hebridean Isle of Lewis. Or one can hear it in the sonorous peals of bells at the stroke of midnight on New Year's morning in cities like Cambridge and Oxford.

---

68. Charles Harris, *Trust Your Eye* (Cambrian Printers, Ltd.: Aberystwth, 2013), 27.

69. Ibid., 31.

70. Ibid., 16.

71. Ibid., 53.

John Eliot Gardiner's recent study of J. S. Bach traces the supreme beauty of Bach's music to the discovery of a certain harmony and mathematical proportion, which is somewhat similar to what Charles Harris says about great classical painting. He says: "For him (i.e. J. S. Bach) invention was an uncovering of possibilities that are already there, rather than something truly original – hence his view that anyone could so as well, provided they were as industrious. God is still the only true creator."[72] Hence, "Perfection for Bach entailed knowledge of 'the most hidden secrets of harmony.'"[73] According to Gardiner, Bach said: "The thorough-bass is the most perfect foundation of music... that results in a well-sounding *Harmonie* to the Honour of God and the permissible delight of the soul."[74] Beethoven described Bach as 'the progenitor of harmony'.[75]

The Old Testament on a few occasions, as we have seen above, speaks of the physical beauty and well-proportioned faces and bodies of such as Sarah, Rebecca, Rachel, Moses, Joseph, Saul, David, Bathsheba, and Absalom, as well as the lovers in the Song of Solomon. Thus Scripture teaches that God created both natural beauty and human beauty, and both of these forms of well-shaped comeliness point upwards to the beauty of God himself.

Augustine defined beauty in this sense of lovely proportion or symmetry, as the harmony between the various elements of an object.[76] Albert the Great combines these aspects of beauty in his definition: 'Beauty consists in the gleaming of substantial or actual form over proportionally arranged parts of matter.'[77] His definition conveys something of the sense of *shekinah*, *kabod*, and 'comeliness' (as conveyed by the Greek: *kalos*).

How can finite creational beauty show us who the infinite Creator is?

We may say of the entire created order what will be said later (following the words of T. F. Torrance of the incarnation of Christ): 'God reveals himself in terms of what is not God.'[78] That is to say that in the incarnation, we see most fully who the Father is, in the created humanity of the Son, and in a similar way, in the entire cosmos we see the shining beauty, stupendous power and brilliant complexity and harmony of the uncreated Light and eternal glory of the Trinity within what is created and temporal.

God is different from his creation; indeed, infinitely so, and yet, he calls it into being, makes space for it, and upholds it in its difference, as a realm in which he will show himself, without either merging with it, or annihilating it. Far from disdaining it, he pours himself out within it to redeem it. And this is where we see him: in creation, in the redemptive

72. John Eliot Gardiner, *Bach: Music in the Castle of Heaven* (Alfred A. Knopf: New York, 2013), 209.

73. Ibid., 216.

74. Ibid., 215.

75. Ibid., 223.

76. See Francesca Aran Murray, *Christ the Form of Beauty: A Study in Theology and Literature* (T & T Clark: Edinburgh, 1995), 211.

77. Albert the Great, *Opusculum de pulchro et bono*, V., 456, quoted in Francesca Aran Murray, op. cit., 211.

78. T. F. Torrance, *Incarnation*, 192.

covenant of grace with Israel and the Church as set forth in Holy Scripture, and above all else, in the Lord Jesus Christ. If granted faith, we see and are transformed by the everlasting beauty of this infinitely glorious God. For all the difference between uncreated Being and created being, and for all the distance between infinity and finitude, God has made a place for us so that what the apostle said to the pagans in first-century Greece – from their own poetry – must be said of us all: 'For in him, we live, and move, and have our being' (Acts 17:28).[79]

But to grasp, in whatever degree, the beauty and glory of the Lord in the created order, in the language of men and in the humanity of Christ, it is necessary to work in terms of *analogy*. That is because the creation is not the Creator, therefore, in order to know him, we have to look through the created order up to him. In other words, when, for example, Psalm 19:1 says, 'The heavens declare the glory of God,' are we to understand that David is saying that the sparkling beauties of the Milky Way are exactly the same as the brightness of the glory of the Being of God? If that be the case, then God himself would be material: perhaps a larger star, or like the theory of the Stoics, a cosmic force of rational, fiery substance, yet still an aspect of the natural realm, and not transcendent to it. But that cannot be right, according to the doctrine of creation given us in Genesis, chapter 1, for his glory was always in action, myriads of ages before the formation of the solar system. And as God himself speaks in Exodus 3:14 to Moses at the burning bush, the 'I AM THAT I AM' depends on nothing outside himself, while everything else directly depends upon him.

Or could it mean that God's glory is so different from that of the stars and galaxies that there is no connection, other than the mere sound of the words? But if that be true, then it would mean nothing to compare these two glories, and hence, we really know nothing of the divine glory when we gaze upon the shining stars in the night sky. If total difference be the case, then why would the writers of Holy Scripture bother to compare God to anything in the created order? It would have absolutely no content.

Or does David mean to say that God's glory is somewhat like that of the beautiful shining stars, but – because he is the creator of them – it could not be exactly the same? That approach certainly seems to be assumed when, in the Psalms, God is compared to a rock, a shepherd, or a hen gathering her chicks under her wings. And this is clearly the case when Christ calls himself 'the door' (John 10:7).

To put it very simply, the history of the doctrine of epistemology (*how knowing is related to being*) indicates three basic approaches to how concepts (or images or visions and prophecies) can convey what they are describing, especially as it comes to what the Bible affirms about the great Creator of all reality. These three different approaches have long been called: (1) *univocal*; (2) *equivocal*, and (3) *analogical*.

(1) Univocal (*with one voice*) assumes that the reality being described (or pictured) is essentially of the same being with those seeing or expressing it.

---

79. This passage is exegeted in detail in vol. 1 of this series, pp. 140-43.

God, for instance, is certainly greater than man who seeks to describe him, but still they are 'under' the same general concept of being. This is a sort of monism that holds to an eternal continuity between the divine and the creaturely; it rejects the biblical doctrine of creation out of nothing, which sees a metaphysical gap between the infinite and the finite; a gap which must be reflected in the way creatures speak of the infinite, so that even their best descriptions cannot be *univocal*. That is because the triune God is not a being, along with the beings of finite things and persons. Rather, he is 'I am that I am' (Exod. 3:14): all things depend on him; he depends on nothing; all beings flow from his creative activity, but he always was, is, and ever shall be. This understanding has to lie behind any accurate usage of human language to express who God is, and that is why the *univocal* cannot be the approach assumed in the Scriptures.

(2) Equivocal (*with the same sound – but with a completely different meaning*): e.g. such as 'knight' and 'night,' which happen to sound alike, but mean completely different things. This assumes a final agnosticism as concerns who or what the divine may be. It (or he) is held to be so different that words or concepts used to describe him get one nowhere.[80] The great twentieth-century scholar of Gnosticism, Hans Jonas, underlined the agnostic basis of Gnosticism: 'The gnostic God...is the totally different, the other, the unknown...this hidden God is a nihilistic conception: no *nomos* [law] emanates from him, no law for nature and thus none for human action as a part of the natural order.'[81]

Similarly, Bishop Demetrios Trakatellis shows in *The Transcendent God of Eugnostos* that the Gnostic god presented by Eugnostos 'has no name' (*Eugnostos* 71, 24-72, 6).[82] Trakatellis further notes that, 'In the *Apocryphon of John*, for instance, the author contends that the supreme God is unnameable because there is no one who existed, before him in order to

---

80. It seems that much of Gnosticism assumed a type of 'equivocalism,' in the sense that God could not really be known, although so many of their remaining writings are so convoluted, that it is hard to be clear on their epistemology. This equivocalism is the case, for instance, in *The Tripartite Tractate* (I, 5): 'This is the nature of the unbegotten one, which does not touch anything else, nor is it joined (to anything) in the manner of something which is limited. Rather, he possesses this constitution, without having a face or a form, things which are understood through perception, which the incomprehensible one transcends. If he is incomprehensible, then it follows that he is unknowable, that he is the one who is inconceivable by any thought, invisible in any thing, ineffable by any word, untouchable by any hand' (James M. Robinson, Director, *The Nag Hammadi Library in English* [Harper & Row Publishers, New York, 1977], 57). Yet, a little later in the same treatise, the Gnostic writer appears to give back (at least partly) what he took away: 'He [also], without falsification, is all of the names.... He it is whom I call the form of the formless, the body of the bodiless, the face of the invisible, the word of [the] unutterable...' (Ibid. , 63). But within a few more lines, the writer is clearly back into the agnostic (equivocal position): 'He is neither divided as a body, nor split up into the names which he has. He is now this, now something else, with each item being different. Yet he is entirely and completely himself...' (Ibid.). It would be difficult to give any content to these dialectical games, which are based on the denial of a clear revelation from God as to who he is.

81. Hans Jonas, *The Message of the Alien God & The Beginnings of Christianity: The Gnostic Religion*, Third Edition (Beacon Press: Boston, MA, 2001), 332.

82. Demetrios Trakatellis, *The Transcendent God of Eugnostos: An Exegetical Contribution to the Study of the Gnostic Texts of Nag Hammadi With a Retroversion of the Lost Original Greek Text of Eugnostos the Blessed*, Translated by Charles Sarelis (Holy Cross Orthodox Press: Brookline, MA, 1991), p. 42.

name him' (*Apocryphon of John II, 1:3, 16-17*).[83] In other words, if God is unnameable, anything we say about him is equivocal.

Any reading of Holy Scripture will indicate, even to a child's mind, that this 'equivocal' approach is **not** the one used by the inspired writers of Holy Scripture. Isaiah's 'Thus saith the Lord' involves a particular content with true information about what the transcendent God is announcing through his prophet to his needy creatures in the finite realm. For example, what God calls 'sin' is not so different from what seventh-century B. C. Israelites knew to be sin, that there is no similar meaning. The threatened judgments are based on the fact that the sinful people knew precisely what God was telling them through the prophet. It was not an equivocal message, for in that case, they could not have been fairly brought into judgment. Or, to go back to Psalm 19:1, David definitely thinks that the beauty of the stars in the evening sky do tell us something important about who God is, and so, he cannot have been speaking in an *equivocal* way.

(3) Analogical (*it is alike in some ways, and different in some ways*).[84] The great theologians, such as St. Thomas Aquinas, have explored analogy in careful detail (see *Summa Theologiae* I.13.3-5). Thomas considers analogy to be 'the application of a concept to different beings in ways that are simply diverse from each other and are only the same in a certain respect, *simpliciter diversa et eadem secundum quid*,' as E. L. Mascall states it.[85]

St. Thomas distinguishes between analogy *duorum ad tertium* and analogy *unius ad alterum* (in *Summa Theologiae* I.xiii.5c and *Summa Contra Gentiles* I.xxxiv). Analogy *duorum ad tertium* does not really work for correct speech about God, for as Mascall points out, this would be 'attributing the same predicate to God and to a creature, [but] there is no being antecedent to God to whom the predicate can apply more formally and properly than it applies to him.'[86] Therefore, the alternative is the right one: *unius ad alterum*. This 'is founded not upon diverse relations which each of the analogates bears to a third, but upon a relation which one of them bears to the other.'[87] He continues:

> In this case the predicate belongs formally and properly to one of the analogates (which is thus not merely *an* analogate but is the *prime* analogate), and only relatively and derivatively to the other...In its theological application, where the analogates concerned are God and a creature, the relation upon which the analogy is based will be that of creaturely causality; creatures are related to God as to his effects...the perfections which are found formally in various finite modes in creatures exist *virtually* in God, that is to say, that he is able to produce them in his creatures...[88]

---

83. Quoted in *Ibid.*, 44.

84. See the helpful discussion of analogy in D. B. Hart, op. cit., 62, 72, 234-35, 247, etc.

85. E. L. Mascall, *Existence and Analogy* (Libra Books, Darton, Longman & Todd Ltd.: Norwich, 1966), 100.

86. Ibid., 101.

87. Ibid.

88. Ibid., 102.

St. Thomas notes that the analogies given to creatures are 'proportional' to God's perfect knowledge of himself in the Logos, and the Logos enlightens us creatures who bear God's image.[89] By that means, we can share in God's knowledge of himself, *analogically*. That is, we do not know the substance of God; our finite knowledge cannot be sufficient to grasp his infinite Being. Yet he has given us metaphors or analogies by which we may truly, though never exhaustively, grasp him (such as Shepherd, Rock, and Light). God is like our fathers and shepherds; he is like mighty rocks and beautiful luminaries, but he is also different, with an infinite difference. God transcends these analogies, but gives them so that we may truly grasp who he is, insofar as is appropriate for creatures. John Calvin called this process of God's stooping low to help us understand who the infinitely great One is, God's merciful 'accommodation' to our human weakness. He compared it to a nurse prattling over the crib of a baby. What God says in Scripture, or what he shows in nature, is not the measure of his all-surpassing greatness, yet these things are truly connected to who he is.[90]

The prime analogy

Ephesians 3:14, 15 speaks of 'the Father...of whom the whole family in heaven and on earth is named...' This means that human parenthood and children in some sense participate in a crucial aspect of the trinitarian life. That is surely the prime *analogy*, from which all other analogies given in creation by means of the Logos are finally rooted.

Bavinck states this point clearly:

> Since here on earth we walk by faith and not by sight we have only an analogical and proportional knowledge of God. We do not have a 'direct or proper idea' of God, but 'an indirect or derived idea,' an idea which is derived from the creaturely realm, but which, though inadequate, is not untrue, in as much as the creature is *God's creature* and hence reveals something of his excellencies.... In its epistemology Scripture, which is theological from beginning to end and derives everything from God, in spite of this fact, rather because of it, ascends to God *from the plane of the universe*, Isa. 40:26; Rom. 1:20. Just because everything is *from* God, everything points back *to* God.[91]

Hence, the Fatherhood and Sonship of God, the glory and beauty of his being and works, are to be discerned *analogically*. That is the constant assumption of the Scriptures, and thereby we know God in truth, but not in infinite fulness. The distance of his infinity always makes room for the reality of our finite experience of him; his distance and difference from us are therefore good news, not bad news.[92]

---

89. Hans Urs Von Balthasar states that 'This is the more true when the realm of the archetypes – the world of ideas, which is the *Logos* of God – becomes man and along with the archetype of man, represents in himself the archetype of the entire cosmos as well' (*The Glory of the Lord – I – Seeing the Form*, 220).

90. John Calvin, *Institutes*, I. xiii.1.

91. H. Bavinck, *The Doctrine of God*, 134.

92. Etienne Gilson summarizes the centrality of analogy in *The Spirit of Medieval Philosophy*:

The prime analogy, given us in the Son who is the Logos (cf. John 1:1-8), is the divinely offered way for us mortals to participate in the immortal glory and beauty of the self-giving of the triune God (2 Pet. 1:4). This is exhibited in Christ's highly priestly prayer in John 17: 'I have manifested thy name unto the men which thou gavest me out of the world; thine they were, and thou gavest them me; and they have kept thy word...'; 'And all mine are thine, and thine are mine; and I am glorified in them...'; 'And the glory which thou gavest me I have given them; that they may be one, even as we are one...' (John 17:6, 10, 22).

How do we reach the Triune Beauty?

Our access to the beauty of the triune God is only through the incarnate Son. Von Balthasar explains: 'The conclusion to be drawn from all this is that, just as we can never attain to the living God in any way except through his Son become man, but in this Son we can really attain to God in himself, so too, we ought never to speak of God's beauty without reference to the form and manner of appearing which he exhibits in salvation history.'[93]

In the words of Jonathan Edwards:

> By this sense of the moral beauty of divine things, is understood the sufficiency of Christ as a mediator; for 'tis only by the discovery of the beauty of the moral perfection of Christ, that the believer is let into the knowledge of the excellency of his person, so as to know anything more of it than the devils do: and 'tis only by the knowledge of the excellency of Christ's person, that any know his sufficiency as a mediator.[94]

This prepares us to think of what Christ, the Father's eternal Son, has brought to us sinful humans in his incarnate person and saving work as Messiah of Israel and Saviour of the world. He has come down to share with us his knowledge of the Father in the Holy Spirit.

III. When Christ Comes Down to us, He brings the Beauty of the Trinity with Him

This is where Christology is rooted: the Father gifts the Son with a world and a bride (the church); the Spirit perfects the creation of the world and the creation of the bride, and the Son gives back these divine gifts to the Father in the fellowship of the Spirit. That is the life of the Holy Trinity: loving, giving and receiving, and giving back the precious gift in infinite love. The world and church, in their appropriate ways, are informed by the Logos, who from the eternal heart of the Father forms and enlightens all of which

---

'In a Christian universe, in which beings are created by Being, every creature is a good and an analogue of the Good. At the root of all this order of relations there lies, therefore, a fundamental relation of analogy which rules every derived relation subsequently set up between creature and Creator' (p. 285).

93. Von Balthasar, op. cit., 124.

94. Jonathan Edwards, *Religious Affections*, ed. John E. Smith (Yale University Press: New Haven, 1959), 125-26.

he is the agent both of creation and of redemption (John 1:3-5, 9). 'The Word was made flesh and dwelt among us' (John 1:14) so that the glory he always had with the Father might be manifested to us (John 17:5-6). In manifesting the divine glory in himself, he causes his people to realize that the glory came from the Father (John 17:7-8), and in the process of sharing in the Son's knowledge of the Father, the people of God are united to the Father through the Son (John 17:21), so that they too share in that glorious beauty of life with God (John 17:22).

What a zeal the Son had for his Father's glory, and what a zeal the Father had for his Son's glory! We see this zeal in the Gospel of John at a major turning point in Christ's ministry, when, on Palm Sunday, he is facing being glorified in death. Jesus prays: 'Now is my soul troubled; and what shall I say? Father, save me from this hour: but for this cause came I unto this hour. Father, glorify thy name. Then there came a voice from heaven, saying, I have both glorified it, and will glorify it again' (John 12:27-28). It is as though we are overhearing the voices of the economical Trinity saying the same thing as they did (and do) in the ontological Trinity: each Person is determined to glorify the other!

The zeal of Father and Son to glorify one another is the same when Christ goes out into the night at the conclusion of the Last Supper: 'Therefore, when he was gone out, Jesus said, Now is the Son of man glorified, and God is glorified in him. If God be glorified in him, God shall also glorify him in himself, and shall straightway glorify him' (John 13:31-32). But ages before the Passion week, the Father had shaped the entire created order in the interests of the cosmic headship of his eternal Son, who would be both agent of creation (John 1:3), and then its agent of redemption, as the Apostle Paul writes:

> Giving thanks unto the Father...who hath delivered us from the power of darkness, and hath translated us into the kingdom of his dear Son: In whom we have redemption through his blood, even the forgiveness of sins: Who is the image of the invisible God, the firstborn of every creature: For by him were all things created, that are in heaven, and that are in earth, visible and invisible, whether they be thrones, or dominions, or principalities, or powers: all things were created by him, and for him: And he is before all things, and by him all things consist. And he is the head of the body, the church: who is the beginning, the firstborn from the dead: that in all things he might have the pre-eminence (Col. 1:12-18).

The beauty of the Lord in the Book of Revelation

The Book of Revelation takes an overview of the history and meaning of the creation, and in so doing, it focuses attention on Christ, from beginning to end. In the first three chapters of the Apocalypse, the risen Christ is the center of the Church. In chapter four, he is the center of the activity and purposes of the Throne of God in glory. In chapter five, he is the one who opens the Lamb's book of life, in which are the predestinated purposes of God, including the salvation of all the elect. In Chapters six to nineteen, 'the King of saints' (Rev. 15:3) is orchestrating all that happens within the nations, from his resurrection to his return. In chapter 20, he is in charge of all the details of 'the first resurrection' (that period – also known as 'the millennium', when multitudes from the Gentile nations pass from death to spiritual life, by faith in the preaching of the Gospel of Jesus. This period takes place between the first and second comings of Christ). In chapters twenty and twenty-one, the Lamb is the center of eternal glory, which he shares with all his people for evermore.

Revelation often shows how the glory that flows over from one Person of the blessed Trinity to the others, also finally encapsulates the people of God. For instance, 'the four and twenty elders' (representing Old Testament Israel and New Testament Church) join the four living heavenly creatures as they give '...glory and honour and thanks to him that sat on the throne, who liveth for ever and ever, The four and twenty elders fall down before him that liveth for ever and ever, and cast their crowns before the throne, saying, Thou art worthy to receive glory and honor and power: for thou hast created all things and for thy pleasure they are and were created' (Rev. 4:9-11). They came to see the glory, and it functioned, as it were, as the agent that made them Christians, as they beheld the Father's glory in the face of Jesus: 'But we all with open face beholding as in a glass the glory of the Lord, are changed unto the same image from glory to glory even as by the Spirit of the Lord' (II Cor. 3:18).

At the end of space/time history, we shall see, with the heavenly creatures and the saints of all ages above, that every aspect of creation has pointed to Christ's glory, and that he turns it all back to the glory of Father and Spirit. It is the same with the written Word, which has been given by Father, Son and Holy Spirit: every part of it one way or another points to the same divine trinitarian glory. From the Old Testament prophets all through the New Testament, the glory that Christ should achieve through his sufferings has been set forth, as Peter tells us:

> Of which salvation the prophets have inquired and searched diligently who prophesied of the grace that should come unto you: Searching what, or what manner of time the Spirit of Christ which was in them did signify, when it testified beforehand the sufferings of Christ, and the glory that should follow. Unto whom it was revealed, that not unto themselves, but unto us, they did minister the things, which are now reported unto you by them that have preached the gospel unto you with the Holy Ghost sent down from heaven; which things the angels desire to look into (I Peter 1:10-12).

The necessity of sensibility

As the Holy Scriptures in their detailed ways lead us up to Christ, so from the other direction, we may say, with St. Jerome, that 'Christ is the key to the Scriptures'.[95] That is, the Old and New Testaments lead us to Christ, and then, with faith in Christ, in the fellowship of the Holy Spirit poured

---

95. Jerome takes the passage in Revelation 5, where only the Lamb can take the saving action to open the Book of Life, and applies it in an unusual way. He says that only Christ can enable us to understand the Scriptures (cf. *In Is.* 29, 11 – 332A). See Pierre Jay, *L'Exégèse de Saint Jerome d'Àpres son 'Commentaire sur Isaie'* (Etudes Augustiniennes: Paris, 1985), 388.

out on the Church, we can make sense of the Scriptures, which would otherwise be closed. And with that in mind, we seek together the face of the Lord through the Word and Spirit; that is, it is only in union with Christ that we know Christ and understand his words. Union with Christ (which brings us into his knowledge of the Father) comes about with regeneration. Regeneration gives us the ability *to perceive* who God is.

It is a strong emphasis in Edwards' teaching on beauty that 'sensibility' is necessary in humans in order to see the beauty of God's Being, and then to receive it. It takes the New Birth in order to grasp it and to be grasped, and transformed by it: 'The first effect of the power of God in the heart in REGENERATION is to give the heart a divine taste or sense; to cause it to have a relish of the loveliness and sweetness of the supreme excellency of the Divine nature...'[96] Elsewhere he explains:

> Spiritual understanding primarily consists in this sense, or taste of the moral beauty of divine things; so that no knowledge can be called spiritual, any further than it arises from this, and has this in it. But secondarily, it includes all that discerning and knowledge of things of religion, which depends upon and flows from such a sense. When the true beauty, and amiableness of the holiness or true moral good that is in divine things, is discovered to the soul, it as it were opens a new world to its view.[97]

This saving insight granted to believers, is a result of their graciously granted union with Christ in his humanity, which was baptized in the same Spirit that he communicates to his church. Commenting on a statement in Athanasius' Third Festal Letter, 'We will become partakers of Christ if we hold fast to the Spirit' (3.4), Khaled Anatolios writes: '...the incarnate Word enables us to receive the Spirit through his own reception of the Spirit in his humanity. Through the correlated activity of Son and Spirit, we become "worded" and "sons" in the Son and thus are incorporated into the Son's stance of self-offering to the Father.'[98]

In his *Charity and Its Fruits*, Edwards shows that the difference between 'the faith' of devils and that of true believers is that demons see only God's greatness, wisdom, and omnipotence, '...yet they see and feel nothing of his loveliness.'[99] No doubt, Edwards is thinking of James 2:19: '... the devils also believe, and tremble.' But in the miracle of regeneration: 'It is this sight of the divine beauty of Christ that bows the will and draws the hearts of men.'[100] This is another way of expressing the teaching of Christ to Nicodemus: '...Except a man be born again, he cannot see the kingdom of God' (John 3:3). But once you see it, you wish to invite the world (in the words of David): 'O taste and see that the LORD is good: blessed is

---

96. Jonathan Edwards, 'A Treatise on Grace,' in *Selections from the Unpublished Writings of Jonathan Edwards of America*, ed. A. B. Grosart (Edinburgh, 1865), quoted in Delattre, op. cit., 4.

97. J. Edwards, *Religious Affections*, 273.

98. Khaled Anatolios, *The Development and Meaning of Trinitarian Doctrine: Retrieving Nicea* (Baker Academic: Grand Rapids, MI, 2011), 148.

99. Edwards, *Charity and Its Fruits*, 135.

100. J. Edwards, 'True Grace,' *Works*, 4, 469-70, quoted in Delattre, op. cit., 205.

the man that trusteth in him' (Psalm 34:8). That is the prayer with which this second volume is written, and it is the spirit in which Joseph Conder (1789-1855) composed this hymn:

Thou art the Everlasting Word,
　　The Father's only Son;
God manifestly seen and heard,
　　And heaven's beloved One!

In Thee most perfectly expressed,
　　The Father's glories shine:
Of the full Deity possessed,
　　Eternally divine.

True image of the Infinite,
　　Whose essence is concealed;
Brightness of uncreated light.
　　The heart of God revealed:

But the high mysteries of Thy Name
　　An angel's grasp transcend:
The Father only – glorious claim! –
　　The Son can comprehend:

Throughout the universe of bliss
　　The centre Thou and sun,
The eternal theme of praise is this,
　　To heaven's beloved One:

Worthy, O Lamb of God, art Thou,
　　That every knee to Thee should bow!

Therefore, in the next section (our first chapter) we study how Old and New Testaments witness to Christ, including the giving of his names and titles, in preparation for the setting forth of his Person and work. As the Lord has taken every detail into account in ordering all aspects of creation to speak of his Son, so must we seek to examine, in our necessarily limited way, the details – minor and major – concerning the Bible's witness to who Christ is. The same God who ordered creation to point above all else to Christ in his beauty, also gave his inspired Word in such a way that all of its varied, and yet harmonious parts, set forth Christ, as Jesus himself stated: 'Search the Scriptures, for in them ye think ye have eternal life; and they are they which testify of me' (John 5:39).

Throughout the New Testament witness, we shall always be meeting the blessed Trinity, for as Jonathan Edwards said: 'God is glorified within Himself these two ways: 1. By appearing or being manifest to Himself in His own perfect idea, or in His Son who is the brightness of His glory. 2. By enjoying and delighting in Himself, by flowing forth in infinite love and delight towards Himself, or in His Holy Spirit. [Misc. 448].'[101]

---

101. Delattre, op. cit, 155.

Who the Triune God is, in himself, and then towards us, is the truest expression of all beauty. This vision of a Christ who comes forth to us from the beautiful and beatific life of the Trinity, and lifts us up to share in it by divine grace, has motivated the writing of this volume. And if several of the Church Fathers and Reformers were right, prophetic foreshadowings of that vision can be traced in a number of the Messianic Psalms. One of them, Psalm 45, foresaw the coming of the beautiful Saviour from the heart of God, so as to take us back up to him:

> Thou'rt fairest of all men;
> > Grace in thy lips doth flow:
> And therefore blessings evermore
> > on thee doth God bestow.
>
> Of myrrh and spices sweet
> > a smell thy garments had,
> Out of the iv'ry palaces,
> > whereby they made thee glad.
>
> They shall be brought with joy,
> > and mirth on every side,
> Into the palace of the King,
> > and there they shall abide.[102]

---

102. Psalm 45:2,8,15, from *The Scottish Metrical Psalter*.

PART ONE

THE TRINTARIAN CONTEXT
OF THE PERSON AND WORK OF CHRIST

In light of the Father's testimony to the Son, given us through the Scriptures which are inspired by the Holy Spirit, we consider the witness of Old and New Testaments to Christ (ch. I); the Names and Titles of Christ in Old and New Testaments (ch. II); Crucial passages on the Lord's Incarnation, Atonement, Resurrection and Ascension: John 1:1-18; Philippians 2:5-11; Hebrews 1:1-4, and Revelation 5:1-14 (ch. III), which prepare us for the accurate expression of their teaching in the Church's doctrine of the Hypostatic Union of the two natures of Christ in one Person (ch. IV). Chapter V discusses significant details of the Church's further understanding of the Hypostatic Union through the meaning of anhypostasia, enhypostasia, two wills, the communication of idioms, the communion of natures, Christ's human development, Mary as Theotokos, and the 'extra Calvinisticum.' Chapter VI considers the epistemology of Immanuel Kant, which for much of the world since his time, constitutes the dividing line between believing and non-believing accounts of Christology, and even when not specifically mentioned, is often an underlying issue in any interpretation of the person and work of Christ. Chapters VII to X survey the 'first state' of the incarnate Christ: his Humiliation, and Chapters XI and XII study the 'second state': his Exaltation.

CHAPTER I

THE WITNESS OF OLD AND NEW TESTAMENTS TO CHRIST

The first confession of the Church is that Jesus Christ is Lord. Lord, and other names, take us immediately back to the preparation for his coming in the Old Testament, which points the way to his being understood as agent of creation, last Adam, and primal image of God. He can be grasped only in the context of the history of Israel, as Head of the New Covenant, as Prophet, Priest, and King, and as victor over Satan and all the powers of evil. When we face the Lord Jesus Christ, we are brought face to face with the Triune God. In Christ we see what the being and actions of the eternal Trinity are like in space and time.

'Jesus Christ is Lord'

'Jesus Christ is Lord' (Rom. 10:9) is the first confession of the Christian Church, and one that can only be made by the power of the Holy Spirit, who comes from the Father through the Son (cf. I Cor. 12:3). The very name 'Christ' means 'anointed one,' and takes us back into the Old Testament, without which we can never make sense of him whom to know is eternal life (cf. John 17:3).

The Old Testament Scriptures prepared over the long ages for their fulfillment in Christ, the Messiah, who, as the New Testament clearly reveals, is 'one God, and one mediator between God and man, the man Christ Jesus' (I Tim. 2:5), who was born 'in the fullness of the time' (Gal. 4:4). Here in chapter I, we study the background of the Old Testament preparation for Christ, from the work of creation, to the person of Adam, and especially through the history of Israel.

Old Testament Preparation for the Incarnation

Lessons from the risen Christ on the road to Emmaus

In his post-resurrection appearance to Cleopas and another disciple on 'Easter Sunday' afternoon on the way to Emmaus, the risen Lord dealt with their consternation over the suffering and death of him 'whom they had trusted would redeem Israel'(Luke 24:21). The brutal defeat of the very one who was to restore the Kingdom of God in Israel seemed to disqualify him from successful completion of that much longed-for mission. Yet after that bitter disappointment, strange things had happened, for 'certain women of our company' found his tomb empty and were told by angels that he was alive (Luke 24:22-24).

The risen Christ, who had not yet revealed his identity, took them to the Old Testament scriptures to show that the promised Messiah first had to suffer, and only then enter into his glory (Luke 24:26). That is to say, the messianic expectations of that time (even among the disciples) had grasped only one side of the scriptural truth about Messiah, the true King of the Kingdom: before he was manifested as the 'conquering lion of the tribe of Judah'(Rev. 5:5), he must first fulfill his office as suffering 'Lamb of God that taketh away the sins of the world,' as John the Baptist had announced at the beginning of Jesus' public ministry upon his baptism in the Jordan River (John 1:29).

'And beginning at Moses and all the prophets, he expounded unto them in all the scriptures the things concerning himself' (Luke 24:27). This seems to indicate that he took them through the entire Old Testament canon in order to show them how his incarnate life, suffering, death and glorious physical resurrection were already set forth by Moses and the other inspired writers of what was at that time the only Scriptural record. How we would like to have overheard that conversation! Paul's preaching in the synagogues of the dispersion must have been similar, for he mentions the necessity of Christ's first having to suffer, then enter into his glory (cf. Acts 17:2-3).

Christ as Agent of Creation

Yet we certainly get strong hints of what the Lord must have pointed out that afternoon as we study the way the New Testament writers employ the Old Testament scriptures to show us who Jesus is and what his work involved. John 1:3 indicates that Christ, the Son of the Father, was the very agent of creation, while Colossians 1:16-17 states it in even more detail: 'For by him were all things created, that are in heaven, and that are in earth, visible and invisible, whether they be thrones, or dominions, or principalities, or powers: all things were created by him, and for him; And he is before all things, and by him all things consist.' Hebrews 1:2, 10 tell us that '[God] hath in these last days spoken unto us by *his* Son, whom he hath appointed heir of all things, by whom also he made the worlds... [unto the Son he saith] and, Thou, Lord, in the beginning hast laid the foundation of the earth; and the heavens are the works of thine hands.' Revelation 4:11 summarizes the entire history of the cosmos in terms of the pleasure of the incarnate Lord: 'Thou are worthy, O Lord, to receive glory and honour and power; for thou hast created all things, and for thy pleasure they are and were created.'

Church Fathers, Medieval Christian scholars, and later Reformers understood the plural name of God (אֱלֹהִים) that takes a singular verb (בָּרָא in the Qal stem) to have been a sort of prophetic hint of the Trinitarian activity in the original creation. And they argued similarly for a Trinitarian reference in the consultative form of the verb 'let us make' immediately prior to the creation of mankind in the divine image (Gen. 1:26). That is certainly not the reading of rabbinical scholarship, but it has a long history in the church! In this regard, it is instructive to hear echoes of the debate between Justin Martyr, the Christian apologist, and the Jewish scholar, Trypho, on this matter as far back as the second century A.D.[1]

Creation by means of 'wisdom' and the interpretation of Proverbs 8:22

Some Church Fathers made much of the pre-incarnate Christ as the wisdom of God, through whom God the Father made the worlds. But this was not without its downside, as the fourth-century Arians, who denied the eternal pre-existence of Christ, used the passage in Proverbs 8:22 concerning the connection of wisdom with the divine work of creation to argue that, if Christ is wisdom, then he is subordinate to the Father and is finally a sort of higher creature. Basil the Great replied that the translation of Proverbs 8:22 should not be 'the Lord created me as the beginning of his ways for all his works,' but 'the Lord *possessed* me as the beginning of his ways for all his works.'[2] 'Possessed' is definitely a possible option for translation, but the weight of the evidence, surveyed below, tends towards 'created.'

Athanasius gives an exegetical survey of this verse in *Contra Arianos*.[3] He accepts the verb as meaning 'created', but argues that it refers to the created humanity of Christ, which was essential to our salvation. Similarly, Gregory Nazianzus accepted 'created' as the operative verb in Proverbs 8:22. But then he attempted to explain it so as to retain the eternal existence of the Son, who is often called 'wisdom'.[4]

---

1. Justin Martyr, *Dialogue with the Jew Trypho*.

2. Basil, *Against Eunomius* 2.20.

3. See Athanasius, Athanasius also suggests that Prov. 8:22 (as in the LXX) could be thought of as the 'created' humanity of Christ, which is essential for our salvation: *Contra Arianos*, 2:18-44.

4. Gregory of Nazianzus writes in his *Fourth Theological Oration, Which is the Second Concerning the Son (XXX) II:* In their eyes the following is only too ready to hand 'The Lord created me at the beginning of His ways with a view to His works.' How shall we meet this? Shall we bring an accusation against Solomon, or reject his former words because of his fall in after-life? Shall we say that the words are those of Wisdom herself, as it were of Knowledge and the Creator-word, in accordance with which all things were made? For Scripture often personifies many even lifeless objects; as for instance, 'The Sea said' so and so; and, 'The Depth saith, It is not in me;' and 'The Heavens declare the glory of God;' and again a command is given to the Sword; and the Mountains and Hills are asked the reason of their skipping. We do not allege any of these, though some of our predecessors used them as powerful arguments. But let us grant that the expression is used of our Saviour Himself, the true Wisdom. Let us consider one small point together. What among all things that exist is unoriginate? The Godhead. For no one can tell the origin of God, that otherwise would be older than God. But what is the cause of the Manhood, which for our sake God assumed? It was surely our Salvation. What else could it be? Since then we find here clearly both the Created and the Begetteth Me, the argument is simple. Whatever we find joined with a cause we are to refer to the Manhood, but all that is absolute and unoriginate we are to reckon to the account of His Godhead. Well, then, is not this 'Created' said in connection with a cause? He created Me, it so says, as the beginning of His ways, with a view to His works. Now, the Works of His Hands are verity and judgment; for whose sake He was anointed with Godhead; for this anointing is of the Manhood; but the 'He begetteth Me' is not connected with a cause; or it is for you to shew the adjunct. What argument then will disprove that Wisdom is called a creature, in connection with the

The most reasonable approach seems to lie in the consideration that this remarkable piece of poetry in Proverbs 8 is a meditation on the relation of God to the wisdom by which he created the world and is not intended to be a precise statement of the relationship of the Lord to one of his attributes, or (in Trinitarian terms) of the relationship of the Father and the Son in the work of creation. Rather, it is suggestive, evocative, and 'inner-connective' in the way of poetry. In that context, wisdom can be thought of as a sort of characteristic of God, or even a companion of God in his work. Something like that seems to be the case in *Sirach* 24:1-28, where Wisdom is 'the breath of God,' created before everything else, and also connected to the Shekinah glory and the Law (Torah). Philo also spoke of wisdom as the 'beginning and image of God' (*De Leg. All.* I.43), by whose agency the world was completed (*De Fuga* 109), and wrought by divine wisdom (*Heres* 199).

So, when God in wisdom created the cosmos, it could poetically be said that the first thing he brought forth was wisdom, without one expecting to find in this poem (in terms of later 'prosaic' doctrinal teaching) precise formulations of distinctions within the Godhead that would have to wait until the coming of Christ and the outpouring of the Holy Spirit. As B.B. Warfield wrote: 'The revelation [i.e. of the Trinity] in word must needs wait upon the revelation in deed…'[5] James Dunn summarizes the background of wisdom in Judaism as it prepared the way for Christological teaching:

> What pre-Christian Judaism said of Wisdom and Philo also of the Logos, Paul and the others say of Jesus. The role that Proverbs, ben Sira, etc. ascribe to Wisdom, these earliest Christians ascribe to Jesus… Paul seems to make the identification explicit in so many words when he proclaims 'Christ the power of God and the wisdom of God' (I Cor. 1:24; also 1:30).[6]

And Larry Hurtado points out the parallel structure of word and wisdom in *Wisdom of Solomon* 9:1-2 as an illustration of this process.[7]

Yet it is significant that Irenaeus, the greatest Biblical theologian of the second century, does not use Proverbs 8:22 to point to Christ, nor does Cyril of Alexandria, the great theologian of the fourth century. One has to study other passages than Proverbs 8 to answer such questions.[8]

Two Adams

The Old Testament sets forth Adam as head of the human race (cf. Genesis 1:27-28; 2:18-25, and possibly Hosea 6:7, if one translates 'Adam' as the

---

lower generation, but Begotten in respect of the first and more incomprehensible?

5. B. B. Warfield, 'The Biblical Doctrine of the Trinity' in *Biblical Foundations*, 91. Yet, as he points out, as the Old Testament advanced over the years, there was increasingly a 'hypostatization' or 'personification' of such realities as word, breath, and wisdom, in which God and some of his activities (or attributes) are to some degree both identified and distinguished.

6. James D. G. Dunn, *Christology in the Making: A New Testament Inquiry into the Origins of the Doctrine of the Incarnation* (Wm B. Eerdmans: Grand Rapids, [1980] 1996), 167.

7. Larry Hurtado, *Lord Jesus Christ*, 366.

8. For a study of the relationship of late Jewish concepts of wisdom and Christ's preexistence, see Martin Hengel, *The Son of God: The Origin of Christianity and the History of Jewish-Hellenistic Religion*, transl. John Bowden (Philadelphia: Fortress, 1976), 69-74.

specific person, rather than rendering it as the generic – 'humankind'). Genesis 3 makes clear that all our true problems – alienation from God and from one another, death and judgment – go back to our first father's 'original sin' (Gen. 3:6-20). This adamic theme is taken up particularly by the Apostle Paul in Romans 5:12-21 and I Corinthians 15:21-22, 44-49. He presents Christ as the Last Adam, who recapitulates the fallen person and work of the First Adam. 'For if by one man's offence death reigned by one; much more they which receive abundance of grace and of the gift of righteousness shall reign in life by one, Jesus Christ... For as by one man's disobedience many were made sinners, so by the obedience of one shall many be made righteous' (Rom. 5:17, 19). 'And so it is written, the first man Adam was made a living soul; the last Adam was made a quickening spirit' (I Cor. 15:45).

Dunn points out '...how Hebrews presents a classic statement of Adam Christology in Heb. 2:6-18... Christ as the one in whom God's original plan for man finally (or eschatologically) came to fulfillment – that is in Christ the exalted-after-suffering one (the last Adam).'[9]

The comparison and contrast between the two Adams in a soteriological sense was explored more fully by the great second-century theologian, Irenaeus of Lyon, than by any other. Irenaeus says that as the first Adam had led the human race astray, so the Word comes as the last Adam to bring it back to God. Irenaeus writes with a Trinitarian understanding, 'the Word arranging after a new manner the advent in the flesh, that he might bring back to God that human nature which had departed from God.'[10]

> For I have shown that the Son of God did not then begin to exist, being with the Father from the beginning; but when he became incarnate, and was made man, he commenced afresh the long line of human beings, and furnished us, in a brief comprehensive manner, with salvation; so that what we had lost in Adam – namely, to be according to the image and likeness of God – that we might recover in Christ Jesus.[11]

He had to be true flesh because it was Adam (a fleshly being) who had sinned and whose race needed redemption:

> ...and because death reigned over the flesh, it was right that through the flesh it should lose its force and let man go free from its oppression. So *the Word was made flesh* that through that very flesh which sin had ruled and domesticated, it should lose its force and be no longer in us.[12]

Irenaeus continues, 'He [God the Father] sent his creative word, who in coming to deliver us, came to the very place and spot in which we had lost life.... and hallowed our birth and destroyed death, loosing those same fetters in which we were enchained.'[13]

---

9. Dunn, op. cit., 208.

10. Irenaeus, *Adversus Haereses* 3.10.2.

11. Ibid., 3.18.1.

12. Irenaeus, *Demonstration of the Apostolic Preaching* 31.

13. Ibid. 38.

Dominion

The dominion given by the Lord to Adam over the rest of the created order (Gen. 1:28) is celebrated by David in Psalm 8. Yet Hebrews 2 puts the actual carrying out of this dominion by fallen mankind into a redemptive, Christocentric context (Heb. 2: 5-9).

The Image of God

The original creation by God of humankind in his own image is taken up by the New Testament as really having been in the image of Christ, the Son of God, who, in due season, through his redemptive person and work does all that is necessary to restore us twisted ones back into the beauty of the original divine image (cf. Ephesians 4:24 and Colossians 3:10).

Although much of his teaching was rejected by the church, nonetheless many of the Ante-Nicene fathers took the same line as Origen in positing a necessary difference between the original image of God (Christ) and mankind, who are 'in his image':

> He [the antichristian philosopher Celsus] failed to see the difference between what is 'in the image of God' (Gen. 1:27) and His image (Col. 1:15). He did not realize that the image of God in the firstborn of all creation, the very Logos and truth, and further, the very wisdom Himself, being 'the image of his goodness' (Wisd. of Sol. vii.26), whereas man was made 'in the image of God,' and furthermore, every man of whom Christ is head is God's image and glory (I Cor. 11:3,7).[14]

Hence, Christ is the Father's true and original image, whereas mankind are copies of the Son's likeness. Christ, then, is the only one who is able to restore the original image of God back to those in whom it was twisted by sin.[15]

John Calvin denies any substantive difference between 'image' and 'likeness,'[16] but still teaches that Christ is the original image, of which man is the copy. After referring to the image of God having been imparted to the newly created Adam, he adds:

> All men unanimously admit that Christ was even then the image of God. Hence whatever excellence was engraved upon Adam, derived from the fact

---

14. Origen, *Contra Celsum* VI. 63, translated with notes by Henry Chadwick (Cambridge University Press: Cambridge, 1980), 378.

15. Barth, in 3/2 Section 41, seems to interpret the parallelism between 'image' (צֶלֶם) and 'likeness' (דְּמוּת) of Genesis 1:26 in this fashion:

> But this is more simply expressed if we go back immediately to the object of this copy and pattern of this imitation, to God Himself, and therefore translate *tselem* as 'original' and *Demuth* as 'prototype.' At any rate, the point of the text is that God willed to create man as a being corresponding to His own being – in such a way that He Himself (even if in His knowledge of Himself) is the original and prototype, and man the copy and imitation.

Whether the parallelism between 'image' and 'likeness' actually carries this difference, I am not sure, but at least his overall point is well taken that Christ is the true and original image of God, and mankind are copies or likenesses of that image of him 'through whom all things were created' (cf. John 1:3).

16. Calvin, *Institutes* I.xv.3.

that he approached the glory of his Creator through the only-begotten Son. 'So man was created in the image of God' [Gen. 1:27]; in him the Creator himself willed that his own glory be seen as in a mirror. Adam was advanced to this degree of honor, thanks to the only-begotten Son.[17]

Calvin also teaches the restoration of the effaced image in mankind in and through the redemption of Christ:

> There is no doubt that Adam, when he fell from his state, was by this defection alienated from God. Therefore, even though we grant that God's image was not totally annihilated and destroyed in him, yet it was so corrupted that whatever remains is frightful deformity. Consequently, the beginning of our recovery of salvation is in that restoration which we obtain through Christ, who also is called the Second Adam for the reason that he restores us to true and complete integrity... the end of regeneration is that Christ should reform us to God's image.[18]

Saint Thomas Aquinas, however, does not teach that the original image of God is in Christ, but rather, following Saint Augustine, that the whole Trinity *is* the image.[19]

Much of the main thrust of the New Testament is on the divine intention to restore the image (whether one takes it primarily of Christ, or of the whole Trinity). James Dunn puts 'image of God' in an eschatological context, in terms of Christ's appointment as the Last Adam:

> More significant is the eschatological thrust of the most closely related passages – the transformation of believers into the image of Christ or of God as the goal of the whole process of salvation which climaxes in resurrection (2 Cor. 3:18-5.5; compare particularly Rom. 8:29; I Cor. 15:49; also Phil. 3:21). In this motif the image which Christ bears (or is) is that of the last Adam, Christ as fulfilling the original purpose God had in making man to be his image (Gen. 1:26).[20]

Some far-fetched references

For the sake of space, I refrain from mentioning some of the untenable and far-fetched references (in my viewpoint) made by some Church Fathers to Christ in the Old Testament, such as the claim of Justin Martyr and others that the LXX version of Deuteronomy 30:15 (cf. Justin's *First Apology*, c. 32) was speaking of Christ reaching out his hands on the cross, or the *Letter of Clement of Rome*, stating that the scarlet cord of Rahab pointed to the blood

---

17. Ibid., II.xii.6.

18. Ibid., I.xv.4.

19. 'Thomas does not actually indicate any awareness that certain Greek Fathers held that man is the image of the divine Son. His reply to this theory is largely a paraphrase of Augustine's refutation of a similar theory whose origin Augustine does not bother to name [de Trin. 12.6.7]. Thomas follows Augustine's careful exegesis of Genesis 1:26-27, by which he shows that God the Trinity made man to the image of God the Trinity [Thomas, S. T., q.93, a.5, ad 4m].' See: D. Juvenal Merriell, *To the Image of the Trinity: A Study in the Development of Aquinas' Teaching* (Pontifical Institute of Medieval Studies: Toronto, 1990), 201.

20. James D.G. Dunn, *Jesus, Paul and the Law: Studies in Mark and Galatians* (Westminster/John Knox Press: Louisville, KY, 1990), 97.

of Christ (c. 12), or the bells on the priests' robes prefiguring the movement of the apostles (*Dialogue with the Jew Trypho*, xl). There is more than enough substantial material reaching forward to Christ in the Old Testament to keep us from creatively manufacturing allegorical prefigurements of the Lord, much as some of the apologists loved doing so!

Typology and Allegory

What is in view here is the difference between *typology* and *allegory*. In brief, *typology* (as used by the Church Fathers), in discovering an analogy between events or persons in the Old and New Testaments, points out that the same operation of God's providence is displayed in the Old Testament *type* and the New Testament *antitype* (or *archetype*). Paul does this in I Corinthians 10, where he sees a typological analogy between 'the baptism' of the children of Israel in the sea unto Moses (vv. 1, 2) and baptism unto Christ. The author of the Epistle to the Hebrews draws a typological connection between the Old Testament tabernacle and the human nature of Christ, thus explaining the one by the other.

Allegory, however, speaks of one thing in terms of its meaning something else, with very little control over the derivation of the meaning, and at times very little concern for the reality or historicity of that which is allegorized. The Christian apologists did a great deal of this, and, as Jean Daniélou suggests, were probably influenced by the allegorization of the Homeric stories as carried through by the Middle Platonists.[21] Philo Judaeus used allegory to make biblical stories acceptable in the Hellenistic culture. He was heavily followed by such as Origen of Alexandria, who, rather than relying on the literal meaning of the text, put forward three levels of interpretation: the literal, the moral and the spiritual. These three were supposedly like the human body, soul, and spirit. This methodology gave his imagination free reign in coming up with 'spiritual' meanings. To a lesser degree, Augustine made some use of allegorism. At the time of Augustine's conversion, he had been somewhat influenced by Origen as well.[22] Hence, the 'School of Alexandria' tended to allegory, which the rival 'School of Antioch' rejected in favor of typology, in a more sober sort of exegesis. Theodore of Mopsuestia, for instance, argued that '[o]ne ought to learn the sense of what is written... there is only a single sense in all of the divine scriptures' (*Fragments syriaque*, 13/17-18).[23] McLeod explains:

> First, Theodore required that a true type had to be acknowledged as such in Scripture...Theodore maintains that it is this that distinguishes a type from an allegory. For an allegory's meaning is derived not from within Scripture, but

21. In the West, Jean Daniélou points out that Hippolytus of Rome always has a pejorative sense when he speaks of allegory. See: Jean Daniélou, *Message évangelique et culture héllénistique* (Paris, 1961), 73-101.

22. György Heidl, *Origen's Influence on the Young Augustine. A Chapter of the history of Origenism* (Gorgias Press: Piscataway, NJ, 2003).

23. Quoted in Frederick G. McLeod, S.J., *The Roles of Christ's Humanity in Salvation: Insights from Theodore of Mopsuestia* (The Catholic University of America Press: Washington, DC, 2005), 35.

from the imaginative speculations of the exegete. This indicates, moreover, that the type and its archetype (or its antitype), which constitute the two ends or poles of a relationship, must both be historical realities related in the Scriptures.[24]

It is not strictly true to history to say that the East followed allegory while the West followed typology in interpreting the Scriptures. That probably became a general tendency, yet the great Western Fathers Hilary, Augustine and Jerome used both typology and allegory, whereas the Eastern Father Cyril of Alexandria was critical of allegory.[25] His works *Glaphyra* and *De Adoratione* criticize allegory in favor of typology. Following the Church Fathers, John Calvin rightly states that '[a]llegories ought not to go beyond the limits set by the rule of Scripture, let alone suffice as the foundation of any doctrines.'[26] In his *Commentary on Galatians*, Calvin interprets Paul's statement in reference to Abraham's two wives, 'Which things are an allegory' (Gal. 4:24), as really being a *type*, rather than a true allegory: 'Sinai is called Hagar, because it is a type or figure, as the Passover was of Christ.'[27]

The key point of typology is based on the historical/revelational analogy between what God was already doing in Israel and what he would do in Christ. That is to say, God did things in Israel that were analogous to what he would do in Christ. Exodus and Passover, for instance, were setting forth a pattern in Israel's history in analogy to what would be accomplished in the death and resurrection of Christ. This was not allegory (fictitious stories invented to covey some kind of spiritual truth, which would need to be allegorized), but historical truth that presaged – in its *sensus literalis* – what would literally be accomplished in the Incarnate Christ through his cross and empty tomb. These types were not accidental, but rather were anchored in the long-term providence of God to accomplish redemption for his people.

A historically disconnected 'accidental' allegory, for example, is brought forward by Justin Martyr in his *Dialogue with the Jew Trypho*, where he says that 'the bulls of Bashan' (a reference to Psalm 22:12) referred to the Pharisees of Jesus' day (ciii)! On the contrary, the New Testament itself uses sober typology to show how Christ was foreshadowed in the Old, and fleshed out in the New Testament. Hosea 11:1, which says 'Out of Egypt have I called my son,' is taken by Matthew to refer to the bringing of the Christ child by Joseph and Mary out of Egypt back to Nazareth (Matt. 2:15). The underlying point here is that Israel (who came out of Egypt under Moses) proved to be a false son, whereas the Incarnate Son of God would be the obedient son that the Father always wanted; he would do this on behalf of Israel and the Church.

24. McLeod, op. cit., 49.

25. See A. Kerrigan, *St. Cyril of Alexandria's Interpretation of the Old Testament* (Rome, 1952).

26. John Calvin, *Institutes of the Christian Religion* II. v. 19, Battles translation (Philadelphia: The Westminster Press, MCMLX), vol. 1, 339.

27. John Calvin, *Commentaries on the Epistles of Paul to the Galatians and Ephesians*, Pringle translation (Edinburgh: Calvin Translation Society, MDCCCLIV), 139.

Likewise, the brass serpent in Numbers 21:9 that Moses was instructed to fashion and then put on a pole, so that the snake-bitten sinners who looked to it could be healed, prefigures Christ. Jesus told Nicodemus that those who looked to the one who would be 'lifted up' would receive eternal life (John 3:14-15). This is true typology: anchored in the analogies placed by God in the history of redemption, pointing beyond themselves to something infinitely greater, and yet still historically and literally true. Cyril of Alexandria said that, in his person, Christ transformed types into truth.[28]

After the sixth century, typological preaching tended increasingly to displace allegorical preaching in the Church, both East and West. A good illustration of this in the West is the famous preacher of the sixth century, Caesarius of Arles, whose Scriptural interpretation is typological rather than allegorical, as was that of the more famous John Chrysostom in the East.[29] Yet to this day one still finds some allegorical preaching in Eastern Orthodoxy, Roman Catholicism, and Evangelical Protestantism; this is the case especially when preachers deal with the Old Testament.

The advantages of typology over allegory have been explored in the Enlightenment period (in the late eighteenth century) by Johann G. Hamann, both critic and friend of Immanuel Kant. Hamann reflected deeply and widely on the difference between typological and allegorical interpretation, and followed the typological mode, as in his comments on how God in Christ fulfills the land purchased by Jacob in Genesis 33:19 (*Biblical Meditations* I. 38), or the entire Mosaic economy as a type of 'transcendent history'(*Golgotha and Scheblimini* III. 308).[30] But Christian commentators in most of the Middle Ages neglected typology in favor of allegory, with the notable exception of Saint Thomas Aquinas.[31]

---

28. Cyril of Alexandria, *Glaphyra* (PG 69:89).

29. For the preaching of Caesarius, see the three-volume translation by M.M. Mueller: *Saint Caesarius of Arles: Sermons*, 3 vols. (The Catholic University of America Press: Washington, DC: vol. 1, 1956, vol. 2, 1963, vol. 3, 1972). For a helpful analysis of the preaching of Chrystostom, see Jaroslav Pelikan, *The Preaching of Chrysostom*, (Fortress Press: Philadelphia, PA, 1967).

30. See the study of Hamann's typology by Karlfried Grunder, *Figur une Geschichte: Johann Georg Hamann's 'Biblische Betraachtungen' als Ansatz einer Geschichtsphilosophie* (Freiburg/Munich: Verlag Karl Alber, 1958), especially pp. 134-143.

31. In the early Medieval period, especially with Saint Jerome, there were several modes of interpretation beyond typological and allegorical, although some of them were seldom used (as compared to the mainstays: typology and allegory). The earlier Fathers, and especially Jerome, at times spoke of 'literal sense,' "historical sense,' 'spiritual sense,' and (on occasion) 'tropological sense' and 'anagogical.' These senses are discussed in Pierre Jay, *L'Exégese de Saint Jerome d'Apres son 'Commentaire sur Isaie"*(Etudes Augustiennes: Paris, 1985), chapters 3 and 4 (pp. 127-333). See also *The Cambridge History of the Bible: The West From the Fathers to the Reformation*, Edited by G. W. H. Lampe (Cambridge: At The University Press, 1969), where it points out that, with Jerome: 'In general the exegesis proposed is confined to two senses, the literal and the spiritual...The literal is also called the historical,...The spiritual sense also receives other names. It is called *anagoge* and *tropologia* but without any precise difference in application' (vol. 2, pp. 89-90).

Christ and the History of Israel

Broader context in which the history of Israel is to be seen[32]
The context of the establishment of the people of Israel is found in the worldwide sin and cosmic alienation following on from the fall of Adam in Genesis 3, down to the judgment of the flood of Noah in Genesis 6-9, the table of nations in Genesis 10, and the disruption and scattering of humanity at the Tower of Babel in Genesis 11. Men and women were created social beings in communion with God himself. But sin broke that communion and damaged the social bond, both vertically and horizontally. The bond between male and female was ruptured, as well as the bond of intimate communion with the Lord.[33]

Sin can be thought of as rupture between what we ought to be and what we actually are. Even man's relationship with nature was damaged by sin. The massive increase of violence within the descendants of Adam brought the devastating judgment of the universal Flood, whose catastrophic marks remain in the once-pressurized deposits of our oil and coal beds, and in the masses of seashells on top of some of the highest mountains. The consequences of sin are not merely 'spiritual,' but also intensely physical. Human self-rehabilitation efforts such as the Tower of Babel (intended to be the integrating center of a humanist empire) actually led to further disintegration, because mankind's fallen nature always tends towards disruption.

Only God can reverse this disintegration of Babel, for, as Johann Georg Hamann noted, 'The confusion of language was a work of God to disperse man; the gift of the same a work of the Holy Spirit to unite man. We hear not only our tongues, but we hear the miraculous work of God speaking in the same.'[34]

The only solution to this universal disruption lies in the recreation of the bond between God and mankind, as indicated by the first promise of the Gospel to our first mother, Eve, in Genesis 3:15: 'And I will put enmity between thee and the woman, and between thy seed and her seed; it shall bruise thy head, and thou shalt bruise his heel.' The splitting off of humanity from service to Satan would be part of bringing it back into redeeming fellowship with God. God himself would have to accomplish

---

32. Much of this material is a direct paraphrase of class notes given by Professor T. F. Torrance in the 1960s and 70s at the University of Edinburgh, where I sat under him as a very appreciative student. Years later, after I became a teacher of theology myself, he gave me permission to reprint some of these notes for my own classes year by year. Hence, I am making use of these printed notes here, and I also add in some of my own thoughts. But I wish to point out the recent, happy publication of most of Torrance's printed class notes, plus other material, by his nephew, Dr. Robert T. Walker, in the two grand volumes: *Incarnation: The Person and Work of Christ* (2008), and *Atonement: The Person and Work of Christ* (2009). Where I make reference to these two volumes, as I do very frequently, all quotations or paraphrases will be marked and footnoted. But some of this preliminary material is not found in exactly the same form in either of the two books, though the essence of it is to be found in *Incarnation*.

33. Much of this material, in a slightly different form, is found in T. F. Torrance, *The Incarnation*, pp. 39-40.

34. Johann Georg Hamann, *Works* [*Samtliche Werke, historisch-kritische Ausgabe*], ed. Josef Nadler (Vienna: Herder, 1949-1957), I. 220.

this recreating of the bond by providing 'the seed'. Galatians 3 identifies this seed as the descendant of Abraham according to the flesh, the Lord Jesus Christ (vv. 16-20). That is one reason Christ told the woman of Samaria that 'salvation is of the Jews' (John 4:22), and why Paul considered Abraham the father of the faithful (cf. Romans 4 and Galatians 3).

Therefore, in the context of mankind's sin and inability, God himself must condescend to mankind in order to remove the alienation from both sides, thereby restoring humans to communion with God and to loving relationships with one another. For this to happen, '[…] the destruction of the power of evil, and a recreation of the bond between God and man,' is necessary.[35] Torrance explains further:

> How is mankind to be reconciled to God? There are two possible ways. The way of Cain in which man offers of the fruits of personal labour to God, the way of man is from man to God. Man provides a personal offering, a personal sacrifice. The way of Abel is one in which God provides the sacrifice, the sacrifice of another. Abel followed God in his sacrifice of animals to cover – in Old Testament language to atone for – Adam and Eve's sin and shame. Abel let God provide the sacrifice and offered it to God. So in Abraham, who would offer his best, his only son, we see that his offering is displaced by God who himself provides the lamb (Gen. 22:10-14). Substitution and free grace are identical…That adumbration of God's way of redemption is worked out more fully with Abraham, Isaac, and Jacob. It is the way in which God comes in pure grace to gather frail humanity into covenant and communion with himself, and even provides for man a covenanted way of response to God's grace.[36] Man responds by faith, but in faith relies upon a divinely provided way of approach and response to God in the covenant.[37]

So the history of Israel is the story of God coming down to lift man up. This history is the pre-history of the Incarnate Word of God. That Word was forming in Israel a womb for the birth of Christ. Torrance mentions three lines of thought in the formation of this matrix for the ultimate birth of Christ, that is, of how the nation of Israel foretold the story of Christ: (1) If one is to make a thing, tools are necessary, (2) There has to be developed a community of reciprocity, and (3) There must be an organic relationship.

(1) If one is to make a thing, one needs tools to give it shape.[38]

These (conceptual) 'tools' are intellectual analogies or categories to shape the apprehending of the knowledge of God in the human mind. The question is always asked: how can a finite human mind ever grasp the infinite God? Much of the massively influential philosophy of Immanuel Kant taught that God is in the separated, infinite realm of the noumenal, and that since we are in the realm only of the finite and phenomenal,

---

35. Torrance, op. cit., 39.

36. On 'a covenanted way of response,' see also T. F. Torrance, *The Mediation of Christ*, revised edition (Edinburgh: T & T Clark, 1992), p. 74ff.

37. Torrance, *The Incarnation*, 40.

38. Ibid., 41.

therefore we cannot really know him as he is.[39] This separation of the noumenal from the phenomenal was made almost inevitable by the prior separation of the mathematical-mechanical-empirical phenomena from their created reality as phenomena rendered accessible to us by the variety of our qualitative and meaningful sense perceptions. However, Torrance responded as follows:

> God refused to allow our limitations and weaknesses to inhibit his purpose of love and redemption. He condescended in incredible humility to find a way of entering within our beggarly weakness and poverty, to find a mode of divine entry into our finite and moral existence, in order from within as creator and saviour to restore us to complete fellowship with himself, both in knowing and in being.[40]

In this wonderful condescension to our finitude, the Lord provided in the order of creation, as reflected in human language, as well as supremely in his self-revelatory Word, creational analogies and categories such as Father, Son, shepherd, sacrifice, etc. One of the chief 'tools' for apprehension of God by all humanity was his choosing the race of Israel in whose life and history he showed his grace.

> Hence God selected one race from among all the races of mankind, one of the smallest, and, as Moses said, most beggarly and contemptible of all races, in order to make that race the very instrument of his redemptive purpose to reveal himself to every people and to save all humanity...[the people of Israel] were the most stubborn and stiff-necked people under the sun (Exod. 34:9). They disobeyed God at every moment in his saving purpose...
>
> And so God took this stubborn people, as a potter might take the worst, and lumpiest and most resistant and intractable clay, in order to put it upon the wheel for moulding and shaping into an earthen vessel designed to contain heavenly treasure... He used their very stubbornness in order to train them.[41]

Hamann, the famous friend and critic of Kant, wrote along these same lines in his *Biblical Meditations*:

> I can recognize my own crimes in the history of the Jewish people, for there I see my own life as I am reading their story, and I keep thanking God for his mercy upon his people, for their example builds me up in the same hope. Above all else, it has been in the Books of Moses where I made this rare discovery that the Israelites, no matter how intractable they appear to us in certain instances, were only waiting upon God for what his divine will would do for them. Hence they recognized with profound ardor their disobedience, as no sinner had ever done. And yet they did not fail very quickly to forget their repentence. Nonetheless, in the anguish of that repentence, they were

---

39. See chapter 6 of this volume concerning Kant's epistimology, which has a dichotomy between noumenal and phenomenal.

40. T.F. Torrance, op.cit., 40.

41. Ibid., 42.

imploring God to send a Saviour, a Mediator, without whom they would never be able to fear and love God as they should.[42]

Particularly in Luke 2, we see a faithful remnant in Israel who gladly recognized who Jesus was:

> ...the Son of God come in the flesh, the redeemer of Israel, and the light to lighten the Gentiles – Zechariah, Anna, Simeon, and John the Baptist, and who more than the blessed virgin Mary, and then one after another, the twelve disciples, and many others, who acknowledged that this was indeed the Christ, the Son of the living God, the saviour of the world.[43]

Without the history of Israel, one has no conceptual tools with which to grasp the meaning of the Son of God in the flesh. 'Apart from the context of Israel we could not even begin to understand the bewildering miracle of Jesus.'[44] How could we understand the cross without the Levitical system and the Day of Atonement? As the accounts of Christ's passion in all four Gospels show, we need the deliverance out of Egypt and the Passover of Exodus, Isaiah 52 and 53, Psalms 22 and 69, and Zechariah 9 to get a handle on what is happening to the Redeemer in our place. We need the prophets, we need King David and the others, we need the High Priests to grasp what the Incarnate Son of God is doing for us as our true prophet, priest, and king.

(2) A Community of Reciprocity

God was working in Israel to create a community of reciprocity, in which his Word evoked a response back to God. This is the basis of how we learn both to hear God speaking to us and to speak to God. A marriage is a relationship of reciprocity, as is the larger family, and Israel is both God's child (as we see in Exodus 4:22-23, which gives us the significance of the death of the firstborn son) and God's covenanted wife (as we see at large in Hosea). This is typical of the loving, giving, and receiving within the ontological Trinity. Through all of Israel's history, God was preparing a people who would hear his Word and respond rightly as a true child. In his mighty providence, he used even the bad responses of Israel to penetrate their life more deeply, so that the Word would come more fully to them, and through them to all nations. In due season, all the families of the earth would come to be blessed in Abraham (Gen. 12:3). This people will be 'a light to the Gentiles... [God's] salvation to the end of the earth' (Isa. 49:6).

(3) An Organic Relationship

This relationship between God and Israel is not only conceptual or intellectual, but also an organic bonding, which ties Israel into sharing in,

---

42. Pierre Klossowski, *Les Méditations bibliques de Hamann* (Éditions de Minuit: Paris, 1948), 122,123. My translation.

43. Torrance, op. cit., 43.

44. Ibid., 44.

a mode appropriate for humans, the life of God. This organic bonding was a covenanted relationship, profoundly different from the other nations, so that Israel was 'a peculiar people', set apart from the other Adamic tribes of the earth. Through God's Word, with its promises and law, and through the cult (or worship), God worked into their existence a knowledge of the way of response that he would ultimately provide in the One whom he elected to fulfill that covenant, in a way that Israel on its own never could do.

The organic relationship between God and his people is often presented in Scripture in terms of a grapevine. It is significant to study here the connection between the vineyard that did not produce good fruit in Isaiah chapter 5, and Christ who takes that image up and shows himself to be the true vine, with his Father as the husbandman (John 15:1); a vine that brings forth 'more fruit' (John 15:2) and 'much fruit' (John 15:5), by virtue of its abiding in Christ, the true vine, who gives fruitful sap to the branches.

Christ thus fulfilled the covenant into which Israel had long been called, as (a) head of the new covenant, as (b) prophet, (c) priest, and (d) king/shepherd, all of which offices were adumbrated in the Old Testament. And from the fall of mankind and the first promise of the Gospel, through the experience of patriarchs, kings, and prophets, we find an evil adversary, Satan, the accuser, constantly opposing with his malignant darkness the light of the kingdom of God. Finally, Christ as (e) 'the coming one'; the Messiah alone, will be able to defeat Satan, and even use Satan's sinful plots to further the victorious kingdom of God.

This leads us to consider the relationship between God and Israel as illustrated in the following:

(a) The Head of the New Covenant

Covenant is a major concept in the Old Testament. The way it develops within the old economy and the way it is interpreted within the new shows that it is arranged by God. The Triune God carries through the Covenant, but Jeremiah 31 and Hebrews 8 give special reference to the Head of the New Covenant, who, as its Mediator, is both God and man together at the same time, thereby fulfilling both sides of this covenant.

In the first volume of this series, I briefly surveyed the biblical teaching on covenant from Genesis to Revelation, and need not repeat that here,[45] except for amplifying two points: (i) The Covenant of Abraham, and (ii) The New Covenant.

(i) The Covenant of Abraham

Let us first note here how the quintessential form of the Covenant of Grace, the Covenant with Abraham (e.g. cf. Genesis 12, 17, 21), requires someone, some 'head' of the covenant administration, who will be like Abraham in faith (cf. Gen. 15:6); indeed, who will be the very 'seed' of

---

45. cf. Kelly, op. cit., chapter 6, 'The Triune God Makes Himself Known in the Covenant of Grace,' pp. 387-444.

Abraham (cf. Gal. 3), but also greater than Abraham, e.g. John 8:53: 'Art thou greater than our father Abraham...?', in answer to which Christ says: 'Before Abraham was, I am' (v. 58). Paul interprets the faith of Abraham in God as a resurrection faith, leading to justification (cf. Rom. 4:24-25). Along similar lines, the writer of the Epistle to the Hebrews mentions Abraham's faith in God's ability to raise the dead (cf. Heb. 11:17-19). Abraham is placed in a long line of heroes and heroines of the faith, who somehow were 'looking unto Jesus', who was truly 'the author and the finisher of the faith' as the ultimate head of the covenant of faith, which is the covenant of grace (cf. Heb. 12:1-2), rather than of works (cf. Gal. 3).

As G. Vos explains the connection between Abraham and Christ:

> [Abraham's faith]... trusts in [God] for calling the things that are not as though they were. This does not, of course, mean that the objective content of the patriarch's faith was doctrinally identical with that of the New Testament believer. Paul does not commit the anachronism of saying that Abraham's faith had for its object the raising of Christ from the dead. What he means is that the attitude of faith towards the raising of Isaac and the attitude of faith towards the resurrection are identical in point of faith and able to confront and incorporate the supernatural.[46]

Jean-Marc Berthoud, in his recent volume on the Covenant of God throughout Holy Scripture, amplifies this point clearly.[47] He shows that the judgment of the flood did not solve the true problem of corrupt mankind (cf. Genesis 8:21). He shows that the dispersion of the nations at the tower of Babel still did not solve the problem of human corruption. It would only be Christ in the flesh, the true descendent of Abraham, who would be able to redeem lost humanity from its corruption, death, and judgment. What God did in the covenant with Abraham was a preparation for his glorious reversal of human sin, death, and judgment.[48]

(ii) The New Covenant

The New Covenant, which will be the grand fulfillment of all the earlier covenants, both in redeeming lost mankind and binding together in union and communion the Lord and his people, is set forth in Jeremiah 31:31-37 and commented on by Hebrews 8:6-13 and 10:1-18. Having studied these passages in the previous volume, I wish to underscore only one point here in terms of Christology: the head (or 'carrier through') of the New Covenant had not yet arrived when Jeremiah was writing – 'Behold, the days come' (Jer. 31:31). Jeremiah and the pious ones in Judah with him were looking forward to some new, supernatural agent to come. Hebrews 8 and 10, I Corinthians 11, and II Corinthians 3 tell us who this agent was. And what he did in coming was all for the benefit of his church, which in

---

46. Geerhardus Vos, *Biblical Theology: Old and New Testaments* (Edinburgh, Banner of Truth Trust, 1975), 85,86.

47. Jean-Marc Berthoud, *L'alliance de Dieu à travers l'Écriture sainte: Une théologie biblique* (Messages: L'Age D'Homme: Lausanne, 2012).

48. Ibid., 162-64.

a mysterious way is somehow in spiritual continuity – notwithstanding temporary disruptions (cf. II Corinthians 3 and Romans 11) – with Old Testament Israel.

Covenant theology has always marked the believing community, and an expectation of covenantal mercy was present before the New Testament era. Matthew Black shows how the concept of New Covenant passed into the Qumran community, as evidenced by the Dead Sea Scrolls:

> The name itself 'New Covenant' (*berith hadhasha*) occurs at least twice in the Qumran literature [CD viii.15; ix.8]… Again and again the writers dwell on the wonder of the divine forgiveness in God's 'Covenant of mercy,' which brings the whole conception into line with the basis of Jeremiah's New Covenant, 'I will forgive their iniquity' (xxxi.34). Entry into the New Covenant took place at a solemn assembly or convocation of the sect, and the *Manual of Discipline* has preserved two accounts of such a ceremony of 'entering into the New Covenant.[49]

Dr. Black does not suggest any direct borrowing from this practice in Qumran by the early Christians, although at least he shows that concepts of a New Covenant were current in various strands of Judaism in the first two centuries before Christ.

In the words of Herman Ridderbos:

> It is on account of this fulfillment of the prophecy of the New Covenant in the Christian church that all the privileges of the Old Testament people of God pass over to the church. To it, as the church of Christ, the pre-eminent divine word of the covenant applies: 'I will be their God, and they shall be my people…' (II Cor. 6:16ff.)… The more one views the Pauline epistles from this vantage point, the richer the materials prove to be that characterize the New Testament church in its continuity with ancient Israel on the one hand, and as the church of the New Covenant qualified by the forgiveness of sins and gifts of the Spirit on the other.[50]

In other words, the Old Testament is a preparation for the coming of the Mediator of the New Covenant. He fulfills the various covenants of the old economy in his person and work. In him we have both continuity with the old forms of the covenant, and an open door to the fullness of what God is doing in the future of redemption.

(b) Prophet

The exercise of prophecy goes back into the early strands of Israel's history. Jude 14 tells us that 'Enoch, the seventh from Adam' prophesied (of the Lord's coming). Abraham was considered a prophet (Gen. 20:7). Moses, the chosen mouthpiece of God, through whom the law was given on Sinai, and writer of the five books of Moses, as well as self-sacrificing mediator for a sinning people (cf. Exod. 32), spoke of himself as a prophet

---

49. Matthew Black, *The Scrolls and Christian Origins* (Thomas Nelson: London, 1961), 91,92.

50. Herman Ridderbos, *Paul: An Outline of his Theology,* translated by John R. deWitt (Wm. B. Eerdmans Publ. Co.: Grand Rapids, 1975), 336, 337.

(Deut. 18:15). Samuel, 'the seer,' established schools of the prophets before the coming of David to the kingship (see I Samuel at large). From time to time till the end of the Old Testament era, God was raising up prophets to call the priesthood, kings, and people back to true faith and repentance, so that their worship would not be an empty sham, but 'in spirit and in truth' (e.g. Hosea 1 and Isaiah 1).

Moses, in particular, teaches that an ultimately authoritative and 'sealing' prophet was to come, who would be like him: 'The LORD thy God will raise up unto thee a Prophet from the midst of thee, of thy brethren, like unto me; unto him ye shall hearken... I will raise them up a Prophet from among their brethren, like unto thee, and will put my words in his mouth; and he shall speak unto them all that I shall command him. And it shall come to pass, that whosoever will not hearken unto my words which he shall speak in my name, I will require it of him' (Deut. 18:15, 18, 19).

Thus, Moses points forward from his own time – the final prophet was to be looked for; he had not come yet. Some passages in the New Testament identify 'that Prophet' with Christ, the Messiah of Israel. John the Baptist was asked if he were 'that prophet,' and he denied it: 'Art thou that Prophet? and he [John the Baptist] answered no... Philip findeth Nathanael, and saith unto him, We have found him, of whom Moses in the law, and the prophets, did write, Jesus of Nazareth, the son of Joseph' (John 1:21, 45).

The first-century crowds seem to have discerned (at least for a time) who the prophet was. After the miraculous feeding of the five thousand, they said, 'This is of a truth that Prophet which should come into the world' (John 6:14). Acts 7:37 directly refers to this same text of Deuteronomy 18 and applies it to the risen Christ.

But, though it is not yet our subject in this section on the Old Testament preparation for Christ, Hebrews 1:1-2 shows us that while Christ was *like* the other prophets, more importantly, he was nevertheless *different*: 'God, who at sundry times and in divers manners spake in time past unto the fathers by the prophets, hath in these last days spoke unto us by his Son, whom he hath appointed heir of all things, by whom also he made the worlds...' That is to say, the previous holy prophets *spoke* the Word, but Christ Himself *is* the Word (as we shall see in some detail later when considering John 1:1-18).

(c) Priest

Some form of priesthood, at least in the sense of offering sacrifice for sin, goes back to the earliest part of the Old Testament. From the gates of the Garden of Eden (Gen. 3:21), when the Lord slew animals to provide coats of skins for our first parents, to the time of Noah, with his extra pairs of clean animals for sacrifice (Gen. 7:2, 8:20-22), down through patriarchal times, with sacrifices made by Abraham (Gen. 15:9-18), sacrifices were regularly made to God by his people.

But in the revelation given to Moses by the Lord on Mount Sinai (Exod. 12-13, 24-32, 37-40, and Leviticus, at large, [cf. Hebrews 8-10]), the priesthood and cult were regularized until the ultimate sacrifice of Calvary, when the veil of the Temple was rent in twain from top to bottom, thus signifying that the way into the holiest was now made open to all of God's people (cf. Matt. 27:51 and Heb. 9:8).

The High Priest of Israel represented God to the people, and the people to God. He bore the names of the twelve tribes of Israel upon his breastplate when he went once a year into the holy of holies to confess the sins of the people as their appointed representative, and when he came out, he was authorized to pronounce the Aaronic benediction upon them: 'The LORD bless thee, and keep thee: The LORD make his face shine upon thee, and be gracious unto thee: The LORD lift up his countenance upon thee, and give thee peace' (Num. 6:24-26).

As he went into the holy place, he took a bowl of blood, 'first, for his own sins, and then for the sins of the people' (Heb. 9:7). This Aaronic priest 'was a figure for the time then present…that could not make him that did the sacrifice perfect, as pertaining to the conscience' (Heb. 9:9). He was a type, or pointer, to a more perfect priest (not of 'the order of Aaron,' but 'the order of Melchizedek,' the mysterious priest/king of ancient Salem, unto whom Abraham paid tithes; cf. Gen. 14, Ps.110, Heb. 6:19-7:28). His authority did not come from Levitical descent (for he lived long before Levi's birth), but directly from the Lord's providential appointment (Heb 7:1-28). Hence, Melchizedek was a type of the eternal Christ, who came, not of the tribe of Levi, but of Judah (Heb. 7:14-17).

While the Old Testament Levitical priests died *from being priests*, Christ died *as our priest*, and thus his priesthood is unchangeable (cf. Heb. 7:22-24). As John Owen writes: 'He died *as a priest*, they died *from being priests*. He died as a priest because he was also to be a sacrifice; but he abode and continued not only vested with his office, but in the execution of it, in the state of death…. Nor did the apostle say that he did not die, but only that he "abideth always" [Heb. 7:24].'[51]

Because of the total sufficiency of his atoning death, God raised him from the dead, so that 'he ever liveth to make intercession for his saints' (Heb. 7:25). He does this not in the earthly tabernacle, but in that highest place of all, in God's immediate presence in heaven, upon which the tabernacle in Israel was originally patterned (Heb. 9:23).

What Owen means is this: Levitical priesthood was, by definition, temporal. When one high priest died, his son or other representative had to take his place to carry on the work. But Christ's supreme priesthood is eternal. His death did not cause him to cease from being priest so that another would have to replace him. Indeed, his death was at the center of his priesthood. He is our eternal priest before, during, and after his death.

The great twelfth-century Western theologian, Peter Lombard, brought out well the connection of the death of the Aaronic high priest and the setting free of unintended killers from the various 'cities of refuge' dotted throughout Israel of old: 'And so great things were granted to us in the

---

51. John Owen, *Commentary on the Epistle to the Hebrews vol. 5: Exposition of Hebrews chapters 6:1–7:28* (Edinburgh: The Banner of Truth Trust, [reprint 2010]), 517.

death of the only-begotten, so that we should be allowed to return to the fatherland, just as formerly, at the death of the high priest, those who had fled to the city of refuge could now safely return to their own lands [cf. Num. 35:25-28; Jos. 20:6].'[52]

Wonderful as that Aaronic priesthood is, the endless 'Melchizedek' priesthood of Christ accomplishes even more. He has not merely relieved us from the penalty of the banishment of guilt, but he has actually brought us into the peaceful position of sitting down with the Lord in his kingdom: 'But this man, after he had offered one sacrifice for sins for ever, sat down on the right hand of God; from henceforth expecting till his enemies be made his footstool. For by one offering he hath perfected for ever them that are sanctified' (Heb. 10:12-14). And so, believers are, by that miraculous grace, already 'seated with him in heavenly places' (Eph. 2:6).

Athanasius the Great describes the High Priesthood of Christ in this light:

> ...when He took on Him flesh like ours; which moreover, by Himself offering Himself, He was named and became 'merciful and faithful,'—merciful, because in mercy to us He offered Himself for us, and faithful, not as sharing faith with us, nor as having faith in any one as we have, but as deserving to receive faith in all He says and does, and as offering a faithful sacrifice, one which remains and does not come to naught. For those which were offered according to the Law, had not this faithfulness, passing away with the day and needing a further cleansing; but the Saviour's sacrifice, taking place once, has perfected everything, and is become faithful as remaining for ever. And Aaron had successors, and in a word the priesthood under the Law exchanged its first ministers as time and death went on; but the Lord having a high priesthood without transition and without succession, has become a 'faithful High Priest,' as continuing for ever; and faithful too by promise, that He may hear. Or, answer, and not mislead those who come to Him. This may be also learned from the Epistle of the great Peter, who says, 'Let them that suffer according to the will of God, commit their souls to a faithful Creator.' For He is faithful as not changing, but abiding ever, and rendering what He has promised.[53]

Here we find that Athanasius sees the same truth that John Owen would note thirteen hundred years later: 'the Levites died from being priests, whereas Christ died as our priest.'

(d) King/Shepherd

The kingdom of God, while never limited to the nation of Israel (nor to the church, later), was intimately bound up with its development. Over the strong protest of the noble prophet, Samuel, Israel chose a king (cf. I Sam. 8).[54] Yet God used their desire to be like the rest of the nations to

---

52. Peter Lombard, *The Sentences: Book 3: On the Incarnation of the Word*, translated by Giulio Silano (Pontifical Institute of Medieval Studies: Toronto, Ontario, 2008), 77.

53. Athanasius, *Contra Arianos*, II. 9.

54. The sermon of John Calvin on I Samuel 8 is remarkable in its insight. In 1982, I translated the Latin into English: John Calvin, *Sermon XXVIII*, from 31 July 1562, (on I Samuel 8), published

prepare them in his wise providence for the true king of the kingdom, the 'king of kings and the lord of lords' (Rev. 19:16). For God is a king, even THE king, and 'his kingdom ruleth over all' (Psalm 103:19). At times, even pagan nations came to see this truth. The greatest pagan king of his own time, Nebuchadnezzar of Babylon, finally came to this confession: 'Now I, Nebuchadnezzar praise and extol and honour the King of heaven, all whose works are truth, and his ways judgment: and those that walk in pride he is able to abase' (Daniel 4:37).

Ridderbos, in *The Coming of the Kingdom*, shows the centrality of the saving grace of the covenant God in the history of Israel. He argues that many of the synoptic parables of Jesus are ways of setting forth the ancient Jewish kingdom hope in a renewed, Christological setting (as the ancient symbol of vine or vineyard, the sheep and shepherd, as well as such more contemporary analogies as a steward and master, or a son and a father).[55]

He finds much of Christian apocalyptic language pointing in this same direction:

> The 'Messianic woes' tradition indicated that this suffering and vindication would be climactic, unique, the one-off moment when Israel's history and world history would turn their great corner at last, when YHWH's kingdom would come and his will be done on earth as it was in heaven. The central symbolic act by which Jesus gave meaning to his approaching death suggests strongly that he believed this moment had come. This would be the new exodus, the renewal of the covenant, the forgiveness of sins, the end of exile. It would do for Israel what Israel could not do for herself. It would thereby fulfill Israel's vocation, that she should be the servant people, the light of the world.[56]

Throughout the Old Testament, in the Psalms and the Prophets, Israel was looking for an ideal king to come, who would accomplish a victorious work for the kingdom, that David and Solomon had – at the best – only been able to foreshadow. To take only two references out of hundreds in the Old Testament, God through the prophet Nathan promises to build King David a house (a line of kingly descent):

> And when thy days be fulfilled, and thou shalt sleep with thy fathers, I will set up thy seed after thee, which shall proceed out of thy bowels, and I will establish his kingdom. He shall build an house for my name, and I will establish the throne of his kingdom for ever. I will be his father, and he shall be my son. If he commit iniquity, I will chasten him with the rod of men, and with the stripes of the children of men: But my mercy shall not depart away from him, as I took it from Saul, whom I put away before thee. And thine house and thy kingdom shall be established for ever before thee; thy throne shall be established for ever (II Samuel 7:12-16).

---

in *Calvin Studies Colloquium*, eds. Charles Raynal and John Leith (Davidson, NC: Davidson College Presbyterian Church, 1982).

55. Herman Ridderbos, *The Coming Kingdom* (Presbyterian and Reformed: Phillipsburg, New Jersey, 1962).

56. Ridderbos, *Paul: An Outline of his Theology*, 596-597.

Psalm 89 meditates on the future blessings promised to come through a king like David, who will be established in the covenant (vv. 20-37). Amos 9:11 prophesies that the Lord will raise up the fallen tabernacle of David, and this is referred to as the victorious work of the crucified, risen, ascended Christ and his church by James at the apostolic council, in the context of the church's spreading of the good tidings of salvation to the Gentiles:

> And to this agree the words of the prophets; as it is written, After this I will return, and will build again the tabernacle of David, which is fallen down; and I will build again the ruins thereof, and I will set it up; that the residue of men might seek after the Lord, and all the Gentiles, upon whom my name is called, saith the Lord, who doeth all these things (Acts 15:15-17).

Hence the Old Testament ends without the messianic king, the royal seed of David, having yet to come. But many in Israel had been encouraged by the prophets to look for him. Thus, the last book in the Old Testament, Malachi, portrays this kingly descendant of David in terms of the Lord himself, the messenger of the covenant, suddenly appearing: 'Behold, I will send my messenger, and he shall prepare the way before me: and the Lord, whom ye seek, shall suddenly come to his temple, even the messenger of the covenant, whom ye delight in; behold, he shall come, saith the LORD of hosts' (Mal. 3:1).

Furthermore, the most frequently quoted Old Testament reference in the New Testament, Psalm 110, speaks of this figure as being both son of David and Lord of David (to be considered in detail later). Jesus tells the Pharisees that it is he who is both son of David and Lord of David (cf. Matt. 22:41-46). But the Pharisees' viewpoint of the coming messianic king was so different from who Christ actually was that it led to his death (which in the predestined providence of God helped to establish his true kingdom forevermore – cf. Acts 4:26-28).

Part of the deep longing for this divine and human figure sprang from Israel's knowledge of the shepherd-like function of the coming king. But this deep desire had been shifted in a military/political direction in the thought of the Pharisees, Sadducees and Herodians before the time of Jesus.

The King as Shepherd

None I have read has expressed more beautifully the Old Testament background of the shepherd-kingship of Christ than T. F. Torrance:

> Behind this of course lies the Old Testament concept of the shepherd king applied to *Yahweh* in his relation to Israel, and the promise of the messianic shepherd when God will set up his servant David over the forsaken and oppressed sheep of his people. The Psalms are full of this concept but also the prophets, and several of the prophetic passages are clearly in the mind of Jesus and the evangelists, especially Ezekiel 13 and 34; Jeremiah 23 and 31; Isaiah 40; Micah 4 and 5; Zephaniah 3 and Zechariah 10–13. In these

passages we find the divine judgment spoken against the false shepherds who do not feed the flock and are no shepherds, and who reject the true shepherds. We also find the picture of the true shepherd whom God will raise up to gather his sheep together as a whole and individually, giving great care to the hurt and weak, and the young and the lost. We also see a picture of the sheep scattered because there is no true shepherd, so that they become a prey to the beasts of the field; and then we see the picture also of a future shepherd whose life will be violently taken away, for the shepherd and the sheep will be smitten and many will perish, though a remnant will be saved by the word of the Lord. All that is undoubtedly in our Lord's mind, and the evangelists see it clearly and draw it out, for example in Matthew's emphasis upon the thirty pieces of silver for which Judas betrayed Jesus [Matt. 26:14-16; cf. 27:3-10], and which has reference to the betrayal and rejection of the good shepherd in Zechariah 11.

That is how Jesus regarded his life and faithfulness toward mankind, as the shepherd of the sheep, the shepherd who calls his sheep by name and leads them into the fold of salvation, the shepherd who does not run when the wolf comes, and who lays down his life for the sheep. As such, Jesus looks upon the multitudes of men and women as the disinherited and lost, and he pours out his life in compassionate service, standing in the gap where there is no shepherd, and taking their hurt and their troubles to himself...[57]

'The Lord [who] is my Shepherd' of Psalm 23 is met most fully in the incarnate person and work of the Good Shepherd in John chapter 10. Peter tells us that this Good Shepherd is also 'the chief shepherd' (I Peter 5:4), and the Epistle to Hebrews calls him 'that great shepherd of the sheep' (Heb. 13:20). Without the Old Testament portrayals of shepherd, as well as king, we could never grasp the crucial New Testament testimony to who our Incarnate Lord is as head of his church, as shepherd and king.

(e) Messiah's victory over Satan, the accuser

From the primeval temptation and fall in the Garden of Eden (Gen. 3), through the murder by Cain of Abel (Gen. 4), through the wickedness and violence that led to the flood (Gen. 6), and the disruption of sinful humanity at the Tower of Babel (Gen. 11), through Abraham's lies (Gen. 12), Jacob's duplicity (Gen. 27), through the Satanic persecution of Job (Job 1), through the grumbling of the people against Moses (e.g. Exod. 16; Num. 11), through their unbelief that prevented them from entering the Promised Land in the early part of the wilderness journey (Num. 13 and 14 and Deut. 1), and then their orgiastic adultery with the young women of Moab (Num. 25), the time of the Judges, on through Saul's shameful, demonized demise (I Sam. 28–31), and David's fall into adultery and murder (II Sam. 11 and Ps. 51), and his sinful numbering of the people (II Sam. 24), not to mention the idolatrous worship of the split-off Northern Kingdom (I Kings 12 and 13), and the final caving in to idolatry in the once-faithful South (Jeremiah and Ezekiel, at large), through the Seleucid and then Roman occupation of restored Palestine, which was the case in the time of Christ, we discern a dark shadow behind all these

---

57. T. F. Torrance, *The Incarnation*, 130,131.

attempts to destroy the holy Kingdom of God in Israel, so as to replace the worship of God with that of Satan.

The head of the evil kingdom unleashed his attacks in renewed fury with the birth of the Messiah. Although, by divine revelation in a dream, Joseph and Mary and the Christ-child escaped to the safety of Egypt, King Herod had all the children in the region of Bethlehem murdered, so as to wipe out the baby Messiah (Matt. 2:16-18). At the beginning of Christ's ministry, Satan fiercely tempted him to avoid the Father's way of obedience to the cross as the true mode of establishing the kingdom of love and light, and instead to worship Satan, who vainly offered him the entire world (Matthew 4; Mark 1; Luke 4).

The evil one never left Christ alone for very long. He influenced Simon Peter to forbid the Lord from going to the cross (Matt. 16:22-23), and later would 'sift Peter' (Luke 22:3). He entered into Judas Iscariot before his betrayal of the Master (John 13:27), and somehow – all unseen – motivated the enmity and brutality of the Garden of Gethsemane and Cross of Calvary. But God Almighty never allowed the evil being to go any further than to accomplish the divine purposes for salvation of Israel and the world (cf. Acts 4:25-30, quoting Psalm 2, and fulfilling the basic principle of Psalm 76:10: 'Surely the wrath of man shall praise thee; the remainder of wrath shalt thou restrain'). And we shall later see how the mission of the seventy sent out by Christ with the good news to Israel began 'the fall of Satan like lightning' (Luke 10:18). Colossians 2:14-15 demonstrates how the instrument so urged on by Satan became his total downfall: 'Blotting out the handwriting of ordinances that was against us, which was contrary to us, [Christ] took it out of the way, nailing it to his cross; and having spoiled principalities and powers, he made a shew of them openly, triumphing over them in it.'

One cannot but admire the quaint saying of Peter Lombard that the Redeemer…

> set a mouse-trap for Satan, which was his own cross, and he set his own blood as if bait for him. It was not a debtor's blood that he shed and by which the devil departed from his debtors. Christ shed his own blood so that he might erase our sins… for it was by nothing else than the bonds of our sins that he bound us [he refers to Prov. 5:22; 2 Tim. 2:25-26]. These were the captives' chains. Christ came and *bound the strong one* [Matt. 12:29] by the bonds of his passion; he entered *into his house*, that is, in those hearts in which the devil had made his abode, and took out *his vessels*, that is, ourselves, which the devil had filled with his bitterness…[58]

Without employing the figure of a 'mousetrap,' Thomas Boston (of early eighteenth-century Scotland) made a similar point:

> …Christ ruined the devil's empire by the very same nature that he had vanquished, and by the very means which he had made use of to establish and confirm it. He took not upon him the nature of angels, which is equal

---

58. Peter Lombard, *Sentences*, vol. 2, 79.

to Satan in strength and power; but he took part of flesh and blood, that he might the more signally triumph over that proud spirit in the human nature, which was inferior to his, and had been vanquished by him in paradise. For this end he did not immediately exercise omnipotent power to destroy him, but managed our weakness to foil the roaring lion. He did not enter the lists with Satan in the glory of his Deity, but disguised under the human nature which was subject to mortality. And thus the devil was overcome in the same nature over which he first got the victory.... As our ruin was effected by the subtility of Satan, so our recovery is wrought by the wisdom of God, who takes the wise in their own craftiness.[59]

The Gospel of Mark indicates that the first beings in Christ's ministry to recognize that he was the Son of God were the demons (Mark 1:22-27). These evil beings realized that Christ had come 'to torment them' (Mark 5:7; Matt. 8:29) as part of the battle he was waging, that would ultimately fulfill the longings of Old Testament Israel for deliverance from their true enemy.

Stephen A. Dempster in *Dominion and Dynasty* points out who the real enemy of the people of God is:

Jesus reconstructed the battle which had to be fought as the battle against the real enemy, the accuser, the satan. He renounced the battle that his contemporaries expected a Messiah to fight, and that several would-be Messiahs in that century were only too eager to fight. He faced, instead, what he seems to have conceived as the battle against the forces of darkness, standing behind the visible forces (both Roman and Jewish) ranged against him.[60]

We shall later see how this battle was, and will continue to be, victorious – that 'through death he might destroy him that had the power of death, that is the devil; and deliver them who through fear of death were all their lifetime subject to bondage' (Heb. 2:14-15). Revelation shows the grand denouement of all this age-long battle, with a definite day, divinely appointed, on which the devil, death and hell shall be cast into the lake of fire (Rev. 20:10, 13-14).

Saint Symeon the New Theologian shows how this battle is to be won:

The Son and Logos of God did not become man to be believed in, or to be glorified, or that the Holy Trinity and Godhead should be theologized, but 'that he might destroy the works of the devil' (I John 3, 8; cf. Heb. 2:14-15), and when the works of the devil are destroyed in those who believe in him, then the mysteries of theology and of Orthodox dogma are entrusted to him. For if those who have not been liberated from the works of the devil by the manifestation of the Son and Logos of God... are forbidden to enter the temple of the Lord and pray to God, how much more are they forbidden to read and explain Holy Scriptures?[61]

---

59. Thomas Boston, *The Beauties of Boston: A selection of his writings*, Edited by Samuel McMillan (Christian Focus Publications: Inverness, 1979), 76.

60. Stephen A. Dempster, *Dominion and Dynasty* (InterVarsity Press: Downer's Grove, Ill, 2003), 605.

61. Symeon the New Theologian, *Oration* 10, 3.

Question and Answer 32 of the 1563 Heidelberg Catechism happily
convey this point of the Messiah as victor for the Christian life:

> Question 32. *But why art thou called a Christian?*
> Answer. Because by faith I am a member of Christ, and thus a partaker of
> his anointing; in order that I also may confess his name, may present myself
> a living sacrifice of thankfulness to him, and may with free conscience fight
> against sin and the devil in this life, and hereafter, in eternity, reign with
> him over all creatures.

The Westminster Larger Catechism shows how in our daily prayers, we
are instructed by Christ to call for the continual application of his once-
for-all victory over the kingdom of evil to be applied in our own lives and
times:

> *Question 191*: 'What do we pray for in the second petition?
> *Answer*: 'In the second petition (which is, *Thy kingdom come*), acknowledging
> ourselves and all mankind to be by nature under the dominion of sin and
> Satan, we pray that the kingdom of sin and Satan may be destroyed, the
> gospel propagated throughout the world, the Jews called, the fullness of
> the Gentiles brought in; the church furnished with all gospel-officers and
> ordinances, purged from corruption, countenanced and maintained by the
> civil magistrate; that the ordinances of Christ may be purely dispensed,
> and made effectual to the converting of those that are yet in their sins,
> and the confirming, comforting, and building up of those that are already
> converted: that Christ would rule in our hearts here, and hasten the time of
> his second coming, and our reigning with him for ever: and that he would
> be pleased so to exercise the kingdom of his power in all the world, as may
> best conduce to these ends.'

This mighty victor over the powers of evil that sought to destroy the
universe in general, and humankind in particular, was able to win the
battle of the ages, because he possessed in deepest reality and fulfilled,
with infinite fullness and efficacy, all the names and titles ascribed to him
through the Old and New Testaments. His incarnate life fulfills all these
names and titles, and he carries everything to its successful conclusion in
unbroken fellowship with the Father, and in the power of the Holy Spirit.
Our next chapter will take us through the most significant ones of these.

CHAPTER 2

NAMES AND TITLES OF CHRIST
IN OLD AND NEW TESTAMENTS

The Holy Trinity names himself in Old and New Testaments in order to reveal to us who he is. Having already surveyed the names God gives himself in the Old Testament (in volume 1), here we focus on the names given to the Lord Jesus Christ in both Testaments, but with emphasis on the New. We look at the constituent parts of his main title: Lord, Jesus, and Christ. We consider him as Son of God and Son of Man, Logos, and then look at the seven (or eight) 'I am' sayings in the Gospel of John. These names and titles will be put into a biblical context in the next chapter, which expounds four major passages relating who he is (ch. III).

The first appendix to this chapter discusses massive research done by Jacques Masson in the 1970s that sought to fit together the genealogies of Matthew and Luke.

Biblical Significance of Names

We serve a God who names himself. That is why the names and titles of Christ from Old and New Testament are so crucial to an understanding of who he is. Genesis 1:1 begins with the name of the Creator of the cosmos: *Elohim*. We have previously surveyed several of his divinely revealed names: *YHVH, El Shaddai*, and others.[1] The Old Testament begins without any discussion of the possibility of God's existence, but rather with his revealing of his name and activity. It is essentially the same in the New Testament, which is largely devoted to the person and work of the eternal Son of God incarnate. None of the four Gospels begin with any 'foundational' discussion of why and how God can exist. Rather, all of them start, in different ways, with what D. Bonhoeffer called 'the Who question': who is this Jesus Christ?[2] All the glad tidings of the new phase of the Covenant of Grace flow from that divinely revealed reality, a supreme reality which is given a name by God.

Matthew begins with 'the book of the generation of Jesus Christ, the son of David, the son of Abraham' (Matt. 1:1). There follows a genealogy

---

1. See Kelly, *Systematic Theology*, vol. 1, 279-285, 293, 294.

2. Dietrich Bonhoeffer, *Christology* (Collins: Fontana Library: London, 1966).

taking the Incarnate Christ back to Abraham (father of Israel), through David (cf. Matt. 1:17). Here we have several names or titles which identify the one whose being and activity the Gospel will unfold.

Mark simply starts with 'The beginning of the Gospel of Jesus Christ, the Son of God' and then draws a connection between the Old Testament prophet mentioned by Isaiah (Mark 1:2-3, quoting Malachi 3:1 and Isaiah 40:3) and the New Testament prophet, John the Baptist.

Luke begins by declaring his purpose in writing his Gospel (Luke 1:1-4) and then relates the supernatural conceptions of John the Baptist (Luke 1:5-25; 57-80) and Christ, Virgin-born son of Mary, as announced by the holy archangel, Gabriel (Luke 1:26-38). Chapter 2 takes us through his holy birth, his family's flight into Egypt, their return to Israel, and his presence in the Temple of Jerusalem at age 12. Luke's third chapter, after conveying the preaching of John the Baptist, then gives another genealogy of Christ's human ancestry, taking us through Abraham (which is as far as Matthew goes) and back to Adam. We will discuss in an appendix the relationship of these two genealogies.[3] By definition, these two genealogies are full of names, leading up to the person of supreme importance, whose name was given to him by God through the archangel (cf. Matt. 1:21). And throughout Gospel and Epistle, the subject of the fulfilled covenant is provided with many names, given by the Spirit through the writers of the sacred text.

A Biblical Name is not Accidental

If we receive Old and New Testaments as divine revelations, then it is clear that God is in charge of the naming concerning the person of his incarnate Son. And this is in accordance with the lordship of God. As Barth writes:

> In the Bible the name of a person or thing is not an accidental appendix or a sign of recognition, but is something that designates the nature and function of the person or thing in question, thus corresponding to it. Jesus is not called Jesus without reason. Judas is not called Judas without reason. Every person or thing is what its name implies… For this reason the naming of a thing is never an incidental act in the Bible. It is always a decisive act, as is presupposed even where it is not expressly mentioned. To give a thing a name is thus an act of lordship…[4]

This lordly naming is also an act of true divine and human knowledge, as well as an act of the will.

Gregory Nazianzus rejoices in how the names attributed to Christ in the Scriptures exalt his Lordship as One of the Trinity, who came to redeem the world:

> For we have learnt to believe in and to teach the Deity of the Son from their great and lofty utterances. And what utterances are these? These: God—The

---

3. See Appendix 1 at the end of this chapter.

4. Karl Barth, *Church Dogmatics*, III/1, 124.

Word—He That Was In The Beginning and With The Beginning, and The Beginning. 'In the Beginning was The Word, and the Word was with God, and the Word was God,' [John 1:1], and 'With Thee is the Beginning,' [Ps. 110:3], and 'He who calleth her The Beginning from generations,' [Isa. 41:4]. Then the Son is Only-begotten: The only 'begotten Son which is in the bosom of the Father, it says, He hath declared Him,' [John 1:18]. The Way, the Truth, the Life, the Light. 'I am the Way, the Truth, and the Life;' and 'I am the Light of the World.' [John 8:12; 9:5; 14:6]. Wisdom and Power, 'Christ, the Wisdom of God, and the Power of God,' [1 Cor. 1:24]. The Effulgence, the Impress, the Image, the Seal; 'Who being the Effulgence of His glory and the Impress of His Essence,' [Heb. 1:3 R.V.] and 'the Image of His Goodness,' [Wisdom 7:26.] and 'Him hath God the Father sealed.' [John 7:27]. Lord, King, He That Is, The Almighty. 'The Lord rained down fire from the Lord;' [Gen. 19:24]. and 'A sceptre of righteousness is the sceptre of Thy Kingdom;' [Ps. 45:6], and 'Which is and was and is to come, the Almighty' [Rev. 1:8.]—all which are clearly spoken of the Son, with all the other passages of the same force, none of which is an afterthought, or added later to the Son or the Spirit, any more than to the Father Himself. For Their Perfection is not affected by additions. There never was a time when He was without the Word, or when He was not the Father, or when He was not true, or not wise, or not powerful, or devoid of life, or of splendour, or of goodness.[5]

Why such a variety of Names?

While Gregory the Theologian has properly given an overall impression of who Christ is, taken from many biblical names, somewhat more careful attention to the particular names given to Christ in the New Testament texts is called for in order to understand the bearings of the texts themselves. John Owen said it well concerning the reason for the variation of names used of the Redeemer in the Epistle to the Hebrews:

> Sometimes he [the writer of Hebrews] calls him Jesus only, sometimes Christ, sometimes Jesus Christ, sometimes the Son, and sometimes the Son of God. And he had respect herein unto the various notions which the church of the Jews had concerning his person from the prophecies and promises of the Old Testament. And he useth none of them peculiarly but when there is a peculiar reason for it...[6]

Or, as Cyril of Jerusalem said over a thousand years before Owen, the rich variety of the ministries flowing from the person of Christ is why he, although one subject, has so many names.[7] The variety of names teaches us important truths about God, though none of them can convey fully who he is. In his arguments against the Arian Eunomius (who denied the significance of the distinct names of God), Basil the Great pointed out that every one of God's names demonstrates (though never fully) something that he is, or something that he is not.[8]

---

5. Gregory Nazianzus, *Oration XXIX*. 17.

6. John Owen, *Exposition of Hebrews*, vol. 6. Chapters 8.1–10.39 (Edinburgh: The Banner of Truth, 2010 reprint), 260.

7. Cyril of Jerusalem, *Catechetical Orations*, X.4.

8. Basil, *Against Eunomius*, I.10.

As one looks at some of his most frequently applied names and titles in the New Testament, one cannot but be struck by how early in the life of the Christian Church Jesus of Nazareth was worshiped as God. We have already seen this in Larry Hurtado's *Lord Jesus Christ*,[9] and it is much the same in Richard Bauckham's article 'Worship of Jesus' in the Anchor Bible Dictionary which similarly demonstrates the early church's worship of Christ as divine.[10] The Christian believers considered themselves as monotheistic as the Jews, but a profound change came in their view of Jesus.[11]

In the words of Larry Hurtado: 'I have proposed that in this development we have what amounts to a new and distinctive 'mutation' or variant form of the monotheistic practice that is otherwise characteristic of the Jewish religious matrix out of which the Christian movement sprang.'[12]

Barth summarizes the New Testament attitude to Jesus as a whole:

> In attestation of this understanding of the man Jesus the New Testament tradition calls Him the Messiah of Israel, the *kyrios*, the second Adam come down from heaven, and, in a final approximation to what is meant by all this, the Son or the Word of God. It lifts him right out of the list of other men, and as against this list (including Moses and the prophets, not to mention all the rest) it places Him at the side of God.[13]

We shall enter into these details as we work our way through the various names and titles (or 'identifications' in terms of Old Testament types) applied to Christ in the New Testament text. We begin with the fullest name of the incarnate Son of God: (1) Lord Jesus Christ (to which Hurtado's 2003 volume is devoted). Then we consider other major New Testament appellations: (2) Son of God, (3) Son of Man, (4) *Logos* ('Word'), and (5) the seven 'I AMs' of John's Gospel.

(1) Lord Jesus Christ

(a) Lord (Κύριος)

We have previously studied the widespread usage of *adhonai* [אֲדֹנָי] and *kyrios* [κύριος] in Old Testament Hebrew, the Greek of the LXX version, and in the New Testament.[14] The briefest summary of the word usage here must suffice. The LXX translated *adhonai* as *kyrios*, and the New Testament uses *kyrios* as a title for God, 'just as does the Jew.'[15] 'In the LXX *kyrios*

---

9. See D. Kelly, *Systematic Theology*, vol. 1, 449-450.

10. See *Anchor Bible Dictionary*, ed. David N. Freeman (New York: Doubleday, 1992), vol. 3, 812-819.

11. N. T. Wright discusses this profound change for the Jews who were converted to Christ in *The New Testament and the People of God* (Fortress Press: Minneapolis, 1992), 457.

12. Hurtado, op. cit., 2.

13. K. Barth, *Church Dogmatics*, IV/1, 160.

14. D. Kelly, op. cit., 292-93.

15. See ibid., 292, quoting George A. F. Knight, *A Biblical Approach to the Doctrine of the Trinity* in 'Scottish Journal of Theology Occasional Papers,' No. 1 (Edinburgh: Oliver & Boyd, 1953), 19.

occurs over 9,000 times…'[16] Colin Brown noted 'the substitution of the title *adonay* for the proper name Yahweh.'[17] 'Where *kyrios* stands for *'adon* or *'adonai* [i.e. in the LXX] there has been genuine translation, but where, on the other hand, it stands for Yahweh it is an interpretative circumlocution for all the Heb. text implies by the use of the divine name: Yahweh is Creator and Lord of the whole universe, of men, Lord of life and death. Above all he is God of Israel, his covenant people.'[18] I. Howard Marshall agrees that the LXX usage of *kyrios* was a rendering of the Hebrew *Adon* and the equivalent of Yahweh.[19]

After his exaltation, Jesus was widely confessed as *kyrios*:

> The confessional cry used in worship, *kyrios Iesous*, Jesus (is) Lord, no doubt originated in the pre-Pauline Hellenistic Christian community. This confession is one of the oldest Christian creeds, if not the oldest. With this call the NT community submitted itself to its Lord, but at the same time it also confessed him as ruler of the world (Rom. 10:9a; I Cor. 12:3; Phil. 2:11…)… All powers and being in the universe must bow the knee before him…'[20]

Kyrios is reserved for the True God

Kittel summarizes the usage of *kyrios*:

> In the religious sphere, then, *kyrios* or *ho kyrios* is reserved for the true God, and apart from unimportant periphrases of the name in figurative speech, it is used regularly, i.e. some 6,156 times, for the proper name (Yahweh) in all its pointings, and in the combination (*Yahweh Tsabaot*) or in the short form (*Ya*)… Thus *kyrios* is best understood by looking at the original name, *Yahweh*.[21]

A careful reading of the Gospels will indicate that Jesus was not often called *kyrios* during his earthly ministry. Jesus does use the title to refer to himself in Mark 2:28: 'The Son of Man is Lord of the Sabbath,' and in Matthew 7:21-22: 'Not every one that saith to me, *kyrie, kyrie*, shall enter the kingdom of heaven' and 'On that day, many will say to me, *kyrie, kyrie*, did we not prophesy in thy name?…' At times, the vocative, *kyrie*, can simply mean a title of respect: 'Sir' (as in Mark 12:9 or Luke 16:3). But in Mark 2 and Matthew 7, it means far more: the context refers to Jesus' lordship over entrance into heaven.

And that is certainly the case in Matthew 22:41-46, where Christ put a question to the Pharisees concerning the identity of the messiah (for whom they waited): 'What think ye of Christ? whose son is he? They say unto him, *The son* of David. He saith unto them, How then doth David in spirit call him Lord… how is he his son?' Here, Christ is referring to the leading

---

16. Kelly, op. cit., 292, quoting *New International Dictionary of New Testament Theology*, Colin Brown, gen. ed. (Grand Rapids: Zondervan, 1986), 511.

17. Ibid.

18. Ibid.

19. I. Howard Marshall, *The Origins of New Testament Christology*, 99.

20. Ibid., 293.

21. Kelly, op. cit., 293,294, quoting *Theological Dictionary of the New Testament*, edited by Gerhard Kittel; trans. and ed. G. W. Bromiley (Grand Rapids: Wm. B. Eerdmans, 1965), vol. 3, p.1062.

messianic Psalm 110 (v. 1). The Psalm contained an ontological reference
to deity – it is God himself who exercises messianic lordship, not normally
in view in the messianic expectations during the time of Christ. Yet Christ
appropriates this divine reference to himself, in this roundabout way with
the religious leaders of Israel.

Christ's lordship was shown in the manner of his teaching. Rather than
quote a long list of rabbis, or even the prophetic phrase, 'Thus saith the
Lord,' he taught them 'as one having authority'. That was particularly
the case after the Sermon on the Mount (Matt. 7:29). How often he said:
'Ye have heard it said by them of old time...But I say unto you...' (e.g.
Matt. 5:27-28). Jesus 'taught as one that had authority, and not as the
scribes' (Mark 1:22). A man from outside the covenant people of Israel,
a Roman centurion, perceived the lordly authority of Jesus: '...but say in
a word, and my servant shall be healed. For I also am a man set under
authority, having under me soldiers, and I say unto one, Go, and he goeth;
and to another, Come, and he cometh...' (Luke 7:7-8). Jesus himself noted
with wonder that the centurion's faith in his lordship went far ahead of
what he had so far found in Israel (Luke 7:9).

After the resurrection of Christ, his anointed witnesses constantly
call him *Lord* (κύριος). Now the Holy Spirit has been poured out from on
high, thereby enabling them to see this truth about the crucified one (cf.
John 16:7-15, and I Cor. 12:3). The risen Lord gave his church the great
commission to take the Gospel to all the world on the basis that 'all power
(or authority) is given unto me in heaven and on earth' (Matt. 28:18). He
now sits at the right hand of the Majesty on high' (Heb. 1:3), and is head of
the Church (Eph. 5:23). He exercises highest power over all the visible and
invisible world, as 'the head of all rule and authority' (Col. 2:10). By his
resurrection, he was 'declared to be the Son of God with power' (Rom. 1:4).
He is sovereignly seated in 'the midst of the throne', where he exercises
authority over all affairs in heaven and on earth (Rev. 7:17). All people
and angels will stand before his judgment seat at the last (II Cor. 5:10). He
now has power to grant eternal life to those whom the Father has given
him (John 17:2).

From that throne he poured out the Holy Spirit upon his waiting
church (cf. Acts 1; 2:33). In view of Christ's authority in granting the
baptism with the Holy Spirit (in this case to a Gentile), Peter makes
an equivalence between the Lord Jesus Christ and God the Father
(Acts 11:15-17). Hence, Christian believers prayed to Christ (e.g. as Saul
of Tarsus upon his conversion in Acts 9:5-6, and later in the matter of the
healing he requested in II Corinthians 12:8, and the closing prayer of the
first Christian martyr, Stephen, in Acts 7:59-60). The Christian believers
sang praises to the Lord (Eph. 5:19), and called on his name in worship (I
Cor.1:2). The beloved apostle shows that even the praises of the heavenly
realm are now directed to the enthroned Lamb (cf. Rev. 5:8-14; 7:9-17, etc.).
According to Peter, from his exalted position as Prince and Saviour, Christ
gives 'repentance to Israel and forgiveness of sins' (Acts 5:31), as well as
to the Gentiles (Acts 11:18).

The great passage by Paul on the humiliation and exaltation of Christ (to be discussed in Chapter 4) ends with the words: 'Wherefore God hath highly exalted him, and given him a name which is above every name; that at the name of Jesus every knee should bow, of things in heaven and things in earth, and things under the earth; and that every tongue should confess that Jesus Christ is Lord, to the glory of God the Father' (Phil. 2:9-11). Paul teaches that the coming resurrection of all flesh will be in terms of the power of Christ, and for believers, analogous to his glorious body (I Cor. 15:21-22; 45-49). Hence, final judgment is committed by the Father into the hands of his Son, according to Paul's preaching on the Areopagus in Athens (Acts 17:31).

Questions by some modern scholars on the Jewish originality of Jesus as kyrios

Such comes from a plain reading of the New Testament's teaching on Jesus as Lord. Yet much twentieth century scholarship in Western Europe (followed, as always, in America) argued in various ways that originally in the early church (or large parts of it), Jesus was not understood to be Lord. William Bousset advanced this position early in the century, holding that the title *kyrios* was not used by the Palestinian, Aramaic-speaking Christians, but by Hellenistic churches in the diaspora who spoke Greek.[22]

Rudolph Bultmann took over Bousset's concept of the Hellenistic background of Jesus as *kyrios* in his massively influential New Testament scholarship.[23] He especially sought to ground the early Christian concept of Jesus as Lord in the Greek mystery religions (and Gresham Machen was not slow to point out the lateness of Bousset's sources on this matter). Bultmann found the roots of this 'myth' in Gnosticism (influenced by the mystery religions), especially the myth of the Gnostic redeemer.[24] Bultmann relegates to the nursery of Gnostic religion, not only Jesus as kyrios, but other items, such Pauline terms as 'spiritual' ($\pi\nu\epsilon\upsilon\mu\alpha\tau\iota\kappa\sigma\varsigma$) and 'end' ($\tau\epsilon\lambda\sigma\varsigma$).[25]

But as James Dunn pointed out: 'However, since the publication of Bultmann's *Theology* it has become increasingly evident that his formulation of the myth is an abstraction from later sources. There is nothing of

---

22. William Bousset, *Kyrios Christos: A History of the Belief in Christ from the Beginnings of Christianity to Irenaeus* [original German, 1913, English translation by J. Seely] (Nashville: Abingdon, 1970). The New Testament scholar, first of Princeton Seminary, then of Westminster, J. Gresham Machen, answered several assertions of Bousset (particularly drawing attention to the late dating of material that Bousset claimed to be from the early Church) in *The Origin of Paul's Religion*. Machen, however, had relatively little effect on the study of titles of Christ (including Lord) after the publication of his book. However, Craig Blomberg has covered some of the same ground, dealing with more recent sources, in which he indicates the general lateness of much of the rabbinical material that has often been suggested to have been parallels to the Gospels. He speaks of this procedure (as in Strack and Billerbeck - 1922-61) as involving 'an anachronism' in Blomberg, op. cit., 65, and states that this sort of work needs updating.

23. See Bultmann's *The Theology of the New Testament*, vol. 1, ch. 1.

24. Ibid., vol. 1, 166f.

25. R. Bultmann, *Jesus and the Word*, transl. L.P. Smith and E. H. Lanterno (New York: Scribner's, 1958), 172,182.

any substance to indicate that a Gnostic redeemer myth was already current at the time of Paul.'[26] N. T. Wright gives an entire chapter to the unlikelihood that there was any Gnostic religion before the second century A.D., or more specifically, a Gnostic Redeemer-myth.[27]

On the contrary, in addition to the preaching of Peter and Paul in Acts, where (as we have just seen) Jesus is frequently proclaimed to be *kyrios* by the earliest Jewish Christians, I Corinthians 16:22 uses a phrase from the worship of the early Christians: *Marana tha*. It is Aramaic, and calls Jesus 'Lord' (*Mar*), and apparently prays for him to come.[28] This prayer for his coming is like the one (in Greek) in Revelation 22:20: 'Even so, come Lord Jesus.'[29] Similarly, Matthew Black explored the meaning and connections of *marana tha* in relation to Jude 14–15 and I Enoch.[30] Such references make it clear that the early church saw Jesus as Lord, and that he bears the prerogatives of God almighty.

(b) Jesus

'Jesus' was a normal human name within Israel. 'The name borne by Jesus is in the first instance an expression of his humanity...'[31] The angel Gabriel told the Virgin Mary to give this name to her divinely conceived Son: '... and thou shalt call his name JESUS: for he shall save his people from their sins' (Matt. 1:21). 'This shows that the important thing in the name [יְשׁוּעָה] is the verb [יְשׁוּעָה] which means to help.'[32] This personal name [יְשׁוּעָה] 'seems to have come into general use about the time of the Babylonian exile in place of the older *yeshua*... It is the oldest name containing the divine name Yahweh, and means "Yahweh is help" or "Yahweh is salvation".'[33] Cyril of Alexandria speaks along these lines of the significance of the name of Jesus: 'The very name of Jesus shows specifically how he is truly, and by nature, the Lord of the universe' [i.e. God saves].[34]

'Jesus' refers to his divine mission of salvation that only God could accomplish. Yet it is a historical name, based on that of Joshua, who led God's people into the Promised Land.

Hence, he is one of us, a true human person, yet on mission from God, and conceived by God in the womb of the Virgin. The meaning of this human name of the Messiah has not been contested by scholars, and

---

26. James Dunn, op. cit., 99.

27. N. T. Wright, *The New Testament and the People of God*, chapter 14 (pp. 418-43).

28. See Oscar Cullman, *The Christology of the New Testament* (London: SCM, 1963), 209.

29. See C. F. D. Moule, *The Origin of Christology* (Cambridge: Cambridge University Press, 1977), chapter 2, and Wolfhardt Pannenberg, *Systematic Theology* translated by G. W. Bromiley (Wm. B. Eerdmans: Grand Rapids, 1991), who also sees it as a prayer for Christ's return, p. 266.

30. Matthew Black, 'The Maranatha Invocation and Jude 14–15 (I Enoch 1:9)' in *Christ and Spirit in the New Testament* (Cambridge: Cambridge University Press, 1974), 189-98.

31. *Theological Dictionary of the New Testament*, ed. by Gerhard Kittel, trans. G. W. Bromiley (Eerdmans: Grand Rapids, 1965), vol. III, 287.

32. Ibid., 289.

33. *New International Dictionary of New Testament Theology*, Colin Brown, ed. (Exeter: The Paternoster Press, 1975), vol. II, 330-31.

34. Cyril of Alexandria, *Commentary on the Incarnation of the only Son* 3 (PG 75, 1373 B).

much less has been written on it than on such theologically laden terms as Christ, Son of God and Son of Man.

(c) Christ
'Christ' was originally a title, which came from 'to anoint' (χρίω), hence 'the anointed one' (ὁ Χριστός). In the LXX, 'Christ' translates into Greek the Hebrew word cluster around *mashach* [מָשַׁח] (or the substantive [מָשִׁיחַ]). Historical examples of anointing are seen in royal anointing, as Saul in I Samuel 9:16; David in I Samuel 16:3, 12; Solomon in I Kings 1:34; and the unnamed king anointed by God in the messianic Psalm 45 (v. 7). The high priest was also anointed by having oil poured from a horn or vessel on to his head, as in I Chronicles 29:22 and Leviticus 4:3. Anointing can refer to enablement for service by descent of the Spirit of God, or (not unrelated) to consecration, as this action avails in the spiritual realm to set the anointed servant apart.

So, Christ was a title that eventually became a personal name. Yet, even so, the sense of the title still carried its 'messianic' weight. Hence, N. T. Wright denies the assumption that, with the Apostle Paul, the messianic title had lost its power, as it passed over into a personal name:

> Many have tried to argue that Paul, writing within twenty or so years of Jesus' crucifixion, already used the word *Christos* as a proper name, with its titular significance ('Messiah') being swallowed up by other theological meanings. I believe this to be mistaken…. The truth is simpler…Paul, in company with all other very early Christians actually known to us (as opposed to those invented by ingenious scholars), believed that Jesus was indeed the true Messiah, and held that as a central identifying mark.[35]

Messianic Longing
In the developing revelation of the Old Testament, one finds definite elements of 'messianic longing.' The descent of the Davidic kingship continued to be a basis of hope for the future, as, for example, 'the anointed of the Lord' is looked forward to in Lamentations 4:20 and Habakkuk 3:13. This Davidic royal descent is often taken up and expanded in various Psalms (2:2, 6; 21:9-13; 89:19ff.; 110:1,3ff.; 132:11ff.).

The messianic longing involved in some types of anointing is in some texts related to the promise of God to David through Nathan that his house will last forever (I Sam. 7:14). Isaiah 9:5ff. speaks of the adoption of a new ruler by the Lord: this adopted one will be final and perfect. Micah 5:1-3 speaks of the birth of the messianic Son of David, the anointed one, and predicts that it would be in Bethlehem.

In the development of revelation, Messiah is characterized by lavish possession of the Spirit (Isa. 11:2). Three pairs of concepts are used to describe this state (compare Hebrews 1:9, where Christ is anointed 'with the oil of gladness above his fellows'): 'the spirit of wisdom and understanding, the spirit of counsel and might, the spirit of knowledge and of the fear

---

35. N. T. Wright, *Jesus and the Victory of God*, 486.

of the Lord' (Isa. 11:2). Messiah comes 'out of the stem of Jesse' (David's father, and Christ's ancestor) – Isaiah 11:1.

This messianic reign will be beyond all human kingdoms in dignity, power, and greatness (Isa. 3–5). God's power will be seen within it (Ezek. 17:24). Its greatness will extend to the ends of the earth (Micah 5:5). Through him paradise will be regained (Isa. 11:6-9). The afflictions of the last times will be overcome with the accession of Messiah (Isa. 16:4ff.).

Yet as we see the Messiah in the New Testament, he is poor and rides on a donkey (prophesied in Zechariah 9:9). In light of all that had been promised concerning the messianic kingdom, even before his crucifixion, John the Baptist was not the only one to be disappointed. It was John who had 'anointed' through baptism the Messiah, yet from prison he sent word to Jesus asking whether he were really the Messiah (Matt. 11:1-19).

G. Vos comments on the concerns lying behind this inquiry:

> In it [John's question] the Old Testament once more, as it were, voices its impatience about the tarrying of the messiah. But as there, so here, the impatience centred on one particular point, the slowness of God's procedure in destroying the wicked. John had been specifically appointed to proclaim the judgment-aspect of the coming crisis. Hence a certain disappointment in the procedure of Jesus.[36]

John the Baptist had baptized Jesus (the Lord's 'anointing' as Messiah) in terms of the Old Testament preparation for him. Vos explains:

> In Malachi, a prophetic book from which…so much of John's imagery is taken, we find in chapter 3 verse 1 the distinction of the three stages in the eschatological advent, as it were, in preformation: first we have 'I send my messenger and he shall prepare the way before me'; this messenger was (in the fulfillment) John the Baptist; it covers therefore the public ministry of Jesus preceded by John's; in regard to it John could say: 'after me comes a man.' But in the same passage of Malachi, the Lord, before whom the messenger goes to prepare His way, is in the immediate sequel called 'the Messenger of the *Berith*, whom ye desire'; this refers to the figure otherwise called 'the Angel of Jehovah' [who, John says in his second affirmation, 'came before me']…But in the prophet there is also an intimation of the third clause: 'He was before me,' because 'the Lord whom ye seek,' and who is come to His temple, is through apposition identified with the Angel of the *Berith*…[37]

Christ's Messiahship Different from the Jewish conception of his contemporaries

Herman Ridderbos shows the profound difference between what Christ was actually doing as Messiah and what much of the contemporary Jewish public was anticipating:

> … there can be no doubt that Jesus' announcement of the future was not in the stream of the Jewish nationalistic expectations found, e.g., in the

---

36. G. Vos, op. cit., 313.

37. Ibid., 323.

Psalms of Solomon. It must much rather be viewed as the continuation of the transcendent and apocalyptic predictions of the future in the prophecies of the Old Testament and the expectations based on the latter.[38]

Whereas what Jesus was and did severely disappointed most of Israel, his life was a delight to the Father's heart: 'I do always those things which please the Father' (John 8:29); 'This is my beloved Son in whom I am well pleased' (Matt.3:17), and 'Thou art my beloved Son, in whom I am well pleased' (Mark 1:11). The ugliness of Israel's rejection of its Messiah is far outweighed (in terms of the glorious weight of the *kabod*) by the beauty of the Father's approbation of his Son during his life, and of his raising him from the dead by the Father's glory (Rom. 6:4).

Within the hidden plan of God, the defeat on the cross was the beginning of the triumphal uplifting of true messianic king (cf. Acts 4:27,28; Luke 12:50, and John 12:23-33). According to Paul: 'Jesus Christ our Lord…was made of the seed of David according to the flesh; and declared to be the Son of God with power, according to the spirit of holiness, by the resurrection from the dead…' (Rom 1:3-4).

Augustin Lemann – a Jewish scholar converted to the Roman Catholic Faith in the latter part of the nineteenth century – very ably shows that the Jews of the time of Jesus Christ chose, to a large extent, the glorious, triumphant Messianic prophecies of the Old Testament (addressed to the Second Coming of the Messiah) as against those relating to the Suffering Servant (applicable to his First Coming).[39] The intensely nationalistic vision of many Jewish parties at that time blinded them to the suffering servant passages in favor of triumphal messianic predictions. However, that messianic triumph did arrive, but not in the way the first-century Jewish leadership had anticipated.

The bodily resurrection proves who Jesus is. Kittel's *Dictionary*, in agreement with Paul, shows how the resurrection confirmed Christ's true messiahship (although differently from what had been expected):

The Easter event has plainly related Israel's Messianic expectation to Jesus. Jesus of Nazareth is the promised and expected Messiah. If He does not conform to the ordinary conception of the Messiah, God Himself has accredited Him as the Messiah at Easter. A decisive reconstruction of the term is thus accomplished in combination with the history of Jesus. Along these lines, the Messianic designation, *Christos*, becomes a name, for *Christos* is Jesus. In the non-Palestinian world, where the word *Christos* was not understood, it became a sobriquet attached to the name of Jesus or doing duty for it. By means of this commonly used name the unmistakable uniqueness of Jesus is emphasized.[40]

38. Herman N. Ridderbos, *The Coming of the Kingdom* (Presbyterian and Reformed Publishing Company: Philadelphia, PA, 1962), 36, 37.

39. Augstin Lemann, *Histoire complète de l'idée messianique chez le peuple d'Israël* (reprint: Éditions Saint-Rémi, Cadillac, 1909).

40. Walter Grundmann, 'Χριστος' in *Theological Dictionary of the New Testament*; ed. Kittel (Eerdmans: Grand Rapids, Mi.), 540.

(2) Son of God

The major issue between the early Church and Judaism, between the Church and various early heresies such as Gnosticism and Arianism, between Islam and Christianity, and between Christianity and the eighteenth-century European Enlightenment and its intellectual descendants down to the present (especially the different mutations of both Protestant and Roman Catholic Modernism) has always been this basic confession of faith: Jesus Christ is the incarnate Son of God.

The full deity of the Son, as Dr. George Dragas writes,

> ...appears strikingly in the primitive creedal symbol of the Fish, which enshrined the early Church's confession of IXΘYE = Jesus, Christ, God's Son, Saviour. Indeed to be received into the Christian Church one had to make this confession, 'I believe that Jesus Christ is the Son of God' (Acts 8:37), which implied the other confession, which was finally universalized, the proper name of God, the Father Son and Holy Spirit.[41]

Varied Biblical uses of 'Son of God'
G. Vos in *The Self Disclosure of Jesus* shows that in Scripture the title 'Son of God' can be used in four different ways:

(1) In a **nativistic** sense, because a creature of God owes his existence to the immediate creative activity of God, as in Luke 3:38, where Adam is called 'son of God', and his son Seth is called 'son of Adam'. In Exodus 4:22, Israel is called God's son (although there is a covenant adoption here, in addition to the original creational relationship); in Malachi 2:10, the concepts of sonship both by creation and also by covenant are brought together, and in Acts 17:28-29, quoting the pagan poet Aratus of Soli, Paul tells the Greeks at Athens that 'we are the offspring of God'.

The second appendix to this chapter addresses the issue of the term 'Son of God' in Bible Translation for Muslim people groups.

(2) In a **moral-religious** sense, in which context 'son of God' can refer to man as the particular object of God's loving care, such as Israel in Exod. 4:22. In the New Testament, believers are the sons of God by birth (cf. John 1:12,13; 3:3), or by adoption (cf. Rom. 8:14; Gal. 3:26; 4:5).

(3) In a **messianic** sense, the Davidic king is designated the son of God (II Sam. 7:14). Psalms 2 and 110 point to the son of God as some higher reality than a mere earthly king who reigns and then passes into the dust.

(4) In a **theological** sense, as in John's prologue (cf. John 1:1-18) – to be expounded presently,[42] Jesus, the Logos, is 'Son of God' because he is God

---

41. George Dragas, 'The Eternal Son: (An Essay on Christology in the Early Church with Particular Reference to Saint Athanasius the Great)' chapter 2 in *The Incarnation: Ecumenical Studies in the Nicene-Constantinopolitan Creed A.D. 1981*, edited by Thomas F. Torrance. (The Handsel Press: Edinburgh, 1981), 16.

42. See chapter 3 of this volume.

from all eternity. He partakes of the divine nature, as such (cf. Rom. 8:3; Gal 4:4). In the Epistle to the Hebrews, where the high priestly ministry of the Lord is described, these two titles are brought together: Jesus and Son of God (thus pointing to the two natures of Christ).[43]

It is, of course, in the last sense that the New Testament affirms Jesus Christ to be the Son of God. If this title had only been used in one of the first two senses, Christ would not have been crucified for the blasphemy supposedly involved in his answer to the High Priest at his first trial:

> …And the high priest answered and said unto him, I adjure thee by the living God, that thou tell us whether thou be the Christ, the Son of God. Jesus saith unto him, thou hast said: nevertheless I say unto you, hereafter all ye shall see the Son of man sitting on the right hand of power, and coming in the clouds of heaven. Then the high priest rent his clothes, saying, he hath spoken blasphemy; what further need have we of witnesses? Behold, now ye have heard his blasphemy. What think ye? They answered and said, He is guilty of death (Matt. 26:63-66).

Son of God in the Synoptic Witness

In the synoptic Gospels, the title 'Son of God' is not frequently employed, although it is definitely found in these Gospels. Mark 1:1 shows that Christ is the Son of God, and Matthew 16:16 understands Peter's confession of Jesus Messiah in the high sense of his being Son of God. Normally – with a very few exceptions – in the synoptics (as we just saw in Matthew 26 above) – Jesus does not use this title to describe himself, although he does say the same thing in other ways. Certainly in Matthew 11:27 Jesus unveils the highest and most intimate inner knowledge between himself and the Father, the fullest knowledge and love between God and God. This divine and exclusive knowledge puts the Son in a position to reveal the Father (v. 27) and to offer the most wonderful rest to those who will come to God through him (vv. 28-30).

J. Jeremias has shown that Jesus' addressing God as *Abba* (an intimate word for 'Father') in his prayers was a strong indication of his sonship.[44] Although James Barr perhaps properly pointed out that 'Abba does not mean "Daddy"',[45] N. T. Wright comments that, nonetheless, Jeremias never actually claimed that it literally meant 'Daddy', and that Barr himself acknowledges 'that Jeremias' wider argument remains valid'.[46]

But other voices do ascribe 'Son of God' to Christ in the synoptic witness. It is used of him at his baptism (Mark 1:11; Luke 3:22). The evil one attacked him in the wilderness temptations on the basis that he was the Son of God (Matt. 4:3 and Luke 4:41). Satan was tempting Christ to put forth his divine power prematurely, so as not to go through the divinely appointed work of human obedience in our place, which alone would

---

43. Geerhardus Vos, *The Self Disclosure of Jesus*, (Eerdmans: Grand Rapids, Mi., 1954), 141f.

44. J. Jeremias, *The Prayers of Jesus*, English transl. (SCM: London, 1967), 11-65.

45. James Barr, 'Abba isn't Daddy' in *Journal of Theological Studies* 39:28-47.

46. N. T. Wright, *Jesus and the Victory of God*, 649, n. 132.

prepare the way for the putting forth of the divine majestic power in his exaltation.

At the baptism, God the Father confesses Christ to be his Son, speaking with a heavenly voice that was audible at the River Jordan (Mark 1:11). Especially in Mark's Gospel, the demons recognize Jesus as the Son of God (e.g. Mark 1:24; 3:11, and 5:7). Again at his transfiguration on the mount, God himself speaks and names Jesus as his beloved Son (cf. Mark 9:7; Matt. 17:5; Luke 9:35). As Christ died, even the Roman centurion recognized him as Son of God (Mark 15:39).

Son of God in the Gospel of John

The general reserve on public usage of 'Son of God' in the synoptics is emphatically not the case in John. As G. E. Ladd shows, 'It is obvious that Jesus' sonship is the central Christological idea in John, and that he writes his Gospel to make explicit what was implicit in the synoptics. The Gospel is written that men may believe that Jesus is the Messiah; but more than Messiah, He is the Son of God (John 20:31).'[47]

The prologue to John (1:1-18) teaches the eternal co-existence and co-equality of the Word (Logos) with the Father, and this Word is identified in verse 18 as the Son of God.[48] In John 1:14, John states that 'we beheld his glory, glory as of the only-begotten[49] of the Father.' In John's Gospel, John the Baptist confesses that Jesus is the Son of God (John 1:34). And John 3:16 and 18 call him God's only-begotten Son.

In Mark, Jesus calls God 'Father' only four times; in Matthew, twenty-eight times, but in John, Jesus speaks of God as Father 106 times. According to George E. Ladd:

> Jesus' sonship stands apart from all other sons. This is supported by the fact that Jesus never speaks of God as 'our Father' in such a way as to place Himself on the same relationship to God as His disciples. On the contrary, He sets His sons apart when He says to Mary, 'I am ascending to my Father and to your Father, to my God and your God' (John 20:17)... As the Son, Jesus claims to possess an exclusive knowledge of the Father. No one has seen the Father except Him who is from God; He has seen the Father (6:47). As the Father knows the Son, so the Son knows the Father (10:15). Here as in Mt. 11:27, the knowledge the Son has of the Father is the same direct, unmediated knowledge the Father has of the Son. The knowledge the Son has of the Father stands in contrast to the ignorance of other men (17:15).[50]

As Martin Hengel writes, above all the other titles: 'Son of God connects the figure of Jesus with God.'[51]

---

47. George Eldon Ladd, *New Testament Theology* (Eerdmans: Grand Rapids, Mi., 1993), 283.

48. We deal with the translation issue concerning 'only-begotten' Son immediately below.

49. In our exposition of John 1:1-18, we will discuss the textual issue surrounding 'only-begotten' *Son* or only-begotten *God* (see chapter IV of this volume).

50. Ladd, op. cit., 284.

51. Martin Hengel, *The Son of God*, Engl. translation (London: SCM, 1976), 61.

In the fourth century, Gregory Nazianzus brought out some of the profound theological ramifications of this exclusive Trinitarian relationship by means of metaphors taken from relationship, mind, and speech, which we with our human psychology can, to a certain degree, grasp:

> In my opinion He is called Son because He is identical with the Father in Essence; and not only for this reason, but also because He is Of Him. And He is called Only-Begotten, not because He is the only Son and of the Father alone, and only a Son; but also because the manner of His Sonship is peculiar to Himself and not shared by bodies. And He is called the Word, because He is related to the Father as Word to Mind; not only on account of His passionless Generation, but also because of the Union, and of His declaratory function. Perhaps too this relation might be compared to that between the Definition and the Thing defined, since this also is called Λόγος. For, it says, he that hath mental perception of the Son (for this is the meaning of Hath Seen) hath also perceived the Father, and the Son is a concise demonstration and easy setting forth of the Father's Nature. For every thing that is begotten is a silent word of him that begat it.[52]

John shows that the Son has power to confer life as does the Father (5:21). As the Father has life in himself, so he has granted the Son to have life in himself (5:26). Jesus not only mediates eternal life, but does so as one of the Persons of the Godhead (cf. John 1:18 and 14:6-7). The Christ is 'above all,' testifies John the Baptist, for 'he came down from heaven' (3:31). A few verses later, John adds: 'The Father loveth the Son, and hath given all things into his hand' (v. 35). And John tells us that final judgment is given to the Son (5:22-23). And until that day, he reigns over all.[53]

He who exercises the highest Lordship is infinitely generous in what he gives. That is a chief characteristic from the very heart of the Trinity, for the greatest gift of the Triune God is the gift of himself.

Christ as the 'Only-begotten Son'

Two of the most influential Church translations over the centuries have translated μονογενὴς (monogenes) as 'unigenitus' (the Vulgate) and 'only-begotten' (the Authorized or King James Version). John applies this adjective to Christ in John 1:14; 1:18; 3:16; 3:18, and also in I John 4:9. In the LXX this term is used to translate the Hebrew [יהיד] yahid, which generally conveys the sense of 'only' child, as in Judges 11:3 (Jephthah's only daughter), or Psalm 25:16 (the lonely suffering person mentioned in the Psalm). It is used in the New Testament for such as the deceased 'only' son of the widow of Nain (Luke 7:12); Jairus' daughter (Luke 8:42); Isaac, the son of Abraham, whom he was called on to offer up in sacrifice to God (Heb. 11:17); and one or two other incidents. It usually bears the meaning of having only one child (although in the case of Abraham, he had another son, but only one son of covenant promise).

---

52. Gregory Nazianzus, *Fourth Theological Oration, Which is the Second Concerning the Son* (XXX) 20.

53. Oscar Cullman expounds the Son's present authoritative reign as *kyrios*, with special reference to the life of his church. See Cullmann, *The Early Church: Studies in Early Church History and Theology*, A. Higgins, ed.(Philadelphia, 1956), 104-140.

It also can bear the sense of 'beloved,' and at times the LXX translates *yahid* as ἀγαπητος (as with Isaac in Genesis 22:2, 12, 16). This sense is conveyed of Christ in Colossians 1:13 as 'the Son whom he loves'. And John 3:16 conveys the wonder of the unique Son of God's love being given by the Father to a world who hated him.

Yet only-begotten is not the only possible translation, and in most cases has been replaced by 'unique' in modern translations (such as the NIV). Father Raymond Brown argues with extensive scholarship that what the AV renders as 'only-begotten' (μονογενὴς actually comes from γινομαι ('to become') rather than from γενναω ('to be born').[54] Thus, many prefer the translation 'unique,' which, textually speaking, is a valid rendering, and takes nothing away from the eternal relationship of the Son of God to his Father.

The conservative evangelical scholar of New Testament Greek, A.T. Robertson, preferred the translation 'only born', and held that it said more about the eternal relationship of the Son to the Father than to his birth in the incarnation:

> μονογενὴς ('only born' rather than only begotten) here refers to the eternal relationship of the Logos (as in John 1:18), rather than to the Incarnation. It distinguishes thus between the Logos and believers as children (τέκνα) of God ... John clearly means to say that 'the manifested glory of the Word as it were the glory of the Eternal Father shared with His only Son.'[55]

Granted that although many other passages in John and elsewhere in the New Testament clearly teach the eternal Father/Son relationship,[56] it does seem to me that John 1 is more specifically referring to his birth in the incarnation (although his being eternally begotten by the Father is the background and value of his human birth). Even though I cannot affirm that he is irrefutably in the right textually, I am sympathetic theologically with Jacob Van Bruggen's reasons for preferring the older translation 'only-begotten' (and all translations are to some degree theological interpretations, and necessarily so). I would add that the *unigenitus* is fundamental to the identity of the Person of the Son, with regard to his Father and to the Holy Spirit.

> When the Bible calls Jesus the μονογενὴς Son of God, it means that He alone is the *natural* Son of God. He is distinguished from believers as natural children are distinguished from adopted ones. The phrase 'only-begotten Son of God' is really a summary of Psalm 2:7, where God the Father says to Christ: '...Thou art my Son; this day have I begotten thee.' This Psalm is quoted and applied to Christ in Acts 13:33 and Hebrews 1:5; 5:5. On the basis of Psalm 2, the ancient church saw the unique character of Christ's sonship in His divine life. The translation **only** weakens the spiritual insight into the unique sonship of Christ, and threatens the spiritual understanding of the unity of the Father and the Son.[57]

---

54. Raymond E. Brown, *The Gospel according to John (1-X11)* (New York: Doubleday, 1966), 13.

55. Archibald T. Robertson, *Word Pictures in the New Testament*, Vol V (Nashville: Broadman Press, 1932), 13-14.

56. See D. Kelly, *Systematic Theology*, vol. 1, chapters 4 and 7.

57. Jacob Van Bruggen, *The Future of the Bible* (Nashville: Thomas Nelson, 1978), 134,135.

Likewise the statement of the Nicene-Constantinopolitan Creed that the Spirit proceeds from the Father is essential to the Personal identiy of the Holy Spirit within the Trinity.

But whether μονογενὴς is rendered 'only begotten,' 'only,' or 'unique,' Gregory Nazianzus summarizes with biblical fidelity precisely what the New Testament means by this Father/Son relationship:

> ...Father is not a name either of an essence or of an action... But it is the name of a relation in which the Father stands to the Son, and the Son to the Father. For as with us these names make known a genuine and intimate relation, so, in the case before us too, they denote an identity of nature between him that is begotten and him that begets...[58]

The authority of the Gospel of John

Before we go on to other New Testament witnesses to Christ as the Son of God, it seems proper here to give some attention to the functional rejection of the Gospel of John as a true representative of Christ's life and words. For well over a century this has been a debated issue in much of New Testament theology. That is to say, if John is not taken as read, then much of the evidence for Christ's divine Sonship is at a stroke removed.

In the limitations of this volume, and also with my own lack of scholarly expertise in Johannine studies, it cannot be my purpose to discuss in any detail why I hold to the authority and historicity of the Gospel of John. The nineteenth-century work of J. B. Lightfoot, *Internal Evidence for the Authenticity and Genuineness of Saint John's Gospel,* is still of significance, and more recently Neill and Wright[59] and Martin Hengel[60] help bring us up to date, as well as later reconsiderations of the more radical scholar, John A. T. Robinson.[61] And other significant sources must be considered immediately below.

For example, James Dunn writes:

> No one can dispute the vast differences between the discourse style in the Fourth Gospel and Jesus' teaching recorded in the Synoptics. The point is that the style is *so consistent* in John...and *so consistently different* from the Synoptics that it can hardly be other than a Johannine literary pattern largely imposed upon it. The best explanation still remains that the Johannine discourses are meditations or sermons on individual sayings or episodes from Jesus' life, but elaborated in the language and theology of subsequent Christian reflection.[62]

But as a humble believer, I would simply ask: how does he know this? How can he be so certain that the discourses of John were fabricated at a much later time by the early Church? John A. T. Robinson may have

---

58. Gregory of Nazianzus, *Oration* XXIX.16.

59. Stephen C. Neill and N. Thomas Wright, *The Interpretation of the New Testament:1861-1986,* second edition (Oxford: Oxford University Press).

60. Martin Hengel, *The Johannine Question,* English transl. John Bowden (London: SCM, 1989).

61. John A. T. Robinson, *His Witness is True: A Test of the Johannine Claim* in his *Twelve More New Testament Studies* (London: SCM, 1985).

62. James D.G. Dunn, *Christology in the Making,* 30.

been right, that all the books of the New Testament were written *before* the Fall of Jerusalem in 70 A.D.[63] If so, that would not have left much time for 'pious' imagination and fabrication! But even if an early date is not the case, it has yet to be shown that the differences in John come from unhistorical inventions by the author.

Certainly, the Christian Church has, from the beginning, accepted John as part of its canon. As we saw in the earlier volume, God reveals his truth within a chosen community of faith, and believers are never to stand off the ground he has given to make himself known.[64] In John 10, Jesus says, 'My sheep hear my voice, and I know them, and they follow me...' (v. 27). It is impossible to apologize for perceiving and following the Shepherd's voice in the Gospel of John!

Of course, from ancient times, it has been understood that there are significant differences between John and the Synoptics, but that provides no grounds for denying the historicity of either. Craig Blomberg has shown that their varying approaches share alike a high selectivity, depending on what each evangelist wished to emphasize: '...Matthew, Mark and Luke, no less than John, are highly selective in what they record and are theologically motivated in structuring their Gospels.... Whatever does not fit into the structures determined by those criteria is simply omitted...'[65]

Blomberg adds: 'Once one recognizes similar principles of selection at work in the redaction of each of the Synoptists, John does not appear particularly more or less historical than they, especially when we recognize that what the Synoptics share counts as only one independent witness and not three...'[66]

For all the differences among the Gospels, both Craig Blomberg and D. A. Carson have extensively studied the *interlocking* traditions between John and the Synoptics.[67] And these interlocking traditions explicate one another, rather than contradict one another, and therefore cannot be said to indicate that one Gospel is less reliable than another.

Probably the most glaring difference between John and the Synoptics was held by much of nineteenth and twentieth-century scholarship to be their supposedly dissimilar presentation of who Christ is. Hence a very different Christology was said to constitute an unbridgeable gap between John and the Synopticcs.

But D. A. Carson has wisely warned against overemphasizing the Christological difference between John and the Synoptics: '... though the Christological distinctiveness of John's Gospel should not be denied, it should not be exaggerated.... The Synoptic Gospels present in seed form the full flowering of the incarnational understanding that would develop

63. See John A. T. Robinson, *Redating the New Testament* (Westminster Press: Philadelphia, 1976).

64. Kelly, *S. T.*, vol. 1, 16-37.

65. Craig Blomberg, *The Historical Reliability of John's Gospel* (InterVarsity Press: Downers Grove, Illinois, 2001), 54.

66. Ibid., 285.

67. See Blomberg, op. cit., 53-56, and D. A. Carson, *The Gospel According to John* (Inter-Varsity Press: Leicester, England, 1991), 49-58.

only later; but the seed is there, the entire genetic coding for the growth that later takes place. If John lets us see a little more of the opening flower, it is in part because he indulges in more explanatory asides that unpack for the reader what is really going on.'[68]

I must gladly enroll myself in the company of Peter Lombard, when he wrote (following Saint Ambrose): 'We believe fishermen, not dialecticians.'[69] And I invite others to join me.

God the Son in the Writings of Paul

Rather than speaking of 'God the Son', the Apostle Paul in general directly calls the Lord Jesus Christ 'God,' and it is clear from the context that he means 'the Son of God'. He writes to this effect in Romans 9:5: 'Whose are the fathers, and of whom as concerning the flesh Christ came, who is over all, God blessed for ever. Amen.'

However, some translations (such as the Revised Standard Version) have inserted a period after flesh, so that the doxology is ascribed only to the Father, thereby removing the word 'God' from Christ. But as we know, periods and commas, etc. were not in the original manuscripts. Translators have to decide what seems the most probable structure of the sentence.[70] When we read 'according to the flesh', we expect a contrast on the other side, and this seems to be 'God over all'. The contrast is hence between the human background of Christ in Israel and his full deity. The relative clause 'who being' refers to an antecedent, which in this case can only be Christ, for this name (Rom. 9:5) comes directly before the relative clause, thus identifying Christ as 'God over all' (Rom. 9:5). Also, the blessing (εὐλογητὸς) comes after both the Father and Christ, rather than first, before the Father only. This indicates that it is intended to refer to both.

This is not unprecedented elsewhere in the New Testament, for Revelation 5:13 ascribes such blessing to Christ, the enthroned Lamb of God: 'And every creature which is in heaven, and on the earth, and under the earth, and such as are in the sea...heard I saying, Blessing, and honour, and glory, and power, be unto him that sitteth upon the throne, and unto the Lamb for ever and ever.'

The same direct ascription of full deity to Christ occurs in Titus 2:13: 'Looking for that blessed hope, and the glorious appearing of the great God and our Saviour Jesus Christ.' In the Greek text, there is only one article before 'the glorious appearing [or, the appearing of the glory] of the great God and our Saviour, Jesus Christ.' This one definite article indicates that 'God and Saviour' is referring only to one person: the Lord Jesus Christ. It is Christ who will come on the last day, not the Father. Thus, while maintaining a distinction between God the Father and Christ, Paul is denominating Christ, the Father's Son, as God.

Paul also attributes Godness, or at least equality with God the Father, to Christ in II Thessalonians 1:12: 'That the name of our Lord Jesus Christ may

---

68. D. A. Carson, op. cit., 57.

69. Peter Lombard, *The Sentences*, vol. 3, 93.

70. See p. 34 above, on the point of theological conviction necessarily influencing translation.

be glorified in you, and ye in him, according to the grace of our God and the Lord Jesus Christ.' If (as is textually possible) one assumes the reading to have only one article, 'according to the grace of *[the]* our God and Lord Jesus Christ,' then it more clearly points out a single person: 'our God and Lord, Jesus Christ.' Hence, H. Ribberbos takes II Thessalonians 1:12 as an ascription of deity to Christ, and he refers to R. Bultmann, who also does so.[71] Yet on the other hand, Paul often sees a twofold source of grace, as in I Thessalonians 1:1 and II Thessalonians 1:2, so that could be the meaning in II Thessalonians 1:12. But even if so, the twofold source of grace would be two coordinated persons, who in the nature of the case must each be assumed to be God, else they could not be the same source.

In Paul's instruction to the Ephesian elders in Acts 20:28, he tells them 'to feed the church of God, which he hath purchased with his own blood.' This plainly means that the one who shed his blood to save his people is God. There is no significant textual problem here,[72] and yet the plain sense of it was already causing offense as far back as the time of the Church Fathers: how could one put God and blood immediately together, without transgressing the transcendence of God? But the Fathers answered that the God we know from Holy Scripture is the one whose Son (as much God as the Father is God) came into the flesh to die for our sins. Instead of being ashamed of it, they gloried in it!

In the development of Patristic theology in the third and fourth centuries, such statements as 'blood of God' would come to be known under the rubric of *communicatio idiomatum* (i.e. communication of 'idioms' – that is 'characteristics' that are proper to one nature, rather than to another).[73] Gregory of Nyssa was typical of other orthodox Fathers of the fourth century when he wrote:

> In the Lord Christ, because of the full union of the divine and human natures, we can exchange their names and call human what is divine, and divine what is human. That is why the Apostle Paul says that 'The Lord of glory was crucified' (I Cor. 2:8). And that is why he gives the name of Jesus to the One before whom every knee shall bow, of things in heaven, and things on earth, and things under the earth (Phil. 2:10).[74]

The basic concept is that both the 'idioms' or 'characteristics' of the human nature and the divine nature can be directly attributed to the Person (but not directly to the other nature). Hence, the one Person of the Lord Jesus Christ, who has two natures, is the subject of the acts of both natures. He is God the Son, who took on human nature, in which he, the God/man, shed his own blood for our sins.[75]

---

71. Herman Ridderbos, op. cit., 68, referring to Bultmann, *Theology of the New Testament*, 129.

72. Other than some manuscripts reading 'the church of the Lord,' the oldest ones, such as Codex Vaticanus and Sinaiticus read 'church of God.'

73. e.g. See Tertullian, *Of the Flesh of Christ*, v; Cyril of Alexandria, *De incarnatione Unigeniti* (PG 75.1244); Athanasius, *Contra Arianos*, III. 31. (See Chapter V of this volume).

74. Gregory of Nyssa, *Against Apollinarius* 2 (PG 45, 1277A).

75. John Calvin discusses this with clarity in *Institutes* II.14.1-4, where he says: 'Thus, also, the

We will postpone discussion of Philippians 2:5-11 for a few pages, for it will require much more exegetical detail. As we shall see there, the Apostle Paul teaches the same high view of Christ as God become man.

(3) Son of Man

This title was Jesus' preferred way to speak of himself. It is found about fifty times in the four Gospels. It was never attributed to him by others. The New Testament no longer uses it after the death and resurrection of the Lord, except for Acts 7:56, which probably means that it was he alone who used it (rather than having been 'invented' later by the 'early Church,' as postulated by the Form Critical theory). Instead of the Church later foisting the title back onto Jesus, it makes sense to believe that, in his own lifetime, he was using 'Son of Man' in terms of the original text in Daniel 7, which would have been perfectly comprehensible to his Jewish audience.

Richard Bauckham shows the basic methodology of Form Criticism:

> Although the methods of form criticism are no longer at the center of the way most scholars approach the issue of the historical Jesus, it has bequeathed one enormously influential legacy. This is the assumption that the traditions about Jesus, his acts and his words, passed through a long process of oral tradition in the early Christian communities and reached the writers of the Gospels only at a late stage of this process…Mark's Gospel was written well within the lifetime of many of the eyewitnesses, while the other three canonical Gospels were written in the period when living eyewitnesses were becoming scarce, exactly at the point in time when their testimony would perish with them were it not put in writing…But the period in question is actually that of a relatively (for that period) long lifetime.[76]

In that context, what N.T. Wright notes is reasonable. He mentions the irony of such a procedure, in that scholars who easily see the Daniel 7 background of 'Son of Man' assume that his audience did not also see it, so that,

> …this meaning has been both wished onto Jesus by pious scholarship, eager to find vestiges of a supernatural glory for the incarnate son of god, and snatched away from him by less pious scholarship, convinced that Jesus could not have spoken thus of himself. The whole debate has suffered the consequences of a failure to read Daniel 7 as it was read in the first century… The phrase, in its context, *could* be taken in the first century to refer to the Messiah; I have argued that Jesus did take it, and use it like that.[77]

Scriptures speak of Christ: they sometimes attribute to him what must be referred solely to his humanity, sometimes what belongs uniquely to his divinity; and sometimes, what embraces both natures but fits neither alone. And they so earnestly express this union of the two natures that is in Christ as sometimes to interchange them. This figure of speech is called by the ancient writers "the communicating of properties"' (II.14.1).

76. Richard Bauckham, *Jesus and the Eyewitnesses: The Gospels as Eyewitness Testimony* (Wm.B. Eerdmans: Grand Rapids, 2006), 6,7.

77. N. T. Wright, *Jesus and the Victory of God*, 516,518,519.

'Son of Man' then does not simply mean 'Christ was a man' (although it certainly includes that). Over the centuries, the popular concept in the Church has been that 'Son of God' refers to his divine nature and 'Son of Man' refers to his human nature. While it is biblically correct and necessary to hold that the one person, Christ, has at the same time a divine and a human nature, that is not the main point of this term. The main provenance of the title comes from the prophecy of Daniel, chapter 7. In a vision of what lies in the future for the four world empires already predicted in chapter 2, generally understood to be Babylon, Medo-Persia, Greece, Rome, one succeeding another, a supernatural figure is presented in chapter 7, who overcomes all human empire as he comes from Almighty God to judge with divine glory and to establish an unmovable kingdom forever (cf. Dan. 7:9-14). This figure, the Son of Man from God's glorious and mighty presence, is very much like the description John gives of the risen Christ in the Apocalypse (Rev. 1:7, 13-18, and 5:6-14). This connection between prophecy and unveiling of the Son of Man is united in Christ's taking to himself of this very title in his humiliation before being revealed as the glorious Son of Man in his exaltation.

The once popular paraphrase/translation of Scripture, *The Living Bible* by Kenneth Taylor, caught this significance, when it frequently rendered 'Son of Man' (in the context of Jesus' usage) as 'the heavenly one'. That will definitely not always accord with the way Jesus used it, but it has an important and defining place in the cluster of meaning around this phrase.

Three main contexts where 'Son of Man' is used

It is generally pointed out by experts in this field that there are three main contexts where Son of Man is used: (a) statements that were part of Jesus' ministry (e.g. Mark 2:10, 28; Luke 7:34; 9:58; 19:10); (b) statements relating to his suffering and resurrection: (e.g. Mark 10:45; Luke 17:24, 25; 22:48; 24:7; John 3:14; 6:53; 8:28; 12:23; 13:31); (c) statements relating to his future comings: (e.g. Matt. 10:23; 19:28; 24:30; 25:31; Mark 8:38; 13:26; 14:62; Luke 12:8-10, 40; 17:22-30; 18:8).[78]

a) e.g. Luke 9:58 shows the stupendous contrast between the high and heavenly one and the poverty and humility of his earthly ministry: 'And Jesus said unto him, Foxes have holes, and birds of the air have nests; but the Son of man hath not where to lay his head.' After the conversion of Zacchaeus, where the sinless one had entered the home of a highly disregarded sinner, Jesus said: 'For the Son of man is come to seek and to save that which was lost' (Luke 19:10).

b) e.g. John 3:14 speaks of the Son of Man being lifted up on the cross as the way to salvation/healing, as the brass serpent in the wilderness healed the disobedient Israelites as they looked upon it: 'And as Moses lifted up the serpent in the wilderness, even so must the Son of man be lifted up.'

---

78. e.g. see A.J.B. Higgins, *Jesus and the Son of Man* (London, 1964); I. Howard Marshall, *The Origins of New Testament Christology* (Downers Grove, 1976), and C.F.D. Moule, *The Origins of Christology* (Cambridge: Cambridge University Press, 1977).

c) e.g. Matthew 19:28 shows the once humbled Son of Man on the throne of glory: 'And Jesus said unto them, Verily I say unto you, that ye which have followed me in the regeneration when the Son of man shall sit in the throne of his glory, ye also shall sit upon twelve thrones, judging the twelve tribes of Israel.'

Although the prophecy of Daniel 7 did not reveal any hint of the grief and brokenness of the cross, Jesus the Son of Man had to experience it first, 'and then to enter into his glory' (Luke 24:26). But that grief was set forth in other Old Testament passages, such as Psalms 22 & 69, and Isaiah 52 & 53. His death as Son of Man would be followed by his victorious resurrection precisely as Son of Man (in line with what Daniel foresaw): 'And he began to teach them, that the Son of man must suffer many things, and be rejected of the elders…and be killed, and after three days rise again' (Mark 8:31). Six verses further down, Mark 8:38 speaks of the coming of the Son of Man 'in the glory of his Father with the holy angels.'

The only time 'Son of Man' is used after the ascension of Christ is at the martyrdom of Stephen, when he was given a look into the heavenly realm, where he was soon going: 'But he, being full of the Holy Ghost, looked up steadfastly into heaven, and saw the glory of God, and Jesus standing on the right hand of God, and said, Behold I see the heavens opened, and the Son of man standing on the right hand of God' (Acts 7:55-56). This is very near to what Daniel saw in Daniel 7. The state of humiliation is all past; exaltation is now his glorious experience, which he shares with his saints.

Hebrews shows just how he shares this divine glory with his people. Hebrews 2:6-8 takes over Psalm 8, and puts its divine gift of dominion originally granted to humanity over the created order into the context of the coming of the Son of Man into our human nature (Heb. 2: 11, 14, 16); his atoning death in our nature (2:9-10), followed by his lifting up of our cleansed humanity into everlasting glory, in which he has brought many sons to glory (Heb. 2:10-15). The completed work of the Son of Man included glorious victory over the devil, who long loved tormenting people with fear of death (2:14-15).

Is 'the Son of Man' Corporate?

Some scholars have held that Daniel's Son of Man is not one person, but a corporate entity; in particular, the righteous in Israel.[79] N. T. Wright discusses different options on this figure, as reflected in I Enoch (62 and 71), and draws together several messianic types, such as the descriptions in Daniel, Psalm 110, (probably) Zechariah 12:10, Psalm 2, Isaiah 11, and Isaiah 40–55.[80] He holds these references to lead finally to the Messiah, not to a corporate figure. Although the New Testament teaches the corporate union between Christ and his people (as in Romans 6:3-6; Galatians 2:20; John 15, etc.), the actual Son of Man is an individual, historical figure:

---

79. e.g. see M. D. Hooker, *The Son of Man in Mark* (London: SCM, 1967). See also 'Is the Son of Man really soluble?' in *Text and Interpretation: Studies in the New Testament Presented to Matthew Black*, ed. E. Best & R. McL. Wilson (Cambridge: Cambridge University Press, 1979), 155-168.

80. N. T. Wright, *Jesus and the Victory of God*, 625, 626.

one who lived a holy life, was crucified, and was raised victoriously from the dead. On the basis of who he was, his people are personally and corporately united to him in the Holy Spirit, and as such partake of all the benefits of his person and work. Most of the passages in the Gospels where Son of Man is used would not make sense unless they have reference to an individual person, rather than a corporate entity.

The Final Kingdom of the Son of Man
James Denney places the kingdom of Daniel's Son of Man as the righteous successor of the previous four world dominions:

> The prophet [Daniel] sees four great beasts come up from the sea and reign in succession. But they have their day; the dominion they exercised is taken away from them; it is transferred – and here the vision culminates – to one like a son of man. The brute kingdoms are succeeded by a human kingdom, the dominion of selfishness and violence by the dominion of reason and goodness; and this last is universal and everlasting...When Jesus defined it and made it his own...He intimated to those who were able to understand it his consciousness of being head of a new, universal, and everlasting kingdom... The wild beasts had had their time; now the hour had come for the dominion of the human; man claimed his sovereignty in Jesus. This is the root idea in the name, Son of Man...[81]

Yet it must be added (and Denney would have never denied it) that this succession of failed worldly kingdoms is profoundly based upon Old Testament Jewish concepts. As Ben Witherington writes:

> Jesus' message was about the coming of God's Dominion...He referred to himself as the enigmatic Son of Man of Daniel 7 and the Enoch literature. He presented himself as the embodiment of God's wisdom, Wisdom come in the flesh. In all these regards Jesus was presenting a religious worldview thoroughly grounded in the Hebrew Scriptures.[82]

The Son of Man's Kingdom of Peace Brought in by Violence
Furthermore, a careful reading of the Gospel accounts of the preparation for the passion of Christ will indicate that the Son of Man's kingdom of love and peace could only come through the hatred and violence that was to be visited upon him. T. F. Torrance shows in detail that Christ knew what he was doing in actually provoking the events that would lead to his crucifixion (cf. Luke 12:50 – 'But I have a baptism to be baptized with; and how am I straitened till it be accomplished!') and was in charge of what was happening (cf. John 10:17-18 – 'Therefore doth my Father love me, because I lay down my life, that I might take it again. No man taketh it from me, but I lay it down of myself. I have power to take it again. This commandment have I received of my Father').[83]

---

81. James Denney, *Studies in Theology* (Hodder and Stoughton: London, 1895), 36, 37.

82. Ben Witherington, *The Jesus Quest: The Third Search for the Jew of Nazrareth*, Second Edition (InterVarsity Press: Downers Grove, IL, 1997), 40.

83. T. F. Torrance, *The Incarnation*, 48-55, 148-56.

These facts about what Jesus thought he was doing are precisely contrary to the assumptions held by so many in the first 'Quest' for 'The Historical Jesus,' as summarized by Albert Schweitzer:

> In the knowledge that He is the coming Son of Man [He] lays hold of the wheel of the world to set it moving on that last revolution which is to bring all of ordinary history to a close. *It refuses to turn, and He throws Himself on it.* Then it does turn; and crushes Him. Instead of bringing in the eschatological conditions, He has destroyed them. The wheel rolls onward, and the mangled body of the one immeasurably great Man, who was strong enough to think of Himself as the spiritual ruler of mankind and to bend history to His purpose, is hanging upon it still. That is His victory and His reign.[84]

But if that were the case, it is a fair question to raise: why had the Christian Church been in existence for some 1,900 years, when Schweitzer was searching for its failed leader? Would he have really bothered to do so if Christ had been nothing but another long-slain, deluded prophet?

Ben Witherington gets right to the point as he responds to John Dominic Crossan's *The Historical Jesus*,[85] a book even more skeptical, if possible, than Schweitzer's, noting that 'If, as Crossan maintains, all of Jesus' followers deserted him, and were ignorant of the sequel other than that Jesus was crucified, it is frankly unbelievable to me that there would have arisen a continuing Jesus movement at all. There would have been no church without Easter.'[86]

The tragic result of so much otherwise brilliant nineteenth and twentieth-century scholarship that took the impossibility of his resurrection as a foundational premise for interpreting Jesus Christ was a self-imposed blindness that could never locate him. D. Staniloae has accurately analyzed what happened:

> Those who tried to eliminate everything that surpasses the exclusive humanity in Christ were not able to reconstruct the definite image of a historic Christ in the purely human sense of the word. They were not able to do that not only because they could not use other sources, by which, according to their method, the rejection of what that method considered to be eliminated from the New Testament image of Christ as not being purely human could have been established, but also due to the fact that the disciples themselves could not capture the Person of the Teacher within a human outline even before his Resurrection. Even then he remained for them a being always beyond all human dimensions, notwithstanding his supremely human closeness to them. They needed the key that is the Resurrection even to be able to complete, to fully understand, and to clearly formulate this divine character of their Teacher, who seemed to them, even before his Resurrection, as surpassing what the strictly human dimensions could hold.[87]

---

84. Albert Schweitzer, *The Quest of the Historical Jesus: A Study of its Progress from Reimarus to Wrede* (London: A. & C. Black [1906] 1954), 368-69.

85. John Dominic Crossan, *The Historical Jesus: The Life of a Mediterranean Jewish Peasant* (San Francisco: Harper/SanFrancisco, 1991).

86. Witherington, op. cit., 77.

87. Staniloae, op. cit., 43, 44.

But the Scriptures tell us that the Son of Man, that son of David, who 'hid not his face from spitting' (Isa. 50:6), as he willingly laid down his life to a shameful death, was 'declared to be the Son of God with power, according to the spirit of holiness, by the resurrection from the dead' (Rom. 1:4).

(4) Logos (Word)

A careful discussion of the significant description of who Christ is in relation both to God and to the created order will be temporarily postponed, so as to avoid repetition. It will be opened up in the exposition of the prologue to the Gospel of John.[88]

(5) The seven 'I AM' sayings of the Gospel of John, plus one more

As we have seen earlier, when Jesus calls himself 'I AM,' he is identifying himself with YHWH: the Name by which God revealed himself to Moses at the burning bush (Exodus 3) as the salvation of Israel. Thus, Jesus is God Almighty, God eternal; the God of the Covenant of Grace, and at the same time, come in the flesh, fully man.[89] Much of chapters 2 through 11 of John's Gospel is based upon seven miracles, which are signs of who Christ is. Either before or after these defining miracles, Jesus says 'I am' as a way of explaining what these miracles meant as to his identity and salvation. And in other cases he calls himself 'I am' in the context of major discourses, and at his final crisis in Gethsemane.

I will here list, rather than explicate, these seven 'I am' sayings of Christ, as they will be expounded in various aspects of the 'States of Christ' later. These 'I am' sayings show the meaning of his signs in a fallen world, and point to its redemption by the One 'Who is.'

1. After the miracle of the feeding of the five thousand, Jesus seeks to turn the desires of the multitude from merely physical bread to that relationship which will give them eternal life: 'For the bread of God is he which cometh down from heaven, and giveth life unto the world. Then they said unto him, Lord, evermore give us this bread. And Jesus said unto them, **I am the bread of life**: he that cometh to me shall never hunger: and he that believeth on me shall never thirst' (John 6:33-35). This saying seems to be based in Isaiah 55:1, 'with respect to the eschatological salvation brought about by the Word of God' as D. A. Carson points out.[90]

2. After his forgiveness of the woman taken in adultery (which in spite of its absence in some of the oldest manuscripts, I assume – with the church fathers, and with a majority of other ancient manuscripts – to have actually happened), Jesus says: 'Then spake Jesus again unto them, saying, **I am the light of the world**; he that followeth me shall not walk in darkness, but shall

---

88. See Chapter III of this volume.

89. See Kelly, *S. T.*, vol. 1, 279-292.

90. D. A. Carson, op. cit., 28.

have the light of life' (John 8:12). 'Light is Yahweh in action, Ps. 44:3...The coming eschatological age would be a time when the LORD himself would be the light of his people (Is. 60:19-22; cf. Rev 21:23-24).'[91]

3. In order to warn his sheep against false shepherds, who wish to rob them, rather than save them (John 10:1) Jesus says: 'Verily, verily [the Old Testament word for affirmation of God's covenant: i.e. 'Amen'], I say unto you, **I am the door of the sheep**' (v. 7). 'In vv. 1-5, Jesus the shepherd enters the sheep pen through the gate, here he is the gate...Here the watchman has disappeared, and the only flock in the enclosure belongs to the shepherd who serves as the gate.'[92]

4. Continuing the contrast of his ministry to that of false shepherds, who fleece the sheep, Jesus says: '**I am the good shepherd**: the good shepherd giveth his life for the sheep' (John 10:11). He indicates that as shepherd, he is in the highest relationship of mutual knowledge with the Father (v. 15). This relationship of knowledge and love between Shepherd/Son and Father will lead him to lay down his life, and also to take it up again (vv.17-18). 'Far from being accidental, Jesus' death is precisely what qualifies him to be the good shepherd – a point presupposed in Hebrews 13:20, which acknowledges Jesus to be "that great Shepherd of the sheep." And by his death, far from exposing his flock to further ravages, he draws them to himself (12:32)'.[93]

5. Shortly before he raised Lazarus from the dead after four days in the tomb, Jesus said to Martha: '**I am the resurrection and the life**: he that believeth in me, though he were dead, yet shall he live' (John 11:25). D. A. Carson notes with insight the message of Jesus to Martha in this saying: 'Jesus' concern is to divert Martha's focus from an abstract belief in what takes place on the last day, to a personalized belief in him who alone can provide it. Just as he not only gives the bread from heaven (6:27) but is himself the bread of life (6:35), so also he not only raises the dead on the last day (5:21, 25ff.) but is himself the resurrection and the life. There is neither resurrection nor eternal life outside of him.'[94]

6. In answer to Thomas' question about how one could know the way to the Father's house where Jesus was going (John 14:5), Jesus replies: '**I am the way, the truth, and the life**: no man cometh unto the Father, but by me' (v. 6). 'Only because he is the truth and the life can Jesus be the way for others to come to God, the way for his disciples to attain the many dwelling places in the Father's house (vv. 2-3), and therefore the answer to Thomas' question (v. 5). In this context Jesus does not simply blaze a trail, commanding others to take the way that he himself takes: rather, he *is* the way.'[95]

7. At the beginning of his discourse on the relationship of believers to him in terms of the analogy of a vine and its branches, Jesus said: '**I am the true vine**, and my Father is the husbandman' (John 15:1). In addition to Isaiah 5, Psalm 80 seems to be in the background of meaning here. 'The true ...

---

91. Ibid., 338.

92. Ibid., 384.

93. Ibid., 386.

94. Ibid., 412.

95. Ibid., 491.

vine, then, is not the apostate people, but Jesus himself, and those who are incorporated in him...if they wish to enjoy the status of being part of God's chosen vine, they must be rightly related to Jesus.'[96]

I add one more to the traditional list of seven. This statement of 'I am' is not in the same genre as the seven sayings for they are all found in the heart of Christ's doctrinal discourses. This one is not a formal exposition of who he is, as are the other seven, but rather is 'overheard' in the hour of his passion in Gethsemane. But I include it (without claiming that it is in the category of the seven traditional 'I am' statements), because of the stupendous power that came forth when it was uttered. In a mighty way, it too shows us who this Jesus is, and explicates his relation to the Father.

8. When the officers from the chief priests and Pharisees came to arrest Jesus in the Garden of Gethsemane upon his betrayal by Judas, Jesus asked them whom they were seeking (John 18:2-4). Then occurred a supernatural event that knocked the officers to the ground with the mere mention of a name from the Lord. 'They answered him, Jesus of Nazareth. Jesus saith unto them, I am. And Judas also, which betrayed him, stood with them. As soon then as he had said unto them I am, they went backward, and fell to the ground' (vv. 5-6). It appears that at the mention of the divine name, which is that of YHWH, 'I am that I am,' a surge of deity ran through the manhood of our Lord; a beam of the uncreated light broke through the darkness of the very night where Satan was so active, and overwhelmed the enemies of God and his incarnate Son. The theory of Schweitzer, Renan[97] and others, including the popular 1970s' rock opera 'Jesus Christ Superstar,' that the deluded Jesus was now being broken under the control of the powers of evil is shown to be a delusion itself. The great 'I AM' was in direct control of it all, willingly choosing to lay down his life 'a ransom for many' (Matt. 20:28); 'no man could take it from him' (John 10:18).

In a certain sense, most of what the various names and titles of the LORD Jesus Christ convey can be, one way or another, included under the seven, (perhaps plus one) 'I ams' of John. As Matthew tells us, following the annunciation of Gabriel, he is Jesus (YAHWEH) who will save his people (1:21), and following Isaiah 7:14, he is 'Emmanuel... God with us' (Matt 1:22-23).

Should the Church call the Lord 'Yahweh' in its preaching and praying?
In the last third of the twentieth century, I have noticed an increasing tendency (at least among Protestant preachers) to speak of God, in preaching and in prayer, by the Name 'Yahweh.' While I would not argue that this is necessarily improper, I do wonder why we should have to depart from the centuries-long English tradition of rendering the Name JHVH, or YHWH, as 'Lord'? And that was also the tradition in the Medieval Latin tradition (i.e. JHVH is generally rendered in the Vulgate as *Dominus*).

---

96. Ibid., 514.

97. E. Renan, *La Vie de Jésus* (Paris: Michel Levy Frères, 1863).

An obvious problem with addressing God as 'Yahweh' is simply that we do not know how it originally sounded, for the Hebrew was not *pointed* (i.e. *supplied with vowels*, by means of placing certain signs under the consonants, which alone were in the original text) in the ancient manuscripts, before the work of the Masoretes.[98] That is certainly not enough to preclude our using this term in church, but – to me at least – it makes the practice a bit questionable for liturgical usage. Secondly, why depart from the Latin and English liturgical tradition? Again, sounding out the name of JHVH (YHWH) in church is not wrong, but is it really worth doing so? Also, the reticence of both ancient and modern Judaism from pronouncing the 'Tetragrammaton' would bear some weight with me.

I appreciate what Dr. Patrick D. Miller wrote on this matter:

> I would argue there is no inherent claim in Scripture that the name of God is not to be pronounced. But substitutions for the name, even as the Bible substitutes the term 'God' for the name, and uses it as a name, may properly represent the invocation and proclamation of the name of God. As for the actual vocalization and pronunciation of the Tetragrammaton (YHWH) by Christians, Robert Jenson's counsel in this regard is simple and wise: 'Jewish feeling in this matter should be honored by Christians; the recent fashion of pronouncing the name in lectures and from the pulpit is deeply regrettable.' It is important to observe that Jenson's comment in this regard is a matter of counsel and is not a theological argument (Jenson, *Systematic Theology* I:44 n. 12).[99]

Other 'I am' statements

In other words, the 'I am' sayings demonstrate that he is God in his fullness, dwelling in human flesh, thereby accomplishing our salvation. For instance, as Craig Blomberg points out, several verses after Christ's saying, 'I am the light of the world' (John 8:12) some crucial Old Testament allusions appear, that show the Son's identity in being with the Father. Jesus says to the Jewish authorities who were denying him: '"If you do not believe that I am, you will die in your sins" (John 8:24). ...there is a veiled allusion to Isaiah 43:10, in which Yahweh himself declares, "I am he..." But by 8:58 a clear reference to Exodus 3:14 ("I am that I am") is heard, "I tell you the truth...before Abraham was born, I am" (John 8:58).'[100]

In sum, the Old Testament foreshadows his names and titles, and sets forth in both type and event who he is and what he achieves, while the

---

98. However, on the other hand, the great Jewish theologian of the Middle Ages, Rabbi Moses Maimonides (often called Rambam) did actually discuss its pronunciation: 'They [the Priests, when reciting the Priestly Blessing, when the Temple stood] recite [God's] name – i.e., the name *yod-hei-vav-hei*, as it is written....' [In the Masoretic text, there is a distinction between 'what is written in the actual text' (the *Ketibh*), and what is generally read out loud (the *Qere*), which is noted in the margin. Thus, Ramban is stating that *in this* case, with the Tetragrammaton, it would have been sounded out the same way *it is* written in the text – author's addition]. He added that it could be pronounced only in the Temple, but elsewhere, another of God's names, such as Adonai is recited. See *Mishneh Torah* Maimonides, Laws of Prayer and Priestly Blessings, 14:10. For further details, see Maimonides, *The Guide to the Perplexed*, vol. I, chapter 62.

99. Patrick D. Miller, *The Ten Commandments* (Westminster John Knox Press: Louisville, Kentucky, 2009), 115.

100. Craig Blomberg, op. cit., 143.

New Testament displays his infinitely perfect fulfillment of them all. The 'I am' sayings, and other titles ascribed to him in the Scriptures, are the outflow of the inner-trinitarian relations between Father, Son, and Spirit. They demonstrate the beauty of God's holiness, glory and love. Precisely how the Old Testament foreshadowings are brought to their fullness by God in the flesh will be seen in the next chapter which expounds four crucial passages from the New Testament.

APPENDIX 2.1

THE GENEALOGIES OF JESUS CHRIST

The Gospels of Matthew (1:1-17) and Luke (3:23-38) each give genealogies of Jesus Christ, which are in some ways compatible, and in other ways are different in detail. These similarities and differences have long been recognized, and have been commented on (in writing) since the time of the Apologists (i.e. second and third centuries). From that time to the present, scholars have taken very different approaches to the genealogies. Until the European Enlightenment (eighteenth century), except for a few opponents of early Christianity (such as Celsus, who critiqued these genealogies – c. A.D. 120, and whom Origen answered),[1] most believers have accepted them as basically valid, but have been faced with the problem of how then to reconcile them.

In the last three centuries, those in the more liberal tradition have assumed that while there is probably some value in them, their details cannot be taken seriously as literal history. On the contrary, they have held that these genealogical lists may have been made up at a later time, such as by the early Judeo-Christian communities, and thus include some historical facts, and a considerable measure of imaginative invention.

To the best of my knowledge, the most careful, scholarly, and coherent study of the complex details of both the genealogies of Matthew and Luke comes from a Roman Catholic French scholar, l'Abbé Jacques Masson: *Jésus Fils de David Dans les Généalogies de Saint Mathieu et de Saint Luc.*[2] This appendix offers a brief summary of his findings, which represent decades of close research in both ancient and modern sources.

His basic goal was to see if each of the various generations in the two genealogies is credible, and if it is possible to harmonize the different accounts in Matthew and Luke.[3] He seeks to do so by providing five closely related studies (or 'Parts'):

I. The credibility of the genealogies from David to Jechoniah and Neri.
II. The father of Salathiel (to whom Matthew and Luke ascribe different

---

1. Origen, *Contra Celsum* II.32.

2. *Dissertatio ad Lauream in Facultate S. Theologiae apud Pontificiam Universitatem S. Thomae in Urbe* (Tequi: Paris, 1981).

3. J. Masson, op. cit., 3.

fathers: Jechoniah (by Matthew), and Neri (by Luke)). III. The credibility of the two genealogies from Salathiel to Jacob and Heli (the list in Matthew descends from ancestor to descendant, and names Jacob as father of Joseph, while that in Luke ascends from descendant to ancestor, and lists Heli as father of Joseph). IV. Details concerning the father of Joseph: Jacob, according to Matthew, and Heli, according to Luke. V. In what sense Jesus Christ is called 'Son of David' even though both of his genealogies are those belonging to his foster-father, Joseph, rather than to those of his mother, the Virgin Mary.

I. The credibility of the genealogies from David to Jechoniah and Neri

Matthew gives three series of fourteen generations each, from Abraham to David, from Solomon to Jechoniah, and from Jechoniah to Joseph (and Jesus) (Matt. 1:17). This series leaves out some generations, which Luke fills in from other perspectives, as we shall see. It has been suggested that Matthew employs the mnemonic device of fourteen either because he found fourteen generations between Abraham and David, or because the numerical value of the name David amounted to fourteen (i.e. ד = 4 + ו = 6 + ד = 4 = 14).[4]

To get fourteen generations, it was necessary for Matthew to omit some names: particularly those of three kings, who were related to the evil queen-mother, Athaliah, sister of idolatrous King Ahab of the Northern Kingdom. Hence, Matthew omits the names of King Ahaziah, Joash, and Amaziah, who come between King Joram and Uzziah [Ozias – as in the LXX] (both of whom he does list – Matthew 1:8-9). Masson argues that this suppression was not a mistake, but was deliberate, perhaps because Matthew did not want the Messiah connected to a family that by Mosaic law was cursed to the third or fourth generation,[5] owing to their alliance with the polytheistic house of Omri.

Abraham Park, a Korean minister and scholar, has also written extensively on these genealogies. In particular, he discusses the omitted generations in Matthew's account.[6] Like Masson, Park ascribes the omission of these four evil rulers to their massive sins against the covenant.[7]

There are other omissions. Between Salmon (one of the Israelite spies to Jericho) and Jesse (father of David, some four centuries or so later), there are only two names (Boaz and Obed – cf. Matt. 1:5), and these are insufficient to cover so many years.[8] The names given between Phares (son

---

4. Ibid., 132.

5. Ibid., pp. 116-24.

6. See Abraham Park, *The Unquenchable Lamp of the Covenant: The First Fourteen Generations in the Genealogy of Jesus Christ* (Periplus Editions: Singapore, 2010), Chapter seven (pp. 78-81), and *God's Profound and Mysterious Providence as Revealed in the Genealogy of Jesus Christ from the Time of David to the Exile in Babylon* (Periplus Editions: Singapore, 2011), Chapter 20 (pp. 208-32).

7. A. Park, *God's Profound and Mysterious Providence*, 220-232.

8. Masson, op. cit., p. 127.

of Judah, born before Jacob's sojourn in Egypt) and Naason (living at the time of the Exodus – cf. Matt. 1:3,4) are too few.[9] But these omissions are not the same things as mistakes; rather, they represent deliberate choices to fit with the overall purpose of Matthew.

Masson traces this same overarching purpose in the mention of 'the brothers of Jechoniah' in his second series of fourteen generations. For reasons that I will not discuss here, Masson changes 'the brothers of Jechoniah' to 'the brothers of Joiaquim' (cf. Matt. 1:11).[10]

Matthew's overall purpose is this:

> Saint Matthew needed to emphasize the end of the earthly reign of the house of David. Well, all of the sons of Josiah ('the brothers of Joiaquim') took the throne [one after another]. It was with them that the earthly Davidic royalty was extinguished forever. Saint Matthew also mentions that all of them were the final representatives of this earthly royalty in Israel: Joiaquim and his brothers, and Jechoniah. As it turned out, Matthew emphasizes the tragic nature of the events that led to the fall of the royalty and the deportation to Babylon. He also emphasizes the fulfillment of the messianic promises in Jesus, Son of David and Messiah.[11]

Masson reasonably suggests that the reason why Matthew lists four women: Tamar, Rahab, Ruth and Bathsheba (the last two, or possibly three of them, of foreign origin, in the second series of his genealogy – cf. Matthew 1:3,5,6) is for a precise purpose: '…he wished to show that Jesus, the son of David, was the heir of the messianic promises.'[12] All four of them were important to the line of descent in the tribe of Judah.[13] All of them were worked upon by the Holy Spirit, as was the Virgin Mary.[14]

The number of generations in Luke is different from that in Matthew

Masson shows that there is no serious reason to think that Luke is working with a symbolical number of generations, as was Matthew. Whereas Matthew lists three series of fourteen generations each (cf. Matt. 1:17), Luke does not specifically state the number of generations, other than listing the names, from Jesus back to God, creator and father of Adam (cf. Luke 3:23-38).[15] Luke lists twenty names between Nathan, son of David, and his descendant, Neri (cf. Luke 3:27-31), whereas Matthew lists only eighteen (*if one adds in* the three omitted kings) between Solomon, brother of Nathan, and his descendant, Jechoniah, father of Salathiel (cf. Matt. 1:7-12). But Luke names Salathiel's father as Neri (Luke 3:27).[16]

---

9. Ibid., p. 128.

10. Ibid., pp. 43,45; 49-63; 133-43; 233-35.

11. Ibid., 141 (my translation).

12. Ibid., 159.

13. Ibid., 190-98.

14. Ibid., 200-05.

15. Ibid., 214-15.

16. Ibid., 218.

Masson explains this difference of two generations, and shows that it does not invalidate either genealogy.[17] This means that if Neri is the father of Salathiel, then Salathiel is descended from Nathan, while if Jechoniah is his father, then Salathiel is descended from Solomon.

Hence, at first glance, Matthew seems to trace the lineage of Jesus through Solomon (son of David), while Luke seems to trace it through Nathan (another son of David). But as we shall soon see, a more careful look at the genealogical facts will correct this first impression. This highly significant matter is discussed in Part II of Masson's work.

Similarly, Dr. Abraham Park suggests that 'God had omitted the time of spiritual darkness (most of the 430 years in Egypt and about 300 years from the period of the judges) from the genealogy of Jesus Christ. By so doing, God is demonstrating that the purpose of Jesus Christ's genealogy is not to record a complete list of all generations in the fleshly lineage, but to record the lineage of faith that reveals God's administration in the history of redemption.'[18]

II. The father of Salathiel

In brief, according to Matthew's genealogy, *Jechoniah* is the father of Salathiel (from whom Christ descends through Zorobabel) – cf. Matthew 1:12, whereas according to Luke's genealogy, Neri is the father of Salathiel (from whom Christ descends through Zorobabel), cf. Luke 3:27. Jechoniah is descended from David's son Solomon while Neri is descended from David's son Nathan. Therefore, we must ask: is Salathiel descended from Solomon (as according to Matthew), or from Nathan (as according to Luke)?

Masson notes that while Jechoniah (whom Matthew lists as descendant of David's son, Solomon) is attested in the Old Testament as the father of Salathiel, and of several other sons (cf. I Chronicles 3:17-24), Neri (whom Luke says is descended from David's son, Nathan) is nowhere mentioned in the Old Testament.

However we explain Neri, it is not likely that his name was a free invention by Luke. Luke had available to him several historical/ genealogical sources in addition to the lists in the Old Testament, as Masson comments, 'The author of the genealogy of the first Gospel, and Saint Luke, almost certainly made use of private sources, such as family archives, or consulted genealogical documents conserved in the Temple, as Josephus mentions (cf. Josephus, *Contra Apionem* I.37)...'[19]

But even if the name of Neri did, as is most likely, come directly from ancient archives, how could he and Jechoniah both be the father of Salathiel? Masson then provides the most reasonable solution, in light of the Jewish customs and legal structures of that time: one of the 'fathers' of Salathiel is the natural father, and the other is the legal father. If so, which was which?

---

17. Ibid., 219-32.

18. A. Park, *God's Profound and Mysterious Providence*, 211.

19. Masson, op. cit., 236, 417.

Masson shows that Jechoniah was not the natural father of Salathiel. An important oracle of Jeremiah (ch. 22:22-30) pronounced a curse on this last reigning king of the Jews. At the center of this divine curse was that Jechoniah would be childless (and thus have no direct descendant to take the throne):

> As I live, saith the LORD, though Coniah [i.e. Jechoniah] the son of Jehoiakim king of Judah were the signet upon my right hand, yet would I pluck thee thence; And I will give thee into the hand of them that seek thy life, and into the hand of them whose face thou fearest, even into the hand of Nebuchadnezzar king of Babylon, and into the hand of the Chaldeans… Thus saith the LORD, write ye this man childless, a man that shall not prosper in his days: for no man of his seed shall prosper, sitting upon the throne of David, and ruling any more in Judah (Jer. 22:24-25, 30).

Neri, according to the research of Masson, was in fact the natural father of Salathiel, and Salathiel was the father of Zorobabel (as we shall later see). Neri was:

> [T]he son of Melchi, a descendant of David by Nathan. He was more distantly connected to the throne, being the member of a cadet branch of the royal line. However, it is very likely that he would have been an eventual successor of the throne of Judah, and was connected to Jechoniah by other ties, which are difficult to discern at this stage of our discussion…[Even so], he seemed to be the most likely, or at least one of the most likely, to receive eventual access to the throne-line of David and to the promises of God.[20]

Masson shows that Ezekiel (ch. 17) and Zechariah (ch. 12) see the line of Nathan (rather than Solomon) as carriers of the royal Davidic line into the future.[21] If that is correct, then Salathiel, continuer of the throne line, was descended *physically* from Neri, yet is counted in I Chronicles 3 and Matthew 1 as son of Jechoniah (or, as Jeremiah calls him, the childless 'Coniah'). Masson explains that Salathiel is the *legal* son of Jechoniah. He then shows the impossibility of his having become his son through a levirate marriage (in which the wife of a male who died without descendants can marry a relative of her late husband, who then 'raises up seed' in the name of the deceased kinsman – cf. Deuteronomy 25 and the book of Ruth).[22] But that could not have worked in the case of Jechoniah.

Rather, Salathiel became the legal son of Jechoniah by *adoption*. Masson argues that the kind of adoption relevant in the Old Testament was a kind of 'special adoption' – i.e. *deficiente filio* – 'in the absence of a son, the son-in-law, that is, the husband of the daughter who would be the heir, obtains by adoption, all the rights of a son: name and inheritance.'[23] Masson shows why Jechoniah would have been interested in such a legal and biblically allowable transaction:

---

20. Ibid., 301.

21. Ibid., 303-314.

22. Ibid., 314-20.

23. Ibid., 335-36.

Jechoniah was the successor of David, charged with continuing the messianic line till the Messiah announced by God should come…But Jechoniah had been condemned by divine oracle to end his life without a successor…Yet he could not have been disinterested in the future of this Davidic line, and in the permanence of his name, according to the possibilities offered in the Law… Since Jechoniah was the legal father of Salathiel, it signifies that during his lifetime he sought to assure that he would have a legal line of descent through the only way possible: adoption.[24]

This appendix cannot enter into the details of how this type of biblically allowed adoption – *deficiente filio* – would have worked in this case.[25] But in briefest compass, Masson proposes that Jechoniah had given his daughter in marriage to Salathiel, and that Salathiel was a near relative to him in the female line of descent.[26]

This explains the validity of Matthew's attribution of Jechoniah as father of Salathiel:

> …[he is his father] legally, by the type of adoption known as *deficiente filio*. Matthew introduces into his genealogy a *new element: legal paternity*. And if Saint Matthew has given the natural descent from David to Jechoniah, after Salathiel, all of the descendants of Jechoniah are legal descendants, in the feminine and dynastic line (because this is in accordance with biblical law).[27]

If that is correct, then – contrary to what many have supposed – it is not the case that Matthew is giving the line of descent through Solomon, while Luke is giving it through Nathan. 'Both give the genealogy of Jesus through his attachment to Salathiel, son of Neri, descendant of Nathan. Saint Matthew calls "Jechoniah" the father of Salathiel, which he really is in a legal sense, by means of adoption *"deficiente filio."*'[28]

Yet there are still differences between the lines given by Matthew and Luke *after* Salathiel. Masson suggests that the key to resolving these differences is found in the use that Matthew makes of legal descent and that Luke makes of natural descent.[29] This is discussed by Masson in his Part III.

III. The credibility of the genealogies from Jacob and Heli [i.e. each one listed as the father of Joseph in the different genealogies] to Salathiel

We cannot enter in this brief appendix into the complexities of how this is worked out, and refer the interested reader to Masson.[30] It is appropriate though to note the goal of Matthew in his 'legal' genealogy:

---

24. Ibid., 338-40.

25. Ibid., 340-53.

26. Ibid., 348-49.

27. Ibid., 351.

28. Ibid.

29. Ibid.

30. Ibid., 356-416.

Saint Matthew attained his goal, and showed that Jesus, a descendant of David, the successor of Jechoniah, was thus the successor of David, and the heir to the Davidic promises. Saint Luke for his part attached Saint Joseph, from father to son, to king David, and showed that Saint Joseph was an authentic descendant of David.[31]

This leads us to consider the next major question, which is discussed in Masson's next Part:

IV. The Father of Saint Joseph

Matthew lists Joseph's father as Jacob (cf. Matt. 1:16), and Luke gives him as Heli (cf. Luke 3:23). If that is correct, then which one is the legal father, and which is the natural father? Masson shows that:

> By way of Elioud-Esli [which he considers to be the same person],[32] the genealogy of Jesus is carried by Saint Matthew through Eleazar, the ancestor of Matthan, the father of Jacob, leading to Joseph; but Saint Luke takes the line through Naum, probably the brother of Eleazar, and finally ends up with Joseph, son of Heli, son of Matthat… Once again, we find ourselves facing two fathers for one man, as was the case with Salathiel.[33]

But instead of assuming this to be a contradiction, there is a more likely approach. We should remember that both Matthew and Luke had not only the Old Testament genealogies, but also private sources, which at that time were still extant before the burning of the Temple. And in addition to that, there was still the living memory of relatives of Christ. It is therefore far more likely that Matthew and Luke both knew what they were doing with these genealogies, and worked with them in accordance with their different purposes. The ascription of ignorance to either of them does not fit what we know of the Jewish culture at that time.

> [When Matthew and Luke were being written]… relatives of Christ were still alive, members of his family whom the Gospel speaks of as his 'brothers,' his 'sisters,' or at least, as close relatives and friends of the family. The great care with which the Jews sought to keep their genealogy readily available…is well known. Also one can assume that Saint Matthew and Saint Luke would have had available for consultation the genealogical registers conserved in the family of Joseph. Can we imagine that these private documents, carefully kept available, would have diverged on the name of the father of Saint Joseph, and that, after the death of Christ, but within the lifetime of the apostles, people would already have forgotten the immediate ancestors of the Saviour?[34]

Instead of being contradictory, the two genealogies are complementary: one (Matthew) gives the *legal* descent, the other (Luke) gives the *natural*

---

31. Ibid., 415.

32. Ibid., 407-411.

33. Ibid., 417.

34. Ibid., 417-18.

descent. But if this is true, by what means was Saint Joseph made the *legal* descendant of Jacob (in accordance with Matthew's genealogy)?

Masson refers to a letter of Julius Africanus (third century) which stated that he had visited relatives of Christ in Palestine, and asked them about this seeming contradiction of Joseph having two fathers.[35] According to their explanation, the natural father of Joseph was Jacob, who died, and then Joseph was adopted by Heli, Jacob's half-brother.[36]

But Masson believes that while there is an element of truth in these family traditions, they are not exactly correct, in part owing to the loss in A.D. 70 of the archives in the Temple (over a century and a half before Africanus visited these relatives of the Lord). He believes that the element of truth is that 'Joseph is the issue of Jacob and Heli by a levirate marriage.'[37]

This would have been possible, because Masson finds that 'Jacob and Heli both descended from the two sons of Judah (who is not otherwise mentioned in Scripture), who was one of the sons of Hananya-Joanna, the son of Zorobabel...'[38] Abiud (probably the older brother) was one of them (cf. Matt. 1:13), and the other (probably younger) was an earlier Joseph (cf. Luke 3:26). The details are as follows:

> Faithful to the same principle [i.e. of *legal* descent], and to the Jewish manner of procedure, Saint Matthew needed to attach Elioud-Esli to his legal father, Achim [cf. Matt. 1:14], and by him to the kings of Judah. Hence, Elioud-Esli, although he was the son of Nagge, according to the flesh [cf. Luke 3:25], was attached by Abiud, Judah, Hananya-Joanna, Zorobabel, and Salathiel to Jechoniah, and to the kings of Judah. Saint Luke, on the contrary, retained Nagge, the father of Elioud-Esli, according to the flesh, and led up to David by way of Nathan, in passing through Neri.
> The two lines issuing from Judah were thereby reunited, so that Jacob and Heli had a common ancestor, Elioud-Esli: Jacob by Matthan, descended from Eleazar, the eldest son of Elioud-Esli; Heli through Matthat descended from Naum, another son of Elioud-Esli. This common ancestor provides us with the necessary postulate to explain the descent of Joseph from Jacob and Heli by means of the levirate law.[39]

Since Luke gives the natural fathers, and Matthew gives the legal fathers, it is more likely that Heli (from Luke's list) is the natural father, and Jacob (from Matthew's list) the legal one.[40] Joseph seems to have been from a levirate marriage, since they were closely related, and had a male ancestor in common.[41] In sum, '[t]he presence of two fathers for Saint Joseph makes one postulate a *legal* father; the levirate law is a possible and highly likely explanation; it is, moreover, the only reliable, and the most ancient

---

35. Ibid., 420.
36. Ibid., 421.
37. Ibid., 439.
38. Ibid., 455.
39. Ibid., 456.
40. Ibid., 457.
41. Ibid., 458.

proposal.'[42] In other words, Jacob and Heli were both descended from Elioud some two centuries earlier. If Jacob, as seems to have been the case, died without male descendants, then his wife married his relative, Heli, who raised up seed for him (namely, Joseph, foster father of Jesus).[43]

This research brings us to Masson's final Part:

V. Jesus, Son of David

This fifth section summarizes the 'legal' proof of the Davidic descent of the foster father of Christ: Joseph.

> The two lists of Saint Matthew and of Saint Luke, at first glance contradicting one another, show us that in fact Joseph was the son of David in two different manners: according to nature, he was a descendant from David through Heli, Naum, Nagge, Judah, Salathaliel, Neri, and Nathan [i.e. in Luke's account]. According to the law [i.e. Matthew's account], he is descended from David through Jacob, Eleazer, Achim, Abiud, Salathiel, Jechoniah, and Solomon...[44]

> It is by means of Joseph that Christ inherited the title of Son of David... Joseph may thus be considered the 'father' of Jesus, and since it is not a matter of *natural* fatherhood, it can only mean a *legal* paternity...[45]

God Almighty, not Joseph, was the true Father of Jesus. Masson, in company with all Christian believers, recognizes that God, the heavenly Father, begat Christ, through the power of the Holy Spirit in his miraculous working within the Virgin Mary (cf. Matt. 1:18-25; Luke 1:26-38).[46]

The genealogy given by Matthew is particularly addressed to Jewish Christians, and with that context in mind, traces the Lord's descent *legally*, through Jechoniah and Solomon. On the other hand, Luke is addressed to Hellenistic believers, who were less likely to have understood rules of Jewish descent, and so he gives the line of *natural* descent through Nathan.

I believe that the concluding remarks of l'Abbé Masson are fair and well-grounded in careful genealogical and historical research:

> The two genealogies do not therefore differ in any decisive points, and their divergences only seem to be such. Instead of contradicting one another, they complement one another. Each one goes back to David in a normal way: that is, first by legal descent (according to Jewish law – which considers it to be a reality), or by natural descent, according to the otherwise universal way of procedure... The two genealogies are not lists invented by their author, or later constructions of the primitive Christian community. We are in the presence of texts that are truly credible: the information they give us rests upon a solid basis. They are true to history, and demonstrate that Jesus is truly descended from David, in accordance with both of the two genealogies.[47]

---

42. Ibid., 468.

43. Ibid., 469.

44. Ibid., 475.

45. Ibid., 479.

46. Masson devotes a section to a discussion of the genealogy of the Virgin Mary, which I will not go into here (cf. ibid., 483-511).

47. Ibid., 516.

APPENDIX 2.2

THE ISSUE OF TRANSLATING DIVINE FAMILIAL TERMS FOR MUSLIM LANGUAGE COMMUNITIES

Does it matter whether modern translations of the New Testament render 'Son of God' accurately, or replace it with another term, which may be less offensive to Muslims? We shall see that it does, and that this issue of 'Son of God' enters into the very substance of the Gospel. And we shall also see that there are trends abroad in the community of evangelical missionary translators that are failing to identify with precision that Jesus Christ is the eternal Son of God. This should be a matter of great concern to all Christian people, who are wishing to convey the saving truth of God to every tribe, tongue and nation.

Here are two illustrations of why the Church should be concerned over the direction some translation projects have taken:

In the 1990, W/SIL [Wycliffe Bible Translators and Summer Institute of Linguistics] participated in the production of the 'Stories of the Prophets' Arabic New Testament audio dramas[1] translating the Greek *pater* as 'rabb' (used with the non-familial meaning 'Lord' throughout the *Qur'an*) instead of a word closer to English 'father.' Examples of word replacement solutions in particular verses include:[2]

(a) Luke 1:32, 35 – 'Son of the Most High' and 'Son of God' become 'the awaited Christ'.
(b) Luke 4:3 – 'If you are truly the Son of God' becomes 'If you are truly the Messiah of the most high God.'
(c) Luke 4:9 – 'the Son of God' becomes 'the Messiah of God'.
(d) Luke 6:36 – 'your Father is merciful' becomes 'God is merciful'.
(e) Luke 11:2 – 'Father' in the Lord's Prayer becomes 'Our loving heavenly Lord'.
(f) Luke 11:13 – 'the heavenly Father' becomes 'the Lord of the world'.
(g) Luke 24:49 – 'I will send the promise of my Father upon you' omits 'of my Father'.
(h) Matthew 28:19 – 'in the name of the Father, the Son, and the Holy Spirit' becomes 'in the name of God, and his Messiah and the Holy Spirit'.[3]

---

1. 'Divine Familial Terms: Answers to Commonly Asked Questions,' *Wycliff.org*. March 30, 2012, http:www.wycliffe.org/SonofGod/QA.aspx (accessed April 2012).

2. Adam Simnowitz, 'How Insider Movements Affect Ministry: Personal Reflections,' in *Chrislam: How Missionaries Are Promoting an Islamized Gospel*, ed. Joshua Lingel, Jeff Morton and Bill Nikides (Garden Grove, CA: i2 Ministries, 2011), pp. 206-207.

3. 'A Call to Faithful Witness – Part One – Like Father, Like Son: Divine Familial language in

That General Assembly Committee notes that, 'In response to complaints, expansion of this audio series has ended, and some of the debated recordings have been withdrawn from SIL-affiliated web sites. However, some problematic recordings remain available.[4] W/SIL staff members have also issued conflicting statements about whether the dramas should be considered a sort of Bible or not.'[5]

The Assemblies of God dealt with this issue in April 2012, in a report: 'The Necessity for Retaining Father and Son Terminology in Scripture Translation for Muslims', and I quote their 'Appendix D' to that committee report:[6]

Examples of specialized 'translations' for Muslims

The following include any non-literal renderings for Father and Son terminology, including 'Son of God' and 'son of God':

Verse	NASB	Back Translation	Original Language
Gospel Of Matthew	Son of God	'God's representative'	Turkish (Incil-i Serif'in Yuce Anlami – Havari Matta'nin Kaleminden)
Gospel Of Matthew	Father	Protector/Helper	Turkish (Incil-i Serif'in Yuce Anlami – Havari Matta'nin Kaleminden)
Matthew 6:9	'Pray, then, in this way: 'Our **Father** who art in heaven, Hallowed be Thy name.	And when you pray then pray in the following manner, saying, 'O our **guardian** whose throne has encompassed the heavens, blessed [be] your name, the exalted.	**Arabic** The True Meaning of the Gospel of Christ (aka, The Lighthouse, An Eastern Reading of the Gospels and Acts, 2008)
Matthew 6:9	Pray, then, in this way: 'Our **Father** who art in heaven, Hallowed be Thy name.	O our **sustainer** (parvardigaar) that you are at the great throne, may your holy name be honored	**Baluchi/Balochi** Injil Sharif (aka Greek-Balochi NT, 2nd ed., 2001)

Bible translations – A Partial Report (Part one of two parts) of the AD Interim Committee on Insider Movements to the Fortieth General Assembly of the Presbyterian Church in America' May 14, 2012 (Office of the Stated Clerk of the General Assembly of the Presbyterian Church in America).

4. See alambiya.net and sabeelmedia.com (accessed April 2012).

5. 'Face Check: Biblical Missiology's Response,' p. 6 (accessed April 2012). This paragraph and its references are taken from 'A Call to Faithful Witness,' p.39.

6. 'The Necessity for Retaining Father and Son Terminology in Scripture Translations for Muslims,' Contributors: Ben Aker, Jim Bennett, et al. for the General Assembly of the Assemblies of God (April 2012), pp. 51-59.

Matthew 28:19	Go therefore and make disciples of all the nations, baptizing them in the name of the **Father** and the **Son** and the **Holy Spirit**	Cleanse them by water in the name of **God, his Messiah** and his Holy Spirit.	**Arabic** The True Meaning of the Gospel of Christ (aka, The Lighthouse, An Eastern Reading of the Gospels and Acts, 2008)
Matthew 28:19	Go therefore and make disciples of all the nations, baptizing them in the name of the **Father** and the **Son** and the **Holy Spirit**	and baptize them with water in the name of **God** and **His Messiah** and the Holy Spirit.	**Arabic Baghdadi** (Lives of the Prophets aka Stories of the Prophets, an audio panoramic Bible)
Matthew 28:19	Go therefore and make disciples of all the nations, baptizing them in the name of the **Father** and the **Son** and the **Holy Spirit**	wash (*ghusul*) in the name of the **sustainer** (*parvardigaar*), in **my name that am his beloved** (*habeeb*), and in the **holy spirit's name** [it is no trifling matter that 'name' is repeated three times, contrary to the Greek. This is the same thing that is done by Jehovah's Witnesses in the New World Translation in order to deny the unity of the singular name of the Father and the Son and the Holy Spirit.	**Baluchi/Balochi** Injil Sharif (aka Greek-Balochi NT, 2nd ed., 2001)
Matthew 28:19	Go therefore and make disciples of all the nations, baptizing them in the name of the **Father** and the **Son** and the **Holy Spirit**	Now go to all the nations and train [islamic] disciples to me and make them purify themselves by [islamic ritualistic] washing unto repentance to the name of the Protector, his Representative (or, deputy, agent) and the Holy Spirit.	**Turkish** (Incil-i Serif'in Yuce Anlami – Havari Matta'nin Kaleminden)
Mark 1:1	The beginning of the gospel of Jesus Christ, the **Son of God.**	Here begins the biography of the unique **Son of God** (the unique beloved of God).	**Arabic** The True Meaning of the Gospel of Christ (aka, The Lighthouse, An Eastern Reading of the Gospels and Acts, 2008)

Mark 1:1	The beginning of the gospel of Jesus Christ, the **Son of God.**	Beginning of the Injil of Isah Masih. [**Son of God** is not translated at all]	**Baluchi/Balochi** Injil Sharif (aka Greek-Balochi NT, 2nd ed., 2001)
Mark 1:11	and a voice came out of the heavens: 'Thou art My beloved **Son**, in Thee I am well-pleased.'	At his exiting from the water, he saw the heavens had split [open], and the Spirit of God descended upon him as a dove, and a voice was heard from heaven and it said, 'You are my beloved **Son** (the beloved chosen one), and with you I am well pleased.'	**Arabic** The True Meaning of the Gospel of Christ (aka, The Lighthouse, An Eastern Reading of the Gospels and Acts, 2008)
Mark 1:11	and a voice came out of the heavens: 'Thou art My beloved **Son**, in Thee I am well-pleased.'	From heaven a voice came, that 'you are my beloved (habeeb), I am happy with you.' [**Son** is not translated]	**Baluchi/Balochi** Injil Sharif (aka Greek-Balochi NT, 2nd ed., 2001)
Mark 1:11	and a voice came out of the heavens: 'Thou art My beloved **Son**, in Thee I am well-pleased.'	As soon as he came out of the water, he saw – the sky had opened up and Ruhul Kuddus was coming down towards him appearing like a pigeon. And a voice chanted from the heaven: 'You are my beloved **Masih**, I am very much pleased with you.' (Masih has been replaced by either, **'God's Uniquely-Intimate Beloved Chosen One'** or **'God's Uniquely-Intimate Beloved One'** in the revised edition).	**Bengali** (Injil Sharif, 2005 ed.)

Mark 9:7	Then a cloud formed, overshadowing them, and a voice came out of the cloud, 'This is My beloved **Son**, listen to Him!'	Suddenly a cloud covered them and gave them a voice from heaven saying, 'This is my beloved **Son** (the beloved Messiah), he is the one you must listen to and obey!' Then they turned around and they did not find [anyone] except Isa.	**Arabic** The True Meaning of the Gospel of Christ (aka, The Lighthouse, An Eastern Reading of the Gospels and Acts, 2008)
Mark 9:7	Then a cloud formed, overshadowing them, and a voice came out of the cloud, 'This is My beloved **Son**, listen to Him!'	a voice came from the cloud that, 'this is my beloved (habeeb), obey his words.' [**Son** is not translated]	**Baluchi/Balochi** Injil Sharif (aka Greek-Balochi NT, 2nd ed., 2001)
Mark 9:7	Then a cloud formed, overshadowing them, and a voice came out of the cloud, 'This is My beloved **Son**, listen to Him!'	At that point, a white cloudlet came and covered them, and from that cloud, these words were pronounced, 'This is my beloved **Masih**, you listen to what he says.' Instantly they looked around but couldn't find anybody with them except Isah. (Masih has been replaced by either, **'God's Uniquely-Intimate Beloved Chosen One'** or **'God's Uniquely-Intimate Beloved One'** in the revised edition).	**Bengali** (Injil Sharif, 2005 ed.)
Mark 14:36	And He was saying, 'Abba! **Father**! All things are possible for Thee; remove this cup from Me; yet not what I will, but what Thou wilt.'	And he cried out, 'O **my Lord**, you are the Almighty over everything, put this cup of sorrows far from me; however, O Lord, may it be what you want, not what I want.'	**Arabic** The True Meaning of the Gospel of Christ (aka, The Lighthouse, An Eastern Reading of the Gospels and Acts, 2008)

Mark 14:36	And He was saying, 'Abba! **Father**! All things are possible for Thee; remove this cup from Me; yet not what I will, but what Thou wilt.'	in place of 'Abba, Father' **sustainer** (parvardigaar) is used	**Baluchi/Balochi** Injil Sharif (aka Greek-Balochi NT, 2nd ed., 2001)
Mark 14:36	And He was saying, 'Abba! **Father**! All things are possible for Thee; remove this cup from Me; yet not what I will, but what Thou wilt.'	He said, 'Oh **Rabbul Alamin**, everything is possible for you. Take this glass away from me. Nonetheless, let it not happen in accordance of my wish, but according to your wish.' [Rabbul Alamin is Arabic for 'Lord of the worlds' and is one of the titles of God in the First Sura of the Quran which is also repeated in their 5 daily prayers]	**Bengali** (Injil Sharif, 2005 ed.)
Mark 14:61	But He kept silent, and made no answer. Again the high priest was questioning Him, and saying to Him, 'Are You the Christ, the **Son** of the Blessed One?'	However, Isa – his peace be upon us – kept his silence and remained speechless. Then the high priest turned to him a second [time] with the question, saying, 'Are you the Messiah, **Son of God (beloved of God)**, the blessed and exalted?'	**Arabic** The True Meaning of the Gospel of Christ (aka, The Lighthouse, An Eastern Reading of the Gospels and Acts, 2008)
Mark 14:62	But He kept silent, and made no answer. Again the high priest was questioning Him, and saying to Him, 'Are You the Christ, the **Son** of the Blessed One?'	Isah said, 'I'm he. You will see **Ibnul Insan** to sit to the right of The Almighty and to come along with the cloud of the sky.' [Ibnul Insan is Arabic for '**Son** of Man'.]	**Bengali** (Injil Sharif, 2005 ed.)

Luke 1:32, 35	[32]'He will be great, and will be called the **Son** of the Most High; and the Lord God will give Him the throne of His father David;' [35] And the angel answered and said to her, 'The Holy Spirit will come upon you, and the power of the Most High will overshadow you; and for that reason the holy offspring shall be called the **Son of God**.	The Spirit of God will come down upon you and this thing is the proof that this child is the awaited **Christ** who will rule forever.	**Arabic Baghdadi** (Lives of the Prophets aka Stories of the Prophets, an audio panoramic Bible)
Luke 1:32, 35	[32] 'He will be great, and will be called the **Son** of the Most High; and the Lord God will give Him the throne of His father David;' [35] And the angel answered and said to her, 'The Holy Spirit will come upon you, and the power of the Most High will overshadow you; and for that reason the holy offspring shall be called the **Son of God**.	He will be great among all the people and he will be the king, **God's caliph**, the exalted. And God will give him the throne of the prophet David, his great [lit. first] grandfather. The spirit* of God will descend on you and from his power [that] you see, you will bring forth a boy [who] will be the awaited king from God, he who will be **God's awaited caliph**. *contrary to standard Bible translations in Arabic, spirit of God is given a feminine adjective	**Arabic Urbed** (Lives of the Prophets aka Stories of the Prophets, an audio panoramic Bible)

Luke 1:32, 35	[32] 'He will be great, and will be called the **Son** of the Most High; and the Lord God will give Him the throne of His father David;' [35] And the angel answered and said to her, 'The Holy Spirit will come upon you, and the power of the Most High will overshadow you; and for that reason the holy offspring shall be called the **Son of God.**	his name (laqab) will be the **beloved** (habeeb) of almighty God. ...he will be called **God's beloved** (habeeb) [**Son** is not translated]	**Baluchi/Balochi** Injil Sharif (aka Greek-Balochi NT, 2nd ed., 2001)
Luke 1:32, 35	[32] 'He will be great, and will be called the **Son** of the Most High; and the Lord God will give Him the throne of His father David;' [35] And the angel answered and said to her, 'The Holy Spirit will come upon you, and the power of the Most High will overshadow you; and for that reason the holy offspring shall be called the **Son of God.**	He will become great and will be called **the Son who comes from Allah** the Most High. Allah, our God, will give him the throne of David, his ancestor. The angel replied, 'Ruh Allah will come upon you and the power of Allah the Most High will over/ envelop you. Because the child who will be born will be called holy, the Son who comes from Allah.	**Indonesian (Bahasa)** (Kitab Suci Injil)

Luke 1:32, 35	[32] 'He will be great, and will be called the **Son** of the Most High; and the Lord God will give Him the throne of His father David;' [35] And the angel answered and said to her, 'The Holy Spirit will come upon you, and the power of the Most High will overshadow you; and for that reason the holy offspring shall be called the **Son of God**.	He will be great and will be called the **prince of God** Most High. God, our Lord will grant the throne of David, his ancestor to him, The angel said, 'Holy Spirit will descend upon you, and the power of the Most High will overshadow you. Therefore, the holy child to be born will be called the **prince of God**.	**Malay ("Shellabear revision')** (My Kitab Suci)
Luke 3:38	…Adam, the **son of God**	…Adam **whom God created**	**Arabic** The True Meaning of the Gospel of Christ (aka, The Lighthouse, An Eastern Reading of the Gospels and Acts, 2008)
Luke 3:38	…Adam, the **son of God**	…God **created Adam**	**Baluchi/Balochi** Injil Sharif (aka Greek-Balochi NT, 2nd ed., 2001)
Luke 3:38	…Adam, the **son of God**	…Adam **was from God**	**Dari** http://gospelgo.com/q/Dari%20Bible%20-%20New%20Testament.pdf
Luke 3:38	…Adam, the **son of God**	…Adam, **child/ offspring of God** (the typical word for 'son' is not used while in the rest of the genealogy it is present)	**Sorani-Kurdish** Injili Sorani (Kurdish NT (Sorani) or NKV, 1999)
Luke 9:35	And a voice came out of the cloud, saying, 'This is My **Son**, My Chosen One; listen to Him!'	…they heard a voice from heaven saying: 'This is the beloved **Messiah** whom I have sent, so listen to Him and obey Him.'	**Arabic Baghdadi** (Lives of the Prophets aka Stories of the Prophets, an audio panoramic Bible)

Luke 11:2	And He said to them, 'When you pray, say: **Father**, hallowed be Thy name. Thy kingdom come.	When you pray, say: Our **loving, heavenly Lord**	**Arabic Baghdadi** (Lives of the Prophets aka Stories of the Prophets, an audio panoramic Bible)
John 20:31	but these have been written that you may believe that Jesus is the Christ, the **Son of God**; and that believing you may have life in His name.	...Isa is the Messiah, the **Son who comes from God**.	**Indonesian (Bahasa)** (Kitab Suci Injil)
Romans 1:7	to all who are beloved of God in Rome, called as saints: Grace to you and peace from God our **Father** and the Lord Jesus Christ.	The word 'Father' is **skipped** in this verse: God's peace be upon you, His mercy and blessings* through our master Jesus (Isa) Christ. *A distinct Islamic phrase is used here.	**Arabic Urbed** (Lives of the Prophets aka Stories of the Prophets, an audio panoramic Bible)
Romans 8:14-17	[14] For all who are being led by the Spirit of God, these are **sons of God**. [15] For you have not received a spirit of slavery leading to fear again, but you have received a **spirit of adoption as sons** by which we cry out, '**Abba! Father!**' [16] The Spirit Himself bears witness with our spirit that we are **children of God**, [17] and if **children**, heirs also, **heirs of God** and fellow heirs with Christ, if indeed we suffer with Him in order that we may also be glorified with Him.	**Completely skipped.** Only 4 of the 39 verses in this chapter were rendered (vv. 10-11, 34, 37)	**Arabic Urbed** (Lives of the Prophets aka Stories of the Prophets, an audio panoramic Bible)

Romans 8:14-17	[14] For all who are being led by the Spirit of God, these are **sons of God**. [15] For you have not received a spirit of slavery leading to fear again, but you have received a **spirit of adoption as sons** by which we cry out, '**Abba! Father!**' [16] The Spirit Himself bears witness with our spirit that we are **children of God**, [17] and if **children**, heirs also, **heirs of God** and fellow heirs with Christ, if indeed we suffer with Him in order that we may also be glorified with Him.	14 …they are **God's friends** (dost). 15 – we are **God's friends** (dost)…'O **sustainer** (parvardigaar). 16 – we are **God's friends** (dost). 17 – if we are **God's friends** (dost)…	**Baluchi/Balochi** Injil Sharif (aka Greek-Balochi NT, 2nd ed., 2001)
Galatians 1:16	to reveal His **Son** in me, that I might preach Him among the Gentiles, I did not immediately consult with flesh and blood,	God, the praised and exalted, revealed His **caliph** in me so that I preach His message among the foreigners	**Arabic Urbed** (Lives of the Prophets aka Stories of the Prophets, an audio panoramic Bible)
Galatians 2:20	"I have been crucified with Christ…by faith in the **Son of God**…	I, in the old life was crucified with my master Christ…by the faith of the **caliph of God**…	**Arabic Urbed** (Lives of the Prophets aka Stories of the Prophets, an audio panoramic Bible)
Galatians 2:20	I have been crucified with Christ…by faith in the **Son of God**…	here in place of 'Son of God' is '**God's beloved** (habeeb) 'Eesaa' [**Son** is not translated]	**Baluchi/Balochi** Injil Sharif (aka Greek-Balochi NT, 2nd ed., 2001)
Galatians 2:20	I have been crucified with Christ…by faith in the **Son of God**…	I have been crucified with Al-Masih… because of faith in the **Son who came from Allah**…	**Indonesian (Bahasa)** (Kitab Suci Injil)

Galatians 3:26	For you are all **sons of God** through faith in Christ Jesus.	For this reason, you, oh Galatians, whether you were sons of Jacob or not, today you have become **members of God's household**	**Arabic Urbed** (Lives of the Prophets aka Stories of the Prophets, an audio panoramic Bible)
Galatians 3:26	For you are all **sons of God** through faith in Christ Jesus.	…you are **God's friends** (dost)…	**Baluchi/Balochi** Injil Sharif (aka Greek-Balochi NT, 2nd ed., 2001)
Galatians 4:4-7	[4] But when the fulness of the time came, God sent forth His **Son**, born of a woman, born under the Law, [5] in order that He might redeem those who were under the Law, that we might receive the **adoption as sons.** [6] And because you are **sons**, God has sent forth the Spirit of His **Son** into our hearts, crying, 'Abba! **Father!'** [7] Therefore you are no longer a slave, but **a son**; and if **a son**, then an **heir through God.**	Completely skipped	**Arabic Urbed** (Lives of the Prophets aka Stories of the Prophets, an audio panoramic Bible)
Galatians 4:4-6	[4] But when the fulness of the time came, God sent forth His **Son**, born of a woman, born under the Law, [5] in order that He might redeem those who were under the Law, that we might receive the **adoption as sons.** [6] And because you are **sons**, God has sent forth the Spirit of His **Son** into our hearts, crying, 'Abba! Father!'	[4] When the time was fulfilled, God sent **the Son who came from him**. He was born of a woman and was under the Law (Taurat). [5] The reason was so he could redeem every person who was under the law and so we could receive the rights of a child. [6] Because you have become his children, God sent the Spirit of **the Son who comes from him** to go into our hearts and cry, 'Ya Abba, ya Bapa.'	**Indonesian (Bahasa)** (Kitab Suci Injil)

How the Church translates the Word of God into the various languages is of essential importance in communicating the Gospel from age to age, and from culture to culture. It is a significant part of obedience to Christ's Great Commission to take the Gospel to every tribe throughout the world. The Church has from the beginning of its world-wide mission taken with utmost seriousness this command to translate the written Word into different languages with exquisite accuracy, knowing with Paul that if 'Christ died for our sins according to the Scriptures, and was raised again the third day from the dead according to the Scriptures' (I Cor. 15:3, 4), then specific – and accurate words – must be employed to convey the saving message into whatever language is being used.

Accuracy in language is always necessary, because behind the saving Gospel is the Bible's presentation of who the God is who saves us eternally through what he became and did within history. The Lord Jesus Christ, who died for our sins and rose for our justification (Rom. 4:25), is none less than the eternal Son of God. We have frequently discussed in this volume how his eternal Sonship is essential to his saving work. Indeed, we could say that the defining doctrine of Christianity is the Holy Trinity: Father, Son, and Holy Spirit, electing and creating, redeeming and applying that redemption to all the people of God. As Basil the Great has shown, the Christian life is basically transformative knowledge of God the Father, through God the Son, in God the Holy Spirit.[7]

Therefore, knowing that God the Father has a Son, and has sent him to save our fallen humanity, and has sent down the Holy Spirit to apply to us all that the Son accomplished in his life, death and resurrection for us, is the very heart of authentic Christian Faith. Simon Peter affirmed in his confession that became the rock foundation of the Church: 'Thou art the Christ, the Son of the living God' (Matt. 16:16). Had there been no confession of the Son of God, there could have been no church, and the church, founded on the prophets and apostles, is the ground where God reveals his truth, and brings a lost humanity from darkness into his marvelous light. Thus, the believing confession of the Christ as the Son of God is not peripheral matter for Christian outreach, for Paul says: 'That if thou shalt confess with thy mouth the Lord Jesus, and shalt believe in thine heart that God hath raised him from the dead, thou shalt be saved' (Rom. 10:9), and soon adds: 'So then faith cometh by hearing, and hearing by the word of God' (Rom. 10:17). The conclusion is obvious: in order to confess Jesus as Lord to our salvation, people need to know who he is as the Son of God and Savior of the world.

Athanasius taught that the Father/Son relationship is the basis for the Church's thinking through, and then formulating, the doctrine of the Trinity.[8] The Church did so, because the Trinity enters into the structure and content of the salvation of the world. The reality of Christian redemption is directly based upon the truth of God as three distinct persons in one Being. 'For God so loved the world that he gave his only begotten Son,

---

7. Basil, *De Spiritu Sancto*, 18.47.

8. Athanasius, *Contra Arianos*, 3.3.

that whosoever believeth in him should not perish, but have everlasting life' (John 3:16).

But if the Father does not have a Son, then God must be something like an impersonal monad, or dark, massive force, and if God is a formless, impersonal monad, or hidden faceless power, then he is not love, and, in that case, no one would have come down from him to save us (for a non-person would not have a person to send to us, and there would be no love to motivate him to any plan of salvation). In such a dreadful case, within the dark force, there would be neither Son, nor Holy Spirit, and thus there would be no church, no Gospel, no Christian salvation.

That is why in our translations of the Scriptures of the New Testament, we must never countenance the replacing of the word 'Son' with something like 'wisdom' or 'word.' But that is beginning to happen in some evangelical quarters, and since it so enters into what the Puritans called 'the vitals of religion', in this volume on Christology we must look at this translation movement carefully.

I. The history of the controversy

The late 1960s and early 1970s saw the rise of studies in contextualization in foreign missions. Initially the term 'contextualization' focused primarily on the external and visible trappings of Christian expression, but over time some mission strategists began to extend the concept of contextualization to include aspects of belief and its expression, resulting in the growth of controversy over principles, methods, and practice. Concurrent with this growing movement and related to it was a focus on culture, such that courses in cultural anthropology became a required part of missionary training. Richard L. Heldenbrand, an American missionary in France in the 1980s, discussed the direction contextualization was then taking in *Christianity and New Evangelical Philosophies.*[9]

Fuller Seminary's School of World Mission showed a particularly strong focus on cultural anthropology and on viewing cultural issues as central concerns for evangelism, especially among Muslims. Such distinguished scholarly figures as Charles Kraft, Donald McGavran, Dudley Woodberry, and Ralph Winter, all associated with Fuller, are well known for their focus on the role of cultural concerns in contemporary missiology. While much that these scholars said needed to be heard by a self-satisfied church, some aspects of it certainly appear to have been taken too far (as in the previous two groups of illustrations). That is, with some of them, or perhaps with some of their followers, the focus on culture and anthropological training came to outweigh theological concerns in certain areas, with the result that much of the driving force for missions came to be based on social science, instead of theology or Biblical revelation, although theology and revelation were never formally denied.

In the late 1970s and early 1980s a new phenomenon, known as the 'Insider Movement,' emerged among Muslims who had been evangelized

---

9. Richard L. Heldenbrand, *Christianity and New Evangelical Philosophies*, (Words of Life: Warsaw, IN 2003).

by western missionaries. As with all religious or spiritual movements, there was a wide variety of expression in the movement, but one thing that seemed to unite the various expressions of it was the focus on people turning to Christ within the context of their own cultural setting, *including the religious orientation of their culture.*

Many evangelicals became alarmed at what seemed to them to be syncretistic tendencies of this 'Insider Movement.' The Jesus to whom at least some of these Muslims were turning was not all that different from what Islam already affirmed of him, which is that he is the Messiah and a prophet. It will come as no surprise that not all of those who affirmed their allegiance to him as his followers within this movement acknowledged the Trinity or acknowledged that Jesus was in fact God's Son, and that God was his Father. If that be the case, then this movement is a serious aberration from historic Biblical Christian Faith.

But even very knowledgeable missiologists find it difficult to verify precisely what these Insider converts really believe, and how many of them actually exist, in large part because of the understandable secrecy that has surrounded this movement, owing, presumably, to security concerns, to which we Christians in relatively free societies must not be unsympathetic. Because of the lack of access to such insider communities, and the absence of verifiability regarding what actually happens on the field in those closed societies, supporting constituencies in the home countries have had to rely for information on reports from the practitioners of this methodology that has led to the Insider Movement.

And that is a major problem: while it is good to respect necessary privacy in the interests of security in generally anti-Christian areas, this not unexpected lack of verifiability and accountability has allowed some serious issues to go unchecked. And one of these pressing issues is the way that critical biblical terms are being translated. No doubt, the most important of these words requiring translation are the divine familial terms 'Father,' 'Son,' and 'Son of God.' We have seen above how these words constitute the very heart of the Gospel, and therefore are always non-negotiable.

Sometime about the mid-1990s, some missionary Bible translators working among Muslims began avoiding using these terms (such as Son of God) on the grounds that they can be so scandalous to some Muslims that they refuse to read material that contains them. The idea that God could have a son is fundamentally opposed in the Qur'an, which very clearly states that God does not beget, nor does he have any relationship which would result in procreation, and anathematizes anyone who would dare to say that Jesus is the Son of God (Qur'an 4:165; 5:18; 6:101; 9:30; 19:35; 88-92; 17:111; and 23:91).

In addition, a number of Muslim imams have often taught their people that Christians believe in a Trinity of God, Mary, and Jesus, who was procreated physically through a sexual union of God and Mary. It appears that many in the 'Insider Movement' hoped they could avoid this kind of terrible misunderstanding and misrepresentation of the Biblical presentation of the Trinity in many mosques by replacing the New Testament textual references to 'Son of God' with something like 'Word of God' or 'Wisdom of God'.

This approach to translation among predominantly Muslim language groups was later termed 'Muslim Idiom Translation' (MIT),[10] and the stated underlying premise was that it is much more effective to use terms that Muslims are familiar with, and avoid 'ecclesiastical' terms that are confusing to them. An unstated underlying premise, however, is that the religious understanding of many Muslims is so shaped by their language and its culture that it is not possible successfully to introduce new and different concepts that would challenge their prevailing view of God, such as the Biblical teaching that God has always had a Son, and that Fatherhood/Sonship is an essential part of the identity of the One true God. Apparently many of the evangelical leaders of this outreach to Muslims definitely assume that clearly following the New Testament and the historic Church in presenting Christ as the eternal Son of God would lead to automatic rejection of Christian teaching.

Another way to say this is that it seems to assume that Muslims are somehow incapable of having their previous theological system shattered in the light of fuller truth, based on new information that challenges their original belief system. Among some of these leaders of the Muslim Insider Movement, there would appear to be relatively little expectation that the people reading the translated Scripture are likely to learn new concepts, or to change their mode of thinking in a profound way.

It would appear then that the human culture (in this case, various types of Islam) has, in the estimation of some of these missionary Bible transla-tors, become so all-prevailing that presumably, the best that one can hope for is that by using terms that do not directly confront or challenge their existing worldview, the people can be gradually brought to hold views that are more in line with what the Bible teaches, and to do so without necessarily making a dramatic break with their culture, including its reli-gious understandings.[11] That is why many of them do not want to give an accurate translation of Christ as the Son of God, and wish to replace 'Son' with something like 'Word' or 'Wisdom' because the latter terms seem to avoid the offence caused by misrepresentations of the doctrine of the Trin-ity by many in the mosque.

Though it would be inaccurate to say that all practitioners of MIT (i.e. Muslim Idiom Translation) are also in step with the Insider Movement, or that all those who hold and promote Insider Movement assumptions and methodologies favor the MIT approach, there seems to be a considerable degree of overlap between the two groups, with the most vocal advocates of MIT being in many cases sympathetic with the Insider Movement and vice versa. What this means is that for those who accept both the Insider

---

10. See Rick Brown, John Penny and Leith Gray, 'Muslim-idiom Bible translations: Claims and facts," *St Francis Magazine*, Vol 5, No 6 (December 2009).

11. For examples of objectionable renderings see http://www.change.org/petitions/lost-in-translation-keep-father-son-in-the-bible.

Movement and MIT as valid paradigms, it is not a concern to them if a movement grows up that does not relate to the larger church or to historic Christianity, because in their estimate, both the Church and Christianity are expressions of culture. As has often been said by some who are of that persuasion, it is not *religion* that saves, it is Jesus that saves, so people who want to follow Jesus do not necessarily need to change their religion and culture (which are seen as component parts of one indivisible whole) in order to be saved. But the Church must ask: who is this Jesus?

Metaphor or core theology?

Another presupposition of the MIT practice is the notion that divine familial terminology is metaphorical. That is, the terms 'Father' and 'Son' are an analogy that have their root and basis in human relationships, and are employed metaphorically by God and the writers of Scripture to describe some aspects of the relationship between two of the persons of the Trinity.[12] Here the bias of dependence on social science is seen again, involving, in this case, linguistics.

The Church has always held that the relation between the first and second persons of the Trinity is an eternal Father-Son relation, meaning that it is not a metaphor. That is, it is rooted in the eternal reality of inter-trinitarian relationships in eternity, not in human relationships. While it is true that in Scripture the royal son was metaphorically described as standing in a father-son relation to God (2 Samuel 7:14; Psalm 2:7), that does not mean that the Davidic Messiah, the ultimate royal son, was to be considered the Son of God in a metaphorical sense *only*. Unfortunately, most of what was published in discussion of this issue focused only on the term 'Son of God,' leaving out the much more commonly used terms 'Father' and 'Son,' an omission that lends itself to ignoring the bigger picture of Christ's relationship to the Father as eternal Son. Whether intentional or not intentional, this neglect of the larger picture on the part of at least some of those who were hoping to convince others of the validity of the practice has led to a disastrous logical consequence. That is, if the term 'Son of God' is a metaphorical equivalent for 'Messiah,' then the logical corollary to that is that the eternal Word became the Son of God at the incarnation.

While this claim is not clearly stated in so many words in the missiological literature advocating the MIT practice, it is there and it is recognizable as such. Private reports of unpublished internal writings among practitioners of MIT confirm that in fact, this is a tenet that is held or was once held by at least some of those who advocate the MIT practice. Such a belief is manifestly outside the boundaries of Christian orthodoxy, particularly as spelled out at the Council of Constantinople in AD 381, which anathematized bishop Marcellus of Ancyra for exactly that teaching.

Further problems will also ensue from this notion that the term 'Son of God' is equivalent to 'Messiah,' for the logical implication of that

---

12. See for example Rick Brown, 'Why Muslims are repelled by the term "Son of God,"' 2007, *Evangelical Missions Quarterly* Vol 43 No 4 (2007).

understanding is that the eternal Word became the Son at the incarnation. Such ideas clearly imply a deficient, indeed, non-Biblical understanding of the Trinity. It may not be far from the ideas deemed heretical by the Adoptionists (as condemned in Tertullian's *Adversus Praxean* - c. 217 A. D.). That kind of concept held that Jesus Christ was a man whom the Father adopted (perhaps at his birth, or baptism, or resurrection). What is precluded in this heretical thinking is that God is an eternal Trinity of co-equal Persons in one Being. Or the idea could be something like the Modalism that was also condemned as heretical by the Church: that is, God is unipersonal, and comes at one time as Father, another time as Word, and another time as Spirit. One hopes that the translators would not wish to go in these heretical directions, but the point here is that some of their translations could lead readers into such erroneous thinking, and that is why the Church cannot accept such inaccurate renditions.

In sum, some of the translations listed earlier in this Appendix do not present the Biblical Triune God. They do not confront us with the eternal Trinity whom we meet in the Great Commission of Christ in Matthew 28, in the birth narratives of Jesus in Matthew 1 and 2, and in Luke 1 and 2; in the Trinitarian passages in Paul's discussion of spiritual gifts in I Corinthians 12:4-6, and in Galatians 4:4-6, in Ephesians 4:4-6, in the Apostolic Benediction in II Corinthians 13:14, and at the baptism of Jesus (Matt. 3:16,17; Mark 1:8-11; Luke 3:21-22; John 1:29-34), in Revelation 1:4-5, and in many another passage of Holy Scripture.[13]

Using different terminology for divine familial terms was first advocated in the late 1980s and early 1990s, and the practice was underway in earnest by the mid-1990s, though not without opposition from some within the Bible translation movement even at that early stage. Opposition, however, was minimal because the practice was largely unknown, with almost nothing being published about it until about the year 2000, when Rick Brown of SIL began to advocate the use of alternative terminology.[14] Although Brown never referred to his affiliation with SIL in the published articles, that affiliation was known in missionary Bible translation circles. His advocacy of the MIT practice drew its credibility with some people from the excellent reputation that SIL has always had for its

---

13. See Rick Brown, 'Presenting the deity of Christ from the Bible,' *International Journal of Frontier Missions* 19:1, 2001. 'What Jesus said clearly indicates his divinity. If we add to this the doctrine that God is one, which Jesus affirmed in Mark 12:29, then it indicates his deity, because the inescapable conclusion is that Christ is not a separate god but is an incarnation of an aspect of the one God, namely his Wisdom-Word' (p.23). 'Isaiah uttered another important messianic prophecy in 52:7 to 53:12. Here he describes the savior as God's servant (52:13; 53:11), his righteous one, but also as his arm (52:10; 53:1; cf. Ps. 98:1–2; John 12:38; Rom. 3:25). We understand that an arm does not act on its own but is a part of a person, the part that interacts physically with the world' (pp.21-22). 'And they (Muslims) can discover that 'God's Word' refers to God's own wisdom and power expressed to mankind. The resolution of the partnership dilemma then comes when they realize that if Jesus is God's right arm, the incarnation of his Word and Wisdom, then he is part of the one God and not a separate god or partner' (p.23). 'For the Christians of the first four centuries, what we now call 'the Trinity' was usually expressed as God, his Word (or his Son), and his Holy Spirit' (p.26).

14. Rick Brown, 'The 'Son of God': Understanding the Messianic Titles of Jesus,' *International Journal of Frontier Missions*. 17(1): 41–52, 2000.

solid pioneering work in linguistics and translation theory and practice. With hundreds of PhDs in its ranks and over 40,000 published works in its bibliography, SIL's expertise has long been trusted by many.

Two things are worth noting though. One is that these articles appeared in missiological publications, but not in theological or exegetical journals, nor were the concepts brought before theological faculties for discussion, despite the fact that they dealt with critical Christological and theological issues. Secondly, with over 5,000 members in its ranks, one would expect SIL to have a much broader range of experts writing on the subject than actually did. Other than a few articles that Rick Brown coauthored with several others (writing under pseudonyms), no one else from SIL other than Rick Brown published on this topic, and no other view was published by any SIL member until 2010 (though that author was still not identified as a member of SIL, and was relatively unknown). In fact, other than Rick Brown almost no one from any organization published on the subject, leaving him a virtual monopoly of viewpoint. Perhaps those who practiced the MIT approach sensed that publishing on this topic would raise questions and challenges that they preferred to avoid. But for whatever reason, Rick Brown was almost completely alone in addressing the issue.

The fact that there were no divergent views expressed within SIL was due largely to the fact that the vast majority of SIL members had no knowledge of the controversial practice until the publication of the first news article about it, which was in *Christianity Today* in February 2011. This article was followed by several shorter articles, as well as by several feature articles in *World Magazine*.[15]

The response of SIL through its Wycliffe affiliate agencies was to assert that people who do not work in Bible translation and are not familiar with the Biblical languages or with the languages into which translation is being done, and are not familiar with the linguistic challenges of Bible translation, cannot understand or appreciate many translation decisions that are made by people with many years of training and experience. It is implied that they should trust the experts. While it is true that SIL has both expertise and many years of deservedly good reputation, the argument was severely inadequate for several reasons.

One is that the MIT practice dealt with a core theological issue, one in which even people without expertise in linguistics and translation can sense that something important is amiss. Secondly, there were people with expertise, training and experience both within SIL and outside of it who strenuously objected to the practice. There have also been a number of principled objections from Christian pastors and leaders in Asian countries in the last several years. For example, the Bible Society of Pakistan severed ties with SIL over this issue in 2011. That Bible Society certainly understands the biblical languages, the nature of translation, their own

---

15. Collin Hansen, 'The Son and The Crescent' *Christianity Today*, Feb 2011, and Emily Belz, 'Inside Out' *World Magazine*, May 7, 2011; Emily Belz, 'Holding Translators Accountable,' *World Magazine*, Sept. 26, 2011; and Emily Belz, 'The battle for accurate Bible translation in Asia,' *World Magazine*, Feb 25, 2012.

national languages, and the differences between Islam and Christianity quite well. This fact was known to leaders in SIL, but apparently was not taken into consideration when its affiliate Wycliffe organizations pled their case, asking for the trust of their supporting constituency and critics based on the argument that the experts should be allowed to make such decisions and not be challenged.

Bridging the Divide conference

In June of 2011 a Bridging the Divide conference was held on the campus of Houghton College in New York. The conference had emerged from the concern by several missiologists on both sides of the Insider Movement controversy that real discussion of the substantive issues was being outweighed by the polemical tone of articles in various missiological publications. The organizers of the conference wanted to bring the two sides together in face-to-face communication in an environment that promoted respectful listening and response. Approximately fifty people attended the first conference to discuss issues, but very little substantive change of viewpoint was reported by either side. In fact, almost nothing of substance was actually agreed upon, with the significant exception of a statement about Bible translation that even Rick Brown, the primary proponent and apologist of the MIT approach, signed. The statement reads as follows:

> We affirm:
> * God is moving globally in a variety of ways to draw Muslims to Christ,
>
> * The primacy of the Word of God for all aspects of faith and practice guided by the Spirit of God for the people of God, and
>
> * Practicing fidelity in Scripture translation using terms that accurately express the familial relationship by which God has chosen to describe Himself as Father in relationship to the Son in the original languages.

Not long afterwards this affirmation was adopted by Wycliffe Bible Translators US and published on its webpage. However, one must understand that Wycliffe US and SIL are not the same organization, though most of the members of Wycliffe US are members of SIL. While SIL and Wycliffe US have close ties, what Wycliffe US affirms does not automatically bind SIL, because the leaders and boards of directors of the respective organizations are not the same, and a fairly sizeable portion of the membership of SIL are not members of Wycliffe US, but are members of other Wycliffe organizations.

Critical response by the PCA and Assemblies of God

A few weeks after the Bridging the Divide conference in Houghton the Presbyterian Church in America convened its annual general assembly. One of the items for discussion was a resolution entitled 'A Call to Faithful Witness,' which addressed both the Insider Movement and the question of Bible translations that did not accurately represent the divine familial terms of 'Father,' 'Son,' and 'Son of God' (quoted at length earlier in this Appendix). The resolution was presented by a pastor who had also been at Bridging the Divide, and who had been concerned about Insider Movement issues and MIT issues for years. The resolution was passed overwhelmingly, almost unanimously, with the few negative votes being opposed to the fact that the resolution called for a study committee. Apparently few, if any, opposed the resolution in principle. The study committee has chosen to present its results in two parts. The first part, which was completed and presented to the PCA General Assembly in June of 2012, deals knowledgably with the translation question, but issues a strong call for translation agencies to use the normal terms for 'Father' and 'Son' that occur in the language, which are the 'biological' terms. It also calls for congregations to be careful and wise about which translation projects they support financially.[16] (The second portion of the report of the committee's work, which comments on the Insider Movement, is due to be presented at the 2013 General Assembly.)

In April of 2012 the Assemblies of God, after several unproductive meetings with leaders of SIL, issued a similar statement (also referred to in this Appendix).[17] They also determined that AoG missionaries who had been seconded to SIL would no longer be supported, but then decided to postpone implementing that decision until a report from a panel to be named by the World Evangelical Alliance was received and evaluated (see below). That report, which was initially expected to be available in December of 2012, was postponed until April of 2013, and as of the time of this writing has not yet been issued.

Meanwhile, despite the expression of agreement by Wycliffe Bible Translators US with the principles stated at Bridging the Divide, including the commitment to use 'terms that accurately express the familial relationship by which God has chosen to describe Himself as Father in relationship to the Son in the original languages,' the controversy was not settled within SIL, nor externally with its critics. Consequently the organization's leadership convened a conference in August of 2011 in Istanbul, Turkey, to address the issue of translating divine familial terms. Several dozen SIL members were in attendance, along with a small handful of outside observers. Commitments to the various sides run deep, however, such that even the statements that were agreed upon in principle by all the attendees of the Istanbul conference were naturally interpreted in significantly different ways by the different sides, and no real resolution of the controversy occurred. Several months later three articles appeared in *IJFM* and *Missions Frontiers*, authored by Rick Brown, who had been at Bridging the Divide and at Istanbul, and two of his colleagues.[18] In these articles Brown and his colleagues acknowledged

---

16. For a summary report on the Ad Interim committee's findings, see http://theaquilareport. com/at-the-pca-general-assembly-ad-interim-study-committee-on-insider-movements- overwhelmingly-approved/, accessed Feb 24, 2013.

17. 'The necessity for retaining father and son terminology in scripture translations for Muslims,' April 2012, http://www.fatherson.ag.org/download/paper.pdf (accessed Feb 24, 2013).

18. Brown, Rick, Leith Gray, and Andrea Gray, Translating Familial Biblical Terms: An Overview of the Issue.' *Mission Frontiers*, October 20, 2011; Brown, Gray, and Gray, 'A New Look at

that 'Messiah' was not an adequate substitute for 'Son of God.' However, the assertion was made that, unlike biblical Hebrew and Greek, many languages of the Middle East do not have a way to translate 'Father' and 'Son' that do not communicate biological reproduction and which differentiate between biological fatherhood (or sonship) and what they called *social* fatherhood (or sonship), and that the use of divine familial terms in the Bible designate social fatherhood and sonship. Suggestions were made for remedying this presumed problem, including the use of simile: he is *like* a son to God.

The negative reaction to these articles was swift and strong. Some forcefully challenged the contention by the authors that Greek and Hebrew vocabulary actually makes such distinctions between biological father or son and a social father or son. Brown, et al, had in fact not given any supporting data, either for the languages of the Middle East they were supposedly describing, nor for biblical Hebrew or Greek, and no citations were provided from the vast existing literature of biblical scholarship and lexicography that would indicate that such a distinction exists in biblical Hebrew and Greek. It appeared, at least to some, that the argument had been newly devised for the sake of providing a loophole for taking exception to the policies agreed upon at Bridging the Divide and at Istanbul.

Online change petition

From at least one group the reaction was especially strong, eventually resulting a few months later in an online change petition in January of 2012. That petition outlined the history of the problem, and called for the agencies implicated in this practice to cease and desist from what they had been doing. The petition cited denials of wrongdoing by spokespersons from these translation organizations, and gave forceful counter-arguments to these denials in great factual detail. These sponsors of the petition had previously been in communication on multiple occasions with Rick Brown and SIL during and since the Bridging the Divide conference, and reported that they had become frustrated with what they viewed as a lack of substantive response by SIL. They also reported frustration with the fact that the articles were supposed to have been a statement of retraction that Rick Brown had agreed to make when he was at Bridging the Divide. In the view of those who sponsored the petition the retraction was inadequate, and was further neutralized by the fact that even though Brown and the other authors did acknowledge that 'Messiah' was no longer considered an acceptable translation for 'Son of God,' they seemed to reintroduce through the back door what they had supposedly ushered out the front door, providing rationale and strategies for avoiding the use of clear familial terms, that is, the equivalents for 'Father' and 'Son' that naturally occur in the languages in question.

It has also been noted that though the argument for avoiding familial language has largely been made on the basis of linguistics, this problem is found in a wide range of language groups, many of which have nothing in common with one another linguistically, but *do* hold in common a Muslim belief system. So the conflict is from all appearances *not* linguistic in nature, as has so often been claimed, but religious. In other words, language is not the impermeable barrier that it has been claimed to be.

The posting of the change petition was also a reaction to the publication of a translation of the Gospel of Matthew in Turkish that had been posted online, in which 'Father' had been translated as 'guardian' or 'protector,' and 'Son' had been translated as 'representative.'[19] The translation had been done in conjunction with personnel from Frontiers, with advice from an SIL translation consultant. SIL defended itself by saying that it did not publish the book, and that the SIL consultant was only one voice among many. However, it was done in conformity with what SIL's Rick Brown had been advocating for many years, and in keeping with what SIL's primary entity working among Muslim language groups endorses. And while it was not published in print by SIL, it was published online by Sabeel Media, which is a company in the US that is supported by SIL and staffed by SIL personnel. SIL itself views posting a book online as online publishing, so its claims not to have been responsible for the publication of this translation only further angered those who had challenged SIL to stop the practice, and who believed on the basis of statements from Wycliffe US and SIL that no more translations of this sort would be published until a further examination of the larger issue was held.[20]

The change petition eventually garnered over 14,000 signatures from a number of countries around the world, mostly from the US, Canada, and the UK, but also from a variety of other countries. A few of the signatories were theologians, some were pastors in the countries where the disputed translations had been published, and even a very few were SIL members.[21]

Attempting to resolve the controversy through accountability to the broader church

Soon it became evident that Wycliffe and SIL were losing credibility, and that even a good portion of their own members were quite concerned over what was being done, so the two organizations agreed to ask the World Evangelical Alliance to form a panel to study the matter and issue a statement on it. Dr. Robert Cooley, President Emeritus of Gordon Conwell Theological Seminary, was appointed to chair the committee. Other scholars were appointed to the committee from various parts of the world, and representing a range of disciplines including missiology, biblical studies, systematic theology, historical theology, Islamic studies, and linguistics. The report of this panel was published in April of 2013.[22]

19. See Belz, 'The battle for accurate Bible translation in Asia.'

20. For further details see http://biblicalmissiology.org/ 'Wycliffe, SIL, Frontiers Translation Issues.'

21. http://www.change.org/petitions/lost-in-translation-keep-father-son-in-the-bible

22. The original report may be accessed at http://www.worldea.org/images/wimg/ files/2013_0429-Final%20Report%20of%20the%20WEA%20Independent%20Bible%20

There has not been enough time (as of this writing – in Spring of 2013) to know how much influence this important report may have on Bible translation., but it seems likely that what has been known as the MIT approach to Bible translation may not continue as it has in the past. For one thing, even the most ardent proponents of translating 'Son of God' as 'Messiah' have conceded that the two are not in fact synonyms. More importantly, a number of people in the Bible translation movement itself are aware of the issues and are unhappy with their own organizations for practicing this approach. Their expressions of concern will no doubt have an impact on policy. That the MIT approach went unchallenged for so long was due largely to the fact that it was unknown, not only to the supporting constituency in the sending countries, but also even to many of the members of the organizations actually engaged in it. Churches and Christian leaders, both in the sending countries as well as in the Muslim areas where the Bible translation work in question was being carried out, have spoken out vocally against the practice. Financial support for Bible translation projects has declined significantly over the last year and a half, though it is unclear whether that is due primarily to economic trends or due to disillusionment with the agencies involved. No doubt both are factors.

Time will tell what the outcome of the controversy will be, but meanwhile one would hope that a new level of resolve to translate faithfully and accurately, without compromise with religious syncretism, will develop within those organizations that have been implicated in the controversy. One would also hope that Bible translation agencies would commit to a deeper level of responsiveness to the concerns and input of the broader church, and that the independence and lack of transparency that have characterized translation work in the Muslim world previously will become a thing of the past.

II. Principles in conflict

To understand the controversy over translating divine familial terms, it would be helpful to look at some principles that have emerged as underlying the problem. In other words, how did the practice of missionary Bible translation get from where it once was to where it is today?

Social science and theology

One of the first principles that emerges is the dependence by missionaries on social science, including linguistics, to the near exclusion of concern for theology. While cultural anthropology and linguistics are valuable tools in church planting and missionary Bible translation, they cannot usurp the place of systematic and biblical theology for the simple reason that theology is based on revelation, whereas the social sciences are not.

For most of its history of very faithful pioneer work in Bible transla-tion, SIL has avoided recruiting people with degrees in theology to do translation work. The reason for this was that theologically trained people

Translation%20Review%20Panel.pdf.

were often too inflexible for pioneer translation work, leaning too strongly toward a literalness that is for the most part unintelligible to new readers in newly written languages. What made this approach workable for so many decades was the fact that the vast majority of those translators came from theologically sound church backgrounds, so that even if they did not have formal training in theology, they still had sound instincts for what should and should not be done. However, as western culture has changed, and theological standards in what are supposedly evangelical denominations have declined, new recruits, the majority of whom still hail from North America and Western Europe, bring certain tendencies of theological thinking that characterize postmodernity. What might have been unthinkable a generation ago may go without comment with at least some translators, translation consultants, and area administrators. Just as some church planters are looking heavily to cultural anthropology for the 'keys' to the response of a culture to the gospel, so also some translators have looked to linguistics as the primary key to communicating the message of the Bible.

It also needs to be said that avoiding Father-Son language in translation will result in a seriously deficient view of God, and as a natural consequence of that deficiency there will be a seriously deficient understanding of what salvation entails. In the gospel we learn that the Son of God became the Son of Man so that the sons of men could become the sons of the living God. Because we as believers are sons, God has sent forth the spirit of his Son into our hearts, by which we cry Abba, Father (Gal 4:6).[23] Scripture that mutes or hides the eternal Father-Son relationship between the first and second persons of the Trinity also fails to communicate the great privilege that believers have of being God's very own children. The Muslim understanding of God requires that Muslims be servants of God, but never would they become sons. It is worth noting that a hunger for a heavenly Father is what has driven some Muslims to investigate the gospel, and becomes one of the most precious experiences they have when they have received it and their identity as a child of God begins to form and grow.

Atomistic approach to the text of Scripture

A second tendency observable among some missionary Bible translators is to be atomistic with the text.[24] Whereas biblical theology and systematic theology provide a big picture of what is being conveyed in the Bible's message, linguistics focuses on the bits and pieces of each text and how it is to be communicated in the receptor language. Both are needed, but where either is absent deficiencies will occur in a translated text. Much of the discussion about the translation of divine familial terms appears to have missed the bigger picture that should be relatively apparent even to

23. See Dave Garner, 'A world of riches,' http://www.reformation21.org/articles/a-world-of-riches.php

24. See comments by D. A. Carson, *Jesus the Son of God: A Christological Title Often Overlooked, Sometimes Misunderstood, and Currently Disputed* (Crossway: Wheaton, Il, 2012), pp.107-08.

the lay reader, which is that Jesus really is God's dearly beloved Son, and that that fatherhood and sonship are core components of how they relate to one another. These are theological non-negotiables. The general lack of theological training among the majority of Bible translators, coupled with their very thorough training in linguistics leaves them vulnerable to looking at texts atomistically instead of holistically.

Transparency and accountability

Another problem that has become apparent in this debate is the lack of transparency and accountability that has existed in the world of missionary Bible translation for predominantly Muslim-language communities. While translators have claimed that critics don't understand 'meaning based translation' and prefer a too literal approach, the fact is that what appears to have been being practiced was not meaning-based translation at all, but rather an avoidance of the real meaning of the text. Since Islam strongly denies the possibility of God being Father and of Jesus being Son, any attempt to use wording that sidesteps that basic tenet of biblical truth must be misguided, and missing the main point. Claiming that making substitutions for divine familial language is 'meaning-based translation' that non-specialists cannot understand does not make it so. There needs to be a very open transparency on the part of translation agencies with regard to their work, including provision being made for verifiability. Claiming that this is impossible due to security concerns is not going to be acceptable any longer; any translation that appears to deviate from core theological truth with regard to key biblical terms must be closely scrutinized, both from within and from outside of the translation organization involved in a particular project. Asking others to simply trust the skill and expertise of dedicated and well-trained translators is not sufficient; anyone can err, and because the cost of error with key theological terms is enormous, controls and accountability must be practiced in Bible translation. Most evangelical mission agencies subscribe to the financial policies and standards of the ECFA, and go to considerable expense and effort each year to conduct open audits and to provide the results of those audits to interested parties. The same diligence and openness could and should be done for any area of potential impropriety in the operation of a Christian organization. Allowing impartial external scrutiny and providing objective evidence from neutral parties that rigorous standards and controls have been maintained, whether financial or theological, helps to keep an organization from falling into error and provides a ready way to demonstrate its integrity.

Results orientation

One final principle that seems to underlie the current translation controversy is simply the proclivity that our age has for getting results. In reading the literature where Insider Movement and MIT methodology are advocated, one quickly sees that these methodologies grew, at least in part, out of impatience with the lack of response to the gospel among

Muslims that has characterized the history of Muslim missions. While it is good to be zealous to see results among the world's enormous Muslim population, care must be taken to insure that any positive response they give to the gospel they receive is based on a gospel that is faithful to the witness of the New Testament and to the witness of the Church throughout history, and unites them in belief and fellowship to believers in Christ in other times and places. Any witness that is less than that will serve them very poorly and will fail to offer the truth that can provide salvation for their souls.

It is of highest importance ever, and at any cost, to continue to communicate accurately and faithfully the apostolic Gospel, based in Holy Scripture and in the historic Christian Tradition. The deepest charity for Muslims, as for all others, is 'to speak the truth in love,' for their greatest treasure will be to find the Father 'who to know is eternal life, and His Son whom He hath sent' (John 17:3). Sometimes the discovery of the saving truth requires the shattering of previous conceptual molds, and through such shattering of blinding conceptions, the light of the love and truth of who God is shines out in beauty and transformative power.

CHAPTER 3

CRUCIAL PASSAGES ON THE LORD'S INCARNATION AND ATONEMENT

The testimony of the Father and the Spirit to the Son of God is found in the Scriptures of the Old and New Testaments. As Saint Augustine said: 'The New is in the Old concealed, and the Old is in the New revealed.'[1] We have already looked to some degree at the witness of the Old Testament to the coming Christ, who in the New Testament is most clearly revealed. After long years of Old Testament prophecy, 'the Lord,' whom Old Testament saints and sages were seeking, 'suddenly appeared in his Temple' (Mal. 3:1). The Lord is therefore most clearly manifested in the New Testament, after his incarnation and saving life and works among men, and after the outpouring of the Spirit upon the Church at Pentecost. The Triune God himself bore thorough witness to what the incarnation means in the various writings of the New Testament. More than once the heavenly Father said: 'This is my beloved Son, in whom I am well pleased' (cf. Matt. 3:17; Mark 1:11, etc.). To the Father's words of approbation, the Holy Spirit added his personal presence (cf. Matt. 3:16; Mark 1:10). In John 16, Jesus told of how the Spirit would speak, not of himself, but of the Lord, and that he would glorify Jesus (16:13-14). A careful look at some central New Testament passages will enable us to grasp more clearly and fully the Trinitarian testimony to the incarnate Son of God.

In this chapter we look in some detail at four definitive passages that convey the Gospel message of Christ's incarnation, death, resurrection, and ascension: John 1:1-18; Philippians 2:5-11; Hebrews 1:1-4, and Revelation 5:1-14. These four texts accord in their overall teaching concerning: (1) The eternal Deity of Christ; (2) His Incarnation; and (3) The redemption he wrought. The details and the overarching coherence of these scriptural texts finally require expression in something like the Church's classical teaching on the divine and human natures together at the same time in the one person of Christ, which will be studied in Chapter IV.

We are told in Revelation 13:8 that Christ is 'the Lamb slain from the foundation of the world'. According to the Holy Scriptures, everything

---

1. Augustine, *Quaest. 73 in Exod.*

that God was doing in Israel was a preparation for the glorious accomplishments of the incarnate life, death, resurrection, and enthronement of this once-suffering Lamb, the now victorious 'Lion of the tribe of Judah' (Rev. 5:5), in 'the fullness of the time' (Gal. 4:4). All that was prepared in the Old Testament was manifestly fulfilled in the New, so that now we await the final dénouement of all human and cosmic history in 'the marriage supper of the Lamb' (Rev. 19:7, 9). 'Happy' will be those who are called to it (Rev. 19:9)!

In this chapter we look carefully at four definitive passages on who the Lord Jesus Christ is in his eternal state, incarnation, death, victory, and continuing ministry of redemption. We survey these passages from different parts of the New Testament (Gospel, Epistles, and Apocalypse), with particular reference to how all history finds its happy fulfillment in who he is as our incarnate Savior, and what he has freely made available to sinners, who are lost and condemned without him. In these texts we see the Holy Trinity putting forth his light and glory as John sets forth the Son in the realm of space and time.

(1) John 1:1-18

¹In the beginning was the Word, and the Word was with God, and the Word was God.

²The same was in the beginning with God.

³All things were made by him; and without him was not any thing made that was made.

⁴In him was life; and the life was the light of men.

⁵And the light shineth in darkness; and the darkness comprehended it not.

⁶There was a man sent from God, whose name was John.

⁷The same came for a witness, to bear witness of the Light, that all men through him might believe.

⁸He was not that Light, but was sent to bear witness of that Light.

⁹That was the true Light, which lighteth every man that cometh into the world.

¹⁰He was in the world, and the world was made by him, and the world knew him not.

¹¹He came unto his own, and his own received him not.

¹²But as many as received him, to them gave he power to become the sons of God, even to them that believe on his name:

¹³Which were born, not of blood, nor of the will of the flesh, nor of the will of man, but of God.

¹⁴And the Word was made flesh, and dwelt among us, (and we beheld his glory, the glory as of the only begotten of the Father,) full of grace and truth.

¹⁵John bare witness of him, and cried, saying, This was he of whom I spake, He that cometh after me is preferred before me: for he was before me.

¹⁶And of his fulness have all we received, and grace for grace.

¹⁷For the law was given by Moses, but grace and truth came by Jesus Christ.

¹⁸No man hath seen God at any time, the only begotten Son, which is in the bosom of the Father, he hath declared him.

The theme of the prologue

The *Logos* (Word) is the theme of the prologue quoted above (John 1:1-18), and the prologue is the key to the entire Gospel of John. Thus, the 'Logos' is the key to the book. It is the key to the book as an overture is to certain types of classical music (as, for example, the overture to Handel's 'Messiah', providing in prospect musical themes that will be developed in the main work).

Who is the Word (*Logos*)?

I shall argue that John's concepts were firmly rooted in the Old Testament, rather than in Greek Platonic or Stoic philosophy, which also made much of 'logos'. Yet the Platonists, Stoics and John all have in common the idea of 'word' as an underlying reality connected to reason or rationality.

The Jewish philosopher Philo's works were published some fifty years before the time of John. Philo sought to interpret the term 'logos', which was so frequently used in the Old Testament, in light of the synchronic Greek usage, both Platonic and Stoic. Philo employed logos some 1,400 times in his writings.[2] Plato thought of logos as something like a thought in the mind of God, whereas the later Stoics considered it to be a sort of material reality: a rational, fiery substance pervading the universe, but especially 'concentrated' in minds. James Dunn seems to be correct in stating that Philo's thought is closer to that of Plato, though with considerable developments. 'Philo quite often speaks of the Logos as though a real being distinct from God, who acts as intermediary between God and the world...Philo's thought...is a unique synthesis of Platonic and Stoic world-views with Jewish monotheism.'[3]

Only a few typical illustrations of Philo's usage of logos need be given here. In *De Confusione Linguarum*, he speaks of the Logos as being 'God's image' (XX), and says that 'The Word (Logos) is the eldest-born image of God' (XXVIII). In *De Migratione Abrahami* he calls the *logos* 'the house of God' (Loeb translation, pp. 173-175), and that 'antecedent to all in existence is the Logos, which the Helmsman of the universe grasps as a rudder to guide all things on their course' (I). Later in this work he comes up with the famous phrase of the *logos* as being *logos endiathetos* ('word in the mind') and *logos prophorikos* ('uttered word') (VIII). This was taken over by such Church Fathers as Theophilus of Antioch and Tertullian. In *Quis Rerum Divinarum Heres Sit* he calls logos 'the invisible, seminal artificer, the divine Word, which will be fitly dedicated to its Father' (XXIV). Elsewhere he compares the Logos to the High Priest, 'who lives in us as the monitor of our soul and understanding' (*De Fuga et Inventione* XIX).

It has never been demonstrated that John either knew or used Philo, nor has it ever been disproved. It is clear, however, that at a later time the Church Fathers made much use of him. John's understanding of Logos was different from Greek philosophy's (particularly the Stoic, materialistic

---

2. According to G. Mayer, *Index Philoneus*, 1974, *logos*.

3. James D. G. Dunn, *Christology in the Making*, 220, 221.

version) in two important ways: (1) In Greek philosophy, Logos is finally part of the created, or natural, realm; something less than God. (2) In Greek philosophy, the Logos is finally impersonal, not a distinct person. John's prologue is different on these two points: (1) for John, Logos is the source of rationality, and exists outside of creation, and (2) He is a person.

Instead of crediting Philo as the source of John's concept of Logos, R. Bultmann held that, because of similarities with the figure of wisdom in Sirach, some kind of 'early Gnostic' context was its background.[4] But, as N. T. Wright answers:

> [W]e must insist on a large difference between the worlds of Jewish wisdom and early Gnosticism. In Sirach, the figure of Wisdom comes to live, permanently, among humans, more specifically in the Temple at Jerusalem. In Gnosticism, the redeemer-figure comes down to the world of humans, but only in order to return from that wicked sphere to his own true home. The background to the Johannine prologue in wisdom thought is evidence, not of its leaning in the direction of early Gnosticism, but of its emphatically Jewish and world-affirming orientation.[5]

New Testament *Logos* and Old Testament *Dabar*

I think that T. F. Torrance is right in seeing the Old Testament itself as the direct source of John's teaching on Logos. He shows that 'word' (or *Logos*) as used in the New Testament has its roots in the Hebrew *dabar*.[6] He relates *dabar* to *debir*, the 'word house': that is, the holy of holies in the Tabernacle: John was clearly thinking of the Old Testament tabernacle, the moving tent of meeting, as it was called, the place where God and man met and God revealed himself to man…behind the inner court there was the Holy of Holies, the *debir* and within the *debir* there was the ark and within the ark there was lodged the word of God, the law (I Kings 8:9; cf. Exod. 24:12). This was known as the ten words, the *debarim*…The tabernacle enshrined the word of God, the word that made Israel's history. But all through Israel's pilgrimage that word was hidden in the *debir*.[7]

John's prologue will soon show us that the Word hidden in the 'word house' of the tabernacle comes forth as the fullness of personal reality, as one who is both eternal God and enfleshed man at the same time. Saint Athanasius in *Contra Gentes* demonstrates the eternal, personal of this Word, while showing him not to have his divine origin within the created order (in opposition to the Arians of his day, who held the Word to be a creature).

[6] Who then could it be, save His Word? For to whom could God be said to speak, except His Word? Or who was with Him when He made all created Existence, except His Wisdom, which says, Prov. viii. 27: 'When He was

---

4. Rudolph Bultmann, 'The History of Religious Background of the Prologue to the Gospel of John,' trans. John Ashton in *The Interpretation of John*, ed. John Ashton. Issues in Religion and Theology, no. 9 (Philadelphia: Fortress, 1986), 208.

5. N. T. Wright, *The New Testament and the People of God*, 415.

6. See the discussion in T. F. Torrance, *The Incarnation*, 58-61.

7. Ibid., 59.

making the heaven and the earth I was present with Him?' But in the mention of heaven and earth, all created things in heaven and earth are included as well.

[7] But being present with Him as His Wisdom and His Word, looking at the Father He fashioned the Universe, and organised it and gave it order; and, as He is the power of the Father, He gave all things strength to be, as the Saviour says, Joh. v. 19; Col. i. 16: 'What things soever I see the Father doing, I also do in like manner.' And His holy disciples teach that all things were made 'through Him and unto Him;'

[8] and, being the good Offspring of Him that is good, and true Son, He is the Father's Power and Wisdom and Word, not being so by participation, nor as if these qualifies were imparted to Him from without, as they are to those who partake of Him and are made wise by Him, and receive power and reason in Him; but He is the very Wisdom, very Word, and very own Power of the Father, very Light, very Truth, very Righteousness, very Virtue, and in truth His express Image, and Brightness, and Resemblance. And to sum all up, He is the wholly perfect Fruit of the Father, and is alone the Son, and unchanging Image of the Father.[8]

In other words, the Scriptures show that the Son (Logos) is not a mere creature, but the mighty agent of creation; one with the Father and Spirit from all eternity. He is the head of the cosmos, and true image of the Father. His eternal being is on the side of God, not on the side of created things. He did, most amazingly, deign to become a creature, while still remaining God, and that is what the Arians sought to deny.

John 1:18 makes clear the identity of the Logos: it is: 'the only begotten Son, which is in the bosom of the Father...' Hebrews 1:1-2 also affirms that the Son is the one by whom God has spoken...' In other words, the Word of God is the Son of God. He is a person – the self-communication of the personhood of God, the absolute, the infinite. Personal knowledge of the one true God follows directly from knowing his Son. To see Jesus, the Word of God made man, in faith is to look directly into the being of God, for as Karl Barth said, 'There is no wordless existence in God.'[9] Or, to paraphrase Hilary, God's being is eloquent, not mute: 'The Word is a reality, not a sound; a being, not a speech; God, not a nonentity.'[10]

Epiphanius says in his *Panarion*:

'Because God is in Thee' (Isa. 45:14). In whom would we say that God is except in the Word of God the Father? And indeed, the Son is truly God [the] Word and in him one knows the Father, according to his words: 'He who hath seen me, hath seen the Father' (John 14:9), and 'I have glorified thy name upon the earth' (John 17:4).[11]

---

8. Athanasius, *Contra Gentes*, III. 46.

9. Barth, *Church Dogmatics* I/1, 414.

10. Hilary, *De Trinitate* II.15.

11. Epiphanius, *Panarion* 57.7.4 in *Die Grieschischen christlichen Schriftsteller der ersten drei Jahrhunderte*: K. Holl, ed. (Leipzig, 1922), 31, p. 352, 14-17)

The Word in Eternity

'In the beginning was the Word.' The language of John 1:1 at this point reflects Genesis 1:1 ('In the beginning, God created...'), for in the LXX the same two words are used: ἐν ἀρχῇ. But John's account reveals the Word by whom the heavens and earth were created, as B. F. Wescott writes: 'Genesis takes us to the beginning of creation, but John takes us beyond the beginning, to dwell on that which was when time and finite being began its course.'[12] John's prologue recalls the first creation of the cosmos. In addition to the phrase ἐν ἀρχῇ ('in the beginning') of verse 1, we see in verse 4 'life,' 'light,' and 'darkness,' all found also in the creation narrative of Genesis. The point here of John 1 is to assert the eternity of the Word: as we shall see, he was with God and was God before anything at all was created. That is, he shares God the Father's attribute of eternality. In that sense, John takes us further back than even Genesis 1.

Leon Morris, quoting Archbishop William Temple, notes that ἐν ἀρχῇ can mean (1) at the beginning of history, and (2) at the root of the universe. Both meanings are probably contained in the 'beginning' of John's prologue. That is, there was never a time, nor a thing – whether flea or archangel – which did not depend on him for its very existence.[13]

There are two Greek terms that relate to existence: εἰμί ('to be') and γίνομαι ('to become'). The finite verb ἦν ('he was'), used in the phrase 'In the beginning *was* the Word' (John 1:1), is the imperfect form of the verb εἰμί ('to be'). This is verb is consistent with the concept of eternal existence, whereas the verb γίνομαι – 'to become' is used of the Word's becoming flesh (John 1:14), and hence indicates historical, creational coming into being from nothing. Εἰμί is suitable to express the eternal being of the Word, while γίνομαι suits his historical becoming.

James Dunn states that:

> Here we have moved beyond any thought of the Logos as created, even the first created being (contrast Prov. 8:22; Sir. 24:8f.; Philo, *Leg. All.* III.175; *Ebr.* 31). Rather the point is made with emphasis that *everything* that came to be, came to be through the Logos (v. 3).[14]

Cyril of Alexandria in his *Commentary on John* says:

> But to the word ἀρχῇ he fitly annexes the *was*, that He may be thought of as not only of renown, but also before the ages. For the word *was* is here put, carrying on the idea of the thinker to some deep and incomprehensible generation, the ineffable generation that is outside of time. For that *was*, spoken indefinitely, at what point will it rest, its nature being ever to push forward before the pursuing mind, and whatever point of rest any might suppose that it has, *that* it makes the starting point of its further course? *The Word* was then Ἐν ἀρχῇ that is in sovereignty over all things, and possessing the dignity of the Lord, as being by nature from it. But if this be true, how

---

12. B. F. Wescott, *Commentary on John's Gospel* (John Murray: London, 1894), 2.

13. Leon Morris, *The Gospel According to John* (William B. Eerdmans: Grand Rapids, Mi, 1995) 65.

14. James Dunn, op. cit., 240.

is He any longer originate or made? And where the *was* wholly is, how will the 'was not' come in, or what place will it have at all as regards the Son?[15]

'And the Word was with God'

The first verse of John's prologue further identifies the Logos as having always been 'with God.' A. T. Robertson shows that this preposition with the accusative case (πρὸς τὸν θεόν) implies more than the idea of 'with' that one finds in the preposition πρός. There are other prepositions that John could have used: μετά or παρά for example. But πρός is consistent with the idea of being 'face to face'.[16] In human terms, he suggests that the concept might be like two men standing on each end of a log looking at each other, but of course that is not to be literally applied to the Trinity.[17] Some commentators take preposition (πρός) to refer to the Son's being 'faced towards the Father'. It may also mean 'the presence of one person with another,' as in Matthew 13:56; Mark 6:3, etc. B. F. C. Atkinson in *The Theology of Prepositions* sees in this preposition 'a sense of intimacy and communion, that at the same time implies separate [that is, distinct] personality.'[18] It is close to the Hebrew פָּנִים (*panim*) found for example in the Aaronic benediction, 'Lift up the light of thy countenance upon us...' And no doubt the concept of personality ultimately comes from the idea of *panim*.

And the Word was God

This phrase 'the Word was God' is the culmination of verse 1 on the eternal and personal identity of the Word. Leon Morris says:

> Nothing higher could be said. Language cannot assist us in making any more clear a statement about the divinity of Jesus. All that may be said about God may fitly be said about the Word. John is not merely affirming that there is something divine about Jesus. He is affirming that He is God, and doing so emphatically, as we see from the word order in the Greek.[19]

The Greek reads: καὶ θεὸς ἦν ὁ λόγος. A very few translations (such as *The New World Translation* of the Jehovah's Witnesses) have said that because θεός has no article, it therefore does not mean the full, personal Godhead, but merely a certain divine quality, far less than God. But there are widely accepted criteria to determine whether a noun without the article means mere quality or not.

E. C. Colwell states the rule concerned here: 'A definite predicate nominative has the article when it follows the verb. It does not have the

---

15. Cyril of Alexandria, *Commentary on John*, transl. E. B. Pusey (Library of the Fathers, 43,48 (1874/1885): online edition), Book I. chap. I, p.5.

16. A. T. Robertson, *A Grammar of the Greek New Testament in Light of Historical Research*, (Hodder and Stoughton: London, 1919), 625.

17. Ibid., 572.

18. B. F. C. Atkinson, *The Theology of Prepositions* (Tyndale Press: London, n.d.), 19.

19. Morris, op. cit., 68.

article when it precedes the verb. In John 1:1, θεός precedes the verb.'[20] There are a few, but not very many, exceptions, and there is nothing in this context to make us believe that this phrase deviates from the general rule.[21] Or, as D. A. Carson states it: 'Syntactically, the question does not turn simply on the presence or absence of the article, but on the presence or absence of the article with definite nominative predicate nouns preceding a finite copula...'[22]

Then there is the question of the order in which most of the versions in other languages have rendered καὶ θεὸς ἦν ὁ λόγος. In English, French, German, etc., 'the Word' is put first (i.e. 'And the Word was God'). Why not the other way around? Here is the general rule: To determine the predicate, if two nouns are connected by the verb 'to be,' the articular one is the subject; the anarthous one is the predicate nominative.

Thus, in our text, ὁ λόγος is the subject: 'The Word was God.' The massive importance of this is that it settles the question of whether the Word was of the very substance of God, and indeed, God himself. It takes someone as big as God to remove sins and transform the created order. No lesser being could accomplish it!

The Word and Creation

John 1:3-5: 'All things were made by him; and without him was not any thing made that was made. In him was life; and the life was the light of men. And the light shineth in darkness; and the darkness comprehended it not.'

John now moves from the identity of the Word (Logos) of God to the divine work of creation. The Word is the means of bringing all things into existence. '**All things**' (in Greek: πάντα without the article) refers to individuality; that is, 'every single thing that exists' was brought into being by the Logos. '**Were made by him**': 'by' renders the Greek preposition διά, which (when used with the genitive case, as here) means 'through.' To say 'through' the Word implies that the Father is the source of the creative action, and the Son is the agent that the Father uses.

This is also the teaching of Paul in I Corinthians 8:6. There, the apostle teaches that creation is the work of both the Father and the Son: 'But to us there is but one God, the Father, of whom are all things, and we in him; and one Lord Jesus Christ, by whom are all things, and we by him.' In a different context – that of controversy with the Pharisees over Christ's healing of a man on the Sabbath – John reports Jesus as saying something that indicates the mysterious union in the work of both Father and Son: 'My Father worketh hitherto, and I work' (John 5:17).

---

20. E. C. Colwell, 'A Definite Rule for the Use of the Article in the Greek New Testament,' *JBL* 52 (1933), 12-21.

21. D. A. Carson discusses the complexities and limitations of formulating 'overall' rules for Greek grammar in *Exegetical Fallacies* (Baker Book House: Grand Rapids, 1990), 86-88.

22. D. A. Carson, *Commentary on John*, 37.

Scriptural View of Creation

John, in Hebraic fashion, often states facts, first positively, and then negatively (somewhat like the antithetical parallelism of the Psalms). Hence he says here in verse 3: 'without him was not anything made that was made.' We see in John's teaching on creation, as also in that of Genesis 1 and 2, these three implications:

(a) **That creation (or matter) is not eternal**; it was brought into being through the Logos out of non-existence. Once there was absolutely nothing but the Triune God: no matter, no 'natural forces,' no 'space,' no time: only the eternal God. Then through the agency of the Word, the Father brought everything into being.

(b) **This natural realm that was thus brought into being is not inherently evil**; it is God's good work. Genesis 3 and Romans 5 tell us how the world was devastated by evil and sin, in and through the fall of Adam, which gives the background of what John says in verse 5 about 'the darkness' in which the light of the Logos still shines. Yet although it is fallen, the world, including the various aspects of the physical, was created good, and is still to be respected and appreciated: both in light of its original divine creation and in light of its redemption through the same Word through whom it was created (cf. vv. 12-17).

(c) **That the cosmos was not made by some inferior being** (like the Gnostic 'demiurge', a being far below God, and of questionable activity), but was planned and brought into being by the one eternal God, the Father and the Son (and in Genesis 1:2 the Spirit of God is spoken of as 'brooding over the waters' of the new, as yet undifferentiated, creation). Thus, this physical world, albeit fallen from its original purity and beauty, would be a place where God himself, in the person of his eternal Son, would 'come unto his own' (John 1:11).

'He came unto his own' (εἰς τὰ ἴδια) – verse 11 – that is to say, 'to his own things,' or 'to his own home.' These are the same words used of John's future care for Mary, as Jesus had requested on the cross: 'And from that hour that disciple took her *into his own house*' (John 19:27). He had made this world, and it was proper for him to be in it, yet it rejected him. John will go on to show us that it was by means of this very rejection of the Son of God that the world was redeemed.

Saint Irenaeus of Lyon (in the second century) saw that the redemption of humanity had to be by none less than the agent of its creation. That is why he suggested that the historical Christ was the prototype God had in mind when he created the first human being. Christ was the complete and perfect man who was going to appear on earth and whom the Creator foresaw by creating Adam according to this future prototype. As a result, Adam was created after the model of the Word who, as Christ, was going to assume in time human nature and to appear on earth as a perfect man.[23]

---

23. See Irenaeus, *Adversus Haereses*, IV. xxxviii, 1,3.

Life

John 1:4 moves from creation of all things in general, to creation of life. Reference to ζωή ('life') is a frequent characteristic of John's writings; the term is used 36 times in his Gospel. The Book of Revelation, also believed to have been written by John, uses it 17 times, and no other writer utilized it as often. The term ζωή often refers to 'eternal life'. We see here, two chapters before John 3:16, that the gift of eternal life is through God's Son. But here in the Prologue, ζωή is used in its broadest sense of 'life'. Leon Morris states: 'It is only because life is in the Logos that there is life in anything on earth at all. The basic source of life is in the Father, who has life in himself. But the Father gave to the Son to have life in himself, so attention is directed to him.'[24]

Light

'And the life was the light of men' (verse 4). 'Light' (φῶς) could be understood to include both (1) intelligence and (2) moral sensibility. Mankind is endowed intellectually and morally by God through the Logos, both by birth as a person in God's image, and also all through the experience of life in God's created realm.

Mankind, created in God's image, can make sense of God's created realm, because, as Origen pointed out, when God created space and time out of nothing, he impregnated this realm with rational order; that is, with intrinsic intelligibility by means of the agency of the divine Logos.[25] Origen also held that basic moral principles were implanted by the Logos in the minds of humans, and that these are in accordance with what is written in the Scriptures.[26] This is to say that the universe was created by the agency of the Logos, and our minds were created through his agency, in his own image, so that we may grasp what the one in whose image we are created has made. This intellectual aspect of light that comes from the Logos is emphasized by D. A. Carson. He notes that in most cases, when John mentions 'light', he means the revelation 'which people may receive in active faith and be saved'.[27] But he adds: 'If 1:4, by contrast, is read in the context of the first three verses, it is more likely that the life inhering in the Word is related not to salvation but to creation. The self-existing life of the Word was so dispersed at creation that it became the light of the human race...'[28]

We might consider Psalm 36:9 to have been a sort of prophecy when it said: 'In thy light shall we see light.' And the request articulated in the Aaronic benediction would find one aspect of its fulfillment here (though the plenitude of the desired face-to-face knowledge of God goes far beyond the light of creation, without being separate from it): 'The Lord

---

24. Leon Morris, op. cit., 73.

25. e.g. see Origen, *De Principiis* 1:3:8; 3:5:6.

26. See Henry Chadwick's edition of Origen, *Contra Celsum* I.4 (Cambridge University Press; Cambridge, 1965), 8,9.

27. D. A. Carson, *Commentary on John*, 119.

28. Ibid.

bless thee, and keep thee; The Lord make his face shine upon thee, and be gracious unto thee: The Lord lift up his countenance upon thee, and give thee peace' (Num. 6:24-26).

(1) This endowment of light makes humankind human, giving them an ability to understand much of the world around and above them, so as to make considerable sense of the work of the agent of creation. Appropriately, it is the Logos who shines into the minds of humankind so they can grasp the created order. In the seventh century, Maximus the Confessor describes how the Logos continually brings mankind, the crown of God's creation, insofar as they cleave to the Lord and are one spirit with him, to a sort of 'universal simplicity' of vision:

> It is in him [i.e. the Logos] as the Creator and Maker of beings that all the principles of things both are and subsist as one in an incomprehensible simplicity. Gazing with a simple understanding on him who is not outside it but thoroughly in the whole of reality, it will itself understand the principles of beings and the causes why it was distracted by divisive pursuits before being espoused to the Word of God. It is by them that it is logically brought safe and sound to him who creates and embraces all principles and causes.[29]

In an essay on 'The Theology of Light,' T. F. Torrance says:

> It must not be forgotten…that as supreme Light, the Source of all light, God is the Creator not only of sun and moon and stars and all light in the universe, but also of the light of the human mind…Because the uncreated Light of God remains utterly constant and faithful, irrespective of the vagaries of our human actions and conceptions, we are called … to submit our minds freely to the universal claims of his immutable Truth as the ultimate standard for all our conceptions and formulations in human history.[30]

(2) Moral sensibility. As light that exposes darkness, the Logos continually enables humankind to feel an inalienable sense of right and wrong. Although, because of sin, humans 'suppress' this moral accountability to the God who made them (cf. Rom. 1:18), yet they must still dwell with an unseen moral monitor, whether they like it or not.

However, this 'light,' whether pertaining to creation or to the moral monitor speaking within, is not yet the light of salvation. John 3 makes clear that the light of salvation must be conveyed in regeneration (cf. John 3:3, 5). Then we become 'light in the Lord' (cf. Eph. 5:8). The 'darkness not comprehending the light' of John 1 seems to refer to the Fall of mankind and its dark results, which operate in a context of alienation from God. Yet the results of the fall into willful darkness have not totally obliterated humankind's consciousness of reality within and around him, and particularly of his moral obligation to God and his truth. This

---

29. Maximus Confessor, *Selected Writings*, Transl. G C. Berthold and Intro. J. Pelikan for 'The Classics of Western Spirituality' (New York: Paulist Press, 1985), 194,195.

30. T. F. Torrance, 'The Theology of Light' in *Christian Theology & Scientific Culture* (New York: Oxford University Press, 1981), 84.

presupposes that there is something in mankind to which the special revelation of the good news of the coming of Christ in the flesh can appeal. As John Frame says: 'God furnishes the rational structure of the world and of the human mind, so that the two structures are adapted to one another.'[31]

The Word and John the Baptist

'There was a man sent from God, whose name was John. The same came for a witness, to bear witness of the Light, that all men through him might believe. He was not that Light, but was sent to bear witness of that Light' (John 1:6-8).

There is a powerful contrast in the early part of this prologue between the verb 'came' (applied to John in verse 7) and 'was' (applied to the Logos in verse 1). 'Came' (ἦλθεν) is applied first to John in verse 7, and then to the Logos himself in verse 11 (that is, as we shall see, to his human nature in which he came 'unto his own'). But of the Logos alone is it said the he 'was' (that is, eternally existed). Whereas John the Baptist *came* to witness (v. 7) as a created man, the Logos always *was* [ἦν] (v. 1).

'For a witness' (v. 7)

The expression εἰς μαρτυρίαν ('for a witness') is used 14 times in John's Gospel, and its associated verb μαρτυπέω is used 33 times. It is rarely used in the synoptic Gospels. Whereas the synoptics speak of John the Baptist as 'preacher of repentance' and 'baptizer unto repentance', the disciple John calls him 'a witness,' to point beyond himself to the Light. At Christ's baptism at John the Baptist's hands, John the Baptist would say, 'Behold the lamb of God, which taketh away the sin of the world' (John 1:29). He would testify that he saw the Holy Spirit descending upon Jesus at his baptism (v. 32); and that Jesus 'was before him' (v. 30); that Jesus was 'the Son of God' (v. 34).

John 8 makes it plain that John the Baptist was not himself 'the Light'. Because of his fidelity as a true witness to the Lord, John the Baptist would say: 'He must increase, but I must decrease' (John 3:30). A large part of John the Baptist's greatness lay in his constant pointing of people away from himself and his own tremendously powerful ministry to the One whom the Prologue calls 'the true Light' (v.9), whom it identifies as Christ, the eternal Word made flesh.

The Word Incarnate (John 1:9-14)

The incarnation of the Word is the focus of this section. In preparation for it, verse 9 says that he was 'the true light'. That probably means that he is the original light, rather than that he is in opposition to the false light. Thus, all light is an illumination from his original, uncreated light as God, who 'is light, and in him is no darkness at all' (I John 1:5). This uncreated light came into a darkened world, a world which he had

---

31. John Frame, *Apologetics to the Glory of God: An Introduction* (P & R Publishing: Phillipsburg, NJ, 1994), 24.

created. He himself gives the light of creation, intellect, and conscience to all mankind.[32]

Becoming a Child of God

And to those who believe, he gives the light of salvation. Hence he says: 'I am the light of the world: he that followeth me shall not walk in darkness, but shall have the light of life' (John 8:12).

But John 1:10 tells us that the world which he made, and continues to illumine, 'knew him not.' That rejection by the majority will be seen as one of the major themes of his public ministry in the Gospel. The demons themselves (as in Mark) and the woman at the well of Samaria recognized who he was, while the multitudes of his own people Israel did not. Even in face of miracles that the Pharisees could not deny, they still denied his identity as Messiah. That is particularly the case after he raised Lazarus from the dead. The leadership of Israel plainly saw that Jesus was performing miracles: 'What do we? for this man doeth many miracles' (John 11:47). Instead of accepting the light, they decided to put out the light: 'Then from that day forth they took counsel together for to put him to death' (John 11:53).

Nonetheless, some did receive him: 'But as many as received him, to them gave he power to become the sons of God, even to them that believe on his name…' (John 1:12). This 'power' (ἐξουσία) means here the 'authorization to enter a different status.' I John 3:14 speaks of passing from death to life. This is a far more radical change than physical death, for it means passing into a totally new world of salvation. 'To receive him' is defined later in verse 12 as 'to believe on his name'. So all who believed on his name as Messiah could enter into the status of children of God because Christ is the light of salvation to the lost.

Passing into this new world of light and salvation means that one has been 'born again' (as in John 3:3, 5). This same miracle can be spoken of as a 'spiritual resurrection': believers have been raised from the (spiritual) dead. Thus, John 5:25 says, 'The hour is now coming, and now is, when the dead shall hear the voice of the Son of God: and they that hear shall live.' In John 5:28, Jesus speaks of literally raising the physically dead from their graves on the last day, but in verse 25, he is speaking of a spiritual resurrection that occurs when one believes on Christ. Paul prays along these lines that the believers in Ephesus might continue to increase in their experience of the resurrection power of Christ, who has already raised them: 'The eyes of your understanding being enlightened; that ye may know…what is the exceeding greatness of his power to us-ward who believe, according to the working of his mighty power, which he wrought in Christ, when he raised him from the dead…' (Eph. 1:18-20).

Irenaeus describes this process of spiritual resurrection as an effect of the glorious light of the incarnate Christ:

---

32. Basil the Great discusses what it means for the created light to participate in the uncreated light, which upholds it, rather than destroying it, in his study of the six days of creation (Basil, *Hexameron* 6.1ff.).

But his splendor vivifies them; those, therefore, who see God, do receive life. And for this reason, He [although] beyond comprehension, and boundless, and invisible, rendered himself visible, and comprehensible, and within the capacity of those who believe, that he might vivify those who receive and behold him through faith...[33]

Receiving Christ by faith can also be spoken of as becoming 'a new creation'. In it, those who know Christ not merely 'after the flesh', as simply another historical, religious figure, but as their own Lord, become new creations: 'Therefore if any man be in Christ, he is a new creature: old things are passed away; behold, all things are become new' (II Cor. 5:16,17).

John 1:13 uses the concept of new birth of those who receive Christ: 'Which were born, not of blood, nor of the will of flesh, nor of the will of man, but of God.' John 1:12 calls them 'sons of God' (in Greek τέκνα, which means something like the broad Scots word 'bairns,' i.e. the born ones; cf. Greek τέκτειν, 'to be born'). In this 'new birth,' believers are not born of normal human activity in the process of conception, gestation and birth. Thus, the phrase not by 'the will of man' means 'not by the will of the male' (acceptable in its place in natural birth). But humankind, male and female, have to stand aside for this 'birth from above' (ἄνωθεν), for God alone does it. Peter describes becoming children of God in this way: 'Being born again, not of corruptible seed, but of incorruptible, by the word of God, which liveth and abideth forever' (I Peter 1:23). In other words, this is a miracle of creation; it is a miracle of the first order: requiring direct supernatural intervention as great as the creation and resurrection! In the words of Paul: 'For God, who commanded the light to shine out of darkness, hath shined in our hearts, to give the light of the knowledge of the glory of God in the face of Jesus Christ' (II Cor. 4:6).

With such passages in mind, especially in the context of his exposition of God's 'calling the light day' (Gen. 1:5), Saint Basil offered an appropriate prayer for us all:

May the Father of the true light, who has adorned day with celestial light, who has made the fire to shine which illumines us during the night, who reserves for us in the peace of a future age a spiritual and everlasting light, enlighten your hearts in the knowledge of truth, keep you from stumbling, and grant that 'you may walk honestly as in the day' (Rom. 13:13). Thus shall you shine as the sun in the midst of the glory of the saints, and I shall glory in you in the day of Christ, to whom belong all glory and power for ever and ever. Amen.[34]

The true tabernacle
'And the Word was made flesh, and dwelt ('tabernacled') among us, (and we beheld his glory, the glory as of the only begotten of the Father,) full of grace and truth' (John 1:14).

It was not an eternal 'cosmic' principle that became flesh, but the person Jesus Christ, who is the eternal Son of God, who is as 'old' as the

33. Irenaeus, *Adversus Haereses*, IV.xx.5.

34. Basil the Great, *The Hexameron*, II. 8 (quoted from *Nicene and Post-Nicene Fathers*, vol. VIII, 65).

Father. As Athanasius, and then Cyril of Alexandria, write, the Son is like the Father in every respect, except for being Father.[35] God himself, in the person of his Son, who belongs to the eternal inner being of God, 'became flesh,' like us Adamic humans in every respect, except for sin.

Real Humanity

Flesh (σάρξ) in John 1:14 means 'real humanity,' as opposed to Gnostic, Docetic theories that God could never become 'nasty flesh.'[36] Since our fallen flesh needs cleansing and lifting up, Christ (without himself being personally sinful) came all the way down into our frail, condemned condition, our state of mortality, in order to lift us up out of the desperate condition which we could not transcend by ourselves. He took on true Adamic flesh, without personal guilt. This is implied by the term σάρξ.

Irenaeus makes plain the identity of the Adamic nature that Christ assumed. 'But flesh is that which was of old formed for Adam by God out of the dust, and it is this that John has declared the Word of God became.'[37] Elsewhere he writes: 'But the Lord, our Christ, underwent a valid, and not a merely accidental passion; not only was he himself not in danger of being destroyed, but he established fallen man by his own strength, and recalled him to incorruption.'[38] So the same ground that provided the dust for Adam's flesh, cursed by the fall, is promised glory in the new creation and so man is promised a glorious body like that which the Word assumed and glorified through his resurrection. By accepting the flesh of true man, the Word did not become sinful, but rather made sinful man able to accept the Word of God.

Many New Testament passages convey this point. For example, Galatians 4:4-5: 'But when the fullness of the time was come, God sent forth his Son, made of a woman, made under the law, to redeem them that were under the law, that we might receive the adoption of sons.' God the Son assumed the fallen condition of humanity, apart from sin (Rom. 8:3), in order, by coming down where we were in our shame of sin and death, to lift us up to where he was in his glorious light and life with God.

Hebrews 2 shows us that he took on real, human flesh, subject to death: 'Forasmuch then as the children are partakers of flesh and blood, he also himself likewise took part of the same; that through death he might

---

35. Athanasius, *Contra Arianos*, 3.3-6, and Cyril of Alexandria, *Dialogues* III 465 a-d : French translation by Georges de Durand: *Dialogues sur la Trinité* Tome II (Les Editions du Cerf: Paris, 1977), 21.23.

36. *Apocalypse of Peter* for instance, presents Christ as 'a Gnostic docetic redeemer', to quote the introductory words to this *Apocalypse* of James Brashler (in James M. Robinson, op.cit., 339). This literally incredible *Apocalypse of Peter* claims that, at the crucifixion, the real Jesus was 'glad and laughing on the tree,' and the one in whom nails were driven was a fleshly replacement for him (see Robinson, op.cit., 544). One wonders whether such writings had any influence on the Qur'an, such as in the statement, 'They did not kill him, nor did they crucify him, though it was made to appear like that to them…they certainly did not kill him' (Qur'an 4:157)? Timothy Freke and Peter Gandy make such a connection in *The Jesus Mysteries: Was the 'Original Jesus' a Pagan God?* (Random House Digital, 2001), 41.

37. Irenaeus, *Adversus Haereses*, I.ix.3.

38. Ibid., II.xx.3.

destroy him that had the power of death, that is the devil...For verily he took not on him the nature of angels; but he took on him the seed of Abraham' (Heb. 2:14-16).

The Word could not have delivered us fallen descendants of Adam and Eve had he not taken on all that our flesh (or humanity) involves, apart from personal sin (cf. Heb. 7:26). That humanity involves the total personality, including the human psychology or mind. This issue of Christ's psyche came to the fore in the controversy raised by Apollinarius in the fourth century, when he denied that Jesus Christ had a true human mind, or psychology. He accepted that the Logos took on a human body; but not a mind. He claimed that the Logos itself supplanted any human psychology, thereby denying the full incarnation.

A True Human Mind

The Church Fathers saw that if Christ's taking on a human psychology were denied, then only that which he took on (in the theory of Apollinarius, only a human body) would in fact be redeemed. That means that our minds would not be saved! Gregory Nazianzus answered them: τὸ γὰρ ἀπρόσληπτον ἀθεράπευτον ('That which is not taken up is not healed').[39] If Apollinarius had been right, then the whole of human personality, including the fallen mind, was not taken up in the incarnation, and thus was not healed. If that were the case, we who have fallen human minds could never transcend our mortal condition. In sum, when the Logos took on flesh, he took on the whole of what it is to be a human person: body and mind, flesh and spirit.

John describes the stupendous action of the eternal Son assuming human flesh as being like the setting up of the tabernacle in the wilderness; that sacred place in the midst of the camp of Israel, where *God met man* in forgiveness and mercy, holy law and saving grace; where *sacrifice* was made for sin, and then the *benediction* of the peace of God was brought out to the waiting people by the High Priest (e.g. Exodus 40). John says literally that the Word ἐσκήνωσεν ἐν ἡμῖν: that is, 'tabernacled among us.' All that the tabernacle signified by type and shadow, in its structure, and in the worship that was appointed to go on in it, is brought to culmination and full reality in Jesus Christ, the Logos who took on flesh and blood. Jesus Christ is the ultimate meeting place of God and man, where sins are put away, and loving communion is restored.

Maximus the Confessor wrote: 'God, who in his mercy for us has desired that the grace of divine virtue be sent down from heaven to those who are on earth, has symbolically built the sacred tent and everything in it as a representation, figure, and imitation of Wisdom. The grace of the New Testament is mysteriously hidden in the letter of the Old.'[40]

So the Old Testament tabernacle foreshadows Christ, who would himself be the meeting of God and man, where God dwells among his people in peace. John Owen says that what Hebrews 8:2 calls 'the true

---

39. Gregory Nazianzus, *Ep.*, 101.

40. Maximus, *Maximus Confessor: Selected Writings* in *The Classics of Western Spirituality*, Transl. G. C. Berthold, Intro. J. Pelikan (New York: Paulist Press, 1985), 145.

tabernacle' (that is, the original or antitype of the earthly copy) is nothing less that the human nature of Jesus Christ:

> [W]hen he was incarnate, and came into the world, it is said that ἐσκήνωσε, 'he fixed his tabernacle among us,' John i.14… All that old curious structure, for a habitation for God, did only represent his taking our nature upon him, fixing his tent thereby among men…He himself called his *own body* his temple, with respect unto the temple of Jerusalem, which was of the same nature and use with the tabernacle, John ii.19-22. And this he did, because his body was that true, substantial temple and tabernacle whereof he was the minister… That, therefore, wherein God *dwells really and substantially*, and on the account whereof he is our God in the covenant of grace, that, and no other, is the true tabernacle. But this is in Christ alone, for 'in him dwelleth all the fullness of the Godhead bodily,' Col. ii.9. Thus the human nature of Christ is that true, substantial tabernacle, wherein God dwelleth personally.[41]

In order 'to pitch his tent among us', the Word had to become something he was not. The verb ἐγένετο ('he became') is suitable to created beings, beings that come into historical existence from nonexistence. But how can this 'historical genesis' be applied to the eternal being of the Logos? How could he through whom all things had their genesis, himself become subject to genesis?

As Saint Augustine said, 'He became what he was not without ceasing to be what he already was.' That is, he became man (a new experience), without ceasing to be fully God (who he always had been). Two centuries prior to Augustine, Irenaeus of Lyon said it this way: '…the Word of God, our Lord Jesus Christ…did, through his transcendent love, become what we are, that he might bring us to be even what he is himself.'[42]

It is accurately summarized by Symeon the New Theologian:

> God the Word, our creator, came down to earth, in a way that he alone understands and of which he alone is capable. He thus became man, not at all by a mode of human conception, but through the Holy Spirit and the ever-Virgin Mary, as it is written: *And the Word was made flesh and dwelt among us* (John 1:14)…The Son and Word of God, who is also God, took a body from Mary… so as to be a true son of Adam.[43]

The Miracle of Miracles

How this could be, and what it meant was to be the major issue in the first great Council of the Christian Church at Nicaea in A.D. 325, as we shall later see. Fr. Justin Popovitch was right to call the incarnation 'the greatest of all miracles of all worlds'.[44] John Chrysostom said that the incarnation was an act of the love of God greater than the creation of the world.[45]

---

41. John Owen, *Hebrews* Vol. 6, 19.

42. Irenaeus, *Adversus Haereses*, 5, Preface.

43. Symeon the New Theologian, *Discourse* 35:1-2.

44. Justin Popovitch, *Philosophie Orthodoxe de la Vérité: Dogmatique de l'Eglise Orthodoxe*, French transl. [from Serbian] by Jean-Louis Palierne (L'Age D'Homme: Lausanne, 1993), vol. II, 14.

45. John Chrysostom, *Sermons on Hebrews*, Hom. IV.3 (PG 63, 40).

There is no explaining of the 'possibility' of such a miracle of miracles. Without seeking to explain it, Cyril of Alexandria wrote that we must simply remember who God is: 'Do not ask me how the Son of God was born of the Virgin, because wherever God wills it, the order of nature is conquered. He did will it; he was able to do it; he came down, and he saved. Everything obeys God.'[46]

Seeing the Glory

'… And we beheld his glory, the glory as of the only begotten of the Father, full of grace and truth' (v. 14b).

L. Hurtado traces 'the glory' to the shining of the Face of God to his people: 'The Jewish exegetes of the early Christian centuries, who were doing their theologizing at the period of the great Christological controversies in the Church, developed a noun, *shechinah*, from this Hebrew verb, "to dwell," and used it to describe this indwelling of the Face of God in the midst of Israel.'[47]

The Jewish/Christian audience that read the Gospel of John would have immediately thought of the glory-cloud that was over the Tabernacle in the wilderness, and at times came down into the Temple of Jerusalem, as at Solomon's dedication (I Kings 8:10,11). Glory is connected with God's face, and indeed, conveyed its holy brightness to the face of Moses, so that his shining countenance frightened the people when he came down from God's immediate presence on Mount Sinai (cf. Exod. 34:29-35). The Apostle Paul connects this glory that radiated from Moses to the face of Christ, by which, as we behold it in faith, we become transformed into his image 'from glory to glory, even as by the Spirit of the Lord' (cf. II Cor. 3:18). And Hebrews 1:3 (to be studied in detail presently) speaks of Christ as 'being the brightness of [God's] glory…'

Ezekiel saw the glory leaving the soon-to-be destroyed Temple (cf. Ezek.10 and 11). But John sees the glory coming back in him whom Tabernacle and Temple represented: namely, the Word made flesh. Jesus' glory is portrayed throughout John's Gospel, especially in his miracles. The glory was seen after Christ's first miracle of turning water into wine at the wedding of Cana: 'This beginning of miracles did Jesus in Cana of Galilee, and manifested forth his glory; and his disciples believed on him' (John 2:11). It was seen many other times, especially at his resurrecting of Lazarus from the dead: 'When Jesus heard that [i.e. Lazarus' critical illness], he said, This sickness is not unto death, but for the glory of God, that the Son of God might be glorified thereby…Jesus said unto her [Martha], Said I not unto thee, that, if thou wouldest believe, thou shouldest see the glory of God?' (John 11:4, 40).

Yet, perhaps surprisingly to us, John shows that Christ's glory is supremely revealed when he was lifted up on the cross: 'And Jesus answered them, saying, The hour is come, that the Son of man should be glorified' (John 12:23); 'Therefore when [Judas] was gone out [from

---

46. Cyril of Alexandria, *Concerning the True Faith for Queens* 10 (PG 76, 1216 A).

47. Hurtado, op. cit., 44. See also D. Kelly, *Systematic Theology*, vol. 1 for details (463-465).

the Last Supper], Jesus said, Now is the Son of man glorified, and God is glorified in him. If God be glorified in him, God shall also glorify him in himself, and shall straightway glorify him' (John 13:31-32). But after the crucifixion and burial of 'the Lord of glory' (I Cor. 2:8), Paul tells us that 'Christ was raised up from the dead by the glory of the Father' (Rom. 6:4). Thus Christ's high priestly prayer was beginning to be fulfilled, so that his people might behold the glory he had with the Father before the world existed (cf. John 17:24).

Grace and Truth

This glory of the enfleshed Logos is 'full of grace and truth' (John 1:14b). In general, grace originally meant something like 'that which causes joy', and then it came to signify 'goodwill, kindness, unmerited favor.'[48] The term 'grace' (χάρις) is used only three times in the prologue, and nowhere else in John's Gospel. It is Paul who particularly develops the ramifications of grace elsewhere in the New Testament. John directly contrasts 'the law given by Moses' to the 'grace and truth [that] came by Jesus Christ' (John 1:17).

It is not that the law was ever without grace, nor that the grace of God in Christ ever excludes the structure of law (for law expresses the very character of God, and Christian ethics involve obedience to the Lord – cf. John 14:15), but it is rather a matter of emphasis. The law, while providing a mediator and sacrifice for sin, nevertheless focuses on the objective holiness of God, which shows up our Adamic sinfulness, and hence our need of grace. Grace, however, focuses on what God has done for us in his Son that we could never do for ourselves. The 'definition' of grace by the Apostle Paul in II Corinthians 8:9 expresses succinctly what the coming of Christ in the flesh has achieved for sinners who believe: 'For ye know the grace of our Lord Jesus Christ, that though he was rich, yet for your sakes he became poor, that ye through his poverty might be rich.' What John says is not unlike that: knowing who the incarnate Word is, is a receiving of 'grace for grace' out of the divine fullness (John 1:16).

Cyril of Alexandria, with this in mind, writes: 'The law projected toward the beauty of truth… And the truth is Christ, through whom we gained entrance and we arrived close to the Father, raising ourselves, like on a mountain, to the knowledge of truth.'[49] He adds:

> The mountain is interpreted as being the knowledge of Christ's mystery, beyond understanding and beyond everything. Thus Moses brings the people close to the mountain but does not take them up…[W]e gain the perfection and the height in wisdom and knowledge through Christ, not through Moses. The latter [Moses] is a servant and a pedagogue, while the first [Christ], as the Lord of all, was revealed as the giver of perfect knowledge.[50]

---

48. See T. F. Torrance, *The Doctrine of Grace in the Apostolic Fathers* (Oliver and Boyd: Edinburgh, 1948), 1-10.

49. Cyril of Alexandria, *Glaphyra* (PG 69:509).

50. Ibid.

That is, Cyril, and the church in general, believe that by virtue of the Holy Spirit uniting us to the Son's knowledge of the Father, we are – in a way appropriate to creatures – lifted up into God's knowledge of God. There is no experience, and indeed, no state of existence on earth (or in heaven to follow) so wonderful as that!

Grace is accompanied by truth in Jesus Christ. 'Truth' (ἀλήθεια) is used 25 times in John, and is often opposed to lies. It is also closely related to the very being of Jesus ('I am the truth'). Exodus 34:6 seems to lie behind John's formulation of 'grace and truth': 'And the LORD passed by before him [Moses], and proclaimed, The LORD, the LORD God, merciful and gracious, longsuffering, and abundant in goodness and truth...' The incarnate Word is the revelation of both grace and truth, and so of the character of the LORD himself. He was made flesh, so that by this gracious condescension we might know who God truly is.

As Cyril said (immediately above), the truth of the divine character is most beautiful. The glory of the Gospel is that Christ gives us access in his truth and grace to this divine beauty!

The Only Begotten Son

The Authorized Version, the Revised Standard Version and the New International Version read 'the only begotten Son'. But the third edition of the Greek New Testament by the United Bible Societies replaces 'Son' with 'God', thus rendering the phrase: 'the only begotten God.' Some very early textual witnesses and early Church Fathers also have this reading (as Aleph, textual fragments of p66, as well as Irenaeus and Clement of Alexandria and others). Yet other very early witnesses have 'only begotten Son'. The majority of Ancient and Medieval texts also carry the reading 'only begotten Son'. As Edward Hoskyns pointed out, the phrase 'who is in the bosom of the Father' certainly points to Son (υἱός) rather than to God (θεός).[51]

Hence, the Word in the flesh is the final revelation of God (cf. Heb. 1:2): he is superior to John the Baptist (John 1:15); superior to Moses (John 1:17); he supplies all his people's need, where prophecy could not (John 1:16), and he is the only revealer of the God whom no man has seen (John 1:18).

(2) Philippians 2:5-11

[5]Let this mind be in you, which was also in Christ Jesus: [6]Who, being in the form of God, thought it not robbery to be equal with God: [7]But made himself of no reputation, and took upon him the form of a servant, and was made in the likeness of men: [8]And being found in fashion as a man, he humbled himself, and became obedient unto death, even the death of the cross. [9]Wherefore God also hath highly exalted him, and given him a name which is above every name:[10]That at the name of Jesus every knee should bow, of things in heaven, and things in earth, and things under the

---

51. Edward C. Hoskyns, *The Fourth Gospel* (London: Faber & Faber, revised second edition 1947), 154.

earth; [11]And that every tongue should confess that Jesus Christ is Lord, to the glory of God the Father.

The immediate context
In Philippians 2:1-4, we find an exhortation to oneness and humility within the Church. In verse 4, one is to consider the interests of others before one's own interests. In order to do so, selflessness and consideration of others (that is, self-forgetfulness) are called for.

The example of Christ
This Christian selflessness which is to characterize the Christian Church is most perfectly seen in the humiliation of Christ. He is the example of how believers are to behave by renouncing themselves for the welfare of others. Our supreme examples of self-forgetting love, which also enable us to practice this love, are the incarnation and death of the Lord Jesus Christ. As true man, Jesus Christ manifests the fulness of who God is, and thus demonstrates the actions appropriate to God within human relationships.

(a) The pre-incarnate status of Christ (verse 6)
In order to grasp who Christ was from all eternity, and who he became, we must examine what is meant in verse 6 that Christ was 'in the form of God' (ἐν μορφῇ θεοῦ). This designation is essential to the identity of our Saviour and Lord and thus requires our closest attention. Lightfoot in his *Saint Paul's Epistle to the Philippians* says that the term μορφή implies not external 'accidents', but essential attributes used elsewhere of the divinity of the Son (II Cor. 4:4; Col. 1:15; Heb. 1:3), whereas σχῆμα generally has the sense of instability and changeableness (cf. I Cor. 7:31; II Cor. 11:13-15).[52] So, according to Lightfoot, Philippians 2:6 indicates the essential deity of the Son.

Twentieth-Century criticism of Lightfoot on μορφή
Some scholars, however, wrote off this distinction by Lightfoot as nineteenth-century 'Classicism.' It is certainly true that Lightfoot's explanation of μορφή was largely in the context of the Greek philosophers. His research has been challenged since the twentieth century on that basis, as not being as fully cognizant of the biblical word usage as is necessary. For example, Lightfoot's identification of 'form' with 'essence' is not always upheld by the biblical usage of these terms. For instance, in Mark 16:12, the risen Lord appeared in a different 'form' to some of the disciples; yet that could not there mean a change of his 'essence' had occurred.

A more biblical explanation of μορφή?
Ralph Martin went in what he thought was a more thoroughly biblical linguistic direction, by studying the word μορφή in the LXX.[53] There is not

---

52. J. B. Lightfoot, *Saint Paul's Epistle to the Philippians* (London, 1888), 110.

53. R. P. Martin, *Carmen Christi: Philippians 2:5-11 in recent interpretation and in the Setting of Early*

a great deal of data for this usage in the LXX, but he notes, among other considerations, that 'form' (μορφή) can function as 'image' (εἰκών), and holds that these terms, 'form' and 'image,' are interchangeable in the Septuagint.[54] The semantic overlap between these terms could encompass the idea of 'expression of likeness' as outwardly viewed, rather than underlying identity of essence. However, μορφή is not used in the LXX to translate the Hebrew word דְּמוּת ('image'), but it is used one time for צֶלֶם ('likeness') – as in its version of Genesis 1:26-27. Even though there is certainly an infrequent connection between image and likeness in the LXX, nevertheless Genesis 1 says that Adam and Eve were in 'the image and likeness' of God. It does not say that they were 'in the form of God'. But that is precisely what Philippians 2:6 does say about Christ: He was in the form of God.

Reaffirmation of Lightfoot's distinction

Moises Silva's comment on this reputed background of 'form' or 'image' in the LXX is realistic: 'The discussion of LXX backgrounds is often complicated by fuzzy linguistic arguments and by the implication that the various theses expressed are mutually exclusive.'[55]

Therefore, 'form' and 'image of God' do not seem strictly synonymous on the basis of LXX word usage,[56] and so it is uncalled for exegetically to restrict μορφή merely to that which appears outwardly of God, rather than to being a substantial expression of his person. After detailed research, Moises Silva concludes:

> It appears then that Lightfoot (1863:133), although misguided in seeing here a more or less philosophical meaning of 'essence', was *not* off the track in detecting a contrast between 'the true divine nature of our Lord' and 'true human nature'. And it moreover follows that the Philippians passage, although not written for the purpose of presenting an ontological description of Christ, is very much consonant with the Trinitarian formulas of the fourth-century church.[57]

Even if one cannot accept all of Lightfoot's description of what Philippians 2:6 means by μορφή, what the word and verse there convey is not that Christ appears outwardly to be 'in the likeness of God,' but that the reality of what is meant by 'form of God' belongs as much to the Son as to the Father, and hence that the incarnate being and action of the Son reveals who God is. So, while 'form' as used in Scripture does not always definitely connote 'essence' (as in Lightfoot's interpretation from Greek philosophical usage), yet as T. F. Torrance has said: '*Morphe* just means form in the

Christian Worship (Cambridge: Cambridge University Press, 1967), 99-120.

54. Ibid., 108-109.

55. Moises Silva, *Philippians: Baker Exegetical Commentary on the New Testament*, second edition (Grand Rapids, MI: Baker Academic, 2007), 101.

56. See the critique of Martin's ideas at this point by C. F. D. Moule, 'Further Reflections on Philippians 2:5-11,' in *Apostolic History and the Gospel*, eds. W. W. Gasque and R. P. Martin (Grand Rapids, MI, 1970).

57. Silva, op. cit., 101, 102.

ordinary sense, but the sort of form, nevertheless, which corresponds to inner nature.'[58]

Importance of μορφῇ Θεοῦ

B. B. Warfield expresses the meaning of 'form' as the Son possessing the very Godness of the Father:

> The language in which our Lord's intrinsic Deity is expressed, for example, is probably as strong as any that could be devised. Paul does not simply say, 'He was God.' He says, 'He was in the form of God,' employing a turn of speech which throws emphasis upon our Lord's possession of the specific quality of God. 'Form' (*morphe*) is a term which expresses the sum of those characterizing qualities which make a thing the precise thing that it is… When our Lord is said to be 'in the form of God,' therefore, he is declared, in the most express manner possible, to be all that God is, to possess the whole fullness of attributes which make God, God.[59]

That is the stupendous nature of the incarnation! He who is eternal God in the fullest sense became true man without ceasing to be who he always was. That is why Jesus could say to Philip: 'He that hath seen me hath seen the Father' (John 14:9). As we shall see, the cost of his bringing us to the Father was his own willing self-sacrifice. Peter explains: 'For Christ also hath once suffered for sins, the just for the unjust, that he might bring us to God…' (I Peter 3:18).

Equality with God

The last clause of verse 6 underlines the Lord's eternal existence in 'the form of God,' as meaning 'equality with God': '…thought it not robbery to be equal with God.' As Warfield points out, the verb used for 'being in the form of God' is ὑπάρχων, rather than ὤν. ὑπάρχων denotes prior existence in a way that ὤν does not: 'As a present participle it denotes continued action. In both other instances where Paul connects ὑπάρχων with the aorist (II Cor. 8:17; Rom. 4:19), it denotes continuance.'[60]

Continual pre-existence is conveyed in this last clause of Phil. 2:6: οὐχ ἁρπαγμὸν ἡγήσατο τὸ εἶναι ἴσα Θεῷ. That is, the eternally existent Christ 'did not consider equality with God a thing to be seized (or 'held on to').' This clause states incontrovertibly that Christ was 'equal to God'. This is the testimony of other witnesses in the New Testament. Revelation 1:4 describes the risen Christ as 'the one who is, and was and is to come' (that is, he is the eternal 'I am' or YHWH). Romans 9:5 calls him 'Christ, who is over all, God blessed for ever. Amen.' He has always shared the very being of God, and, as he tells us in his high priestly prayer, he has always shared the glory of God (cf. John 17:5). Hence such grammatical details, far from being a clutter of arcane detail, enter into the very heart of the Gospel, and of how it applies to us.

---

58. T. F. Torrance, *The Incarnation*, 74.

59. B. B. Warfield, *Biblical Foundations*, 131,132.

60. Ibid., 132.

As we have discussed in the first volume of this series, Trinitarian theology is simply the necessary development of certain unequivocal New Testament teachings, such as that of the full identity-in-being between God the Father and God the Son, and at the same time, that of their personal distinctiveness.[61] In other words, what Philippians 2 affirms about Christ requires the doctrine of the Trinity, and the glorious news is that we are actually brought to share in the Trinitarian life. As Saint Athanasius said: 'We are allowed to know the Son in the Father, because the whole being of the Son is proper to the Father's being…For whereas the form of the Godhead of the Father is in the being of the Son, it follows that the Son is in the Father and the Father is in the Son.'[62] This is why faith in Jesus Christ lifts us into a saving knowledge of God the Father Almighty, for to know him is life eternal (John 17:3).

A prize not to be held on to

Philippians 2:6b states that the pre-incarnate Christ did not count his equality with God *robbery* (or *a prize to be held on to*). The word translated as 'robbery' in the Authorized Version is ἁρπαγμόν, and is found only here in the New Testament. According to Lightfoot, this word originally signified a piece of plunder or robbery, but later came to mean 'a highly prized possession.'[63] Its meaning here seems to be something like 'to clutch tightly something that is highly valued'. It does not here mean to rob something that one does not have, for Christ always had equality with his heavenly Father. Christ's always having existed in full equality with God is reflected in II Corinthians 8:9: 'For ye know the grace of our Lord Jesus Christ, that, *though he was rich*, yet for your sakes he became poor, that ye through his poverty might be rich.'

When was he rich? He who had nowhere to lay his head (Matt. 8:20), who had to find a coin in a fish's mouth to pay his tax (Matt. 17:27), who had to depend on the generosity of godly women to fund his ministry (Luke 8:1-3), who seemed to own nothing other than a wonderful cloak (which was taken from him by means of gambling at the cross – Luke 23:34), who was buried in a borrowed tomb: when was he rich? It was when he shared with eternal joy the glory of the Father (cf. John 17). It was when, out of the great love he knew as God, 'who is rich in mercy,' he shared in the Father's plan to do all that would be necessary in due time for us to become his (cf. Eph. 2:4-5). Instead of keeping these infinite riches to himself, he made plans with the Father 'to show the exceeding riches of his grace in his kindness toward us…' (Eph. 2:7).

That determination generously and self-sacrificially to share the wealth that was by right always his leads us to:

(b) The lowering of the Incarnation (vv. 7-8)

First, we are told that Christ, although fully God, 'made himself of no reputation, and took upon him the form of a servant, and was made in the likeness of men' (Phil. 2:7).

---

61. See D. Kelly, S.T. vol. 1, chapters 4 and 7.

62. Athanasius, *Contra Arianos* 3.3.

63. Lightfoot, op. cit., 111.

What the Authorised Version translates as 'made himself of no reputation' is in the Greek ἐκένωσε. This verb can be rendered either (1) literally, which would be 'emptied himself,' or (2) metaphorically, which would be more or less the same as the AV: 'made himself of no reputation'; massively humbled himself. There are strong reasons to believe that we should take ἐκένωσε metaphorically, rather than literally.

B. B. Warfield has argued that every place in the New Testament where Paul employs the verb κενόω (from which ἐκένωσε is taken), he uses it metaphorically, not literally. That is its usage in Romans 4:14; I Corinthians 1:17; 9:15; and II Corinthians 9:3. In none of these texts does it mean a literal 'emptying.'

Rather, 'to humble himself,' or 'to make himself of no reputation' is what the Apostle is indicating here. Verse 7 goes on to tell us how 'he humbled himself': 'And took upon him the form of a servant, and was made in the likeness of men.' This means that he lowered himself 'by taking'; by taking 'the form of a servant.' The verb rendered 'taking' is λαβών. It is the aorist participle, denoting simultaneous action, which means: 'when he lowered himself, it was by taking the form of a servant.' There is no suggestion in the text of his emptying out any of his divine attributes, but a paradox is stated here: 'he 'emptied' (i.e. lowered) himself by taking something to himself'; that is, the form or manner of being of a servant. Upon his incarnation, he remained in the form of God as Lord of all, but also took on the nature of a servant in his humanity. Rather than literally 'emptying out' anything he was, he added something: the form of a servant.

Warfield states that 'the term "form" here, of course, bears the same full meaning in the preceding instance of its occurrence in the phrase "the form of God." It imparts the specific quality, the whole body of characteristics by which a servant is made what we know as a servant.'[64]

The Kenotic Theory

Especially in the nineteenth century, interpreters in Germany, then later in Britain and America, took ἐκένωσε literally, as though the eternal Son of God had emptied himself of his divine attributes while he was in the flesh. Thomasius of Erlangen taught that, as incarnate, Christ abandoned such divine attributes as omnipotence and omniscience, but kept the attributes of love and holiness.[65] British theologians such as P. T. Forsyth[66] and H. R. Mackintosh[67] held to forms of this theory that were somewhat more consistent with the deity of Christ than that of some of the Germans,[68]

---

64. Warfield, op. cit., 135.

65. See Thomasius, *Christi Person und Werk* , vol. 1 (Erlangen, 1886).

66. P. T. Forsyth, *The Person and Place of Jesus Christ* (London: Hodder and Stoughton, second ed., 1910).

67. H. R. Mackintosh, *The Doctrine of the Person of Jesus Christ* (Edinburgh: T & T Clark, second ed., 1913).

68. See the discussion of the development of the kenotic theology in Germany in Karl Barth, *Church Dogmatics* IV/1, 180-183.

although no forms of this theory seem to have any significance in contemporary scholarship.[69]

We may mention three major criticisms of the Kenotic theory.

(i) Archbishop William Temple showed that the agent of creation, who is affirmed by the New Testament still to 'hold all things together' (cf. Col. 1:16, 17), did not give up his cosmic functions during the incarnation:

> What was happening to the rest of the universe during the period of our Lord's earthly life? ...[this would be] to assert that for a certain period the history of the world was let loose from the control of the Creative word, and 'apart from Him' very nearly everything happened that happened at all during thirty odd years, both on this planet and throughout the immensities of space.[70]

(ii) The Kenotic theory gives us less than a genuine union in which Christ is at the same time both God and man. Donald Baillie said:

> The Kenotic Theory appears to me to give us a story of a temporary theophany, in which He who formerly was God changed Himself temporarily into man, or exchanged his divinity for humanity... He had been God, but now He was a man. If taken in all its implications, that seems more like a pagan story of metamorphosis than like the Christian doctrine of Incarnation, which always found in the life of Jesus on earth, God and man in simultaneous union – the Godhead 'veiled in flesh' but not changed into humanity. Surely the relation between the divine and the human in the Incarnation is a deeper mystery that this.[71]

Baillie helped put an end to the prevalence of this theory in Britain when he pointed out that Kenoticism makes the incarnation only temporary:

> Thus on the Kenotic Theory ... He is God and man, not simultaneously in a hypostatic union, but successively – first divine, then human, then God again ... It seems to leave no room at all for the traditional catholic doctrine of the permanence of the manhood of Christ, 'who being the eternal Son of God, became man, and so was, and continueth to be God and man in two distinct natures, and one person, forever' (Westminster Shorter Catechism, Q. 21).[72]

(iii) The Kenotic theory robs the mediatorship of Christ of its value. The fact that Christ is able to represent God to man, and man to God in his infinitely valuable person and work depends upon his continuing to be God and man at the same time. As James Muller writes:

> If Christ lay down His divine attributes or ceased for a time to exist in a manner equal to God, His self-humiliation loses its soteriological significance and His conciliatory work of grace its saving power. For He was not very

---

69. But see *Exploring Kenotic Christology: The Self-Emptying of God*, C. Stephen Evans, ed.

70. William Temple, *Christus Veritas* (London: Macmillan, 1926), 142.

71. Donald Baillie, *God Was in Christ* (New York: Charles Scribner's Sons, 1955), 96.

72. Ibid., 97.

God and very man then, no true mediator between God and man. Christ without divine attributes is not God-man, but only man.[73]

D. Staniloae shows that Cyril of Alexandria answers far ahead of time nineteenth-century theories of kenosis:

St. Cyril refutes in anticipation the Protestant kenotic theories of the nineteenth century, according to which the Son of God gave up – through the incarnation, for the time of his life on earth – the divine omnipotence, omnipresence, knowledge and consciousness: 'How did he become poor [cf. II Cor. 8:9]? By the fact that being God by his nature and the Son of God the Father, he became man and was born with the body from the seed of Adam, putting on the measure fit for a servant, namely that which is human. For he who did not consider it disdainful to become like us, how would he give up those [divine attributes] by which one knows that he became like us for us?'[74]

Barth writes that if Christ were not fully God in his fully human state, then the atonement he accomplished would not be efficacious:

God is always God even in His humiliation. The divine being does not suffer any change, any diminution, any transformation into something else, any admixture with something else, let alone any cessation. The deity of Christ is the one unaltered because unalterable deity of God. Any subtraction or weakening of it would at once throw doubt upon the atonement made in Him. He humbled Himself, but He did not do it by ceasing to be who He is. He went into a strange land, but even there, and especially there, He never became a stranger to Himself. The word ἐκένωσε in Phil. 2:7 certainly does not mean this…[75]

J. Jeremias and others have suggested that 'emptying himself' was a way of drawing upon the language of 'the servant of the Lord' (*ebed Yahweh*) of Isaiah 53.[76] Ralph Martin discusses this suggestion, without finding it convincing.[77] We note two of the objections (among others) he raises to this identification:

There is no allusion to the personal benefits which the Servant's work makes available (cf. Isa liii. 4f., 11 f.). In Christian terminology, there is no hint of *propter nos et propter nostram salutem* [for us and for our salvation]. Advocates of the *'Ebed Yahweh* background explain this omission by saying that the application of Christ's work to men is implied…But … if the author wanted to show that Christ was the fulfillment of the Servant, he should have left as implicit only what stands out most clearly in the fourth song

---

73. James Muller, *Commentary on Philippians* (Grand Rapids: Eerdmans, 1955), 84.

74. Dumitru Staniloae, *The Experience of God: Orthodox Dogmatic Theology: vol. 3. The Person of Jesus Christ as God and Savior*, translated and edited by Ioan Ionita (Holy Cross Orthodox Press: Brookline, Massachusetts, 2011), 106, quoting Saint Cyril of Alexandria, *Response to the Combating of Anathemas*, anat. 12.

75. K. Barth, *Church Dogmatics* IV/1. 179,180.

76. J. Jeremias, *Studia Paulina*, p. 154 (quoted in Ralph P. Martin, *Carmen Christi*, 182).

77. Ralph P. Martin, *Carmen Christi*, 182-196. Latin translation mine.

– the Servant's sin-atoning ministry. And there is no explicit mention of obedience in Isa. liii.[78]

The real issue is what Christ accomplished in his 'making himself of no reputation,' while remaining fully God. Had he been less than God in his humiliation, the sins of the human race would not have been atoned for. Although it challenges our normal conceptions of God to state that he could remain fully God under such abuse and abnegation, so much the worse for our preconceptions of God. Indeed, our concept of God and his glory is certainly challenged by the teaching in John that the glory of God was manifested when the Son of God was lifted up on the cross (John 12:23, 27-28; 21:19)!

It took this lowering of God to restore the lost creation, and in so doing, to shine forth the glory of God's judgment and mercy together. In the words of Psalm 85:10: 'Mercy and truth are met together; righteousness and peace have kissed each other.' They met in invisible embrace at the cross of Calvary, to our eternal benefit.

(c) The humiliation of the Incarnate Christ (verse 8)

Philippians 2:8 shows the ultimate humiliation of the Incarnate Christ: 'And being found in fashion as a man, he humbled himself, and became obedient unto death, even the death of the cross.' After the initial lowering of the Son of God into the flesh, there is the further humbling of himself (ἐταπείνωσεν ἑαυτὸν).

As E. Kasemann points out, this emphatic 'himself' indicates the voluntary nature of this lowering. He contrasts this to the *Ebed Yahweh* songs of Isaiah, and shows that with Christ, the emphasis is upon what he did, not simply what he was.[79] The nadir of his humiliation was the death to which he submitted himself on the cross. We must postpone the discussion of the immense accomplishment of his atoning death and descent into hell, when he 'bound the strong man' (cf. Luke 11:20-22) and 'spoiled principalities and powers' (cf. Col. 2:15). His 'lifting up' on the cross was already the beginning of his exaltation (cf. John 3:14).

In the words of Saint Athanasius, commenting on Philippians 2:9-10: 'For as Christ died and was exalted as a man, so as man he is said to take what as God he ever had, that the grace thus given might come to us. For the Word did not suffer loss in taking a body in order that he should seek to receive grace, but rather he even deified what he put on, and more than graciously gave it to mankind' (*Contra Arianos* 1.42).

Staniloae shows that, contrary to the way we normally think, the very weakness of the death of the Son of God was at the same time the putting forth of hidden infinite power, as we see from the results of that death:

---

78. Ibid., 213.

79. E. Kasemann, 'A Critical Analysis of Philippians 2:5-11' in *God and Christ. Existence and Province (Journal for Theology and Church,* 5), English Transl. (New York, 1968); quoted in R. P. Martin, op. cit., 178.

In the East the acceptance of death before God is understood as strength. That is why the death Jesus suffered is at the same time an occasion for manifesting the power through which death is conquered by the Son of God in the body and with the collaboration of the strengthened body. For the body too can be strong in bearing sufferings through the power given to it by the Son of God on behalf of the divine nature. Thus there is no contradiction between the power given to the human nature in performing healings and the power of endurance. It is in the power of enduring sufferings that the body becomes interiorly capable of being an instrument of healings and of his Resurrection as the last step in that direction. Therefore, by accepting this humbling of the body, the Word of God simultaneously strengthens it.[80]

Gregory of Nyssa sees clearly that Christ's voluntary humiliation is a sign of infinite power rather than an indication of weakness:

> But this his descent to the humility of man is a kind of superabundant exercise of power, which thus finds no check even in directions which contravene nature ... In like manner, it is not the vastness of the heavens, and the bright shining of its constellations, and the order of the universe, and the unbroken administration over all existence that so manifestly displays the transcendent power of the Deity, as this condescension to the weakness of our nature...[81]

Gregory goes on to point out that although his coming down 'to the lowly level of our nature' might 'raise the expectation that death would overcome him,' precisely the opposite happened. Instead, who Christ really was shown forth in majestic power after he entered the realm of death.[82]

(d) The exaltation of Christ and his recognition as Lord (Phil. 2:9-11)

The main subject of the action in this section is God the Father; He takes charge: 'Wherefore God also hath highly exalted him, and given him a name which is above every name' (v. 9). 'Lohmeyer...has shown that the Exaltation has to do with the cosmic lordship of Christ, who is installed as Lord of the universe and not simply as cultic Lord of the Church...'[83] His exaltation is the fruit of his humiliation; that is, he came first as suffering lamb, and then as conquering lion of the tribe of Judah.

The exalted name he was given is of such a nature that all things: in heaven, on earth, and under the earth, bow down to it. The heavenly beings: angels and the world of spirits (cf. Eph. 6:12); things on earth: all of its inhabitants, past and present (cf. Rev. 5:12,13); and things under the earth (Rev. 6:12-17; 20:10-15), all must bow low in utter submission to his name. That name is YHWH – 'Jehovah'; 'I AM THAT I AM.' The name Jesus means that 'Jehovah (or YHWH) saves' (Matt. 1:21).

'All that the Old Testament predicates of Yahweh – that He is exalted far above all demonic powers and idols and is worthy to receive the

---

80. Staniloae, op. cit., 110.

81. Gregory of Nyssa, *The Great Catechism*, vol. V in *A Select Library of the Nicene and Post-Nicene Fathers* (Eerdmans: Grand Rapids, 1994), 494.

82. Ibid.

83. Lohmeyer, *Philipper*, p. 97, quoted in Ralph P. Martin, op. cit., 235.

homage of the whole creation and that His name is all-excelling… – is applied to the exalted Christ at the behest of God Himself.'[84]

(3) Hebrews 1:1-4

[1]God, who at sundry times and in divers manners spake in time past unto the fathers by the prophets,

[2]Hath in these last days spoken unto us by his Son, whom he hath appointed heir of all things, by whom also he made the worlds;

[3]Who being the brightness of his glory, and the express image of his person, and upholding all things by the word of his power, when he had by himself purged our sins, sat down on the right hand of the Majesty on high:

[4]Being made so much better than the angels, as he hath by inheritance obtained a more excellent name than they.

Hebrews 1:1-2 states that the Son is the last word that the Father speaks to this world. All the inspired revelation of the Old Testament was a preparation for him, and found its full meaning and culmination in him. 'God's previous spokesmen were His servants, but for the proclamation of His last word to man He has chosen His Son.'[85]

F. F. Bruce points out from this passage seven facts about the Son of God, 'which bring out His greatness and show why the revelation given in Him is the highest that God can give':[86]

God appointed him 'heir of all things' (v. 2). This recalls Psalm 2:8: 'Ask of me, and I will give thee the nations for thine inheritance, and the uttermost parts of the earth for thy possession.' Like Philippians 2:10, his possession includes all things: in heaven, on earth, and under the earth.

Through Him, God 'made the worlds' (v. 2). The Greek word for 'worlds' (τοὺς αἰῶνας) can mean 'the ages' (as translated in Heb. 11:3), but also includes the entire universe of space and time. As John 1:3 demonstrates, the Logos was the agent of creation.

Although Jesus is introduced as the divine Son (v. 2a), the functions attributed to him are those of the Wisdom of God; he is the mediator of revelation, the agent and sustainer of creation, and the reconciler of others to God. Each of these Christological affirmations echoes declarations concerning the role of divine Wisdom in the Wisdom of Solomon (cf. Wis. 7:21-27).[87]

He is the 'effulgence (ἀπαύγασμα) of God's glory' (v. 3); that is, the brightness and outshining of who God essentially is. The Wisdom of Solomon describes Wisdom as:

84. Ralph P. Martin, op. cit., 245,246.

85. F. F. Bruce, *Commentary on the Epistle to the Hebrews* (London: Marshall, Morgan & Scott, 1964), 3.

86. Ibid., 3-9.

87. William L. Lane, *Word Biblical Commentary: Hebrews 1-8, 47A* (Word Books: Dallas, TX, 1991), 12.

... a breath of the power of God,
And a clear effluence of the glory of the Almighty;
...an effulgence from everlasting light,
And an unspotted mirror of the working of God,
And an image of His goodness (Wisdom 7:25f. ERV)[88].

Christ is not merely a reflection of God, but he is the true radiance of the eternal light. As we confess in the Nicene Creed, he is 'light from light.' 'The writer [of Hebrews] appears to have borrowed a word employed in the LXX to describe the relationship between Wisdom and the eternal, divine light... to express the relationship he believed existed between God and the Son.'[89] Lane adds: 'If the formulation of v. 3a owes something to the vocabulary and concepts of Alexandrian Judaism, it has been thoroughly assimilated and refashioned by a distinctly Christian thinker...'[90]

Athanasius stated that as God is eternal light, so his Son is the eternal radiance of God. This means that Christ himself is eternally light, without beginning or end.[91]

He is the true image of God: 'the express image of his person...' **(v. 3)**. The Greek word χαρακτήρ is used only here in the New Testament. It implies the hard impression made in a soft substance, like a metal ring impressed into wax, so that it shows the substance of who God really is.[92] To see Christ is to see the Father's true character. Athanasius makes the same point: '...he [Christ] is the express image of the Father's ὑπόστασις, and light of light, and true power and image of the being of the Father.'[93] John Calvin writes: '...[God] has in him [Christ] stamped for us the likeness [cf. Heb. 1:3] to which he would have us conform.'[94]

He upholds all things 'by the word of his power' (v. 3). 'The creative utterance which called the universe into being requires as its complement that sustaining utterance by which it is maintained in being.'[95] As Paul says of Christ: 'In him all things consist (or hold together)' (Col. 1:17).

John Calvin sees the divinity of Christ set forth in Hebrews 1:3: '... to govern the universe with providence and power, and to regulate all things by the command of his own power [Heb. 1:3], deeds that the apostle ascribes to Christ, [which are] the function of the Creator alone. And he not only participates in the task of governing the world with the Father; but he carries out also other individual offices, which cannot be communicated to the creatures.'[96]

---

88. As quoted in Bruce, op. cit., 5.

89. Lane, op. cit., 13.

90. Ibid.

91. Athanasius, *Contra Arianos* 1.13.

92. John Calvin criticizes the propriety of thinking of the word picture of 'stamp,' fearing that it does not convey the sense of the 'distinct personality' of the Son. Yet that being said, Calvin still affirms 'that the very hypostasis that shines forth in the Son is in the Father' (cf. Calvin, *Institutes* I. 13.2). Also, in another direction, where he himself uses the image of 'stamp,' see Calvin, III.6.3 – below.

93. Ibid., 1.9.

94. John Calvin, *Institutes* III.6.3.

95. Lane, op. cit., 6.

96. Calvin, op. cit., I.13.12.

He has made purification of sins: (καθαρισμὸν τῶν ἁμαρτιῶν ποιησάμενος) – v. 3c. This statement is different from the Wisdom tradition: 'There is no association of divine Wisdom with sacrifice in order to procure cleansing from sin…The source of this solitary reference to the accomplishment of Jesus' earthly life in the exordium is thus not the wisdom tradition but reflection on the incarnation and the cross.'[97]

Lane comments further that 'The purification of the people was… achieved by blood in an act of expiation (cf. Lev. 16:30)…That the writer to the Hebrews draws upon this conceptual framework for interpreting the death of Christ is confirmed by chaps. 9 and 10, where the categories of defilement and purgation are foundational to the argumentation.'[98]

Athanasius teaches that Christ as both Son and High Priest offers himself as a propitiatory sacrifice for us.[99] Gregory Nazianzus emphasizes the necessity of the Son being *homoousios* ('of the same substance') with the Father so that he was thus able to bear away in himself all our evil, crucifying our sins with himself.[100]

'The Wondrous Exchange'

John Calvin terms this miraculous transaction 'the wonderful exchange' (*mirifica commutatio*):

> This is the wonderful exchange which, out of his measureless benevolence, he has made with us; that, becoming Son of man with us, he has made us sons of God with him; that, by his descent to earth, he has prepared an ascent to heaven for us; that, accepting our weakness, he has strengthened us by his power; that, receiving our poverty unto himself, he has transferred his wealth to us; that, taking the weight of our iniquity upon himself (which oppressed us), he has clothed us with his righteousness.[101]

Martin Luther had spoken similarly, years before Calvin, in his 1520 *Treatise on Christian Liberty*.[102] He further developed this concept in his *Sermon on the Sacrament of the Body of Christ and on the Brotherhoods*.[103]

He sat down on the right hand of the majesty on high (v. 3d). 'Each of the participial clauses of v. 3 is dependent upon the finite ἐκάθισεν, which grammatically provides the main assertion of vv. 3-4… it establishes that the acts of purifying and sitting down were temporarily sequential…'[104]

The fact that only the final High Priest could at last 'sit down' after he purged our sins is reflected in the furniture in the Holy of Holies of the Tabernacle. In that sparse inner sanctum, there was no chair; no seat

---

97. Lane, op. cit., 15.

98. Ibid.

99. Athanasius, *Contra Arianos* 1.41.

100. Gregory Nazianzus, *Oration* 4.5f.

101. Calvin, *Institutes* IV.17.2.

102. Martin Luther, *Treatise on Christian Liberty* in *Werke* WA VII. 54f.

103. See M. Luther, *Werke* WA II. 743ff.

104. Lane, op. cit., 15.

for the High Priest to take after finishing his work on the yearly Day of Atonement. That is because his work was not finished. It would have to be repeated the next year, and the morning and evening sacrifices would carry on day by day. But when Christ, the Great High Priest, purged our sins, he 'sat down'; all was finished, 'once for all' and hence, forever.

But Christ did not take his seat in the Temple of Jerusalem (although by the earthquake at his crucifixion, the veil that separated the Holy of Holies from the outer courts was split down the middle, from top to bottom, thus giving access to the holy presence for all believers). Rather, he took his seat 'at the right hand of the Majesty on high'. This recalls Psalm 110:1, which is the only other biblical reference to someone being seated on the Throne of God. This seat is the place of supreme Lordship: that of 'the King of Kings and Lord of Lords'.

'The majesty on high' – μεγαλωσύνη – is a periphrastic way of speaking of God Himself (as in Hebrews 8:1). 'Enthronement at "the right hand of the divine Majesty" asserted the supreme exaltation of the Son without compromising the rank and rule of God the Father...'[105]

F. F. Bruce summarizes the position:

> Thus the greatness of the Son receives sevenfold confirmation, and it appears, without being expressly emphasized, that He possesses in Himself all the qualifications to be the mediator between God and men. He is the Prophet through whom God has spoken His final word to men; He is the Priest who has accomplished a perfect work of cleansing for His people's sins; He is the King who sits enthroned in the place of chief honor alongside the Majesty on high.[106]

Christ's superiority to the angels (Heb. 1:4)

Christ's new name which is exalted above the angels is mentioned elsewhere (Phil. 2:9; Eph. 1:20; I Pet. 3:22). 'In v. 4 the superior name is almost certainly the acclamation 'my son' of Ps. 2:7 quoted in v. 5...'[107]

The main point of the contrast between Christ and the angels seems to be that of a parallel to verses 1-2a, 'where revelation through the prophets is contrasted with the ultimate word spoken through the Son. The angels in verse 4 are the counterpart to the prophets in verse 1.'[108] Hebrews 2:2 refers to the word spoken by angels, and elsewhere it is taught that the law had been received by Moses through the angels (cf. Acts 7:38-39, 53; Gal. 3:19, and various references in intertestamental literature, listed by Lane).[109]

The chapter continues with various quotations from the Old Testament (Heb. 1:5-14) 'for two specific reasons – to show (i) that the final message of God, communicated by the Son, is safeguarded by even more majestic sanctions than those which attended the law, communicated by angels (cf. Ch. 2:2f.), and (ii) that the new world over which the Son is to reign

---

105. Lane, op. cit., 16.

106. F. F. Bruce, op. cit., 8.

107. Lane, op. cit., 17.

108. Ibid.

109. Ibid.

as Mediator far surpasses the old world in which various nations were assigned to angels for administration (Ch. 2:5).'[110]

To emphasize Christ's superiority with the history of revelation before his coming, the adjective 'better' is used thirteen times in Hebrews (6:9; 7:7, 19, 22; 8:6 (bis); 9:23; 10:34; 11:16, 35, 40; 12:24). The renewed awareness of the superiority and supremacy of Christ would have strengthened the resolve of the Jewish Christians as they were facing opposition. The affirmation of Christ's supremacy in this part of Hebrews is much like the teaching of John 3:31-32: 'He that cometh from above is above all: he that is of the earth is earthly, and speaketh of the earth: he that cometh from heaven is above all. And what he hath seen and heard, that he testifieth…' Hence, whether in John 3 or Hebrews 1, Jesus Christ is the Father's last word: the only sure way of salvation and eternal life.

(4) Revelation 5:1-14

[1]And I saw in the right hand of him that sat on the throne a book written within and on the backside, sealed with seven seals. [2]And I saw a strong angel proclaiming with a loud voice, Who is worthy to open the book, and to loose the seals thereof? [3]And no man in heaven, nor in earth, neither under the earth, was able to open the book, neither to look thereon. [4]And I wept much, because no man was found worthy to open and to read the book, neither to look thereon. [5]And one of the elders saith unto me, Weep not, behold: the Lion of the tribe of Juda, the Root of David, hath prevailed to open the book, and to loose the seven seals thereof.
[6]And I beheld, and lo, in the midst of the throne and of the four beasts, and in the midst of the elders, stood a Lamb, as it had been slain, having seven horns and seven eyes, which are the seven Spirits of God sent forth into all the earth. [7]And he came and took the book out of the right hand of him that sat upon the throne. [8]And when he had taken the book, the four beasts and four and twenty elders fell down before the Lamb, having every one of them harps, and golden vials full of odours, which are the prayers of saints. [9]And they sung a new song, saying, Thou art worthy to take the book, and to open the seals thereof: for thou wast slain, and hast redeemed us to God by thy blood, out of every kindred, and tongue, and people and nation: [10]And hast made us unto our God kings and priests: and we shall reign on the earth. [11]And I beheld, and I heard the voice of many angels round about the throne and the beasts and the elders: and the number of them was ten thousand times ten thousand, and thousands of thousands: [12]Saying with a loud voice, Worthy is the Lamb that was slain to receive power, and riches, and wisdom, and strength, and honour, and glory, and blessing. [13]And every creature which is in heaven and on the earth, and under the earth, and such as are in the sea, and all that are in them, heard I saying, Blessing, and honour, and glory, and power, be unto him that sitteth upon the throne, and unto the Lamb for ever and ever. And the four beasts said, Amen. [14]And the four and twenty elders fell down and worshipped him that liveth for ever and ever.

---

110. Bruce, op. cit., 9.

A Hymn of Praise

Revelation 5 sounds out a hymn of praise that rings down from heaven. It is yet another New Testament presentation of the person and work of Christ. This fifth chapter of Revelation needs to be taken together with chapter 4, for both chapters express the joy of the inhabitants of heaven over what God has done and will be doing on the earth.

To grasp the heavenly hymn's view of Christ, we note three related points: (1) How this hymn of praise fits into the structure of the Book of Revelation (chs. 4, 5, and 6); (2) The theme of the hymn of praise (Rev. 5:9, 12, 13); and (3) Who is singing this hymn (Rev. 5:8-14).

How this Song fits into the structure of Revelation (chs. 4, 5, and 6)

The basic structure of this larger section of Revelation is that chapter 4 presents a vision of God's throne at the beginning of that chapter, by which it is made clear that God is in complete control of absolutely everything. Then at the end of chapter 4, all heaven is full of praises, because of him who is running all things.

Similarly, chapter 5 presents the vision of God's Book. It is the book of history; the Lamb's book of life. This βιβλίον is 'on the open palm of the right hand'.[111] R. H. Charles takes it to be 'a book-roll…the idea in our text is that with the opening of each successive seal a part of the contents of the book-roll is disclosed in prophetic symbolism.'[112]

In it are the purposes of God, from the foundation of the world until the final consummation when all the elect are gathered together. It is in the context of a vision of the scroll or book being opened as a prelude to the working out of God's predetermined purposes, and of their being concluded, in prospect of which all heaven bursts forth into hymns of praise. That is especially the case in chapter 6, which focuses on the activities of the Lamb.

The Theme of the Song (Rev. 5:9, 12-13)

Revelation 5: 9, 10 and 12 express the theme: 'Thou art worthy to take the book, and to open the seals thereof: for thou wast slain, and has redeemed us to God by thy blood, out of every kindred, and tongue, and people and nation; and hast made us unto our God kings and priests: and we shall reign on the earth…Worthy is the Lamb that was slain to receive power, and riches, and wisdom, and strength, and honour, and glory, and blessing…'

Its theme is the Lamb of God. Through the Lamb (a most unusual name for a governor), the government of the throne and the carrying out of the Book are accomplished, and that is, for all who believe in him, very good news.[113]

---

111. R. H. Charles, *A Critical and Exegetical Commentary on The Revelation of St. John* (ICC – Edinburgh: T & T Clark, 1920), vol. 1, 136.

112. Ibid., 137.

113. One wonders if John's consistent use of *arnion* – the diminutive of lamb – could possibly be meant to underline the strange juxtaposition of concepts: mighty governance and little lamb? A juxtaposition that overturns our normal human ways of thinking.

The Lamb of God is the Theme of the Song

It is natural that the Lamb of God should be the center of this song, because he is the center of the Book of Revelation itself. In Chapters 1 to 3, he is in the center of the church, as he is walking in the midst of the candlesticks. Revelation 5:6 says that 'he is in the midst of the throne...' The phrase used here for 'in the midst of,' ἐν μέσῳ, is a Hebraism.'[114] That is to say, it is not necessary to take it literally, but it does make an important point: He is seated at the right hand of God, 'symbolizing power and authority.'[115] His power is shown to be going forth in the world as Revelation chapter 6 progresses.

In the later part of chapter 6 and in following chapters, we see that history is centered on what the Lamb is doing. The events of history are not accidental, although from our earthly viewpoint they may often seem to be so. The Lamb is the center of everything that he is allowing to happen. He is riding forth, 'conquering and to conquer.' In Chapters 21 and 22, the Lamb is the center of eternal glory. After the heavens have rolled back like a scroll, and the sands of time have flowed down, so that we are at last into the glorious consummation, the Lamb is in the center of heaven. There they need no sun, moon or stars, because the Lamb is the light. They need neither temple nor tabernacle, because the Lamb, whom both represented, is there in his embodied and glorified Person to be worshiped. The words taken from Samuel Rutherford and turned into a hymn express this picture of Revelation 21–22 another way: 'The Lamb is all the glory of Immanuel's Land.'

Why the Lamb is Worthy

Who Could Open the Book? Verses 2 through 7 show us the unique, incomparable worthiness of the one the heavenly choir is singing about. He is the only One who could have offered himself up to be slain and thereby to redeem the world. In verse 2, a mighty angel states a question that seems to baffle the Apostle John: 'Who is worthy to open the scroll [or book] of coming history so as to unseal its seven seals?' To understand the significance of this question, we must understand the function of seals, which are seldom used in the modern culture of electronic communication. 'Seals were wax or clay blobs placed where the scroll ended and often further sealed with a signet ring to make the document official. The purpose of the seals here is to keep the contents secret until the time of fulfillment, a common apocalyptic theme (Dan. 8:26; 12:9).'[116] This image of sealed books is found in earlier Jewish apocalyptic, as in I Enoch 47:3; 81:1-3; 106:19; 107:1.

But what is in the Book? There are several options, but Osborne seems correct when he summarizes them: '[I]t summarizes the whole of biblical truth, beginning with the foreshadowing of the plan in the OT and the progressive unveiling of it in Christ. It was the death of Christ that

---

114. Ibid., 136.

115. Grant R. Osborne, *Revelation: Baker Exegetical Commentary on the New Testament* (Baker Academic: Grand Rapids, MI, 2008), 247.

116. Osborne, op. cit., 248.

anchored God's redemptive plan, and the rest of Revelation describes the events that will bring that plan to completion.'[117]

This sealed scroll seems likely to include, though perhaps not exclusively, 'the Lamb's book of life.' This book of life is mentioned several times in Revelation (3:5; 13:8; 17:8; 20:12, 15; 21:27). It includes the names of all who will be redeemed. However, Revelation 5 itself does not specifically name 'the book' as 'the book of life', but it is reasonable to assume that it at least includes it. To be written in the Lamb's book of life is to be assured of pardon for sins, and thus of eternal life. Hence, we can understand his intense desire to have the book opened. But who can open that book?

The Worthiness of the Lamb

The seer on Patmos 'wept much' (v. 4) since no one in all creation was found who was worthy to open that book. But then he sees something that makes him rejoice (v. 5). That worthy person is described as 'a lamb that was slain' (v. 6). Later, Revelation 13:8 will speak of him as 'the lamb slain from the foundation of the world'. Earlier, in Revelation 5:5, John called him 'the lion of the tribe of Juda, the root of David' (alluding to the true humanity he took through the Jews, as descendant of David, who as king, represented the quality and status of 'lion'; hence 'lion of the tribe of Judah'). He is described as having 'seven horns' and 'seven eyes', which are 'the seven Spirits'. The number seven generally speaks of perfection. 'Horn' symbolizes power (cf. Num. 23:22; Deut. 33:17; I Sam. 2:1; I Kings 22:11; Ps. 75:4; 89:17) or kingly dignity (Ps. 112:9; 148:14; Zech. 1:18; Dan. 7:7,20; 8:3ff.). He is 'the all-powerful warrior and king.'[118] But his worthiness is more than his power, though inclusive of it.

'The worthiness (ἀξιότης) is the inner ethical presupposition of the ability (ἱκανότης) to open the book.'[119] Osborne shows that five of the six uses of ἄξιος ['worthy'] in this book occur in these two chapters. God himself is 'worthy' in 4:11. In 5:2-4 he seeks a 'worthy' stand-in to 'open the scroll and break the seals.' There is only one such 'worthy,' the slain Lamb, who is celebrated first in terms of the reason for his 'worthiness' (5:9,10), and then the results, as he like God is given a sevenfold acclamation (5:12; 4:11).[120]

Yet more is required than moral purity (necessary though that is) to equip this worthy figure for his opening the book of redemption. He must be able to represent both God and man in his one person. This is at least hinted at in chapter 5, in his possessing 'seven eyes' and 'seven spirits' (Rev. 5:6). The 'seven eyes' seem to refer to the lamb's omniscience. Seven eyes are attributed to JHWH in Zechariah 4:10. Revelation 3:1 identifies the seven eyes with the seven spirits 'of which the Lamb is Lord and Master'.[121] Hereby he is identified as Yahweh (v. 6), and in verse 5 he was identified as man, being of 'the tribe of Juda, the root of David.'

---

117. Ibid., 249.

118. Charles, op. cit., 141.

119. Ibid., 139.

120. Osborne, op. cit., 251. Greek gloss mine.

121. Ibid., 142.

'The holy one of Israel' alone was infinitely holy, he alone was both God and man in one person, so that the shedding of his blood availed to cleanse all sin. Hence they sing: 'Worthy is the Lamb that was slain!'

Why Our Redeemer Had to be both Man and God at the Same Time
An old hymn says:

> No angel could his place have taken,
> high, of all the high, though he;
> The loved one on the cross forsaken
> was one of the Godhead three.[122]

No other could his place have taken. No angel could have done it (because they do not live in the flesh, which is what needs to be redeemed), and no mere descendant of Adam could have done it, for they are all encompassed with sin. Only a sinless one could have done it. He had to be identified with God, so that his suffering would be great enough to erase the stain of infinite sin, and so God sent his Son, who is the second person of the Trinity, 'God of God,' into human nature, so that he could fully and truly represent in it our humanity. For sin to be forgiven, it had to be punished in the very place where it was committed; that is, in human nature, but for the atonement to be sufficient, it had to be that of an infinitely worthy person: one identified with God, as well as with humanity.

Praise the Cleansing Blood!
Now in this heavenly song to the Lamb, which is echoed in Revelation 5:9-12, we are given two *marks of the Lamb's worthiness*, which constitute two lasting *grounds for praise*. First, he was slain for us; secondly, on the basis of his having been slain, he has redeemed us by his shed blood.

First, the Lamb is worthy because 'He was slain (ἐσφάλης)' (5:9).

> Nowhere else in the NT is ἐσφάλης used of the death of Christ, but it occurs four times in this book (5:6, 9, 12; 13:8). Most likely it is drawn from Isa. 53:7 LXX, 'like a lamb to the slaughter,' and depicts the sacrificial death of Christ…'the Lamb that was slain from the creation of the world' (13:8). Second, his sacrifice 'ransomed' (ἠγόρασας) people for God. 'Jesus' death has been a 'ransom' payment through which God has 'purchased' people for himself (see I Cor. 6:19-20; 7:23; 2 Pet. 2:1; Rev. 14:3-4)…The 'blood' of the Lamb here is the payment rendered to 'buy' people for God.[123]

In both Old and New Testaments, sacrifice by blood is at the heart of setting people free from their bondage to sin. Hebrews 9:22 says that 'without the shedding of blood there is no remission of sin.' On the basis of his shed blood, he alone is worthy to open the book (Rev. 5:2). Jesus has conquered '…primarily not through military might, though that is

---

122. James M. Gray, 'O Listen to Our Wondrous Story,' 1904.

123. Osborne, op. cit., 260.

to come, but through his sacrificial death (5:6, 9, 12).'[124] 'A lamb as it had been slain' (v. 6) clearly marks out his wounds as what avails to open this book of life. As John the Baptist had said at his baptism, 'Behold the lamb of God that taketh away the sin of the world' (John 1:29, 35). The image of the slain lamb takes us back through the whole sacrificial system of the Old Testament, with lambs slain at the morning and evening sacrifices, and particularly back to the Passover lamb slain after the children of Israel came victoriously out of Egypt.

Hebrews shows how it would finally take more 'worthy' blood to remove the sins of the people than what could be offered by animal sacrifices. Those sacrifices were acceptable temporarily 'to cover sin', but more would be needed to complete the actual taking away of sin: 'For if the blood of bulls and of goats, and the ashes of an heifer sprinkling the unclean, sanctifieth to the purifying of the flesh: how much more shall the blood of Christ, who through the eternal Spirit offered himself without spot to God, purge your conscience from dead works to serve the living God?' (Heb. 9:13, 14). Thus, Hebrews 9:23 says: 'It was therefore necessary that the patterns of things in the heavens should be purified with these; but the heavenly things themselves with better sacrifices than these.' The blood of the worthy lamb constituted the final and total offering for all sin: 'But this man, after he had offered one sacrifice for sins for ever, sat down on the right hand of God…For by one offering he hath perfected for ever them that are sanctified.' (Heb. 10:12,14).

Who is Singing this New Song? (Rev. 5:8-14)
Heaven is singing 'a new song' (Rev. 5:9).

> In Isa. 42:10… the 'new song' is eschatological and connected to the appearance of the 'servant of Yahweh' and the 'new things' (Rev. 5:9) God was about to introduce. In 14:3 the 'new song' is linked to the coming of the final kingdom, and here the new song celebrates the basis of God's final act, the sacrificial death of the Lamb.[125]

The song has three parts: the acclamation of the worthy lamb (5:9b), the saving work of the lamb (5:9c), and the benefits for the followers of the lamb (5:10). The benefits of his saving work (5:10) are rooted in Exodus 19:6, God's promise to make Israel a kingdom of priests. This promise is eschatologically fulfilled in the Church, who is the new Israel by faith in Christ.

> Christ's sacrifice has made it possible for all God's people drawn from the nations of the earth to be both royalty and priests in the new kingdom of God…All the promises given to the people of God in the OT are about to be fulfilled, especially those related to the rule of the people of God in the final kingdom, like Dan. 7:18, 22, 27; Ps. 49:14…Through the death of Christ as the final victory over evil, we will be kings serving Christ in authority over his creation.[126]

---

124. Ibid., 254.
125. Ibid., 259.
126. Ibid., 261.

Seven Ascriptions of Praise to the Lamb

This hymn praises Christ with seven acclamations. Four of them praise him for his own attributes (power, riches, wisdom, and strength), and three of them praise the victorious results of the recognition he receives (honour, and glory, and blessing) (v. 12). The attribute 'power' (δύναμις) is always first in the lists of acclamations (Rev. 4:11; 5:12; 7:12; 12:10; 19:1). 'Most likely here it emphasizes the sacrificial death of the Lamb as the "power" by which the forces of evil have been "conquered" (5:5; cf. 12:11; 17:14).'[127]

'Riches' (πλοῦτον) appears only in Revelation 18:7, where people mourn over the destruction of 'Babylon' with its immense wealth. But this shows that true riches are found in Christ, 'in whom are the riches of the glory of this mystery': namely 'Christ in you, the hope of glory' (Col 1:27). The Lamb is praised for 'wisdom', which is also ascribed to God in Revelation 7:12. Christ is 'the wisdom of God' (σοφίαν) (I Cor. 1:24,30). Colossians 2:3 says that 'all the treasures of wisdom and knowledge' are hidden in him. 'Strength' (ἰσχύν) is close to the meaning of 'power,' and in Revelation 7:12 it is ascribed along with δύναμιν to God (as it is here in 5:12 to the Lamb). This pair of words probably emphasizes the omnipotence of God and the Lamb, by which he overcomes the dragon, who is 'not strong enough' (Rev. 12:8).

The last three ascriptions of praise describe the worship of the Lamb. Τιμή (honor) is paired with δόξα (glory) also in 4:11 to describe the worship of God, and in 5:13 "honor and glory" will be accorded to God and the Lamb together. Thus this depicts the exaltation and honor that the Lamb receives from the heavenly host.'[128] The last ascription to the Lamb is εὐλογίαν (blessing). It is used 'three times in Revelation, once of the "praise" of God (7:12), once of the Lamb (here) and once of the two together (5:13). At his triumphal entry into Jerusalem, Christ was greeted with this ascription (Matt. 21:9; Mark 11:9; John 12:13).'[129] 'Blessing' summarizes the heavenly praise accorded to the once-slain, now triumphant Lamb.

Angelic Beings Join in the Song. Two categories of beings are singing this heavenly song: four angelic beings (the four 'living creatures'), other angels, and also the redeemed church. The number of the heavenly host singing in this choir is vast: 'ten thousand times ten thousand, and thousands of thousands' or 'myriads of myriads' (5:11). 'Myriad' was the highest number known in the Hellenistic culture, and the concept goes back to Daniel 7:10.

Israel and the Church Join in the Song. Twelve elders represent the Old Testament tribes of Israel, and twelve represent the twelve Apostles; that is, both phases of the Church: Old and New Testaments are joined together praising the Lamb, who saved them both. Hence, he is the one in whom all history centers. He is in the center of the throne; he breaks the seals and opens the pages of salvation to the unworthy.

---

127. Ibid., 263.

128. Ibid., 263-264.

129. Ibid., 264.

God himself invites us to join this choir through faith in his Son, the Lamb of God, who takes away our sin, and gives us entrance into the kingdom of light, where we may drink of the waters of life freely (cf. Rev. 22:17)!

Summary of the four major passages

The teaching of the passages from John, Philippians, Hebrews and Revelation may be briefly summarized as to their doctrine of the Person and Work of Christ as follows: (1) Christ in eternity; (2) Christ's Incarnation, and (3) the redemption wrought by Christ.

(1) Christ in eternity

John 1 speaks of Christ as 'the Word' (v. 1) who was 'in the bosom of the Father' (v. 18). He was 'with God' and 'was God' (v. 1). He was 'in the beginning with God' (v. 2). He is the only begotten Son of the Father (vv. 14, 18). Philippians 2 says that he was 'in the form of God', thus sharing the very Godness of the Father (v. 6). The same verse states that he was 'equal to God', yet he chose not to hold on to the glories of that eternal equality, in order to redeem his people. Thus, 'he made himself of no reputation'; he 'emptied himself' in a metaphorical, but not literal, sense. He did so, not *by losing* his Godness (which he always had), but *by taking* something which he did not have previously: 'the form of a servant,' all the attributes that make man man, except for personal sinfulness (v. 7).

Hebrews 1 tells us that Christ was 'the brightness of [the Father's] glory, and the express image of his person' (v. 3). Psalm 45:6-7, which speaks of the eternal Throne and scepter of God is ascribed directly to Christ (Heb. 1:8). Revelation 5 attributes to Christ as 'the Lamb' the divine worship of heaven, that which only God himself would be worthy to receive (vv. 12-14). He sits in the midst of the throne, exercising divine power ('horns') and omniscience ('eyes'), with the divine prerogative of sending the Spirit to the earth (v. 6).

This everlasting Christ at a particular point in eternity became the agent of creation. According to John 1:3: 'All things were made by him, and without him was not anything made that was made.' Hebrews 1:2 says that 'by [Christ] he [the Father] also made the worlds.' Revelation 4:11 states the same thing: '…thou hast created all things, and for thy pleasure they are and were created.'

(2) Christ's Incarnation

John 1:14 says that 'the Word was made flesh, and 'tabernacled' among us…' In the words of Augustine, 'He became what He was not, without ceasing to be what He always was.' He who was in 'the form of God' lowered himself by taking on 'the form of a servant' (Phil. 2:6, 7). Hebrews 1:1 states that Christ is the Father's last and final word after the long line of the prophets.

Revelation 5 approaches the incarnation in terms of no one in heaven or earth being worthy enough 'to open the book, and to loose its seals' (vv. 2-4). But One from the midst of the throne of God was able to do so, for in addition to his qualification of possessing the divine prerogatives of the throne, he took on the human nature necessarily involved in his status as 'lion of the tribe of Judah' and 'the root of David' (v. 5). All of this means that he was both God and man at the same time, and from this came the value and victory of his redeeming work.

(3) The redemption wrought by Christ

Philippians 2:8 states that 'he became obedient to death, even the death of the cross.' John 12:23 speaks of his lifting up on the cross as the hour of his glorification (cf. John 13:31-32). Hebrews 1:3 says that 'he by himself purged our sins.' Revelation 5:9 conveys the praises of heaven: '…for thou wast slain, and hast redeemed us to God by thy blood out of every kindred, and tongue, and people, and nation…' Hebrews 1:2-3 implies that only someone so great as the Creator and so worthy as God was able to accomplish this redemption of the order which he had originally created, as Athanasius shows in chapter 1 of *De Incarnatione*. And John 1:18 indicates that the only begotten Son alone was able 'to declare' (to 'exegete' or 'bring out') the Father to us.

This total redemption then is provided for those who believe in him (cf. John 1:12-13). Those who 'receive him' (John 1:12), drink out of his fullness, 'grace for grace' (John 1:16). And near the end of his Gospel, John explains its purpose: 'But these are written, that you might believe that Jesus is the Christ, the Son of God; and that believing ye might have life through his name' (20:31).

Philippians 2 shows that those who confess him as Lord find that God is at work in them 'both to will and to do of his good pleasure' (vv. 11, 13). Revelation 5 indicates that those who join the new song, praising him for his shed blood for sinners, are made kings and priests unto God (vv. 9-10). In the words of Rev. 22:17, to respond to the invitation of the Spirit and the bride to come to Christ is 'to take of the water of life freely.'

These four passages (not to mention a host of others) clearly indicate a plurality of persons within the one being of God; otherwise, these texts would not make sense. The Father sends the Son as redeemer, and from Father the Spirit comes through the Son to apply that redemption: to provide that living water. What the Son accomplishes, and what the Spirit applies is backed up by the infinite fullness of God the Father Almighty, for Son and Spirit are equal with him in their deity, and yet the being of the deity is only one. So the entire Godhead is involved in the redemption of the fallen cosmos.

Christ, the Messiah, the enfleshed Logos, is the one who comes down from highest heaven into a fallen world so as to lift it up to the life of God. To accomplish this 'new creation,' the Son needed to be both God and man at the same time in order to carry through this stupendous redemptive work.

These four crucial passages can only be interpreted in the context of God as Trinity, who always exists as a holy communion of life, light, love and joy within himself. What the Father has done in sending the Son of his love to become incarnate for our salvation, and in breathing forth the Spirit of his Son to unite us to the Father through the Son, is based on the loving and giving of the three distinct persons of the one Godhead from all eternity. That is the basis of the everlasting beauty of who Christ is. The beauty of God is his love; his love is his beauty.

Jonathan Edwards saw the ineffable and ever-living interchange of the divine love as constitutive of the beauty of God, with rare insight:

> And from God, love flows out toward all the inhabitants of heaven. It flows out, in the first place, necessarily and infinitely, toward his only-begotten Son; being poured forth, without mixture, as to an object that is infinite, and so fully adequate to all the fulness of a love that is infinite. And this infinite love is infinitely exercised toward him. Not only does the fountain send forth streams to this object, but the very fountain itself wholly and altogether goes out toward him. And the Son of God is not only the infinite object of love but he is also an infinite subject of it. He is not only the beloved of the Father, but he infinitely loves him. The infinite essential love of God is, as it were, an infinite and eternal, mutual, holy, energy between the Father and the Son; a pure and holy act, whereby the Deity becomes, as it were one infinite and unchangeable emotion of love proceeding from both the Father and the Son. This divine love has its seat in the Deity as it is exercised within the Deity, or in God toward himself.[130]

Although these and many other texts of Scripture set forth the reality of one God in three persons, as the context of any understanding of who Jesus Christ is, providentially it took the theological meditation and profoundly Scriptural work of the Fathers of the Church, especially in the fourth century, that would clarify (as far as the redeemed human mind could ever understand such transcendent truths) two all-important and interrelated realities: that is, the three distinct persons in one substance of the Holy Trinity, and then the union of the two natures in the one person of Christ. The Holy Trinity has been addressed in volume 1 of this work, and now – especially in light of the passages we have just studied – we consider more particularly the Patristic doctrine of the Hypostatic Union of two natures in the one person of Christ.

---

130. Jonathan Edwards, *Charity and its Fruits* (Banner of Truth Trust: London, 1969), quoted from Lecture xvi – 'Heaven, a World of Charity or Love,' 332-333.

CHAPTER 4

THE HYPOSTATIC UNION

Humanity's universal need of a Mediator between their fallen selves and an utterly holy God is deeply embedded in the human conscience, and plainly articulated throughout Holy Scripture. That Mediator, who alone is able to bring God and man together in saving reconciliation and restoration of the lost human race, is competent to this highest of all tasks by being God and man, in two distinct, but unseparated natures, remaining eternally together in one Person after the Incarnation. To save us from our sins, and to bring us eternal life and lasting fellowship with God, the Mediator – the Lord Jesus Christ – had to be at the same time: (1) fully man, in order to accomplish both revelation and reconciliation; (2) fully God, in order to accomplish revelation and reconciliation; and (3)

The appendix to this chapter discusses the early thirteenth century development of the theology of the hypostatic union.

both God and man together at the same time, in order to accomplish revelation and reconciliation.

The finest historical, theological expression of the person and accomplishments of the Mediator is found in the 451 Creed of Chalcedon. It makes a necessary distinction between 'nature' and 'person', and states that the two natures are united together in one person 'without confusion, without conversion, without division, without separation.' We study the question of whether or not the Creed of Chalcedon was an imposition of Hellenistic philosophy upon Christian theology.

The hypostatic (or personal) union of two natures, human and divine, in the one Person of Christ, the eternal Son of God, the Logos, was rightly understood by the Church to be essential to the salvation of the world. In order to be the Mediator between God and mankind, so as to bring them back together, thereby saving lost humanity, Christ had to become a man, while remaining at the same time God.

The Christian Church for the first five centuries of its existence made every costly effort, at times including exile, persecution and martyrdom, with massive biblical and theological reflection, writing, and prayer, to clarify the biblical teaching on this crucial truth, which they saw to be central to the salvation of the lost, the preservation of the Gospel, and the extension of the Great Commission given them by Christ.

Saint Irenaeus Shows the Need of a Mediator

In the late second century, Saint Irenaeus of Lyon showed how essential Christ's mediatorship was over against the heretics of his time, the widespread Gnostics, who lost the Gospel in their confused theories of 'aeons' or extrusions between God and man, as a different 'ladder' to be mounted by pagan practices and secret passwords (known to the 'Gnostics' or those in the know), rather than through the divinely appointed Mediator.

> Therefore...He caused man to cleave to and to become one with God. For unless man had overcome the enemy of man, the enemy would not have been legitimately vanquished. And again: unless it had been God who had freely given salvation, we could never have become a partaker of incorruptibility. For it was incumbent upon the Mediator between God and men, by His relationship to both, to bring both to friendship and concord, and present man to God, while He revealed God to man...Wherefore He passed through every stage of life, restoring all to communion with God.[1]

Irenaeus adds: 'For by no other means could we have attained to incorruptibility and immortality, unless we had been united to incorruptibility and immortality. But how could we have been united unless first, incorruptibility and immortality had become that which we also are...?'[2]

Job cries out for a Mediator

Job, in the early Old Testament, out of his incomprehensible sufferings, seems to have been reaching out towards something like this Mediatorship, when he cried out: 'Neither is there any daysman betwixt us, that might lay his hand upon us both' (Job 9:33). John Calvin interprets Job's longing as a universal need for sinners:

> And yet for all that, we cease not to be separated from him through our sins and iniquities. What must we do then? What remaineth more? That Jesus Christ put himself betwixt us: Jesus Christ must be seen to be our daysman, not to pass judgment upon the majesty of God, nor to set God at the bar with us: but to be the means to reconcile us to God, and to draw us after him as our head, to knit us in such wise unto God, as we may be all one in him, as the Scripture speaketh (John 17:11,21-22). And hereupon let us learn to humble ourselves and say, Lord, we come unto thee, not to plead, or to presume upon anything that is in us or in our own persons: but because

---

1. Irenaeus, *Adversus Haereses*, III. 18.7.

2. Ibid., III.19.1.

thou art favourable to us, and because thou art willing to receive us for thy Son Jesus Christ's sake.[3]

'Daysman' or 'umpire' is in Hebrew *môkîach* [מוֹכִיחַ] like 'judge.' In the LXX it is rendered μεσιτης ('Mediator'), and this is the only place in the LXX where this word is found. Thus, it may possibly have been a background to the New Testament usage of 'Mediator.'

I Timothy 2:5 sets forth a Mediator

The Apostle Paul sets forward in I Timothy 2:5 the very thing that Job, along with all who suffer in a world of sin, have longed for: the one mediatorship of the Lord Jesus Christ: 'For there is one God, and one mediator between God and men, the man Christ Jesus.'

This proclamation of the mediator is in a section of Chapter 2 (vv. 1-7), directing the congregation to pray 'for all men'. Paul calls for petitions, prayers, intercession and thanksgiving for everyone (v. 1), including kings and those in authority, that 'we might lead a quiet and peaceable life in all godliness and honesty' (v. 2). These prayers for all are good in the Lord's sight (v. 3), for they are grounded in God's purpose, which is 'for all men to be saved, and to come to the knowledge of the truth' (v. 4). God's will to save all is shown in the one Mediator whom God sent between himself and humanity (v. 5), the one who gave himself a ransom for all (v. 6), which person and ransom Paul was chosen for the mission of proclaiming to the Gentiles at the right time (v. 7).

In particular, Christ's mediatorship is opened up by verses 5 and 6 as follows: (a) One God, (b) One Mediator, and (c) One Ransom.

(a) One God – 'There is one God…'

P. H. Towner is in company with leading scholars when he traces this phrase as 'a formulaic abbreviation of the *Shema* (Deut. 6:4) that goes back to the Jewish mission and polemics of Diaspora Judaism against the many gods of the Gentiles…(cf. I Cor. 8:6).'[4] Yet he properly adds that his use of the phrase in Romans 3:29-30 to support Gentile access to divine justification explains this text (cf. Gal. 3:20; Eph. 4:5-6).[5] That is, rather than primarily stating a prohibition against polytheism (which, of course, *is* prohibited), it is saying that Jews and Gentiles can get to the one, true God in exactly the same way. That way is through the one Mediator.

(b) One Mediator – '…and one mediator between God and men, the man Christ Jesus…'

'Mediator' means something like 'one who stands in the middle' and brings two parties together. It may well mean more than that, but at least, it does encompass the concept of reconciling offended parties. Paul

---

3. John Calvin, *Sermon XXXVII on the Ninth Chapter of Job* (The Banner of Truth Trust, 1574 Facsimile Edition: Edinburgh, 1993), 174.

4. Philip H. Towner, *The Letters to Timothy and Titus: The New International Commentary on the New Testament* (Wm. B. Eerdmans: Grand Rapids, MI, 2006), 180.

5. Ibid.

in Galatians 3:19 seems to employ the term 'mediator' with reference to Moses, who mediated the law of God. That is, he would bring together a holy God and sinful humanity in the context of the revelation of the character of God. Part of that revealed Law was the sacrificial system, which provided the way for sins to be covered in God's sight.

The author of Hebrews speaks of Christ as our heavenly High Priest and Mediator (Heb. 8:6; 9:15; 12:24). In that context he is the 'mediator of the new covenant.' He does all that is necessary from both the side of God and the side of man for the gracious promises of that Covenant to be fulfilled, as Jeremiah 31 describes: '...I will put my law in their inward parts, and write it in their hearts; and I will be their God, and they shall be my people...for I will forgive their iniquity, and I will remember their sins no more' (vv. 33-34).

This one mediator is 'a man': 'the man Christ Jesus.' Although Old Testament terms are used to describe him ('Christ,' his office as anointed Messiah, and 'Jesus,' his Jewish name), he is here called 'the man,' rather than 'the Jew' (although he was that). This means that he is the one way both for Jew and for Gentile; thus, for all who will be saved of all humanity.

I Timothy 2:5 does not specifically state that this man was also God, but Paul goes on to say so in the very next chapter: 'God was manifest in the flesh' (3:16). Hence, taken together, these two chapters indicate that the one Mediator was both man and God at the same time. That, as we shall see, was the only way he and he alone could be the one Mediator between God and man. However, I Timothy 2:5 focuses on his humanity, for that would be where the work of reconciliation must primarily occur, though never in separation from his deity.

(c) One Ransom for all

To carry through his work as mediator, 'he gave himself a ransom for all'. 'Ransom' (ἀντίλυτρον) comprises the words λύτρον – a ransom price paid for release of a person from bondage, and ἀντι – in exchange for. In Matthew 20:28, the Son of Man gives his life 'a ransom for many' (cf. Mark 10:45). In Galatians 2:20, Paul says that 'he loved me and gave himself for me,' and in Ephesians 5:2, Christ 'gave himself for us.' Romans 4:25 states in the passive voice that which these earlier references put in the active: 'who was delivered for our offences...' The active voice stresses the voluntary nature of Christ's ransom (cf. John 10:18: 'No man taketh my life from me, but I lay it down of myself...'), while the passive stresses the giving nature of God the Father in this ransom (cf. John 3:16: 'For God so loved the world that he gave his only begotten Son...'). In his self-giving as our ransom, Jesus expresses the heart of the Trinitarian life, in which from all eternity each Person gives himself to the others, in a mysterious 'mutual indwelling.' In taking on our flesh and giving himself to be our ransom, he shows us who God is, as the one who 'spared not his own Son, but freely gave him up for us all' (Rom. 8:32).

The nature of this divinely provided ransom is elsewhere described as that of substitutionary atonement: 'Christ died for our sins' (I Cor. 15:3). Life was given for life, in accordance with the Old Testament sacrificial system (especially described in Leviticus), in which both the sin offering and the whole burnt offering foreshadowed the expiatory sacrifice of the Son of God, as well as the offering of his holy life on our behalf. Thus occurred what John Calvin called 'the wondrous exchange,' in which Christ takes our place, that we might take his place.[6] Paul more fully explicates the meaning of the ransom in II Corinthians 5:21: 'For he hath made him to be sin for us, who knew no sin; that we might be the righteousness of God in him,' and in II Corinthians 8:9: 'For ye know the grace of our Lord Jesus Christ, that though he was rich, yet for your sakes he became poor, that ye through his poverty might be rich.' The infinite benefits of this ransom were at the infinite value of Christ's shed blood ('…without shedding of blood is no remission,' Heb. 9:22).

The substitutionary ransom was a price paid 'for all.' The significance of 'all' is to be seen in the framework of the one God and one Mediator, who opens the way heaven-ward to both Jew and Gentile. God is the God of both Jew and Gentile (Rom. 3:29), and his Gospel is 'to the Jew first, and also to the Greek' (Rom. 1:16). Thus, God will have 'all men' to be saved (I Tim. 2:4), and he will have them all prayed for (I Tim. 2:1-2).

Yet as Hermann Ridderbos writes:

> Even the most universal pronouncements of the apostle, therefore, in which he speaks of the redemptive will of God with respect to all men, and of his own universal commission as apostle and teacher of the gentiles, are never to be detached from belonging to Christ, and form the unconditional requirement of faith (cf. I Tim. 2:4, 7; 4:10; cf. v. 8). For this reason in the parallel between 'the many,' 'all,' and 'all men,' who through Adam have been constituted sinners and through Christ have been justified , etc. (cf. Rom. 5: 15, 18, 19; I Cor. 15:22), it is not a question of equal numbers of persons, but first of 'the many' (or 'all') who by virtue of descent have been comprehended in Adam, then of 'the many' ('all') who belong to Christ by faith. For it is only in Christ, who by God has been made a stone of stumbling and a rock of offense, as well as a foundation by whom none shall be put to shame, that Jew and Greek, slave and free, male and female, have become the new unity, the one new man (Gal. 3:28; Eph. 2: 15); in him, the people of God, Israel, circumcision, promise, sonship, and heirship receive their new definition and content; therefore in him, too, is the only and utterly decisive criterion of what may be called by the name of Israel (cf. Rom. 9:33).[7]

Saint Irenaeus (quoted above) expressed the main thrust of the New Testament teaching on the one mediatorship of Christ, thus setting the tone for the Church to follow over the centuries, as it worked out the details of the hypostatic union of the two natures in the one person of Christ. Specifically, Christ the only true Mediator had to be (1) fully man, (2) fully God, and (3) both man and God at the same time in order to accomplish his eternally purposed work of redemption for the lost human

---

6. Calvin, *Institutes* IV.17.2.

7. Herman Ridderbos, *Paul: An Outline of His Theology*, translated by John Richard DeWitt (Wm. B. Eerdmans Publ. Co.: Grand Rapids, MI, 1975), 340-41.

race.[8] (4) Once we summarize these three co-existent truths, then we must consider *the almost universally accepted* formula given to the Church by the Council of Chalcedon in A.D. 451 as to the reality of two natures in one person, and the question of the influence of Greek philosophy upon it.[9]

John Calvin, leading theologian of the sixteenth-century Reformation, did substantial work on the hypostatic union of the two natures in Christ, largely in the interests of Christ's mediatorship. W. Pannenberg rightly says that Calvin 'interpreted the doctrine of the two natures itself through the mediator concept'.[10] That is confirmed in what Calvin writes in his 1559 *Institutes*:

> Here we cannot excuse the error of the ancient writers who pay no attention to the person of the Mediator, obscure the real meaning of almost all the teaching one reads in the Gospel of John, and entangle themselves in many snares. Let this, then, be our key to right understanding: those things which apply to the office of the Mediator, are not spoken simply either of the divine nature or of the human.[11]

To be mediator, then, these things were necessary at the same time:

(1) Christ had to be fully man

If Christ had not become truly man, we could not have been saved. *The Belgic Confession* clearly stated that our salvation depends upon the true humanity of Christ.[12] Athanasius had written centuries before: 'That then which was born from Mary was according to the divine Scriptures human by nature, and the body of the Lord was a true one; but it was this, because it was the same as our body, for Mary was our sister inasmuch as we are all from Adam.'[13]

T. F. Torrance shows the necessity of this:

> The very fact that God became man in order to save us, declares in no uncertain way that the humanity of Christ is absolutely essential to our salvation…In the language of the Epistle to the Hebrews, 'he had to be made like his brethren' (Heb. 2:17)…
>
> Christ's humanity signifies the objective actuality of God's coming and presence in the very same sphere of reality and actuality to which we human beings belong. If Jesus Christ were not man as well as God, that would mean that God had not actually come all the way to man, that he had not really got a foothold in our creaturely world, as it were, within the time series in which we are…[14]

---

8. Here I will be following the work of T. F. Torrance, both in his (1960s) unpublished class notes, and wherever possible, his 2008, *Incarnation*, edited by Robert T. Walker.

9. See footnote 35 for the Oriental Orthodox Churches who did not accept Chalcedon, but still were fairly close to its affirmations.

10. Wolfhart Pannenberg, *Jesus – God and Man* (London: SCM Press, 1968), 124.

11. Calvin, *Institutes* II. 14. 3.

12. *The Belgic Confession*, Article 19.

13. Athanasius, *Letter to Epictetus*.

14. T. F. Torrance, *Incarnation*, 185.

John Calvin makes the same basic point:

> The situation would surely have been hopeless had the very majesty of
> God not descended to us, since it was not in our power to ascend to him.
> Hence, it was necessary for the Son of God to become for us 'Immanuel, that
> is, God with us' (Isa. 7:14; Matt. 1:23), and in such a way that his divinity
> and our human nature might by mutual connection grow together...Even
> if man had remained free from all stain, his condition would have been too
> lowly for him to reach God without a Mediator...Therefore, lest anyone
> be troubled about where to seek the Mediator, or by what path we must
> come to him, the Spirit calls him 'man,' thus teaching us that he is near us,
> indeed, touches us, since he is our flesh...Who could have done this had
> not the self-same Son of God become Son of man, and had not taken what
> was ours as to impart what was his to us, and to make what was his by
> nature ours by grace? Ungrudgingly, he took our nature upon himself to
> impart to us what was his, and to become both Son of God and Son of man
> in common with us...[15]

Following Torrance, we note that Christ's humanity is essential for: (a)
revelation, and (b) reconciliation.

(a) Christ's humanity essential for revelation
The only way we can know who God really is, is for Christ to have taken
on our human nature in order to show us the heart of the Father.

> The astounding thing is that the eternal Word by whom all things were
> created became a creature, became man, certainly without ceasing to be that
> eternal Word, and therefore by his very creatureliness constitutes the act of
> revelation...Because the eternal has become temporal, men and women can
> know the eternal truth in creaturely form, the eternal truth in time.[16]

Jesus Christ is accessible to us through his true humanity. When on earth
he lives in a body in our space/time series; he exists in a web of personal,
familial, social, economic and political relationships, as we do; he speaks
with a human voice that can be understood by other humans. He shares
our experiences; he uses our thought-forms, linguistic conventions, and
grammar. He is so truly human that nearly always he did not appear to
be divine; he could be passed by on the road as any other man. He did
not keep himself 'at arm's length from us' by being frightening, openly
'otherworldly' or bizarre. His words and actions bring him within our
human range. His full humanity welcomes us to come, for he says: 'Come
unto me, all ye that labour and are heavy laden, and I will give you rest.
Take my yoke upon you, and learn of me; for I am meek and lowly in
heart: and ye shall find rest for your souls' (Matt. 11:28-29). In John 10:27
the Good Shepherd says: 'My sheep hear my voice, and I know them, and
they follow me...' And in John 6:63 he says: 'the words that I speak unto
you, they are spirit and they are life.'

---

15. Calvin, *Institutes* II.12.1,2,3.

16. Torrance, op. cit., 186.

God gives himself in the incarnation of the Son so that we can know him truly in and through Christ. Ever remaining God, he takes on our genuine humanity so that we humans can apprehend the transcendence of God through that graspable humanity.

Maximus the Confessor shows that it is only through Christ, who came to us as a true man, that we can make sense of everything else: 'Christ is the measure of all persons and of all things, and one must neither measure nor explain Christ by anything whatsoever or by anyone whatsoever, but only by Christ himself, who the measure of all and the explanation of all.'[17]

(b) Christ's humanity essential for reconciliation

The full reality of Christ's humanity is essential to our being reconciled to God. Its perfection is the basis of the perfection of Christ's atonement. As T. F. Torrance writes:

> The humanity of Christ is also essential to God's act of *reconciliation*, for the actuality of atonement is grounded upon the fact that in actual human nature it is God himself acting on our behalf. Thus any docetic view of the humanity of Christ would mean that God only appears to act within our human existence, or that his acts are only of tangential significance, that they do not really strike into the roots of our existence and condition, and have no relevance to our need. Atonement is real and actual only if and as the mediator acts fully from the side of man as man, as well as from the side of God as God. If the humanity of Christ is imperfect, atonement is imperfect, and we would then still be in our sins.[18]

John Calvin, while placing pre-eminent emphasis on Christ's atoning death for our reconciliation, at the same time understands the holy life he lived as an obedient human to have entered into 'the price of our liberation':

> Now someone asks, How has Christ abolished sin, banished the separation between us and God, and acquired righteousness to render God favorable and kindly toward us? To this we can in general reply that he has achieved this for us by the whole course of his obedience. This is proved by Paul's testimony: 'As by one man's disobedience many were made sinners, so by one man's obedience we are made righteous' [Rom. 5:19]. In another passage, to be sure, Paul extends the basis of the pardon that frees us from the curse of the law to the whole life of Christ: 'But when the fullness of time came, God sent forth his Son, born of woman, subject to the law, to redeem those who were under the law' [Gal. 4:4-5]. Thus in his very baptism, also, he asserted that he fulfilled a part of righteousness in obediently carrying out his Father's commandment [Matt. 3:15]. In short, from the time when he took on the form of a servant, he began to pay the price of liberation in order to redeem us.[19]

---

17. Maximus the Confessor, *Questions (and Responses) to Thalassius*, 60.

18. Torrance, *Incarnation*, 186.

19. Calvin, *Institutes*, II.xvi.5.

The necessity of Christ's humanity to our salvation is why Saint Irenaeus so emphasizes the real humanity which the Lord took on, rather than an unreal, or non-Adamic flesh, proposed by many of the Gnostics:

> But if he pretends that the Lord possessed another substance of flesh, the sayings respecting reconciliation will not agree with that man. For that thing is reconciled which had formerly been in enmity. Now, if the Lord had taken flesh from another substance, He would not, by so doing, have reconciled that one to God which had become inimical through transgression. But now, by means of communion with Himself, the Lord has reconciled man to God the Father, in reconciling us to Himself by the body of His own flesh, and redeeming us by His own blood, as the apostle says to the Ephesians, 'In whom we have redemption through his blood, the remission of sins…' [Eph. 1:7]. And in every epistle, the apostle plainly testifies, that through the flesh of our Lord, and through His blood, we have been saved.[20]

(2) Christ had to be fully God

If Christ had not always existed as God, and if he had not remained fully God in his incarnation, his salvation, revelation and reconciliation would not have been God's own work, and we would still be in darkness and sin. Following again T. F. Torrance, we note three points about the deity of Christ as essential to our redemption: (a) Christ's deity is the guarantee that salvation is the work of God, (b) His deity is essential for revelation, and (c) His deity is essential for salvation.

(a) Christ's deity is the guarantee that salvation is the work of God

God himself must come down to our race in Jesus Christ's human nature, while still remaining eternally God. This stupendous coming down to earth 'to tabernacle among us' (John 1:14), and yet somehow remaining in the bosom of the Father (cf. John 1:18) is the way he conveys to sinners full and eternal pardon. In the words of Torrance:

> If the humanity of Christ is the guarantee of the action of God *among humanity*, revealing himself and reconciling sinners to himself, the deity of Christ is the guarantee that his work of revelation and reconciliation is not hollow and empty and unreal on its objective side; it is the guarantee that in Jesus Christ we have to do with the *full reality of God* himself. What Jesus does in forgiveness is not just the work of man, but the work of God, and is therefore of final and ultimate validity. Only God against whom we sin can forgive sin, but the deity of Christ is the guarantee that the action of Christ in the whole course of his life is identical with the action of God toward us. It is not something of God that we have in Christ, but God himself, very God of very God…
>
> If Christ is not God, then the love of Christ is not identical with God's love, and so we do not know that God is love…If Christ is not God, then we do not have a descent of God to man…The dogma of the deity of Christ means that our salvation in Christ is anchored in eternity: that it is more sure than the heavens.[21]

---

20. Irenaeus, *Adversus Haereses*, V.14.3.

21. Torrance, *Incarnation*, 187,188.

Calvin explains:

> Therefore, by his love God the Father goes before and anticipates our
> reconciliation in Christ. Indeed, 'because he first loved us' [I John 4:19], he
> afterward reconciles us to himself. But until Christ succors us by his death,
> the unrighteousness that deserves God's indignation remains in us, and is
> accursed and condemned before him. Hence, we can be fully and firmly
> joined with God only when Christ joins us with him.[22]

(b) Christ's Deity is essential for Revelation

The Lord Jesus Christ had to be truly God in order for his teaching and
actions to be as true as God himself is true. Torrance explains:

> ...its reality as revelation of God is grounded on the reality of God's presence
> in it, the reality of God's act of self communication in and through it; that
> is, it is grounded on the identity between revelation and God the revealer.
> The humanity of Christ guarantees the actuality of revelation, but the deity
> of Christ guarantees its nature as revelation of *God*. Jesus Christ is the Son
> of the Father, and as such he *is* the revelation he brings...
>
> Any weakening in the affirmation of the deity of Christ here results in
> indecision and uncertainty, and it is because of this weakness that people are
> engulfed in relativity, and are not sure about what they believe. How then
> can we know that they are not right and we are wrong? Such uncertainty is
> the inevitable outcome of doubts and clouded vision of the deity of Christ.
> When the deity of Christ is denied, his humanity is denied as well, for the
> bond between Jesus in his humanity and the Father is broken and then Jesus
> is made out to be a liar. But if Jesus is cut adrift from the truth, then we are
> all hopelessly at sea. Thus the full reality of Christ's deity is essential to
> revelation, and faith, for the reality of revelation is grounded in the reality
> of the action and presence of God in Christ, on the identity of his revelation
> with God's self-revelation.[23]

One can readily see the correctness of what Torrance says in the various
'Quests' for the Historical Jesus. Torrance's point was that if you deny
Christ's deity, then you lose his humanity. His deity is so central to his
being as the revelation of God to humankind, that to attempt to hold on
merely to his humanity is methodologically impossible, for the ancient
documents that witness to him are, on that assumption, not reliable. If they
testify falsely to his deity, who could reasonably use them to demonstrate
anything historically certain (or at least, not very much) concerning his
humanity?

On the contrary, as we saw in volume 1, the Scriptures were given
in the context of the faith and life of Israel and then of the Church. It is
impossible to interpret them properly outside the community of faith, as
has been the case since the eighteenth-century Enlightenment. One of the
clearest illustrations of the manifest failure of this kind of procedure is
found in the Jesus Seminar, discussed in the first volume. In some respects

---

22. Calvin, op. cit., II. xvi. 3.

23. Torrance, *Incarnation*, 188,189.

(though not all), a majority of the scholars of the Jesus Seminar were following the theology of Rudolph Bultmann, who though technically a part of the Church, functionally worked outside its context of historical faith.[24] Indeed, Bultmann writes off the basic worldview given us by divine revelation as 'mythological,' and in its stead, tries to find out who Jesus is in terms of certain aspects of existentialist philosophy, especially that of Heidegger.[25]

The only alternative to God's full revelation of himself in Christ and in his written Word is some form of relativism, which is usually characterized (as it is today) by constantly shifting ideas of what are true 'values.' In the twenty-first century West, these ever-shifting 'values' seem to be derived from the assumptions of an unofficial, inchoate elite, who are committed to various levels of secularistic atheism. Ironically, the vast majority of those who wish to keep in step with the secularistic atheists are not themselves atheists. Many of them are Church people, who do not want to seem 'ethically backwards' (in terms of what is generally called the ethics of 'political correctness'). To maintain their standing with so much of the media, governments and educational realms, they – perhaps half unwittingly – have to work in terms of relativism, lest they be denounced as 'absolutist' or 'intolerant'. This secularist consensus will keep adjusting its agendas, but one thing is unlikely to change: it will remain hostile to biblical Christianity; in fact, it will probably become even less tolerant of the traditional Christian alternative to itself.

Yet the relativists will find their job becoming far more difficult as Islam (which is absolutist) penetrates the populations and institutions of the West. Relativistic secularism will also be set back by the burgeoning supernatural Christianity of the global South, as the massively growing number of evangelical believers, who hold to the absolute authority of Christ and Holy Scripture, overwhelm the shrinking populations of the now aging proponents of Western 'Modernism', with its axiomatic commitment to relativism, which is as uncompromising as any branch of Christian Fundamentalism is about its principles.[26] The day will come when the humanistic relativism which excludes the possibility of divine revelation in and through the Son of God will be replaced by a profoundly different consensus, which claims him as Lord, bows to his Word, and 'in his light sees light.' And as the Holy Spirit works, many who are presently under the sway of relativism will be awakened to saving faith in the Lord and his Word, and will gladly join in the work of reconstructing a moribund culture.

(c) Christ's Deity is essential for Reconciliation
No sinful human can ever be reconciled to a holy God unless Christ, the agent of that reconciliation, is fully God. John L. Girardeau, a nineteenth-

---

24. See Torrance, ibid., 274-290, on 'The modern debate: the views of Rudolph Bultmann.'

25. Ibid., 284-285.

26. See Philip Jenkins, *The Next Christendom: The Coming of Global Christianity* (Oxford University Press: USA, 2011).

century theologian in South Carolina, explained it this way: '...Christ as a divine person energized through his human will... It is this doctrine that grounds the infinite value and sufficiency of the human sufferings of Christ as the substitute of the sinner. As an infinite person he energized through the finite will of his human nature. This imparted infinite merit to his human obedience in life and in death.'[27]

To follow Torrance:

> The full reality of Christ's deity is essential for *salvation*, for the reality and validity of salvation are grounded upon the reality of Christ's deity. Man's salvation must be an act of *God*, else it is not salvation...Everything depends upon the fact that the cross is lodged in the heart of the Father.
>
> It is important to see that if the deity of Christ is denied, then the cross becomes a terrible monstrosity. If Jesus Christ is man only and not also God, then we lose faith in God and man. We lose faith in God because how could we believe in a God who allows the best man that ever lived to be hounded to death on the cross – is that all that God cares about our humanity... Put Jesus Christ a man on the cross, and put God in heaven, like some distant god imprisoned in his own lonely abstract deity, and you cannot believe in him, in a god such that he is monstrously unconcerned with our life, and who does not even lift a finger to help Jesus. But if you deny the deity of Christ you also lose faith in man, for that would mean that mankind is such that when they see the very best, the very highest and truest the world has ever known, they crucify that man in spite, and will have nothing to do with him except to hate him. Put God in heaven, and Jesus on the cross only as a man, and you destroy all hope and trust, and preach a doctrine of the blackest and most abysmal despair. Denial of the deity of Christ destroys faith in God and in man, and turns the cross into the bottomless pit of darkness. But put God on the cross, and the cross becomes the world's salvation. The whole gospel rests upon the fact that it is God who became incarnate, and it was God who in Christ has reconciled the world to himself.[28]

The various forms of Deism, which by definition cannot have God on the cross, 'reconciling the world unto himself' (cf. II Cor. 5:19), are left with a vacuum as concerns redemption of a sinful world. Historically, they have sought to fill this spiritual vacuum with different 'candidates'. With the eighteenth-century Enlightenment, they may simply deny that humankind is radically fallen, and with Pelagius of the fifth century seek to solve the problems wrought by sin in terms of superficial moral self-help, as a species of religious 'good works', of which all are really capable. Or more likely, in our twentieth and twenty-first century context, they may deny the significance of personal sinfulness in order to concentrate on the unjustness of societal structures, calling for revolution, to be followed by some kind of strong central statism. Some of the late twentieth century South American 'liberation' theology tended in that direction, following in their own 'theistic' way the earlier pathway of Euro-Communism. With the failure of Marxism, many whose hopes for redemption were

---

27. John L. Girardeau, *Discussions of Theological Questions* (Sprinkle Publications: Harrisonburg, Virginia, 1986), 396.

28. Torrance, op. cit., 189,190.

lodged in it have gone in other directions, not least that of radical forms of environmentalism.[29]

The replacements for redemption by Christ will always be unsuccessful, and hence will keep mutating. It may not be so important here to point them out, or even to critique them, as it is to be aware of their folly in wishing to replace the one way of salvation established by the eternal Godhead, and instead to bow in adoration to the God-man, the only possible Mediator between God and man, the man Christ Jesus (I Tim. 2:5), for he is the one 'who gave himself a ransom for all, to be testified in due time' (v. 6). In doing this, we obey the Messianic Psalm 2: 'Kiss the Son, lest he be angry, and ye perish from the way, when his wrath is kindled but a little. Blessed are all they that put their trust in him' (v.12).

(3) Christ had to be both man and God *at the same time* in order to save humanity

Our salvation is not accomplished simply by God alone (i.e. apart from our humanity), or simply by man alone (operating independently from God), but always and only by Godhead and manhood together, at one time, in the one Person of the Lord Jesus Christ. Chapter 8 of *The Westminster Confession of Faith* states clearly why the Godhead and manhood are essential at the same time, in the same person, to the saving work of revelation and reconciliation:

> The Son of God, the second person in the Trinity, being very and eternal God, of one substance and equal with the Father, did, when the fullness of time was come, take upon Him man's nature, with all the essential properties and common infirmities thereof, yet without sin: being conceived by the power of the Holy Ghost, in the womb of the virgin Mary, of her substance. So that two whole, perfect, and distinct natures, the Godhead and the manhood, were inseparably joined together in one person, without conversion, composition, or confusion. Which person is very God, and very man, yet one Christ, the only Mediator between God and man.

> The Lord Jesus, in His human nature thus united to the divine, was sanctified and anointed with the Holy Spirit, above measure, having in Him all the treasures of wisdom and knowledge; in whom it pleased the Father that all fullness should dwell; to the end that, being holy, harmless, undefiled, and full of grace and truth, He might be thoroughly furnished to execute the office of a mediator and surety. Which office He took not unto Himself, but was thereunto called by His Father, who put all power and judgment into His hand, and gave Him commandment to execute the same.[30]

Torrance fills out the details:

---

29. See an article in *The Wall Street Journal*, Tuesday, January 18, 2011, by Patrick Moore, founding member of Greenpeace, on the politics of the environmental movement (in 'Notable and Quotable' from *The Vancouver Sun*, Jan. 7, 2011). He notes that after the collapse of Euro-communism, many of its people moved into the environmental movement, bringing their neo-Marxist agendas with them.

30. *Westminster Confession of Faith*, VIII. 2,3.

... [T]he humanity of Christ has no revealing or saving significance for us apart from his deity, and his deity has no revealing or saving significance for us apart from his humanity. The doctrine of Christ is the doctrine of true and complete humanity in full union with true and complete deity, and it is in that *union* that the significance of both revelation and reconciliation lies. It is such a union that the presence of full and perfect deity does not impair or diminish or restrict the presence of full and perfect humanity. It is such a union that true Godhead and true humanity are joined together in Jesus Christ in such a way that they cannot be separated, and yet that they can never be confused, in such a way also that one does not absorb the other, nor do both combine to form a third entity which is never divine nor human. In the hypostatic union, God remains God and man remains man, and yet in Christ, God who remains God is for ever joined to man, becomes man and remains man. In this union God has become man without ceasing to be God, and man is taken up into the very being of God without ceasing to be man.[31]

The simultaneous co-existence in one person of deity and humanity are essential to: (a) Revelation, and (b) Reconciliation.

(a) Revelation

We humans cannot understand 'the tongues of angels', and so in the incarnation, the God/man came to live in our humanity, partly so he could speak in a human tongue that humans could make sense of. Because his human nature is united to his eternal deity, what the incarnate one says is exactly what God says.

In the words of T. F. Torrance:

> The incarnation of the Word means that the Word assumes human form and approaches us from within the actual forms of human life in the only way which we can understand...There, within human nature, God reveals himself as God in terms of what is not God, in terms of what is man. He speaks to us in a human voice, in human language, and in human thought forms...
>
> No, not even in Jesus can we get across from man to God, unless in Jesus Christ there is hypostatic union between him and God, unless the human forms and speech and acts of Jesus are predicates of the one divine person [cf. Col. 2:3]. It is only because Christ is himself personally God that his human speech and human actions, and his human forms of thought, are also divine revelation...[32]

(b) Reconciliation

God in Christ came to us as true man, and the verity of his manhood was not compromised by its coexistence with his eternal deity. On that basis, we may be reconciled to God, rather than destroyed by the burning holiness of God, which would be the case apart from the divine/human Mediator.

> In Jesus Christ, God has come in the humble form of a servant, veiling his divine majesty, for we could not look on the face of God and live. If God came openly in his glory and majesty, we would be smitten to the ground

---

31. Torrance, op. cit., 191-92.

32. Ibid., 192.

in sin and death; the last judgment would be upon us, with no time to repent, no opportunity for personal decision in faith. The very humanity of Christ is the veiling of God; the flesh of sin, the humiliation and the form of a servant, the death of Christ all veil God – and so God draws near to us under that veil in order to reveal himself, and save us. It is sometimes asked if God could not reveal himself to us apart from or without Christ, without the humble form of a servant. But if revelation were to take place apart from the veiling of Christ, or in a form totally unknown to us, it would disrupt the conditions of our world and of our humanity, and instead of saving us, it would mean our disintegration...

The humanity of Christ is the actuality of God's presence among man, but his humanity holds mankind at arm's length from God, in order to give them breathing space, time, and possibility for surrender to God's challenge in grace, time for decision and faith in him...[33]

Torrance then shows what the deity and humanity together in the one person of Christ accomplished for our reconciliation:

The hypostatic union is also the objective heart of reconciliation, in atonement. The unassumed is the unhealed, but in the hypostatic union God the Son has sinlessly assumed our flesh of sin into oneness with himself. In so doing he has judged sin in the flesh and made expiation for our sin in his own blood shed on the cross, and so has worked the hypostatic union right through our alienation into the resurrection where we have the new humanity in perfect union with God, and in that union we are given to share.[34]

The Westminster Confession of Faith expresses it as follows:

This office the Lord Jesus did most willingly undertake, which that He might discharge, He was made under the law, and did perfectly fulfil it, endured most grievous torments immediately in his soul, and most painful sufferings in His body; was crucified, and died; was buried, and remained under the power of death; yet saw no corruption. On the third day He arose from the dead, with the same body in which He suffered, with which also He ascended into heaven, and there sitteth at the right hand of the Father, making intercession, and shall return to judge men and angels at the end of the world.

The Lord Jesus, by His perfect obedience, and sacrifice of Himself, which He, through the eternal Spirit, once offered up unto God, hath fully satisfied the justice of His Father; and purchased, not only reconciliation, but an everlasting inheritance in the kingdom of heaven, for all those whom the Father hath given unto Him.[35]

The eighth chapter of *The Westminster Confession* (from the Puritan parliament in the 1640s) takes over directly the teaching of the Council of Chalcedon to set forth the oneness of the person of the Mediator in

---

33. Ibid., 194.

34. Ibid., 195.

35. Chapter VIII, 4-5.

two natures.[36] In doing so, it is in the company of *nearly the whole Church*, East and West, which relied upon the fifth century formula of this fourth ecumenical council.[37]

Most traditional Protestants Affirm Chalcedon

The same reliance upon Chalcedon is true throughout the magisterial Reformation of the sixteenth century, as we see in the Lutheran *Formula*

---

36. Chapter VIII, 2: 'So that two whole, perfect, and distinct natures, the Godhead and the manhood, were inseparably joined together in one person, *without conversion, composition, or confusion.*' We shall study the significance of these negative statements immediately. But for the present, we note that while the original Chalcedonian formula has 'four alpha privatives' (or negations about how the two natures are united): *'without confusion, without conversion, without division, without separation,'* the Westminster Confession reduces them to three negatives: *'without conversion, composition, or confusion.'* The meaning is not in the least changed by Westminster, but rather the two Chalcedonian negatives: *'without division and without separation'* are included in one term that encompasses them both: *'without composition.'* That is, the two natures are not the combination of parts or elements of a whole (which would mean that they were *divided* and *separated*).

37. Some portions of the Church in the Middle East did not accept Chalcedon, including the Coptic Church. It may be that part of the problem in their resistance to Chalcedon was terminological: especially the concepts of nature and person, and it is possible that in the end of the day they were not too far from what Chalcedon meant. Iain R. Torrance carefully works through these issues in *Christology After Chalcedon: Severus of Antioch and Sergius the Monophysite* (Wipf and Stock Publishers: Eugene, Oregon, 1998), especially pp. 3-19. See also: John S. Romanides, Paul Verghese, Nick A. Nissiotis, eds., *Unofficial Consultation Between Theologians of Eastern Orthodox and Oriental Churches*, Aarhus, Denmark, 11-15 August 1964. Papers and Minutes. *The Greek Orthodox Theological Review*, vol. 10, No. 2, Winter 1964-1965, entire issue. More recently, through the auspices of the World Council of Churches, a Communique was issued from Anba Bishoy Monastery in Egypt, by representatives of both Eastern Orthodox and Oriental Orthodox Churches affirming an essential closeness on the Hypostatic Union by those who have always accepted Chalcedon (Eastern Orthodoxy) and by those who have historically rejected it (Oriental Orthodox). It says, among other affirmations: 'The Logos, eternally consubstantial with the Father and the Holy Spirit in his divinity, has in these last days become incarnate of the Holy Spirit and Blessed Virgin Mary Theotokos, and thus became man, consubstantial with us in his humanity, but without sin. He is true God and true man at the same time, perfect in his divinity, perfect in his humanity. Because the one she bore in her womb was at the same time fully God as well as fully human we call the Blessed Virgin Theotokos. When we speak of the one composite (*synthetos*) hypostasis of our Lord Jesus Christ, we do not say that in him a divine hypostasis and a human hypostasis came together. It is that the one central hypostasis of the Second Person of the Trinity has assumed our created human nature in that act uniting it with his own uncreated divine nature, to form an inseparably and unconfusedly united real divine human being, the natures being distinguished from each other in contemplation (*theoria*) only. The hypostasis of the Logos before the incarnation, even with his divine nature, is, of course, not composite. The same hypostasis, as distinct from nature, of the incarnate Logos, is not composite either. Jesus Christ is one eternal hypostasis who has assumed human nature by the incarnation. So we call that hypostasis composite, on account of the natures which are united to form one composite unity. It is not the case that our Fathers used *physis* and *hypostasis* always interchangeably, and confused the one with the other. The term hypostasis can be used to denote both the person as distinct from nature, and also the person with the nature, for a hypostasis never in fact exists without a nature. It is the same hypostasis of the Second Person of the Trinity, eternally begotten from the Father who in these last days became a human being and was born of the Blessed Virgin…We agree in condemning the Nestorian and the Eutychian heresies. We neither separate nor divide the human nature in Christ from his divine nature, nor do we think that the former was absorbed in the latter and thus ceased to exist. The four adverbs used to qualify the mystery of the hypostatic union belong to our common tradition – without commingling (or confusion) (*asyngchytos*), without change (*atreptos*), without separation (*achoristos*), and without division (*adiairetos*). Those among us who speak of two natures in Christ do not thereby deny their inseparable, indivisible union; those among us who speak of one united divine-human nature in Christ do not thereby deny the continuing dynamic presence in Christ of the divine and the human, without change, without confusion' in *Growth in Agreement: Reports and Agreed Statements of Ecumenical Conversations on a World Level, 1982-1998*, edited by J. Gros, H. Meyer, W. G. Rusch (WCC Publications, Geneva; Wm. B. Eerdmans Publ. Co.: Grand Rapids, MI, 2000), 192-193.

of Concord (1576, with revisions in 1584). In its 'Epitome' it accepts the Apostle's Creed, Nicene Creed, and the 'Athanasian' Creed, and it rejects 'all heresies contrary to them' (Article II).[38] It states, under Article I – 'Original Sin': 'And the Son of God, by a personal union, has redeemed this nature, yet without sin…' (Article II).[39] It gives an essentially Chalcedonian definition of the hypostatic union in Christ in Article VIII – 'Of the Person of Christ,' Affirmative, sections I- XII,[40] and Negative, sections I-XX.[41] Section XII of Article VIII specifically denies the Nestorian and Eutychian heresies.[42]

It is the same with the Anglican *Thirty-nine Articles of the Church of England* (1563 and 1571). In Article II – 'Of the Word or Son of God, which was made very Man,' it is affirmed that in the Incarnation through the substance of the blessed Virgin, the eternal Word of the Father, 'took Man's nature…so that two whole and perfect Natures, that is to say the Godhead and Manhood, were joined together in one Person, never to be divided, whereof is one Christ, very God, and very Man…'[43]

The French Reformed *Confession of La Rochelle* (1559) affirms: 'We believe that in one person, that is, Jesus Christ, the two natures are actually and inseparably joined and united, and yet each remains in its proper character: so that in this union the divine nature, retaining its attributes, remained uncreated, infinite, and all-pervading; and the human nature remained finite, having its form, measure, and attributes…' (Article XV).[44]

The Belgic Confession (1561) is also Chalcedonian in its doctrine of the Incarnation: 'We believe that by this conception the person of the Son is inseparably united and connected with the human nature; so that there are not two Sons of God, nor two persons, but two natures united in one single person; yet each nature retains its own distinct properties…' (Article XIX).[45]

The Chalcedonian doctrine is found in the Baptist adaptation of *The Westminster Confession of Faith* (1677 and 1688 in London, and in Philadelphia in the early eighteenth century). It essentially takes over whole and entire the eighth chapter of *The Westminster Confession* 'Of Christ the Mediator,' which, as we saw above, teaches the Chalcedonian formulation on the hypostatic union.[46]

The Methodist Articles of Religion (drawn up by John Wesley, and adopted by the American Methodists in 1784) is also Chalcedonian in its confession concerning Christ: 'The Son, who is the Word of the Father,

38. *The Formula of Concord* in Philip Schaff, *The Creeds of the Evangelical Protestant Churches* (London: Hodder and Stoughton, 1877), 91-180.

39. Ibid., 99.

40. Ibid., 147-154.

41. Ibid., 154-159.

42. Ibid., 153-154.

43. Ibid., 488.

44. Ibid., 368,369.

45. Ibid., 404.

46. See *A Faith to Confess: The Baptist Confession of 1689, rewritten in Modern English* (Carey Publications: Haywards Heath, Sussex, 1982 reprint), Chapter 8: 'Christ the Mediator' (pp. 27-30).

the very and eternal God, of one substance with the Father, took man's nature in the womb of the blessed Virgin; so that two whole and perfect natures – that is to say, the Godhead and manhood – were joined together in one person, never to be divided, whereof is one Christ, very God and very man...' (Article II).[47]

The Calvinistic Methodists in Wales affirmed the hypostatic union during the early years of their movement (as part of the Evangelical Revival of the 1740s). Their leaders issued this statement in 1750: *Ymddiddan Rhwng Methodist Uniongred ac un Camsyniol* ('Dialogue Between an Orthodox and an Erroneous Methodist'). Among other points, it states of Christ 'that the union of two natures (human and divine) in one Person remains, so that our Lord was God-man in the womb, God-man on the cross, God-man in the grave.'[48]

(4) The formula of the Council of Chalcedon concerning the union of two natures in one person

Chalcedon was the fourth ecumenical council. The first council, that of Nicea (A.D. 325), had affirmed that Jesus Christ is truly God (*homoousios tw patri*), against the Arians, who held that Christ was finally a creature; a mere man, although a very remarkable one. The second council took place in Constantinople (381), and affirmed that Jesus Christ is perfectly man, against the Apollinarians, who denied that he had a human mind. The Council of Ephesus (431) was third. It affirmed that Jesus Christ is one person, against the Nestorians, who were thought to have divided Christ into two persons.

Following, to a large degree, the famous 'Tome' of Leo of Rome, the Fathers of Chalcedon stated:

> Following the holy fathers, we all teach with one accord one and the same Son, our Lord Jesus Christ perfect in Godhead and perfect also in humanity, truly God and also truly man, being of a reasonable soul and body, of one being with the Father as touching his Godhead, and also of one being with us as touching his humanity, being like unto us in all things except sin, begotten of the Father before all times according to his Godhead, and also in the last days born for our sake and for our salvation, of the virgin Mary, the bearer of God, according to his humanity, one and the same Christ, the Son, Lord, only begotten of two natures, without confusion, without conversion, without division, and without separation (ασυγχυτος, ατρεπτος, αδιαιπετος, αχωριστος); the differences of natures not being removed by their union, but rather the propriety of each being preserved and concurring in one prosopon and in one hypostasis so that he is not divided or separated into two prosopa but in one and the same only begotten Son, God the Word, Lord Jesus Christ, even as the prophets of old and Jesus Christ himself taught us concerning him, and the creed of our fathers that has been handed on to us.

---

47. Ibid., 807.

48. Quoted from Eifion Evans, *Bread of Heaven: The Life and Work of William Williams, Pantycelyn* (Bridgend, Wales: Bryntirion Press, 2010), 118,119.

The distinction of 'nature' from 'person'.

Since the crucial issue here is how the two natures are united in one person, we must first seek to understand how the Fathers of Chalcedon distinguished nature from person. Competent studies in the development of historical theology all point out that it took until about the fourth century before there were widely accepted words for person and nature, much less clear definitions of them. That does **not** mean that the realities expressed by those terms were not distinguished by the fathers before the fourth century; it only means that it took a long time, and not a little controversy, to work out phraseology that would be generally received as accurate expressions in both East and West.[49]

For instance, the Creed of Nicea, and the Synodical Letter (written the year after the 381 Council of Constantinople) used the terms *hypostasis* (or 'person') and *ousia* ('being' or 'substance') interchangeably. However, by the time of the *Tomus ad Antiochenos* (362), largely based on the work of the Cappadocians, a general consensus was reached in which the Holy Trinity was understood to be one divine *ousia* and three divine *hypostaseis*. Hence, the 382 Synodical Letter of the Fathers of Constantinople states that the Father, Son, and Holy Spirit possess: 'a single Godhead and power and … three most perfect *hypostases* or three perfect *prosopa*, so that there exists no place here for the disease of Sabellius wherein the *hypostases* are confused, with the result that their peculiar characteristics too are destroyed.'[50]

Frederick G. McLeod accurately remarks:

> By distinguishing the Greek word *ousia* (substance and, in the context, the same as 'nature') from both *hypostasis* and *prosopon*, the fathers insisted on the necessity of making a distinction between 'substance/nature' on the one hand and both *hypostasis* and *prosopon* on the other. They affirm in fact that these two latter words are approximate in meaning (though *hypostasis* is said to be 'most perfect' and *prosopon* only 'perfect').[51]

In brief, then, 'nature' (or 'substance') comes to be distinguished from 'person'. 'Nature can be thought of as a set of 'idiomatic' ('peculiar,' 'distinguishing' or 'characteristic') qualities that make that nature what it is (whether human or divine), whereas 'person' is the 'who' through whom the peculiar qualities of that nature are manifested. The 'who' (or the person) is characterized by self-consciousness, which is not true of the nature in and by itself, until it is expressed through the person, in which it is established.

Staniloae clarifies this significant issue:

---

49. Protopresbyter George Dion. Dragas illustrates the clear distinctions already being made by Athanasius in the first third of the fourth century, which indicate a grasp of the differences that would later be 'codified' by the Church, in *Saint Athanasius of Alexandria* (Orthodox Research Institute: Rollinsford, NH), chapter 2 – 'The Relation of Nature to Grace in the Writings of St. Athanasius' (pp. 25-78).

50. Tanner, Norman P., ed., *Decrees of the Ecumenical Councils I: Nicea I to Lateran V* (Washington, DC: Georgetown University Press, 1990), 28.

51. Frederick G. McLeod, op. cit., 148.

The person is a unique 'who' that exists and knows himself as the subject of
a nature or a complex set of qualities out of which he can bring forth acts
that are always new, and in which he supports and receives the acts of
other personal and impersonal factors. The unique 'who' of the person is in
consonance with the complexity of this set of qualities which is manifested in
the person's own acts and in which he receives the acts of others. When seen
as unity, this complexity is a person; when seen as a complex set of qualities,
it is nature. But this complex set of qualities cannot be seen as standing
by itself. It subsists in a unitary 'who' or as a unitary 'who' … It is worth
mentioning that the Hypostasis must not be understood as a basis different
from the two natures, but as a mode of concrete existence that penetrates
them completely through its hypostatic characteristic by uniting them.[52]

As Torrance has written, this hypostatic union is entirely unique. 'It is not a
personal union in our common sense of the word "personal," which involves
a mutual relation between personalities, but personal only in the sense that
it is grounded in the one unique person of God the Son. It is "personal"
because it is "in the person of the Son" – that is the meaning of hypostatic.'[53]

The Fathers had to combat the Nestorian theory (or at least, attributed
to him and his followers) that Jesus Christ's incarnation involved the
combination of a human person and a divine person, since that precludes
incarnation, and hence, salvation, for God did not really become man. They
also had to fight the theory of those in the line of Eutyches, who held that
the divine and human natures merged into one another to become 'a third
thing,' for in that case, divinity is demoted into something else, and humanity
finally disappears, so that in both cases, sinful humanity is not saved.

The Chalcedonian formula probably comes as close as humans can
to stating in a biblically balanced way that God the Son becomes truly
human, without ceasing to be eternally God and, hereafter, always human
in one and the same person, at one and the same time. This is the ground
of our salvation from sin, death, and hell.

This means that the divine Son (the Logos) did **not** take on another
human person, who already had a separate self-consciousness.[54] Rather,
he took on *human nature*. In doing so, it is the eternal Son of God who
consciously – and personally – acts through that human nature, as it truly
subsists in him.[55]

Again, Staniloae's teaching helps make clear a complex matter:

The distinction between Jesus as man and other human persons lies in the
fact that as man he is not an autonomous center of acts and reactions. Rather,
the human center of these acts and reactions is simultaneously their divine
center as well as that of his divine acts. His entire human nature has thus
been centered not outside God, but within God the Word.[56]

---

52. Staniloae, *The Experience of God: Orthodox Dogmatic Theology: Vol. 3. The Person of Jesus Christ
as God and Savior*, 62-63.

53. Torrance, op. cit., 207.

54. We shall discuss this in detail under *anhypostasia* in Chapter 5.

55. We shall study this under *enhypostasia* in Chapter 5.

56. Staniloae, op. cit., 67.

Negative approach of Chalcedon

The Chalcedonian description of the union between the two natures of Christ is stated in negative terms. That is because the fathers sought thereby to avoid major mistakes that the human mind tends to make in attempting to describe how Christ can be God and man at the same time. The fathers never described it positively, for they realized that it is beyond the descriptive powers of the limited human understanding to do so. But what they did do was to set up 'road blocks' to keep believers from going down speculative trails that would lead them into false conceptions of who Christ was; conceptions that would finally destroy the Gospel.

To present a doctrine of Jesus Christ that was based upon the teachings of Holy Scripture, they denied four things about the personal union between the human and divine natures: they are united *without confusion, without conversion, without division, without separation.* We can take these four negatives in two groups.

(a) The first two, 'without confusion, without conversion,' guard against 'extremes of Alexandrian theology'.[57] (Eutyches, who merged divinity and humanity into one nature: 'monophysite,' carried the concepts of the Catechetical School of Alexandria – which emphasized the oneness within the incarnation – to this unbiblical extreme, which was rejected by the Church).

'Without confusion' denies that one nature is mingled with the other, so that like a chemical solution of two different elements, in their mixture they become something different from either. 'Without conversion' denies that one nature is changed (or 'converted') into the other, so that the human is not changed into divinity, nor divinity into the human, hence abandoning their original constitution as human or divine.

The maintenance of the integrity of each nature in the incarnation, 'without confusion, without conversion' is precisely how humanity becomes redeemed. Torrance shows its soteriological significance:

> It was precisely by remaining what it ever was, that the divine nature was able to save and redeem that which it assumed into oneness with itself. On the other hand, in being assumed, healed and sanctified in the incarnate Son, and so elevated to participation in the divine, human nature also suffered no change, but remained truly and fully human. It was precisely by being kept and maintained in union and communion with the divine, that human nature was redeemed as human. Any transubstantiation of human nature would be its dissolution.[58]

(b) The last two, 'without division, without separation,' guard against extremes of the Antiochene School of Theology, which so emphasized the distinction between the two natures that, at its worst, it tended to divide them into two separate persons. (Nestorius and Theodore of Mopsuestia were thought by many to have made this radical misreading of the incarnation).

---

57. Torrance, op. cit., 208.

58. Ibid.

Torrance explains the soteriological significance of the denial of separation between Christ's two natures by Chalcedon, as they state that the union is 'without separation, without division':

> The act of the Son in humbling himself to take upon himself our humanity in the likeness of the flesh of sin and in the form of a servant, without of course sinning himself, and the act of the perfect obedience of the Son to the Father in the whole course of his human life, his whole participation in the life of God, are not two independent acts or events separated from one another. In all their distinctiveness, they are fully and finally and irrevocably united in being the acts of the one person of the incarnate Son of God. It is precisely in the impossibility of their separation that our redemption lies, for it is redemption into unbreakable union and communion with the Father, and the once and for all exaltation of our human nature in Christ, into the life of eternal God. It is because the incarnate Son and the Father are one, and cannot be divided or separated from one another, that our salvation in Christ is eternally secure in the hand of the Father, for no one can snatch us out of his hand.[59]

Is Chalcedon the triumph of Greek Philosophy over the Biblical Witness to Christ?

Particularly since the eighteenth-century Enlightenment, numbers of scholars have held that in the fourth and fifth centuries, especially in the formula of Chalcedon, the bishops of the Church imposed categories of various aspects of Greek philosophy onto the 'originally simple' biblical teaching on the person and work of Christ, and that, therefore, Chalcedon cannot be accepted as a truly biblical representation of who the incarnate Lord is. Adolph von Harnack was typical of many scholars when he said that Christianity was Hellenized by the Church Fathers, although he does credit Athanasius with keeping the Faith from becoming totally Hellenized.[60]

One can respond in several ways to this serious charge. First, the witness of the New Testament was never 'originally simple'. Even if we, with the historical Church – East and West – accept the inspiration of the Holy Spirit in guiding the New Testament writers to a canonical wholeness in their presentation of Christ and the Trinity, still the complexities and depths and heights of whom they reveal Jesus Christ to be always surpass the measures of the most consecrated human minds, even when they think together in submission to the divine text, and in the atmosphere of piety and prayer. That will be as true with the Gospel of Mark as with John, Romans, and Revelation. While it is possible for the humblest person to know Jesus savingly (and millions always have), still who He is can be 'apprehended, not comprehended' (to borrow from saints such as Hilary and Calvin).

Secondly, therefore, the complexity of Chalcedon is no heavier than that of John 1:1-18 or Philippians 2:5-11, or Revelation chapter 5 (as we

---

59. Ibid., 208,209.

60. Adolph von Harnack, *History of Dogma* (English translation 1897), vol. III, p. 194.

sought to demonstrate in our third chapter). Hence, the issue with the four 'alpha privatives' (without confusion, without conversion, without division, without separation) of Chalcedon cannot justly be their complexity, but rather whether in light of the Scriptures, they can be said to be accurate.

Thirdly, then, do the concepts of 'person' and 'nature,' and the four negatives concerning their union, represent the imposition of some kind of Greek philosophy over essentially 'Hebraic' material (as it was reworked in the Greek of the New Testament), or do they fairly go as far as possible in letting the biblical material speak for itself? No one has ever denied that the Church Fathers used Greek words ('nature' and 'person,' etc.), and that these words were employed in their intellectual culture in certain philosophical contexts. But what else could they have done? The *lingua franca* at that time was Greek, and therefore Church documents had to be issued in the language that was most widely understood.

The issue in question is, of course, not that the Church Fathers used Greek, but whether with that linguistic usage they imported pagan Hellenistic concepts onto biblical material. An illustration of this would be found in the Apostle John's usage of Logos (discussed in chapter 3). The true fact that Philo Judaeus widely used it (as did Heraclitus and later Plato) does not in and of itself settle the question of whether the way John employs it is derived from Holy Scripture, and thus, accurately represents who God is (especially in light of the centrality of Word [*dabar*] in the Old Testament).

T.F. Torrance is to the point here:

> On the one hand, the Greek notion of *logos* (*λογος*) was Christianized by being assimilated into the Old Testament notion of the Word of the Lord (YHVH-DABAR) and the New Testament notion of the Word, who was with God and was God, become flesh in Jesus Christ. In contrast to the Greek idea of the logos as an abstract cosmological principle, it was distinctive of Christian theology, that the Logos inheres in the very being of God (ἐνουσιος λογος) and is identical with the Person of the Son.[61]

It is much the same with the terms *nature, substance* and *person*. I have so far not seen it demonstrated that the quite varied connotations of these words in different strands of Greek thought are ever directly taken over into the official thought of the Church (whether with *homoousios* in the Creed of Nicea, or *hypostasis* and *physis* in Chalcedon) *without a shift in meaning*. If one, for instance, surveys such terms in Plato, Aristotle, Philo and the Stoics, and then lays them side by side with how they are used in the writings of Athanasius, Gregory Nazianzus, and the first four Ecumenical Councils, one will find considerable differences.

Radical Differences between Hellenism and Christianity
At the heart of the profound differences, the Greeks (though not Philo) assume an eternal natural realm (no true creation out of nothing) and thus

---

61. T. F. Torrance, *The Trinitarian Faith*, 72.

a continuity between God and nature. They do not have the concept of the biblical Creator/creature distinction. That alone precludes an accurate representation of who Jesus Christ is, *unless one transforms the meaning of the Greek words one is employing*! That is what happened when the Church Fathers took over several words that bore a very different meaning in the context of the varying Hellenistic 'worldviews' that provided their background. In a word, they 'Christianized' these Greek words, rather than 'Hellenized' the teaching of the Scriptures. This is not to deny that they did take over a number of the philosophical concepts surrounding some of the words; it is only to say that they usually Christianized these concepts in light of the divine revelation. Irenaeus, for example, specifies the difference between Greek philosophical theories of Logos and the Christian understanding of the Word of God, showing how the philosophical usage has to be changed in light of the teaching about God in Holy Scripture.[62]

A much later illustration of the re-appropriation of Hellenic vocabulary would be the use of *logoi* ('words' in the sense of 'seminal reasons') by Maximus Confessor, which takes over some ideas found in Stoic (and Philonic) teaching on λογοι σπερματικοι ('spermatic words or reasons') but shapes them in a direction consistent with John 1:1-18. Another would be the use made by many of the third and fourth century Church Fathers of Stoic logic and epistemology.[63]

Certainly, some of the Christian writers later deemed unorthodox, like Origen, took over large blocks of Greek philosophy without shaping and refining it in terms of clear scriptural teaching (as for example, his acceptance of the pre-existence and transmigration of the soul). But more of them were like the orthodox Cappadocian Father, Gregory of Nyssa, who accepted some Platonist ideas that he did not run through the grid of the Scriptures; yet for the most part, he profoundly Christianized the material he subsumed. For example, his teaching on creation (*Hexameron*) is clearly biblical in a way that runs quite contrary to the various strands of Platonism, Aristotelianism and Stoicism of his day.[64]

The Biblical Creator/creation is directly contrary to Hellenistic Philosophy
All of those philosophies were alike in their own ways, in that they were contrary to Genesis, for they assumed the world to have been eternally existent. But in contradiction to all of Greek thought on this point, Athanasius followed Scripture in denying the eternal coexistence of nature with God.[65]

To derive words and concepts from the Hellenistic intellectual culture around them as tools to bring order and coherence into the complexities

---

62. '... but which Logos, for there is among the Greeks one logos which is the principle that thinks, and another which is the instrument by means of which thought is expressed...But since God is all mind, all reason, all active spirit, all light, and always exists one and the same, it is both beneficial for us to think of God, and as we learn from Him from the Scriptures, such feelings and divisions [of operation] cannot fittingly be ascribed to Him' in Irenaeus, *Adversus Haereses* II.28.4.

63. See vol. 1 of this series, pp. 41-46.

64. See Chapter Six- 'St. Gregory of Nyssa' in Georges Florovsky, op. cit., 146-220.

65. Athanasius, *Contra Arianos* 1.29.

of the biblical testimony to the Trinity and Christ was no easy nor quick task. It took over four centuries before the ground had been prepared for the precision of Chalcedon. There were many false starts and sharp controversies, as well as difficulty in mutual understanding between the Greek-speaking East and the Latin-speaking West (until this was largely worked out in 362, after the Council of Alexandria, led by Athanasius).

Georges Florovsky's assessment is realistic:

> The Church fathers had good reason for devoting so much attention to *problems of terminology*. They were trying to find and establish words which would precisely express, and thus protect, the truths of their faith. *Their concern for terminology was not excessive. A word gives outer form to a thought and verbal precision is necessary for the full expression of intellectual conception.* The patristic theologians tried to formulate their creeds with clarity because they hoped to establish the living traditions of the Church by expressing them in a versatile system of theology. This task was not easily fulfilled and theological speculation in the patristic age developed in many different directions. But all coincided in their basic principles and all were united by the common experience of the Church. 'That is the mystery of the Church, that is the tradition of the fathers.'[66]

Determination of the Fathers to speak according to Scripture

We can see how seriously and carefully the Fathers worked on getting the Greek terms they borrowed transformed into useful, biblical concepts. Cyril of Jerusalem (mid-fourth century), for example, was determined not to go beyond the clear implications of the Scriptures. In the summation given by Florovsky:

> For our salvation it is enough for us to know that there is a Father, a Son, and a Holy Spirit. Nothing has been written about anything else, and it is not fitting for us to speculate beyond what can be found in Scripture 'on the essence of the hypostases.' Thus the Trinitarian theology of Cyril is distinguished by its strict adherence to the Bible, and Cyril constantly strives to support his arguments with quotations from Scripture...[67]

Transformation of Greek words in light of God's Triune Being and Act of Creation

By definition, in light of the profound differences between Greek thought and the holy Scriptural testimony to the Trinity, the Greek terms had to be radically adjusted. Florovsky explains why:

> Since the concepts 'essence' and 'hypostasis' were considered to be identical, there was no word sufficient to express the nature of the 'three' which had been left undefined. The concept of 'person' had not been clearly elaborated at this time, and moreover it was tainted because of its use by the Sabellians. The only way to overcome the indefiniteness of Trinitarian terminology was

---

66. Georges Florovsky, *The Eastern Fathers of the Fourth Century*, volume seven in *The Collected Works of Georges Florovsky* (Buchervertriebsanstalt: Belmont, MA, 1987), 35.

67. Ibid., 65.

by distinguishing and opposing the terms 'essence' and 'hypostasis.' It had to be logically demonstrated that these were not just different words, but distinct concepts...

Both terms had to be defined and established within an integral conceptual system. It was not possible to be satisfied with classical philosophical terminology because its vocabulary was insufficient for theology. Classical terms and concepts had to be reshaped. This task was undertaken by the Cappadocians, and first of all by Basil.[68]

Probably the greatest of the Cappadocians, the one known as 'the theologian', Gregory Nazianzus (late-fourth century) is: 'responsible for developing a theological terminology which is close to Western usage through his identity of hypostasis and person τρεις υποστάσεις ή τρία πρόσωπα.'[69]

T. F. Torrance shows the keen awareness among the Church Fathers of having to shift Greek terms so as to 'Christianize' them: 'However, far from a radical Hellenisation having taken place something very different happened, for in making use of Greek thought-forms Christian theology radically transformed them in making them vehicles of fundamental doctrines and ideas quite alien to Hellenism.'[70] He points out that the unbridgeable differences between the Greek philosophical and biblical world views lay in God as Creator of the universe out of nothing:

> ...and as triune in his eternal being, and not least through the doctrine of the incarnation as the personal and saving intervention of God himself in the affairs of mankind, together with the attendant conceptions of providence, judgment and resurrection. This was one of the most significant features of Nicene theology: not the Hellenising of Christianity but the Christianising of Hellenism, a feature for which the Church was peculiarly indebted to Athanasius.[71]

George Dragas gives two chapters of his *Saint Athanasius of Alexandria* to showing, among other matters, how Athanasius takes over and transforms the Greek terms that the Fathers needed to employ into a Christian context.[72] He shows that the differences were between:

> ...two conceptions of God and two conceptions of man and also two conceptions of God's relation to man....Athanasius and the Alexandrian tradition starting with the reality of the inhominized Logos and making it the clue to the doctrine of God and the doctrine of man, developed the differential relationships between *hypostasis* and *ousia* and between the Being of God and the becoming of man and Creation. Insofar as they did this, they

---

68. Ibid., 91.

69. Ibid., 133.

70. T. F. Torrance, *The Trinitarian Faith*, 68. Torrance devotes an entire chapter to the radical differences between Nicene thought and Hellenic thought as regards the notions of *image (eikwn)*, *word (logos)* and *activity (energeia)*.

71. Ibid.

72. George Dragas, *Saint Athanasius of Alexandria*, Chapters 1 ('Inhomination or He Became Man: a Neglected Aspect of Athanasius' Christology') and 2 ('Nature and Grace'), pp. 1-78.

cut across the tension and opened the orthodox path which rests on the truth of the Divine-human Atonement established in Christ and through Christ in the world.[73]

Much later, in the eighth century, we see John of Damascus carefully sifting through Greek terminology so that he could adjust it to express the details of who Christ is according to the Scriptures. He particularly works through the necessary shift in meaning of such crucial words as 'nature' (*phusis*), 'species' (*eidos*), 'genus' (*genos*), 'hypostasis' (*hypostasis*), and 'essence' (*ousia*), and several others, in his lesser known work, *Dialectica*.[74] He is well aware of what he has to be doing, and this is also seen at large in his most famous work, *De Fide Orthodoxa*.[75]

We may fairly summarize the matter of the Greek terminology used in Chalcedon as follows. Many key words that were useful and needful for the task of expressing, in their own day the good news of who the Son of the Father is, and what he has become **For further development of the** and done for lost humanity, were **doctrine of the hypostatic union** thoughtfully and critically taken over **in the Medieval West, see the** by the Church Fathers. These were **appendix following this chapter.** employed in a thoroughly different context or worldview: that of Christian theology, which reposes on the testimony of the Old and New Testaments.

Hellenistic Philosophy did not know 'the mystery of personal being'

The most basic difference between the Greek philosophical concepts and Christian doctrinal beliefs, concerned the transcendent being of God, who eternally existed in a blessed communion of three persons in one substance, and who had created the world by the word of his power out of nothing. Unlike the way he was perceived in Greek and Eastern thought, God was neither dependent on the world, nor an aspect of it.[76] Nor was he a lonely monad, needing some kind of completion from outside. We could not expect ancient Hellenistic philosophy to have realized that God was more than a solitary monad, for as Florovsky appositely states: '*The classical world did not know the mystery of personal being and in the classical languages there was no word which exactly designated individual personality.*'[77] They could not have known before the Church brought the glad tidings into their culture of the Father sending the Son in the incarnation, and then the outpouring of the Spirit at Pentecost.

But the Church and its teachers now knew and wanted all others to know! Hence, instead of looking to a bare monad, Irenaeus sets forth the

---

73. Ibid., 16-17.

74. *Dialectica* 30 (P.G. XCIV).

75. See for instance, chapter III.

76. Irenaeus briefly summarizes this foundational concept that divides Greek philosophy from biblical revelation: 'For system does not spring out of numbers, but numbers from a system; nor does God derive his being from things made, but things made from God' in *Adversus Haereses* II.24.1.

77. Florovsky, op. cit., 32.

rich diversity of the inner life of God: 'In the first place, [we must] believe not only in the Father, but also in his Son now revealed; for he it is who leads man into fellowship and unity with God.'[78] Later he adds: 'For with him [the Father] were always present the Word and Wisdom, the Son and Spirit, by whom and in whom, freely and spontaneously he made all things...'[79] Similarly, in the fourth century, Hilary similarly stated that 'God is not solitary'.[80]

In a passage that one wishes had been expanded, nineteenth-century Calvinist, John L. Girardeau, raises this question about the mysterious richness of God's inner life: 'Is it venturing too far to say that as all the persons of the Godhead have one and the same spontaneous essence, each person appropriates that essence and energizes peculiarly through it in his peculiar relation to the other persons?'[81] He was not far from what the Fathers of the Church had called *perichoresis* (or 'mutual indwelling' of the three members of the Trinity within one another, while retaining their distinct personalities). The reality of the Triune God has been the great contribution of Biblical faith to the world, and the way we are brought into the saving reality of who God is, is through faith in Christ, in the power of the Holy Spirit. That knowledge constitutes salvation (John 17:3).

Creation and Incarnation exclude Deism

Unlike Enlightenment thought, with its deistic assumptions, God always kept his creation open to himself, so that he could intervene in it as he saw fit, for the Father had originally created 'all things through the Word in the Spirit,' as Athanasius said.[82] And he entered his own handiwork supremely in the miracle of the incarnation, when God the Son became truly man without ceasing to be eternal God. Basil the Great termed this presence of God in the creation 'the royal freedom of the Spirit'.[83] Karl Barth described it as 'the freedom of the Spirit of God' (who makes Christ continually real to the Church) to be present to the world.[84] That freedom establishes the Son's life, death, resurrection, ascension, intercession and second coming as saving actions, constituting the fallen world on a new basis where it could be redeemed from the inside out.

Irenaeus shows that these divine actions form the basis of the universal Church's 'rule of truth'.[85] He further shows that this universal rule of truth

---

78. Ibid., IV.13.1.

79. Ibid., IV.20.1.

80. Hilary, *De Synodis* 37.

81. John L. Girardeau, op. cit., 427.

82. Athanasius, *Ad Serapionem* 3.5.

83. Basil, *On the Spirit* xix. 48 in vol. VIII of Nicene and Post-Nicene Fathers (p. 30).

84. "The Spirit of God is God in his freedom to be present to the creature, and so to create this relation and thereby to be the life of the creature. And God's Spirit, the Holy Spirit, especially in revelation, is God himself in that he can not only come to man but also be in man, and thus open up man and make him capable and ready for himself, and thus to complete his revelation in him' in Barth, *Church Dogmatics* I./1, 450.

85. 'The Church, though dispersed throughout the whole world, even to the ends of the earth, has received from the apostles and their disciples this faith: in one God, the Father Almighty,

is a faithful summary of Holy Scripture: 'Since, therefore, the tradition from the apostles does thus exist in the church, and is permanent among us, let us revert to the Scriptural proof furnished by those apostles who did also write the Gospel, in which they recorded the doctrine regarding God, point out that our Lord Jesus Christ is the truth, and that no lie is in him.'[86]

But contrary to the Holy Scriptures which leave the world constantly open to the interventions of God, a certain type of deistic disjunction between 'the spiritual world' and 'the physical world,' separated by a '*chorismos*' ['disjunction'] is important to the thought of Plato, and a rather different,[87] though not unrelated, type of deistic disjunction is found in the thought of Immanuel Kant in the late eighteenth century, with his restriction of God's being to the realm of 'the noumenal' and that of man and nature to the realm of 'the phenomenal'. According to this still prevalent Kantian disjunction, mankind cannot know who God ('the noumenal') really is in himself, although Kant never denies God's existence.[88]

Above all else, the incarnation of Jesus Christ has bridged the gap that Plato and Kant held to separate God and humankind. In him we truly know God, and in him God saves and uplifts us to share in his own beatific life, a fact in which Irenaeus rejoices:

> For God is powerful in all things, having been seen at that time indeed, prophetically through the Spirit, and seen too, adoptively through the Son; and he shall be also seen paternally in the kingdom of heaven, the Spirit truly preparing man in the Son of God, and the Son leading him to the Father, while the Father too, confers incorruption for eternal life, which comes to every one from the fact of his seeing God. For as those who see the light are within the light, and partake of its brilliancy, even so, those who see God are in God, and receive of his splendour. But his splendour vivifies them; those, therefore, who see God, do receive life…[89]

Maker of heaven and earth and the sea, and of all things that are in them; and in one Christ Jesus, the Son of God, who became incarnate for our salvation; and in the Holy Spirit, who proclaimed through the prophets the dispensations of God and the advents, and the birth from a virgin, and the passion, and the resurrection from the dead, and the ascension into heaven in the flesh of the beloved Christ Jesus, our Lord, and God, and his manifestation from heaven in the glory of the Father 'to gather all things in one,' and to raise up anew all flesh of the whole human race, in order that to Christ Jesus, our Lord and God, and Saviour and King, according to the will of the invisible Father, 'every knee should bow, of things in heaven, and things in earth, and things under the earth, and that every tongue should confess' to him, and that he should execute judgment towards all, that he may send 'spiritual wickedness,' and the angels who transgressed and became apostates, together with the ungodly and unrighteous, and wicked and profane among men, into everlasting fire; but may, in the exercise of his grace, confer immortality on the righteous, and holy, and those who have kept his commandments, and have persevered in his love, some from the beginning, and others from their repentance, and may surround them with everlasting glory' in *Adversus Haereses* I.10.1.

86. Irenaeus, op. cit., III.5.1.

87. In his *Prolegomena to any Future Metaphysics*, intended to be an introduction to *Critique of Pure Reason*, Kant says that Plato left the world of sense for an empty ideal realm, to which the mind had no definite connection, although he agrees partly with Plato's theory of the *a priori* nature of mathematics, B, 16.

88. See chapter VI of this volume for further discussion of Kant's epistemology and its relation to the biblical doctrine of Christ.

89. Irenaeus, op. cit., IV.20.5.

Later, Basil the Great expounds the same theme:

> We understand by Way that *prokope* [cf. Luke 2:52 – on Christ's human advancement] to perfection which is made stage by stage, and in regular order, through the works of righteousness and the illumination of knowledge, ever longing after what is before, and reaching forth unto those things which remain, until we shall have reached the blessed end, the knowledge of God, which the Lord through himself bestows on them that have trusted in him. For our Lord is an essentially good Way where erring and straying are unknown, to that which is essentially good, to the Father. For no one, he says, comes to the Father but through me. Such is our way up to God through the Son.[90]

The Fathers of Chalcedon, working on the basis of the transformed terminology and concepts that Athanasius, the Cappadocians, Cyril of Alexandria and others had previously made available, probably came as close as the redeemed human mind could ever come to expressing with clarity and scriptural fidelity the saving reality of our Mediator's existence as one person in two natures, which constitutes the heart of the Gospel, is our way to the Father, and is the basis of the Church's preaching and mission to the end of time.

Gnostic Heresies represent true Hellenization of Christian concepts

On the contrary, if one wants to see real examples of the total Hellenization of certain forms of 'Christianity', they are not hard to find. Harnack spoke in this fashion, calling Gnosticism 'the acute secularising or hellenising of Christianity.'[91] Irenaeus,[92] Hippolytus,[93] Tertullian,[94] Epiphanius,[95] and others stated frequently that Gnosticism represented

See appendix 2 for a discussion of some of the historical and contemporary applications of Chalcedon.

the transmutation of elements of divine revelation about Christ into totally pagan philosophical thought and life.

---

90. Basil, *De Spiritu Sancto* 16.39.

91. Adolph von Harnack, *History of Dogma*, vol. 1, p.227.

92. See Irenaeus, *Adversus Haereses* 2.14.1-6.

93. Hippolytus traces Gnostic thought to the materialism of Greek philosophy in *Philosophumena* I.9; V.6,9,16-24,32,47; VII.2,13,17, etc. and in Books V–IX exposes some 33 Gnostic sects, seeing them as the later development of pagan concepts.

94. Tertullian called the Greek philosophers 'the patriarchs of heretics' in *De Anima* 3, and speaks similarly in *De Presc.* 7.

95. Epiphanius devotes the earlier parts of his *Panarion* to tracing and refuting some 80 heretical sects. He says that they all descend from 'five mothers': (1) Barbarism, (2) Scythianism, (3) Hellenism, (4) Judaism, and (5) Pythagoreanism – *The Panarion of Epiphanius of Salamis*, Book I (Sects 1-46), translated by Frank Williams (Brill: Leiden, 1997), 4-7. What he says about the authors of Greek mythology would be typical of his view of other pagan writings: 'For the Greek authors, the poets and chroniclers, would invoke a Muse when they undertook some work of mythology. A Muse – not God – their wisdom was demonic, 'earthly, and not descended from above,' as scripture says' (p. 12).

In general, the anti-Gnostic Christian fathers emphasized the Greek philosophical elements lying at the roots of Gnosticism, but they were also aware of other sources. Epiphanius, as we saw immediately above, mentioned not only Greek philosophical thought, but also 'Barbarism,'[96] 'Scythianism,'[97] 'Hellenism'[98] and elements of Judaism.[99] Hippolytus discussed pagan sources as far afield as Celtic Druidism and Indian Brahmanism.[100]

The discoveries of the massive literary remains of Gnosticism at Nag Hammadi in 1945 has, to some degree, confirmed the wide range of sources of thought, and the general correctness of what the Church Fathers reported on the Gnostic shape of theology, hostile though they were to the heretics.[101] Hans Jonas, the great twentieth-century expert on Gnosticism, saw a major aspect of it as a Christian heresy, but also affirmed the existence of a *pre-Christian Jewish* and a *Hellenistic pagan* Gnosticism.[102] However varied its sources, Gnosticism was 'a product of syncretism',[103] and took its bearings from a wide variety of pagan constructions. For all its bewildering developments, it was clearly pagan, not biblical and Christian.

And Athanasius often said that Arianism was its own sort of paganism, which in deistic fashion (although the word was not used by him, the concept is present) so radically separated God from the world, that his Son could not come into it and remain God. Therefore, Christ was only a creature, although the highest of them. In some sense they claimed to worship Christ, whom they said was finally only a creature. This, pointed out Athanasius, was idolatry.[104]

The usage of many aspects of Hellenistic thought, therefore, with all the important technical words it contributed to the development of Christian

---

96. By this Epiphanius refers to the disobedient concepts and lives of fallen humanity between Adam and Noah – *Panarion*, section 1 (pp.13-14).

97. By this Epiphanius refers to the corruption of the original faith between Noah and Abraham, by way of the dispersion of the nations at the Tower of Babel – *Panarion*, section 2 (pp. 15-16).

98. By this he refers to Egyptians, Babylonians, Assyrians and others, some of whose descendants came to ancient Greece, characterized by 'fornication, thinking on idols' (op. cit., section 3.9 – generally pp. 16-18).

99. Here he gives a fairly thin discussion of the line of Abraham down to Moses (op. cit., section 4, pp. 18-19), and immediately jumps back to the origins of Greek mystery religions. Throughout the rest of section 1, Epiphanius goes back and forth between various pre-Christian forms of idolatry.

100. See *Philosophumena* Book I.

101. Frank Williams (translator of Epiphanius' *Panarion*) deems that: 'Insofar as Nag Hammadi is an indicator, Epiphanius may be termed a fairly reliable reporter of the content of certain aspects of that ancient Christian thought which the mainstream judged heterodox. Epiphanius misrepresents the Gnostics less in his account of their content than in what he says of their spirit and motivation' in 'Introduction' to *The Panarion of Epiphanius of Salamis: Book I (Sects 1-46)* (Brill: Leiden, 1997), xxi.

102. Hans Jonas, *The Message of the Alien God & the Beginnings of Christianity: The Gnostic Religion*, Third edition (Beacon Press: Boston, 2005 reprint), 33.

103. Ibid.

104. See Athanasius' comments on Arian idolatry in *Contra Arianos*, where he says that they 'Abandon the worship of the Creator, and then worship a creature and a work' (I.3.8), and suggests that they mimic the Stoics (who were some sort of pantheists): '... resembling the Stoics ... the one drawing out their God into all things' (II. 15.11).

Trinitarian theology, did not represent the transmutation of Christian doctrine into a Greek mould. Rather, the Church Fathers transformed the Greek terms into instruments that, filled with biblical content, were bearers of the doctrine of the Father, the Son and the Holy Spirit: three persons, one God, who have intervened to save a lost humanity through the Gospel.

Wolfson's Theory of the Philonic Background of Trinitarian Theology

Yet one major twentieth-century scholar of late Judaic and early Christian thought, Harry A. Wolfson, believed that Philo Judaeus, rather than Hellenistic philosophers (influenced though Philo was by them), was the main source from which the Church Fathers drew their concepts which they then developed into classical Trinitarian dogma.[105] As a careful scholar, Wolfson distinguished, for example, between Philo's concept of Logos and that of Irenaeus,[106] and shows Tertullian's adaptation of the Platonic theory of ideas in the line of Aristotle.[107]

Still Wolfson suggests that the thought of Philo Judaeus was a greater influence on the development of Christian Trinitarianism than was traditional Hellenistic philosophy. He does not think that the New Testament anywhere clearly presents the three co-equal persons of the one eternal Godhead,[108] and he thinks that many Church Fathers identified 'Logos' and 'Spirit.'[109] Wolfson argues, against clear exegetical evidence (see our chapter 3), that:

> The very fact that as late as the fourth century there were those within Christianity who, despite their acceptance of the Epistles of Paul and the Gospel of John, still argued against the divinity of the preexistent Christ shows that there was nothing in these writings which could be taken as conclusive evidence of a belief on the part of Paul and John that the preexistent Christ was God in the literal sense of the term.[110]

Wolfson believes that the fourth and fifth century Church wrought a 'changed conception' of the origins of the preexistent Christ, so that he became in their thought not merely divine, but God, and that 'the Holy Spirit, now definitely distinguished from the preexistent Christ, though not as yet declared to be God, was recognized as an object of worship and adoration by the side of God and the Logos.'[111] Accordingly, '...the Fathers found themselves confronted with a new problem, the problem

---

105. Wolfson discusses this process of the Fathers taking over, one way or another, and often changing, one way or another, Platonist ideas in his Chapter XIII – 'The Logos and the Platonic Ideas,' in Harry A. Wolfson, *The Philosophy of the Church Fathers: Faith, Trinity, Incarnation*, Third Edition, Revised (Harvard University Press: Cambridge, Massachusetts, 1976), 257-86.

106. Wolfson, op. cit., 263.

107. Ibid., 263-267.

108. He holds that in the fourth Gospel 'there is a Trinity of God, Christ, and the Holy Spirit both after the birth of Jesus and after his resurrection,' but questions whether such a Trinity was thought of before the birth of Jesus (Wolfson, op. cit., 182).

109. Ibid., chapter XI (pp. 183-256).

110. Ibid., 306-307.

111. Ibid., 307-308.

of how to reconcile their new Christian belief in three Gods with their inherited Jewish belief in one God.'[112] In order to handle this problem, Wolfson claims that the Fathers primarily turned to the philosophy of Philo to reconcile one and three.[113]

The Fathers of the Church saw their task differently from the way Wolfson describes it

John Romanides, in a review of this volume of Wolfson, got to the point of the utter difference between what the Fathers were really doing in their biblically-based Trinitarian doctrine, and what Wolfson thinks they were doing:

> Dr. Wolfson misses the very foundations of how the Christians themselves viewed the doctrine of the Trinity. The Fathers of the Church never felt that they were commissioned with the task of philosophically constructing a unity out of three Gods. In claiming that God is neither Oneness, nor Unity, nor Simplicity (Gregory of Nyssa, St. Dionysius the Areopagite) one sees the Fathers laughing at those people who think they can set up an arithmetical idol and call it God. Rather the concern of those Fathers was of a purely soteriological nature. They were interested not in uniting Gods to each other but in being themselves united to God. It is one thing to say that God is One and quite another thing to define God as Oneness, Unity, and Simplicity.[114]

Fr. Romanides rightly says that a realistic interpretation of the Church Fathers must place their work in the conceptual context of Old and New Testaments, rather than that of Philo: 'The unity of the Old and New Testaments is not only of a predictive nature…but involves cosmological, anthropological, soteriological and eschatological considerations which contradict Dr. Wolfson's general approach and make questionable his constant emphasis on Philonic influences in the development of Christian dogma.'[115]

At the heart of this radical difference in context, which is not brought to the fore by Wolfson, are:

> …the implications of the Biblical and patristic doctrine of Creation, especially in its cosmological and gnoseological aspects… and his oversight…conditions his whole approach to the mystery of the Trinity. Like all philosophers and logicians outside the soteriological experience in Christ, he is forced to deal with patristic theology by taking seriously for granted the co-ordination of human concepts concerning numerical unity and simplicity with the divine reality, thereby reducing God to the level of conceptual images.[116]

---

112. Ibid., 308.

113. See especially ibid., chapter XV – 'The Mystery of the Trinity' (pp. 305-63).

114. John S. Romanides, 'H. A. Wolfson's Philosophy of the Church Fathers' in *Greek Orthodox Theological Review* … p. 81.

115. Ibid., 63.

116. Ibid., 80.

To ignore the biblical doctrine of creation precludes understanding of the Fathers

Fr. Georges Florovsky, in a review of Dr. Wolfson's book, also focuses our attention on the defining difference between Greek philosophy (including Philo) and the Church Fathers as consisting in the biblical belief in creation, as opposed to an eternally existent world, of which God is a constituent, co-dependent part.[117] Florovsky refers to Etienne Gilson's *History of Christian Philosophy in the Middle Ages*, which showed that the most radical change wrought by Christian philosophy was the 'contingency of creation.' Florovsky then adds:

> Now, the problem of creation was the main *philosophical problem* in the doctrinal or theological disputes of the fourth century, the main philosophical issue between the Arians and the Nicene Trinitarian Orthodoxy of the Fathers. In his interesting analysis of 'the Mystery of the Trinity' (pp. 305-363) Dr. Wolfson avoids this problem. But this was the *philosophical core* of the whole controversy. Was the concept of God primarily a *cosmological* concept, as it seemed to be in the Hellenic philosophy, Philo included, or did this concept have its own independent content? 'Philonic problems' were superseded at this point by new, properly Christian 'patristic problems'.[118]

The basic issue then and today

The basic issue we face in our twenty-first century is not in principle different from that found throughout the first five centuries of the Christian era, nor from the eighteenth-century European Enlightenment, with its continuing philosophical and theological influence. Holy Scripture and the Church Fathers, for all their differences and disagreements, present us with an eternal God who creates at a specific point all things out of nothing, so that they are dependent on him, rather than his being dependent upon them. Hellenistic philosophy, for all its brilliance and frequent truth, views God as an aspect of the natural realm; ultimately as dependent upon it as it is upon him. These are two radically different worldviews. Both cannot be right, and the decision one makes on this foundational doctrine of creation makes all the difference as to how one understands God, humankind, and salvation.

The very Gospel itself calls us to decide between two utterly contrary world views: a Trinitarian one or a deistic one; a God whom we can personally and savingly know through Christ, who lifts us up to share in his own knowledge of the Father in the Holy Spirit, or an absentee, faceless monad, who – whatever he really is – is not available to reveal himself to us, and in so doing, to transform our lives for time and eternity. To come into saving contact with the transforming truth always requires faith, and the Christian Church has safeguarded and passed down this saving faith for some two millennia. Those who feel unable to get out of the secularist assumptions that blind their eyes from seeing 'the lily of

---

117. G. Florovsky, A review of *The Philosophy of the Church Fathers, vol. 1: Faith, Trinity, Incarnation* in *Religion and Life*, Vol. 26, No. 3, Summer, 451-53.

118. Ibid., 452-53.

the valley, the rose of Sharon, the fairest of ten thousand' are invited by a generous and gracious God to call upon him for the gift of his Holy Spirit, who implants and increases that saving faith (cf. Luke 11:9-13).

If we, by divine grace, do that, then we can join the seventeenth-century English Congregationalist theologian, John Owen, and a countless host of saints of every nation and generation, as they love the Lord in terms of both aspects of his hypostatic union in one person:

> …That we may *love him* with a pure unmixed love. It is true, it is the person of Christ as God and man that is the proper and ultimate object of our love towards him; but a clear distinct consideration of his natures and their excellencies is effectual to stir up and draw forth our love towards him. So the spouse in the Canticles, rendering a reason of her intense affection towards him, says that 'he is white and ruddy, the chiefest of ten thousand;' that is, perfect in the beauty of the graces of the Holy Spirit, which rendered him exceeding amiable. So also Ps. xlv. 2. Would you, therefore, propose Christ unto your affections, so as that your love unto him may be sincere and without corruption, as it is required to be, Eph. vi. 24…consider his human nature, as it was rendered beautiful and lovely by the work of the Spirit of God upon it, before described. Do you love him because he was and is so full of grace, so full of holiness, because in him there was an all-fulness of the graces of the Spirit of God?…You are often pressed to direct your love unto the person of Christ…but this you cannot do without a distinct notion and knowledge of him. There are, therefore, three things in general that you are to consider to this purpose: - 1. The *blessed union* of his two natures in the same person… 2. The *uncreated glories* of the divine nature, whence our love hath the same object with that which we owe unto God absolutely. 3. That perfection and *fulness* of grace which dwelt in his human nature, as communicated unto him by the Holy Spirit…If we love the person of Christ, it must be on these considerations…[119]

William Gadsby put these holy desires to music in his hymn: 'Immortal Honours Rest on Jesus' Head':

> O that my soul could love and praise Him more,
> His beauties trace, His majesty adore;
> Live near His heart, upon His bosom lean;
> Obey His voice, and all His will esteem.

---

119. John Owen, *Works: The Holy Spirit* (Edinburgh: The Banner of Truth Trust, reprint, 2009), vol. III, 187-188.

APPENDIX 4.1

EARLY THIRTEENTH-CENTURY DEVELOPMENT OF THE THEOLOGY OF THE HYPOSTATIC UNION IN THE WESTERN CHURCH

Walter H. Principe has translated four volumes that unfold the remarkable research of four Western Catholic theologians concerning the 'hypostatic theology': (1) *William of Auxerre's Theology of the Hypostatic Union;*[1] (2) *Alexander of Hales' Theology of the Hypostatic Union;*[2] (3) *Hugh of Saint-Cher's Theology of the Hypostatic Union;*[3] and (4) *Philip the Chancellor's Theology of the Hypostatic Union.*[4] According to Walter Principe:

William of Auxerre's theology of the Hypostatic Union is dominated by one central intuition:...'his view of the intimacy or unique closeness of the union of the Son of God with human nature: by reason of the Son of God's assuming human nature the Son of God *is* man and man *is* the Son of God.'[5] He also has much to say about 'the grace of union' between Deity and manhood in Christ.[6]

For **Alexander of Hales**: 'The key philosophical questions for the theology of the Hypostatic Union deal with how the individual is constituted in human nature, and in what way the human individual is distinct from the human person.'[7] Alexander says even more about 'the grace of union' than does William of Auxerre, and connects this 'grace' to the Holy Spirit, who is 'the Gift': 'This[8] is a very vigorous idea of the

---

1. Volume 1: *William of Auxerre's Theology of the Hypostatic Union*, translated by Walter H. Principe (Toronto: Pontifical Institute of Mediaeval Studies, 1963).

2. Volume 2: *Alexander of Hales' Theology of the Hypostatic Union*, translated by Walter H. Principe (Toronto: Pontifical Institute of Mediaeval Studies, 1967).

3. Volume 3: *Hugh of Saint-Cher's Theology of the Hypostatic Union*, translated by Walter H. Principe (Toronto: Pontifical Institute of Mediaeval Studies, 1970).

4. Volume 4: *Philip the Chancellor's Theology of the Hypostatic Union*, translated by Walter H. Principe (Toronto: Pontifical Institute of Mediaeval Studies, 1975).

5. Volume 1: *William of Auxerre...*, 134.

6. cf. Ibid., 105-109.

7. Volume 2: *Alexander of Hales...*, 57.

8. [i.e. a quotation from Augustine]: 'Augustinus, *De vocatione sanctorum*: 'Ea gratia fit ab initio fidei homo quicumque christianus, qua gratia ille homo ab initio factus est Christus,' to which Alexander adds: 'Dicendum quod gratia dicitur ibi Spiritus Sancti virtus, qua conceptus est de

grace of union; in this view it is a grace that made man God in that it is the gift of God as the very efficient activity by which God achieves the union in reality, and not only as God's will to give the gift.'[9] So while Alexander teaches that grace comes to us through the incarnation of Christ, his concern is not so much the activities carried out through the states of Christ, but rather how the natures and person fit together. To that end he discusses the 'communicatio idiomatum' (which he refers to as 'communication of properties').[10]

Hugh of Saint-Cher also concentrates on the issues involved in the *being* of the incarnate Christ, rather than on his salvific *activities* (although he assumes those). In particular, he discusses the three options raised by Peter Lombard in Book III of his *Sentences* concerning how Christ assumed human nature: (1) the Son of God assumed a man; (2) the Son of God assumed the nature of a man, or (3) the Son of God assumed a body and soul not as parts of himself, but as his garment.[11] The first is called the 'Assumptus Theory', the second is called the 'Subsistence Theory', and the third is called the 'Habitus Theory'. The third is considered heretical, the first was generally not followed, while the second (the 'Subsistence Theory') was affirmed as true.

According to Walter Principe:

> The first opinion maintained that Christ is two and that in the triduum [this refers to the 3 days when Christ was in the tomb] of his death he was not a man because there was no union between his soul and body – for this opinion, only such a union would make him man; the second opinion held that Christ is only one, but agreed with the first opinion, and for the same reason, that he was not man in the triduum of his death; the third opinion held that Christ, by assuming a body and soul like a garment, is called man in the sense of being 'humanized' (*humanatus*), and that Christ was man in the triduum in the way that he always was man, that is, as humanized. Hugh adds that although the third opinion is heretical, its teaching about Christ's being man in the triduum falls short of heresy; in his opinion, however, this last teaching is false.[12]

Hugh's support of the second opinion (the 'Subsistence Theory') was in the interests of full salvation coming to the human race:

> I say that the Son of God, at the same moment that he created the body and soul, united them to each other: hence, properly speaking, they were neither united nor separated when he assumed them, but at the same instant that he created and united them to each other, he assumed them…by assuming them he made them at the same time a human nature and a nature that was his own.[13]

Virgine,' ibid., 159.

9. Ibid., 159.

10. Ibid., 209-214.

11. Volume 3: *Hugh of Saint-Cher…*, 59.

12. Ibid., 60.

13. Ibid., 70, quoting Hugh, *Scriptum super Sententiis*, III, 5, 107.

Like his three predecessors listed above, **Philip the Chancellor** gave nearly all of his attention to the questions of being raised by the hypostatic union: i.e. nature, person, with particular reference to 'composed hypostasis'.[14]

> Thus for Philip the Chancellor the 'composed hypostasis' stands forth as his most basic approach to the mode of union in Christ. It expresses for him the twofold aspect of the divine hypostasis of the Word, for it considers him as 'standing under' the two natures, that is, now as a person of divine nature, now as a person of human nature...the divine nature remains totally in act and a whole, whereas the human nature is perfected by being united and by having the divine person in it as its hypostasis.[15]

Like the others, Philip's interest is in how this union takes place, rather than the saving works accomplished in the union. Nevertheless, he holds so strongly to the necessity of a correct understanding of the hypostatic union precisely because it is the way we are redeemed. As Principe says:

> Thus, in summary, once the Incarnation is ordained by God, it is necessary, and although, as an event, it is in itself contingent, it has a certain necessity with respect to God's well-ordered power, that is, with respect to God's ordaining the Incarnation as the wisest means suited to man's redemption.[16]

---

14. Volume 4: *Philip the Chancellor's Theology of the Hypostatic Union* (Toronto: The Pontifical Institute of Mediaeval Studies, 1975), translated by Walter H. Principe, 90-105.

15. Ibid., 105.

16. Ibid., 73.

APPENDIX 4.2

HISTORICAL AND CONTEMPORARY APPLICATION OF CHALCEDON

The abiding importance of the principles of Chalcedon for human liberty in the face of governmental tendencies to exercise control over all aspects of life has been suscinctly underlined by Pierre Courthial of the Reformed Church in twentieth-century France. He sees these principles as the only viable alternative to the attitudes and structures that various forms of what we now call secular humanism has, over the ages, and in different ways, sought to impose on society. He writes:

> The contemporary application of Chalcedon is not only 'theological.' Its [wholesome] foundational bearing is to be found in all domains: cultural, philosophical, political, etc. And its wide-ranging nature is simply because *the salvation* that Jesus Christ brings is *just as universal as is sin*, which has covered everything, and in so doing, has penetrated and corrupted every aspect of created reality.
>
> Since the personal (or hypostatic) union of God and man in Jesus Christ is *unique* and a once-for-all reality, no other man and no other human institution (even the Church, which is the mystical body of Christ; even the State, which has been established by God) has the right to seek some sort of divinity for itself. Since there is a God-man: Jesus Christ, there can be neither a deified Church nor a deified State. *This man alone*: Christ Jesus is truly God, and in him and in his person, since the two natures – divine and human – are united, they are united in a way that precludes either confusion between the two natures, or the transformation of one into the other. How much more is it impossible for this same reason, for such realities as Church, State, science, and work – beautiful and necessary as they are when they are faithful to their calling – to become divinized; it is immoral for them ever to seek to take on Godhood!
>
> It is not only within the ecclesiastical institution (which, by the way, must not be confused with the Church – the mystical body of Christ!), but in all areas of his existence and thought, that mankind needs to be saved; he needs to be saved from the evil one, from sin, and from the corruption of death. Certainly, nothing is by definition profane, for even if everything is sinful in actuality, everything is called to be 'Christified' [i.e. Courthial

means something like: 'to become transformed – in its own appropriate and peculiar way – in terms of the character of Christ']; that is to say to be justified and sanctified in Jesus Christ; this Saviour has the lordly right to say of everything: 'This belongs to me!'

But this 'Christification' of a human reality, in whatever domain it may be, never constitutes deification. In our epoch, where people speak everywhere – with lack of precision – of 'secularization', Chalcedon stands more than ever against all this secularization, and as well, in corollary fashion, is also against every possible and pretended deification. Chalcedon is, more than ever, massively relevant: it teaches us neither confusion (of human and divine), nor transformation (of human into divine), nor separation between that which is of the Creator, and that which is of the creature!

During the first centuries of our Era, the Church faced an imperial State which made itself divine. The worship of Caesar was not at that time an empty theory; there were large numbers of martyrs, who stood against it, [and thereby showed what it was].

During the thousand year Medieval Period, it was the European States who, in their turn, had to stand against a Church which made itself divine; pretending, by the way, to govern by its sovereign pontiff, a State, that was as suzerain over the other States. Today, a growing number of States (whether they are right-wing or left-wing makes no difference to this point!) understand themselves to be in charge of everything: that is, they are becoming more and more totalitarian, with the aquiesence and complicity, and at times – even with the insistence – of a large number of citizens. From this perspective, the State encompasses every domain of human existence, and all humans derive their various rights only from this State alone.

Against all these 'religious' pretensions of a political humanism, as well as that of an ecclesiastical one, Chalcedon directly faces and confesses Him who is Lord, and has, by right, all power in heaven and *on earth* because this person, truly man, is – and He alone – truly God.

The foundation of all the liberties, and of all true and legitimate acts of liberation in every possible realm, is in Him to whom Chalcedon faithfully witnesses on the basis of Holy Scripture. Before Him, all the pretensions of humankind and of human institutions to exercise an *autonomous* authority melt into nothingness.

When Churches, to their own condemnation and detriment, reject Chalcedon, they reject at the same time, the sovereignty of the Triune God and of His Word, over the history of the world and the existence of mankind, and by that token, become complicit with the humanists who wish (and think) that they are 'remaking history' in sovereign fashion, by confiscating the liberties of people and in manipulating their lives.

But on the other hand, the mysterious sovereignty of the thrice holy God *establishes* liberty and the freedoms of mankind, and these liberties proceed only from Him, according to whose eternal and immutable plan, the pretended autonomous and arbitrary sovereignty of humans only tends to *suppress* people's liberties (although they do so in the name of the concept of 'liberty.')

Those 'Christians' who reject Chalcedon will inevitably wind up having only a false Christ, who only has the word Christ; a Christ submerged in temporal history, and confounded with it; a 'Christ' who is no longer the true God who made Himself man, truly man by love and by grace. Instead, they will have 'the man' who is the symbol of an imagined humanity – who makes himself God by pride. Thus, for the true Jesus Christ, for the historical Jesus of the Bible, is substituted some pseudo-Christ of the religion of humanism. This pretended 'demythologization' of Christ Jesus of the Holy Scriptures winds up in fact by replacing the true Christ of Scripture by some form of humanism, according to the ideas and powers of such and such an epoch.

In the one Person of Christ – truly God and truly man – the divine creative and legislative nature is not confounded with that of created and obedient human nature. The perfect law of God is thus revealed to us as much in the sovereignty of Him who ordains as in the obedience of Him who submits Himself to the divine will that He recognizes as being above His own. The union of the *two natures* exists thus in its totality without transformation or confusion.

Our existence as free and responsible men (but not 'autonomous'!) only has reality and makes sense, because they depend, for judgment and for grace, for grace and for judgment, on God alone; hence they do not depend on chance, or necessity, nor on the State or the Church; nothing other than God can deprive us of our dignity as creature-images of God, marred by sin, but called to salvation which is in Jesus Christ.

The contemporary Church finds herself facing a choice: it is between *differing utopian sorts of salvation*, which humanism once again sets before us, and *the salvation* that is offered us and ours, in the Word of God, which is the Christ confessed by Chalcedon.[1]

R. J. Rushdoony, a twentieth-century American theologian of Reformed background, wrote extensively on the implications of Chalcedon as the only antidote to ever-increasing secularist statism. Particularly in his later works (after the 1970s), he wrote from a theonomic perspective (i.e., essentially calling for the imposition of Old Testament Law – except for the Jewish ceremonial law – upon post-New Testament Churches and States). Theonomy has not been accepted by any of the churches in any of the varying historical traditions that I know of. But apart from the theonomic theory, some of Rushdoony's writings do provide a number of insights into the Christian alternative to statism.

In particular, one could mention here two earlier works of Rushdoony that do not yet really appear to have been based on the theonomic theory: *The Foundations of Social Order: Studies in the Creeds and Councils of the Early Church* (Presbyterian and Reformed Publishing Company: Nutley, New Jersey, 1968), and also, his *Politics of Guilt and Pity* (The Craig Press: Nutley, New Jersey, 1970). One aspect of both books is to seek to apply the principles of the Creed of Chalcedon to a healthy balance between order and freedom in human society, in a non-statist way, with reference to the last two thousand years of history, as well as to the contemporary problems of the Post-Enlightenment West.

From a different perspective, which includes much insight, one could mention Colin Gunton's 1992 Bampton Lectures: *The One, the Three and the Many: God, Creation and the Culture of Modernity* (Cambridge University Press: Cambridge, 1993).

---

1. Pierre Courthial, *Ichthus*, No. 116 (1983), 30-32 (my translation).

A very different kind of book – a collection of wide-ranging essays dealing with modern societal problems and combats in the Canton of Vaud (in Switzerland) – was written by Jean-Marc Berthoud: *L'École et la Famille Contra L' Utopie: Les annales d'un combat* (*Messages* L' Age D' Homme: Lausanne, 1997). This volume is a collection of a number of articles that he wrote in various periodicals and reviews (of the French language) from the 1970s to the 1990s. Although they usually deal with particularities (specifically, those in Switzerland), and come from controversies that occurred some decades ago, in the last third of the twentieth century, they are fresh and up-to-date, and applicatory in many another country and culture, because he traces the problems of the late twentieth century in his own homeland down to their roots, and in so doing, seeks to provide answers, especially in terms of who Christ is in Scripture, and the breadth and depth of his Lordship, and in so doing, he – I think – seeks to base his analysis and answers upon the Council of Chalcedon.

Now, he does not give a full historical or theological discussion of Chalcedon (though he could well have done so), but in his grasp of its teaching that humanity and deity are united in the one Person of Christ, without transformation of one into the other, or without separation of one from the other, he illumines the bitter roots of many modern societal diseases, and offers a gracious alternative (that is, at the same time, presented always vigorously and sometimes combatively). It is a presentation that, in general, is relevant in all countries.

In his leadership of 'L'Association de Parents chrétiens', he led over the years its concerned parents and other members, who were committed to the authority of Holy Scripture, in thinking through and answering the secularist and immoralist direction in which Switzerland (like the rest of Western society) was traveling. His essays are grouped within three parts of the book: I. *The Family*, II. *The School*, and III. *The Foundations of Society*.

A typical comment that shows his Chalcedonian theology (and the social order it has engendered) is the following (in the context of the family as a divinely created institution):

> ...The diversity in unity, which characterizes all the creatures of God and all aspects of his creation, is equally proper to human thought itself. For this thought, and the languages in which it is expressed, is constituted in an equilibrium that is constantly found in its concepts – which have a universal character – tied to realities that are quite particular and concrete. These realities, at the same time, both one and diverse, specifically reflect the nature of the Creator God. For the God of the Bible, the Triune God, is One [in Being] and exists in Three [distinct] divine Persons, and this Oneness and Trinitarian [co-existence] is without confusion, without transformation, without separation, without division, to borrow terms from the Council of Chalcedon. If even the nature of man, which is a living image of God, makes us understand why biblical anthropomorphisms (by means of which God is compared to man), are an integral part of Revelation, it [naturally] causes us to pay close attention to the bearings of the text of the Epistle to the Ephesians

which we have just cited, and which attest to the character - to express its true meaning - *familial*, reposing on eternal relationships between the three Persons of the divine Being (p. 5).

It is doubtful that all of our readers will agree with all that he says, but in these 'Tracts for the Times', they will find – I believe – the authentic spirit of the Council of Chalcedon in terms of the challenges of our own generation.

CHAPTER 5

QUESTIONS RAISED BY THE HYPOSTATIC UNION

Granted that the Incarnation of the Son of God is, as some have called it, 'the miracle of miracles,' in which the eternal One enters into time and becomes part of it, while remaining eternal, can we be surprised that we are confronted on every hand with mysteries that stretch the normal categories of the time-bound human mind? Given the absolute uniqueness of the hypostatic union of a divine and a human nature in one person, in which God the Son becomes man while at the same time remaining God, and thus the Creator becomes a creature without ceasing to be the agent of creation, it can come as no surprise that such a stupendous event altogether surpasses the limits of our human understanding (though it does not go against it), and raises profound and difficult questions, perhaps among the most complex concepts that have ever passed through the human mind. The Church as part and parcel of her doctrinal and missional task, has over the centuries sought to answer, as best she could, on the basis of Holy Scripture and relevant Creeds, the most central of these questions. In this chapter we shall address a number of these questions, and the Church's answers, drawn from her long meditation on many passages of Scripture: (1) 'extra-Calvinisticum'; (2) *Theotokos*; (3) anhypostasia; (4) enhypostasia; (5) communicatio idiomatum; (6) communio naturarum; (7) two wills in Christ; (8) the temptability of Christ, and (9) the ignorance of Christ. We must also look at (10) major Christological heresies that disturbed the Church, and were answered by her: such as (a) Ebionitism; (b) Docetism; (c) Gnosticism, and (d) Apollinarianism. Some of these heretical ideas have a way of periodically returning, and thus we need to remember what was and is involved in defective views of Christ, as a way of continual fidelity to 'the faith once delivered,' a fidelity that enlightens and enlivens the daily presentation of the Gospel to the world. This good news brings those who believe it to share in the peace and beauty of the life of the Trinity.

I. 'EXTRA-CALVINISTICUM'

This is a way of asserting that while 'Immanuel' is 'God *with us*,' during the time he is with us, *he remains truly and fully God.* Therefore, he does not abandon his cosmic functions during the time when he is with us as truly and fully man. Here, we may well exclaim with Paul: 'For we know in part, and we prophesy in part...' (I Cor. 13:9)! And we remember that our limited human minds are never the measure of the all-surpassing greatness of God's being.

This word was coined by some of the sixteenth-century Lutherans: 'the Calvinistic extra,' to indicate Calvin's teaching that something about the second Person of the Trinity was not fully included in the incarnate flesh of Christ: that is, there was an 'extra' reality that was not reducible to the body of Christ during his incarnation. Of course, John Calvin, as we shall see, did not originate this ancient teaching; he found it in the Church Fathers of the early centuries, and he and they believed that it was set forth by various New Testament passages. As Heiko Oberman rightly stated: 'What would later be called the *extra calvinisticum* –the existence of the second *person* of the Trinity *et extra carnem*...[was] erroneously seen as an innovation on the part of John Calvin...' [1]

Calvin described it as follows:

> Although the boundless essence of the Word was united with human nature into one person, nevertheless we do not imagine there to be any enclosing of the Word in it. The Son of God descended miraculously from heaven, yet without abandoning heaven; was pleased to be conceived miraculously in the virgin's womb, to live on earth, to hang on the cross, in such a way that he always filled the world as from the beginning.[2]

Biblical references

The last verse in the Prologue to John's Gospel (John 1:18) clearly implies that the Logos remains transcendent (or *'extra'*) to the body Christ took on: '...the only begotten Son, which is in the bosom of the Father, he hath declared him [i.e. 'exegeted' him, or 'brought him out']'. In other words, the Logos (Son) truly 'brings out' the reality of the Father by means of his incarnation, yet all the while he is incarnate upon earth, he still abides with the Father in heaven. He is fully and truly incarnate, but at the same time remains transcendent.

The same assumption is conveyed by Colossians 1:15-17: 'Who is the image of the invisible God, the firstborn of every creature: for by him were all things created, that are in heaven, and that are in earth, visible and invisible...And he is before all things, and by him all things consist.' 'Consist' seems to mean here 'hold together' [συνεστηκεν]. The Logos, or Son of God, always holds the elements of the world together, even during his incarnation. Archbishop William Temple raised the right question

1. Heiko A. Oberman, *The Harvest of Medieval Theology* (The Labyrinth Press: Durham, North Carolina, 1983), 265.

2. John Calvin, *Institutes*, II.13.4.

concerning the consequences of denying this mystery: what would have happened to the universe, which is held together by the Second Person of the Trinity, if he had abandoned his cosmic functions during the incarnation?[3]

We have previously made reference to various passages in the Church Fathers of the early centuries which convey their teaching of what became known as 'extra-Calvinisticum', and need not repeat it all here,[4] beyond one apposite quotation from Athanasius: 'Thus even while present in a human body and Himself quickening it, He was, without inconsistency, quickening the universe as well, and was in every process of nature, and was outside the whole, and while known from the body of His works, He was none the less manifest from the working of the universe as well.'[5]

Also, the same section of our volume I discusses T. F. Torrance's explanation of the Lutheran resistance to this mystery in terms of their 'container' (or 'receptacle') notion of space. But on the contrary, the Church Fathers, and Calvin in their train, held that God is related to space not spatially, but in terms of power.[6] And Christ, remaining God even while he has become man, is primarily related to bodies and space, not in terms of their limitations, but in terms of his continuous, infinite power. That kind of never-diminishing, infinite greatness was essential to the work of the salvation of the lost human race from the inside out, and to the glorious renewal of the entire cosmos from the inside out.

As the leading theological textbook of the Medieval universities (from the twelfth century until the Reformation), Peter Lombard's *Sentences* summarizes succinctly the transcendence of the Word to his incarnate body:

THAT THE WHOLE CHRIST IS EVERYWHERE, YET NOT WHOLLY, JUST AS HE IS WHOLE MAN OR GOD, YET NOT WHOLLY. In any case, the whole Christ was at the same time in hell, in heaven, and everywhere. For that eternal person was not greater where he had both body and soul united to himself than where he had only one of them; nor was he greater where he had both together or only one of them united to himself, than where he had neither of them. And so Christ was whole and perfect everywhere. – AUGUSTINE, IN THE *EXPOSITION OF FAITH AGAINST FELICIAN*. Hence Augustine: 'Christ did not abandon the Father when he came into the Virgin: he was everywhere whole, everywhere perfect. And so at one and the same time he was whole in hell, whole in heaven. In the netherworld, he was the resurrection of the dead; in the heavens, he was the life of the living. Truly dead, truly alive: in him, the acceptance of mortality drew our death, and the Godhead did not give up life.'[7] 'And so

---

3. William Temple, *Christus Veritas* (London: Macmillan Co., 1934), 42ff.

4. Douglas Kelly, *Systematic Theology*, vol. 1, 218-21.

5. Athanasius, *De Incarnatione* 17. 2.

6. For details, see T.F. Torrance, *Space, Time, and Incarnation* (Oxford University Press, 1969)

7. While Lombard thought he was quoting Augustine, the reference actually came from Vigilius of Thaspe, *Contra Felicianum*, c. 14, according to Giulio Silano, translator of Book 3 of Peter

the Son of God did not bear death in his soul, nor suffer it in his majesty; but only by participation'[8] in infirmity 'was the King of glory crucified'.[9]

II. THEOTOKOS (GOD-BEARER)

This compound Greek word (God-bearer) helped the church grasp, to some degree, how the eternal Logos (or Son) took on human flesh in the womb of the Virgin, while still remaining God, between his miraculous conception and birth, and ever afterwards, as our divine/human mediator. The Gospels of Matthew and Luke show that the transcendent Logos took on true human flesh through the miraculous action of God within the womb of the Virgin Mary (cf. Matthew 1:18-25; Luke 1:26-56; 2:21). Without specifically using the word θεοτοκος here, Athanasius conveys the same point: 'For being Himself Mighty and Artificer of everything, He prepares the body in the Virgin as a temple unto Himself, and makes it His very own as an instrument, in it manifested, and in it dwelling.'[10]

The ecumenical councils of Ephesus (431) and Chalcedon (451) introduced the formula θεοτοκος, as Karl Barth shows, to maintain at the same time both the true deity of Him whose Father is God, not any man, and also the true humanity of him who was born of Mary, who bore the God/man (and was thus *Godbearer*):

> But it was the second motif [i.e. his true humanity], the identity of Him born of Mary with Him born of the Father in eternity (in opposition to the Nestorian distinction of a twofold Christ) that led to the subsequent dogmatizing of the formula θεοτοκος, *Dei genitrix*, at the Council of Ephesus in 431…confirmed by the Council of Chalcedon in 451.[11] What is expressed by *θεοτόκος* cannot be better described than in Luther's words: *Peperit (Maria) non separatum hominem, quasi seorsim ipsa haberet filium et seorsim Deus sum Filium. Sed eundem quem ab aeterno Deus genuit, peperit ipsa in tempore* (*Enarr. 53, cap. Esaiae* 1550 E. A. *ex op. lat.* 23, 476). Luther himself, therefore, had no hesitation in using this description of Mary; not only in his exposition of the Magnificat (1521) but also in his sermons we continually find incidental use of 'mother of God.' Zwingli, too, (*Christ. fidei expos.* 1536), declares expressly: (*virginem) deiparam θεοτόκος appellari justo vocabulo et iudicamus et probamus*. It is different with Calvin, who, so far as I see, rejects Nestorianism and insists that in Luke 1:43 *virgo ipsa mater Domini nostri appellatur* (*Instit.* II. 14.4), but even in his explanations of this passage (*C. R.* 73, 35; 74, 106 f.) avoids, if he does not contest the *θεοτόκος* or any similar expression about Mary. Lutheran

---

Lombard's *The Sentences: On the Incarnation of the Word* (Pontifical Institute of Mediaeval Studies: Toronto, 2010), 95, note 1.

8. Vigilius of Thaspe, ibid., c. 16.

9. Augustine, *De Trinitate*, bk. 1. c13 n. 28, quoted in Silano's translation of Book 3 of *The Sentences* (op. cit.), 95, 96.

10. Athanasius, *De Incarnatione* 8. 3. But Athanasius does mention Mary as 'God-bearer' in *Contra Arianos* III. 33.

11. For the relevant sentence of these Councils, see *Anathema* of Cyril, *can.* 1, in Denzinger No. 113 (for that of Ephesus), and Denzinger No. 148 (for that of Chalcedon).

and Reformed Orthodoxy took sides with Luther and Zwingli and in spite of obvious difficulties in confessional tactics expressly validated the use of θεοτοκος to express the *duplex nativitas* in question.[12]

Calvin's reserve was almost certainly in reaction to the medieval develop-ment of the cult of Mary which threatened to displace the centrality of Christ in the Gospel. Again, what Barth says is to the point:

> It is admitted that the first four centuries do not know either the later dogma of Mary or the later worship of Mary. 'During the first four centuries, alike in the doctrine and in the worship of the Church, the person of Mary as such 'stands' even further in the background' (Scheeben, op. cit. p. 474 f.). Even the θεοτόκος of the Council of Ephesus attributed to Mary absolutely no 'co-operation' in the work of redemption (against F. Heiler, *R. G. G.*, III, 2015).
>
> But all that changed. What had been an annexe to Christology (for that is how the θεοτόκος must be conceived) became the chief proposition of an ever-expanding special 'Mariology' and the dogmatic justification of a luxuriantly unfolding liturgical and ascetic practice with legendary accre-tions. And there is no doubt that the change meant a twisting both of the New Testament witness and of the sound Christological tradition of the first four centuries. However we interpret it, in increasing measure men began to listen to the voice of a stranger, not to the voice of the Word of God, the founder of the Church…[13]

The use of the term θεοτόκος in reference to Mary is, I think, a valid theological statement to express the results of the Virgin Birth through the womb of the highly favored Mary. But we need to keep in mind what Leontius of Byzantium stated, that 'the Holy One who, being born of her, also sanctified her.'[14] Saint Thomas Aquinas did not teach the immaculate conception of the Virgin.[15] In the next century (fourteenth), Duns Scotus did teach this, although he was not the first to have suggested it, for it was mentioned in ninth-century Spain by Paschius Radbertius.[16] In 1992, a Roman Catholic theologian (Canon Roland Walls) and a Protestant theologian (Prof. James B. Torrance) discussed their understanding of what Duns Scotus meant by the immaculate conception.[17]

Pope Alexander VII declared in 1661 in his bull, *Sollicitudo omnium Ecclesiarum* that the Virgin Mary had been kept from the stain of original sin. Pope Pius IX declared her immaculate conception to be an official dogma of the Catholic Church in *Ineffabilis Deus* in 1854. Pope Pius XII declared the bodily assumption of the Virgin Mary in 1950.

---

12. Barth, *Church Dogmatics* II/1, 138,139.

13. Ibid., 141.

14. Leontius of Byzantium, *Adversus Nestorium*, book VI (PG 86a: 1720d).

15. See Thomas Aquinas, *Summa Theologica* III. Q. XXVII 'Of the Sanctification of the Blessed Virgin,' English translation (London: R. & T. Washbourne, Ltd., 1914), 1-18.

16. Paschius Radbertius, *Concerning the Birth of the Virgin* I (PL 120, 1371 C, 1372 A).

17. James B. Torrance and Roland C. Walls, *John Duns Scotus in a Nutshell* (Edinburgh: Handsel Press, 1992).

Without wishing to take anything away from the honors deserved by the highly graced Virgin, I am unable to affirm these Marian additions, since they are not found in the New Testament, and are no part of the proclamation of the apostolic Gospel; indeed, I fear that they can tend to remove the emphasis from Christ himself, and from the one way of salvation offered through faith in him alone. If the imagination of Christians is not constantly tested by the light of the Holy Scriptures, the Gospel can become obscured by a multitude of additions. While this is not so bad as the Modernist Protestant tendency to obscure (or actually lose) the Gospel by subtractions (e.g. denial of the Virgin Birth and bodily resurrection), still it will not withstand the plain teaching of the written Word of God, and should, therefore, not be a part of the official teaching of the Christian Church.

What G. C. Berkouwer observes seems fair and accurate:

> The Reformers did not object to the exalted position of Mary, her unique motherhood as the blessed one among women, but they looked upon the idea of 'cooperation' that played such an important part in the Roman view as the obfuscation of salvation and a devaluation of the divine grace in Jesus Christ. And even if they had been able to get acquainted with the stress laid on the *subordination* of Mary to Christ later on, their fundamental protest would not have been weakened by it.[18]

Nonetheless, with those reservations in view, I am unable to disagree with an important observation in the *Documents of the Second Vatican Council* (much as I have to disagree with many aspects of its teaching) that 'Mary is a model of the Church' (quoting Saint Ambrose), especially in the sense of her profound faith and humble obedience to the Lord, when she replies to the annunciation of the holy angel: 'Behold, the handmaid of the Lord; be it unto me according to thy word' (Luke 1:38).[19] That submissive attitude to the Word of God is always the way forward for every Christian, and for the entire Church to the end of the age.

III. ANHYPOSTASIA

When the Son of God became Immanuel, he did not join himself to a previously existing human person. This is the basic meaning of *anhypostasia*. The word means *'not person'*; that is, the human nature assumed by the Logos had no separate, or previously existing personality before the miracle of the incarnation, when his human nature came into existence for the first time in union with God the Son.[20] The seventeenth century Swiss Reformed theologian Heidegger described it as:

---

18. Gerrit C. Berkouwer, *The Conflict with Rome*, Translated under supervision of David H. Freeman (Philadephia, PA: The Presbyterian and Reformed Publishing Co., 1958), 164, 165.

19. See *The Documents of Vatican II*, Walter M. Abbott, General Editor (Geoffrey Chapman: London-Dublin, 1966), 92.

20. *Anhypostasia* is listed in G. H. W. Lampe's *A Patristic Greek Lexicon* (Oxford: At the Clarendon Press, 1978), as having been used among the Church Fathers, and bearing the meaning (among other possibilities) of 'without independent existence,' p. 164.

The assumption of the human nature into the person of the Son of God, whereby the *Logos*, the Son of God, in the very moment of formation and sanctification assumed the human nature void of an hypostasis of its own into the unity of its own person in order that there might be one and the same hypostasis of the *Logos* assuming and of the human nature assumed, outside of which it neither ever subsists, nor can subsist.[21]

This cuts out any form of adoptionism of a previously existing human person. T. F. Torrance adds this comment:

When the Word was made flesh, God and man were so related that Jesus came to exist as man only so far as he now exists as God. In other words, there is only one Christ, one mediator, one Lord, only one person in Jesus Christ the incarnate Son of God. This one person means that his human nature had *no independent subsistence* or *hypostasis*, no independent centre of personal being….the human nature of Jesus never existed apart from the incarnation of God the Son. At the first moment of the existence of his human nature, it was in hypostatic union with his Godhead.[22]

In the same way, Peter Lombard, quotes Fulgentius (whom he misidentifies as Augustine) in order to affirm the *anhypostasia*: 'The same God took human nature into the unity of his person, who, humbling himself through mercy, filled the womb of the undefiled Virgin from whom he would be born. And so the same God took into his person *the form of a servant* [Phil. 2:7], that is, the nature of a servant.'[23] Also: 'For God the Word did not take the person of a man, but the nature of a man.'[24]

The Puritan John Owen wrote similarly in the seventeenth century concerning Christ's human nature: 'In itself it is anhypostatos – that which hath not a substance of its own, which should give it individuation and distinction from the same nature in any other person. But it hath its subsistence in the person of the Son, which thereby is its own.'[25]

His Oxford colleague, Thomas Goodwin, stated that although Christ became man, '*that man was never a person of itself*, but subsisted from the first in the personality of the second Person: so that Son of Man was never called or accounted a Son of God, of himself, as such; but his Sonship was that of the Person, which he was taken up into.'[26]

D. Staniloae shows how the meaning of the anhypostasia constitutes for our self-centered humanity such good news:

The distinction between Jesus as man and other human persons lies in the fact that as man he is not an autonomous center of acts and reactions. Rather, the human center of these acts and reactions is simultaneously their divine

---

21. Heidegger, XVII, 36, in H. Heppe, *Reformed Dogmatics*, 427.

22. T. F. Torrance, *Incarnation*, 229.

23. Fulgentius, *De fide ad Petrum*, c. 2, n. 28, quoted in P. Lombard, book 3, translated by Silano, p. 18.

24. Fulgentius, op. cit., c. 17 n 58, quoted in ibid.

25. John Owen, *Works*, vol. I, 233.

26. Thomas Goodwin, *Works*, I, *Exposition of Ephesians*, Pt. 1, 26.

center as well as that of his divine acts. His entire human nature has thus been centered not outside God, but within God the Word.

Among human beings there walked a man who is no longer centered in himself, but within God, being – as a Person – identical with God. The relationships of other human beings with this fellow of theirs are not relationships lived outside God, but they are relationships with God himself. Because this Hypostatic center, which surpasses all human centers, has a power attracting toward God and irradiating good, it is our center. A Personal human center that is simultaneously divine has been placed for eternity in the midst of creation.[27]

IV. ENHYPOSTASIA

As Immanuel, the Son of God remained as truly personal as he had been through all eternity, but now that personhood is lived out in human nature. This Greek terms means something like 'made personal within' – that is, the humanity of Christ assumed in his incarnation is given personal quality within the Son, or Word of God. 'At the first moment of the existence of his human nature, it was in hypostatic union with his Godhead. That is, the human nature from the first moment of its existence had its *hypostasis* or personal subsistence *in* the personal subsistence of God the Son. That is the meaning of *en-hypostasis*.'[28]

According to T. F. Torrance (just quoted above), the concept of *enhypostasia* was already used by Cyril of Alexandria in *Contra Theodoretum*.[29] Torrance also indicates that Leontius of Byzantium in the sixth century, in his work against both Nestorians and Eutychians, brought into focus the concept of *enhypostasia*; that is, the human nature of Christ is established in the Person of the Son, and noted that this concept was passed down by John of Damascus' *De Fide Orthodoxa*,[30] further affirmed in Book V of Hooker's *Laws of Ecclesiastical Polity*, and commented on (and drawn together with *anhypostasia*) by the seventeenth-century Reformed theologian, Heidegger (as collected in Heppe's *Reformed Dogmatics*).[31] In the late nineteenth century, Friedrich A. Loofs (1858-1928) conducted research on the significance of the Christological teaching of Leontius, including his understanding of *enhypostasia*.[32]

Karl Barth made considerable usage of the two interrelated concepts of anhypostasia and enhypostasia in his *Church Dogmatics* I/2, and since the time of Barth, these two concepts have been given far more attention than in the Patristic and Medieval periods. Indeed, Bruce Marshall argues

---

27. Dumitru Staniloae, *The Experience of God: Orthodox Dogmatic Theology: vol. 3. The Person of Jesus Christ as God and Savior*, translated and edited by Ioan Ionita (Holy Cross Orthodox Press: Brookline, Mass., 2011), 67.

28. T. F. Torrance, *Incarnation*, 229.

29. Ibid., 84. See Cyril of Alexandria, *Contra Theodoretum*, P G 76, 397C.

30. John of Damascus, *De Fide Orthodoxa* 3.3-9.

31. Heppe, op. cit. 211-12.

32. Friedrich A. Loofs, *Leontius von Byzanz und die gleichnamigen Schriftsteller der grieschen Kirche* (Leipzig: J. C. Hinrichs, 1887), 67-68.

that it was only in the seventeenth-century discussion of Lutheran and Reformed scholastics that these two *terms* became widely used (although their *content* was to some degree known by theologians from the Middle Age).[33]

After quoting J. Wollebius,[34] Barth shows that '*anhypostasis* asserts the negative' (Christ's human nature has no abstract pre-existence of its own), while '[e]*nhypostasis* asserts the positive' ('The divine mode of being gives it existence in the event of the *unio*, and in this way it has a concrete existence of its own').[35] Then Barth enters into a discussion of the differences between the Lutheran and Reformed theologians on these concepts.[36] We will take note of only one issue in this debate. Barth addresses the misunderstanding of some theologians of *anhypostasia*, as though it meant 'without human personality,' which is not its meaning, as we have seen. *Anhypostasia* is most fully explained in conjunction with its twin concept of *enhypostasia*.[37] It took the Church many centuries to put these two words together, for as Torrance noted: 'The ancient Catholic Church never really came to put *anhypostasia* and *enhypostasia* together in full complementarity in that way.'[38] That conjunction would await the sixteenth-century Reformation and the Protestant Orthodoxy that followed it in the seventeenth century (although the content of the truths, if not the precise joining of the words, was always recognized in the Church).

With this later development in view, T. F. Torrance has expressed the central significance of these two related concepts with especial reference to the latter:

> **Enhypostasia asserts**: because of the assumption of humanity by the Son, the human nature of Christ is given existence in the existence of God, and co-exists *in* the divine existence or mode of being (*hypostasis*) – hence *enhypostasis* ('person *in*,' that is, real human person *in* the person of the Son). This means that Jesus had a fully human mind, will, and body, and was in complete possession of all human faculties…[39]

Later, Torrance takes the two concepts together:

> The *anhypostasia* stresses the *general* humanity of Jesus, the human nature assumed by the Son with its *hypostasis* in the Son, but *enhypostasia* stresses the *particular* humanity of the one man Jesus, whose person is not other than the person of the divine Son. Therefore from the *enhypostasis* we have to go back again to the *anhypostasis* and say this: while the Son of God assumed our human nature, and became fully and really like us, nevertheless his full and

---

33. Bruce Marshall, *Christology in Conflict: The Identity of a Saviour in Rahner and Barth* (Oxford: Basil Blackwell, 1987), 194-195.

34. J. Wollebius, *Christ. Theol. Comp.*, 1624, O *c.* 16 *can.* 4,3.

35. Karl Barth, *Church Dogmatics*, I/2, 163.

36. Ibid., 163-165.

37. Ibid., 163-164.

38. Torrance, *The Incarnation*, 84.

39. Ibid.

complete human nature was united to God in a unique way (hypostatically in one person) as our human nature is not, and never will be. Therefore he is unlike us, not unlike us as to the humanity of his human nature, but in the unique union of his human nature to the divine nature in the one person of God the Son. (This is the baffling element in the virgin birth, which tells us that while it is our very human nature he assumed, he did not assume it in the way we share in it, because he took it in a unique relation with his deity). But it is upon the unique, hypostatic relation of his human nature to his divine nature, that the truth of our human nature depends, for it is as we share in his human nature, which is hypostatically united to God, that we are in union and communion with God.[40]

V. COMMUNICATIO IDIOMATUM

The Lord Jesus Christ carries out what are appropriate actions for divine nature and for human nature during his earthly life, through his one incarnate person. The formula of Chalcedon stated that 'the distinction of the natures is in no way destroyed because of the union, but rather the peculiarity [*idioma*] of each nature is preserved.' D. Staniloae rightly pointed out that 'It is due to the common Hypostasis that both the essential unchangeability of the two natures is maintained, communication by means of which their separation is avoided.'[41] That means that each nature, both human and divine, does what is proper to it in communion with the other, through the Person, without being separated from the other.

It took the Church some centuries to work out the precise terminology by which one could correctly attribute the predicates of human properties to the divine person. According to John N. D. Kelly, the rules for doing so were developed out of the twelve anathemas that Cyril of Alexandria directed against Nestorius.[42] A modified form of these rules was issued in the Pact of Reunion that both Cyril and John of Jerusalem signed in 433.[43] The Eastern Orthodox appear to have worked this out in a similar manner by the Third Council of Constantinople in 680-81.[44]

Torrance describes this 'communication of idioms' (or peculiar properties):

> ... because the divine and human natures, acts and qualities are predicated of the one person of Christ, the qualities and acts predicated of the one person in virtue of his divine nature as Son of God, may be predicated of Christ under his human appellation as Son of Man, or son of David. Likewise, acts and qualities predicated of the one person of Christ in virtue of his human nature, may be predicated of Christ under his divine appellation as Son of

---

40. Ibid., 230.

41. Staniloae, op. cit., 90.

42. Cyril of Alexandria, *Against Nestorius* in *A Library of the Fathers of the Holy Catholic Church* (Oxford: James Parker, n.d.), 10.

43. J. N. D. Kelly, *Early Christian Doctrines* (San Francisco: Harper, 1978), 329. For the text of the *Formula of Reunion* see T. H. Bindley, *The Ecumenical Documents of the Faith* (Westport, Conn.: Greenwood Press, 1950), 221.

44. See P. Schaff, *The Creeds of the Greek and Latin Churches* (London: Hodder and Stoughton, 1877), 72.

God. That is because the one person shares equally in the names, properties, acts and experience of both natures…[45]

This 'communication of personal properties' from each nature to the one person is of greatest consequence for Christ's working out of our salvation, in that it required both God and man together at one and the same time to accomplish this infinitely valuable feat. Many passages in the New Testament assume this communication, and show how it gains the salvation of the lost human race.

Fr. Justin Popovitch has drawn several of these texts together:

> It is because of the unity of the Hypostasis, who is the bearer of two natures, that one attributes to the Lord Christ as God the names, the properties and the energies which belong to him according to his humanity, and that one attributes to him reciprocally as man the names, the properties and the energies which belong to him according to his divinity. It is for this reason that Holy Scripture frequently attributes to his divine nature the properties of his human nature, and on the other hand, she often attributes to his human nature the properties of the divine nature. It is in this way that Holy Scripture speaks of the Lord Christ as: '[they]… crucified the Lord of glory' (I Cor. 2:8), and describes him as follows: '… the church of God, which he hath purchased with his own blood' (Acts 20:28); 'And killed the Prince of life…' (Acts 3:15); '… the second man is the Lord from heaven' (I Cor. 15:47); '…we were reconciled to God by the death of his Son…' (Rom. 5:10); 'He [God] that spared not his own Son, but delivered him up for us all' (Rom. 8:32); 'Though he were a Son, yet learned he obedience by the things which he suffered; And being made perfect, he became the author of eternal salvation unto all them that obey him…' (Heb. 5:8, 9). In the same manner the same Scriptures often attribute to the Lord Jesus as Son of Man and as man, the properties which belong to his divine nature, such as: omnipresence ('And no man hath ascended up to heaven, but he that came down from heaven, even the Son of man which is in heaven' – John 3:13); the power to forgive sins (Matt. 9:6; Mark 2:10; Luke 5:24); the eternal divine Sonship (Matt. 16:13, 16); judgment upon the world on the last day of Judgment (John 5:27; Matt. 19:28); the divine glory (John 17:3); divine omnipotence (Matt. 26:64); divine worship (Phil. 2:7-11).[46]

After the Reformation, different understandings of the 'communicatio idiomatum' developed between the Reformed and the Lutherans. The Reformed followed more closely the earlier Catholic teaching that the properties of the two natures coincide in the one person, and only in that way can they be attributed to the other nature. That is, the divine properties are not to be *directly* attributed to the humanity, nor are the human properties to be *directly* attributed to the deity, but rather *indirectly* or *mediately*, in and through the one person in whom each nature is personally established.

Torrance shows the great importance of this understanding for avoiding theories of the transmutation of human nature into deity that violate the biblically foundational Creator/creature distinction:

---

45. Torrance, op. cit., 209-210.

46. J. Popovitch, op. cit., vol. 2, 170-171, (my translation).

God became man in Christ, but man did not, or did not also, become God. In the assumption of man into unity with the divine being, human nature was not divinized, but only raised into union and communion with God. If the divine Son assumed human nature into unity with himself only then to divinize it, then that would mean that he had no sooner condescended to be our brother, than he broke off that brotherhood – the idea of a divinization of the human nature thus makes nonsense of the incarnation and reconciliation.[47]

Lutheran dogmatic teaching, however, went in another direction. It held to a *direct* communication of divine properties to the human nature, and a *direct* communication of human properties to the divine nature (rather than *mediately* through the person, as with the Reformed view). This innovation within Lutheran theology came from Martin Luther's literal interpretation of Christ's words of institution of the Lord's Supper: 'This is my body.' For Christ's body to be literally present in the celebrations of this sacrament on earth, Luther suggested that his risen body was ubiquitous.[48]

In his long and complex discussion of 'This is my body', Luther appears to teach an elevation of Christ's human nature to a sort of exalted status far above what we understand as normal humanity: 'If God and man are one person and the two natures are so united that they belong together more intimately than body and soul, then Christ must also be man wherever he is God. If he is both God and man at one place, why should he not be both man and God at a second place…a third, fourth, or fifth, and so forth, at all places…If we wish to be Christians and think and speak rightly about Christ, we must regard his divinity as extending beyond and above all creatures. Secondly, we must assert that though his humanity is a created thing, yet since it is the only creature so united with God as to constitute it one person with the divinity, it must be higher than all other creatures and above and beyond them, under God alone...since this humanity also is beyond the creatures, it must be wherever God is, without fail…it must be at least in person God and thus exist everywhere that God is.'[49]

Two leading Lutheran theologians after this time, John Brentz and Martin Chemnitz, gave rather different accounts of the 'communicatio idiomatum', as it was said to affect the ubiquity of Christ's human nature. John Brentz held that Christ's two natures were somehow merged into a common person. Hence he taught that divine properties extended to the human nature, including omnipresence: 'Because of this the body of Christ fills the whole universe. The technical term for the omnipresence of Christ's human nature is *ubiquitas*, ubiquity. Because of this ubiquity the body and blood of Christ are present in the Eucharist.'[50]

47. Torrance, op. cit., 222-223.

48. See the discussion of the direction in which this led Lutheran theology in A. B. Bruce, *The Humiliation of Christ: In Its Physical, Ethical and Official Aspects* (Edinburgh: T. & T. Clark, 1876), 85.

49. Martin Luther in *Luther's Works, Volume 37, Word and Sacrament III* (Fortress Press: Philadelphia, 1961), Edited by Robert H. Fischer, 229-230.

50. Alar Laats and Kadri Lääs, 'The Concept of the Communication of the Majesty in the

Martin Chemnitz does not seem to have gone so far, for he held that Christ's human nature is always localized. He held that the 'communicatio idiomatum' was not a permanent extension of divine attributes to the humanity, but rather a use of the human nature by the divine in modes that exceed human limitation.[51] He uses the ancient Patristic concept of *perichoresis* to try to explain the relationship of the two natures (which concept was normally reserved by the Catholic and the Reformed for the intra-Trinitarian relationships): 'Because of the intimate personal union the natures are in some way in communion with each other. Through their mutual interpenetration (περιχωρησις) there takes place the communication of the attributes of the two natures in Christ.'[52]

These two varying streams of thought were, to a degree, brought together by the 1576 *Formula of Concord* (which was considerably influenced by Chemnitz).Their similar affirmations were listed, although their differences were not discussed.[53] W. Pannenburg points out that before that period of time, both Calvin and Melanchthon (Luther's immediate successor, and 'Preceptor of Germany') had agreed with the traditional Catholic teaching of the real transfer of attributes from the two natures of Christ to his person.[54]

The standard doctrinal survey of Lutheran theology by H. Schmid lists three kinds of 'communication of properties' in Lutheran thought:[55]

(i) *The genus idiomaticum* is a reciprocal communication of characteristics by which the properties of either nature belong to the whole person of Christ, so that one can say that 'God died', and 'the man Christ Jesus is almighty'.

(ii) *The genus maiestaticum* which is a communication of the divine majesty to the human flesh assumed by Christ. 'Here the Lutherans affirmed there is no reciprocation, no *genus tapeinoticum*, whereby the divine nature is humbled through the communication to it of properties from the human nature of Christ.'[56]

It is this second aspect that Martin Chemnitz emphasizes. In *The Two Natures of Christ*, he writes: '… we say that the communication of majesty really took place not only in the person but also in the assumed nature, just as the power of shining and burning is communicated to heated iron in a true and actual way, yet without commingling, conversion, or equation.'[57] This last clause shows that Chemnitz was definitely seeking

Theology of Martin Chemnitz,' in Trames, 2002, 6 (56/51), 1, 64 (*Journal of the Humanities and Social Sciences* # 1, 2002).

51. R. L. Ottley, *The Doctrine of the Incarnation* (London: Methuen, 1911), 115.

52. Laats and Lääs, art. cit., 65.

53. *Formula of Concord*, Article VIII. 5.

54. Wolfhart Pannenburg, *Jesus – God and Man* (London: SCM Press, 1968), 298.

55. H. Schmid, *Die Dogmatik* :English translation. *The Doctrinal Theology of the Evangelical Lutheran Church*, 2nd Eng. edition, revised according to the 6th German edition (Philadelphia: Lutheran Publication Society, 1889), 319ff.

56. Torrance, op. cit., 224.

57. Martin Chemnitz, *The Two Natures in Christ* (St. Louis, MO: Concordia Publishing House, English edition 1971), translated by J. A. O. Preus.

to keep within the bounds of Chalcedon, although not all were agreed that he had been successful.[58] Chemnitz had written to that purpose in an earlier chapter of *The Two Natures of Christ* (ch. 4): 'The hypostatic union...is a work of the entire Trinity by which the divine nature in the person of the Son alone assumed from the Virgin Mary a true human nature without transmutation and confusion. The two natures are inseparably connected and from them and in them is established one person in the incarnate Christ, in whom the assumed nature subsists and is sustained.'[59]

(iii) *The genus apotelesmaticum* indicates the co-operation of the two natures in the work of redemption. This is fairly close to the Reformed understanding of the *communicatio idiomatum*. Torrance notes that:

> ...it is the second, even apart from the first, which horrified the Reformed theologians. In a real sense, of course, and not just metaphorically, we must say that God died, and that the man Jesus is almighty, but there are important senses in which we cannot say these things. We must say that God was directly present and active in the death of Christ, and that the Son of God suffered and bore the judgment of our sins in the death of Christ on the cross. We must also say that the human nature is assumed into unity with the divine being of the Son, and that there is now a man on the throne of God...but can we say that the human nature as such is so interpenetrated by divine majesty and power and all the divine attributes, that, in point of fact, its human properties are swallowed up or nullified in the divine – as for example, in the doctrine of the ubiquity or immensity of the body of Christ?[60]

The major problem here is that if Jesus' humanity directly took on divine attributes in itself, then it was no longer fully human, and in that case could not really represent us in what he was doing on the cross, the empty tomb, and on the Father's throne. Instead of representing lowly humankind, he would represent some 'third thing,' somewhere between God and man, though not fully either God or man, and thus our humanity, as such, would not have been atoned for and then lifted up into resurrection life. Hence we humans would still not have been redeemed as humans if his humanity had become merged or transmuted into something else.

Torrance pointed out the negative direction in which this kind of thinking can go, if taken to its logical conclusions (which the original orthodox Lutherans certainly did not do, nor did these faithful Christians foresee where it might lead):

> What kind of humanity is this, to which all the divine attributes can be described? Have we not compromised the true and complete humanity of Christ...then who can stop short of applying all the divine attributes to the humanity of Jesus, and not apply them to humanity in general? Indeed, that is exactly just what German idealistic theology and philosophy did do, so

58. See a fair assessment of this in Laats and Lääs, art. cit., 63-78.

59. Chemnitz, *The Two Natures in Christ*, 72.

60. Torrance, op. cit., 224.

that it is very difficult indeed to dissociate that deification of man which we find in nineteenth century German philosophy, from the Lutheran doctrine of the incarnation in the sixteenth and seventeenth centuries with its attribution of divine properties to human nature.[61]

Theodore Beza, the immediate successor of Calvin in Geneva, wrote to the Lutherans on this point, seeking to demonstrate the serious errors that could follow from this kind of direct communication of divine attributes to the human nature, rather than to the person of Christ.[62] In the same vein, the great antagonist of the Protestant Reformation, Cardinal Robert Bellarmin, also wrote against Lutheran theory of direct communication of divine idioms to the humanity of Christ, with particular reference to their theory of the ubiquity of the body of Christ.[63] The Puritan John Owen wrote that 'to affix unto the human nature divine properties, as ubiquity or immensity, is to deprive it of its own.'[64]

Karl Barth discusses what he calls 'the unfortunate controversy which arose out of the Eucharistic conflict and in the sixteenth and seventeenth centuries separated the Lutheran and Reformed Schools in respect of the ubiquity of the human nature of His body.'[65] He states that:

> ...the Lutherans did not take seriously enough the distinctions and the Reformed did not take seriously enough the connexion between the stages of the circle...The Lutherans ignored the fact that the Reformed for their part did not altogether disregard or deny the connexion, while the Reformed ignored the fact that the Lutherans did not altogether disregard or deny the distinctions, the trouble on both sides being a failure to take the one aspect or the other seriously enough, or to make it sufficiently clear to what extent they meant to do so.[66]

Barth then suggests a possible way forward by accepting that 'the whole Jesus Christ is here in Israel and the Church, but also in the world in another way.' He would make a distinction with the Reformed by saying: 'He is there properly and originally and here symbolically, sacramentally, spiritually,' and with the Lutherans: 'He is here no less than there, but really present both there and here, in both places the whole Christ after His divine and also after His human nature.'[67]

---

61. Ibid., 224-225.

62. Jill Raitt, *The Eucharistic Theology of Theodore Beza. Development of the Reformed Doctrine* (American Academy of Religion: Chambersburg, 1972).

63. See Christian David Washburn, *St. Roberto Bellarmino's Defense of Catholic Christology against the Lutheran Doctrine of Ubiquity* (UMI electronic books, Amazon.com), 2004.

64. John Owen, *Works*, I. 238.

65. Karl Barth, *Church Dogmatics*, II/1, 487.

66. Ibid.

67. Ibid., 490.

VI. THE COMMUNION OF NATURES –
COMMUNIO NATURARUM

The deity and humanity of Christ are so intimately joined together in one incarnate person, that while retaining their distinctly divine and human characteristics, the life-force and actions of that unique communion achieve the redemption of all who are united by faith and the Holy Spirit to him. Hence, *communion of natures* is a way of saying that in order to redeem our fallen humanity, Christ became one of us, yet without sin, and lived a holy life within it, atoned for sin within it, and was raised from the dead in his humanity (always joined – without transmutation – to his deity), ascended to the Father's throne in his glorified humanity, intercedes there within our nature, feeling all our exigencies (cf. Heb. 4:15,16), and will come as a man to judge the world (Acts 17:31). Throughout the continuing history of redemption, humanity and deity have been joined together in the one person of Christ, as the Chalcedonian doctrine states: 'without change, without confusion, without division, without separation.'

Chalcedon was following, in a more terminologically precise way, the basic teaching of Saint Athanasius, who had charted the course in the previous century:

> Whence it was that, when the flesh suffered, the Word was not external to it; and therefore is the passion said to be His: and when He did divinely His Father's works, the flesh was not external to Him, but in the body itself did the Lord do them. Hence, when made man, He said John x. 37, 38, 'If I do not the works of the Father, believe Me not; but if I do, though ye believe not Me, believe the works, that ye may know that the Father is in Me and I in Him.' And thus when there was need to raise Peter's wife's mother, who was sick of a fever, He stretched forth His hand humanly, but He stopped the illness divinely. And in the case of the man blind from birth, human was the spittle which He gave forth from the flesh, but divinely did He open the eyes through the clay. And in the case of Lazarus, He gave forth a human voice as man; but divinely, as God, did He raise Lazarus from the dead; and it became the Lord, in putting on human flesh, to put it on whole with the affections proper to it; that, as we say that the body was His own, so also we may say that the affections of the body were proper to Him alone, though they did not touch Him according to His Godhead. If then the body had been another's, to him too had been the affections attributed; but if the flesh is the Word's (for 'the Word became flesh'), of necessity then the affections also of the flesh are ascribed to Him, whose the flesh is. And to whom the affections are ascribed, such namely as to be condemned, to be scourged, to thirst, and the cross, and death, and the other infirmities of the body, of Him too is the triumph and the grace. For this cause then, consistently and fittingly such affections are ascribed not to another, but to the Lord; that the grace also may be from Him, and that we may become, not worshippers of any other, but truly devout towards God, because we invoke no originate thing, no ordinary man, but the natural and true Son from God, who has become man, yet is not the less Lord and God and Saviour.[68]

---

68. Athanasius, *Contra Arianos*, III. 32.

The Reformed theologians, in line with Chalcedon, understood there to be an *indirect* union between the two natures. As Heppe wrote: 'There was a *unio immediata* between the human nature and the person of the Son, but a *unio mediata* between the divine and human natures through the Spirit.'[69] Torrance points out what the seventeenth century orthodox Reformed wished to accomplish through this careful terminology:

> In that way, the Reformed theologians sought to speak of an active communion between the natures without teaching a doctrine of mutual interpenetration between the natures, which is precisely what the Lutheran conception of mutual communion or participation led to. The Lutheran theologians therefore spoke of a *communio* or *communicatio naturarum* in which there was in the person of Christ a mutual participation of the divine and human natures, through which the divine nature, by participating in the human nature, permeates, perfects and inhabits it, and so appropriates it to itself, while the human nature by being made participant in the divine, is permeated by it, perfected and inhabited by it. This relation was called mutual penetration...[70]

The same difficulties raised by both Roman Catholic and Reformed theologians against the Lutheran theory of 'communicatio operationum' would be the case with their concept of 'communio naturarum', and needs no repetition here, but it is appropriate to mention the three aspects of the Reformed doctrine of 'communicatio naturarum' as found in H. Heppe:[71]

(i) Communicatio gratiarum

> What is meant here is that from the first moment of his life, his properties as God and man, and the communication of the properties of his divine and human natures, effectively entered into operation step by step with his developing human life – and here we think especially of the graces of the knowledge, will and power in which Jesus increased and grew, growing in knowledge, and learning obedience. It is at the baptism of Jesus, when he was anointed for his ministry and consecrated for his sacrificial life and death as the suffering servant, that we are surely to think of this growth and increase as reaching its culmination.[72]

(ii) Communicatio idiomatum

This has just been discussed, and here one merely re-emphasizes the Reformed (and before them, the ancient Catholic) teaching that the idioms proper to each nature are not directly attributed to the other nature, but to the person. Thus, each nature in communion with the other carries out what is proper to it in its direct relationship to the person.

---

69. H. Heppe, op. cit., 431.

70. Torrance, op. cit., paraphrasing H. Schmid, op. cit., 316f.

71. H. Heppe, op. cit., 434-447.

72. Torrance, op. cit., 225.

(iii) Communicatio operationum

This indicates that because of the communion between his divine and human natures, the divine acts are acts in his human nature, and the human acts are acts in his divine person. Torrance notes:

> Each nature in communion with the other performs acts appropriate to it, but performs them as acts of the one person who embraces both natures, and is the one subject of all the divine and human acts…It asserts a dynamic communion between the divine and human natures of Christ, in terms of his atoning and reconciling work. It stresses the union of two natures for mediatorial operations in such a way that these works proceed from the one person of the God-man by the distinct effectiveness of both natures.[73]

VII. TWO WILLS IN CHRIST

It seems strange to assert that one well-balanced person could have two wills. But Christ is absolutely unique among humankind and angels, in that he is the God/man, and this is the Scriptural basis of the Church asserting that Christ exercises two wills. John L. Girardeau wrote that 'Through the divine will the person, Christ, energizes divinely; through the human will the person, Christ, energizes humanly.'[74] This mysterious reality lies behind how an utterly holy person could be genuinely tempted (yet without sin), and this reality enters into the lifting up and purifying of the human race. The doctrine of the two wills in Christ helps us make some sense of a great salvational mystery.

We can discern to a certain degree how this theological summary (by Girardeau) of the two wills of Christ works out in his human life. In the life of Jesus we see the struggle of his will as a human to avoid the horrendous suffering of being 'made sin' (II Cor. 5:21), and experiencing God-forsakenness (cf. Ps. 22:1 and Matt. 27:46), culminating in the Garden of Gethsemane (Matt. 26:36-46), in which he comes through to fullest obedience to the will of God: 'He went away again the second time, and prayed, saying, O my Father, if this cup may not pass away from me, except I drink it, thy will be done' (Matt. 26:42).

This indicates that in taking on true humanity, Christ thereby took on a human will which, in his sinless obedience to the Father, he bends to fullest submission to the divine will. Because he possessed a human will, he was involved in intense struggle; a human will was not absent from the eternal Son of God in his assumption of a human nature. Probably because this is mysterious, and thus hard for us to understand, a school of thought in the Church, known as the 'Monothelites' (i.e. 'one will'), maintained that there was only a divine will in the incarnate Lord, and no human will. But this opinion was strongly rejected at the second Council of Constantinople in 680.

---

73. Ibid., 236.

74. J. L. Girardeau, op. cit., 396.

Some three centuries earlier, Gregory of Nazianzus had written that 'the unassumed is the unhealed, but what is united to God is saved. If only half Adam fell, then what Christ assumes and saves may be half also; but if the whole of his nature fell, it must be united to the whole nature of him who was begotten, and so be saved as a whole.'[75] Cyril of Alexandria said much the same: 'What has not been taken up has not been saved.'[76]

The mysterious reality of two wills in the incarnate Christ is discussed, perhaps as clearly as a human mind can manage it, by Maximus the Confessor as follows:

> The double nature of the Lord Jesus manifests itself naturally and logically by a double will and a double energy. Possessing human nature, the incarnate Word also possesses in it a will, because human nature cannot exist without a will. The natural will is that force which desires what is in accordance with its nature, which contains in its essence all the particularities that constitute that nature, and according to which it is always natural to desire. This is not the same thing as having natural will and desire, since it is not the same thing to have by nature the faculty of speaking and the actual fact of speaking. As man, the incarnate Word had by nature a will, which was in itself put into motion and governed by the divine will. For his proper characteristic is to will nothing which is opposed to God. In so far as he was man, the Saviour possessed a human will by nature, which his divine will governed, and which his human will never opposed.[77]

Maximus adds: 'He possesses, at the same time and in the fullest sense, the essence, the will, and the energies, both fully divine and fully human.'[78] 'In the hypostasis of the incarnate Word of God, the difference between the two united natures remains whole and entire; no change nor any confusion affects the two natures: neither their essences, nor their wills, nor their energies, nor anything which they possess.'[79]

We can state this mysterious truth in another way. Christ possessed a truly human will, in which he was subject to temptation, but this human will always belonged to the person of the incarnate Son of God. In exercising his human will, he never denied who he always was as God. But this immense feat was not accomplished apart from titanic struggle, which presumably would not have been the case had he possessed only one will. As a real man, he had to *choose* to do the will of the Father, even at infinite cost to himself. There would have been no painful choice if Christ had possessed only one will.

In his comments on Matthew 26:39: 'Nevertheless, not as I will, but as thou wilt,' John Calvin writes: 'This passage shows plainly enough the gross folly of those ancient heretics, who were called Monothelites, because they imagined that the will of Christ was but one and simple;

---

75. Gregory of Nazianzus, *Epistle 101.*

76. Cyril of Alexandria, *In. Jn., MPG* 74, 89CD.

77. Maximus the Confessor, *Opuscules théologiques et polemiques*, PG 91, 45 D-48 A. B. D.

78. Ibid., 80 BC.

79. Ibid., 97 A.

for Christ, as he was God, willed nothing different from the Father; and therefore it follows, that his human soul had affections distinct from the secret purpose of God.' [80]

VIII. THE TEMPTABILITY OF CHRIST

The Scriptural teaching that the incarnate Christ lived his human life so that he was 'tempted, yet without sin' raises the profoundest questions and takes us into the realm of mystery. But the Church has always accepted both Christ's temptability and his victory over sin and the devil, because as our covenant head, he is representing us humans, who so often fail, thereby lifting us into his victory over all evil powers. Hence this doctrine is of no small importance for us.

The clear teaching of the Gospels is that Jesus Christ was tempted to sin, and yet their equally clear teaching is that he resisted all sin, living a perfectly holy life without the least stain of sin. How to hold these two truths together is challenging to our limited understanding, as is so much else in the full biblical presentation of who Christ is.

Although Christ had no sin within himself, yet he was able to be tempted. To be tempted to sin is **not** the same thing as to commit sin. We see this from Hebrews 2:18: 'For in that he himself that suffered being tempted, he is able to succour them that are tempted'; and Hebrews 4:15: 'For we have not an high priest which cannot be touched with the feeling of our infirmities: but was in all points tempted like as we are, yet without sin.'

Christ was not tempted on account of any indwelling sin, for he had none, as we see from John 14:30: '...for the prince of this world cometh, and hath nothing in me.' He was therefore not driven by the lust which entices all the other sons and daughters of fallen Adam. James 1:14-15 shows how we are driven from within to commit sin: 'But every man is tempted, when he is drawn away of his own lust and enticed. Then when lust hath conceived, it bringeth forth sin: and sin, when it is finished bringeth forth death.' Nor was he dragged down by the indwelling sin that we all feel, described by the Apostle Paul in Romans 7, that urges us to do what we hate (Rom. 7:15-21). On the contrary, for all his true humanity, Scripture makes it plain that 'he was holy, harmless, undefiled, separate from sinners' (Heb. 7:26). And Jesus could say to the Pharisees, 'which of you convinceth me of sin?' (John 8:46).

The eighth chapter of Romans, which follows immediately the struggle with indwelling sin of the seventh chapter, points us in the right direction to understand the temptations of Christ: 'For the law of the Spirit of life in Christ Jesus hath made me free from the law of sin and death. For what the law could not do, in that it was weak through the flesh, God sending his own Son in the likeness of sinful flesh, and for sin, condemned sin in the flesh: That the righteousness of the law might be fulfilled in us, who walk not after the flesh, but after the Spirit' (Rom. 8:2-4).

---

80. John Calvin, *Commentary on a Harmony of the Evangelists*, vol. III, 233.

It was as our Mediator, as the head of his Church, that Christ submitted to undergo the fierce onslaughts of the evil one and his demonic hosts. He did this as he was standing in for us, and not because he was inherently pulled towards exaltation of sin over against God. We see this manifested in Christ's temptations in the wilderness (cf. Matthew 4:1-11; Mark 1:12,13, and Luke 4:1-13). Unlike the first Adam, who fell, and Old Testament Israel, who, in their call to live as God's sons, frequently failed to pass the test of obedience to the Lord, the Last Adam showed that the Father's only begotten Son in the flesh put the Father first, denying an easier way offered by the devil, and in so doing, brought his people with him through these temptations into victorious obedience.

Jesus underwent the horrendous temptations to sin against the Father as a true human being, but he would never deny who he was as God the Son; for his humanity, with its temptable will, was established in hypostatic union with the Logos, the Word, the Son. The fact that he would not sin does not lessen the immense conflict he had to endure as our representative in the struggle to overcome evil. We will study in detail the Gospel accounts of Jesus' three temptations under his Active Obedience (Ch. VIII).

IX. THE IGNORANCE OF CHRIST

How God the Son, who is the eternal truth of God, and 'the Light of the World' could at any point, even in his earthly life, be ignorant of something in a world that he had created astonishes us. Yet that is what he himself professes concerning his lack of knowledge, as a man, of the precise date of his second coming.

As with so many other questions raised by a biblical Christology, such as two wills in one person and the temptability of a sinless person, the ignorance of him who is 'God of God' is not easy to be understood. On the one hand, Scripture tells us that Christ is 'the wisdom of God' (I Cor 1:24), the agent of the original creation (John 1:3), and the one into whose hands is committed final judgment (Acts 17:31). He shared the full glory of the Father before the world was (John 17:5), and would have known the entire plan of history from beginning to end. In his earthly ministry, for instance, Jesus knew that there was a coin in the mouth of a fish (Matt. 17:27), that Lazarus had died before he and the disciples came to his house in Bethany, and that the woman of Samaria had had five husbands (John 4:18). Athanasius gave these and other examples of Christ's supernatural knowledge.[81]

On the other hand, the incarnate Christ himself tells us, concerning the time of the last day: 'But of that day and that hour knoweth no man, no, not the angels which are in heaven, neither the Son, but the Father' (Mark 13:32). Luke tells us that 'Jesus increased in wisdom and stature, and in favour with God and man' (Luke 2:52).[82] These two realities (divine

---

81. Athanasius, *Contra Arianos*, III. 37.

82. This concept will be expounded in chapter VIII, under 'The States of Christ': 'Active Obedience.'

knowledge and human ignorance) seem to fit together in this manner. In order to be our Mediator, Christ took on our manhood, and one salient aspect of humanity is that of ignorance of some things.

Hence, Athanasius writes concerning Christ's ignorance of the timing of the last day in terms of the ignorance that inheres in true human nature:

> Now why it was that, though He knew, He did not tell His disciples plainly at that time, no one may be curious where He has been silent; for 'Who hath known the mind of the Lord, or who hath been His counsellor Rom. xi. 34.?' but why, though He knew, He said, 'no, not the Son knows,' this I think none of the faithful is ignorant, viz. that He made this as those other declarations as man by reason of the flesh. For this as before is not the Word's deficiency, but of that human nature whose property it is to be ignorant. And this again will be well seen by honestly examining into the occasion, when and to whom the Saviour spoke thus. Not then when the heaven was made by Him, nor when He was with the Father Himself, the Word 'disposing all things' Prov. viii. 27, LXX nor before He became man did He say it, but when 'the Word became flesh John i. 14.' On this account it is reasonable to ascribe to His manhood everything which, after He became man, He speaks humanly. For it is proper to the Word to know what was made, nor be ignorant either of the beginning or of the end of these (for the works are His), and He knows how many things He wrought, and the limit of their consistence. And knowing of each the beginning and the end, He knows surely the general and common end of all. Certainly when He says in the Gospel concerning Himself in His human character, 'Father, the hour is come, glorify Thy Son Ib. xvii. 1.,' it is plain that He knows also the hour of the end of all things, as the Word, though as man He is ignorant of it, for ignorance is proper to man.[83]

As Mediator, it was Christ's office to carry out his work, not only as God, but also as the God/man; that is, within the limitations of a true human mind. He had to save humanity from the inside out, and that meant being one of us, which includes our ignorance as limited humans. This ignorance is part of his voluntarily choosing to lower himself (cf. Phil. 2:5-11). What he did not know as man, was a matter of choice, in the interests of saving from within the fallen human race. As someone once said: 'it was an economic ignorance, not an ontological ignorance.' Yet it was real nonetheless, although freely chosen by him for the accomplishment of our salvation. And it accomplished its purpose: by it we become 'light in the Lord' (Eph. 5:8). We will never know all that Father, Son and Spirit know, but as fully redeemed image-bearers of the divine, on the basis of all that Christ went through for us, of us too it can be said, 'in thy light shall we see light' (Ps. 36:9).

The Puritan Thomas Goodwin suggested in a famous sermon that after Christ's human ignorance upon earth, he receives the infinite fullness of the Holy Spirit in heaven, thus having 'the Spirit in the utmost measure that the human nature is capable of.'[84] His capacity for knowledge, as our

---

83. Athanasius, *Contra Arianos*, III. 43.

84. Thomas Goodwin, 'The Heart of Christ in Heaven unto Sinners on Earth', taken from *The*

God/man mediator, was hence massively increased upon his ascension, and his love and pity are also enlarged, and all of this he shares with us whom he ushers into the light.[85]

X. CHRISTOLOGICAL HERESIES

The Father has told us in the Scriptures, inspired by the Holy Spirit (II Tim. 3:16), who his Son is, but through the ages there have been contrary voices that seek to deny the divine testimony (as Satan himself did in Eden – Gen. 3:4). These contrary voices rise and fall over the ages, but they are never very far from us (although usually in mutated and updated forms). What they deny and seek to replace is like a devious vandal breaking into a museum, in order to deface a beautiful statue or master painting, by adding in some features, and blotting out others. What is left is not a beautiful portrait or sculpture, but an ugly parody.

It is hard for us who have seen the beauty of the Lord, to know why the 'thief [or vandal] who breaks in' (cf. John 10:8) could ever wish to mar such gracious beauty. There is a certain irrationality about sin that is suggested in one of the New Testament Greek words for it: *anomia*. 'Sin is the transgression of the law' (I John 3:4). The Greek word is *anomia*, which translated literally indicates 'lawlessness'. 'Lawlessness' can mean more than breaking the law, it can imply a sort of irrationality; a craziness that goes, not only against God, but also against one's own highest self-interest. In other words, it does not make sense to us, and cannot be explained. The historical and continuing attacks against the Biblical teaching on who Christ is seem to me to partake of that unexplainable attitude that is suicidal.

That is why the Church has been a vigilant guard of the Scriptural truth about who Christ is (and every other verity set forth in God's written Word). This vigilance has required the Church to confront and clearly oppose false teaching about Christ and his salvation, and all related truths. The Apostle Paul told the Ephesian elders that this would be their continuing task after he had to leave them (Acts 20:28-32). Paul instructs Timothy to 'reprove, rebuke, exhort...' (II Tim. 4:2). Jude instructed the church to 'earnestly contend for the faith which was once delivered unto the saints' (Jude 3). The true church has always continued to execute this task that has never been removed from it.

Our purpose here is to give only the very briefest summary of four of the major Christological heresies that disturbed the early Church for many years: (a) Ebionitism; (b) Docetism; (c) Gnosticism and (d) Apollianarianism.

A. Ebionitism (or Ebionism)
Apparently, the Ebionites, who lived during the late Apostolic era, saw Christianity as a sort of reform of Judaism. They held to a Unitarian view

---

Works of Thomas Goodwin, Vol. IV (James Nichol: Edinburgh, 1862), 121.

85. Ibid., 186.

of God, according to which there was one sovereign God, who had no internal relationships with other co-equal persons. Jesus was a mere man, born of Mary and Joseph. Because of his fulfillment of the Law, he became 'Christ.' They seem to have thought that he was thereby 'adopted' in some sense by God, probably at his baptism. Salvation lay in following him by doing the works of the law.[86] Some have called this approach 'a Christology from below.'

J. Gresham Machen discussed rather fully whether or not Ebionitism was strictly Jewish, or whether it may have had Gnostic elements in it. He leaves it an open question.[87]

B. Docetism

If Ebionitism was 'a Christology from below,' then Docetism was 'a Christology from above.'[88] The Docetists were probably influenced by Gnostic dualism, which viewed the material world as thoroughly bad, created by evil forces and not by God (who was entirely separate from the world). They claimed that since creation is unclean and flesh is inherently sinful, Christ could not have become incarnate in a real body. Rather, he only 'seemed to be' in a body (δοκεω). His human experiences, such as hunger, thirst, suffering and death, and even resurrection were not real for God; they were illusions. Salvation seemed to lie in not being deceived by these illusions of the Gospels, but in somehow escaping the material realm to a higher, spiritual reality, although what remains of their teaching is not very clear on how this was to be accomplished.

Karl Barth perceived that both Docetism and Ebionitism were controlling ideas among the liberal theologians who had taught him:

> In relation to docetic Christology we can think today of the older theological Liberalism influenced by Kant, Fichte and Hegel, and including A. Ritschl, then the structure of 'ebionite' Christology – represented in almost greater than life size in the early Church by Paul of Samosata – is once more typically recognizable in the peculiar Jesus theology which, after the victory of philosophical positivism in a spiritual world, which thought it could live on the alternative to pure empiricism, and deriving from influences emanating from Thomas Carlyle and P. de Lagarde, flourished for a while about the turn of the nineteenth and twentieth-centuries under the leadership of A. von Harnack.[89]

C. Gnosticism

The hydra-headed movement known as Gnosticism left far more writings than the Docetists. They thought that Salvation lay in escaping the inferior

---

86. In the fourth century, for example, Saint Jerome described the Ebionites as still requiring the literal observance of such laws from Deuteronomy as 'not plowing with an ass and ox together' (Deut. 22:10), in his *Commetary on Isaiah*. See Pierre Jay, op. cit., 242.

87. J. Gresham Machen, *The Virgin Birth of Christ* (Baker Book House: Grand Rapids, Michigan, 1971), 18-26.

88. To paraphrase T. F. Torrance's *The Trinitarian Faith*, 60.

89. Karl Barth, *Church Dogmatics*, I/2, 20.

world through various levels or 'aeons,' taking them ever higher than material reality, by means of secret knowledge (γνωσις) attained through the usage of certain passwords and other rituals. The basic approach of Gnosticism has already been discussed in Chapter 4 of this volume, and also in Volume 1 (pp. 240-242; 288-289, and 367-374).

The Gnostics were syncretistic; they seem to have taken elements of Judaism, Christianity, and early Gnosticism, and merged them together into a religious philosophy contrary to both Judaism and Christianity. One of the early Gnostics (sometimes considered a Docetist) was Cerinthus, who was a contemporary of the Apostle John. Cerinthus and his followers taught that there was a supreme God, more or less disconnected from the material world, and that the material world had been created by an inferior power, the Demiurge, who was far below the supreme God, and did not know God. Jesus was not born of a virgin, but of Joseph and Mary. But he surpassed other men in his righteousness, prudence and wisdom. Upon his baptism, Christ descended from the supreme God upon Jesus, enabling him to do miracles. But upon the cross, Christ abandoned Jesus, and was not involved in his sufferings. Saint Irenaeus described this wide-ranging heresy in his second-century *Adversus Haereses* (II. 16. 1).

There was a discovery of Gnostic texts at Nag Hammadi in Egypt in 1945, which included some fifty-two documents (with five of them being duplicates); all of them appear to have been Coptic translations of the original Greek. James Dunn concluded that all of these Gnostic texts were written after the canonical books of the New Testament: 'The more obvious interpretation of the Nag Hammadi documents is that they are all typically syncretistic: they draw bits and pieces of tradition from a wide range of religious influences in the ancient world, including Judaism and Christianity, but including others as well. As such they are totally explainable in terms of what we now know about second and third century Gnosticism.'[90] Ben Witherington gives a lucid discussion of the content and theological approach of this Gnostic library, which includes such documents as the (now) widely known *Gospel of Thomas* and the *Gospel of Philip*, especially in his chapter on *The Mary Magdalene of Myth and Legend*.[91] He shows that:

> ...the Gospel of Thomas should never have been called a gospel, for it has no narrative about the life or death of Jesus, no recounting of miracles, and no prophetic signs. It simply serves up Jesus the talking head. What Thomas's Jesus really wants to accomplish is to be a facilitator so that persons of discernment who are worthy can know themselves, can look deep within themselves, and can thus save themselves by obtaining esoteric knowledge while engaging in ascetical practices.[92]

Craig Blomberg shows the irreconcilable differences between the New Testament Gospels and those of the Gnostics, such as *Thomas*:

---

90. J. D. G. Dunn, *The Evidence for Jesus* (Philadelphia: Westminster Press, 1985), 98.

91. Ben Witherington, *What Have They Done With Jesus?* (Harper: San Francisco, 2006), 27-51.

92. Ibid., 33.

Most of the 'gospels' from Nag Hammadi appear as post-resurrection dialogues (or monologues) of the risen Christ, teaching explicitly Gnostic theology, and bear little resemblance to their canonical namesakes... The *Gospel of Thomas* is formally unique in collecting together 114 relatively unconnected logia attributed to Jesus...[93]

These Gnostic writings draw a certain amount of material from the canonical Gospels, but profoundly subvert them into non-historical stories, such as extrusions of 'aeons' from higher divine sources,[94] and mythological journeys of certain individuals through higher spheres and hostile territories, bringing back information, which conveys secret truths of a new way to be saved, that depends on largely inner experience and the apprehension of arcane information – in general accordance with Gnostic theories, divorced from the historical Person and work of Jesus Christ.[95]

There were many forms of this popular heresy with many variations, but all of them assumed a strict dualism between God and the world; all assumed that creation is bad, and not of God, and that Jesus Christ is not the incarnate Son of God, nor the way of salvation. According to Epiphanius (following Irenaeus[96] and Hippolytus[97]), Simon Magus, mentioned in the Acts of the Apostles as seeking to purchase the power to give the Holy Spirit (Acts 8: 9-25), was thought by many to have been the first Gnostic:

Simon Magus's makes the first sect to begin in the time since Christ. It is composed of persons who do not [believe] in Christ's name in a right and lawful way, but who do their dreadful deeds in keeping with the false corruption that is in them...To the Samaritans he called himself the Father; but to Jews he said he was the Son, though he had suffered without actually suffering, suffering only in appearance.[98]

Only three of the somewhat later representatives of Gnosticism can be mentioned here in any detail, and that only very briefly: (i) Saturninus, (ii) Basilides, and (iii) Valentinus.

(i) Saturninus was the leader of Syrian Gnosticism (under the reign of the Roman emperor Hadrian). He taught that there was a supreme being (the unknown Father), who had created many inferior spiritual beings. Seven angels managed to take a chaotic material mass which they made into a world. The God of the Hebrews was the head of these angels (or perhaps, demiurges). A particular image of light pushed them to create mankind in this likeness (which was far below the supreme light). The

---

93. Blomberg, op.cit., 58.

94. As in *The Tripartite Tractate* and *The Apocryphon of John* (in James M.Robinson, op. cit., 54-116).

95. Some of these suppposed spiritual journeys into the heavenlies are found in *The Dialogue of the Savior*, *The Apocalypse of Paul*, and *Zostrianos* (in James M. Robinson, op. cit., 229-241; 368-393).

96. Irenaeus, *Adversus Haereses*, I. 23. 1-3.

97. Hippolytus, *Haer*. VI. 10. 4, 6.

98. Epiphanius, *The Panarion*, Translated by Frank Williams, op. cit., Section II. 21, I.1 and I.2 (p. 57).

supreme God sent down a sparkle of his divine light into these people, and once they die, this light returns to him. But Satan somehow created another human race which was cursed from the beginning. This evil race did battle with the ones who had a certain amount of light. To deliver the favored race, the supreme God sent down one of the Aeons – Christ –who was for a time clothed in a visible body. He will destroy Satan and his kingdom. Many of the details of how he thought salvation is to be achieved are unclear, for most of his writings were destroyed.

(ii) Basilides came from Alexandria, and was the first Egyptian Gnostic that we know of. He was active in the first quarter of the second century. He taught the existence of a prime source, the supreme God, whose name was Abraxas. This God (or Father) engendered 'the Intellect' (νους), who in turn begat the Word, from whom came Thought, then Wisdom, then Power. These 'ideas' or 'virtues' brought forth angels and archangels, who made the first Heaven. There were three other series, extended to 365 series of spirits. This last large series was composed of seven spirits, each with his own heaven. These spirits or angels created this world and its inhabitants.

The head of these angels was the God of the Hebrews. He sought to show favor to his own people, but other angels raised up other peoples against his. To save the situation, the supreme God sent his first-born Son upon the most spiritual of the people. He appeared to be a man, with a visible body. But on his way to Calvary, he gave over his body to Simon the Cyrenian (who was helping to bear the cross), so that it was Simon who died on the cross, whereas Christ appeared to the crowd to be Simon. Thus Christ, the Son of God, did not die for the sins of the world. To be saved (possible only to those who had a certain spirituality to start with) meant somehow being in touch with the anti-materialist spirits, and with their help rising up through various aeons. Again, how to do so is not clear from his extant writings (quoted in various Church Fathers). But it is clear that faith in the death and resurrection of the incarnate Son of God in our place is not the way of salvation.

(iii) Valentinus was of Jewish origin, born in Egypt. He was apparently brought up as a Christian, but became Gnostic during the second half of the second century. He was probably the most able teacher of all the Gnostic leaders, and seems to have exercised the widest influence among them. He taught the existence of a remote, inconceivable and absolute God, whom he calls 'Depth' (βυθυς). 'Depth' begat 'Thought'(εννοια): sometimes called 'Grace' or 'Silence.' Various 'couples' issued from 'Thought': Mind (masculine) and Truth (feminine). From them came 'Logos' and 'Life' (ζωη), and from them 'Anthropos' and 'Ecclesia' (i.e. mankind and church). They formed several others, which we need not list here. From these original couples came thirty 'Aeons'.

Only the first offspring 'Mind' (νους) had a full knowledge of 'Depth.' The other aeons were jealous, and attempted to advance themselves in various ways that we will not study here. Out of these conflicts amongst the aeons resulted 'matter,' which created the Demiurge. He in turn created the visible universe, including humanity, and became their god. In this created world there are three sorts of beings: the inherently spiritual ones (who are superior), the soulish ones (who are intermediate), and the material ones (who are the lowest). To these differing levels correspond three types of humans: those with a divine soul, those with a material soul, and those with the seeds of a spiritual soul. The first type will inevitably be saved, the second type will inevitably be lost, and the third type can go in either direction, depending on what they do with their wills.

The Gnostic sees salvation as lying in self, rather than in God and his actions. Witherington summarizes this Gnostic soteriology, stating that the Nag Hammadi documents:

> ...see self-knowledge as the essence of salvation, and even appear to urge the worship of human beings. The Gospel of Philip 85:1-4, for example, says, 'God created man and man created God. So it is in the world. Men make gods and they worship their creations. It would be fitting for gods to worship men.' This is not, in fact, a critique of idolatry. It is the divine within human beings that seems to be the ultimate object of worship. Furthermore, the flaws that exist in creation are blamed on some malignant deity – perhaps the so-called Demiurge, which is a lesser god who made the tainted creation. Human sin is not to be blamed for the tainted character of creation. Not surprisingly, in this system of thinking it is ignorance, not sin, that is the ultimate human dilemma.[99]

The body of Jesus was created by the Demiurge, and placed in the Virgin, but taking nothing from her; rather, passing through her 'like water through a tube.' Hence the incarnation is denied; Adam's flesh is not taken on and thus is not redeemed. The plain teaching of Holy Scripture about who Christ is was rejected by Valentinus and his school. They claimed that 'the aeon Christ' came upon Jesus at his baptism, but that at the crucifixion, this Christ returned to 'the Pleroma.' Thus only a mere body, not the incarnate Son of God, suffered and died on the cross. Jesus Christ, therefore, did not accomplish our salvation through his holy life, atoning death and resurrection. The salvation of the 'divine souls' is inevitable; the salvation of the 'soulish ones' depends upon their making proper usage of the right passwords as taught by the Gnostic system, and the 'material souls' are inevitably lost. In fact, the entire material, space/time created order itself is disdained for an ideal realm. In sum, Epiphanius is not exaggerating when he says that the Gnostics have 'invented a new God different from the creator...'[100] This is a travesty of the teaching of the New Testament, and a denial of the revelation given by God in Holy Scripture.

According to Witherington, several of the documents found at Nag Hammadi reflect Valentinian thought, such as 'the Prayer of Paul, the Gospel of Truth, and most importantly...the Gospel of Philip. It is probable that the Gospel of Mary comes from this strain of Gnosticism as

---

99. Witherington, op. cit., 39.

100. Epiphanius, op. cit., 187.

well, though it was not part of the Nag Hammadi collection. It first came to light in 1896 in Cairo.'[101]

Referring not only to the school of Valentinus, but to all of the varied Gnostic documents found at Nag Hammadi, Witherington's statement about the difference between biblical Christianity and Gnosticism is, I think, profoundly correct: 'Though it may be fashionable to suggest that we should be gracious and include the Gnostic texts along with the New Testament as equally valid sources of the truth about early Christianity, the truth is that *both* sources cannot be correct about the historical Jesus…'[102]

Nevertheless, Gnosticism has had a very long career in Western thought. It is generally thought to have done considerable borrowing from some aspects of the Hinduism and Buddhism of the East. Like them, Gnosticism rejects both divine creation and divine revelation. It reappeared in force in the spiritual vacuum left by the European Enlightenment of the eighteenth century, which rejected traditional biblical Christianity, with its emphasis on creation, fall, and redemption through Christ, as witnessed to in the inspired revelation of Holy Scripture. Eric Vogelin has traced the trajectory of modern Gnosticism, with its hostility to the order of created being, where it replaced redemption through Christ with salvation through revolution. It was certainly one of the potent factors in the complex of ideas underlying both French and Russian revolutions; both of which violently opposed traditional Christianity.[103] Theology, and not least Christology, inevitably exercise powerful political and economic ramifications, though it usually takes a century or more to do so after it is widely accepted. The type of political influence it wields, depends of course on the assumptions of the theology.

D. Apollinarianism

This latter heresy was much closer to traditional Christianity than Docetism or Gnosticism, yet denied such a central truth, about Christ at one significant point, that it finally denied the New Testament's teaching on salvation. Apollinarius (died c. 390) was the bishop of Laodicea (c. 360). At first he stood with Nicene orthodoxy and fought against heretical Arianism (which denied the deity of Jesus Christ). In his fight against Arianism, he sought to safeguard the unity of the person of Christ by denying a crucial aspect of his true humanity. To do so, he claimed that Christ did not take on a human mind in the incarnation, but that the divine Logos took the place of a human mind or soul.

In this teaching, Apollinarius read back the limitations of the human understanding onto the being of God. He seemed to have reasoned in this direction: since we cannot fully understand how two natures (human and divine) could function in one person, therefore Christ must not have had such human attributes as a mind and will. In that case, his humanity was

---

101. Witherington, op. cit., 38.

102. Ibid., 34.

103. See my *Systematic Theology*, vol. 1, 240-243, with particular reference to Eric Vogelin's *Science, Politics & Gnosticism*.

not consubstantial with ours. In fact, this Christ has only one nature, and
– as the Church told him – in that case, Christ therefore cannot represent
our humanity.

Fr. Florovsky comments on Gregory of Nazianzus' critique of
Apollinarius: 'It seems to Gregory that the reasoning of the Apollinarians
implies that the intellect is the only property of man which is condemned
and beyond salvation...For Gregory, on the contrary, even if the intellect
is in need of healing, it is the property of man which is most open to
salvation because it has been created in the image of God. "The renewal
of the image" is the goal of redemption and the Word comes to man as an
Archetype to its image.'[104]

Apollinarius' teaching was condemned at the Second Ecumenical
Council in Constantinople in 381 on the grounds that it impaired the
perfect humanity of Christ, owing to the absence of a normal human
mind, and that this full humanity was as essential to our salvation as
his full deity. As we have already seen, Gregory of Nazianzus had said
that 'that which is not taken up is not healed,'[105] and Cyril of Alexandria
that 'the unassumed is the unsaved.'[106] Athanasius the Great had written
earlier, against the teaching of Apollinarius that '[t]he Saviour having in
very truth become man, the salvation is not merely apparent, nor does
it extend to the body only, but the whole body and soul alike, has truly
obtained salvation in the Word himself.'[107]

The inability to know who God truly is, and the consequent inability
to come to him in faith and worship is a common characteristic of all these
Christological heresies, in spite of their considerable differences. That is
one of the reasons why the Church opposed them so strongly. It was true
not only of Ebionitism and Docetism, as well as of Gnosticism, but also of
Apollinarianism. Cyril of Alexandria had pointed out long before that the
inability to come to knowledge of God the Father in rational worship is a
major problem of the heresy of Apollinarius.

In his *Commentary on the Gospel of John*, Cyril expounds the words of
Jesus to the woman of Samaria (in John 4:22-24): 'He does not worship in
that he is Word and God, but having become as we are, he accepted this
experience appropriately in accordance with his economy in the flesh... "You
worship what you do not know, but *we* worship what *we* know." Is it then not
abundantly clear to everyone, that in using the plural number and numbering
himself among those who worship by reason of necessity and servitude, he
speaks like this as one who has come in servile human nature?'[108]

T. F. Torrance comments on Cyril's opposition to the Apollinarians
because their denial of the reality of Christ's human mind short-circuits
our worship in and through him:

---

104. Georges Florovsky, *The Eastern Fathers of the Fourth Century*, volume seven in *The Collected Works*, English translation, (Buchervertriebsanstalt: Vaduz, Europa, 1987), 142.

105. Gregory of Nazianzus, *Epistle* 101.

106. Cyril of Alexandria, *In Jn*. MPG 74, 89 CD.

107. Athanasius, *Ad Epict.*, 7.

108. Cyril of Alexandria, *In Iohannis Evangelium*, MPG LXXIII, 312D-313A.

> Cyril...pointed out that Christ ranged himself among us worshippers as himself a worshipper, for worship was an essential part of his life in the form of a servant: indeed, the office of servant or slave, which Christ assumed for our sakes, is defined in paying worship...That is to say, Cyril stressed the noetic nature of worship in and through the mind of Christ, not the mind of the Logos or the eternal Son, but the human and rational soul of Jesus which in him is inexpressibly united to his divine Mind, but never replaced by it.[109]

The entire Christian Church has understood, from the beginning down to the present day, that only the Christ whom the Scriptures present will get us through to the Father: in saving faith, worship and service on earth, and then on into the eternal glories of heaven in the everlasting joy of the divine presence. Christ is presented in Holy Scripture as both God and man at the same time, upon his incarnation. That is, he has two natures – without confusion, conversion, separation or division – in one person. Our starting point, as Athanasius said, is always the Lord Jesus Christ as 'whole man and God together'.[110] Instead of Docetic, Ebionite and Apollinarian reductionisms, the incarnate Lord is rightly described by Athanasius: 'He was true God in the flesh, and true flesh in the Word.'[111]

As such, he is the head of his church, which he has washed clean in his own blood (I Peter 1:18-20), and raised in his own resurrection (Col. 2:13), and to which he joins all of his people through the Holy Spirit, who unites them to their head in his life, death, resurrection, and victorious ascension (I Cor. 12:13; Rom. 6:3-6; Col. 3:1-4). All of the varying heresies, both ancient and modern, in one way or another have in differing ways sought to preclude this life-giving access to God, and all of them are rightly opposed by the people of God across the ages. In waging the good fight, the people of God have sought to receive fully the testimony that the Father gives to his Son, and thereby they honor the Spirit, who speaks not of himself, but of Christ (John 16:13). The beauty and peace of the Triune God is thereby presented to a broken world.

---

109. T. F. Torrance, *Theology in Reconciliation* (Wipf & Stock: Eugene, Oregon, 1996), 113.

110. Athanasius, *Contra Arianos*, 4. 35.

111. Ibid., 3.41.

CHAPTER 6
THE POST-CRITICAL CHRIST

THE CONTINUING INFLUENCE OF THE EPISTEMOLOGY AND CHRISTOLOGY OF IMMANUEL KANT

Although this volume expounds Christology from within traditional orthodox Christianity, as founded on Holy Scripture, it is appropriate to consider the powerful stream of thought that poured into most churches after the Enlightenment, giving a profoundly different reading of the significance of Christ's person and work; a Christ who is not the same as the one taught in Scripture and believed on for the first seventeen hundred years of church history. More than any other philosopher of the Enlightenment, Immanuel Kant (1728-1804), professor at the University of Konigsberg in East Prussia, shaped the epistemology (and hence the theology) of the Western world from his day until well after the rise of the relativity theory of Albert Einstein in the early twentieth century.

To gain some understanding of lasting influence of the philosophical approach of Kant within the Christian theological tradition since the beginning of the nineteenth century, we must consider (1) his basic epistemology; (2) seek to offer a critique of its central tenets; (3) consider an alternative to his dualistic skepticism, and (4) examine his views of Christology.

I. The Epistemology of Immanuel Kant

Kant seems first to have worked within the rationalist school of thought, going back to Descartes (1596-1650), and to some degree, Leibniz (1646-1716), and especially his follower, Wolff.[1] Although, after his reading of Hume, Kant says that he 'awoke from his dogmatic slumbers' [i.e. dogmatic idealism],[2] and moved in a more empiricist direction (though with important differences from earlier empiricism), still he expresses

---

1. See Kant's reference to Wolff in 'Preface to Second Edition' of *Critique of Pure Reason* (Macmillan and Co.: London, 1934), translated by Norman Kemp Smith, 24. See also his critical reference to the philosophy of Leibniz and Wolff in Ibid., 56, and that of Berkeley on p. 59.

2. Kant mentions this in the introduction to his *Prolegomena to Any Future Metaphysics*, translated with intro. and notes by P. G. Lucas (Manchester, 1953).

in a crucial sense the basic attitude of Descartes. In the general mode of Descartes, Kant makes the mind of man (not God or Scripture or the stable created order) the central concern of his account of how and what we know. A sentence in the 'Preface to the First Edition' is typical: 'I have to deal with nothing save reason itself and its pure thinking; and to obtain complete knowledge of these, there is no need to go far afield, since I come upon them in my own self.'[3]

'Clear ideas' in Descartes; 'pure reason' in Kant

Also in the wake of Descartes, Kant provides his own rather different form of 'clear and distinct ideas.' Instead of 'clear and distinct ideas,' Kant seeks to provide an account of the working of 'pure' reason. By 'pure' he meant that it was not mixed with anything empirical: 'I term all representations *pure* in which there is nothing that belongs to sensation. The pure form of sensible intuitions in general, in which all the manifold of intuition is intuited in certain relations, must be found in the mind *a priori*.'[4] That is, it is 'pure' because it is said to be 'absolutely independent of all experience,' as opposed to *a posteriori* knowledge, which is 'empirical': gained through the experience of the senses, which is thus 'impure,' subject to the limitations and confusion of the senses.[5]

A priori and a posteriori

As we shall see, this 'pure' reason involves the concepts or categories of the human understanding by means of which we process the experiences that come to us through the senses. In other words, according to Kant, *a posteriori* sensations must be processed through *a priori* structures of the mind, which enable them to impose a meaningful form on them, by which they thereby make sense of these 'objects' or 'representations' of perception. 'That in which alone the sensations can be posited and ordered in a certain form, cannot itself be sensation; and therefore, while the matter of all appearance is given to us *a posteriori* only, its form must be ready for the sensations *a priori* in the mind, and so must allow of being considered apart from all sensation.'[6]

A priori categories in the structure of the mind

This inherent structure of the mind (which provides the *a priori* categories) includes such ineradicable concepts as the principle of cause and effect. Kant agrees that Hume had demonstrated that empirical observation of particular events in and of itself cannot prove this principle.[7] Hume had sought to explain away causality by considering it to be merely the habit of the mind as it notices many occasions of events, and held that the

---

3. Ibid., 8.

4. Ibid., 42.

5. Ibid.

6. Ibid., 41-42.

7. As in Kant's 'Preface' to his *Prolegomena*, and second edition of *Critique of Pure Reason*, 35.

mind goes beyond the evidence in considering these closely connected occasions to have been brought about by cause and effect.[8]

As Kant writes: '...the very concept of a cause so manifestly contains the concept of a connection with an effect and of the strict universality of the rule, that the concept would be altogether lost if we attempted to derive it, as Hume has done, from a repeated association of that which happens with that which precedes, and from a custom of connecting representations, a custom originating in this repeated association, and constituting therefore a merely subjective necessity.'[9]

Kant's view of causality in answer to Hume

It was important to Kant to establish some form of valid causality in order to safeguard the scientific achievements of Isaac Newton from a total Humean skepticism, so that things were not disconnected in a sort of nominalistic anarchy. In his 'Preface' to the second edition of the *Critique of Pure Reason*, Kant mentions how his change of reference point from empirical objects to the mind of the observer will enable holding together the research of Copernicus and Newton: 'Similarly, the fundamental laws of the motions of the heavenly bodies gave established certainty to what Copernicus had at first assumed only as an hypothesis, and at the same time yielded proof of the invisible force (the Newtonian attraction) which holds the universe together...'[10]

Thomas Reid and 'common sense' causality

Kant's way of establishing some form of causality was very different from that of Thomas Reid. Reid sought to uphold the truth of causality by positing the 'common sense' deliverances of humanity; that is, axioms that cannot be proven, nor need to be proven, for they have to be assumed as true in order to engage in any kind of reasoning whatsoever (and among these is causality).[11] Hence, Reid argued that the human mind is in touch with external realities, which, in a sense, 'impose themselves' on the mind, rather than the mind, in a certain limited sense, 'creating' them (although Kant never denies that something is already there, though one cannot know it directly in itself. In other words, he does not suggest that the human mind literally creates the sensations it comes to know 'out of nothing'). But the mind is 'creative' of the realities it perceives in a different way.

Unlike Reid, Kant argues for the validity of cause and effect by positing *a priori* categories in the human mind, which impose such concepts as causality on the *a posteriori* experiences presented to the mind through the senses. To achieve this, Kant states that objects must conform to the structures of the mind, rather than vice versa.

---

8. See my discussion of Hume in vol. I of this series, pp. 119-127.

9. Kant, *Critique of Pure Reason* (second edition), 27.

10. Ibid., 18-19.

11. See D. Kelly, *Systematic Theology*, vol. I, 124-127.

We must therefore make trial whether we may not have more success in the tasks of metaphysics, if we suppose that objects must conform to our knowledge. This would agree better with what is desired, namely, that it should be possible to have knowledge of objects *a priori*, determining something in regard to them prior to their being given. We should then be proceeding precisely on the lines of Copernicus' primary hypothesis... A similar experiment can be tried in metaphysics, as regards the *intuition* of objects. If intuition must conform to the constitution of the objects, I do not see how we could know anything of the latter *a priori*; but if the object (as object of the senses) must conform to the constitution of our faculty of intuition, I have no difficulty in conceiving of such a possibility.[12]

In Kant's epistemology then, the mind and language are not transparent lenses through which real, external objects shine, because if they were, we would be 'landed in contradictions': 'If, then, on the supposition that our empirical knowledge conforms to objects as things in themselves, we find that the unconditioned *cannot be thought without contradiction*, and that when, on the other hand, we suppose that our representation of things, as they are given to us, does not conform to these things as they are in themselves, but that these objects, as appearances, conform to our mode of representation, *the contradiction vanishes...*'[13]

Kant's 'Copernican Revolution'
This radical change of reference from external reality itself to the structures of the human mind is what Kant considered as his own 'Copernican revolution'. It is somewhat like Descartes in its spirit, in that Descartes is certain of himself (with his 'clear and distinct' ideas), and Kant is certain of the working of the mind of the person, whose *a priori* structures of reasoning are the filters of otherwise uncertain sensual experiences, which they then bring into the certainty of their organization of these impressions in accordance with the mental nature of the subject.[14] In this way, the emphasis (in this 'Copernican revolution') is on the mind of the person, whose inbuilt capacities make sense of and thereby give structure to what comes to them from outside; not on external reality which imposes itself on him.

We do not know objects outside the mind
In other words, we can know an object only insofar as it conforms to *a priori* categories in the mind, which cause it to be knowable. We do not know the object itself, but can only know it to the degree that it is shaped by the structures of the mind. At certain points, Kant refers to the mind as 'making the object.'[15] In his first *Critique* he writes: 'What objects may be in themselves, and apart from all this receptivity of our sensibility, remains

---

12. Kant, op. cit., 16.

13. Ibid., 18.

14. See Kant's discussion of self-consciousness in his 'Refutation of Idealism' in ibid., especially pp. 138-140.

15. See the discussion in Kant's *Critique of Practical Reason*, II. 7 (English translation, p. 231ff.).

completely unknown to us. We know nothing but our mode of perceiving them…'[16] He adds:

> It is not that by our sensibility we cannot know the nature of things in any save a confused fashion; we do not apprehend them in any fashion whatsoever. If our subjective constitution be removed, the represented object, with the qualities which sensible intuition bestows upon it, is nowhere to be found, and cannot possibly be found. For it is this subjective constitution which determines its form as appearance.[17]

The human mind 'writes laws into nature'

Kant also says that 'The understanding does not derive its laws (*a priori*) from, but writes them into, nature.'[18] The primary way Kant describes this as taking place is by what he calls 'the synthetic *a priori*.' He distinguishes between two types of statements: *analytic* and *synthetic* in section IV of the Introduction to his first *Critique* (second edition):

Analytic and *synthetic* judgments

> In all judgments in which the relation of a subject to the predicate is thought (I take into consideration affirmative judgments only, the subsequent application to negative judgment being easily made), this relation is possible in two different ways. Either the predicate B belongs to the subject A, as something which is (covertly) contained in this concept A; or B lies outside the concept A, although it does indeed stand in connection with it. In the one case I entitle the judgment analytic, in the other synthetic. Analytic judgments (affirmative) are therefore those in which the connection of the predicate with the subject is thought through identity; those in which this connection is thought without identity should be entitled synthetic. The former, as adding nothing through the predicate to the concept of the subjective, but merely breaking it up into those constituent concepts that have all along been thought in it, although confusedly, can also be entitled explicative. The latter, on the other hand, add to the concept of the subject a predicate which has not been in any wise thought in it, and which no analysis could possibly extract from it; and they may therefore be entitled ampliative. Judgments of experience, as such, are one and all synthetic. For it would be absurd to found an analysis on experience…[19]

It is clear that, for instance, the heliocentric thesis of Copernicus and the laws of gravity of Newton are not analytic statements. They are synthetic, for they deal with the deliverances of sensation about nature, and therefore could not be included in the concept A; they lie outside it. They are thus synthetic. Yet they are not merely *a posteriori* concepts, worked up by the senses, and thus uncertain on a nominalistic or empiricist basis. On the contrary they are in an important sense valid and necessary laws, and hence, *a priori*.

---

16. Kant, *Critique of Pure Reason*, 54.

17. Ibid., 56.

18. Kant, *Prolegomena to any Future Metaphysics*, 36.

19. Kant, *Critique of Pure Reason*, 30,31.

This is to say that the raw material of the external world as taken in through the senses (which is the synthetic aspect) is processed and shaped by the mind (which is the *a priori* aspect). As it does this, the mind uses its inbuilt 'forms of intuition' of space and time.[20] In Section 14 of his 'Transcendental Deduction,' Kant explains more fully:

> Now all experience does indeed contain, in addition to the intuition of the senses through which something is given, that is to say, as appearing. Concepts of objects in general thus underlie all empirical knowledge as its *a priori* conditions. The objective validity of the categories as *a priori* concepts rests, therefore, on the fact that, so far as the form of thought is concerned, through them alone does experience become possible. They related of necessity and *a priori* to objects of experience, for the reason that only by means of them can any object whatsoever of experience be thought.[21]

'Synthetic *a priori*'

In this process, the mind uses inbuilt categories of the pure reason, such as quantity and quality.[22] The mind does not actually perceive things 'in themselves,' but rather their appearance to us, which the mind has so conditioned that we do not know their inner reality. Nonetheless, by means of his 'synthetic *a priori*' Kant holds that he has provided for matters such as Newton's mathematical equations, 'necessary and universal' certainty, which is derived '*independently of all experience.*'[23]

An illustration of what he means is seen in his discussion of space:

> Space is nothing but the form of all appearances of outer sense. It is the subjective condition of sensibility, under which alone outer intuition is possible for us. Since, then, the receptivity of the subject, its capacity to be affected by objects, must necessarily precede all intuitions of these objects, it can readily be understood how the form of all appearances can be given prior to all actual perceptions, and so exist in the mind *a priori*, and how, as a pure intuition, in which all objects must be determined, it can contain, prior to all experience, principles which determine the relations of these objects.[24]

Kant illustrates the point by noting that (concerning the categories of relation): 'That the possibility of a thing cannot be determined from the category alone, and that in order to exhibit the objective reality of the pure category of understanding, we must always have an intuition...'[25] That is, there must be some sort of *a posteriori* presentation through the sense to the inbuilt categories of the understanding, which then shapes these presentations into specific patterns. The possibility of empirical experience (geometrical and otherwise) depends directly upon the already existing categories of understanding of the human mind: '...all principles

20. See his 'Transcendental Aesthetic' in ibid., 43-62.

21. Ibid., 79.

22. See his 'Transcendental Analytic,' ibid., 67-105.

23. Ibid., 7.

24. Ibid., 46.

25. Ibid., 144.

of the pure understanding are nothing more than principles *a priori* of the possibility of experience, and to experience alone do all *a priori* synthetic propositions relate – indeed, their possibility itself rests entirely on this relation.'[26]

This synthetic *a priori* body of knowledge is necessarily and universally true because it does not claim to know the actual object of knowledge, [that is, 'as thing in itself'], but only claims to know the forms and principles which 'are limited to mere objects of *experience*' [that is, the appearances of things].[27] This gives us *a priori* knowledge 'absolutely independent of all experience.'[28]

Certainty and necessity depend on the mind, not on external reality

This priority to and independence of empirical experience is important to maintain certainty and necessity, because experience cannot confer these qualities. The two forms of sensible intuition, space and time, do not finally depend on uncertain external experience (although it plays a necessary part in making them aware of such things), but are part of the knowing subject. The concept of causality is also involved in the mind of the knowing subject; it is not dependent on the experiential. That is, pure reason makes synthetic *a priori* judgments only of the forms which inhere in the knower. The content of a phenomenon or appearance is indeed given us by *a posteriori* experience, but the form is built (*a priori*) into the mind as forms of sensibility and concepts of the understanding.[29] It is this 'pure' ('necessary and universal' – i.e. *a priori*) knowledge alone that is certain, and it is able to provide the rational basis of synthetic judgments, which themselves are also certain, although they make use of experiential appearances (or phenomena).

Certain knowledge is restricted to phenomenal realities

This certain knowledge, as developed through the given categories of the mind of the knower is restricted to phenomenal realities. It cannot extend to what these things that are shaped by the knowing mind are in and of themselves. They can be termed 'noumena,' or 'things in themselves,' and as such they are not finally knowable by the mind. They do not involve the mind in actual content, but are 'limiting concepts'; that is, they give the idea of an object apart from its appearance (which is the only aspect of it that the human mind can really know with certainty). 'What objects may be in and of themselves, and apart from all this receptivity of our sensibility, remains completely unknown to us. We know nothing but our mode of perceiving them...'[30]

Realities which go beyond the material are even less knowable by the mind, for the forms of intuition are 'valid only for objects of possible

---

26. Ibid., 148.
27. Ibid., 20.
28. Ibid., 26.
29. Ibid.
30. Ibid., 54.

experience.'[31] To attempt to go beyond material knowledge lands one in irreconcilable self-contradictions (or 'antinomies'). Kant expounded four of these antinomies in his 'Transcendental Dialectic.'[32] In summary, he maintained that '...they detach themselves completely from experience, and make for themselves objects for which experience supplies no material, and whose objective reality is not based on completion of the empirical senses but on pure *a priori* concepts.'[33] In his *Prolegomena*, Kant writes that the noumena 'serve as it were to decipher appearances, that we may be able to read them as experience...Beyond this they are arbitrary combinations, without objective reality, and we can neither cognize their possibility *a priori*, nor verify their reference to objects, let alone make it intelligible by an example.'[34] That is, the mind cannot reach knowledge of anything beyond its experience of the world.

The noumena or 'thing in itself' cannot be known

Kant considers God to be in the category of noumena, or 'thing in itself.' The given categories of the mind do not enable one to know God as an object of one's knowledge (as a phenomenon), for he is beyond such knowledge, and so is a noumenon. I will not discuss here Kant's disproof of what he calls 'only three possible ways of proving the existence of God by means of speculative reason.'[35]

In his 'disproofs' of the theistic arguments, Kant does not claim to have disproven God, but only to have shown that God cannot be proven. Although he cannot be proven, still in his *Religion Within the Limits of Reason Alone*,[36] Kant argues for the high usefulness of God as 'a limiting concept.' Kant considers this limiting concept not to be illogical, and holds that the idea of God is free from contradiction. Still, if one applies the categories of the mind to God, one cannot give knowledge of him, but only provide 'symbols' of the unknown: matters of very vague and unclear content; hence, noumena.

We must consider his views of God in more detail later in this appendix. But before doing so, it is necessary to take a critical look at his basic epistemology, as this determines how he reworks the concept of God, and reduces him to a pale, spectral image, infinitely removed from the Living God of Israel and the Church, as testified in Holy Scripture.

II. A Critique of the *Critique of Pure Reason*

Kant's powerful concept of 'pure reason' which fashions objects by the categories of the mind, and in so doing, imposes its laws onto nature, rested

---

31. Ibid., 60.

32. Ibid., 211-268.

33. Ibid., 267.

34. *Prolegomena to any Future Metaphysics*, 72.

35. Kant, *Critique of Pure Reason*, 277.

36. Kant, *Religion within the Limits of Reason Alone*, translated by T. M. Greene and H. H. Hudson (Glasgow, 1934).

upon a sharp dualism he posited between sensibility and intellect. This split or dichotomy between what the senses (by means of the structures of the mind) present to us from outside, and what is actually in nature (or transcendent to it), means that the human knower does not finally know the structures of nature, but rather shapes nature through the structures of his mind. Thus, nature does not impose itself on our knowing, rather, we impose our knowing on nature. Priority is with the knower, not with the realities of nature.

Kant's dualism and skepticism

This dualism is based on a kind of agnosticism, or skepticism, both as to what we can perceive from nature (as in science), and as to what we can know about the Creator and Redeemer God (as in theology and personal devotion). Those who followed in Kant's path, had to abandon most of what the Holy Scriptures teach about God, our knowing of him, and our salvation through his grace. It largely turns from the traditional faith based on the revelation of God in history and Scripture, and replaces it with a different kind of faith: the assumed structures and power of the autonomous human mind. That is why there is such a hiatus between much of pre-Kantian and post-Kantian theology.

Kant's epistemology has been critically addressed both (1) by his own philosophical contemporaries – on the basis of how language works, and also (2) by distinguished physicists in the twentieth century – on the basis of how science knows reality and advances its research. Let us consider these in turn.

(1) A critique of Kant on the basis of how language works

Johann Georg Hamann (1730-1788) was a fellow Prussian, and personal friend of Immanuel Kant, much as he disagreed with his epistemology. While Hamann, like his neighbor in Koningsberg, Kant, is not easy to read, still one can appreciate major points he raises against Kant's thought, questioning the validity of his fitting reality into the mind (thereby making reality dependent on the structures of the mind), rather than considering the mind to be a receptive channel through which, by the normally reliable use of our five senses, we know what is outside us, so that external reality has priority over the mental structures of the human knower.

Hamann denies Kant's split between sensibility and intellect

To help establish this point, of the priority of external reality over the categories of the 'pure' intellect, Hamann denies the foundational Kantian split between sensibility and intellect. W. M. Alexander notes Hamann's two basic objections to Kant's division between reason and experience:

> A. The supposed dichotomy between experience and the pure reason invites the reason to overvalue its formal certainties and to make this kind of 'knowledge' the norm and model for all knowledge. In effect the knowing subject is given a sovereign authority.

B. This dichotomy is actually impossible, or at least cannot be demon-strated.[37]

Hamann deals with these two points (in reverse order from the above):

The possibility of human knowledge of objects of experience *outside of* and *before* all experience, and after this, the possibility of a sensible intuition *before* all experience, and after this, the possibility of a sensible intuition *before* all perception [*Empfindung*] of an object, belong to the *concealed mysteries* of an object, the task of solving which – not to speak of the solution – has yet to be given to a philosopher. The content and form of a transcendental Doctrine of Elements and Method are based upon this double *impossibility* and upon the *formidable* [*machtigen*] *distinction* between analytical and synthetical judgments: for besides the proper [*eigentumlichen*] distinction between reason as an *object* or *source* or also *way* of *knowledge*, there is yet a more universal, sharper and purer distinction, by virtue of which reason serves as the basis of all objects, sources and ways of knowledge, and is itself none of the three, and consequently also has need neither of an empirical or aesthetic, nor logical or discursive concept, but consists merely in subjective conditions, under which can be thought *everything, something* and *nothing* as object, source or way of knowledge, and as an infinite maximum or minimum, can be *given*, or if need be, *taken* as an immediate intuition.[38]

Sensibility and intellect are already joined together in language

Hamann shows that this improper split between reason and sensibility is already joined together in the language that we all have to use. John R. Betz writes:

In other words, whereas Kant's philosophy divided the phenomenal from the noumenal, the sensible from the intelligible, and subsequent to 'this unnatural and unholy divorce' (in Hamann's phrase) could offer only a tenuous connection by means of synthetic judgments a priori, Hamann repeatedly points out that the actual living unity of these elements, which reason subsequently sunders, is already *given* in language.[39]

On this crucial point, Gwen Griffith-Dickson writes:

In his [i.e. Hamann's] view, the central question of Kant's first *Critique*, the very possibility of *a priori* knowledge and of pure reason, depends on the nature of language. In a passage full of subtle allusions to Kantian passages and terms, he writes:

Indeed, if a chief question does remain: *how is the power to think possible?* – The power to think *right* and *left, before* and *without, with* and *above* experi-ence? then it does not take a deduction to prove the genealogical priority

---

37. W. M. Alexander, *Johann Georg Hamann: Philosophy and Faith* (Martinus Nijhoff: The Hague, 1966), 102.

38. Hamann, *Samtliche Werke, historisch-kritishce Ausgabe*, ed. Josef Nadler (Vienna: Herder, 1949-1957), III. 283, 284, quoted in Alexander, op. cit., 103.

39. John R. Betz, *After Enlightenment: Hamann as Post-Secular Visionary* (Wiley-Blackwell: West Sussex, 2009), 232,233.

of language … Not only the entire ability to think rests on language … but language is also the *crux of the misunderstanding of reason with itself*. (Hamann, III. 286: 1-10).[40]

According to Hamann, Kant's 'pure reason' was not pure

This neglect of the crucial place of language in human understanding enabled Kant vainly to imagine that his construction of the pure categories of the human reason was totally free and disconnected from the history of human thought and culture. But the truth was otherwise. Hamann believed that Kant's 'pure' reason was not really pure. As Betz points out:

> … the *Critique* is precisely *not* pure; it itself is a product of tradition, and he exposes the hypocrisy, saying, 'But since the whole content can be nothing but form without content, was none more expedient than the product [*Gemachte*] of the scholastic art form, and was no schematism purer than the synthesis of the syllogistic apodictic tripod?' In other words, the supposed purity of Kant's principles notwithstanding (whose miraculous birthing apart from any impregnation by experience or tradition Hamann equates with a kind of parthenogenesis), Kant has borrowed not only from Aristotle's logic, but even from the scholastic tradition he rejects. This is why in general Hamann accuses the tradition of modern philosophy, beginning with Descartes, of blatant hypocrisy: it claims to be laying a new foundation for the sciences, but it does so disingenuously, building with the materials of the philosophies that preceded it…the unacknowledged dependence upon tradition, which Kant has covered up.[41]

Rationalism is also based on faith

Wittgenstein, after Alexander Koyré and Étienne Gilson,[42] showed similarly that Descartes did not derive his 'distinct and clear' ideas out of the air, or out of his own mind, but from within a linguistic and cultural tradition.[43] The rationalistic tradition within which Kant was working held as a sort of 'faith premiss' the unproven assumption that human reason is autonomous: it is explained by itself; it is not dependent on tradition, nor on a language community, nor on divinely given revelation, nor on external reality imposing itself on the human knower. 'Hamann could assert that "faith," not rational grounds, underlies his contemporaries' high valuation of reason. Thus even the enthusiastic advocates of impartiality and "reason," who are also skeptics about "blind faith," have ultimately only faith as the ground for their convictions.'[44]

Alexander summarizes Kant's necessary dependence upon 'faith': 'Faith' belongs to the natural conditions of our powers of knowing, to

---

40. Gwen Griffith-Dickson, 'Johann Georg Hamann' in *Stanford Encyclopedia of Philsosphy* (copyright 2007 by Gwen Griffith-Dickson *gcgriffithdickson@blueyonder.co.uk*), 10.

41. Betz, op. cit., 240.

42. See Étienne Gilson, *Études sur le role de la pensée médiéval edans la formation du système cartésien* (Vrin: Paris, 1930), and Alexandre Koyré, *Essai sur l'idée de Dieu et les preuves de son existence chez Descartes* (Leroux: Paris, 1922).

43. See D. Kelly, *Systematic Theology*, vol. 1, p. 248.

44. Gwen Griffith-Dickson, art. cit., 8.

the basic drives of our souls (III. 190). It is ubiquitous in the being and reasoning of man. '*Facta* rest upon faith' not less than does 'every common proposition.' 'Knowledge on the basis of faith is fundamentally identical with the *nil in intellectu*.'[45] Nothing is a matter of knowledge which is not first a matter of faith, just as nothing is in the understanding which was not first in the senses. 'The soul can as little live without faith as the body without the provisions of nature' (I. 287).[46]

Hamann rightly states that just as faith enters into acceptance of a divine revelation (which is criticized by Kant as landing one in the 'contradictions' attendant upon attempting to describe the 'noumena'), so also faith enters into the acceptance of one's own 'knowing existence': '"Our own existence and the existence of all things outside of us must be believed and in no other way can be known" (II. 73). It is not that the *cogito, ergo sum*, is not "true," but that it is a contentless and meaningless abstraction…The real content, basis and object of faith is now inaccessible to man; it must be given to him.'[47] But Kant does not see nor admit that his position also depends upon a faith starting-point.

Hence, instead of being a 'pure' product of the autonomous mind, disconnected from previous tradition, Kant's 'synthetic *a priori*' is as much based on a certain kind of *faith* as is the Church's trust in the validity of divine revelation, although Kant never seems to have realized this faith-foundation of his epistemology. Betz summarizes the point:

> Hamann's point, however, is that faith cannot be bracketed out even for methodological purposes, since it is involved from the outset in all our reasoning. What is more, as Hamann profoundly grasped, the very attempt to separate reason from faith (and from the testimony of history and the senses) is ultimately inimical to reason itself, since reason is suddenly forced to do what it cannot, however much, like Sisyphus, it might try: namely, ground itself.[48]

(2) A Critique of Kant on the Basis of Scientific Methodology

Although Albert Einstein had read (as a precocious teenager) Kant's *Critique of Pure Reason*, he later found the progress of physics leading him in a contrary direction to Kant's split between autonomous reason and empirical reality.[49] Einstein stated in 1922 that he had come to differ from Kant on the question of the *a priori*.[50] In 1931 in a commemorative volume on Sir James Clerk-Maxwell, Einstein wrote that 'The belief in an external world independent of the perceiving subject is the basis of all natural science.'[51]

---

45. *Nihil est in intellectu quod non antea fuerit in sensu*. (Gildermeister, V. 505, note 1), quoted in Alexander, op. cit., 44 [Nothing is in the intellect which was not first in the senses.]

46. Ibid., 44-45.

47. Ibid., 45.

48. Betz, op. cit., 238.

49. Stanley L. Jaki, *The Road of Science and the Ways to God: The Gifford Lectures, Edinburgh, 1974-1975 and 1975-76* (Real View Books: Port Huron, Michigan, 2005 reprint), 184.

50. Ibid., 185.

51. Albert Einstein, 'Clerk Maxwell's Influence on the Evolution of the Idea of Physical

Albert Einstein rejects Kant's denial of the comprehensibility of the world

In 1951, Einstein spoke of 'the miraculous character of man's ability to comprehend the world.'[52] A year later he wrote:

> You find it surprising that I think of the comprehensibility of the world (insofar as we are entitled to speak of such world) as a miracle or an eternal mystery. But surely, a priori, one should expect the world to be chaotic, not to be grasped by thought in any way. One might (indeed one *should*) expect that the world evidenced itself as lawful only so far as we grasp it in an orderly fashion. This would be a sort of order like the alphabetical order of words. On the other hand, the kind of order created, for example, by Newton's gravitational theory is of a very different character. Even if the axioms of the theory are posited by man, the success of such a procedure supposes in the objective world a high degree of order, which we are in no way entitled to expect a priori. Therein lies the 'miracle' which becomes more and more evident as our knowledge advances.[53]

In this same letter, Einstein raised the question of whether the mysterious ability of the human mind to grasp accurately objective facts of the universe (which were already there without needing to be structured by the *a priori* categories of man's intellect) implies the existence of God, who, in that case, would be thought to have made the universe to be comprehensible. Einstein clearly does not wish to take this step, much as he has undercut the Kantian positivism, which thought it had finally excluded the Deity. He adds in his 1952 letter to Solovine:

> And here is the weak point of positivists and professional atheists, who feel happy because they think that they have preempted not only the world of the divine but also of the miraculous. Curiously, we have to be resigned to recognizing the 'miracle' without having any legitimate way of getting any further. I have to add the last point explicitly, lest you think that weakened by age I have fallen into the hands of priests.[54]

The intelligible universe is not the creation of the mind

As Jaki comments, 'Such a universe was not the creation of the mind, nor could its high degree of order be expected a priori. The orderly world was something given. Moreover, Einstein, the scientist, knew that the specific form of that order could not be derived a priori if the need for experimental verification was to retain any meaning. Finally, Einstein, the philosopher-scientist, perceived that such a train of thought was not only a road of science but it also came dangerously close to turning at the end into a way to God.'[55]

Reliability,' in *The World as I See It* (New York: Covici-Frede, 1934), 60.

52. A. Einstein, in a letter of January 1, 1951, to Maurice Solovine in *Lettres à Maurice Solovine* (Paris: Gauthier-Villars, 1956), 102, quoted in Jaki, op. cit., 192.

53. Einstein to Solovine in ibid., 115, quoted in Jaki, op. cit., 193.

54. Einstein to Solovine, op. cit., 115, quoted in Jaki, ibid.

55. Jaki, ibid.

Although Einstein finally refused to move from the mysterious comprehensibility of the cosmos to its mysterious Creator, at very least his research demonstrated that the world is not dependent for its existence and knowability on the mind of man, and in this powerful insight, he broke the long hold of Kant's skeptical dualism on the advancement of true knowledge. Jaki writes:

> Any resort to Kantian epistemology in order to escape the full logic of a realist metaphysics is discredited not only by the marvel which modern science provokes about the mind's understanding of the world in general. Modern science also served notice that contrary to Kant's precepts the mind's success with reality has a far greater measure of selectivity than the one permitted by Kant's a priori categories.[56]

Throughout much of his significant work that shows a profound similarity of approach to objective knowledge (in a realist sense) of both classical theology and leading strands of modern physics, T. F. Torrance shows that the latter had to depart from Kant's skeptical dualism to achieve the kinds of advancements we now think of as part and parcel of science.

Einstein moves away from Kant's skeptical dualism

> The really decisive advance, however, was due to Einstein himself, in the establishing of mathematical invariances in nature irrespective of any and every observer, in which he was able to grasp reality in its depth. This was decisive not only because it broke through the idealist presuppositions stemming from Kant but because it broke through the positivist concept of science.[57]

Torrance draws together a number of Einstein's statements summarizing his understanding of an objective science, free from the Kantian 'legislative reason'[58]:

> 'Physics is an attempt conceptually to grasp reality as it is thought independently of its being observed.'[59] Science of any kind is possible only in so far as it rests upon 'a faith in the simplicity, i.e. the intelligibility, of nature.'[60] Hence what the scientist tries to do is to find the simplest possible set of concepts and their inter-connections through which he can achieve as far as possible a complete and unitary penetration into things in such a way as to grasp them as they are in themselves in their own natural coherent structures. 'Our experience hitherto justifies us in believing that nature is the realisation of the simplest conceivable mathematical ideas... In the limited nature of the mathematically existent simple fields and the simple equations possible between them lies the theorist's hope of grasping the real

---

56. Ibid., 259.

57. T. F. Torrance, *Reality and Scientific Theology*, 21.

58. The following paragraph is taken directly from T. F. Torrance, op. cit., 134,135.

59. A. Einstein, 'Autobiographical Notes,' in P. A. Schilpp, *Albert Einstein: Philosopher-Scientist* (New York, 1949), 81.

60. A. Einstein, ibid., 63.

in all its depth.'[61] The scientist is activated by a wonder and awe before the mysterious comprehensibility of the universe which is yet finally beyond his grasp.[62] This wonder and awe are sustained by religion. 'His religious feeling takes the form of a rapturous amazement at the harmony of natural law, which reveals an intelligence of such superiority that, compared with it, all the systematic thinking and acting of human beings is an utterly insignificant reflection.'[63]

All of this indicates that Kant's regulative *a priori* structures of the mind which supposedly legislate what forms external reality as reported through the sense may take is precisely **not** the way that science works. Torrance writes elsewhere:

> Scientific procedure will not allow us to go beyond the boundary set by the object, for that would presume that by the inherent powers of our own 'autonomous reason' we can gain mastery over it. We have to act within the limits imposed by the nature of the object, and avoid self-willed thinking. It would be uncontrolled and unscientific procedure to run ahead of the object and prescribe just how it shall or can be known before we actually know it, or to withdraw ourselves from actual knowing and then in detachment from the object lay down the conditions upon which valid knowledge is possible. As against all loose arbitrary thinking, or rather romancing, of that sort… It keeps its feet on the ground of actuality.[64]

If Kant's attempted separation of faith from reason, and of the structures of the intellect from the data of sensibility is not grounded in reality, nor justified by the way language works and the way science makes progress, then how can we give a fair account of the way the mind can accurately grasp realities outside it? One does not have to look far to find an alternative to Kant's dualist skepticism, for it has always been assumed by the common sense of mankind, and has to be employed even by those who deny it.

III. An Alternative to Kant's Skeptical Dualism

Hamann argued, as we have seen above, that intellect and sensibility are already joined together in the language that we all use.[65] He held that the entire ability to think rests on what we automatically assume about language (see Hamann's *Werke*, III. 286).[66] Against Kant's views of the legislative *a priori* powers of the autonomous mind, Hamann held that '*Sounds* and *letters* are therefore pure forms a priori…'[67] He stated that: 'Since our way

---

61. A. Einstein, *The World as I See It*, 136, 137f; *Ideas and Opinions*, 274ff.

62. A. Einstein, *Out of My Later Years*, 30, 60.

63. A. Einstein, 'The Religious Spirit of Science,' *Ideas and Opinions*, 40, Cf. also 'On Scientific Truth,' ibid., 262.

64. T. F. Torrance, *Theological Science* (London: Oxford University Press, 1969), 26.

65. See p. 269 of this chapter.

66. See ibid.

67. Hamann, *Werke*, III. 286, quoted in Alexander, op. cit., 73.

of thinking is based upon sense impressions and the perceptions connected with them, so an agreement of the organs of feeling with the mainsprings of human speech can be supposed as quite probable.'[68]

According to Hamann, language is *a priori* to reason

Betz says that this is the crucial point in Hamann's critique of Kant: 'In other words, for Hamann language, with all its a posteriori qualities, is *prior* to reason.'[69] And as John 1 tells us, language comes from him who is 'the Word'. A God who speaks and knows creates a people in his image who also speak and know (in accordance with their own creaturely capacities). Hamann states it this way, as he describes the Garden of Eden:

> Every phenomenon of nature was a word, – the sign, symbol and pledge of a new, mysterious, inexpressible but all the more intimate union, participation and community of divine energies and ideas. Everything the human being heard from the beginning, saw with its eyes, looked upon and touched with its hands was a living word; for God was the word.[70]

The Logos creates and makes the world intelligible

That is, from a biblical/theological point of view, we have been created through the agency of the divine Logos so that to some real degree we share in his Logos ('light of reason' – cf. John 1:9), are thereby enabled to grasp truly (though never exhaustively) the realities of the universe which have been made by the same Logos. It is a willful obstruction of the light of reason he continually imparts to us to split in a Kantian fashion our knowing and what we know. This is not the case in the normal usage of language, and it is not the case in the advancement of modern science. Hamann held that this unnatural dualism and skepticism ultimately came, not from a close observation of the workings of the mind, nor from a close observation of empirical reality, but rather from a theology that was alien to the Christian tradition.

This theology of Kant was Deism. Its authority was not Holy Scripture, but – as Kant writes in *Religion within the Limits of Reason Alone* – 'universal human reason' which he held to be 'the supremely commanding principle.'[71] In his famous article on 'What is Enlightenment,' Kant had made it clear that the traditional creeds of the Christian tradition, and the Scriptures on which they were based, were external authorities to which progressive thinkers were no longer to be bound. Instead, Kant called on them: 'Dare to use your own understanding.'[72]

---

68. Ibid., II. 123 in Alexander, ibid.

69. Betz, op. cit., 251.

70. Hamann, *Werke*, 32: 21-30, quoted by Gwen Griffith-Dickson, 'J. G. Hamann' in *Stanford Encyclopedia of Philosophy*, 9.

71. Kant, *Religion within the Limits of Reason Alone* (1793), English trans. by T. M. Greene and H. H. Hudson (New York: Harper, 1934), 152.

72. Kant, 'What is Enlightenment' in James Schmidt, ed., *What is Enlightenment: Eighteenth Century Answers and Twentieth Century Questions* (Berkeley: University of California Press, 1996), 58-64.

The dogmas with which Kant replaced those of Christianity must be considered later (under section IV), but for the present, we concentrate on the question as to how the mind knows reality. In replacing Christianity, Kant necessarily had to replace its ancient epistemology (that God has created man's trustworthy sense perceptions and the human mind to use language and to know what is outside it). But how does the traditional Christian epistemology give an account of the validity of its knowledge of reality?

How our minds know reality, according to Christian epistemology

First, it believes that the God of order who spoke worlds into existence made them intelligible and orderly (for all their amazing complexity), so that they can be intelligibly perceived by his image-bearers. As T. F. Torrance writes:

> We cannot argue at any point from forms of thought to objective structures in being, even though they arise in our minds under the pressure of those structures, but neither can we make any progress in grasping and interpreting those structures apart from the forms of thought to which they give rise in us. On the other hand, we do have to assume the reality and rational accessibility of those structures in testing or establishing the forms of our thought about them.[73]

Polanyi points out 'the structural kinship between subject and object'

Michael Polanyi has discussed this:

> … correspondence between the structure of comprehension and the structure of the comprehensive unity which is its object, or a structural kinship between subject and object…The intrinsic unity of form and being in the object of this knowledge means that it is only through mental penetration into the form inherent in the object together with intelligent interpretation of it that the human knower can bring its inherent intelligibility to rational expression, but since that intelligibility is inherent in being, his knowing of it must rest on the compulsive ground of that being and not upon himself.[74]

The priority of faith in the knowledge of reality

Thus, instead of Kant's 'autonomy of reason,' the human knower starts out with a faith in something greater than he; something given, something outside himself, that in a certain sense 'imposes itself upon him.' 'Faith' means that one cannot prove it in the form of a syllogistic argument, but there are other ways to know truth than by syllogisms (although these have their proper place).

Discussing Einstein's discovery that 'light has a unique metaphysical status in the universe,'[75] T. F. Torrance states: 'Thus while in the logical

---

73. T. F. Torrance, *Reality and Scientific Theology*, 61.

74. Torrance paraphrases Polanyi's *The Tacit Dimension*, 30ff. in *Transformation and Convergence in the Frame of Knowledge*, 85.

75. See F. S. C. Northrop, with reference to a conversation with H. Weyl in 1927, *Man, Nature and God* (1962), 206 (referred to in Torrance, op. cit., 260).

sense such an order in the universe is neither verifiable nor falsifiable, it remains the most persistent of all our scientific convictions for without it there could be no science at all: hence we do not believe that there is or could be anything that can ultimately count against it...'[76]

Einstein, following Sir James Clerk Maxwell, held to the priority of fundamental belief.

> In his essay on Clerk Maxwell's influence, he insisted in sharp contrast to the positivist and conventionalist tradition [that owes much to Kant's skeptical dualism – ed.], that 'The belief in an external world independent of the perceiving subject is the basis of all natural science,' but along with that belief went another belief in the intrinsic comprehensibility of the universe. These are beliefs...[that] are not open to logical derivation or proof for they are prior to logical reasoning and have to be employed as premises in any attempted proof...Belief of this kind, Einstein claimed, is and always will remain the fundamental motive for all scientific work.[77]

'Faith' or fundamental axioms need no proof, but have to be assumed

These basic beliefs are like fundamental axioms, that even to be denied, still have to be used. They do not need proof, for they are essential 'givens' for any use of the mind in whatever direction it seeks to go. Michael Polanyi has addressed this question in detail (as in his Gifford Lectures: *Personal Knowledge*).

T. F. Torrance comments:

> No human intelligence, Polanyi claimed, however critical or original, can operate outside such a context of faith, for it is within that context that there arises within us, under compulsion from the reality of the world we experience, a regulative set of convictions or a framework of beliefs which prompts and guides our inquiries and controls our assessment of the evidence. They are the ultimate beliefs or normative insights grounded in reality on which we rely...Unless our minds are informed by prior intuitive contact with reality which we have in this way through our basic beliefs they flounder about in fruitless surmises...[78]

Although we are not able to say exactly how 'concepts are correlated with experience',[79] our whole lives have been lived on the basis of its reality. It is an axiom that needs no proof. It is the same with the ability of normal language to convey true information concerning the external and internal worlds. Not to accept this is what Torrance speaks of as a prime error: 'The first error we may speak of in the mode of Wittgenstein as a radical failure to understand the nature of language as a transparent medium through which we allow the objective realities to show through.'[80]

---

76. T. F. Torrance, *Transformation and Convergence in the Frame of Knowledge*, 257.

77. T. F. Torrance, *Christian Theology & Scientific Culture*, 57-58.

78. Ibid., 64.

79. To quote Torrance, *Transformation and Convergence* (Wipf & Stock: Eugene, Oregon, 1998), 77.

80. T. F. Torrance, *Theology in Reocnstruction* (SCM Press: London, 1965), 57.

Wittgenstein on the impossibility of picturing the relation of words to what is represented

What Wittgenstein had noted was that language works in conveying external facts, even though we cannot state in words exactly how language conveys external reality: '…what we cannot represent in language is the relation of language to the external facts – that is, in the language of Wittgenstein, we cannot produce a picture of the relation of a picture to that which is pictured.'[81]

In sum, Kant's skeptical dualism between intellect and the senses, which keeps us from knowing either 'things in themselves' and especially transcendent realities, is, in my view, a sophisticated philosophical invention, intended to clear the field both of the God of the Bible and of traditional Christian dogma. Kant's epistemology, which focuses on the inbuilt structures of the legislative reason of the autonomous knower, raises far more problems than it solves. It cannot make sense of language, and would short-circuit the advancement of science, in so far as its assumptions are followed. It was not proven by Kant and his followers: it was a faith.

Does Kant's 'faith' make more sense than the alternative?

But is there not a better faith? Is it not far better to follow the basic axioms necessary for all healthy reasoning, axioms which are consonant with the way normal minds work, and with the way science goes forward, and are – according to the Prologue to John's Gospel – the reflections of the Creator Logos in the minds of his image-bearers? But to do so inevitably confronts people with their Creator, and that is a price that some tragically lose everything to keep from paying.[82]

IV. Kant's 'Christology'

Since the thought of Immanuel Kant has had such deep and wide influence on the Western Christian tradition from the early nineteenth century to the present time, it is appropriate to see how he has impacted the doctrine of Christ, especially in the Protestant world. Not only Schleiermacher[83] and the German idealist stream of thought,[84] but also French,[85] British[86] and American scholars (from the nineteenth-century Social Gospel of Walter Rauschenbush to the long since defunct 'God is Dead' theologians of the 1960s, such as Paul Van Buren, down to the 'Jesus Seminar' leaders of the 1980s and '90s) have followed him, in various degrees (usually accepting, in

---

81. A reference to L. Wittgenstein, *Tractatus Logico-philosophicus* 4.01f, 4.12f in T. F. Torrance, *Theological Science*, 183.

82. 'For what is a man profited, if he shall gain the whole world, and lose his own soul? Or what shall a man give in exchange for his soul?' Matthew 16:26.

83. See the discussion of Schleiermacher in H. R. Mackintosh, *Types of Modern Theology* (London: Charles Scribner's Sons, 1937), 31-100.

84. e.g. James Richmond, *Faith and Philosophy* (London: Hodder and Stoughton, 1966), 54-71.

85. Ibid., 44-45.

86. e.g. John MacQuarrie, *Principles of Christian Theology* (New York: Scribner, 1966).

their own way, Kant's dichotomy between intellect and sensibility; between phenomenal and noumenal) so that through many of these church leaders, the traditional doctrine of Christ has taken a very different turn since Kant.

It is not my purpose here to trace the influence of Kant on the changing religious scene of the Protestant Churches of the West, for that would be a volume itself, one that I am not competent to write. Here I pursue the much more modest goal of briefly surveying what Kant himself seems to have taught about the person and work of Christ, keeping in mind that what he said has shaped most of the established or 'main-line' churches of Western Europe and America as they teach who Christ is.

Kant never names 'Jesus Christ,' but speaks of him in other ways

To speak of Kant's 'Christology' may appear strange to those who have read his major works, for he never brings himself to write either the name Jesus or Christ. Yet he does deal, in his own round-about way, with the Son of God[87] and with the one he calls 'the wise teacher of rational religion,'[88] and 'the personified idea of the good principle.'[89] Perhaps surprisingly, he actually rebukes Feuerbach (who to a degree followed Kant) for his denigration of the motives of the death of God's Son in the infamous *Wolfenbuttel Fragments*.[90] Thus, without using the name 'Christ,' Kant definitely sets forth a certain kind of Christology.

God is a 'limiting concept'

The Christology of Kant is, of course, taught in the context of his views of God and of religion, which in turn are based on his epistemological separation between phenomenal and noumenal, for – according to this concept – the mind is unable to understand anything beyond empirical experience. In general, God and religion are placed in the noumenal, which cannot be known directly by the human mind.[91] God, for instance, is 'a limiting concept'; that is, a certain awareness of God is 'regulative' for our thought, but not 'constitutive.' In other words, the concept of God 'regulates' or helps make sense of the totality of our thought processes, but is not 'constituted' by positive content that is knowable by us: 'To take the regulative principle of the systematic unity of nature as being a constitutive principle, and to hypostatize, and presuppose as a cause, that which serves, merely in idea, as the ground of the consistent employment of reason, is simply to confound reason.'[92]

---

87. Kant, *Religion Within the Limits of Reason Alone*, English translation by Greene and Hudson (New York: Harper and Brothers: reprint ed. 1960), 54.

88. Ibid., 78.

89. Ibid., 54-55.

90. Ibid., 77.

91. In his 'Transcendental Dialectic,' Kant lists four 'antinomies' that occur if one attempts to grasp the content of the noumenal (or that which exceeds sense experience as interpreted through the structures of the mind). One of these antinomies is the following: although the existence of the world calls for 'a being that is absolutely necessary,' yet no such being exists (*Critique of Pure Reason*, 224).

92. Ibid., 314.

The place of 'transcendental ideas'

Such regulative principles as God, freedom, and immortality have their place, if not taken too far as concerns content: 'I understand by idea a necessary concept of reason to which no corresponding object can be given in sense-experience. Thus the pure concepts of reason...are *transcendental ideas*. They are concepts of pure reason, in that they view all knowledge gained in experience as being determined through an absolute totality of understanding. Finally, they are transcendent and overstep the limits of all experience; no object adequate to the transcendental idea can ever be found within experience.'[93]

So on this basis, how far does Kant think we can take the concepts of God and of the Son of God? We consider here (1) the existence of God; (2) the authority (or source) for beliefs about God and his will, and (3) how to interpret traditional Christian dogma.

(1) Kant's approach to the existence of God

I will not enter the details of how Kant disproves what he considers to be the three classical theological arguments for God's existence, but offer only the briefest outline.[94] He considers there to be only three ways of proving the existence of God by speculative reason: (a) the *physico-theological* proof; (b) the *cosmological* proof, and (c) the *ontological* proof.[95]

In brief, (a) the *physico-theological* (or *teleological*) proof starts from a consideration of the mode in which the sensible world exists, a world which seems to demonstrate finality, from there one moves backwards to God, who is the final cause. Similarly, (b) the *cosmological* proof, starts with empirical reality and moves backwards to God, who causes it. But Kant holds that both (a) and (b) are actually based on (c) the *ontological* proof, which states that in the idea of a most perfect being, his existence is necessarily included. Kant argues that it is begging the question to conclude that a being exists merely from its concept. He holds that existence is not a predicate:

> '*Being*' is obviously not a real predicate; that is, it is not a concept of something which could be added to the concept of a thing. It is merely the positing of a thing, or of certain determinations, as existing in themselves...If, now we ... say 'God is,' or 'There is a God,' we attach no new predicate to the concept of God, but only posit the subject in itself with all its predicates, and indeed posit it as being an *object* that stands in relation to my *concept*. The content of both must be one and the same; nothing can have been added to the concept, which expresses merely what is possible, by my thinking its object (through the expression 'it is') as given absolutely.[96]

Then Kant adds a famous illustration that being is not a predicate:

---

93. Ibid., 174.

94. See under 'Transcendental Dialectic,' Book II, Chapter III – 'The Idea of Pure Reason' (*Critique of Pure Reason*, 269-305).

95. Ibid., 277.

96. Ibid., 281.

Otherwise stated, the real contains no more than the merely possible. A hundred real thalers do not contain the least coin more than a hundred possible thalers...My financial position is, however, affected very differently by a hundred real thalers than it is by the mere concept of them (that is, of their possibility)...the conceived hundred thalers are not themselves in the least increased through thus acquiring existence outside my concept.[97]

Stanley L. Jaki, I think, accurately points out Kant's erroneous reasoning here:

Kant's two objections to the ontological argument show him a poor reasoner. They are based on his failure to perceive the conceptual difference between infinite and finite being. Concerning the latter, be it Kant's hundred thalers or the perfect island of Gaunilo (Anselm's first critique), the existence of a thing is wholly extrinsic to the concept of it, but not in the case of an infinite, that is, infinitely perfect being.[98]

Kant's critique of (b) the *cosmological* proof (i.e. if anything exists, a necessary being also must exist'), is said by Copleston to be 'singularly unconvincing':

Or, rather, it is convincing only on one assumption, namely that the argument based on experience brings us, not to an affirmation of the existence of a necessary being, but only to the vague *idea* of a necessary being. For in this case we should have to look about, as Kant puts it, for a determining concept which would include existence in its content, so that existence could be deduced from the determined idea of a necessary being. If, however, the argument based on experience brings us to the affirmation of the *existence* of a necessary being, the attempt to determine *a priori* the necessary attributes of this being has nothing to do with the ontological argument, which is primarily concerned with deducing existence from the idea of a being as possible, and not with deducing attributes from the idea of a being the existence of which has already been affirmed on grounds other than possibility.[99]

Kant, while denying the validity of (a) the *teleological* (or *physico-theological*) proof, accords it more respect than the others: 'The proof always deserves to be mentioned with respect. It is the oldest, the clearest, and the most accordant with the common reason of mankind.'[100] He adds: 'I therefore maintain that the physico-theological proof can never by itself establish the existence of a supreme being, but must always fall back upon the ontological argument; and the latter therefore contains (in so far as a speculative proof is possible at all) *the one possible ground of proof* with which human reason can never dispense.'[101]

---

97. Ibid., 282.

98. Jaki, op. cit., 121. See also Douglas Kelly, *Systematic Theology*, vol. 1, 70-76 for fuller details.

99. Copleston, *A History of Philosophy*, vol. 6, 'Modern Philosophy,' Part II, Kant (New York: Image Books, 1960), 91-92.

100. Kant, op. cit., 293.

101. Ibid., 294.

Kant explains:

> The physico-theological argument can indeed lead us to the point of admiring the greatness, wisdom, power, etc., of the Author of the world, but can take us no further. Accordingly, we then abandon the argument from empirical grounds of proof, and fall back upon the contingency which, in the first steps of the argument, we had inferred from the order and purposiveness of the world...Thus, the physico-theological proof, failing in its undertaking, has in face of this difficulty suddenly fallen back upon the cosmological proof; and since the latter is only a disguised ontological proof, it has really achieved its purpose by reason alone – although at the start it disclaimed all kinship with pure reason and professed to establish its convictions on convincing evidence derived from experience.[102]

But Kant himself seems to be begging the question here: he reduces the teleological argument (that perceives design in the real world with which we have to do) to the structure of our minds which shape sense experience to such a degree that we cannot finally get beyond the constitutive human mind to perceive such things as intelligent design in the real world beyond us. As T. F. Torrance has written in answer to this procedure of short-circuiting the real world so that all we are left with is another form of the ontological argument (which argument, as we argued above, Kant has not properly understood):

> These are beliefs [i.e. the reality of the external world and the inherent comprehensibility of the universe] that have to be assumed and put to the test, but they are not open to logical derivation or proof for they are prior to reasoning and have to be employed as premises in any attempted proof. There could be no science without belief in the inner harmony of the world or without the belief that it is possible to grasp reality with our theoretical constructions. Belief of this kind, Einstein claimed, is and always will remain the fundamental motive for all scientific work.[103]

Kant accepts one 'proof' for God's existence

Having rejected three basic proofs for God's existence, Kant then goes on to formulate a proof which he thinks has validity in light of his dualist assumptions: the moral argument. In his *Critique of Judgment* Kant wrote that this moral argument alone 'only establishes the Being of God sufficiently for our moral destination, i.e. in a practical point of view.'[104] He proceeds in terms of what the moral consciousness says is good.

'Good' is defined as 'duty'

In his *Groundwork of the Metaphysics of Morals*, Kant says that 'It is impossible to conceive of anything in the world, or indeed out of it, which can be called good without qualification save only a good will.'[105] Kant

---

102. Ibid., 297.

103. T. F. Torrance, *Christian Theology & Scientific Culture*, 58. See a discussion of this in D. Kelly. op. cit., 96-98.

104. Kant, *Critique of Judgment*, Translated by J. H. Bernard (London, 1932).

105. Kant, *Groundwork of the Metaphysics of Morals*, translated by T. K. Abbott (London, 1909),

defines the good, when applied to the will, as acting for the sake of duty. By this 'good' he means a human will, for he terms the divine will as 'holy' to avoid speaking of God 'performing his duty.' But humans are to perform their duty, and this means acting out of reverence for the moral law, and this law is universal.

The 'categorical imperative'

After making certain distinctions that need not detain us here, Kant says that 'good,' or acting out of duty requires this attitude: 'I am never to act otherwise than so that I can also will that my maxim[106] should become a universal law.'[107] Kant calls this will to obey the universal law for duty's sake the 'categorical imperative.' Since our wills are not necessarily holy (as is God's), they are under the commands which come through pure practical reason. This moral command puts us under an imperative. This type of imperative is not a *hypothetical* (or problematic) imperative (e.g. if you wish to learn, you must go to school). Rather, it is an apodictic (or categorical) imperative: 'The categorical imperative, which declares an action to be objectively necessary in itself without reference to any purpose, that is, without any other end, is valid as an *apodictic* imperative.'[108]

This categorical imperative is characterized by oneness and universal range: 'There is, therefore, only one categorical imperative, and it is this: *Act only on that maxim through which you can at the same time will that it should become a universal law.*'[109]

The autonomy of the will

But what is the source of this universal law? 'In Kant's view, the will of man considered as a rational being must be regarded as the source of the law which he recognizes as universally binding. This is the principle of the autonomy, as contrasted with the heteronomy of the will.'[110]

On this autonomous basis, Kant states in his *Religion within the Limits of Reason Alone* that: 'So far as morality is based upon the conception of man as a free agent who, just because he is free, binds himself through his reason to unconditioned laws, it stands in need neither of the idea of another Being over him, for him to apprehend his duty, nor of an incentive other than the law itself, for him to do his duty.'[111]

In other words, morality does not need to be traced back to the character of God, for that would be 'heteronomous.' Yet morality still constitutes a moral proof of God in that the idea of God gives 'a special point of focus

---

sixth edition, 9.

106. According to Kant's terminology, a *maxim* is a subjective principle of volition (e.g. one type of maxim is the desire to obey universal law as such), as contrasted to *principle* (a basic objective moral law, grounded in the pure practical reason).

107. Ibid., 18.

108. Ibid., 32.

109. Ibid., 38.

110. Copleston, op. cit., 121.

111. Kant, *Religion within the Limits of Reason Alone*, 3.

for the unification of all ends.'[112] It is only the idea of the highest good (or *summum bonum*), or God, who can unite both duty and happiness.[113]

An illustration of how Kant's moral proof works

An illustration of how Kant believes this moral proof would work to demonstrate the reality of his kind of limited God is given as he leads 'a well-disposed man' (such as Spinoza, according to Kant's second edition of *Critique of Judgment*), 'who is firmly convinced that there is no God and no future life':

> We may thus suppose a well-disposed man who is firmly convinced that there is no God and (what, in regard to the object of morality, comes to the same thing) no future life either; how will he judge concerning his own inner determination to an end by means of the moral law, which in practice he reveres? He demands no advantage to himself from obedience to it, either in this world or in another; rather does he disinterestedly will merely the establishment of the Good towards which that holy law directs all his faculties. But his striving is limited; and from Nature he can expect indeed an occasional coincidence, but never a regular conformity according to constant principles with the end which he notwithstanding feels himself bound and impelled to bring about. Deceit, violence, jealousy will always prevail around him, though he himself is honest…and the other well-disposed men whom he encounters will, notwithstanding all their deserving to be happy, yet, through the indifference of Nature, be subject to all the evils of want, sickness, and untimely death…and cast back them who would believe that they were the final purpose of creation into the abyss of the purposeless chaos of matter whence they were drawn. Thus the end which this well-disposed man had, and was bound to have, before his eyes in following the laws of morality, he must assuredly give up as impossible of attainment; or else, if he wishes to remain still faithful to the moral vocation whereof he is inwardly conscious, and not to suffer the feeling of reverence, inspired in him directly by the Moral Law, and urging him to obey it, to be weakened by disbelief in the reality of the only ideal end adequate to its sublime demands – a weakening which cannot but involve damage to the moral sentiment – he must, as he quite well can, since there is nothing essentially contradictory in the assumption, assume, from a practical point of view, that is to say, in order to form for himself at least a conception of the end presented to him as a moral duty, the existence of a Moral Author of the world, that is, of God.[114]

But this God, whom Kant has proved by means of the autonomous moral sense of mankind, is a severely reduced figure from the Lord God Almighty of Old and New Testaments! The eternally self-existent Trinity, who reveals himself as 'I am that I am,' who depends on nothing outside himself, and on whom all things directly depend bears very little relation to the Kantian deity, who somehow is a regulative concept of the categories of the autonomous human intellect! In a word, Kant's God is not the infinite God of traditional Judaism and Christianity, but the largely finite

---

112. Ibid., 5.

113. Ibid.

114. Clement C. J. Webb, *Kant's Philosophy of Religion* (Oxford: at the Clarendon Press, 1926), 83-84.

God of the eighteenth-century European Enlightenment. Functionally, Kant replaces the aseity of God (his self-existence) with the autonomy (self-law) of the human will. These are irreconcilable differences as to who is in charge!

Naturally, the Son of God suffers, at the hands of Kant's philosophy, the same incredible reduction to a 'limiting concept'. So does the authoritative Word that Israel and the Church had always held to be of the highest, absolute truth for information about God and his will.

(2) The authority (or source) for beliefs about God and his will
Kant's philosophy does not see mankind as inherently obligated by virtue of creation to obey the voice of its Creator, as he has spoken in his revealed Word. Instead, 'he does not need the idea of another Being over him...':

> So far as morality is based upon the conception of man as a free agent who, just because he is free, binds himself through his reason to unconditioned laws, it stands in need neither of the idea of another Being over him for him to apprehend his duty, nor of an incentive other than the law itself, for him to do his duty.[115]

Kant functionally replaces the authority of Holy Scripture with human reason
Oswald Bayer shows what has happened in Kant as regards the former authority of Holy Scripture:

> In Kant the authority hitherto accorded to Scripture is assumed by the authority of reason. This can easily be shown point by point: *auctoritas, infallibilitas, perfectio, perspicuitas,* and *efficacia,* above all the power of self-interpretation, of criticism, of autonomous judgment, and the power to establish norms – all of these effective modes and attributes of Holy Scripture, which can only be effective modes and attributes of the Triune God, are ascribed by Kant to reason – albeit, in the final analysis, not to theoretical, but to practical reason.[116]

Copleston shows the direction that this shift in final authority takes in Kant:

> But any idea of a unique revelation of religious truths, and still more of an authoritarian Church as custodian and accredited interpreter of revelation, is rejected by Kant. I do not mean that he rejected altogether the idea of a visible Christian Church, with a faith based on the Scriptures; for he did not. But the visible Church is for him only an approximation to the ideal of the universal invisible Church, which is, or would be, the spiritual union of all men in virtue and the moral service of God.[117]

---

115. Kant, op. cit., 3.

116. *Auctoritat und Kritik: Zur Hermeneutik und Wissenschatfstheorie* (Tubingen: Mohr-Siebeck, 1991), 44, quoted in Betz, op. cit., 190, note 5.

117. Copleston, op. cit., 136.

(3) How Kant interprets Scripture and Christian Dogma

The traditional Lutheran and Reformed principle of interpretation (based in many ways on Saint Augustine, who relied (in part) on the Seven Rules of the Donatist, Tychonius) was that Scripture is to be interpreted by Scripture. Kant's principle of interpretation is vastly different: 'We must then interpret Scripture by the principles of natural religion; and this exposition of Scripture by natural religion is what we are to understand by the Spirit of God which guides us into all truth.'[118]

Kant re-interprets the Scriptures, rather than attacking them

Kant did not directly attack the authority of the Scriptures; rather, he re-interpreted them in terms of the religious philosophy of the Enlightenment. And what he does with Scripture, he does with the traditional dogmas of Christianity, as Copleston shows:

> But it is perhaps worth noting, that he shows a strong tendency to strip away, as it were, the historical associations of certain dogmas and to find a meaning which fits in with his own philosophy. Thus he does not deny original sin: on the contrary, he affirms it against those who imagine that man is naturally perfect. But the ideas of an historical Fall and of inherited sin give place to the conception of a fundamental propensity to act out of mere self-love and without regard to the universal moral laws…In this way Kant affirms the dogma in the sense that he verbally admits it while at the same time he interprets it rationalistically…[119]

How Kant re-interprets the Person and Work of Christ

This rationalistic re-interpretation of Scripture and traditional dogma is nowhere more evident than in what Kant makes of Christ. Colin Brown has shown how Kant reduces the historical Christ to *The Personified Idea of the Good Principle*:

> *Mankind* (rational earthly existence in general) *in its complete moral perfection* is that which alone can render a world the object of a divine decree and the end of the creation. With such perfection as the prime condition, happiness is the direct consequence, according to the will of the Supreme Being. Man, so conceived, alone pleasing to God, 'is in Him through eternity' (John 1:1-2), the idea of him proceeds from God's very being; hence he is no created thing but His only-begotten Son, 'the *Word* (the *Fiat!*) through which all other things are, and without which nothing is in existence that is made' (John 1:3) (since for him, that is, for rational existence in the world, so far as he may be regarded in the light of his moral destiny, all things were made). 'He is the brightness of his glory' (Heb. 1:3). 'In him God loved the world' (John 3:16), and only in him and through the adoption of his disposition can we hope 'to become sons of God' (John 1:12), etc.
>
> Now it is our universal duty as men to *elevate* ourselves to this ideal of moral perfection, that is, to this archetype of the moral disposition in all its purity – and for this the idea itself, which reason presents to us for your

---

118. Webb, op. cit., 138.
119. Copleston, op. cit., 136-137.

zealous emulation, can give us power. But just because we are not the authors of this idea, and because it has established itself in man without our comprehending how human nature could have been capable of receiving it, it is more appropriate to say that this archetype has *come down* to us from heaven and has assumed our humanity (for it is less possible to conceive how man, by nature *evil*, should of himself lay aside evil and *raise* himself to the ideal of holiness, than that the latter should *descend* to man and assume a *humanity*, which is in itself, not evil). Such union with us may therefore be regarded as a state of *humiliation* of the Son of God (Phil. 2:6-8) if we represent to ourselves this godly-minded person, regarded as our archetype, as assuming sorrows in fullest measure in order to further the world's good, though he himself is holy and therefore is bound to endure no sufferings whatsoever. Man, on the contrary, who is never free from guilt even though he has taken on the very same disposition, can regard as truly merited the sufferings that may overtake him, by whatever road they come; consequently he must consider himself unworthy of the union of his disposition with such an idea, even though this idea serves him as an archetype.[120]

Although full of traditional Christological references from Holy Scripture, Kant's re-interpretation of the significance of Christ essentially turns him into a disembodied, humanistic moral idea, flowing from the autonomous concepts of the rationalistic mind. He is thereby no longer the God/man: 'the one mediator between God and men, the man Christ Jesus, who gave himself a ransom for all, to be testified in due time' (I Tim. 2:5-6). According to this view, he is not the incarnate Son of God, who still exists in two natures: divine and human, in one person, who by means of his person and work in and through the hypostatic union saves forever all his people.

Therefore, Kant's Christology is a species of infinite reductionism in which the embodied Second Person of the Holy Trinity disappears into a moralistic idea that is not threatening to proud human autonomy. But willfully to lose who Christ really is, is to lose everything worth being and having, and that loss is eternal, if not repented of.[121]

Followers of Kant's re-interpretation of Christ

Kant's re-interpretation of Christ with its widely followed reductionism has been carried on in many schools of thought from his time to the present day. Without expounding the history of this humanistic misinterpretation of Christ, we need only mention a few of its followers: Harnack's reduction of the truth about Christianity to 'the Fatherhood of

---

120. Kant, *Religion within the Limits of Reason Alone*, 54-55, quoted in Colin Brown, *Jesus in European Protestant Thought 1778-1860* (Baker Book House: Grand Rapids, Michigan, 1985), 62.

121. See John 8:24b: '...For if ye believe not that I am he, ye shall die in your sins.' But there is another way set before us: 'If we confess our sins, he is faithful and just to forgive us our sins, and to cleanse us from all unrighteousness' (I John 1:9). If we do that, then the happy condition of Jeremiah 9:23-24 will become true for us: 'Thus saith the LORD, Let not the wise man glory in his wisdom, neither let the mighty man glory in his might, let not the rich man glory in his riches: But let him that glorieth glory in this, that he understandeth and knoweth me, that I am the LORD which exercise lovingkindness, judgment, and righteousness, in the earth: for in these things I delight, saith the LORD.'

God, the brotherhood of man, and the infinite value of the human soul' through his *What is the Gospel*, widely followed, first in liberal circles in Germany, and then throughout the Western world; the pathetic, broken apocalyptic figure of the merely human Jesus, traced by Albert Schweizer in his *Quest for the Historical Jesus*; the Social Gospel in North America, with its replacement of eternal salvation by forcible statist socialism; the humanistic, existentialist Jesus of Rudolph Bultmann, who – not unlike Kant – 'demythologizes' Christ and his miracles into symbols of one's 'authentic self-existence'; the American Protestant Modernism of Harry Emerson Fosdick in the 1920s and '30s, as exemplified in his notorious sermon, 'Shall the Fundamentalists Win?'; the British radical skepticism of Bishop John A. T. Robinson's *Honest to God* in the 1960s; the revolutionary, this-worldly Jesus of radical Roman Catholic Liberation theologians, and the alienated, skeptical and cynical teacher of the 'Jesus Seminar.'

Possibly the most influential theologian of the twentieth century was Karl Barth. Certainly he was heavily influenced by Kant, especially in Barth's earlier writings. But Barth sought to escape the philosophy of the Enlightenment in which he had been trained. His interaction with the Church Fathers, the Medieval Scholastics (particularly Saint Anselm), and then the sixteenth-century Protestant Reformers, and the seventeenth-century Reformed Orthodox theologians (especially as conveyed in H. Heppe's *Reformed Dogmatics*) helped lead him in a different direction.[122]

Yet, having read much of Barth over the years, and having rejoiced in many areas of his teaching, still I have found it difficult to make sense of his dialectical methodology (even in his later phase), and wonder how much of both Kant and Hegel may remain in this methodology. In particular, the way Barth renders his account of the traditional doctrines of the inspiration of Holy Scripture, of creation, of election and reprobation, and of such crucial matters as the bodily resurrection of Jesus Christ, and universal salvation goes in a very different direction from the classical Christian reading of these pivotal truths on the basis of a straightforward exegesis of Scripture, in the context of the historic Creeds and Councils of the Church. It seems doubtful to me that he was necessarily following Kant in any direct manner on these issues (on most of which Kant did not speak), but rather he spoke to an Enlightenment culture which had been heavily influenced by Kant, and it seems to me that he spoke to it in a way far more acceptable to its assumptions than did the traditional preaching and teaching of the historic Christian Churches.

Whether or not his dialectical method owed much to Kant and Hegel is beyond my limited knowledge, but as a humble believer, I have found it difficult to make sense of how – with one hand he can clearly present

---

122. T. F. Torrance, for instance, discusses the major shift from the early Barth to the later Barth in terms of his leaving the Kantian-type dialectic between time and eternity. Torrance states that other leading twentieth century theologians such as Bultmann, C. H. Dodd, Reinhold Niebuhr, and Paul Tillich remained in the older, Kantian dialectic. See: T. F. Torrance, *The Incarnation*, 272-274.

a doctrine in its traditional reading – and then within a few pages, take it away with the other hand, and re-interpret it within a mode that often (though certainly not always) seems suited to the culture that has followed the Enlightenment.

All of the theologians mentioned above, and some more than others, owe much to Kant, and without him their thought would not have been possible (though one would not wish to blame Kant for all the directions in which some of them have gone, nor could one assert that Kant is equally present in their thought). Some of them may well take their re-interpretation of Christology further than Kant would have, but even so, many of them have heard his basic message clearly. Some may well have resisted Kant, and others gladly affirmed his epistemology. For those who followed Kant, one must note that they do not deliver the message of Holy Scripture and of the historic Christian Creeds and Confessions. Kant and the Scriptures cannot both be right.

One must decide whether to follow the Biblical Christ or the Christ of Kant

The decision one makes as to which one to follow: the Living Christ of Scripture, or the pale, vapid 'limiting concept' allowed by Kant and his school, does not depend on one's intellectual quotient and educational level. It does not depend on whether one seeks to be in touch with the legitimate concepts and concerns of the modern world (always a divinely given duty), for the defining issue between the followers of the Biblical Christ and the Kantian post-critical Christ is not the willingness to reach out to the modern world (something they both share in their own quite differing ways), but rather: what constitutes the truth for the world in all ages?

Along these lines, it is a serious begging of the question at issue to assume that the skeptical dualism of Immanuel Kant lies at the foundations of the scientific advancements of the modern world, for as we sought to show above, modern physics since Clerk Maxwell, Faraday and Einstein had to go in a precisely contrary direction from the critical assumptions of Kant. If by 'modern world' one means 'modern science,' Kant cannot validly be said to be its true pioneer. So, clear thinking will indicate that a desire to speak intelligibly on the behalf of the Lord to the modern culture, far from requiring one to accept Kantian philosophy, calls for the contrary; it calls for the assumption (and practice) of a realist and unitary (not dualist) theory of knowledge; one that accords with the way the mind normally works; one that has made possible the advancement of science; one that accords with the truth claims of Holy Scripture.

But the plain truth is that something else (even beyond an objective demonstration of reality) is required for us to be willing to face the facts that will lead us in the right direction.[123] Jesus has told us exactly what it

---

123. Or to speak more accurately: 'Someone' needs to accompany the objective demonstration of every theological truth in order for it to be effective: that is, the Holy Spirit. For example, see I Thessalonians 2:13: 'For this cause also thank we God without ceasing, because, when ye received the Word of God which ye heard of us, ye received it not as the word of men, but as it is in truth, the word of God, which effectually worketh also in you that believe.'

is: it is nothing less than a miraculous intervention of God into alienated human life – the miracle of the new birth, wrought by the Holy Spirit. For Jesus said, 'Except a man be born again, he cannot see the kingdom of God' (John 3:3). It is a miracle, but at the same time, it is also a gracious and sincere call to anyone who will listen. Unto this good hour, the door is still open to all who will hear the word of faith: 'That if thou shalt confess with thy mouth the Lord Jesus, and shalt believe in thine heart that God hath raised him from the dead, thou shalt be saved' (Rom. 10:9). It is a matter of exercising faith in God's own testimony to his Son: 'So then faith cometh by hearing, and hearing by the word of God' (Rom. 10:17).

If this seems impossible for us to do, let us remember that 'With men this is impossible; but with God all things are possible' (Matt. 19:26), and that the down-coming of the Holy Spirit alone is able to awaken us to this saving faith. We may boldly claim the promise of Jesus for the Holy Spirit to assist us in exercising a faith that is beyond our natural powers, for he promised: 'If ye then, being evil, know how to give good gifts unto your children: how much more shall your heavenly Father give the Holy Spirit to them that ask him?' (Luke 11:13).

May many who read these words come to sing with the nineteenth-century Scottish minister and hymn writer, Horatius Bonar:

I came to Jesus, as I was,
Weary and sick and sad;
I found in Him a resting place,
And He has made me glad.

PART TWO

THE HUMILIATION OF CHRIST

CHAPTER 7

THE STATES OF CHRIST

When the Apostle Paul instructs his son in the faith, Timothy, concerning the foundational truths on how to live and minister for God, he says: 'This is a faithful saying, and worthy of all acceptation, that Christ Jesus came into the world to save sinners; of whom I am chief' (I Timothy 1:15). The foundation of the mission of the church is always what the Son of God came into the world to do for it, what it could never do for itself. What he did and what he lived out as man in our place has traditionally been spoken of by the teachers of the church as 'the two states of Christ'. It is through the accomplishments of these two states of the Redeemer that the world is redeemed, and so they have been held forth in the hearts of God's people, the pulpits of the church and the witness of the redeemed through the ages. They take us to the heart of Biblical Christology, and in them the beauty of the Lord shines out at every turn, especially as its Trinitarian pattern shines forth. All through the events of Christ's incarnation, in giving himself to and for a lost humanity, he is always giving himself to the Father in love and obedience, always operating in the power of the Spirit, and always being affirmed by the Father and anointed by the Spirit. Thus, in the details of these states, and the steps within them, we find the salvation the Father eternally planned, provided for us through his Son, and applied by his Spirit.

These 'Two States' of Christ are (I) his Humiliation and (II) his Exaltation.

By way of outline:

In this seventh chapter, after considering the creedal and confessional background of the doctrine of the two States, at present we look only at the first 'stage' of his Humiliation: (1) his Incarnation, under which we consider (a) his Virgin Birth (in this chapter), and (b) his Active Obedience, or Life of True Sonship (in chapter eight).

The other 'stages' of his Humiliation follow in the ninth and tenth chapters: (2) Suffering, (3) Death, (4) Burial, and (5) Descent into Hell. The ninth chapter deals both with: (2) his suffering, and also with (3) his death, but only up to the crucifixion. Chapter ten listens to his seven words from the cross, and goes on to look at (4) his burial, and (5) his descent into hell.

His Exaltation is expounded in chapters eleven and twelve. Its steps or stages are discussed in chapter eleven (the Resurrection), and then in chapter twelve, his Ascension, Session, and Return.

Before opening the discussion of the two states, we must survey the development of the concept of 'states of Christ' in the Church. The historic church, at an early stage of its existence, needed to summarize the basic facts about how the incarnate Christ accomplished our salvation, as a guide to its faith and preaching. Early on, the church developed a sort of conceptual, doctrinal outline to inform the basic faith of its congregations, and to guide the preaching of its leaders.

The Creedal Background of the Doctrine of the Two States of Christ

From the time of the Apostles Creed (probably by the late second century) unto the present, the Christian Church has gathered much of its worship and teaching around what in later centuries would come to be called *'the States of Christ.'* The ancient Creed confessed God as Father and Creator; Jesus Christ, his only Son as our Lord; and then recites the most significant stages of his experience for us: his conception by the Holy Spirit and birth of the Virgin Mary; his suffering under Pontius Pilate; his crucifixion, death, and burial; his descent into hell (added somewhat later); his resurrection on the third day; his ascension into heaven; his sitting on the right hand of God; and his coming from there to judge the living and the dead. The Creed has other clauses, but for the purposes of this chapter, we shall concentrate at present only on those 'stages' in the incarnate experience of our Lord between his conception and descent into Hades.

It is difficult to pinpoint the date of the Apostles Creed, but the 'Interrogatory Creed of Hippolytus' seems to be dated around the year 215. It asks these questions:

Do you believe in God the Father All-Governing [*Pantokratora*]?

Do you believe in Christ Jesus, the Son of God, Who was begotten by the Holy Spirit from the Virgin Mary, Who was crucified under Pontius Pilate, and died (and was buried) and rose the third day living from the dead, and ascended into the heavens, and sat down on the right hand of the Father, and will come to judge the living and the dead?

Do you believe in the Holy Spirit, in the holy Church, and (in the resurrection of the body [*sarkos*])?[1]

---

1. John H. Leith, *Creeds of the Churches* (Anchor Books: Doubleday & Company: Garden City, NY, 1963), 23.

Hence, both the Apostles Creed and Hippolytus (not to mention theological statements from several other early Church writers, such as Ignatius, Justin Martyr, Irenaeus and Tertullian) set in order what would much later be termed the two 'states' of Christ, and also some, if not all, of the various 'stages' or 'steps' in those overall life experiences of the Redeemer. Some of their preliminary discussions of 'the states of Christ' are found in their various expositions of 'the rule of faith' (or 'rule of truth'), which originally came from the baptismal formula.[2]

Medieval Developments leading to the doctrine of the Two States

Without employing the precise categories of the two states of Christ with their subsections, leading theologians in the Middle Ages, usually referring to Saint Augustine, did expound most of these stages of the life and work of the Redeemer, in one way or another. Peter Lombard does so in several distinctions of volume three of *The Sentences: On the Incarnation of the Word*. In 'Distinction XV,' Lombard discusses 'Man's defects which Christ assumed in his human nature,' including ignorance and sorrow.[3] 'Distinction XVI' deals with Christ's taking on our mortality,[4] and XVII discusses his two wills in light of his prayer for 'the cup to pass from him'.[5] 'Distinction XVIII' expounds what Christ has merited for us through his obedience unto death.[6] 'Distinction XIX' shows how the Mediator redeemed us from the devil and sin.[7]

Substantial work was done in the Latin-speaking Western Church during the early thirteenth century, but it was generally directed to questions involved in the *being* of the Mediator (as God and man: two natures in one person), rather than his saving *activities* (although these are certainly assumed). Some of this very serious theological discussion is summarized in Appendix I to chapter four.

Later in the thirteenth century, Saint Thomas Aquinas also devotes much of his Christological attention to the issues of the being of Christ: how the two natures are united in the one person of Christ. Yet he does say more than his predecessors about several aspects of Christ's redeeming actions, as for instance, in Book Four of his *Summa Contra Gentiles*: especially chapter 54, where he states the argument that 'it was suitable for God to be made flesh,' and chapter 55, where he responds to 'Arguments previously set down against the suitability of the incarnation.'[8] But in his later masterpiece, *Summa Theologiae*, Thomas moves in a direction that foreshadows the fuller study of the sixteenth-century Reformation scholars on what would come to be called the 'States of Christ'.

---

2. See D. F. Kelly, *Systematic Theology*, vol. 1, 426-35.

3. Peter Lombard, *The Sentences: On the Incarnation of the Word*, Book 3, translated by Giulio Silano, pp. 57-65.

4. Ibid., 66-67.

5. Ibid., 69-72.

6. Ibid., 72-77.

7. Ibid., 78-84.

8. Saint Thomas Aquinas, *Summa Contra Gentiles: Book Four: Salvation* (Notre Dame: University of Notre Dame Press, 1957), Translated with notes by Charles J. O'Neil, pp. 228-46.

Part III of his great work is given to an exposition of Christology, where he deals with both the *being* and the *actions* of the Redeemer, from Questions XXVII to LIX. Thomas covers the Lord's birth, holy life, temptations, teaching, miracles, transfiguration, passion, death, burial, descent into hell, resurrection, ascension, session, and final coming as judge. From time to time, this volume will make reference to some of this teaching from volume III, which, for the most part, is the common heritage of all the churches.

Reformational Developments concerning the Two States

Without employing the term 'States of Christ', John Calvin still covers all the saving actions within the hypostatic union with much more emphasis on the divine/human *activity* than had been the case before the sixteenth-century Reformation. The sixteenth chapter of Book II of his *Institutes of the Christian Religion* largely follows the order of the Apostles Creed as his basic outline.

I believe that Karl Barth was right to point out the major difference in emphasis between the earlier theology of the Church with its close study of the *two natures* of Christ, and the later, largely post-Reformation development of the *two states* of Christ.[9] He saw certain beginnings of this change both in Lutheranism and in some of the Reformed theologians (although I would wish to add that a certain element of this change in emphasis towards the saving activities of Christ goes back to Saint Thomas):

> In the older Lutherans this doctrine [i.e. the two states of Christ] forms a great excursus in the doctrine of the human nature of Christ, which as they understood it was not merely exalted in the incarnation but actually divinized...For them *exinanitio* meant that for a time, for the period of His life up to and including death, the God-man denies Himself that divinization of His humanity (either by concealment or by genuine renunciation), but then reassumes it with the *exaltation* which begins with His triumphant descent into hell.[10]

Then he looks at the rather vague beginning of a closer attention to the two states among the Reformed:

> The older Reformed writers described the two states rather obscurely as the humiliation and exaltation of the divine Logos, and with them the doctrine is simply left in the air, following that of the work of Christ but not organically related to it. It was brought in for the sake of completeness, but on their presuppositions it had only an incidental application. If our presentation is right, then at least the doctrine of the humiliation and exaltation of Christ does acquire a place and function in line with its scriptural and factual importance.[11]

---

9. Karl Barth, *Church Dogmatics* IV/1, 132-35.

10. Ibid., 132.

11. Ibid., 133.

But later Reformed exponents of Christology did give a much more thorough exposition of the two states of Christ. By 'state' (*status*) they meant something like his 'estate': that is, the profoundly changed conditions through which he had to live, once he became incarnate, in order to accomplish his divine mission for our salvation. Francis Turretin (1623-87) devoted his 'Ninth Question' to 'The Twofold State of Christ': 'the one of emptying and humiliation; the other of exaltation and majesty...'[12] The seventeenth-century Reformed scholars sought to summarize the teaching of the New Testament on the redemptive work of Christ in its wholeness, by showing that each of these two 'states' has several 'stages' within it.

Wonder of the Divine Condescension

We shall look presently at the first state and its stages as traditionally listed in the Reformed Tradition. But first, it is important to note the wonder of the divine condescension to human sin and rebellion that is to be found in both the state of humiliation and the state of exaltation, with all their stages. The coming of God in Christ to us is necessarily set in the context of the fallenness of rebellious human nature, which God humbled himself in order to enter as one of us in order to redeem us. That in itself is wonder enough, but there is more to make us marvel. To appreciate the wonder of God's stooping down to us broken and condemned creatures, when we were still his enemies, his coming must also be set in the context of the stupendous brilliance of the wisdom of God, which infinitely outshone the craftiness of Satan.

Wilhelmus à Brakel, seventeenth-century Dutch Reformed theologian, celebrates the splendor of God's brilliance in the coming of Christ into our race to be humbled and exalted:

> No one could be Surety and bring man to God but He who was God and man in one person. The Son of God first had to be personally united to the human nature before sinful man could be restored into friendship and union with God. Behold, how great a work it is to save a sinner! What manifold wisdom was required to have conceived such a remedy! All the holy angels together could not have conceived such a remedy as God has conceived and revealed. They are desirious to look into this, but they shall never be able to comprehend it...[13]

The Humiliation of Christ

We now look at his first state, with its five traditional 'stages' or 'steps': His Humiliation involves five stages: (1) Incarnation, under which we include both (a) Virgin Birth and (b) 'Active Obedience'; and then (2) Suffering, (3) Death, (4) Burial, and (5) Descent into Hades.

---

12. Francis Turretin, *Institutes of Elenctic Theology, Vol. Two: Eleventh Through Seventeenth Topics*, Translated by G. M. Giger, Ed. by J. T. Dennison (Phillipsburg, NJ: P & R Publishing, 1994), 332.

13. Wilhelmus à Brakel, *The Christian's Reasonable Service*, Translated by Bartel Elshout and Edited by Joel R. Beeke (Reformation Heritage Books: Grand Rapids, Michigan, 1999 reprint), vol. 1, 511.

(1) Incarnation

'Incarnation' is a Latin-based word, which in Anglo-Saxon would possibly be expressed as 'enfleshment.' Some questions and answers from the Westminster Larger Catechism summarize the term in biblical fashion:

> The estate of Christ's humiliation was that low condition, wherein he for our sakes, emptying himself of his glory, took upon him the form of a servant, in his conception and birth, life, death, and after his death, until his resurrection. (Q. 46)

> Christ humbled himself in his conception and birth, in that, being from all eternity the Son of God, in the bosom of the Father, he was pleased in the fullness of time to become the son of man, made of a woman of low estate, and to be born of her; with divers circumstances of more than ordinary abasement. (Q. 47)

Thus, the Larger Catechism properly considers even his incarnation as a man to be an aspect of his humiliation, in the sense of coming into an infinitely lower status of life as a creature: he who was the agent of creation! The incarnation made possible his sufferings, death, burial, and descent into Hades.

In this chapter (seven), under the incarnation, we consider: (a) his virgin birth, and – in chapter eight – (b) his active obedience (or life of sonship).

His Virgin Birth

The state of Christ's Humiliation first took place in his incarnation, through the miracle of the Virgin Birth. Two passages in the New Testament clearly announce his virgin birth, and others may imply it, or at least, are fully consistent with it.

The first account of the Virgin Birth is found in Matthew 1:18-25:

> Now the birth of Jesus Christ was on this wise: When as his mother Mary was espoused to Joseph, before they came together, she was found with child of the Holy Ghost. Then Joseph her husband, being a just man, and not willing to make her a public example, was minded to put her away privily. But while he thought on these things, behold, the angel of the Lord appeared unto him in a dream, saying, Joseph, thou son of David, fear not to take unto thee Mary thy wife: for that which is conceived in her is of the Holy Ghost. And she shall bring forth a son, and thou shalt call his name JESUS: for he shall save his people from their sins. Now all this was done, that it might be fulfilled which was spoken of by the prophet, saying, Behold a virgin shall be with child, and shall bring forth a son, and they shall call his name Emmanuel, which being interpreted is, God with us. Then Joseph being raised from sleep, did as the angel had bidden him, and took unto him his wife: And knew her not till she had brought forth her firstborn son; and he called his name JESUS.

We are told here that through the agency of the Holy Spirit, the virgin Mary had become pregnant, without the intervention of any human male, before she and Joseph were married. God sent his angel to explain this to Joseph, and he was instructed to name him 'Jesus' (related to *Joshua*: Jehovah [JHVH or YHWH] saves). His name also means 'Emmanuel' (God with us), and thus, 'He will save his people from their sins.'

The accounts of both Matthew and Luke give the Holy Spirit a special prominence in the miraculous conception that leads up to the virgin birth. Karl Barth shows the biblical logic of this:

> But why is it precisely God the Holy Spirit who is named here? ... The Holy Spirit is God Himself in His freedom exercised in revelation to be present to His creature, even to dwell in him personally, and thereby to achieve his meeting with Himself in His Word and by this achievement to make it possible ... The very possibility of human nature's being adopted into unity with the Son of God is the Holy Ghost....[14]

Prophecy of Isaiah 7:14

Isaiah 7:14 was somehow a prophecy of this virgin birth, which would bring about salvation. The text from Isaiah may have been, in part at least, an instance of typology, in which by the time of the birth of a child of a woman, who was still a virgin, the land would know a certain kind of salvation: deliverance from enemies.

It is significant that the prophecy was made to Ahaz, a member of the house of David, which carried the messianic line. The true and final fulfillment of the promise would be long after the preliminary fulfillment in the time of Ahaz and Isaiah. Only that descendant of David, who was also the Lord of David, could be its fulfillment for all the people of God in all ages (cf. Psalm 110:1).

Yet it may be even more directly prophetic of the birth of Christ than this example of typology, for what Isaiah offered was a *sign*: something far out of the ordinary. The ordinary birth of a son to a young woman who becomes married in the future (which is all that the typological interpretation requires) seems rather less than a special sign. In this regard, as has often been pointed out, the Hebrew word in Isaiah for 'virgin' is *almah*. It could mean either 'virgin' or merely 'young woman.' But when the Hebrew text was translated into Greek in the third century B.C. (the LXX version), the translators used the specific Greek word for 'virgin' (παρθενος). Apparently they understood it to have been predicting a miraculous kind of birth. And certainly that is the way that Matthew 1:23 takes it.[15]

---

14. Karl Barth, *Church Dogmatics*, I/2, 198, 199.

15. J.Gresham Machen discusses carefully the word usage of *almah* in the Old Testament. He writes: 'It has been urged, indeed, on the one hand, that the Hebrew language has a perfectly unmistakable word for 'virgin' *bethulah* and that if 'virgin' had been meant that word would have been used. But as a matter of fact, there is no place among the seven occurences of *álmah* in the Old Testament where the word is clearly used of a woman who was not a virgin [Prov. xxx.19 and Cant. vi.8]. It may be readily admitted that '*almah* does not actually indicate virginity, as does *betulah*; it means rather 'a young woman of marriageable age.' But on the other hand one may well doubt, in

Jerome in his fourth-century *Commentary on Isaiah*, after a thorough discussion of the difference between the Hebrew words for 'young woman' and 'virgin,' emphasizes the sign value of the Virgin Birth. Had it merely been a conception and birth through a young woman, he argues, it would not have been a sign.[16]

As J. Gresham Machen asks:

> ...Why should an ordinary birth be regarded as a 'sign"? The word naturally leads us to think of some event like the turning back of the sun on Hezekiah's dial, or the phenomena in connection with Gideon's fleece. But it is not merely the use of this one word which would lead us to expect something miraculous in that which the prophet proceeds to announce. Equally suggestive is the elaborate way in which the 'sign' is introduced. The whole passage is couched in such terms as to induce the reader or hearer a sense of profound mystery as he contemplates the young woman and her child.[17]

However, the following question has often been raised: Matthew 1:23 quotes only part of the prophecy of Isaiah 7:14 ('A virgin shall conceive'), but what about the other part of the same prophetic announcement (in verses 15 and 16: 'Butter and honey shall he eat, that he may know how to refuse the evil, and choose the good. For before the child shall know to refuse the evil, and choose the good, the land that thou abhorrest shall be forsaken of both her kings?') Verse 17 then goes on to speak of things that will occur during what seems to be a time near that in which the prophet was speaking to King Ahaz.

Since Matthew 1:23 quotes only the prophecy of Isaiah 7:14, it can be assumed that he knowingly drew it out from the historical context that immediately followed it. He only claimed the relevance of that verse for the Virgin Birth of Christ. But, believing as we do in the inspiration of the Scriptures, can we still make any sense of this separation of one verse from the others? J. Gresham Machen has suggested two possible answers:

> In the first place, it may be held that the prophet has before him in vision the birth of the child Immanuel, and that irrespective of the ultimate fulfilment the vision itself is present.
>
> I see a wonderful child whose birth shall bring salvation to his people; and before such a time shall elapse as would lie between the conception of the child in his mother's womb and his coming to years of discretion, the land of Israel and of Syria shall be forsaken.[18]

Machen suggests a second line of reasoning:

---

view of the usage, whether it was a natural word to use of anyone who was not in point of fact a virgin....If a married woman were referred to in Is. vii.14, it does seem as though some other word than '*almah* would naturally be used.' In J. Gresham Machen, op. cit.,288, 289.

16. Quoted in Pierre Jay, op. cit., 198.

17. Machen, op. cit., 290,291.

18. Ibid., 292.

In the second place, one may hold that in the passage some immediate birth of a child is in view, but that event is to be taken as the foreshadowing of a greater event that was to come. Does an immediate reference to a child of the prophet's own day really exclude the remoter and greater reference that determines the quotation in the first chapter of Matthew?[19]

That sort of miraculous prophecy, literally foretelling with accuracy events that will occur hundreds of years later, should be readily accepted by those who know the Triune God. God inhabits eternity, in which time is merely a stitch, although it has reality and significance, but always in light of eternity. God is the creator and master of time, not its servant. As Boethius said in the sixth century, God is not subject to the time series of past, present, and future, for all of these are 'spread out before him' in an eternal present, in which all are ever ready for him to work on as he sees fit. If such a God exists, then it should not be difficult for us to understand that God foresees and foretells his prophets what his plan will bring about ahead of time: as with Isaiah and the Virgin Birth some six hundred years later. To reject out of hand the prophetic details given concerning the incarnation and all the events coming after it as impossible is simply to attempt to read back human limitations onto God, which is a failure to have met the true and living God.

But a door of grace is open to those who wish the leave the darkness of 'Enlightenment' unbelief, by looking up to the place of light. The same Isaiah says:

> Lift up your eyes on high, and behold who hath created these things, that bringeth out their host by number: he called them all by names by the greatness of his might, for that he is strong in power; not one faileth…Hast thou not known? hast thou not heard, that the everlasting God, the LORD, the Creator of the ends of the earth, fainteth not, neither is weary? there is no searching of his understanding…But they that wait upon the LORD shall renew their strength; they shall mount up with wings as eagles; they shall run, and not be weary; and they shall walk, and not faint (Isa. 40:26, 28, 31).

The second account of the Virgin Birth is found in Luke 2:3-14, 21

> And all went to be taxed, every one into his own city. And Joseph also went up from Galilee, out of the city of Nazareth, into Judea, unto the city of David, which is called Bethlehem; (because he was of the house and lineage of David:) To be taxed with Mary his espoused wife, being great with child. And so it was, that, while they were there, the days were accomplished that she should be delivered. And she brought forth her firstborn son, and wrapped him in swaddling clothes, and laid him in a manger; because there was no room for them in the inn. And there were in the same country shepherds abiding in the field, keeping watch over their flock by night. And, lo, the angel of the Lord came upon them, and the glory of the Lord shone round about them, and they were sore afraid. And the angel said unto them, Fear not: for behold I bring unto you good tidings of great joy, which shall be to all people. For unto you is born this day in the city of David a Saviour, which

---

19. Ibid.

is Christ the Lord. And this shall be a sign unto you; Ye shall find the babe wrapped in swaddling clothes, lying in a manger. And suddenly there was with the angel a multitude of the heavenly host praising God, and saying, Glory to God in the highest, and on earth peace, good will toward men… And when eight days were accomplished for the circumcising of the child, his name was called JESUS, which was so named of the angel before he was conceived in the womb.

Luke's account agrees in detail with that of Matthew: Mary's pregnancy was owing to the direct intervention of God in his gracious purposes of salvation. She had replied to the angel at the annunciation: 'how shall this be, seeing I know not a man?' (Luke 1:34). The angel replied: '… The Holy Ghost shall come upon thee, and the power of the Highest shall overshadow thee: therefore also that holy thing which shall be born of thee shall be called the Son of God' (v. 35). Here we have the involvement of the entire Trinity: the power of the Highest (the Father), the Holy Ghost, and the Son of God. Any who consider the virgin birth to be impossible will do well to consider whether or not they know who the Triune God is!

Some of the higher critics, as might be expected, came up with the theory that the Birth Narrative of Luke was a later addition to the full Gospel of Luke. But J. Gresham Machen long ago did serious research demonstrating that Luke 1:5 to 2:52 are in no sense an addition to the original Gospel.[20]

The Holy Trinity and the Virgin Birth

Peter Lombard shows the involvement of the Trinity in the miraculous conception:

> … the Son does nothing without the Father and the Holy Spirit, but the operation of these three is one, undivided, and in no way dissimilar, and yet the Son took on flesh, and not the Father or the Holy Spirit. Nevertheless it was the Trinity which worked this taking on of flesh, as Augustine says in the book *On Faith to Peter*: 'We were reconciled *through* the Son alone according to the flesh, but not *to* the Son alone according to the divinity. For the Trinity reconciled us to itself by that same Trinity making the Word alone flesh.'[21]

Luke relates the same identity of the firstborn Son as did Matthew: 'A Saviour which is Christ the Lord' (v. 11), and also the name given him in the annunciation of the birth to the virgin Mary by the holy angel: JESUS (v. 21). But in Luke we are shown something more of the divine glory that was showed forth at his birth (vv. 13-14).

---

20. J. Gresham Machen, *The Virgin Birth*, 45--61.

21. The author whom Lombard quotes was not Augustine, but Fulgentius, *De Fide ad Petrum*, c. 2, n. 23, quoted in Peter Lombard, *The Sentences*, vol. 3: pp. 5,6.

Other New Testament Intimations of the Virgin Birth?

John 1:13

T. F. Torrance has argued that the original text of John 1:13 was in the singular. The text, as we have it now, says (beginning with verse 12): 'But as many as received him, to them gave he power to become the sons of God, even to them that believe on his name; Which were born, not of blood, nor of the will of the flesh, nor of the will of man, but of God.' Torrance believes that the original text said: not 'which [or who] *were* born…,' but 'who *was* born…' Thus, if he is right, the verb was *singular*, not *plural*, in the first manuscripts. He writes:

> What about the MSS (manuscript) evidence? All the main MSS give the plural reading except the Verona Old Latin, a MSS significantly of Ephesian origin [i.e. where John later lived] which gives the singular. These are all 5th century MSS. But there is considerable patristic evidence going back to the second and third centuries, Tertullian, Irenaeus, Justin Martyr, *Epistola Apostolorum*, and Hippolytus, Clement of Alexandria – that is, all the available patristic evidence has John 1:13-14 in the singular at that date…evidence for the singular is also given by Ambrose and Augustine, and ambiguously by Leo the Great (who uses the plural as well as the singular), and many codices, such as 10, 14, 36, 37, etc…
>
> Tertullian, however gives us explicit comments upon the text at this point [in his *De Carne Christi*, chapters 19 and 24], where he remarks that the Valentinians had corrupted their text making the singular into a plural (they did not like the idea of the virgin birth), whereas all other texts were in the singular. That is a most impressive weight of evidence for the singular reading, all twice as old as the oldest of our main codices. According to Harnack[22] the singular is the true text, a judgment which is being increasing by followed by scholars…[23]

In other words, if the original text is singular, then it refers to the virgin birth of Jesus Christ. But, as D. A. Carson says, none of the existing Greek manuscripts of John's Gospel actually have this text in the singular.[24]

Galatians 4

Torrance notes that,

> Paul uses the verb γενναν of human generation, but when in that very context he speaks of Jesus, he avoids the word γενναν and uses the word γινεστηαι (Gal. 4:4). In other words, in reference to Jesus' birth he refuses to use the only word the New Testament uses of human generation. Every time Paul speaks of human birth he uses γενναν, but not once when he speaks of Jesus.

---

22. A. Harnack, *The Date of the Acts and of the Synoptic Gospels*, English transl. by J. R. Wilkinson (London: Williams & Norgate, 1911), 148.

23. Torrance, *Incarnation*, 90, 91. Torrance lists Wolfgang Harnish (who succeeded Bultmann in Marburg), as having said that the singular was the true reading, according to an article by P. L. Hofrichter, in an article in FZB 31, 1978, pp. 155f; and in a monograph about the prologue of John's Gospel, entitled *Das Urchristliche Logosbekenntnis*, 1986: in a note (16) in ibid., 92.

24. D. A. Carson, *Commentary on John* (Eerdmans: Grand Rapids, Mi., 1991), 138-39.

Every time Paul wants to refer to the earthly origin of Jesus he uses the word γινεσθαι (Rom. 1:3; Phil. 2:7; Gal. 4:4). That is the strongest disavowal of birth by ordinary human generation in regard to the birth of Jesus. 'God sent forth his Son made (γενομενον) of a woman, made (γενομενον) under the law …that we might receive the adoption of sons… (Gal. 4:4).[25]

Torrance rightly points out that the RSV translation fails to show the difference Paul makes between γενναν ('born' – true of all humans) and γινεσθαι ('made of a woman' – hence reserved for the supernatural birth of Christ). The RSV rendering is '*born* of woman, *born* under the law,' whereas the AV (or KJV) is more accurate: '*made* of a woman, *made* under the law.'[26] I suspect that this understanding of Galatians 4:4 is a stronger testimony for the Virgin Birth than Tertullian's statement about the singular verb in the original text of John 1:13. Yet, either or both could be true.

How much can we know about the 'how' of the Virgin Birth?

The most direct answer to this question is: very little. Matthew, Luke, and John (if one takes the original text to have been in the singular – 'who was born') tell us no more than that the Holy Trinity was involved in this miraculous conception and birth. But they do not tell us 'how.' John Calvin states the simple truth here: 'As God, in publishing his miracles, keeps back from us the means of His working, so on our part we must adore with restraint, what He wishes to keep hidden from us.'[27]

Some speculation on the origin of the blood of Christ

There has been some speculation on this matter: by speculation, I mean going beyond the chaste reserve of the text (unless, assuming John refers to the virgin birth, one takes 'who was not born of blood' – literally, *bloods* – in a rather literal fashion). But this speculation is not well-grounded scripturally or theologically, and no one as far as I know in the main tradition of the various churches has followed it.[28]

---

25. Torrance, op. cit., 93.

26. Ibid., 93, note 28.

27. Calvin, *Harmony of the Gospels*, vol. I, 28 (on Luke 1:35).

28. M. R. De Haan, in his book *The Chemistry of the Blood* (Grand Rapids: MI: Zondervan Publishing House, 1943), speculates that original sin passes down through the blood rather than the physical body (p. 31). He then argues that the male sperm brings the blood into existence, and that therefore since God is the Father of Christ's human nature, his blood was sinless (pp. 31-33). But this separation between blood and physical body does not seem to be indicated either in Scripture or in medical science. Instead, Romans 5:12-21 indicates that our sinfulness is related to our having been in Adam as our representative or 'head' when he sinned. That, of course, does not exclude the possibility that the sinfulness of fallen humanity passes down through the genetic pool, but the weight of the emphasis of Romans 5 is on Adamic representation having brought us into a stage of sin, guilt and death, rather than the fallenness of the genetic stock, although it would seem that both can be true at the same time.

It appears that John Calvin held both to the causal factor of Adam's representational headship, and also to the resulting corruption of the stock of his descendants, though with considerable causal priority to the principle of representation. Hence, Calvin understood (a) Adam to have represented us as our head, but at the same time, in the line of Augustine, also taught (b) that Adam's fall vitiated the genetic stock.

Warning of Saint John Chrysostom on Speculation

We know wonderfully well the beneficent results of the virgin birth, but not its 'mechanism'; not its 'how.' No doubt, we will do well to heed a warning issued in a Homily of Saint John Chrysostom (on Matthew 5:2):

> Do not try to go beyond what is said; do not ask: how did the Holy Spirit work within the Virgin? If it is impossible to explain exactly how children are conceived and grow in natural conditions, how much less could we possibly explain how such things take place under the marvelous operation of the Holy Spirit...Let those who desire to explain so high a generation be ashamed... for neither the archangel Gabriel nor the evangelist Matthew were able to say anything further about this conception by the Holy Spirit. How, and in what precise manner the Holy Spirit proceeded, was never explained by them, nor could it have been.[29]

Beneficent results of the Virgin Birth

We may simply summarize the benefits of the virgin birth, accompanied by a few necessary comments:

(1) It was the way the eternal Son of God chose to come into the human race. Barth discusses this divinely chosen mode of entry:

(a) Calvin makes it clear that Adam represents us by appointment of God as the head of the human race, and that from this representational principle comes our implication in the guilt of the fall: 'For the contagion does not take its origin from the substance of the flesh or soul, but because it has been so ordained by God that the first man should at one and the same time have and lose, both for himself and for his descendants, the gifts that God had bestowed upon him' (Calvin, *Institutes* II. I. 7)

(b) But Calvin also holds that the fall of Adam vitiated the Adamic stock. 'For so Adam at his first creation received both for himself and for posterity the gifts of divine favour, so by falling away from the Lord he in himself corrupted, vitiated, depraved, and ruined our nature. Having been divested of God's likeness, he could not have begotten seed but like himself. Therefore we all have sinned because we have all been imbued with natural corruption, and so are become wicked and perverse' (John Calvin, *Commentary on Romans,* 5:12).

One of the most careful exegetical/theological discussions of this entire matter is that of John Murray: 'The Imputation of Adam's Sin' (John Murray, *'The Imputation of Adam's Sin,'* [reprinted in] *Justified in Christ,* K. Scott Oliphant, Ed. [Christian Focus: Fearn, Scotland, 2007], 203-94). He argues in favor of 'immediate imputation' of Adam's sin to all his posterity from a close grammatical construction of Romans 5:12-19. He notes: (i) *The immediate conjunction of the sin of Adam and the death of all* (cf. Rom. 5:12, 15, 17); (ii) *The immediate conjunction of the sin of Adam and the condemnation of all* (cf. Rom. 5:16, 18); (iii) *The immediate conjunction of the sin of Adam and the sin of all* (cf. Rom. 5:12, 19); (iv) *The analogy supports immediate imputation* (cf. the entire parallel in Rom. 5:12-19). For more, see Murray, *The Imputation of Adam's Sin,* 265-70.

Murray concludes: 'It may not be strictly accurate to say that we become depraved by natural generation. It is true that *in* the act of generation we become depraved. This is true because it is by generation that we come to be as distinct persons. In this sense it would not be improper to say that we become depraved by natural generation. But natural generation is not the reason why we are conceived in sin...But the *reason* why we are naturally generated in sin is that, whenever we begin to be, we begin to be as sinful because of our solidarity with Adam in his sin' (Murray, *The Imputation of Adam's Sin,* 291).

No doubt, it is always best not to go beyond the plain teaching of the scriptural text, which tells us that somehow through the miraculous action of the Holy Spirit of God, the humanity that Christ assumed was preserved from all sin: both of blood and of body. Calvin wrote: 'For we make Christ free of all stain not just because he was begotten of his mother without copulation with man, but because he was sanctified by the Spirit that the generation might be pure and undefiled...' (Calvin, *Institutes* II. 13. 4). That is sufficient for us to know.

29. J. Chrysostom, *Homily on Matthew V. 2* (PG 57, 42).

It means that God Himself – acting directly in His own and not in human fashion – stands at the beginning of this human existence and is its direct author. It is He who gives to man in the person of Mary the capacity which man does not have of himself, which she does not have and which no man could give her. It is He who sanctifies and ordains her the human mother of His Son. It is He who makes His Son hers, and in that way shares with humanity in her person nothing less than His own existence…This is the miracle of the Virgin Birth…comparable with the miracle of the empty tomb at His exodus from temporal existence.[30]

Hilary of Poitiers beautifully contrasts the status of the eternal Son of God in heaven with that of his birth of the Virgin Mary:

What worthy return can we make for so great a condescension? The One Only-begotten God, ineffably born of God, entered the Virgin's womb and grew and took the frame of poor humanity. He Who upholds the universe, within Whom and through Whom are all things, was brought forth by common childbirth; He at Whose voice Archangels and Angels tremble, and heaven and earth and all the elements of this world are melted, was heard in childish wailing. The Invisible and Incomprehensible, Whom sight and feeling and touch cannot gauge, was wrapped in a cradle… We were raised because He was lowered; shame to Him was glory to us. He, being God, made flesh His residence, and we in return are lifted anew from the flesh to God.[31]

John Calvin says that this was the way that Christ 'took what was ours as to impart what was his to us, and to make what was his by nature ours by grace.'[32] He then adds:

Therefore, relying on this pledge, we trust that we are sons of God, for God's natural Son fashioned for himself a body from our body, flesh from our flesh, bones from our bones, that he might be one with us [Gen. 2:23-24, mediated through Eph. 5:29-31]. Ungrudgingly he took our nature upon himself to impart to us what was his, and to become both Son of God and Son of man in common with us…[33]

(2) The doctrine of the Virgin Birth safeguards Christ's true humanity as much as it does his true deity.

It means that the Son of God took on real human nature from the substance of the virgin Mary: from the egg that she contributed in the miraculous action. Through her, a descendant of King David, the incarnate Lord 'was made of the seed of David according to the flesh…' (Rom. 1:3). Through Mary, Christ 'takes on' 'the seed of Abraham' (Heb. 2:17). It had to be human flesh, and Jewish flesh that the Lord took on, for as he told the woman at the well of Samaria: 'Salvation is of the Jews' (John 4:22). The Savior had to be a descendant of Adam, of Noah, of Seth, of Abraham, of

30. Karl Barth, *Church Dogmatics*, IV/1, 207.

31. Hilary, *De Trinitate* II. 24.

32. Calvin, *Institutes* II. 12. 2 (Battles' translation).

33. Ibid., Battles' translation.

Judah, of David to accomplish the long-planned purposes of redemption for God's people. It was the contribution of the blessed Virgin Mary that made possible the entrance of the eternal Word into the historical messianic line and, with it, the fulfillment of the promises of God throughout the Old Testament.

Barth shows the importance of this affirmation of true humanity through Mary in the ancient creedal tradition, which specifically rejected the Gnostic (Valentinian) theory that Christ had received nothing from his mother (having taken on 'a heavenly body'), but merely passed through her like a tube, like water going through an aqueduct.[34] Had Christ not received his humanity through the substance of Mary, he could not have represented humanity, as we see in the scriptural texts quoted above. In that case, our humanity would not be saved, and for that reason, the Church always did battle for the truth of what Christ received from the Virgin. For them it was not a theoretical issue; it entered into the salvation of the world.

Most of the Ecumenical Councils of the undivided Church (except for the first one – i.e. Nicea – which had to assert clearly the full deity of Christ, against the Arians) devoted their energies to defending and explicating the full humanity of Christ. His humanity seemed harder to be accepted and apprehended than his divinity. Thus, Constantinople (381) affirmed his perfect humanity, against the Apollinarians (who denied his human mind); Ephesus (431) affirmed that Jesus Christ is one person, against the Nestorians who divided him into two persons; Chalcedon (451) affirmed that there are two distinct natures in one person, which are united 'without confusion, conversion, division, or separation,' against Eutychians and Monophysites. Constantinople (680) taught that Jesus Christ possessed a human will as well as a divine will, against the Monothelites. 'As we look back upon the development of Patristic Christology, we can see that the danger point lay ultimately in attacks not against the deity of Christ, but against his full humanity.'[35]

(3) The human nature taken on by the Son of God in the miraculous conception was safeguarded from any taint of sin by the action of the Holy Spirit.

If De Haan is right, it may have had something to do with the original formation of the blood coming from supernatural intervention of God, apart from the action of any human male (cf. John 1:13 – 'born… not of *blood*, nor of the will of the flesh, nor of the will of the *male*, but of God'). But that is a speculation: reverent, yet going beyond the text, in a way that Chrysostom would presumably been unhappy with, and a speculation that no other – that I am aware of – in the whole Christian tradition has ever suggested! However, the important point is that the sanctity of the human nature taken by the Son of God is made perfectly clear in the Scriptures.

---

34. Karl Barth, *Church Dogmatics*, I/2, 185-186.

35. Torrance, op. cit., 199.

John Calvin writes: 'We make Christ free of all stain not just because he was begotten of his mother without copulation with man, but because he was sanctified by the Spirit that the generation might be pure and undefiled as would have been true before Adam's fall.'[36]

Reformed theologian John L. Girardeau follows the general Calvinist tradition in ascribing the sinlessness accomplished through the Virgin Birth to the implications involved in the the headship of Adam over the human race, and, within that context, to Christ's **not** being represented by Adam, and **not** being subject to the principle of parental propagation. That is, Christ's not having had a human father absolved him of the guilt that belongs to all who are represented by Adam through normal parental propagation.[37] Girardeau says with insight that 'Christ was not represented in Adam; on the contrary, he represented Adam...Not having been representatively guilty, he could not have been inherently depraved.'[38]

(4) The Holy Trinity accomplished this action apart from any human capabilities; apart from 'the will of the male.'
In the words of Karl Barth:

> In the *ex virgine* there is contained a judgment upon man…In other words, human nature possesses no capacity for becoming the human nature of Jesus Christ, the place of divine revelation. It cannot be the workmate of God… The virginity of Mary in the birth of the Lord is the denial, not of man in the presence of God, but of any power, attribute or capacity in him for God.[39]

Barth shows, I think, sharp insight in suggesting that much of the resistance of liberal religious thought to the virgin birth may be human pride, which perhaps underlies their refusal of biological mystery: '… it rests upon a fundamental circumvention and conjuring away of this mystery, and upon a consciousness of human control over God, which necessarily has to be described as pride rather than humility.'[40]

Fallen or Unfallen Flesh?
To the best of my knowledge, the Christian Church up to the nineteenth century taught that because of the miracle of the holy conception and virgin birth, Christ took on human nature that was not tainted with sin. In that sense, it was not fallen in the same way that all the rest of the descendants of sinful Adam bore a fallen nature. But since the time of **Edward Irving,**

---

36. John Calvin, *Institutes of the Christian Religion*, II. 13. 4.

37. '…the first sin was committed by Adam as a person, representing the persons of his posterity. As in accordance with the principle of federal representation, his guilt is derived to his descendants through the channel of parental propagation, it follows that as Christ was born out of the line of ordinary generation, the guilt of Adam, in his first sin, could not have been derived to him' (Girardeau, op. cit. 403).

38. Ibid., 406-407.

39. Karl Barth, *Church Dogmatics*, I/2, 188.

40. Ibid., 131.

a once famous Scottish minister and theologian, some major theologians have held that Christ took on fallen humanity, although in taking it on, they have taught that he thereby sanctified it from the beginning. The first one to have taught this viewpoint, Edward Irving, was deposed from the Church of Scotland in 1833, on the charges of having denied the sinlessness of Christ.

Yet Irving definitely taught that Christ never committed sin.[41] But at the same time, he held that the flesh of Christ was mortal and corruptible, 'through its participation in a fallen nature and a fallen world.'[42] He believed that unless Christ had taken on fallen flesh, he would not have met us sinful humans where we are, and could not have redeemed us from our fallenness.

Nearly a century later (1938), **Karl Barth** accepted the basic thesis of Irving (and also the same thought from Gottfried Menken in 1812) that Christ took on fallen flesh, apparently by way of a book by H. R. Mackintosh of Edinburgh University in 1931.[43] Barth also lists some other theologians who, he said, held to some form of Christ's fallen flesh, such as Hermann Bezzel and H. F. Kohlbrugge.[44] Barth writes:

> The same doctrine [i.e. of Gottfried Menken who taught that Christ took on human nature as it was after the Fall] was delivered about 1827 by the Scottish theologian Edward Irving… [and then quotes Irving]: 'The point of issue is simply this, whether Christ's flesh had the grace of sinlessness and incorruption from its own nature or from the indwelling of the Holy Ghost…I say the latter…It was manhood fallen which He took up into His Divine person, in order to prove the grace and the might of Godhead in redeeming it, (cited by H. R. Mackintosh, *The Doctrine of the Person of Jesus Christ*, 1931, p. 277)…[45]

T. F. Torrance has made the concept of the fallen humanity that Christ, according to this line of theology, took upon himself an important aspect of his theology. He writes:

> If the Word of God did not really come into our fallen existence, if the Son of God did not actually come where we are, and join himself to us, and range himself with us where we are in sin and under judgment, how could it be said that Christ really took our place, took our cause upon himself in order to redeem us?[46]

But Torrance is always at pains to assert the full holiness and sinlessness of the incarnate Christ. Thus he adds:

> He entered into complete solidarity with us in our sinful existence in order to save us, without becoming himself a sinner. However, while we must say

---

41. *The Collected Writings of Edward Irving*, vol. V (London, 1865), 137.

42. Ibid., 126.

43. Mackintosh himself, however, rejected Irving's position in *The Doctrine of the Person of Christ*, 276-77.

44. Barth, op. cit., 154-55.

45. Karl Barth, *Church Dogmatics* I/2, 154.

46. T. F. Torrance, *Incarnation*, 62.

all that about the flesh that the Word assumed, we must also say that in the very act of assuming our flesh, the Word sanctified and hallowed it, for the assumption of our sinful flesh is itself atoning and sanctifying action... by remaining holy and sinless in our flesh, he condemned sin in the flesh he assumed and judged it by his very sinlessness.[47]

Although influenced by Edward Irving, Torrance takes a different position to explain the sinlessness of Christ. Duncan Rankin brings this out:

> In response to Barth's commendation to Edward Irving for his doctrine of Christ's sinful humanity, Torrance recoils, siding instead with H. R. Mackintosh and the body of Scottish opinion that the Holy Spirit was not needed to make Christ impeccable. Christ's humanity was made pure by his person, Torrance proposes. In his more mature Christology, this sanctification of Mary's fallen seed by the divine person – treated using his well-developed anhypostatic and enhypostatic rubrics – kept original sin from the Saviour and makes impossible the Roman Catholic doctrine of the immaculate conception.[48]

The Greek Fathers

Torrance believed that the Greek Church Fathers also held that the Logos assumed a fallen human nature (although sanctifying it in doing so). In light of his massive knowledge of the Church Fathers, I am very hesitant to dissent from his teaching on this point. However, in spite of my hesitancy, I must say that in my own reading over the years, I have not yet found a passage in the Fathers that clearly shows they taught Christ's participation in fallen flesh. That of course does not mean that some of them may not have said so.

The significant statement by Gregory Nazianzus, so frequently referred to by Torrance, that 'the unassumed is the unredeemed' was stated in the context of the controversy with the Apollinarians, who denied that Christ took on a human mind (or psychology). If Christ did not become fully human, including both body and mind (or soul), then mankind is not fully redeemed by him. But I am not aware that Gregory ever actually said that Christ had to take on *fallen* humanity in order to redeem us sinners. Rather, he had to take on humanity in its *fullness*.

What is the teaching of Holy Scripture on this issue? It affirms that Christ takes upon himself full and true human nature in order to save us. To do so, Saint Paul writes in Romans 8:3 that God sent his own Son 'in the likeness of sinful flesh.' If he believed that Christ had in fact taken on fallen flesh, this would have been the perfect place to have said so, but that is not what he says. The way he states it here definitely seems to indicate that although Christ's flesh was like our flesh, still it was not sinful.

---

47. Ibid., 62,63.

48. W. Duncan Rankin, *Carnal Union With Christ in the Theology of T. F. Torrance* (Ph.D. dissertation, Edinburgh University, 1996, unpublished), 118.

A Latin Christian Writer

Tertullian (early third century in North Africa) said that what Christ's incarnation and atonement had abolished was not *carnem peccati* (the flesh of sin), but *peccatum carnis* (the sin of the flesh).:

> We maintain moreover that what has been abolished in Christ is not *carnem peccati*, but *peccatum carnis* – not the material thing, but its condition; not the substance, but its flow ... Now in another sentence he says that Christ was 'in the likeness of sinful flesh' [Rom. 8:3] ... but he means us to understand like to the flesh which sinned, because the flesh of Christ, which committed no sin itself, resembled that which had sinned – resembled it in its nature, but not in the corruption it received from Adam; whence we also affirm that there was in Christ the same flesh as that whose nature in man is sinful. In the flesh therefore, that sin has been abolished, because in Christ that same flesh is maintained without sin, which in man was not maintained without sin. Now it would not contribute to the purpose of Christ's abolishing sin in the flesh, if he did not abolish it in that flesh in which was the nature of sin... then you say, if he took our flesh, Christ's was a sinful one. Do not however, fetter with mystery a sense which is quite intelligible. For in putting on our flesh, he made it his own; in making it his own, he made it sinless.[49]

But that is not to ignore that Christ did totally submit to the inherent requirement on descendants of fallen Adam to carry out the whole law that is binding upon sinful humanity, even in its most exacting require-ments. He specifically came into our place to do so, as Paul writes in Ga-latians 4:4-5: 'But when the fullness of the time was come, God sent forth his Son, made of a woman, made under the law, To redeem them that were under the law, that we might receive the adoption of sons.'

Nor is it to ignore that Jesus Christ submitted to the penalty for the sin of Adam and all of his descendants, in that 'he hath made him to be sin for us, who knew no sin, that we might be made the righteousness of God in him' (II Cor. 5:21), and indeed, was made a curse: 'Christ hath redeemed us from the curse of the law, being made a curse for us: for it is written, Cursed is every one that hangeth on a tree' [quoting Deut. 21:23] (Gal. 3:13).

Adamic Flesh

For this action of immense grace to have happened, it is clear that Jesus Christ took on Adamic flesh, in the sense of its being mortal, for he willingly submitted to death in the body: 'For the wages of sin is death: but the gift of God is eternal life through Jesus Christ our Lord' (Rom. 6:23). If he died in his human nature, then in that sense his assumed nature was mortal, and hence *in that sense* shared in the situation that obtained after the fall of Adam. This mortality could be explained either as inherent in his having taken on post-Adamic flesh in his incarnation, or it could be explained as an exchange that occurred towards the end of his ministry, as the sinless one took on himself our sins, rather than a description of the humanity he assumed.

---

49. Tertullian, *Car. Chr.*, xvi.

But Hebrews 2:14-17 seems to indicate that Christ specifically took on a mortal human nature with the purpose of dying in it, and thereby delivering it from the power of death. We are told here that Christ 'took not on him the nature of angels, but the seed of Abraham...' (Heb. 2:16). The Greek verb rendered in the Authorised Version as 'took on him' is ἐπιλαμβανομαι. It can mean literally 'to seize or lay hold of something,' or metaphorically 'to take on or to assume.' The Authorised Version employs the metaphorical sense, although the literal sense would also be a valid translation.[50] But either way, here is the point of Christ's having 'assumed' or 'seized' human nature: angels do not die; their nature is immortal, but humans, after the fall of Adam, which brought death (cf. Gen. 2:17; Rom 6:23; Rom. 5:12), do die. Christ in his incarnation identified himself with those whose nature is mortal, for they have the price of death to pay for their sin. When Hebrews says that Christ took on the seed of Abraham, it is naming someone who lived after the fall of Adam; someone whose nature, therefore was mortal. That is what Christ took upon himself.

Without being personally sinful in any way whatsoever, Christ took on mortal flesh in a stupendous action of grace by which he would pay a price ('the wages of sin is death') that he did not owe, in order to deliver those who did owe a price that they could not pay.

John Calvin describes it in a moving way, in terms reminiscent of Irenaeus of Lyon:

> ...we cannot be condemned for our sins, from whose guilt he has absolved us, since he willed to take them upon himself as if they were his own. This is the wonderful exchange [*mirifica commutatio* in Latin] which out of his measureless benevolence, he has made with us; that, becoming Son of man with us, he has made us sons of God with him; that, by his descent to earth, he has prepared an ascent to heaven for us; that, by taking on our mortality, he has conferred his immortality upon us; that, accepting our weakness, he has strengthened us by his power; that, receiving our poverty unto himself, he has transferred his wealth to us; that, taking the weight of our iniquity upon himself (which oppressed us), he has clothed us with his righteousness.[51]

In the second century, Irenaeus holds the same facts together: true Adamic flesh and personal sinlessness:

> If then anyone allege that in this respect the flesh of the Lord was different from ours, because it indeed did not commit sin, neither was deceit found in his soul, while we, on the other hand are sinners, he says what is the fact. But if he pretends that the Lord possessed another substance of flesh, the sayings respecting reconciliation will not agree with that man. For that thing is reconciled which had formerly been in enmity. Now if the Lord had taken flesh from another substance, He would not, by so doing, have reconciled that one to God which had become inimical through transgression. But now, by means of communion with himself, the Lord has reconciled man

---

50. For both literal and metaphorical approaches to ἐπιλαμβανομαι, see J. A. L. Lee, *A History of New Testament Lexicography* (New York: Lang, 2003), 129,130, 136.

51. John Calvin, *Institutes*, IV. 17. 2.

to God the Father, in reconciling us to himself by the body of his own flesh, and redeeming us by his own blood, as the apostle says (quoting Eph. 1:7; 2:13; 2:15).[52]

In sum, how a sinless one – therefore, one not subject to death – could willingly take upon himself a mortal body, (which *is* subject to 'the wages of sin' which is death), is no easier to explain than how, as Peter says in his second sermon in Acts: '[You] killed the Prince of Life' (Acts 3:15). Is it not a mystery: the Prince of Life lets himself be slain? No one fully understands how death could have been visited upon the Prince of Life, nor how 'the Holy One of Israel' could have taken on a mortal body. In both cases, the proper attitude is to bow our heads and worship, rather than to explain the unexplainable!

(5) The Virgin Birth is the beginning of the re-creation of Adamic humanity, and through that, the renewal of the entire cosmos.
Athanasius ascribed the renewal of humanity to the Virgin Birth and what followed:

> Whence also whereas the flesh is born of Mary Bearer of God (θεοτοκος), He himself is said to have been born, who furnishes to others an origin of being; in order that he may transfer our origin into himself, and that we may no longer, as mere earth, return to earth, but as being knit into this Word from heaven, may be carried to heaven by him.[53]

We, the guilty, diseased and disintegrating members of a justly condemned, created order have become the beneficiaries of this infinite benefit of a new creation, through the chosen Virgin, and the fruit of her womb, who 'came into the world to save sinners...' (I Tim. 1:15). That is why the Church from the beginning has believed and preached as a cardinal aspect of the Humiliation of Christ, his Virgin Birth. That is why she has worked so hard to understand and express it in as clear a doctrine as possible.

---

52. Irenaeus, *Adversus Haereses*, V. 14. 3.

53. Athanasius, *Contra Arianos*, III. 33.

CHAPTER 8

CHRIST'S ACTIVE OBEDIENCE (HIS SONSHIP)

In the beginning, God created Adam to be a loving son, and love is always shown by obedience (cf. John 15:10, 14). Adam failed to render loving obedience, and in due time, God raised up Abraham and Israel to live as his obedient sons, but they too failed. So, 'in the fullness of the time' (cf. Gal. 4:4), God sent his own Son to live a life of deepest and fullest loving obedience. In so doing, the incarnate Son of God obeyed from the heart, in every thought, word and action, all the holy will of the heavenly Father, thereby fulfilling the original intentions of God in his creation of Adam and his posterity. By his active obedience, Christ fulfills the original purpose of the 'Adamic Administration' (or as the Puritans called it, 'covenant with Adam,' 'covenant of life,' 'covenant of works.')[1]

Part of the good news of the Gospel is that Jesus has done, as my covenant representative, all that I ever needed, or ever shall need, to be and to do. This is a liberating truth to the human spirit, which can otherwise be oppressed by constantly unmet obligations.

In the previous chapter we saw that the first stage in the Humiliation of Christ was his incarnation. There (in chapter seven) we considered the first aspect of his incarnation: (a) his virgin birth.

Now, in this eighth chapter we must pursue: (b) his active obedience, or his life of sonship, and its meaning for our salvation. We trace obedience and sonship through the Scriptural history of redemption especially in terms of the Two Adams. We think of the First Adam as a son, Israel as a son, and finally Messiah as the true Son.

In this regard, we note (i) the necessity of Christ's active obedience (or true Sonship) for our salvation, and (ii) the accomplishments of his active obedience (or Sonship) for us. Scriptural evidence will be marshaled to support the concept of Christ's active obedience (Sonship), in our place, as essential to our salvation, opening us up to God and to others.

---

1. Concerning the exegetical and theological details, both pro and con, of this 'covenant' terminology, see the discussion in D. F. Kelly, *Systematic Theology*, vol. 1, chapter 6.

Active Obedience (or Life of Sonship)

It would appear that *the terminology* of 'active' and 'passive' obedience came to the fore during the seventeenth century, especially among British Puritans. However, the concept of Christ's life, and not just his death, playing a significant role in our salvation goes far back in Christian theology. Peter Lombard clearly taught in the twelfth century that Christ's obedient life enters into the salvation of his people.[2] He expounds reasons why 'Christ merited for himself the same things from his conception as through his passion.'[3]

The Reformed Theology traditionally summarized the experience of Christ's incarnation under the concepts: *active obedience* and *passive obedience*. In order to fit into the scheme of the 'Two States' of Christ, one could place his active obedience under his sufferings, as an aspect of them, but the reasoning of John Owen leads me to place it *before* the sufferings of Christ. He writes, 'That the obedience of Christ cannot be reckoned amongst his *sufferings*, but is clearly *distinct* from it, as to all formalities. Doing is one thing, suffering another; they are in diverse *predicaments*, and cannot be coincident.'[4]

Suffering and contest were constantly involved in Christ's life of holy devotion to the Father in our humanity. It is appropriate to consider his active obedience in our humanity as the true Son of the Father immediately after his virgin birth, and prior to the intense sufferings of his final passion, in order the better to see how the miraculous conception and birth prepared the way for the truly cosmic event of the triumphant grace of God, through which Christ as the Last Adam restored all that the first Adam had lost, and thereby fulfilled the original purposes of the creation of humankind in the divine image.

John Calvin expresses it clearly:

> Now since someone asks, How has Christ abolished sin, banished the separation between us and God, and acquired righteousness to render God favorable and kindly toward us? To this we can in general reply that he has achieved this for us by the whole course of his obedience…Thus in his very baptism, also, he asserted that he fulfilled a part of the righteousness in obediently carrying out his Father's commandment [Matt. 3:15]. In short, from the time when he took on the form of a servant, he began to pay the price of liberation in order to redeem us.[5]

Herman Bavinck also teaches that: '…It is totally contrary to Scripture, therefore, to restrict the "satisfactory" (atoning) work of Christ to his suffering…his entire life was…a self offering …as head in the place of his

---

2. Peter Lombard, *The Sentences: Book 3 – On the Incarnation of the Word*, 'Distinction XVIII,' Chapter 2.

3. Ibid., p. 73.

4. John Owen, *Works: Communion with God*, vol. 2, 161.

5. Calvin, *Institutes* II. xvi. 5 (Battles translation).

own.'[6] Thomas Goodwin wrote to the same effect: 'His passive obedience will not suffice unless joined with his active, nor his active do the work, if not followed by his death... since an entire satisfaction of the law is exacted from us, the whole righteousness of Christ, active and passive, ought to be imputed.'[7]

While there can be no strict separation between active and passive obedience, still, for purposes of teaching, it is traditional to look first at the active, and then at the passive obedience. Therefore, in this section we shall concentrate upon Christ's active obedience. Examination of a crucial biblical theme that runs through both Old and New Testaments, may help us grasp the many-sided significance of his active obedience: *the Two Adams*.

The Two Adams

The very first chapter of Genesis begins with God's creation of all things out of nothing, as the crowning act of his creative work, he made and blessed mankind: male and female in his own image (Gen. 1:27). They were given dominion over the rest of the created order (Gen. 1:28-30). Psalm 8:6 says: 'Thou madest him to have dominion over the works of thy hands; thou hast put all things under his feet...' God breathed directly into them the breath of life (Gen. 2:6). Verse 26 of Genesis 1 indicates that there was something different about the creation of the first human pair from all the rest of the animal creation. That verse shows that God entered into 'an executive divine counsel' within himself, since this work was the highest of them all, for humankind alone bore the direct likeness of God. Their creation was a 'crowning of them with glory and honour' (Ps. 8:5).

God created Adam and Eve to enjoy fellowship and the joy of life together with him. The Lord God walked with them in the Garden of Eden (specially planted for their delight) 'in the cool of the day' (Gen. 3:8). This would indicate that God desired a human son (and daughter), who would abide in sweet fellowship with him, loving and obeying him from the heart. Thus he gives them one clear command to be obeyed (and left the rest of the world free and open to them): not to eat of the fruit of one forbidden tree (Gen. 3:3-13).

Adam and Eve willfully chose to disobey God, and took of the forbidden fruit, thus bringing death into the world, and upon themselves and their descendants (cf. Gen. 3:14-19). In the midst of the curse laid upon Satan, (Gen. 3:14), upon Adam and Eve and their descendants (3:16,19), and upon nature itself (3:17-18), God makes the first promise of the gospel to our mother Eve: 'And I will put enmity between thee [Satan] and the woman, and between thy seed and her seed; it shall bruise thy head, and thou shalt bruise his heel' (3:15).

---

6. Herman Bavinck, *Reformed Dogmatics: Sin and Salvation in Christ* , Volume Three, John Bolt, Ed. and John Vriend, Tr. (Grand Rapids, MI: Baker Academic, 2008), 378-379.

7. Goodwin, op. cit., 340, 346, 347.

The Seed of the Woman

The rest of the Old Testament traces this 'seed' of the woman, who would more than undo the damage wrought by yielding to the serpent's temptation. This seed would be brought forth through appointed leaders of the overarching 'Covenant of Grace' – for Genesis 3:15 is a promise of grace; an opening of the covenant that would run through the whole story of redemption, and reach its final culmination only in the 'New Covenant,' whose head, sum, and substance was Christ (cf. Jer. 31; Heb. 8 and 10).[8]

The chosen 'seed of the woman,' and line of the Gospel, passed through Adam's son, Seth, through his descendant, Noah, and through Noah's son, Shem; then through his descendant, Abraham, and onwards through Isaac, Jacob, and the twelve patriarchs, especially Judah (ancestor of David, and through David's line, of Christ himself). From this point of view one could look upon the history of Israel as the way God chose to form within a particular race a line for his Son; a way to reverse the loss suffered in Adam's rebellion from the heavenly Father.

Adam and Abraham

One can look at the call of Abraham as the beginning of the covenantal process in which the Lord calls out a people to be his obedient son, where Adam failed. The grace of God will be operative in this relationship (generally called the covenant of grace), and God's grace reaches its perfect fulfillment in him as 'the seed of the woman' and 'the seed of Abraham.'

It is clear that in one sense Israel was considered 'the son' of God. We see that in the threat made to proud Pharaoh by Moses, to whom God had spoken: 'And thou shalt say unto Pharaoh, Thus said the Lord, Israel is my son, even my firstborn: And I say unto thee, Let my son go, that he may serve me: and if thou refuse to let him go, behold, I will slay thy son, even thy firstborn' (Ex. 4:22-23).

Israel as a disobedient son

The first Adam had failed to be God's loving and obedient son, and so it was with God's corporate son, Israel. Israel grumbled and distrusted in the wilderness. Soon, after the death of Joshua and the elders of his generation, Israel turned to the false gods of the Canaanite culture, and 'every man did that which was right in his own eyes' (Judg. 21:25). There were many times of repentance after seasons of judgment, as we see in the stories related in Judges.

There was a new beginning for Israel when God raised up the prophet Samuel. 'All Israel ... knew that Samuel was established to be a prophet of the Lord. And the Lord appeared again in Shiloh...' (I Sam. 3:20, 21). Towards the end of his prophetic career, in which he had gone about the country, judging matters in light of the Word of God (I Sam. 7:15, 16), the people of Israel insisted on having a king. Samuel protested against it, but the Lord told him to give in to their request (I Sam. 8).

---

8. See Chapter 6 of my *Systematic Theology*, vol. 1, 387-446.

The handsome and imposing young man of the tribe of Benjamin, Saul, was chosen and anointed first king of Israel (I Sam. 9). But he was self-willed, and rushed ahead to make the priestly offering, impatient for Samuel's return. Samuel had to reject Saul from being king (I Sam 13). Eventually Saul suffered sporadic mental derangement, and finally, sought the help of a witch, who was possessed by a familiar spirit (I Sam. 28 and 31). Saul's disastrous career as king prepared the way for the true king of Israel, who would also be the ancestor of the Messiah.

David's kingship and lineage

God had previously chosen through Samuel the shepherd boy from Bethlehem, David, son of Jesse, of the tribe of Judah, to be king. A somewhat obscure prophecy by the dying Jacob seemed to indicate that the true kingship of Israel would be founded in the tribe of Judah: 'The sceptre shall not depart from Judah, nor a lawgiver from between his feet, until Shiloh come, and unto him shall the gathering of the people be' (Gen. 49:10).

David, from Judah, replaced Saul, from Benjamin, and was 'the man after God's own heart' (I Sam. 13:14). God established a firm covenant with David, his chosen, stating: 'Thy seed will I establish for ever, and build up thy throne to all generations' (Ps. 89:3-4). God promised that David's seed would endure forever, and his throne as the days of heaven (Ps. 89:29). God promised through the prophet Nathan that although David's seed could be chastised for iniquity, still his kingdom would endure forever (II Sam. 7:13-17).

The prophets in later years interpreted the fall and captivity of Israel because of their idolatry as a severe, but not final judgment. There would come a time of release and glorious restoration of the disobedient and corrupt people of Israel (cf. Isa. 62 and Jer. 31). God says that he will have mercy upon his 'dear son, Ephraim' (Jer. 31:20). The 'dear son' will be restored through none less than a descendant of David; the one who will occupy the throne forever.

Messiah as the True Son

The most quoted Old Testament passage in the New Testament is Psalm 110, which specifically tells us that David's son is also David's Lord (Ps. 110:1). Jesus applies this to himself (Matt. 22:41-45; Mark 12:35-37; Luke 20:41-44), and Acts 2:34, 35 applies it to Jesus, as does Hebrews 1:13, and 10:12, 13.

It should come then as no surprise to those familiar with the history of Israel, that after God's created son, Adam, failed (for Luke's genealogy calls Adam 'the son of God' – Luke 3:38); after God's adopted son, Israel, failed; even King David, anointed though he was, was marked by many failures. Then God sent the Son of his own heart: his only begotten Son in the flesh, to carry through with impeccable, obedient devotion everything that he wanted in the others; to fulfill all that he ever desired in and through the new head of the human race: the Last Adam.

History of Israel Recapitulated in Christ

In addition to the accounts of the Virgin Birth in Matthew and Luke, the scene of the baptism of Jesus at the hands of John in the Jordan River shows how he fulfills and surpasses every foreshadowing of sonship from the Old Testament: 'and lo a voice from heaven, saying, This is my beloved Son, in whom I am well pleased' (Matt. 3:17). And the same is true in the transfiguration (Matt. 17:1-5): 'This is my beloved Son, in whom I am well pleased; hear ye him' (v. 5). Only by means of the hypostatic union of two natures in one person was Christ able successfully to recapitulate all that sonship toward which the Old Testament was reaching forward in Adam and Israel.

This is also demonstrated in the way Matthew 2:15 interprets the return of Joseph, Mary, and the holy child from Egypt after the death of Herod as a fulfillment of Hosea 11:1, 'Out of Egypt have I called my son.' In a preliminary sense, Israel was the son of God, brought out of Egypt, but the rest of the Old Testament shows how frequently that son rebelled against the Father. Nevertheless, Israel in its historical life foreshadowed the true Son of God: born of the Virgin Mary. What Israel did not carry through, Christ did carry through.

The temptations of Christ in the wilderness, immediately after his baptism, seem to be a contrast with the temptation which Adam and Eve failed (having thought 'my will be done'), and that which Israel failed in the wilderness wanderings, questioning the goodness and providence of the Lord (e.g. Exod. 17:1-7).

Synoptic Accounts of the Temptations

Mark's account of Christ's temptation is very brief, and does not mention the content of the temptations. He states, as do Matthew and Luke, that Satan was the source of them, and that they lasted forty days (Mark 1:12,13). The two other synoptic Gospels give us the number of the temptations (three), and their content, although there is a difference between the order of the last two temptations as reported by Matthew and Luke. As they relate the Biblical quotations used by Jesus and Satan, both of them quote from the LXX (Greek) version of the Old Testament, rather than from the Hebrew of the Masoretic text – and this is fairly typical of much of the New Testament.

Matthew gives the temptations in this order: (1) Turn the stones into bread (Matt. 4:3); (2) Cast yourself down from the Temple (Matt. 4:6) and (3) Worship me and I will give you the kingdoms of the world (Matt. 4:8,9). Luke gives this order: (1) Turn the stones into bread (Luke 4:3); (2) Worship me and I will give you the kingdoms of the world (Luke 4:5-7), and (3) Cast yourself down from the Temple (Luke 4:9-11).

Hence, the difference in the order is: Matthew places last Satan's temptation to Christ to worship him in order to receive the kingdoms of the world, whereas Luke places last Satan's temptation to Christ to cast himself down from the Temple. Following J. Dupont, I will later suggest a possible reason for Luke's order differing from that of Matthew. But first let us consider the larger biblical context of Christ's temptations.

It has from ancient times been noted that the answers of Jesus to the temptations of Satan all come from Deuteronomy (8:3; 6:16, and 6:13). As B. Gerhardsson notes, 'The three decisive replies in the dialogue all are from Deut. 6-8, the deuteronomic exposition of how God allowed his "son" Israel to wander for forty years in the desert that he might discipline and test him.'[9]

Each one of the temptations is related to a specific event in Israel's history as they came through the desert. J. Dupont shows that the quotations Christ draws from Deuteronomy (8:3; 6:16; 6:13) are used in the *inverse* position (i.e. from the later to the earlier), but in that 'backwards' way, Matthew's account of the order of these sayings in answer to each of the temptations actually gives the true historical order of what happened in Exodus: the episode of giving the manna, the miracle of water from the rock after bitter complaint, and the entry into Canaan.[10] Later we must consider the possible reason why Luke varies the order of the second and third temptations for the larger purposes of his Gospel.

(1) First temptation

Jesus fasted for forty days (and Matthew adds, forty nights – Matt. 4:2), and at the end of this period was hungry. There is surely an analogy between Israel's wandering in the desert for forty years, and Jesus'fasting in the desert for forty days. Dupont points out the principle that at times in the Old Testament economy, one day equals a year (as when the spies searched out the Promised Land for forty days - Numbers 14:34; compare Ezekiel 4:1-8). Each of these days stood for a year.[11] This wilderness history is being recapitulated in the temptations of the Messiah of Israel.

The hunger of Christ recalls the distrust and complaining of the Israelites in Exodus 16, after which God started causing the mysterious manna to rain down to serve as the people's daily bread. In the exhortations given near the end of his life, Moses reminded the people of this incident that introduced the provision of the manna, and draws from it the lesson that 'man shall not live by bread alone, but by every word that proceeds from the mouth of God'(Deut. 8:3). Deuteronomy 8:2 states that God was behind this testing, 'as a man chastens his son.' But the 'son,' Israel, failed the test by distrust and complaining.

With Israel's failure in mind, Satan attempted to tempt God's Son to distrust the Father, by encouraging him to employ his supernatural power to turn the stones into bread to satisfy his hunger immediately, rather than waiting on the Lord in the limits of the humanity he had taken on in order to redeem it from the inside out. But Jesus, God's eternal Son, now in the flesh, passes this test, and in so doing answers the evil one in the words

---

9. Birger Gerhardsson, *The Testing of God's Son: (Matthew 4:1-11 & PAR) An Analysis of an Early Christian Midrash* (Wipf & Stock: Eugene, Oregon, reprint of 1966 edition), 11.

10. J. Dupont, *Les Tentations de Jésus au Desert*, in *Studia Neotestamentica 4* (Desclée de Brouwer: Bruges, 1968), 22.

11. Ibid., 15.

of Moses: 'Man shall not live by bread alone, but by every word that proceedeth out of the mouth of God' (Matt. 4:4).

Satan tempted Christ to avoid the sufferings inherent in walking his chosen path as God's trusting Son, and as our Messiah, but Satan failed then and later, for Christ showed that 'my meat is to do the will of him that sent me' (John 4:34). The Son thereby pleased the Father (which was the Son's greatest delight – cf. Psalm 40:8) and in due time, following the other two temptations, Satan gave up for a season and departed, whereupon the Father sent angels, who ministered unto him (Matt. 4:11).

(2) Second Temptation

In Matthew's order of the temptations, Satan leads Jesus up to the pinnacle of the Temple, and tells him to cast himself down, for the Lord would send his angels to bear him up, in accordance with the promise of Psalm 91, which Satan duly quotes. This recalls the episode of Massa, reported in Exodus 17:1-17 (and Numbers 20:1-13), where the thirsty people demanded a sign of God's presence by insisting on an immediate miracle. This incident at Massa seems very different from the call of Satan for Jesus to throw himself down from the Temple, but as Dupont shows, they are alike in that Israel failed in putting God to the test by demanding a miracle, and Satan wanted Jesus also to demand a miracle.[12] The analogy between them is shown in Christ's quotation from Deuteronomy 6:16 (cf. Matt. 4:7 and Luke 4:12): 'Thou shalt not tempt the Lord thy God.'

In refusing to put God to the test, as did Israel in the wilderness, Jesus as our covenant representative shows us the way of true faith through every earthly wilderness with the demands they can place on our self-life; it is trust in God; it is 'walking by faith and not by sight' (cf. II Cor. 5:7). It is utter willingness for God to be God, because he is God, and does not need to keep proving it to us! We frequently fail to trust the Father as we should, but Jesus is our pioneer: 'the author and finisher of our faith' (Heb. 12:2). *In him* we have the victory through the faith that overcomes the world (cf. I John 5:4). He won this gift in our human nature so that he could make it ours in him.

The issue in temptation is that we should remember who God is. As Gerhardsson wrote:

> The acts of JHWH can never be questioned, his way of fulfilling his covenant 'obligations' is in the end above human criticism; man simply has to accept his division of good and evil in trust and obedience; knowing that God is 'righteous' and does not forsake 'the righteous man'... The covenant son will bow before JHWH in love, trust, and obedience, regarding him not as a capricious god of fate, but as a loving Father who, while he can chastise his son with much severity, will never permanently reject him.[13]

---

12. Ibid., 17.
13. Gerhardsson, op. cit., 31.

(3) Third Temptation

Following at this point Matthew's order, the last temptation is when Satan takes Jesus up to a very high mountain, shows him all the kingdoms of the world with their glory, and says he will give them all to Jesus if he will bow down and worship this evil one (Matt. 4:8,9). It is of no consequence for our faith where this 'exceeding high mountain' was located. Many have suggested a connection between Moses being shown by the Lord on Mount Nebo the Promised Land that he was not allowed to enter into, and Christ being shown not just the Promised Land, but all nations of the world (cf. Deut. 34:1-4).[14]

Again, Jesus goes back to Moses' preaching in Deuteronomy to answer Satan. He orders the devil to leave, and then quotes Deuteronomy 6:13: 'Thou shalt fear the LORD thy God, and serve him, and shalt swear by his name' (though Matthew and Luke vary the words slightly from the original Hebrew text – without any change of meaning – as they follow the Greek Version). Verse 13 comes in the midst of a text where Moses is warning the children of Israel as they enter the land, not to worship the false gods of that land:

> Then beware lest thou forget the LORD, which brought thee forth out of the land of Egypt…Thou shalt fear the Lord thy God, and serve him, and shalt swear by his name. Ye shall not go after other gods, gods of the people which are round about you: (For the LORD thy God is a jealous God among you) lest the anger of the LORD thy God be kindled against thee, and destroy thee from off the face of the earth (Deut. 6:12-15).

The New Testament saw Satan behind the gods of this world (2 Cor. 4:4 and Rev. 13:2), so when Moses warned the Israelites not to worship the gods of the Land they were entering, Satan was behind the whole polytheistic system. Thus, Jesus successfully passes the final test that Israel failed, and he does so by rejecting Satan and all the lesser powers he manipulates, in order to worship the Father, and him alone. The success of Jesus in overcoming the last temptation gloriously fulfills the first commandment.

Luke places the second temptation in third place

Luke's order of the temptations puts as the last one, Satan's calling on Christ to throw himself down from the temple (which is second in Matthew's order). The content and conclusions of the temptations in both Gospels is precisely the same, only the order of the second and third ones is different. Why the difference? Most scholars have assumed that the order in Matthew is more likely to be the original one, since it follows so closely the events in Exodus (as conveyed in Jesus' quotations from Deuteronomy). These three quotations by Christ of Moses, as we saw, are in inverse order, so as to fit correctly the historical events set forth in Exodus). This harmony of orders between Matthew's account of the temptations, and the testings related in Exodus does not provide final proof of Matthew's priority, but does seem a reasonable possibility.

---

14. Dupont, op. cit., 18,19.

If that is correct, then why does Luke put what Matthew listed as the second temptation in third place? J. Dupont has suggested that Luke wishes to tie in very clearly the temptations to the final passion of Christ, and does so by putting the call of the evil one for him to jump from the temple as the last test. Dupont writes:

> Luke explicitly presents the devil as an actor in the passion. The history of the passion begins with the betrayal by Judas...Luke adds a significant detail: 'Satan then entered into Judas...' (22:3). [Jesus refers to 'your hour and the power of darkness in Luke 22:53]. 'The hour' of the enemies of Jesus is in reality that of the power of darkness of which they are mere instruments; it is the *Kairos* of Satan.'

Dupont adds that 'Luke sees in the temptations the prelude to the Passion...that Jesus is not merely taken by hostile men, but by the prince of darkness in person.'[15]

Dupont believes that the crucial role Jerusalem played in fulfilling the Old Testament prophecies in the history of redemption is the reason why Luke placed Christ's temptation on the temple in final place. On the Mount of Transfiguration, Moses and Elijah had spoken with Jesus of the 'Exodus' [or 'Decease'] which he should accomplish at Jerusalem (Luke 9:31), and as Jesus was on his way to the holy city, Luke reports that he said: '...it cannot be that a prophet should perish out of Jerusalem' (Luke 13:33). Later, Jesus says in Luke 18:31: '...Behold, we go up to Jerusalem, and all things that are written by the prophets concerning the Son of man shall be accomplished.'

Hence, Dupont concludes that Luke lists the temptation to jump from the Temple last, so as to connect it with the city where Jesus would be crucified, thus fulfilling the Old Testament prophecies:

> Jerusalem is the city where Jesus must 'accomplish his decease' ['exodus'] (Luke 9:31), where he must suffer his passion. It was appropriate that it should be in that place where the temptations concluded and Satan fled from him. It was also there that the devil reappeared, not to further tempt Jesus, but to provoke the ultimate test, of which the temptations were only forerunners.[16]

In all of the temptations (whichever order one follows), Jesus, the Messiah of Israel, showed himself to be the obedient and loving Son of God, thereby restoring our race to the Father's immediate presence, for one can only look face to face upon one who has been loved and obeyed from the heart. While the devil would have us turn our faces eternally away from God, Jesus as our messianic Head has turned us to look upon our heavenly Father forevermore. His going, in our place, through the baptism of repentance and the temptations, prepared him to stand in our place in Gethsemane and on Calvary.

---

15. Ibid., 67.

16. Ibid., 70.

The work of the Messiah of Israel could only have been carried through by the Son of God. Although the Scriptures do not often mention together 'Messiah' and 'Son of God,' it is clear that the task of the one had to be undertaken by the other. Gerhardsson rightly says that '2 Samuel 7... played its part in keeping alive the identification between the Messiah and the Son of God.'[17] In this regard, it is significant that Jesus was tempted both as Messiah of Israel and also as the Son of God. The latter was the basis on which Satan sought to have him disobey the Father: 'If you are the Son of God' (or 'since you are the Son of God') – e.g. Matt. 4:3; Luke 4:3, etc. And fulfilling the appointed tasks of the Messiah was the role only he, who was the Son of God in the flesh, could have undertaken and successfully carried through.[18]

The Anointed One, who definitively rejected Satan in order to be pleasing to God his Father, and to await his will for what must follow, did so for our sakes, as our representative. In him, we have rejected Satan and the gods of a world, darkened by sin and death, in union with the one who is: 'the brightness of his glory, and the express image of his person, and upholding all things by the word of his power, when he had by himself purged our sins, sat down on the right hand of the Majesty on high...' (Heb. 1:3).

Sinclair Ferguson has seen the point here:

> His temptations constitute an epochal event. They are not merely personal, but cosmic. They constitute the tempting of the last Adam...His testing was set in the context of a holy war in which he entered the enemy's domain, absorbed his attacks and sent him into retreat (Matt. 4:11, and especially Luke 4:13). In the power of the Spirit, Jesus advanced as the divine warrior, the God of battles who fights on behalf of his people and for their salvation (cf. Exod. 15:3; Ps. 98:1). His triumph demonstrated that 'the kingdom of God is near' and that the messianic conflict had begun.[19]

At the end of his earthly ministry, the incarnate Son, facing a substitution-ary, God-forsaken death in Gethsemane, unlike the first Adam, said 'Thy will be done' (Matt. 26:42), and, unlike the complaining and distrusting Israel in the wilderness, without reserve committed his spirit into the Fa-ther's hands with his last breath (Luke 23:46). The result of that self-sacri-ficing will and loving trust is 'writ large' in Romans 1:2-3 as the ultimate fulfillment of all the promises of the Gospel: '(... Which he had promised afore by his prophets in the holy scriptures,) Concerning his Son Jesus Christ our Lord, which was made of the seed of David according to the flesh; And declared to be the Son of God with power, according to the spirit of holiness, by the resurrection from the dead.')

Later in Romans 5, and also in I Corinthians 15, the Apostle Paul makes the schema of two Adams: Adam and Christ, crucial to his entire theology of redemption. 'For as by one man's disobedience, many were

---

17. Gerhardsson, op. cit., 23.

18. According to Gerhardsson, op. cit., 23-24: 'The recently discovered Florilegium Fragment from Qumran (4 Q Flor) presents us with a piece of evidence...in it the prophecy of Nathan is interpreted messianically, giving us an explicit statement that the Messiah is called Son of God.'

19. Sinclair Ferguson, *The Holy Spirit* (IVP: Downers Grove, Il., 1996), 48-49.

made sinners, so by the obedience of one shall many be made righteous' (Rom. 5:10); 'For since by man came death, by man came also the resurrection of the dead. For as in Adam all die, even so in Christ shall all be made alive' (I Cor. 15:21-22).

What we must take account of here is that Jesus did **not** go directly from his miraculous birth or from his public baptism straight to the cross of Calvary! Yes, 'In the fullness of the time' (Gal. 4:4) that had been appointed 'before the foundation of the world' (Rev. 13:8) for the great transaction (in Calvin's terms – *mirifica communtatio*), Christ would indeed go to Calvary, but that time was not ripe until he had obeyed the Father in his earthly life for some thirty-three years of constant filial devotion and perfect obedience from the heart. This means that a life of active obedience, a life of perfect filial sonship, was to be lived in its fullness before that hour when the Son would be glorified by the Father on the cross as he poured out his life a ransom for many.

We now consider (i) the necessity of Christ's active obedience for our salvation, and (ii) the accomplishments of his active obedience.

(i) The necessity of Christ's active obedience for our salvation

In traditional confessional Protestantism, most of the emphasis in the doctrine of salvation by Christ has been laid upon his atoning death and resurrection. Yet the significance of his holy life, while generally not receiving the attention it deserved, has not been totally ignored. For instance, this matter was discussed by the fathers of the Westminster Assembly in the 1640s in London. The question was: is the death of Christ alone sufficient for our justification, or is his life necessary as well? The Assembly divines voted strongly in favor of the latter. The *Minutes* of the Assembly state that the arguments of Thomas Goodwin helped win the day for affirming the imputation to believers of the active obedience of Christ.[20] Hence the *Westminster Confession* affirms Christ's active obedience as constituting part of our justification, which is imputed to us by faith (Ch. 9.1).

A fine discussion of the results of the debates in the Assembly concerning his active obedience is found in Jeffrey K. Jue's article 'The Active Obedience of Christ and the Theology of the Westminster Standards: A Historical Investigation.'[21] He argues that a few members of the Assembly (such as Vines and Gataker) opposed the imputation of active obedience out of fear that the concept might lead to antinomianism.[22] But the great majority, probably led by Thomas Goodwin, among others, affirmed the imputation of Christ's active obedience in the justification of believers, although they strongly rejected antinomianism.[23]

---

20. See Chad Van Dixhoorn, 'Reforming the Reformation: Theological Debate at the Westminster Assembly 1643-1652,' 7 Vol PhD diss. Cambridge University, 2004, II. 51; referenced in Mark Jones, *Why Heaven Kissed Earth: The Christology of the Puritan Reformed Theologian, Thomas Goodwin (1600-1680)* (Gottingen: Vandenhoeck & Ruprecht, 2010), 180.

21. *Justified in Christ: God's Plan for us in Justification*, Edited by K. Scott Oliphint (Christian Focus Publications: Fearn, Ross-shire, 2007), 99-130.

22. Ibid., 114-121.

23. Ibid., 121-128.

In Goodwin's 'Of Christ the Mediator,' he devotes three chapters to Christ's active obedience and its imputation to believers.[24] As he comments on Romans 8:4 ['That the righteousness of the law might be fulfilled in us, who walk not after the flesh, but after the Spirit'], he notes:

> There be three parts of justification. *First*, The taking away of actual sin; this is handled in ch. iii. ver. 24, 'All have sinned,' etc. His passive obedience takes away the guilt of actual sin. But, *secondly*, we ought to have an actual righteousness reckoned to us. This is handled in Rom. v. 18, 'As by the offence of one, judgment came upon all men to condemnation; even so by the righteousness of one, the free gift came upon all unto justification of life.' The active obedience of Jesus Christ made many righteous. Justification lies not only in pardon of sin, but in the righteousness of Christ imputed to us, and imputed to us as Adam's sin was.
>
> But the law is not fulfilled yet; for we have corruption of nature in us. The apostle therefore in this Rom. viii. 4, he brings in the *third* part of justification, vis., That Christ came into the world in our nature, and fulfilled the righteousness of the law, in having that nature perfectly holy. And now the righteousness of the law is fulfilled in all parts of it; here is a perfect justification, and we desire no more.[25]

But like earlier historical creeds and confessions of the church, the Westminster divines do not devote much space to the active obedience, but list it before going on to the issues involved in his atoning death. However, Mark Jones shows that owing to the great influence of Thomas Goodwin (quoted above), the *Savoy Declaration* of the Congregationalists, that met soon afterwards, enlarged the section on Christ's active obedience and its imputation, by one strong clause: '... *by imputing Christ's active obedience to the whole law, and passive obedience in his death for their whole and sole righteousness...*' (Ch. 9.1).[26]

Herman Bavinck notes that only a small minority of Protestants ever denied the necessity of Christ's active obedience, such as Karg (Parsimonius), who retracted his opposition in 1570, and Johannes Piscator, who wrote against the concept in a letter of 1604.[27] The vast majority of the Reformed did accept it, as in the Belgic Confession, article 22, which speaks of the Lord 'imputing to us all his merits, and so many holy works, which he has done for us and in our stead.' Yet though the Reformation accepted in principle the redemptive nature of Christ's active obedience as being conveyed to his people, they still did not go very far in expounding it (as compared to their voluminous work on his atoning death).

We see a summary exposition of it in Chapter 8 of the Westminster Confession of Faith ('Christ the Mediator'): 'He was made under the law, and did perfectly fulfill it, endured most grievous torments immediately in His soul, and most painful sufferings in His body...' (par.. 4). 'The Lord Jesus, by His perfect obedience, and sacrifice of Himself...hath fully

---

24. Goodwin, op. cit., chapters XIX – XXI.

25. Goodwin, op. cit., 352.

26. Mark Jones, op. cit., 182.

27. Herman Bavinck, op. cit., 347.

satisfied the justice of the Father...' (par. 5). Similarly, in the Chapter (11) on 'Justification,' his active obedience is definitely taught as part of his action to justify his people, but is not expounded any further than saying: 'Christ, by His obedience and death, did fully discharge the debt of all those that are justified...' (par. 3).

In general, the Westminster Confession considers Christ's active obedience within the context of Covenant. Thus, Chapter 7, 'Of God's Covenant with Man,' states that Adam was in a 'first covenant,' 'a covenant of works,' which works had to be fulfilled for the salvation of humankind to occur: 'The first covenant made with man was a covenant of works, wherein life was promised in Adam, and in him to his posterity, upon condition of perfect and personal obedience' (par. 2).

Covenant of Works

But Biblical Theology in the last century has not accepted that there was ever 'a covenant of works' in the Genesis text. John Murray, a conservative Calvinist, has denied its presence, and has called it rather 'the Adamic Administration,' although he teaches the headship of Adam and the necessary place of full obedience of life to be justified.[28] In place of the concept of the covenant of works binding upon Adam and his posterity, the more recent viewpoint has been that there was a 'covenant of creation,' and that all its phases (including 'the administration of Adam') should be included under the overarching rubric of 'the Covenant of Grace,' although not denying the federal headship of Adam, and its implications for having brought all his posterity into sin and guilt.[29]

One Covenant of Grace

Pierre Courthial, in his *Le Jour de Petits Recommencements* (*The Day of Small Beginnings*), teaches that the Covenant of Grace was in force before Adam sinned, indeed, it was the structural basis of creation. That is to say, grace means more than pardon, and, of course, pardon is applicable only after Adam's fall into sin. Courthial argues, therefore, that God's grace has, in Scripture, two senses: one is benevolence or favor, and the other is merciful pardon. The Covenant of Grace was marked by benevolence *before the Fall*, and merciful pardon *after the Fall*. He points out that God's word to Noah before the Flood in Genesis 6:18, normally translated 'I will establish my covenant with you' actually should be translated 'I will *confirm* my covenant...'[30]

Jean-Marc Berthoud devotes an insightful chapter to 'The Covenant of Creation' (ch. 3) in his recent volume on *The Covenant of God Throughout*

---

28. See John Murray, *The Covenant of Grace*.

29. See my discussion of this in *Systematic Theology*, vol. 1, 391-400.

30. Pierre Courthial, *Le Jour des Petits Recommencements: Essai sur l' Actualité de la Parole (Evangile-Loi) de Dieu* (Messages, L'Age d'Homme: Lausanne, 1996), 6: [Instead of 'I will establish'] 'One can equally well render the Hebrew verb *qum* (which is in the *Hiphil*) 'to ratify' or 'to confirm.' He goes on to argue that 'to confirm' makes better sense that 'to establish' in Genesis chapters 6, 9, and 17, as well as in Exodus 6. This grand book is being translated into English by the Rev. Matthew Miller of Greenville, SC.

the Scriptures (if I may give it an English title at this point, before its translation from French).[31] He shows that Adam and Eve knew the grace of God *even before the Fall*, in the sense of grace as divine benevolence or favor: 'Everything came to them from the grace of God, a grace which enabled them to do all the works which had been ordained for them by God.'[32]

If we keep in mind the original concept of the Covenant of Grace, which (before the Fall of Adam) signified 'grace as divine benevolence', it will help us to make sense of both the created order and the purpose of human life. The created order must be understood in light of the God who made it so that it would be the stage upon which humankind – his image-bearers – would live in fellowship with him.

Following Courthial in particular, I have sought to address the significance of these two senses of grace (i.e. loving condescension and pardon for sin) in chapter 6 of *Systematic Theology, Vol. 1*.[33] If what that chapter says is correct, the fact that God was in covenantal relations with Adam, our first father, and that Adam was to be totally obedient to God, in no sense removes the reality of God's graciousness in this original administration or covenant. God's grace in the sense of beneficence was already in the covenant with Adam without that precluding the necessity of full obedience. Granted these two meanings of grace, it seems to me that the Westminster Confession does not preclude grace from the Covenant of Works.[34]

God's covenant with creation can, in this way, be seen as that of an overarching Covenant of Grace in which the Lord created a son to live in the amity of obedient fellowship with him. Not to do so would have its consequences, but that does not remove the prior fact that the Father wished for a son to love him from the heart, which meant ready and full obedience to the divine will, or – in New Testament terms – 'walking in the light.'

The entire Old Testament shows us that Adam failed; Israel failed. So God, out of love to the world (John 3:16), gave his only begotten Son to stand in for it, and do what it did not do, and now could not do. In terms of the traditional covenant theology, one could say that God's incarnate Son came to pay the penalty of the broken relationship with God (namely, substitutionary death), and – before that supreme climax of love and grace – to keep in its fullness all the righteous requirements of the law. In a certain sense, the substitutionary death keeps us from hell, and the representative obedience takes us into heaven to live forever with God.

(ii) The accomplishments of Christ's Active Obedience

Both Testaments set forward the moral and legal requirements that need to be fulfilled between Adam (and his race) and God (e.g. Genesis 2:16-17;

---

31. Jean-Marc Berthoud, *L'Alliance de Dieu à Travers L'Écriture Sainte: Une Théologie Biblique* (Messages, L'Age d'Homme: Lausanne, 2012), 71-89.

32. Ibid., 72.

33. *Systematic Theology*, vol 1, 387-444.

34. Ibid., 389-390.

Preface to the Ten Commandments in Exodus 20:2 and Deuteronomy 5:1-5; Matthew 5:17-20) and underlying that obedience, is the life of sonship which alone is pleasing to the Father. Since the first Adam, and afterwards Israel, did not live out this loving sonship to the Father, then Christ, the Last Adam, would do so. This is central to the concept of Christ's active obedience, and particularly to its accomplishments.

Christ's Active Obedience is above all else the Life of True Sonship

Two of the early Church Fathers (Athanasius and Irenaeus) provide us the necessary clues to appreciate the one true sonship in which we share by faith: In his *De Incarnatione* (section 13), Athanasius says:

> What then was God to do? or what was to be done save the renewing of that which was in God's image, so that by it men might once more be able to know Him? But how could this have come to pass save by the presence of the very Image of God, our Lord Jesus Christ?... Whence the Word of God came in His own person, that, as He was the image of the Father, He might be able to create afresh the man after the image (par. 7).

He goes on (in section 16) to say:

> For men's mind having finally fallen to things of sense, the Word disguised Himself by appearing in a body, that He might, as Man, transfer men to Himself, and centre their senses on Himself, and, men seeing Him thenceforth as Man, persuade them by the works He did that He is not Man only, but also God, and the Word and Wisdom of the true God (par. 1).

Over a century before Athanasius, Saint Irenaeus of Lyon at several points in his *Adversus Haereses* wrote of Christ having 'recapitulated' our fallen, Adamic humanity, restoring it by his holiness through every stage of life. Irenaeus writes along these lines:

> Being a Master, therefore, He also possessed the age of a Master (i.e. thirty years old), not despising or evading any condition of humanity, nor setting aside in Himself that law which He had appointed for the human race, but sanctifying every age by that period corresponding to it which belonged to Himself. For He came to save all by means of Himself...He therefore passed through every age, becoming an infant for infants, thus sanctifying infants; a child for children, thus sanctifying those who are of this age...a youth for youths...thus sanctifying them for the Lord. So likewise He was an old age man for old men, that He might be a perfect Master for all...sanctifying at the same time the aged also.[35]

These, and other Church Fathers, teach that we are reconciled to God, not only by the saving death of Christ (which they clearly affirmed), but also by his saving life; by his active obedience that does something to our in-turned humanity, to turn it back to God. Hence his life enters into our salvation, as well as his death.

---

35. Irenaeus, *Adversus Haereses* II. 22. 4.

Dumitru Staniloae (1903-1993), has manifested the same insight:

> In this way [incarnation as a true human person] he begins his work of salvation through what he does with his very own human nature. He has not just assumed humanity in order to be our juridical representative, to pay or to suffer in our stead for the offense against God, as is the case in Western theology… 'For you know the grace of our Lord Jesus Christ, that though He was rich, yet for your sakes He became poor, that you through His poverty might become rich' (2 Cor. 8:9). In accord with this, Leontius of Byzantium considers the descent of the Son of God as the only 'remedy' for our disease. 'Through economy, the only wise doctor of our souls has healed the disease of all by receiving within Himself our sufferings.'[36]

Significance of Christ's fulfillment of the Law

Later in his *Christology*, Staniloae again quotes Leontius of Byzantium, and adds a comment:

> According to Leontius, 'If he fulfills the law without having the need to do that (for the righteous have no need of repentance), evidently he does this to fulfill all the righteousness of his *oikonomia* according to the body and to show his divinity in the very act of fulfilling the law; once the bodily nature was lacking the power to fulfill the law, only the divine nature could fulfill it completely.'[37]

Staniloae comments: 'Evidently, it is not about the fulfillment of the law in the sense of an external satisfaction offered to God, but about the fulfillment of God's will and of the requirements of human nature through a life that brings this nature to its true condition by its union with God.'[38]

John Owen summarized Christ's active obedience in terms of fullest keeping of the law on our behalf, as being a successful fulfillment of all its terms, which is by faith imputed to us as one part of our justification:

> First, By the obedience of the life of Christ you see what is intended, – his willing submission unto, and perfect, complete fulfilling of every law of God… Secondly, That this obedience was performed by Christ, not for himself, but for us, and in our stead…Thirdly, Then, I say, this perfect, complete obedience of Christ to the law is reckoned unto us…[39]

We can think of Christ's internal (not merely external) fulfilling of the law and will of God as a sanctification from the inside out of our humanity that was turned away from God. He turns it back around, face to face with the heavenly Father. In *The Mediation of Christ*, Torrance shows us what has happened:

---

36. D. Staniloae, *The Experience of God : The Person of Jesus Christ as God and Savior*, translated by Father, Ioan Ionita (Holy Cross Othodox Press: Brookline, MA, 2011), Vol. 3, 100-102. He quotes Leontius, *Contra Nestor. et Eutych.* (PG 86a: 1321d).

37. Leontius of Byzantium, *Adv. Nest.*, book VI (PG 86a: 1717-20).

38. Staniloae, op. cit., 134.

39. John Owen, *Works, vol.* 2, 161-162.

We are to think of the whole life and activity of Jesus from the cradle to the grave as constituting the vicarious human response to himself which God has freely and unconditionally provided for us. That is not an answer to God which he has given us through some kind of transaction external to us or over our heads, as it were, but rather one which he has made to issue out of the depths of our human being and life, as our own...Jesus Christ *is* our human response to God.[40]

Christ's Sonship and our Sanctification

In this active obedience of sanctification and reconciliation, Christ lives out the life of filial sonship which neither Adam nor Israel ever did. Hence, in addition to the biblical concept of *substitution*, one must add the biblical concept of *representation*. That is what we find in the theology of the Apostle Paul, especially in Romans 5 and 6, which explicate in detail the union of believers with Christ, their covenant head and representative.

This means that as our substitute and representative, as the Last Adam, Christ turns back our humanity from saying with Adam, 'My will be done' (as he succumbed to the temptation of Satan to be as God), to saying 'Thy will be done.' Christ represents us in his true and full humanity by restoring us to God-centeredness. He, in our room and stead, can truly say: 'I do always those things which please him' (John 8:29). He does so especially in his life of prayer. What Mark 1:35 notes of him was, no doubt, typical: 'And in the morning, rising up a great while before day, he went out, and departed into a solitary place, and there prayed.'

In his perfect faith in the Father, in his obedient response to all of God's holy law (cf. Matt. 5:17), he represents us as 'our worship leader' (to quote John Calvin's comments on Christ's priesthood in Hebrews). Thus, through his holy, loving life, we who believe in him are lifted up into the heavenlies, for in him, through union in the Holy Spirit, we have 'access' to God (Eph. 2:18). He takes our humanity with him into heaven in his ascension, so that 'we are seated with him in heavenly places' (Eph. 2:6).

Andrew Murray shows that while our salvation is legally grounded, in accordance with the holy character of God, and what it requires of sinners, it reaches beyond any external legal sense: 'If our salvation was not to be a merely legal one – external... – but an entrance anew into the very life of God, with the restoration of the divine nature we had lost in paradise, it was the Son of God alone who could impart this to us. He had the life of God to give; He was able to give it; He could only give it by taking us into living fellowship with Himself.'[41]

In a covenantal, representative sense, all of Christ's life, including his faith, counted for us, who are united to him in faith and the Holy Spirit. This seems to be confirmed by the Apostle Paul's statement in Galatians 2:20, especially as it is translated in the Authorised Version: 'the faith of the Son of God' (i.e. 'I am crucified with Christ: nevertheless I live; yet not I, but Christ liveth in me: and the life which I now live in the

---

40. Torrance, *The Mediation of Christ*, 90.

41. Andrew Murray, *The Holiest of All: An Exposition of the Epistle to the Hebrews* (Oliphants, Ltd.: London, 1965), 180-81.

flesh, I live *by the faith of the Son of God*, who loved me and gave himself for me.'). Richard B. Hays has given an entire volume to discussing *The Faith of Jesus Christ*.[42] In it he seeks to demonstrate that in terms of Greek usage, the Authorised Version gives us the best translation: it makes most sense to take it as a subjective genitive (i.e. *faith of*, not *faith in*).[43] In that case, it is indeed *the faith of the Son of God*. In that profound sense, our faith is finally grounded in his faith.

Christ's representation of his people in his active obedience is clearly taught in the New Testament. We must examine several relevant passages.

Scriptural evidence for the saving significance of Christ's Active Obedience

Romans 5:12-21
Romans 5:12-21 contrasts the disobedience of the first Adam, which brought guilt and death upon his descendants, with the obedience of the last Adam, which brought pardon and life to all who identify with him through faith. While the emphasis of the passage is upon Christ's death, there are no exegetical grounds for denying the significance of his lifelong, total obedience before that atoning death.

His Circumcision
His circumcision was to fulfill Old Testament law (cf. Luke 2:21), and to do so in our place, as part of his active obedience. I can find no reason to disagree with Saint Thomas Aquinas' exposition of the Lord's circumcision:

> *I answer that*, For several reasons Christ ought to have been circumcised. First, in order to prove the reality of his human nature, in contradiction to the Manichean, who said that He had an imaginary body... Secondly, in order to show his approval of circumcision, which God had ordained of old. Thirdly, in order to prove that He was descended from Abraham, who had received the commandment of circumcision as a sign of faith in Him. Fourthly, in order to take away from the Jews an excuse for not receiving Him, if He were uncircumcised. Fifthly, *in order by His example to exhort us to be obedient...Sixthly, that He Who had come in the likeness of sinful flesh might not reject the remedy whereby sinful flesh was wont to be healed.* Seventhly, that by taking on Himself the burden of the Law, He might set others free therefrom, according to Gal. iv. 4, 5.[44]

His 'Presentation' in the Temple
The same meaning (active, vicarious obedience) would be true of his presentation by his godly parents in the Temple, forty days after his birth.

---

42. Richard B. Hays, *The Faith of Jesus Christ: An Investigation of the Narrative Substructure of Galatians 3:1 – 4:11* (Scholars Press: Chico, California, 1983).

43. Ibid., 167-69.

44. *The 'Summa Theologica' of St. Thomas Aquinas*, Part III, Second Number (QQ. XXVII – LIX), literally translated by Fathers of the English Dominican Province (R. & T. Washbourne, Ltd.: London, 1914), Q. 37, First Article (p. 147).

Staniloae, drawing again from Leontius of Byzantium, writes:

> ...that it was not he who needed this fulfillment of the law [i.e. presentation in the Temple], but his brothers and sisters whom he represented. For he himself was the true purification of sin, and he took away the power of the law...[Leontius writes]: 'Having the strength of purity in his body woven with God, Christ fulfills all the righteousness of the bodily law in order to free the body's nature from the punishment of the law and from curse and to show it worthy of the spiritual existence which he gave to it.'[45]

His Baptism of Repentance

At the beginning of his public ministry, Christ stood in for us in the baptism of repentance, a major event in fulfilling his sonship in a way that Adam and Israel had both failed. John the Baptist knew that he was no sinner, and thus had no need for repentance, but Jesus replied: 'Suffer it to be so now: for thus it becometh us to fulfil all righteousness' (Matt. 3:14-15). This was part of his active obedience, in which he was taking his people through with him into true turning to God in repentance. He had no need to do so for himself; he did it for us.

His Temptations

It is the same with his temptations in the wilderness. We have already seen how it was an epochal event, one that carried through fullest denial of self in order to honor the Father in the same sort of testings where both Adam and Israel had failed. Christ successfully passed those trials on our behalf. He said 'no' to self, and 'yes' to God, where Adam and Israel had yielded to Satan in self-interest. Thereby, Christ is turning our human experience back to God, and doing so on our account.

His Prayers

In his life of prayer to the Father, Christ prays in our place, so that his prayers give validity to ours in his name. In praying, he takes us back to where we were created to live in fellowship with our heavenly Father. While he continues to do this as our mediatorial intercessor in his ascended state, the point here is that he was already doing this during his representation of us during his earthy life. The Gospel of Luke in particular presents scenes from the prayer life of the Lord. Some examples of his praying are seen as follows: when Jesus was baptized, he was praying (Luke 3:21-22); in the midst of a very busy ministry, 'he withdrew himself into the wilderness, and prayed' (Luke 5:16), and similarly, 'went out into a mountain to pray, and continued all night in prayer to God' (Luke 6:12); he took Peter, James and John to the Mount of Transfiguration, and prayed with them (Luke 9:28-29); he prayed ahead of time for Simon Peter's faith to triumph through the attacks of Satan (Luke 22:31-32).

The Gospels also present Jesus' teaching on prayer at large. Jesus gave his church the Lord's prayer (Matt. 6 and Luke 11); he said 'to pray for those

---

45. Staniloae, op. cit., 133, quoting Leontius, *Adv. Nest.* book VI (PG 86a: 1717-20).

who despitefully use you' (Luke 6:28); he told the disciples to pray for the Lord of the harvest to send forth labourers into his harvest' (Luke 10:2); he warned his disciples to pray in order to escape the coming judgments that will try those who dwell on the face of the whole land (Luke 21:36); they were to pray to avoid temptation (Luke 22:40); he taught his people to continue praying when they did not receive a rapid answer (Luke 11:5-13 and 18:1-8).

Our 'worship-leader'

As a crucial aspect of his active obedience Christ worships the Father as our covenant head – in our room and stead, thereby turning us from 'the world, the flesh, and the devil' back to our gracious and holy God. John Calvin calls the risen Christ our 'worship leader' (λειτουργος) in his *Commentary on Hebrews*. While Calvin's comments have reference to the ministry of the risen Lord in heaven, the devotion of his earthly life already played a part in orienting his people 'to lift up their hearts to the Lord'. They are caught up throughout their earthly life in his 'high priestly prayer' for them in John 17, as well as in his heavenly intercessions for them, as in Hebrews chapters 4 and 5. Calvin particularly thinks through Christ's one Priesthood in his commentary on the Epistle to the Hebrews, especially chapters 7 through 10, and he expounds what this means in *Institutes* Book II, chapters 9-11 and Book IV, chapters 14-17.

Calvin teaches that Christ is 'the leader of our worship' (λειτουργος) – Hebrews 8:2, 'the minister of the sanctuary, and of the true tabernacle, which the Lord pitched and not man.' In his incarnation, atonement and coronation, he has fulfilled and replaced the Old Testament priesthood and abides as 'the High Priest over the House of God' (see Heb. 9). This Christ is the sum and substance of our worship, its High Priest, its leader. Or put in covenantal terms, he fulfills the obligations of God towards us and of us towards God as Representative Head of the Covenant of Grace. As Christ 'through the eternal Spirit offered himself' (Heb 9:14), so we still have nothing more nor less to offer in our worship than him.

As Calvin notes in his *Commentary on Hebrews* 6:19, even as in the Old Testament, when the High Priest entered into the Holy of Holies, all Israel entered with him, so in Christ's priestly work 'in the person of one man all entered the sanctuary together.' Even as God accepted Israel in the person of the High Priest bearing the sacrificial blood to the mercy seat, so God accepts all true worshipers as His crucified, risen Son now represents them in the heavenly sanctuary. Our earthly worship only has validity because it is the counterpart of His heavenly worship. In worship, as in justification, sanctification, adoption and glorification, 'we are accepted in the Beloved' (Eph. 1:6).

Commenting on Hebrews 9:11 'of good things to come,' Calvin writes: 'The meaning is, that we are led by Christ's priesthood into the celestial kingdom of God, and that we are made partakers of spiritual righteousness and of eternal life so that it is not right to desire anything better. Christ alone, then, has that by which he can retain and satisfy us in himself.'

This insight, that Christ is always our worship leader, is the continuing ground of vital, biblical worship in its every element and circumstance. The divine worship required of us (and provided for us in our Covenant Head) is not a human work; it is always the work of Christ for us and through us. This bears the closest relationship to the biblical teaching of justification by faith in Christ on the ground of grace alone. We are justified in Christ; we worship in Christ. Worship is not primarily self-expression. Rather it is the groaning, praising and interceding of the Holy Spirit within us, taking us back to the One who sent him to us on the basis of his finished work (see Rom. 8:14-17).

In *The Mediation of Christ*, Torrance describes Christ, both in his active and passive obedience, as *our prayer*. Speaking of the messianic fulfillment of the Tabernacle liturgy, he writes:

> ...Jesus Christ embodied in himself in a vicarious form the response of human beings to God, so that all their worship and prayer to God henceforth became grounded and centred in him. In short, Jesus Christ in his own self-oblation to the Father *is* our worship and prayer...so that it is only through him and with him and in him that we may draw near to God with the hands of our faith filled with no other offering but that which he has made on our behalf and in our place once and for all.[46]

But the fact that Christ himself *is* our worship and prayer does not mean that we do not need to pray ourselves, but precisely the contrary. His prayer life on earth in our place and his continuing intercessions for us in heaven call for, and give supernatural validity to, our intercessions to the Father. That is why, as we have seen, he gave his disciples (and all of the church, for all time to come) the Lord's Prayer (Matt. 6:9-13; Luke 11:1-4). And that is why Paul instructs us 'to pray without ceasing' (I Thess. 5:17).

The Son's Delight to keep the whole Law

The constantly worshiping Christ, through every aspect of his holy life, delighted to keep for us the whole law of God in active obedience to the Father. Psalm 40:8 was the cry of his heart: 'I delight to do thy will, O my God; yea thy law is within my heart' (cf. Heb. 10:7). In John 4:34, the Saviour says: 'My meat is to do the will of him that sent me, and to finish his work.' In Matthew 5:17 he states: 'Think not that I am come to destroy the law, or the prophets: I am not come to destroy, but to fulfill.'

As Galatians 4:4-5 shows us, his being 'made under the law' meant that part of his redemptive activity for us was that he, the author of the law, kept it in spirit and in every detail. He did so at his baptism, when he said to John: 'Suffer it to be so now: for thus it becometh us to fulfil all righteousness' (Matt. 3:15). He did so at the price of immense agony in Gethsemane, as he cries out to the Father: 'Thy will be done' (Matt. 26:42). He, the Holy One of Israel, owed no obligations to the divine law, as though he were not already holy. The Holy One of Israel kept the whole law on our behalf.

---

46. T. F. Torrance, *The Mediation of Christ*, 96-97.

Saint Thomas summarizes the reasons for and benefits of Christ's having kept the law:

> And Christ, indeed, wished to conform His conduct to the Law, first, to show His approval of the Old Law. Secondly, that by obeying the Law He might perfect it and bring it to an end in His own self, so as to show that it was ordained to Him. Thirdly, to deprive the Jews of an excuse for slandering Him. Fourthly, in order to deliver men from subjection to the Law, according to Gal. iv. 4, 5…[47]

The Son fulfilled the prophecies of the Scriptures

Christ in both his active and passive obedience kept the law and fulfilled the prophecies of the Old Testament to the letter; to do so required both a holy life and an atoning death. The Gospel writers, especially Matthew and John, often say of an action in the life or passion of Christ: 'This was done that the Scriptures might be fulfilled…' (e.g. Matt. 1:22; 2:15; 2:17; 2:23; 8:17; 12:17, etc., and John 12:38; 13:18; 15:25; 17:12, etc.). Christ is actively fulfilling the Scriptures: these things were not just *done* to him; he is in active charge (cf. John 10:18: 'No man taketh [my life] from me, but I lay it down of myself. I have power to lay it down, and I have power to take it again. This commandment have I received of my Father').

The Son was the Messiah

Christ speaks of himself as the true temple (John 2:19). He began his preaching ministry at his hometown synagogue by referring to himself as the fulfillment of Isaiah 61. Matthew and Mark relate that on the night of his betrayal Jesus quoted Zechariah 13:7 ('Strike the shepherd, and the sheep will be scattered'), and the four Gospels frequently describe the details of Christ's death as fulfilling such Psalms as 22 and 69.

All that a loving Son ever needed to be, Jesus was; all that the Old Testament Scriptures said had to be done to reconcile a straying humanity with God, Jesus actively and fully carried out. How active was his active obedience, and how active was his passive obedience! Indeed, John Owen (who does accept the concepts of active and passive obedience) states that nevertheless, '…It cannot clearly be evinced that there is any such thing, in propriety of speech, as *passive obedience; obeying is doing*…'[48]

Staniloae has powerfully expressed the astonishing manner in which our union with Christ in his active obedience, as well as in his death, opens our lives towards others:

> On the basis of full solidarity with us – because he is the divine Hypostasis of human nature and as such totally distinct from any hypostasis capable of closing itself off to others – Christ made himself the human center that is no longer subject to any tendency of selfish limitation through free will, but is totally open toward others, giving them, too, this power through their partaking of his nature. He has obtained this victory over sin through the

---

47. Saint Thomas Aquinas, op. cit., 199.
48. John Owen, *Works vol. II, On Communion with God*, 163.

effort of bearing the passions without sliding toward selfish preservation. He has thus achieved through suffering a union with us that remains to be accepted in turn by us, allowing us to assume his victory over the sin of separation.[49]

Thus, our two most pressing needs, reconciliation with God and reconciliation with others, are part and parcel of the active obedience of Christ, finally completed to the full in his vicarious death for us. In conclusion we can say that by grace we have been given the almost incredibly good news: Jesus died for our sins (his passive obedience). But part of those same wonderful tidings is also his active obedience: Christ has turned our nature back to God, has fulfilled every righteous requirement of God in our name, and has lived the life of perfect sonship that our heavenly Father always wanted. In all of these blessings, the Lord has made us to share, as his Holy Spirit unites us to him who is our substitute and our representative. What a happy and loving people we are called and enabled to be!

---

49. Staniloae, op. cit., 149.

CHAPTER 9

THE HUMILIATION OF CHRIST IN THE SUFFERINGS OF HIS LIFE AND DEATH

The eternal Son of the Father 'made himself of no reputation' in order to save us (Phil. 2:5-11). 'Though he was rich, yet for our sakes he became poor, that we through his poverty might be rich' (II Cor. 8:9). Thus, we are saved at the cost of immense humiliation to the Son of God in his human life and death.

In this chapter, we continue the theme of the remaining stages in the humiliation of the incarnate Christ, namely, (1) the suffering during his life. Then we shall move on to consider (2) his passion, in two parts: in this chapter, we go to the point of (a) his crucifixion.

In chapter ten, we listen to (b) the seven last words from the cross, and then discuss: (3) his burial, and (4) his descent into hell. All of these are aspects of his infinite lowering of himself for our salvation out of the fathomless love of God.

Here we enter, as it were, into the holy of holies, and find ourselves in the presence of the infinitely divine love and holiness that has saved us. No other subject requires such close attention by us needy sinners.

I. The sufferings of Christ before the week of his final passion

The weakness and suffering were voluntarily chosen by him who is 'the strength of Israel'

Owing to our own experience as humans, we naturally tend to think of suffering as weakness, in most cases brought on us from outside, by factors largely outside our control. Yet in the case of the incarnate Christ, while the sufferings are no less real and painful than ours (and there is reason to think that they were far worse), still they are in a profound sense very different. Instead of displaying weakness, they are a hidden and carefully reserved measure of the divine strength, accomplishing beneath the surface necessary actions of humanity's redemption, and constituting an avenue to the victorious accomplishment of his redemptive work.

Glimpses of this divine strength, hidden under human weakness, and voluntarily held back for larger purposes, shine forth when Jesus says: 'No man taketh [my life] from me, but I lay it down of myself. I have power to lay it down, and I have power to take it again' (John 10:18), and also when near the cross Jesus asks: 'Thinkest thou that I cannot now pray to my Father, and he shall presently give me more than twelve legions of angels?' (Matt. 26:53). Similarly he spoke to Pilate: 'Thou couldest have no power at all against me, except it were given thee from above...' (John 19:11). That is the case with Jesus' having allowed his good friend, Lazarus of Bethany, to die, when the Lord who could have healed him was away (John 11). His weakness, his sufferings, and his temporal defeats – painful and grievous as they were – all played a divinely orchestrated part in the accomplishment of his redemptive work to enter the darkness and loss of our humanity in order to turn it around and lift it up into the light of God *from within*.

Christ's sufferings and losses were absolutely real; they were dreadful beyond description, but always under the control of the divine plan, as we see from Peter's sermon in Acts 2. There Peter unveils two sides of one reality: God delivered up Christ according to the divine plan, but at the same time, he was crucified out of the worst motivations of wicked people: 'Him, being delivered by the determinate counsel and foreknowledge of God, ye have taken, and by wicked hands have crucified and slain...' (Acts 2:23). The struggles of Christ before these trials and sufferings were long and hard, with an intensity of agony beyond our imagination, yet – as in the Garden of Gethsemane – he submitted to the Father's plan, for it was also his plan (cf. John 17:4, 5, 18, 19).

Staniloae of Romania has expressed this truth in a way that the Christian tradition of the East has seen very clearly:

> In the case of Christ, the initiative of the Son of God to sacrifice himself as man – an initiative that is combined as a response with the sanctifying initiative of the Father – makes Christ as the incarnate Son of God hypostasize, or personalize, the humanity assumed at his birth as man, having imprinted in him the propensity toward sacrifice so that Christ as man could also be sanctified as sacrifice from the very moment of his birth. Thus, from the very beginning of his existence as man, the sanctifying initiative of the Father encountered Christ's propensity as man to offer himself as sacrifice.[1]

That is to say, all that enters into the humiliation of Christ was voluntarily chosen, and all along the way carried out in accordance with the eternal, redemptive purposes of the Holy Trinity. This voluntarily assumed humiliation included not only the hours of his crucifixion, but all of his incarnate life. Herman Witsius expressed this clearly:

---

1. Staniloae, op. cit., 207.

VII. In fine, as *the likeness of sinful flesh*, or the sorrowful and contemptible condition of Christ, runs parallel with the whole course of his life, and he took it upon him *for sin*; so that God did therefore *condemn sin*, and declare it had no manner of right over believers, either to condemn them, or reign over them, Rom. viii.3, it is manifest, that the scripture ascribes the satisfaction of Christ to the whole of his humiliation; consequently, they do not take the scriptures for their guide, who confine it to the sufferings only of those three hours.[2]

And a question of the *Westminster Larger Catechism* speaks of the humility that Christ assumed throughout his life:

> Q. 48. *How did Christ humble himself in his life?*
> Christ humbled himself in his life, by subjecting himself to the law, which he perfectly fulfilled; and by conflicting with the indignities of the world, temptations of Satan, and infirmities in his flesh, whether common to the nature of man, or particularly accompanying that of his low condition.

General Sufferings of Christ Before the Crisis of Passion Week

Life in a humble family

The miraculous Virgin Birth may have caused some difficulties for his parents in the opinion of the general public. The remark of the Pharisees to the adult Jesus may or may not have contained a veiled reference to it: '… we be not born of fornication; we have one Father, even God' (John 8:41). In Mark 6, Jesus returns to his home town to preach in the synagogue of his childhood, and is angrily rejected by the people who had seen him grow up. In that context, commenting on the phrase 'the carpenter, the son of Mary' (Mark 6:3), Ben Witherington writes, 'This suggests, as does the…reading of "son of Mary" as a slur, that Mary was not held in very high esteem in this town…She lived out the role of a normal and good Jewish woman, but she lived with a cloud of suspicion over her head…'[3]

It is certain that his earthly parents were not financially well off. He was born in a stable in Bethlehem; they had to flee to Egypt to escape the murderous intentions of the king. When they returned to Nazareth, Joseph worked as a simple carpenter in order to support what was by then a large family. They had no high standing in the society of that day, although both the foster father and the mother were godly people.

What it was like for a sinless child to live among sinners is something we cannot know. We are all only too comfortable with sin, but what would it have been like for a holy one to dwell in the midst of impurity? The Scottish theologian John Dick thought of it in this way:

> While a child, he was dependent, like other children, upon others; and, although there is no doubt that the blessed Virgin treated him with the

---

2. Herman Witsius, *The Economy of the Covenants Between God and Man: Comprehending A Complete Body of Divinity*, Translated by William Crookshank (Printed for M. Baynes et al.: London, 1822), 215,216.

3. Ben Witherington, *What Have They Done With Jesus?*, 123.

most tender affection, it was impossible that he should not have suffered through inattention, and neglect, and awkwardness of those to whose care he was occasionally committed. Living among imperfect mortals, he must have experienced the effect of their ignorance and irregular tempers, especially while his mental faculties, not being sufficiently matured, nor his bodily strength confirmed, he was not yet qualified to manage himself. His food might have been withheld, when his appetite craved it; his rest might be disturbed by unseasonable intrusions; his mind might be vexed by the peevishness and forwardness of those with whom he associated. These things are only matters of conjecture; but they are by no means improbable, as he was placed in circumstances exactly similar to those in which we find ourselves. It may be thought, indeed, that as the Son of God he would always command profound reverence, and uninterrupted attention to his comfort; but amidst the familiarity of daily intercourse, even his parents might sometimes think of him only as a child; and to his fellow-creatures and neighbours, perhaps, his dignity was unknown. Of this there can be no doubt, that it was humiliating to such a person to be found in a situation in which he was indebted to others for the necessaries of life, and for instruction and protection, and was exposed to the rudeness of the young, and the caprice of the old…Thus the Lord of all was reduced to a level with the lowest of the human race, and literally underwent that part of the curse, which doomed man 'to eat bread in the sweat of his face.'[4]

The only time we see him as a child is when he was twelve years old, visiting Jerusalem with his parents during the Passover season. For all their affection towards him, they do not seem to have understood who he really was, as he sat in the Temple and questioned the doctors of the law, and thereby missed joining the pilgrim group homewards to Nazareth. Yet he submitted to them, and 'increased in wisdom and stature, and in favour with God and man' (Luke 2:52).

Thomas Goodwin reflects upon the lowly vocation of Jesus before his public ministry:

> By a mean calling. Thirty years lived he in a mechanic trade, and that no better than of a carpenter. Now, for him to be hid under chips, who was born to sit upon the royal throne of Israel; for those hands to make doors and hew logs that were made to wield the scepter of heaven and earth; and that he who was the 'mighty counselor' should give his advice only about the squaring of timber; what an indignity, what a cross is this! Do but think with yourselves, what an affliction it would be to a professor of divinity in an university, to a privy counselor, or (much more) to a prince, for thirty years together to be put to cart and plough.[5]

Jesus makes 'progress' (prokope in Luke 2:52)

In his childlike submission to his parents, and in his going through the normal stages of development of childhood and youth – with all the blessing of God upon him – he is doing so *as our head*, taking us with him.

4. John Dick, *Lectures on Theology*, vol. III (Edinburgh: Oliver & Boyd, 1838), Lecture LX, 167-168.

5. *The Works of Thomas Goodwin*, vol. V, 'The Mediator,' 195.

In order to do so he had to come down very low, sharing the limitations of our humanity that require slow growth and development that are not always easy.

Peter Lombard quotes Ambrose to that effect:

>...as it is written: *Jesus made progress in age and wisdom and grace.* How did the wisdom of God make progress? There was a progress of age and a progress of wisdom, but of the human one. That is why he mentioned age, so that you would believe it to be said by reference to man: for age does not pertain to the divinity, but to the body. And so, if he made progress in human age, he also made progress in human wisdom. But his senses made progress; and because his senses did, so did his wisdom.[6]

Among other Eastern Fathers, Cyril of Alexandria spoke of the *prokope*. He explains Luke 2:52 primarily in order to refute the Arians, who denied Christ's deity and claimed that Luke's statement 'he increased in wisdom' proved that he was not truly God, for God has no need of such increase. Cyril counters their argument by pointing out that the need of the God/man to increase was *economical*, not *ontological*. He says:

>He permitted his own flesh, by economy [οικονομικως], to act in terms of the laws of nature that were appropriate to humanity. But that which is appropriate to human nature is '*to progress in stature, in wisdom, and in grace...*' Well, for the economy of our salvation, he allowed the human condition to reign over him. Insofar as God the Word is totally perfect and has need of nothing, and therefore does not need to grow; still, since he became man, he made that which is ours his own...[7]

Hence, as Cyril says in another place, the incarnate Lord took on our limited condition (without ever ceasing to be the God who he always was), in order – in our place – to develop it in the right direction, for '... it is proper to the human spirit that becomes larger, parallel to increase in knowledge, to receive lessons, to make oneself capable of art and science, and to progress gradually towards the knowledge of divine and human things.'[8]

The Gospels show that there was a massive increase in the sufferings of the Saviour during the week of his passion and death, and we shall come to these presently. But even before then, he had been fiercely tempted by Satan, not only during the forty days in the wilderness, but at many points in his ministry. Satan often used others to do it. Hence, when Peter denied that Christ would be put to death and then raised, the Lord replied: 'Get thee behind me, Satan: for thou savourest not the things that be of God, but of men' (Matt. 16:23). The leaders of the Jews attributed his mighty works (which they could not deny) to Beelzebub, the prince of the devils (Matt. 12:24; Mark 3:22; Luke 11:15). Particularly after he raised Lazarus

---

6. Quoting Ambrose, *De incarnationis dominicae sacramento*, c. 7 nn. 71-72, in Peter Lombard, op. cit., 51, 52.

7. Cyril of Alexandria, *That Christ is One* (PG 75, 1332 AC).

8. Cyril of Alexandria, *Concerning the Incarnation of the Saviour* 20 (PG 75, 1453 D – 1456 A).

from the dead, the Pharisees made plans to kill him (cf. John 11:47-57), so that it became necessary for him, during the short time remaining to live, to move about *incognito*.

The emotions of our Savior[9]

During his entire public ministry, we see him suffering the common infirmities of humankind: weariness, hunger, misunderstanding by his own friends (Mark 3:21 – '...for they said, He is beside himself'), and hatred with murderous intent, after he had preached his first sermon in his hometown synagogue in Nazareth (Luke 4:16-30), and their reaction to God's word filled him with anger (Mark 3:5). He was disappointed to see the attendance upon his public ministry dwindling away (John 6:66-69). He had to put up with a traitor in the midst of his disciples (John 6:70-71). He grieved over the hardness of heart of religious leaders who were angry over his healing of a suffering man on the Sabbath day (Mark 3:5). The zeal with which he burned over the pollution of his Father's house must have cost him not a little inward pain. The anger with which he denounced the Pharisees in Matthew 23 surely reflected inward indignation.

Anyone feels it keenly when he or she is ridiculed, and more than once Jesus was the subject of scorn. Sharp and cutting was the ridicule of the official mourners when Jesus, before the miraculous raising of Jairus' daughter, announced that she, instead of being dead, was merely sleeping. Mark 5:40 says that 'they laughed him to scorn.' The hateful mocking and bitter scorning he endured during his trials and upon the cross will be spoken of later in this chapter.

He wept at the death of his good friend Lazarus (John 11:35). His funds were so short that he had to depend on the charity of some godly women for his maintenance (cf. Luke 8:2, 3), and in order to pay his taxes he had to instruct Simon Peter to find a coin in the mouth of a fish (Matt. 17:27). He owned no house or home, and could say: 'The foxes have holes, and the birds of the air have nests; but the Son of man hath not where to lay his head' (Matt. 8:20). He would, near the end of his ministry, lament over impenitent Jerusalem (Luke 19:41). He was, no doubt, very sorry that his closest friends could not stay awake and pray for him (Luke 22:39-46).

Any kind of love is likely to experience pain, and how much more the infinite, divine love in his divine/human person! Mark tells us about Jesus' love for the rich young ruler, who walked away from Jesus after the Lord asked him to 'take up the cross and follow him.' Mark says: 'Then Jesus beholding him loved him...' (Mark 10:21). Although the word 'love' is not used, it must have been in the eyes of Jesus when he looked upon Peter after his betrayal (Luke 22:61). Certainly the eyes of love brought bitter weeping to Peter (Luke 22:62).

John tells that before the feast of the Passover, as Jesus faced the terrible things that lay ahead, he 'knew that his hour was come that he should

---

9. I have learned much from 'The Emotional Life of Our Lord' by B. B. Warfield in *The Person and Work of Christ* (The Presbyterian and Reformed Publishing Company: Philadelphia, 1950), Part One, Chapter IV, 93-145.

depart out of this world unto the Father, having loved his own which were in the world, he loved them unto the end' (John 13:1). Only those who love could have any conception of the painful price of such love, and since none of us could share the fullness of the divine love, we can only bow, worship, and give thanks!

Sorrow in a context of serene joy

Yet we are not to think that his earthly life was one of constant sorrow and grief. Contemplating the certain fruit of his victorious work through his church, he cries out after the return of the seventy from their successful mission: 'In that hour Jesus rejoiced in spirit, and said, I thank thee, O Father, Lord of heaven and earth…' (Luke 10:21). As the God/man, he had been 'anointed with the oil of gladness above his fellows' (Heb. 1:9). The good cheer he gave to his disciples was *his* own good cheer (John 16:33). The joy which he would fulfill in them was *his* joy (John 16:24). The blessed rest to which he invited them was *his* rest (Matt. 11:28-30). The peace he left with his followers was *his* peace (John 14:27). Even facing the horrors of all that the cross entailed, he did so 'for the joy that was set before him…' (Heb. 12:2).

As truly God and truly man in one person, he travailed in a realm of unseen peace, he grieved in a realm of unseen joy, he did battle in a realm of unseen rest, and he went through every tribulation in a realm of unseen cheer. He did all this to raise us up from our grief and sadness, from our anxiety and stress, into his eternal gladness and lasting peace. But what it cost him to do so! Hebrews 4:15 tells us: 'For we have not an high priest which cannot be touched with the feeling of our infirmities; but was in all points tempted like as we are, yet without sin.' Isaiah 53:5 says that 'with his stripes we are healed.'

II. THE HUMILIATION OF CHRIST
IN HIS PASSION AND DEATH

The right interpretation of his final sufferings

As we face the extreme humiliation of our Lord in the tortures, laid upon him by powers both human and demonic, inflicted in their greatest intensity on the Lord during the last week of his life, it is of utmost importance never to forget that when the human nature was reduced to its most miserable status, it was always in closest union with his divine person. His suffering and grief were none the less real, none the less painful, none the less costly, even though they were experienced in the mysterious hypostatic union of the two natures in the one divine person.

Indeed, K. Schilder suggests that the suffering of a sinless person over sin would be far worse than that of the rest of us, who are all sinful ourselves.

> Christ is a human being *in a way very different* from that of other human beings. He is the sinless one. Who can say how intensely or in what manner the discharges of sin, of curse, of suffering, of Satan, and of death affected

Him? ... And what shall we say of Christ's soul, which suppressed nothing, neither God nor devil. We who suppress so much cannot judge of Him.[10]

Without daring to subtract the slightest dreg from the cup of his grief, nevertheless, because of who the New Testament tells us the Lord Jesus Christ really is, we must interpret his sufferings and unspeakable loss in terms of what he knew he was accomplishing.

Hebrews 12:2b gives us the key to interpretation: '...who for the joy that was set before him endured the cross, despising the shame, and is set down at the right hand of the throne of God.' The writer to the Hebrews may have been looking back on John 12 (or at least shared the same perspective we find there), where Jesus was contemplating his final Passover, shortly after he had raised Lazarus from the dead, following which the religious leaders had made a compact to have him killed. Jesus shows that God is in charge of what is taking place, and of what will take place, and that the entirety of his coming passion will be to the glory of Father and Son, through which the Church will be saved.

The famous Puritan theologian, Thomas Goodwin, addressed the eternal joy lying behind Christ's voluntary self-offering, in the context of comments on Proverbs 8:30-31 ['Then was I by him, as one brought up with him: and I was daily his delight, rejoicing always before him; rejoicing in the habitable part of the earth; and my delights were with the sons of men']:

> These delights then were most in this, to think that he should win and gain the love of these accursed rebels whom he himself loved so dearly, and that he should shew his love, by an unheard of way, that should amaze angels and men, to take away their sins, and reconcile them to himself again by the incarnation and death of his Son; and tie them to him by an everlasting knot, which their sins should not untie again, nor separate from that his love... And by all this you see that our salvation was in sure hands, even afore the world was; for God and Christ had engaged themselves by covenant each to other for us, the one to die, the other to accept it for us.[11]

That does not mean that it will not cost him infinite pain, nor does it remove his unspeakable trouble of soul over the dark night of horror he had to endure, nor does it deny that he would have wished for the Father to be glorified and the Church to be saved in some other way, for he cries out to the Father: 'Now is my soul troubled; and what shall I say? Father, save me from this hour: but for this cause came I unto this hour.'

What sacrifice accomplishes

Jesus speaks both to the Father and to his disciples, as it were, in the same breath. He states the lasting principle of fruit-bearing for himself and

---

10. K. Schilder, *Christ in His Suffering* (Grand Rapids, MI: Wm. B. Eerdmans, 1945), Engl. transl. Henry Zylstra, 297.

11. *The Works of Thomas Goodwin* (Edinburgh: James Nichol, 1863), 'Of Christ the Mediator,' Chapter XI, 32-33.

for all who are united to him in his Church: 'Except a corn of wheat fall into the ground and die, it abideth alone: but if it die, it bringeth forth much fruit' (John 12:24). This is the true interpretation of his sufferings: they will inexorably bring forth much fruit. 'Not loving one's life to the death' is God's appointed way to victory (John 12:25-26). That principle was proven true by the holy martyrs: 'And they overcame him by the blood of the Lamb, and by the word of their testimony; and they loved not their lives unto the death' (Rev. 12:11). The very next verse shows where it leads: 'Therefore rejoice, ye heavens…' (v. 12).

Jesus, on the eve of his supreme passion, in tender fellowship with the Father, knew that it was 'the hour' (John 12:27) when the name of the Father would be glorified above anything that had ever happened in all of eternity (John 12:28), and that that supreme glory would come through his death: 'the lifting up of the Son of man' (John 12:32-33). The glorification of the Father would be at the same time the glorification of the Son on the cross, and that horrendous and mysterious and ultimately glorious transaction would achieve nothing less than the salvation of all who will ever ask God for mercy through that atoning death: 'And I, if I be lifted up from the earth, will draw all men unto me' (John 12:32).

The sufferings and death of Christ, then, must be understood in light of what was being accomplished through them in accordance with the eternal purposes of the Triune God. One sees this in Acts 4:25-28, which takes up Psalm 2 and applies it to the saving acts of Christ. These events were not random; they did not represent the triumph of Satan and the evil world system over the only good man who ever lived (as Albert Schweizer's *The Quest for the Historical Jesus* would have it). On the contrary, Psalm 2 concludes with 'the rage of the heathen' being utterly defeated (v. 9) and all bowing to kiss the feet of the Son (v. 12) who has been given by the Father the heathen (who formerly hated him and raged against the Father), and the uttermost parts of the earth for his possession (v. 8). It is in that atmosphere that we must approach the sufferings of the incarnate Son of God on our behalf, and it is entered by humble and grateful faith, beneath the overshadowing of the sovereign and victorious love of God, who has spoken to us in these passages.

Staniloae writes in similar terms:

> By bearing these sufferings Jesus proves himself as 'the strong man,' the man reestablished in his true strength. That is why in Eastern icons the crucified Christ is not Christ fallen to the lowest state of weakness: in the Eastern tradition the cross is conceived of as an occasion to strengthen human nature or the spirit of this nature, not as a simple satisfaction given to God for the offense of the people, a satisfaction expressed in the acceptance of man's self-annihilation, which is understood as an extreme weakness. In the East the acceptance of death before God is understood as strength. That is why the death Jesus suffered is at the same time an occasion for manifesting the power through which death is conquered by the Son of God in the body and with the collaboration of the strengthened body. For the body too can be strong in bearing sufferings through the power given to it by the Son of God on behalf of the divine nature. Thus there is no contradiction between the

power given to the human nature in performing healings and the power of endurance. It is in the power of enduring sufferings that the body becomes interiorly capable of being an instrument and of his Resurrection as the last step in this direction. Therefore, by accepting this humbling of the body, the Word of God simultaneously strengthens it.[12]

Events of the Passion Week

'Palm Sunday'

On what we Christians traditionally call 'Palm Sunday,' Jesus rode triumphantly into Jerusalem to the acclaim of large crowds of people who were gathered there for the Passover festival (cf. Matt. 21:1-9; Mark 11:1-11; Luke 19:29-38; John 12:12-19). John makes it clear that the recent raising of Lazarus had drawn an unusual amount of attention to Jesus, and would have increased the size and the fervor of the crowds in Jerusalem that day (cf. John 11:55-56; 12:9). It had also caused the chief priests and Pharisees to determine to put Jesus to death as quickly as possible, for he was drawing off too many people, and could jeopardize both the position of the religious leadership and of the nation itself in its tenuous relationship with Rome (cf. John 11:47-48).

The large Jerusalem crowds clearly were acclaiming him as messianic king, both with Old Testament words of royal praise: 'Hosanna to the son of David: Blessed is he that cometh in the name of the Lord' (Matt. 21:9), and with Old Testament actions consonant with royalty: 'And a very great multitude spread their garments in the way; others cut down branches from the trees, and strawed them in the way' (Matt. 21:8). The Lord Jesus rode, not walked, into the holy city, albeit not on a kingly white charger, but rather a lowly donkey. He was a king of a very different sort, one whose kingdom was 'not of this world,' as he later told Pilate (John 18:36).

This strange messianic entrance was a precise fulfillment of the prophecy of Zechariah 9:9 (quoted in Matt. 21:4,5). The 'Blessed is he that cometh' is found in the last of the Hallel Psalms, which were traditionally sung after the Passover meal (Psalm 118:26), as would later be done by Christ and his disciples after the Last Supper (cf. Matt. 26:30).

Yet this triumphal entry was also marked by sharp grief in the soul of the Saviour: When the city came into view from the road Jesus was following, he stopped, gazed upon it, and wept over it (Luke 19:41-44). He knew that the hard hearts of most of the crowd would not be softened into faith and repentance, and that in several years their impenitence would draw down dreadful destruction upon them and their children. Instead of gloating over their punishment, the Son of God weeps over it, and in so doing, shows us who God is.

He would repeat essentially the same message to the women of Jerusalem who were following him up the 'via dolorosa' with weeping. In Luke 23:27-31 Jesus tells the women that they should be weeping for themselves and their children, because what he is going through is like

---

12. Staniloae, op. cit., 110.

being a green tree passing through the fire, whereas what their people must go through will be like a dry tree in the burning fire, and thus, far worse!

N. T. Wright points out an Old Testament passage that seems to lie behind this unusual saying, from Hosea 10:1-3, 8, 10, 13-15. For instance, 'They shall say to the mountains, cover us, and to the hills, fall on us...' (Hos. 10:8).[13]

Cleansing of the Temple

Early in the week, Jesus took the radical action that belonged to him as true prophet of 'cleansing the temple' (Matt. 21:1-22; Mark 11:1-25; Luke 19:28-48, and John 12:12-19; 2:13-17). With a whip he overturned the tables of the money changers and drove them out for having made his Father's house a den of thieves.

His cleansing of the temple was an enacted prophecy of the coming destruction of the temple (in A.D. 70). It showed the failure of the various Jewish parties to have fulfilled the will of God in their lives, religion, and politics. It indicated that they and their program must be replaced.

This action, in addition to his strong denunciation of the false teaching of the scribes and Pharisees, the telling of certain parables against them (such as the parables of the Vineyard and of the Marriage Feast), and his Olivet Discourse predicting Jerusalem's coming destruction pressed his all-encompassing prophetic demand for immediate reform into the camp of those who had long been more or less satisfied with the corrupting religious/political synthesis that then obtained in Israel. They had already decided to kill him, and these actions and teachings can only have confirmed them in their resolve.

The Last Supper

The three synoptic gospels place the Lord's Supper in the context of Passover celebration, probably being celebrated on the evening after the day of unleavened bread. But according to Malcolm Maclean:

> The Gospel of John...suggests that Christ was arrested, tried, put to death and taken down from the cross before the Passover meal was held (John 18:28; 19:14)...with the crucifixion of Jesus occurring on the afternoon of 14th Nisan, at the same time as the Passover Lamb was slain. On the evening of 15th Nisan (Friday evening) the official Passover meal would have been held.[14]

Following the research of D. A. Carson, Malcolm Maclean shows that 'It is possible to fit John's details into the Synoptic account, and to interpret the

---

13. N. T. Wright, *Jesus and the Victory of God*, 569 states: ' It is all there: the vine that has become proud and gone to ruin, the judgment on the sanctuary, the rejection of YHWH and of the king... the dire warning to the mothers and their children – and, finally, the death of the king...His own death at the hands of Rome was the clearest sign of the fate in store for the nation that had rejected him...He was the green tree, they the dry.'

14. Malcolm Maclean, *The Lord's Supper* (Christian Focus Publications: Fearn, Scotland, 2009), 15.

evidence as indicating that Jesus arranged for the usual Passover meal to be held.'[15] Carson indicates that the 'Preparation Day' mentioned in John 19:13-14, which speaks of Pilate bringing Jesus out to Gabbatha (Stone of Pavement), on the sixth hour of 'Preparation Day' most probably means 'Friday in Passover Week'.[16]

With this identity of 'Preparation Day' in mind, one can harmonize the chronology of John with the Synoptics as follows:

Thursday afternoon	14 Nisan	two disciples prepare for the Passover
Thursday evening	15 Nisan	Jesus and his disciples eat the Passover
Thursday evening	15 Nisan	Jesus arrested, tried
Friday	15 Nisan	Jesus crucified[17]

This indicates then the highly significant point that Jesus Christ, 'the Lamb of God that taketh away the sin of the world' is actually crucified on the very same day when the Passover lamb was slain in the Temple! That identification of the slaying of the lamb in the Temple at the same hour as the Son of God was crucified on Calvary is discussed in a now standard work by J. Jeremias.[18]

In a later section (Church and Sacraments), we shall study the meaning and application of the Lord's Supper. Here we only mention two facts: (1) It calls to mind the Exodus out of Egypt under Moses, and the slaying of the Passover Lamb with the sprinkling of the blood (cf. Exodus 12-14); (2) It is the ratification of the 'New Covenant.' As Maclean writes:

> The Passover was connected to the old covenant given through Moses by God, when Moses ratified the covenant by the sprinkling of the blood of a sacrificed animal (Exod. 24:8). Jeremiah had predicted that the old covenant would be replaced by a new covenant (Jer. 31:31-34) in which three salvation benefits would be given [God's laws written on believers' hearts; all believers will know God personally; God will forgive their sins].[19]

Jesus said that the cup of wine represented his shed blood for the sins of his people, and that the broken bread represented his body, broken for their sins. Their eating and drinking of these elements was a way of living fellowship with the Lord; a tasting of his salvation, a badge of profession of faith in him, and fellowship with one another in and through him. It was a memorial, a true presence, as it is celebrated, and a looking forward. It represented and conveyed what Jesus was bringing to pass at that time.

What he was doing, in sum, was bringing about the new exodus, as Tom Holland suggests. The background of the Exodus makes sense in light of his meeting with Moses and Elijah on the Mount of Transfiguration,

---

15. Ibid., 16.

16. D. A. Carson, 'Matthew,' *The Expositor's Bible Commentary* (Zondervan: Grand Rapids, MI, 1984), 531-32.

17. Maclean, op. cit., 17.

18. Cf. Joachim Jeremias, *The Eucharistic Words of Jesus* (London: SCM, 1966 [reprint]).

19. Maclean op. cit., 21.

when the topic of conversation in which they apparently encouraged him was 'the exodus [AV – 'decease'] which he should accomplish at Jerusalem' (Luke 9:31). Could it have been that Moses said something like: 'Lord, go through with your final exodus, for the validity of my little exodus depends upon it'? With the appearance of Moses and Elijah to the incarnate Christ, all of the law and the prophets were affirming that the final redemption they set forth depended upon him!

Tom Holland has shown how widespread this thinking was both in the New Testament and in strands of Judaism at the time of Christ:

> The generally recognized New Exodus material in the New Testament is Acts 26:17-18, Galatians 1:3, Colossians 1:12-14 and Revelation 1:5-6. Luke 1-2 reflects the expectations of a group of devout Jews at the time of the birth of Jesus. These were aware of the same traditions that are reflected in the *Damascus Document* found at Qumran.[20]

At the beginning of his ministry Jesus had quoted a text from Isaiah that predicts the new exodus (as had John the Baptist earlier):

> The fact that both John the Baptist and Jesus began their ministries by quoting Isaiah is very significant, the former citing Isaiah 40:3-5 (Luke 3:4-6) and the latter citing Isaiah 61:1-2 (Luke 4:18-19), both passages being New Exodus material. By using these texts they were declaring that the eschatological salvation that Isaiah had predicted was at long last breaking into human history.[21]

The Garden of Gethsemane

After singing a hymn (almost certainly the Hallel Psalms – 114-118), Christ and the disciples went out to the Garden of Gethsemane in order to pray.[22] Here the forces of hell were let loose in fury against the incarnate Son of God in order to go as far as they could in destroying him, and in particular, to deter him from the path of self-sacrifice chosen by him and the Father before all worlds (cf. Rev. 13:8). Jesus described the oppressive spiritual atmosphere of this time as he spoke to the ones who had arrested him: '… but this is your hour, and the power of darkness' (Luke 22:53).

As Christ faces the horror of becoming the sin-bearer, and as such, experiencing God-forsakenness, he goes deep into the old garden of olive trees to cry out to God for help. He also asks his three closest disciples – Peter, James, and John – to stay awake and pray for him as he goes deeper into the privacy of the woods.

The English devotional writer, William Law, posed the right question: why did the one who is God in the flesh feel the need to have the prayer support of a group of his close friends? An answer such as 'to set a good example for us to pray for others' is totally inadequate to enter into the

---

20. Tom Holland, *Contours of Pauline Theology: A Radical New Survey of the Influences on Paul's Biblical Writings* (Christian Focus Publications: Fearn, Ross-shire, 2004), 27.

21. Ibid.

22. Cf. Matt. 26:30; Mark 14:26.

Saviour's time of immensely felt need. I believe that Law is right when he answers: 'It is because the sorrows of a lost soul in hell were opening up in the soul of the Redeemer.' Hell is, above all else, an absence of the sense of the presence of God, and the Saviour is beginning to be identified with the hell that our infinite guilt deserves as he evidently reaches a new stage of mediatorial closeness with us as our sin-bearer.

In Christ's experience in the Garden, we begin to see important aspects of the outworking of the Old Testament concept of 'kinsman redeemer' (or *goel*). T. F. Torrance has drawn the Scriptural testimony together on this concept:

> [It is] derived out of old Israelite family and family-property law. It is the concept of redemption out of bankruptcy, or bondage or forfeited rights, undertaken by the advocacy of a kinsman who is bound to the person in need not only by blood ties, but by a community in property…The most familiar image of this whole conception in the Old Testament is that found in the book of Ruth, in which we see Ruth widowed and stateless and poverty-stricken, redeemed out of her lost and helpless condition by Boaz, her kinsman by marriage…This remarkable conception of redemption is applied by the Old Testament to God himself. In the book of Job and in the Psalms it is applied to the divine salvation of man in distress and anguish, but it is also applied to the redemption by God of Israel out of the bondage of Egypt and out of the captivity of Babylon, and even applied to messianic and eschatological redemption of God's people at the end of time…No human being can stand in the gap, not even a Noah or a Daniel or a Job, and intercede for them, but God and God alone can act as man's *goel*…As this *goel* God enters into the human situation…and so to stand surety for us within our frailty, corruption and lostness and so be the life of our life and redeem us.[23]

The disciples, however, went to sleep and did not give him the prayer support for which he was longing (cf. Matt. 26:45). One can see here a prophetic fulfillment of the strange prophetic description of the Messiah by Isaiah: 'I have trodden the winepress alone…' (Isa. 63:3).

We can never fathom the deep mystery, that although Christ the Son knew from eternity that he would, in the fullness of the time, have to make precisely this sacrifice in order for sin to be forgiven,[24] yet he is intensely struggling with the hope that he might be able to honor God's name and to redeem the church in some other way than by becoming identified with human guilt, and thus become separated from the Father. Christ prayed three times, sounding the depths of the depths, to see if some other way could be found.

We cannot follow him into the dark and deep places he went through in those prayers of agony, especially as the sensible presence of the Father is becoming ever less apprehensible by Jesus. Hebrews 5:7 appears to reflect these prayers: 'Who in the days of his flesh, when he had offered up prayers and supplications with strong crying and tears unto him

---

23. Torrance, *Atonement*, 44-47.

24. cf. Jesus' words in Luke 22:22 – 'And truly the Son of man goeth, as it was determined; but woe unto that man by whom he is betrayed!'

that was able to save him from death, and was heard in that he feared.' Even before the agony of the prayers, Jesus had said to the inner group of disciples: 'My soul is exceeding sorrowful, even unto death...' (Matt. 26:38). So intense was this crying out after the God from whom he must soon enough be separated, that apparently the capillaries under his skin began bursting, so that he sweat great drops of blood (Luke 22:44).

Why an angel helped Christ

The convulsion of soul must have had dreadful effects upon his body, and it is not likely that Jesus could have further withstood it had not the Father sent an angel to strengthen him (Luke 22:43). In this battle of the ages for the holy will of God to be done willingly within human nature, hidden powers of evil are present (for Satan had earlier entered into Judas before this betrayal – Luke 22:3), but at least one holy angel is present to sustain Christ's humanity that is being beaten down far more severely than any of the olives that grew in Gethsemane would ever be crushed beneath the dead weights of the olive press to extract their oil.

K. Schilder believes that the holy angel strengthened Christ precisely so he would *regain the strength* to go through the rest of his ordeal for the salvation of the world, as he actively endured the inspeakable agonies of Calvary:

> Not before that [i.e. the coming of the angel to give new strength], but *precisely* after his coming, Jesus began sweating His own blood. His angel caused that. He sees to it that the Son of man regains the strength of a lion; for only in that way can He die the death of a lamb.... if he is a lion who can shake His mane, who can rise to assert Himself, whose blood courses lustily through his veins in whom the latent Samson is aroused, and if He then gives Himself up to death as voiceless as a lamb, then we can speak of the mediator's strength and the mediator's reward. This angel strengthened the activity of the man Jesus which threatened to lapse into unconsciousness in order that His *active* obedience should keep pace with the *passive*. Jesus' suffering is never allowed to become His fate; it always remains His deed.[25]

This temptation must have been every bit as hard as those in the wilderness; in fact, from the effects on his soul and body, the test in Gethsemane must have been worse. In both cases he required angelic assistance. It is a matter for endless praise (rather than speculation on how the holy one could be so dreadfully tempted[26]) that the Last Adam won where the first Adam failed. The first Adam essentially said (by his actions) 'my will be done,' while the Last Adam specifically said: 'Not my will, but thine be done' (Luke 22:42).

In saying this, the Mediator had by now totally appropriated the principle of substitutionary self-sacrifice, for in Luke 22 he had just spoken concerning what was about to happen in terms of Isaiah 53: 'For I say unto you, that this that is written must yet be accomplished in me, And he was

---

25. K. Schilder, *Christ in His Suffering*, 358-59.

26. See the discussion of 'Christ's temptability' in Chapter V of this volume, section VIII.

reckoned among the transgressors; for the things concerning me have an end.'[27] And in John 12, where he set the tone for his coming passion, he said immediately after his triumphal entry into Jerusalem: 'Verily, verily, I say unto you, Except a corn of wheat fall into the ground and die, it abideth alone; but if it die, it bringeth forth much fruit' (John 12:24). His self-sacrifice would be to glorify the Father's Name (John 12:27-28) by being 'lifted up' in atoning death, (John 12:32), and thereby making the eternal righteousness of God to shine out in the forgiveness of sinners who trust in him, and by that means to come into the light (John 12:36), and into everlasting life (John 12:50).

But for this to happen Christ had to 'become poor' (II Cor. 8:9). He had to 'take upon him the form of a servant…and become obedient unto death' (Phil. 2:7, 8). Such 'making himself of no reputation' (Phil. 2:7) required 'an emptying of self,' and we see part of the cost of such sacrifice of self in his groaning and agonized praying in the Garden. The true fact that as the God/man he would win over sin does not in the slightest remove the terribleness of the temptation, which nearly tore him apart.

What he must have felt is prophetically alluded to in one of the major messianic Psalms (69), one verse of which would be directly applied to Christ on the cross: 'They gave me also gall for my meat; and in my thirst they gave me vinegar to drink' (Psalm 69:21, quoted in Matt. 27:34). A previous verse (Psalm 69:20) unveils how he felt during his passion, presumably both in the Garden and on Calvary: 'Reproach hath broken my heart; and I am full of heaviness; and I looked for some to take pity, but there was none; and for comforters, but I found none.' But the mighty Mediator has won through the churning oceans and blazing fires of temptation; God's predetermined way is the only way to uphold the honor of the Father and to redeem the Church.

Christ's self-offering in Gethsemane

Schilder shows that Christ's victory over Satan in Gethsemane represented the successful offering of his soul to God, and that this was preliminary to his offering his body to God on Calvary:

> In Gethsemane no one touched Him except God alone. Hence in Gethsemane His own soul sacrificed itself to God…In shedding His blood in Gethsemane [i.e. 'sweating great drops of blood'] He is *offering His soul*. In Gethsemane He offered His soul as a sacrifice. And on Golgotha He sacrificed His body… Gethsemane, where the soul offered itself before the body, and Golgotha, where the body offered itself after the soul, are *united* by the invisible work of the Spirit. By the eternal Spirit Christ offered Himself to God blameless.[28]

After the Lord had prayed three different times, always finding his disciples asleep, he says: 'The hour is at hand, and the Son of man is betrayed into the hands of sinners. Rise, let us be going: behold, he is at hand that doth betray me' (Matt. 26:45-46). Judas then betrays him with a kiss.

---

27. Luke 22:37, referring to Isaiah 53:12.

28. K. Schilder, *Christ in His Suffering*, 370- 371.

A sizable contingent of militia has been stationed in the edge of the woods, largely from the high priest and the religious authorities (John 18:12; Matt. 26:47; Mark 14:43; Luke 22:52), but also some from the Roman army. John 'is the only Gospel that even mentions the presence of Roman soldiers at the arrest…'[29] John 18:3 identifies them as 'a band' [of soldiers], according to J. Michaels: '"The band of soldiers" is literally "the cohort," that is, one-tenth of a Roman legion – about six hundred men, obviously an enormous number for such an undertaking.'[30]

One can imagine the reflection of the burning lamps and torches on the burnished shields of the soldiers (John 18:3) as this large military contingent converges on Christ and his disciples in the Garden during the darkness, either very late at night or very early in the morning. Their swords were drawn and spears were at the ready. From a merely human point of view (such as is taken by some of the sentimental humanist 'Lives of Jesus,' like that of E. Renan or A. Schweitzer), it was a pathetic scene in the extreme: in the torchlight one could have seen the tear-stained cheeks of the Savior whose soul and body had just come out of a spiritual bruising more severe than that of any other human up to that time or ever afterward. But without for a moment denying his humiliation, his cries and tears, his brokenness and weakness, we must listen to another side of this drama, given us by the Apostle John, who was there in person.

The 'I AM' speaks

We have already thought about this astonishing factor when considering the 'I Am' sayings of John. When Jesus gives his name to the authorities as they are arresting him, he uses the Old Testament name for God that had sounded out of the burning bush to Moses (Exod. 3:14): 'I AM.' John 18:6 says that when he uttered the holy name of God the whole army was knocked flat on their faces to the ground! A beam of the uncreated light suddenly streamed through the thick darkness of the Judean night; a surge of deity rushed through the manhood of our Lord, and down they all went, flat out before God Almighty!

Here we see that the powers of darkness, and the fallen humans whom they influence, are not finally overpowering the incarnate Son of God. He is willingly allowing them to do it in order for him to save sinners and to carry out the plan of the Father. As he said in John 10:18: 'No man taketh my life from me, but I have power to lay it down of myself. I have power to lay it down, and I have power to take it again.' In all of the dreadful pressure of his praying in the Garden, Jesus had at the deepest level worked back to the principle he had already enunciated in John 10:17: 'Therefore doth my Father love me, because I lay down my life, that I might take it again.' The certainty that he would carry through the sacrifice to the point of his being utterly crushed is now determined within his mind beyond any lingering question. He has sanctified himself at all costs to this transcendent goal,

---

29. J. Ramsey Michaels, *The Gospel of John – The New International Commentary on the New Testament* (Wm B. Eerdmans: Grand Rapids, Michigan, 2010), 889.

30. Ibid., 887.

which he himself had already announced: 'And for their sakes I sanctify myself, that they also might be sanctified through the truth' (John 17:19). Christ, and not the devil, is in supreme charge of every detail.

This is demonstrated when Jesus rebuked Simon Peter, who had cut off the ear of the servant of the high priest in an initial attempt to prevent the arrest of the Lord (Matt. 26:51, 52).[31] Jesus adds: 'Thinkest thou that I cannot now pray to my Father, and he shall presently give me more than twelve legions of angels?' (Matt. 26:53). But Jesus submits to the cross, not because the enemy is stronger, but in order to fulfill the will of God recorded in the prophecies of the Scripture concerning how Messiah is to save the world (cf. Matt. 26:54, 56). The hidden source of strength lies with the Lord, not with his enemies. This is good news, for true and lasting strength lies with the God who is love, and not with the one whose existence functions in hatred and murderous intent!

The Trials of Christ

After his arrest Jesus had to undergo trials before both (a) religious authorities and then (b) civil authorities.

(a) Trials before religious authorities. Religious authorities, with their own courts, had considerable power within the Roman Empire since Rome, in order to hold its vast empire together more effectively, granted a large measure of self-government to its various provinces. Depending on the province, different sorts of courts, some of them religious, were permitted. In Israel, the Jewish Sanhedrin (of seventy-one elders, under the moderatorship of the high priest) exercised considerable sway in settling controversies and keeping the peace. They did not have the power of capital punishment, but they had the authority to recommend it.

Jesus before Annas. Jesus' first trial was more like a hearing. The police who arrested him took him first to the home of Annas, a former high priest, and father-in-law to the current high priest, Caiaphas. It is difficult to tell from the Gospel accounts just what part Annas played in this affair. John 18:24 says that Annas sent Jesus bound to Caiaphas the Chief Priest. It is usually assumed that Annas, an elder statesman and a man of much experience, conducted something like an informal inquest before sending the prisoner on to his son-in-law, who at this time had the judicial authority to pass sentence.

Jesus before Caiaphas and the Sanhedrin. By the time Jesus was taken to Caiaphas' palace, there had been time to assemble a number of the members of the Sanhedrin, who had to be there to make any judicial action legal (Matt. 26:59). Caiaphas began by questioning Jesus about his disciples and his teaching (John 18:19). Jesus answered that his teaching should already be known by his interrogator, since it had been public (John 18:20). Then Caiphas brought in witnesses against the teaching of Jesus, hoping that they could demonstrate that it had been anti-Roman and revolutionary, but their witness did not agree (Mark 14:56-59). This left the high priest baffled.

---

31. Luke adds that Jesus healed the servant's ear: Luke 22:51.

Throughout most of his trial before the Sanhedrin, accused by such false witnesses, Jesus maintained a dignified silence, 'like a lamb before her shearers is dumb, so he openeth not his mouth' (Isa. 53:7). Yet when the high priest adjured him to say whether he was the Christ, then the Lord spoke (Matt. 26:63-64) and affirmed that indeed he was. He at last answered because of the biblical meaning of an oath. To demand an oath brought another important factor into the situation that Jesus faced. As Schilder notes, 'It [the oath] places the Nazarene in the *presence of God*.'[32] That is to say, Christ as God always manifests the presence of God, but the point here is that the Jewish court solemnly understands that, under oath, he is brought into the presence of God in a way that they can comprehend. Schilder adds: 'In God's kingdom every single thing should experience the tension of the presence of God...But in that case everything which refers us to God's presence ought to fill us with a sense of respect, inasmuch as God is in it, sees it, hears it, and judges it.'[33]

Christ and Daniel chapter 7

According to Mark's account, Caiaphas solemnly asked Jesus: 'Art thou the Christ, the Son of the Blessed?' (Mark 14:61). One presumes, after his first two failures, that Caiaphas at last got his heart's desire when Jesus answered him: 'I am: and ye shall see the Son of Man sitting on the right hand of power, and coming in the clouds of heaven' (Mark 14:62).

The triumphantly coming 'Son of Man' is a direct quotation by the Lord from Daniel 7. The incarnate Lord made much use of Daniel, as for instance we see in the apocalyptic sections of Matthew 24, Mark 13, and Luke 21, where he discusses the fulfillment of the prophetic details given Daniel by the angel Gabriel (Daniel 9:24-27). The Jewish court would have been well aware of these references.

The high priest cried out that Jesus had uttered blasphemy, which in the Old Testament was a capital offense (Mark 14:63), and the rest of the court agreed (Mark 14:64). In powerful reaction, the high priest publicly rent his clothing: 'According to Jewish rabbis, blasphemy deserved the practice of rending one's clothes. Eliakim, Shebna, and Joah came to Hezekiah in rent clothes because Rabshakeh, the commander in chief of the army of Sennacherib, had blasphemed the God of Israel (see II Kings 18:37).'[34]

Then, in a manner that was out of accord with their own legal procedure and beneath the dignity of a religious court, the Sanhedrin began spitting on him and slapping him in the face (Mark 14:65). According to Schilder, this was:

> A symbol of defiance, a token which spoke a language very well known to the Jews (Num. 12:14; Deut. 25:9; Isa. 50:6; Job 30:10). Besides, they strike Jesus with their fists. For, according to the meaning of the original text of these various reports, this beating was nothing less than brutal fistcuffing...

32. K. Schilder, *Christ on Trial*, 121.

33. Ibid., 125.

34. K. Schilder, op. cit., 163.

they blindfolded Jesus...They step up to Jesus, strike Him on the face, and then, grinning maliciously, say: Come now, prophesy unto us: who was it that gave you the lusty blow?[35]

But since the Sanhedrin lacked the authority to impose the death penalty, they marched Jesus off to the court of Pilate, the chief civil authority, early the next morning, with strong hopes of getting him sentenced to death very quickly. Pilate had been the procurator, or governor, of Israel on behalf of Rome for some six years. He did not like the Jews, and on one occasion had massacred a number of them (Luke 13:1). Pilate would not, thought Caiaphas, be particularly hesitant to put another troublesome Jew to death.

(b) The civil court: Jesus in Pilate's Hall
Yet Pilate was not so easily manipulated as the leaders of the Sanhedrin had hoped. In proper judicial manner, he asked for the charge against Jesus to be clearly stated (John 18:29). But this confused them at first, so that they were unable to specify capital charges. Instead, they took refuge in the vague presumption that they should automatically be considered to be in the right: 'If he were not a malefactor, we would not have delivered him up unto thee' (John 18:30). Pilate replied that they should leave his court and handle this matter in accordance with Jewish customs, implying that they have no grounds for a capital offense (John 18:31).

But the Sanhedrin officials insisted that they did have such grounds, and reminded Pilate that they were in his court precisely because they lacked the power to put offenders to death (John 18:31). Since they knew that charges of religious blasphemy would not work in the Roman civil court, they quickly changed their charges to something that would work with Pilate. They charged Jesus with treason (Luke 23:2). To support this charge, they first made two false accusations, and then one that was, in a certain sense, true (though, when properly understood, it did not really matter to Pilate).

They falsely charged that 'he was perverting the nation', and that he had forbidden to give tribute to Caesar, which was a lie, as we see from Matthew 22:21, where he instructed his followers to 'render unto Caesar the things that are Caesar's, and unto God the things that are God's.' But their third charge was technically correct, although totally false when wrenched out of its original context and forced into the political maelstrom of that day: '...saying that he himself is Christ a King' (Luke 23:2). Pilate then examined Jesus in private, and when he came back out to the raucous crowd, he announced to them, 'I find no fault in this man' (Luke 23:4). John 18 relates the details of the private interview: Jesus told Pilate that his own kingship was in an utterly different category from the political games of Rome: 'My kingdom is not of this world: if my kingdom were of this world, then would my servants fight, that I should not be delivered to the Jews: but now is my kingdom not from hence' (John 18:36). Jesus

35. Ibid., 175.

explains that the goal of his life (or kingship) is to bear witness to the truth, and Pilate essentially denies that anyone can ever know the truth (John 18:37-38). But in the end, Pilate realizes that Jesus' 'kingship' poses no political threat.

With Pilate's refusal to punish Jesus the crowd grew even more angry, and Pilate grew more uneasy. Pilate tried to get out of his dilemma (i.e. not to offend the Jews, and not to kill an innocent man) in two different ways. First, having heard that Herod, who had jurisdiction over Galilee (where Jesus was from), was in Jerusalem, Pilate decided to send him to Herod for judgment, thus, he hoped, getting the pressure off his own back.

But Jesus stood silent in Herod's court, much to the disappointment of the one who had wickedly put John the Baptist to death and wondered if Jesus were a resurrected form of John (Luke 23:6-10). Perhaps to encourage his cooperation, Herod's men of war abused Jesus, and mocked him as a tacky, would-be king by dressing him in 'a gorgeous robe' (Luke 23:11). Yet for all his superstition and personal corruption, Herod saw through the false charges of the Sanhedrin and sent Jesus back to Pilate, having found no fault in him – an action that restored the strained friendship between the two competing politicians (Luke 23:11-12).

The theological significance of a formal trial

The trial of Jesus before civil authorities in a formal court setting is not without significance for our salvation. Calvin writes:

> To take away our condemnation, it was not enough for him to suffer any kind of death: to make satisfaction for our redemption a form of death had to be chosen in which he might free us by taking our guilt upon himself. If he had been murdered by thieves or slain in an insurrection by a raging mob, in such a death there would have been no evidence of satisfaction. But when he was arraigned before the judgment seat as a criminal, accused and pressed by testimony, and condemned by the mouth of a judge to die – we know by these proofs that he took the role of a guilty man and evildoer.[36]

Back to Pilate

Then Pilate tried a second ploy to keep from killing Jesus, whom he well knew was innocent of any capital crime: he would have him scourged and then released (Luke 23:14-16). In fact, he also tried something else at the same time: according to a custom, the Roman governor could release a criminal at Passover – why not Jesus? But the crowd cried out for Jesus to be crucified and the murderer (in today's terms 'a terrorist'), Barabbas, to be released instead (Luke 23:17-23).

Neither of these ploys worked, so Pilate had to make a decision. Probably his decision was sealed against Jesus when someone from the crowd yelled out: 'If thou let this man go, thou art not Caesar's friend' (John 19:12). A complaint such as that could have meant his impeachment at Rome, and so he went against the advice of his own wife, who had

---

36. John Calvin, *Institutes*, II. 16. 5.

warned him not to harm Jesus because of the dreams she had had (Matt. 27:19). I believe that Schilder is right about this dream:

> ... we can truly say that God intensified Pilate's sense of responsibility to the highest degree by means of this dream. For this dream we thank Him; it will be the reason for which Pilate will be found without excuse in the last day when Jesus will be the judge instead of the accused, and consequently will be the judge of Pilate also. Because of the dream, Pilate will be unable to say: I did not know; or: You did not talk to me *in my own language.*[37]

The Scourging of Christ

Even though Jesus was not to be released, Pilate went ahead with the cruel scourging. An article in the *Journal of the American Medical Association* by a pathologist and two Christian ministers looked at this terrible punishment from a medical point of view:[38]

> Flogging was a legal preliminary to every Roman execution, and only women and Roman senators or soldiers (except in cases of desertion) were exempt. The usual instrument was a short whip (flagrum or flagellum) with several single or braided leather thongs of variable lengths, in which small iron balls or sharp pieces of sheep bones were tied at intervals...For scourging, the man was stripped of his clothing, and his hands were tied to an upright post. The back, buttocks, and legs were flogged either by two soldiers (lictors) or by one who alternated positions. The severity of the scourging depended on the disposition of the lictors, and was intended to weaken the victim to a state just short of collapse or death. After the scourging, the soldiers often taunted their victim.
>
> As the Roman soldiers repeatedly struck the victim's back with full force, the iron balls would cause deep contusions, and the leather thongs and sheep bones would cut into the skin and subcutaneous. Then, as the flogging continued, the lacerations would tear into the underlying skeletal muscles and produce quivering ribbons of bleeding flesh. Pain and blood loss generally set the stage for circulatory shock. The extent of blood loss may well have determined how long the victim would survive on the cross.[39]

This severe flogging so tore into his skin, and muscles, until as someone once said, 'the bones in his back stood out like marble columns in a sea of blood.' This was accompanied by the soldiers' mocking of him by putting a purple robe on him, and a crown of thorns on his head, by spitting upon him, by slapping him in the face with reeds, and bowing their knees sarcastically to simulate honors before a king (cf. Mark 15:16-20; Matt. 27:27-31).

It was this massive loss of blood the previous night that caused Jesus to require help as he was attempting to carry his cross up the hill of Calvary

---

37. Schilder, op cit., 481.

38. "On the Physical Death of Jesus Christ' by William D. Edwards, Wesley J. Gabel, MDiv, and Floyd E. Hosmer, MS, AMI in *Journal of the American Medical Association* (March 21, 1986, Vol. 255, No. 11), 1455-1463. (I do not include the numerous footnotes of the article in this brief quotation).

39. Ibid., 1457.

the next morning (cf. Mark 15:21). In this way, Simon the Cyrenian assisted Jesus in his last painful walk up the 'Via Dolorosa' – 'The Way of Sorrows.' Jesus and the two criminals were brought up the hill of Calvary, or Golgotha, apparently so named because the hill was in the shape of a skull (cf. Mark 15:22). It was outside the holy city of Jerusalem, which was prophetically appropriate because 'Christ is in fellowship with that which is unclean. That which is unclean and is thrown outside of the camp...'[40] His going outside the gates reminds us of the scapegoat in Leviticus (cf. Lev. 16:7-10; 20-22), as he 'laden with sins, died and washed away our uncleanness in his blood. Day of atonement – Good Friday.'[41]

Hebrews 13:11-13 makes a similar point concerning the Old Testament regulations in which the sacrificial animals were to be burned outside the camp (Lev. 16:27): 'For the bodies of those beasts, whose blood is brought into the sanctuary by the high priest for sin, are burned without the camp. Wherefore Jesus also, that he might sanctify the people with his own blood, suffered without the gate. Let us go forth therefore unto him without the camp, bearing his reproach.'

Who is in Charge?

Even in this tragic procession up the 'Way of Sorrows', the suffering Lamb of God, stumbling from loss of blood, not deaf to the hoots and jeers of the mocking crowds by the roadside and well aware of the horrors ahead, was still in charge of the proceedings, hard as that is for human minds to realize. He was not their helpless victim, much as they thought he was. The Son of God in the flesh was knowingly carrying out the plan that he and the Father had before the world was made (cf. Rev. 13:8). This dreadful trip to Calvary had long been planned. 'The Son of man came... to give his life a ransom for many' (Mark 10:45). 'No man taketh my life from me, but I lay it down of myself' (John 10:18). Jesus' own prediction to his disciples early in his ministry concerning his certain passion and death, included the element of divine constraint: 'The Son of man must suffer many things, and be rejected of the elders and chief priests and scribes, and be slain, and be raised the third day' (Luke 9:22).

Behind all of these self-denying actions lies the love of the Father, who 'so loved the world that he gave his only begotten Son, that whosoever believeth in him should not perish, but have everlasting life' (John 3:16). And the Son of the Father voluntarily went through the infinite pains of Gethsemane and Golgotha, for, as John wrote of him, just before the feast of Passover: '...when Jesus knew that his hour was come that he should depart out of the world unto the Father, having loved his own which were in the world, he loved them unto the end' (John 13:1). He whose Spirit inspired Hebrews well knew that: '...now once in the end of the world hath he appeared to put away sin by the sacrifice of himself...So Christ was offered to bear the sins of many...' (Heb. 9:26, 28).

---

40. K. Schilder, *Christ Crucified*, 32.
41. Ibid., 33.

'The lifting up' of Christ

Three crosses were set up on Calvary; Christ was crucified between the two criminals. He was 'lifted up' from the ground on to the cruel cross. Early in John's Gospel, Jesus had said to Nicodemus: 'And as Moses lifted up the serpent in the wilderness, even so must the Son of man be lifted up' (John 3:14). Christ is referring to the brass serpent fashioned by Moses and lifted up on a pole, so that in looking up to it on that pole the complaining Israelites who had been snake-bitten in the wilderness might be saved from death (Num. 21:9). Being 'lifted up' identified the brass snake, and the Lord whom he foreshadowed, with the curse of God, for 'Cursed is every one that hangeth on a tree' (Deut. 21:23, quoted in Galatians 3:13, and there applied to Christ bearing our sins).

Peter Lombard saw this 'lifting up' in terms of propitiation:

> We are also said to be justified by Christ's death in another way, because by faith in his death we are cleansed from sins. Hence the Apostle: *The justice of God is by the faith of Jesus Christ* [Rom. 3:22]; and also: *Whom God has proposed as a propitiator, through faith in his blood* [Rom. 3:25], that is, by faith in his passion, as once those who looked at the bronze serpent hanging from a pole were healed from the bites of serpents [cf. Num. 21:9; Jn. 3:14-15]. In the same way, if we look with right faith upon him who hung from a pole for our sake [Gal. 3:13], we are released from the devil's bonds, that is from sins.[42]

Why would a loving God punish sin?

Before we enter the details of the painful death of Christ, we must remind ourselves of why a holy and loving God must punish sin. Almighty God is under no constraints from any power outside himself, for his own character provides the security of the very structure of the universe which he created. Part of his strength is that he cannot deny himself. Paul writes: 'If we believe not, yet he abideth faithful: he cannot deny himself' (II Tim. 2:13). For God to go against his own character, to deny himself, would mean the total destruction of the universe, and we would not be here to discuss it! Sin constitutes a contradiction against God's own character, and – to speak imaginatively – if he did not deal with it, it would seek to eat him off his throne, and thereby bring all else into utter destruction (of course, infinitely impossible!). It is God's righteous strength that he should punish sin, not an injustice nor a weakness.

In the apposite words of T. F. Torrance:

> If God did not oppose sin, there would be no really objective and ultimate difference between sin and righteousness. Thus the divine opposition to sin is a factor in the qualification of humanity as sinful before God, and especially as guilty before him...Yet that [i.e. holding back his full opposition to sin] was in the very mercy of God, as the cross showed, for the cross reveals that God withheld his final resistance to sin until in Christ, he was ready to do the deed which would also save us from his wrath.[43]

---

42. Peter Lombard, *The Sentences, Book. 3*, op. cit., Distinction XIX, p. 78.
43. T. F. Torrance, *Atonement*, 110.

That is to say, God's holy consistency with himself requires that he should at all times (and throughout an endless eternity) act in accordance with his pure character. His holiness requires the punishment of sin, but at the same time his heart is full of the most tender love for sinners. To bring them back into his immediate favor action must be taken in accordance with who God always is. He cannot deny himself in saving sinners, for that would be the end of all. Indeed, Christ thought so highly of the Father's honor, that he gave up everything for the Father to be honored in the salvation of the Church. His people are called, and through the Holy Spirit enabled, to share in his attitude of devout submission to the thrice holy God.

The sacred transaction among Father, Son, and Spirit in Gethsemane and Calvary, once grasped by the believer, in no sense presents a God who is harsh, nor is it the merely external imposition of standards outside of who God most essentially is, or in any sense alien to the sacred image in which we were made to live and function. On the contrary, Jesus' attitude to the Father in Gethsemane and on Calvary demonstrates the ineffable beauty that reigns within the Trinitarian relations. Jesus' self-offering to the Father as our great High Priest displays the absolute relational beauty of the infinite tenderness of the love of God.

James Henley Thornwell grasps the surpassing loveliness of it:

> There is no room for the remotest suspicion of inexorable rigour when Jesus is seen to be a priest. His death a sacrifice, and the whole transaction an august and glorious act of worship. The position of Jesus is sublime when, standing before the altar, He confesses the guilt of His brethren, adores the justice which dooms them to woe, and almost exacts from God as the condition of His own love that justice should not slacken nor abate. That prayer of confession, that assumption of guilt, that clear acknowledgment of what truth and righteousness demand, make us feel that God *must* strike, that the edict must go forth, Awake, O sword, against my shepherd and the man that is my fellow, saith the Lord of Hosts. Still sublime is His position when with profound adoration of the Divine character, by His own proper act, His own spontaneous movement, He lays His life upon the altar, virtually saying, Take it, it ought to be taken; let the fire of justice consume it; better, ten thousand times better, that this should be than that the throne of the Eternal should be tarnished by an effeminate pity! We feel that death is not so much a penalty inflicted as an offering accepted. We feel that God is glorious, that the law is glorious in the whole transaction, because Christ glorifies them. He lays down His life of Himself; it is His own choice to die rather than that man should perish or the Divine government be insulted with impunity; and although in accepting the offering Justice inflicted upon Him the full penalty of the law, although the fire which consumed the victim was the curse in its whole extent, yet as it was an act of worship to provide it, and especially as that victim was Himself, every groan and pang, every exclamation of agony, amazement and sorrow, was a homage to God which, in itself considered, the Priest felt it glorious to render…His Father was never dearer, never more truly God in His sight, than when He accepted the sacrifice of Himself, the sublimity of the principles involved, and the interest of Jesus in them, are a perfect vindication from every illiberal suspicion…Our world becomes

the outer court of the sanctuary, where a sacrifice is to be offered in which the Priest and the Victim are alike the wonder of the universe – in which the worship which is rendered leaves it doubtful whether the Deity is more glorious in His justice or His grace.[44]

God provides propitiation

Romans 3:24-26 describes how he does so in terms of his providing his own propitiation in the person and work of Christ: 'Being justified freely by his grace through the redemption that is in Christ Jesus: Whom God hath set forth to be a propitiation through faith in his blood, to declare his righteousness for the remission of sins that are past, through the forbearance of God, To declare, I say, at this time his righteousness: that he might be just and the justifier of him which believeth in Jesus.'

We are told by Paul that *propitiation* is the way in which God is able to forgive guilty sinners on the one hand and, on the other hand, simultaneously to retain his own holy integrity. A holy God cannot tell a lie about the guilty. If they are pronounced righteous by him, then something must have taken place so that the new category he says they are in is in accordance with truth and right.

What God himself caused to take place in this miraculous transaction was *propitiation*. John Murray has defined it as follows:

> In the Hebrew of the Old Testament it is expressed by a word which means to 'cover.' In connection with this covering there are, in particular, three things to be noted: (1) It is in reference to sin that the covering takes place; (2) The effect of this covering is cleansing and forgiveness; (3) It is before the Lord that both the covering and its effect take place (cf. especially Lev. 4:35 10:17; 16:30)…It is that sin that evokes the holy displeasure or wrath of God. Vengeance is the reaction of the holiness of God to sin, and the covering is that which provides for the removal of divine displeasure which the sin evokes.[45]

Murray further explains the effects of the propitiation as follows:

> It is one thing to say that the wrathful God is made loving. That would be entirely false. It is another thing to say the wrathful God is loving. That is profoundly true. But it is also true that the wrath by which he is wrathful is propitiated through the cross. This propitiation is the fruit of the divine love that provided it.[46]

It is not we who offer propitiation; on the contrary, as Torrance says: 'The propitiation or expiation is God's own act of grace flowing from his eternal love and mercy…God does not burden us with his wrath, but mercifully bears it himself in the passion of his Son who died for us on the cross.'[47]

---

44. James H. Thornwell, *Collected Writings, Volume 2: Theolgoical and Ethical*, 'The Priesthood of Christ,' 179-180.

45. John Murray, *Redemption Accomplished and Applied* (Wm. B. Eerdmans Publishing Co.: Grand Rapids, MI, 1955), 30.

46. Ibid., 31-32.

47. Torrance, *Atonement*, 104.

To do so, 'God *himself* draws near – he propitiates himself, provides the ground on which man is brought near to God, and provides the offering or sacrifice with which man appears before God in worship.'[48]

A Description of Crucifixion

Dr. William D. Edwards and others in their article in *Journal of the American Medical Association* give a medical description of crucifixion:

> The archaeological remains of a crucified body, found in an ossuary near Jerusalem and dating from the time of Christ, indicate that the nails were tapered spikes approximately 5 to 7 inches long with a square shaft 3/8 of an inch across. Furthermore, ossuary findings and the Shroud of Turin have documented that the nails commonly were driven through the wrists rather than the palms....
>
> When the victim was thrown to the ground on his back, in preparation for transfixion of the hands, his scourging wounds would most likely become torn open again and contaminated with dirt...
>
> Furthermore, the driven nail would crush or sever the rather large sensorimotor or median nerve. The stimulated nerve would produce excruciating bolts of fiery pain in both arms...
>
> The major pathophysiologic effect of crucifixion, beyond the excruciating pain, was a marked interference with normal respiration, particularly exhalation. The weight of the body, pulling down on the outstretched arms and shoulders, would tend to fix the intercostal muscles in an inhalation state and thereby hinder passive exhalation. Accordingly, exhalation was primarily diaphragmatic, and breathing was shallow...As a result, each respiratory effort would become agonizing and tiring, and lead eventually to asphyxia.[49]

These, I believe, are accurate details of what our Lord went through *physically* on our behalf upon the cross, and they would be saying a great deal, even if nothing more were to be added concerning his *spiritual* sufferings. But the accounts of Christ's passion and death on the cross given us in the four Gospels and elsewhere in the New Testament definitely indicate that something far worse than the horrible physical trauma was going on at the same time. As Christ became totally identified with our sins, he experienced what can only be termed as 'the pains of hell': the worst reality that has ever been explained by any human being.

The famous 'Passion Chorale' ('O Sacred Head Sore Wounded'), by Hans Leo Hassler (1564-1612), and set to music by J.S. Bach (1685-1750) gives the only proper human response to such voluntarily endured agony, by the one who 'having loved his own...loved them to the end' (John 13:1):

> O sacred head! sore wounded,
> With grief and shame bowed down,
> Now scornfully surrounded
> With thorns, Thine only crown!

---

48. Ibid., 68.
49. W. Edward et al., art. cit., 1459-1461.

How pale art Thou with anguish,
With sore abuse and scorn!
How does that visage languish
Which once was bright as morn!

Thy grief and bitter passion
Were all for sinners' gain:
Mine, mine was the transgression,
But Thine the deadly pain:
Lo! Here I fall, my Saviour:
'Tis I deserve Thy place;
Look on me with Thy favour,
Vouchsafe to me Thy grace.

The principle of substitution

Through all the sufferings of his entire life, with the culmination in Gethsemane and on Calvary, Christ is standing in for us as our divinely provided *substitute*. The principle of substitution goes back to the earliest strands of the Old Testament. In the Garden of Eden God slew an animal, from which he took skins to cover our guilty parents (Gen. 3:21). A vague sort of substitution was already at work. Abel brought a lamb to the Lord, presumably for purposes of substitution, and the Lord was pleased to accept it (Gen. 4:4). We find Noah offering animal sacrifices in line with the principle of substitution (cf. Gen. 8:20).

Abraham, 'the father of the faithful,' was instructed by God as the covenant of grace was renewed with him, concerning the details of the sacrifices he should now offer (cf. Gen. 15:9-18). These sacrifices pictured the grace God provided through substitution. Immediately after God's deliverance of the enslaved Israelites out of Egypt the Lord gave Moses the details of the Passover sacrifice (cf. Exod. 12). Significantly, it was the blood of the substitute lamb that was slain for each household that was to be smeared on the door posts and lintels, so that the destroying angel of death would pass over those houses while he visited the households of Egypt with the death of their firstborn. The principle of substitution saved the Israelite firstborn, and at the cross of Calvary we discover that the real substitute for them was God's firstborn Son, who is now being offered on that cross to deliver all, from every tribe and tongue, from guilt and sin, if they will look up to him in faith as Christ had told Nicodemus to do (cf. John 3:14-17).

Then in the early part of the Mosaic economy the Levitical system is instituted with its complex rules for sacrifice (cf. Exodus 29, 30, and much of Leviticus). The Levitical economy works on the principle of substitutionary sacrifice. The Epistle to the Hebrews indicates that these sacrifices of bulls and goats, etc. (Heb. 10:4) were foreshadowings of the incarnate Son of God, who would and did offer his body a sacrifice for sin (cf. Heb. 10: 5-7, quoting Psalm 40:6). His once-for-all perfect sacrifice 'takes away the first, that he may establish the second' (Heb. 10:9). After he offers himself, all animal sacrifices are in principle finished: 'For by one offering he hath perfected for ever them that are sanctified' (Heb. 10:14).

In terms of the Epistle to the Hebrews, John Murray saw that:

> Jesus, therefore, offered himself a sacrifice and that most particularly under the form or pattern supplied by the sin-offering of the Levitical economy... We must interpret the sacrifice of Christ in terms of the Levitical patterns because they were themselves patterned after Christ's offering.[50]

The multifaceted aspects of the one supreme substitutionary sacrifice are explored in the next chapter. There we shall see, with Isaiah, that the Man of Sorrow's travail and death accomplish the final pleasure of the Lord and the justification of many (cf. Isa. 53:10-11).

---

50. J. Murray, op. cit., 26- 27.

CHAPTER 10

SEVEN LAST WORDS, BURIAL,
AND DESCENT INTO HELL

Humans normally draw back from death, because they have a sense that it is an enemy; including 'the last enemy' (I Cor. 15:26), and most of them are instinctively aware that beyond it lies some kind of judgment (Heb. 9:27). In that context death is thought to be bad news, for it still whispers the consequences of the divine displeasure over the rebellion of our first parents in the Garden of Eden (cf. Gen 3:19). But the Gospel of Jesus Christ sets before us one death that is good news, for out of the suffering and death of the incarnate Son of God come pardon and eternal life for all who identify with him through faith. In one sense, therefore, he hastened towards it ('I have a baptism to be baptized with, and how am I straitened till it be accomplished' – Luke 12:50), though in another sense, in Gethsemane, for a time, he drew back. It is appropriate then to contemplate in close detail that one death which is a fountain of life to an otherwise condemned humanity.

This chapter continues the theme of (2) the final passion of Christ. The previous chapter studied (1) the sufferings of his life, and then began the consideration of (2) his final passion, reaching the point of (a) his crucifixion.

The present chapter carries on the theme of his final passion, with respect to (b) his seven last words from the cross. Also in this chapter we consider (3) his burial, and (4) his descent into hell.

(2) The Final Passion of Christ (continued)

(b) The Seven Last Words from the Cross
The order of the seven last sayings of Christ on the cross is not absolutely certain, but the sequence traditionally assumed by the Christian Church is probably correct. The seven last words are usually understood to have been spoken in this order: (1) 'Father, forgive them; they know not what

they do'; (2) 'Amen. This day thou shalt be with me in paradise'; (3) 'Woman, behold thy son…'; (4) 'My God, my God, why hast thou forsaken me?'; (5) 'I thirst'; (6) 'It is finished'; (7) 'Father, into thy hands I commend my spirit.' An exposition of these final sayings should help us grasp more about the most significant set of events that ever occurred: the death of Christ, followed in three days by his resurrection.

(1) 'Father, forgive them; for they know not what they do' (Luke 23:34).

John 19:18 tells us that Jesus was crucified between two thieves. Over six hundred years earlier Isaiah had predicted (in the prophetic past tense) that the Suffering Servant of the Lord '…was numbered with the transgressors; and he bare the sin of many, and made intercession for the transgressors' (Isa. 53:12). Now, 'in the fullness of the time,' the Suffering Servant is placed between two transgressors and is 'numbered' with them as a common criminal. In that capacity, 'reckoned with the transgressors,' he is 'making intercession' for them and for others at the foot of the cross. This is apparently the first of his seven last sayings, and its primacy says much about who he is and what the purpose is of his painful death.

The suffering servant

This prayer for forgiveness is properly placed within the experience of the suffering servant as a constituent part of the long-prophesied fulfillment of the covenant sealed in blood. T. F. Torrance explains it:

> The whole conception of the *suffering servant* represents the activity of God whereby he begins to draw together the cords of the covenant in which he had bound Israel to himself as his chosen partner in redemption-history…The great sign of the covenant made with Abraham and Isaac was circumcision, for in it the covenant was cut into the flesh of this people…It was the sign that at last the covenant had to be written into the heart, in the 'crucifixion' of self-will, in the putting off of the enmity of the flesh [Cf. Rom. 8:7f.; Eph. 2:15-16 KJV (RSV 'hostility')].[1]

Christ is praying to the Father for the forgiveness of those who are putting him to death, and probably his prayer goes far beyond those gathered at the cross, and includes the many who resisted him and called for his death. We can fairly soon perceive positive answers to his request to the Father to forgive those who were involved in his persecution and death, for one of the criminals repented and was taken to paradise, after having at first taken part in mocking the Lord (Matt. 27:44), and a few weeks later, not long after the Day of Pentecost, 'a great company of the priests were obedient to the faith' (Acts 6:7).

This prayer of the suffering servant, the incarnate Son of God, for forgiveness of those who 'know not what they do' must go extremely far in both space and time. One assumes that Saul of Tarsus, who viciously

---

1. T. F. Torrance, *Incarnation*, 47-48.

persecuted the early Christian Church, must have been a subject of this prayer for forgiveness, for on his way to Damascus he met the one whom he had persecuted, without recognizing who he really was: '…And he said, who art thou, Lord?…' (Acts 9:5). In I Timothy 1:13 Paul writes of himself: 'Who was before a blasphemer, and a persecutor, and injurious: but I obtained mercy, because I did it ignorantly in unbelief.'

How many more former haters of God have received the mercy and grace to believe in Christ and repent of their sins is known only to God himself. The question here is not whether we have opposed and despised God and his Son in the past, but whether we will seek the grace of being put under the longsuffering mercy of Christ's prayer for forgiveness of his enemies. God never turns back those who seek his grace. The last chapter of the Bible calls us to come to him in order to 'take the water of life freely' (Rev. 22:17). The purchase price of this living water is God's own grace, and it is made available to all who seek it, as the very last verse of Holy Scripture tells us (Rev. 22:21).

The title on the cross

This prayer for forgiveness was prayed under a title that Pilate had chosen to be nailed near the top of the cross, a title that specified the charges against Jesus: 'Jesus of Nazareth the King of the Jews' (John 19:19). The Jewish leadership resented this title and wanted it changed, but Pilate refused (John 19:22). It had been written in Greek and Latin and Hebrew, the three universal languages of that time, to make sure all could read it. Probably Pilate intended to insult the Jews by this title, but it was nevertheless a true prophecy (little though Pilate knew it), in line with Psalms 2, 72, and 110.

Gambling over his garments

It was probably at this stage of his sufferings that Jesus' garments were divided among the soldiers. The Roman soldiers who were on duty for the crucifixion sought to pass away the time once they got the crosses set up by sitting down and playing something like dice. Matthew 27:36 says of them: 'sitting down, they watched him there.' They were gambling in the presence of the greatest transaction in all of eternity. They gambled over who would get the one relatively fine piece of clothing that belonged to Jesus: a seamless garment that was too valuable to be divided.

That too had been predicted in Psalm 22:18: 'They part my garments among them, and cast lots upon my vesture.' Matthew 27:35 quotes this very verse, and said it happened that the word spoken by the prophet (in this case, David) might be fulfilled. A higher hand than that of the Roman dice players is overseeing these seemingly random events, using them to bring the predestined plan of salvation to its divinely intended conclusion. What this originally meant for David we cannot say: perhaps it was related to the deprivations he suffered during Saul's insane persecutions, which kept him far from what was his by right (safety, housing, garments, etc.), but Matthew shows us that it is – in its finality – fulfilled in David's Son.

Jesus was stripped that day that we may be clothed. Out of his nakedness and shedding of blood, soon enough comes the white robes that are given to his saints (Rev. 6:11).

Hateful mockery

Along with the stealing of his clothes goes the hateful mockery of soldiers, chief priests, and other bystanders, including the thieves who were being put to death along with him (cf. Matt. 27:39-44; Luke 23:35-40). K. Schilder suggests that this mockery is different from that which occurred before his trial:

> ...there are more mockers now than there were previously; again, the things for which they blame Christ are not the same for which He was blamed before. But those are not the important differences. The greatest difference between the then and the now is that the mockery of Christ upon Golgotha is a definite and separable moment in the short but violent process of His descent into hell, of His being accused 'without the gate.'[2]

Scripture declares that 'cursed is every one that hangeth on a tree' (Deut. 21:23; Gal. 3:13), and those at the foot of the cross are gratuitously adding in their foul curses, especially in the form of cruel mockery. Who could doubt that the devil is raging around fast and furiously to suggest any and every insult that could be heaped upon the Lord on the cross? Yet again he seeks – through these people – to tempt the Lord to avoid going the full length of dying for our sins: 'If thou be the Son of God, come down from the cross' (Matt. 27:40).

And the temptation was the same when the mockers essentially claimed that his trust in God was not valid unless God delivered him immediately from the cross (Matt. 27:43). But Jesus no more responded to this mocking demand than he did to earlier orders of the Pharisees for a sign (Matt. 12:39). The only sign they will be given will be granted only in the way and at the time that God determines: '...there shall no sign be given to it, but the sign of the prophet Jonah: For as Jonah was three days and three nights in the whale's belly; so shall the Son of man be three days and three nights in the heart of the earth' (Matt. 12:39-40).

One of their nasty insults was truer than they knew: 'He saved others, himself he cannot save' (Matt. 27:42). They meant it in sheer mockery: this so-called physician is false because he cannot heal himself (although they never denied that he had miraculously healed others – cf. John 11:47). But the truth (far beyond their ken) was this: willingly chosen substitution. Peter articulates it: 'Who when he was reviled, reviled not again...Who his own self bare our sins in his own body on the tree, that we, being dead to sins, should live unto righteousness: by whose stripes ye were healed' (I Peter 2:23, 24). John says much the same: 'Unto him that loved us and washed [or 'loosed'] us from our sins in his own blood...' (Rev. 1:5).

---

2. K. Schilder, *Christ Crucified*, 203.

(2) 'And Jesus said unto him, Amen I say unto thee. Today shalt thou be with me in paradise' (Luke 23:43).

At first the one we traditionally call 'the penitent thief' joined the other criminal in mocking Jesus (Matt. 27:44). But he experienced a profound change of heart and mind on his own cross, so that he rebuked the one who was making fun of Jesus: 'Dost thou not fear God, seeing thou art in the same condemnation? And we indeed justly; for we receive the due reward of our deeds: but this man hath done nothing amiss. And he said unto Jesus, Lord, remember me when thou comest into thy kingdom' (Luke 23:40-42).

Biblical significance of 'Amen'

'Amen' is a solemn affirmation of fullest assent to the Word of God. It was used in assenting to the covenant promises of God in the Old Testament. When Genesis 15:6 relates the response of Abraham to God's covenant promise of a seed from his own body, the Hebrew word used signifies 'to amen' the Lord, that is, to consider as fully established, to commit oneself to that promise so that it defines one's life. When Moses is pronouncing the covenant curses to the people as they prepare to start life in the land of promise, they answer with the response, 'Amen.' The Psalms frequently are marked by 'Amen' as the worshiping people honor the Lord and call for his glory to fill the earth (cf. Ps. 72:19).

Paul says that in Jesus Christ 'all the promises of God…are yes, and in him, Amen…' (II Cor. 1:20). John in Revelation 3:14 calls the risen Christ 'the Amen, the faithful and true witness…' K. Schilder noted:

> And He believes that He is being obedient when He, doing the work of the Messiah, opens wide the gate of heaven to a lost son of man who is praying in His ears. Hence He opens the door as a King and nevertheless knows that He is servant…He has the law-book open before His eyes, and the commandments of God in His heart. Thus it was that He uttered His 'amen.' That 'amen' represented the self-control of the servant assuring Himself that the work He had done was compatible with the counsel laid down in the Scriptures.[3]

He who is God's Amen to all the promises of the covenant book of both Old and New Testaments; he who is 'the way, the truth and the life' (John 14:6) pardons this man for all eternity and opens to him the gates of heaven. Later that afternoon Christ ushered the penitent thief into the presence of the heavenly Father. The faith of this thief was already an answer to the prayer of our High Priest who had asked in John 17: 'Father, I will that they also, whom thou hast given me, be with me, that they may behold my glory, which thou hast given me…' (v. 24).

Holy Scripture here, and elsewhere, indicates that those who seek the forgiveness of Christ do not have to wait until the final day of resurrection to be in the presence of the Lord. Jesus said to Martha, 'whosoever liveth

---

3. K. Schilder, *Christ Crucified*, (vol 3), 300.

and believeth in me shall never die' (John 11:26). II Corinthians 5:1-9 shows that when our physical body is dissolved, 'we have a building of God, an house not made with hands' (v. 1), and so we are immediately given new 'clothing' suitable for life in the presence of God (v. 3). Philippians 1:23 tells us that 'to depart is to be with Christ.' Revelation 6:9-11 shows us the souls of the martyrs, very much alive, under the altar in heaven, and talking to the Lord. To that place of bliss and fullness of life Christ took the pardoned criminal who had turned to him in faith. That door is still open (cf. Rom. 10:9 and Rev. 22:17).

(3) 'Woman, behold thy son!' (John 19:26)
John opens the filial heart of the Lord in the midst of his crucifixion, as he makes preparation for his noble mother during the rest of her earthly life: 'Now there stood by the cross of Jesus, his mother, and his mother's sister, Mary the wife of Cleophas, and Mary Magdalene. When Jesus therefore saw his mother, and the disciple standing by whom he loved, he saith unto his mother, Woman, behold thy son! Then saith he to the disciple, Behold thy mother! And from that hour that disciple took her unto his own home' (John 19:25-27).

It has been noted that Mary 'is at the cross, and at the cross *without* Jesus' brothers and sisters.'[4] Many of his family would come to faith later (as James did), but evidently Mary is the only one who believes in Jesus at this time. As we see the Lord turn his mother over to his beloved disciple rather than to a family member, we perceive that the ties of spiritual family become more powerful than those of physical family. Ben Witherington comments:

> Once again we see Jesus addressing Mary simply as 'woman' (*gunai*) here. Rather than disengaging from her and her authority, as he does in John 2, he exercises his authority to integrate her into the family of faith, turning her over to the Beloved Disciple (who clearly is not a member of Jesus's physical family)…We need to consider three things:
>
> 1. As noted earlier, Mark 3:31-35 makes perfectly clear that Jesus, during his ministry, considered his *followers* his primary family – the family of faith, or those who do the will of God.
>
> 2. John 7:5 ('For not even his brothers believed in him') and the verses leading up to it support the Markan stories…in asserting that the brothers of Jesus were unbelievers during the ministry.
>
> 3. We know from Acts 1:14, where Mary is among the disciples in the upper room, that Mary at some juncture joined the inner circle of Jesus's followers. This act of adherence must surely have transpired before that upper room event, and there is no good reason it could not have happened beginning at Golgotha.[5]

---

4. Ben Witherington, *What Have They Done With Jesus?*, 124.

5. Ibid., 125-126.

The prophecy that elderly Simeon gave to Mary at the presentation of the Christ-child at the Temple must now have been reaching its sharpest fulfillment: 'Yea, a sword shall pierce through thy own soul also...' (Luke 2:35).

'Stabat Mater'

From Medieval times, the Church has sung the hymn that recalls what Mary went through:

'Stabat Mater dolorosa juxta crucem lacrimosa, dum pendebat Filius	'The grieving Mother stood weeping by the cross On which hung her Son.
Cuius animam gementem, contristatam et dolentem, pertransivit gladius.'	Her soul wailing, saddened and grieving As if pierced by a sword.'[6]

Schilder comments on this moving scene:

It was for His sake that the sword had originally been thrust through her. He gives the care of His mother into the hands of John. This is the simplest possible meaning of the words. The mother must now give up her own son; for His sake she has been called blessed among women...at His behest she is to have another son in His place.[7]

Jesus' care for his mother as he faces his awful death and descent into hell is one of the brightest illustrations of the principle of Song of Songs 8:6: 'for love is strong as death...' What else would we expect from the God who is love? He obeyed to the end the commandment given through himself to Moses, determining how we treat our parents: 'Honour thy father and thy mother...' (Exod. 20:12). And in taking care of Jesus' bereaved mother, John showed himself to be 'the friend that sticketh closer than a brother' (Prov. 18:24).

(4) 'My God, my God, why hast thou forsaken me?' (Ps. 22:1; Matt. 27:46; Mark 15:34).

Jesus utters this cry of God-forsakenness near the very end of the three hours of darkness that lasted from noon until 3 p.m. (i.e. in Roman timing, from the sixth hour to the ninth hour – Matt. 27:45). The ninth hour (or 3 p.m.) was the hour at which the paschal lamb was slain at the evening sacrifice in the Temple, on this very day.

John the Baptist had proclaimed at Christ's baptism in Jordan: 'Behold the Lamb of God, which taketh away the sin of the world' (John 1:29), and this cry – the fourth word from the cross – shows that the incarnate Son of God is going the last mile in taking away the sin of a fallen world.

---

6. Translation of 'Stabat Mater' by 2010 Naxos Rights International, Ltd.: http://www.naxos. com/cataloque/item.asp?=8.572121

7. K. Schilder, *The Crucifixion*, 347.

He is now doing all that remained to be done to remove the guilt of the sons and daughters of fallen Adam so as to reconcile them completely and eternally to their heavenly Father. In a manner that surpasses our very limited human understanding, something was transpiring in those moments on Calvary to bring to consummate completeness all the activities, and the very being of his holy life and death as the perfect, once-for-all sin offering, in which God 'hath made him to be sin for us, who knew no sin; that we might be made the righteousness of God in him' (II Cor. 5:21).

The first death and the second death

In these words, we see that the Son's experience of forsakenness by the Father who eternally loved him is the major grief in his descending into hell, for above all else, hell is God-forsakenness. In terms of the usage of 'death' in the book of Revelation, we can say that, unlike all other men, Christ died *the second death* before he died *the first death*.

In Revelation death is used in two different ways: first death and second death. The first death is physical death; it is the temporary separation of body and soul (or spirit, or personality). At the moment of physical death, the spirit (or personality) that animates the body is temporarily separated from it, and goes into the realm of departed spirits, while the body begins its return to the dust. For those whose sins are forgiven, the first death holds no terrors; it is an open door into the Christ's nearer presence. Paul is typical of the New Testament testimony: 'Absent from the body, present with the Lord' (II Cor. 5:8), and 'to depart and to be with Christ is far better' (Phil. 1:23). Jesus said: 'Because I live, ye shall live also' (John 14:19b).

But the second death is a different matter; it is not a temporary separation of body and soul, but rather a final, irrevocable and eternal separation of the reconstituted, rejoined body and soul of the unsaved from the Triune God; it is eternity in the lake of fire (which Revelation 20:14 calls 'the second death'), where the torments appropriate to those who hated God and rejected his Gospel are experienced. In the second death, the righteous wrath of God is poured out on those for whom it is proper, on those who would not identify by faith with the Lamb of God who takes away the sin of the world. Upon believers the second death has 'no power' (Rev. 2:11).

Jesus dies the second death first

Jesus on the cross experiences *the second death* (indicated by his cry 'My God…why hast thou forsaken me?') before *the first death* (indicated when he releases his spirit from his body to the Father). He dies the second death first in his total identification with the wickedness and filth of all the guilt brought on by every sin, both original

> The appendix to this chapter discusses various metaphors for the atonement used in Scripture.

and actual, with nothing between that infinite guilt and the righteous wrath of a holy God.

Expounding the second death, Thomas Goodwin writes (after quoting Revelation 20:6):

> And it is the original curse, the fountain of curses; whereas the death of the body, and all miseries of this life, are but the streams. This is the pure curse without mixture, as it is called in the Revelation; the other is the curse in the dregs, mingled and conveyed by creatures. All other curses light upon the outward man first, and upon the soul but at the rebound, and at the second hand, only by way of sympathy and compassion; but the immediate and proper subject of this curse is the soul and spirit…And this is the sum of all curses, and instead of all the rest.[8]

K. Schilder explains the meaning of Christ's cry of dereliction:

> …the fourth utterance from the cross was the turning point of Christ's dying. In making that statement He arrives at the bottomless abysses, and arrives there as Conqueror. That which must follow now is lighter than that which has gone by. First He suffered the pain of hell, and died the eternal, and the spiritual death. But that has gone by now. All that is left for Him to do now is to surrender the body… In this instrument, the tortured instrument in which and by means of it He also as a spiritual man accomplished his hardest work: namely the descent into the affliction of hell… Accordingly, Christ *knew* the suffering of the pain of hell was the severest suffering; He knew that this was the eternal death, the second death. He knew that He had emerged from this second death and He knew that He had not yet been subjected to what the Scriptures call the first death, the dissolution of the body… Very definitely a worse time could not be forthcoming any more.[9]

John Calvin writes about Christ's suffering the second death on the cross:

> If Christ had died only a bodily death, it would have been ineffectual. No – it was expedient at the same time for him to undergo the severity of God's vengeance, to appease his wrath and satisfy his just judgment. For this reason, he must also grapple hand to hand with the armies of hell and the dread of everlasting death…The point is… that we might know not only that Christ's body was given as the price of our redemption, but that he paid a greater and more excellent price in his soul the terrible torments of a condemned and forsaken man…
>
> We see that Christ was so cast down as to be compelled to cry out in deep anguish: 'My God, my God, why hast thou forsaken me?'…This is what we are saying: he bore the weight of divine severity, since he was 'stricken and afflicted' [cf. Isa. 53:5] by God's hand, and experienced all the signs of a wrathful and avenging God.[10]

Samuel Rutherford, a leading theologian of seventeenth-century Scotland and member in the 1640s of the Westminster Assembly, said in one of his sermons that Christ 'paid the first and the second death':

The Lord the Creditor, and Christ, the Cautioner did strike hands together.

---

8. Thomas Goodwin, 'Of Christ the Mediator,' *The Works of Thomas Goodwin*, vol. V, 271, 272.

9. K. Schilder, *Christ Crucified*, 430, 432.

10. John Calvin, *Institutes*, II. xvi. 10, 11 (Battles' translation, pp. 515, 516, 517).

Christ put himselfe in our room, as an hostage, pledge and surety to dye for us, and paid the first and second death, the sum that we were owing, according to a paction between the Lord and Christ...[11]

Where is Hell?

Thomas Goodwin discusses why Christ did not literally have to descend into the fiery pits of hell in order to take on, suffer, and overcome the pain of hell, and in doing so, to destroy its horrendous power.

> That the wrath of God should be thus endured, it is not of absolute necessity that men should be in the place of hell ere they undergo it; it may be endured here. For the devils, being out of that place and in the air, do still endure it, or at least may; as the angels when out of heaven, about their ministration here below, are said to 'see God's face,' Matt. 18:10... For it is God's wrath that is hell, as it is his favour that is heaven... But Jesus Christ's soul could subsist in his body, it being backed with the Godhead, even when filled with God's wrath, as well as when filled with glory, as at the transfiguration. The creatures, like an altar of straw, would have been burnt up by that fire if their souls had been to serve for the sacrifice; whereas this altar of Christ's body was covered with brass (as in the Levitical law), to conserve it from being consumed in ashes.[12]

This is not to deny that Christ did literally descend into the realm of departed spirits, as Peter tells us (I Peter 3:18-21), but that was *after* he had come back from the darkness of hell, and had released his spirit from his body. We shall discuss this passage after the seven words of the cross, under the traditional heading 'He descended into hell,' and under that heading also consider other ideas held within the church on the meaning of his descent into hell.

What is to be underlined here is the fact that the suffering by Christ on the cross of the pains of hell, justly deserved by a sinful humanity, was fully equivalent to what would have been experienced had he literally gone down – body and soul – into 'the lake of fire' (Rev. 20:14-15) – which actually does not appear to be functional until the Last Judgment. Because He is the God/man, and thus infinite in being and holiness, three hours of the intense sufferings of the pains of hell on Calvary are more than equivalent to an endless eternity of grief in the lake of fire, appropriate to all who reject the all-sufficient propitiation provided by God himself. No one who calls out to Christ for mercy need ever fear hell; they will never go to that awful place. If we could speak to the penitent criminal who was on the cross, he would affirm that this is so!

Darkness over the Land

'Now from the sixth hour there was darkness over all the land unto the ninth hour. And about the ninth hour Jesus cried with a loud voice, saying, "Eli, Eli, lama sabachthani?"' (Matt. 27:46; cf. Mark 15:33, 34; Luke 23:44-46).

---

11. Samuel Rutherford, *The Covenant of Life Opened: Or A Treatise of the Covenant of Grace* (Edinburgh, 1655), 248.

12. Thomas Goodwin, op. cit., 280-81.

The cause of this intense darkness that was in place between the time of his cry of dereliction and the words releasing his spirit is unknown to us. It could not have been an eclipse, because 'Easter' coincided with the full moon, and a full moon makes an eclipse impossible, for the moon is directly opposite to the sun. Some have considered it to have been a 'black sirocco', when the air is full of dust in Palestine. Whatever caused it was under the direct control and precise timing of God, for it helped to show that his holy Son was in outer darkness during those hours in his personal experience as our sin-bearer.

Christ had said when he was betrayed by Judas to the high priest: 'This is your hour and the power of darkness' (Luke 22:53). The next to last plague in Egypt was that of intense darkness, followed by the final plague of the death of the first-born. At the greater Exodus, as God's firstborn is dying, all becomes dark as night before the supreme sacrifice. Darkness can serve as a sign of the realm of outer darkness in hell, as it does in Matthew 8:12; 22:13; 25:30, and Jude 13, which says: 'wandering stars to whom is reserved the blackness of darkness for ever.'

The outer blackness of God-forsakeness in hell is the significance of the darkness that fell upon the land during the last three hours of the crucifixion of Christ. It is as though the one who said 'I am the light of the world' is somehow being blotted out in the blackness of the negativity of hell, as he takes on all the darkness of sin that has been committed against the light.

Because he is an infinite person, his suffering of hell for these three hours of outer darkness have been more than sufficient to exhaust all the fires and dark horrors of the infernal realm, as certainly as though a finite person had been consigned to its dread conditions for an endless eternity. As Schilder wrote:

> Now the suffering of Christ receives its infinite value first of all from His Person. His human nature is related to the Person of the uncreated Son of God. However, this suffering must be characterized by an intensity which exacts the utter extremities of His capacity for awful tension. Just as the successive periods of time (three hours) must be subordinate on this occasion to the intensive suffering, everything depends upon the fact that this intensity wholly consumes the Man of sorrows.[13]

The infinitude of Christ's sufferings is, in a certain limited sense, reflected in the darkness that prevailed over the land for the three final hours of his sacrificial life. The description of Schilder does not seem to contain any exaggeration:

> He [God] lays His hand on the suns. His taking away the light is an extension of the worst that human ingenuity can devise for an accursed person. The language which God speaks by means of this darkness is so absolutely devastating, disarming, stripping, erosive, and consuming that the legal sentences of Pilate and the Sanhedrin, and the mocker of

---

13. Ibid., 377.

Golgotha, are as nothing as compared with the language of God which places the exlex ['outlaw'] in the dark...The darkness coincides with the descent of the Son of God into hell...we cannot write of hell unless we have been there...We cannot get beyond the word He used in His own teaching: outer darkness.[14]

The Father never ceased loving his Son during the descent into hell

As we think of the crucified Christ taking on our guilt and bearing away the pains of the hell we all deserve, we must not for a moment imagine that his Father did not love him during this hellish, God-forsaken ordeal. If we could employ human 'time words', and speak anthropomorphically, never had his Father loved him more! Calvin rightly says: 'Yet we do not suggest that God was ever inimical or angry toward him. How could he be angry toward his beloved Son, "in whom his heart reposed" [cf. Matt. 3:17]? How could Christ by his intercession appease the Father toward others, if he were himself hateful to God?'[15]

John Stott writes:

We must not, then, speak of God punishing Jesus or of Jesus persuading God, for to do so is to set them over against each other as if they acted independently of each other or were even in conflict with each other. We must never make Christ the object of God's punishment or God the object of Christ's persuasion, for both God and Christ were subjects not objects, taking the initiative together to save sinners. Whatever happened on the cross in terms of 'God-forsakenness' was voluntarily accepted by both in the same holy love which made atonement necessary. It was 'God in our nature, forsaken of God'.[16]

Although Samuel Rutherford does use the word 'punished' of Christ, still he emphasizes the constant love of the Father toward the Son during this ordeal: 'He punished Christ, who was not inherently, but only by imputation of the sinner, with no hatred at all, but with anger and desire of shewing and exercising revenging justice, but still loving him dearly as his only Son. But on this account Christ must stand in our room.'[17]

Is it immoral for one person to suffer for the sins of another?

We must also remember that it is not immoral for one person to take on the punishment of another, *if* that person willingly agrees to do so. Thomas Goodwin's comments help us here:

---

14. Ibid., 381-383.

15. Calvin, *Insitutes*, II. xvi. 11 (Battles translation, p. 517).

16. John R. W. Stott, *The Cross of Christ* (InterVarsity Press: Leicester, 1989), 151. I would add here that while we would not wish to think of the Father punishing the Son, if that meant he did not have the most tender love towards him during his willingly chosen, holy sacrifice, nonetheless there are too many texts of Scripture that speak of *the penal character of the substitutionary atonement* to deny the clearly *penal aspect* of his loving self-offering to the Father. See section [iii] of Chapter X, Appendix I on 'Penal Substitution'.

17. Samuel Rutherford, *The Covenant of Life*, p. 254.

It is not a thing impossible or unjust for an innocent soul to have the sins of others imputed to it; no more than it is impossible for a sinful soul to have the righteousness of another made over to it. Now, in 2 Cor. v. 21, it is said that Christ 'was made sin, that we might be made righteousness;' and 'not having mine own righteousness,' says Paul, Phil. iii. 9. I say, it is not unjust, and therefore not impossible, in case the party innocent be content to become a surety; as Judah was, Gen. xliii. 9, who was content, if Joseph should detain his brother, Benjamin, to take that sin and evil upon him… And the ground is, because though his own acts make him not a sinner, yet his own covenant and consent do make him a surety; and so oblige him to the other's guiltiness and punishment, and wholly to bear the blame…and so was Christ. It was by his own compact and agreement.[18]

God forsaken by God

How far may we humans enter into the profound mystery of the Son somehow being forsaken by the Father, who loved him from all eternity? Martin Luther has been often quoted as saying somewhere: 'How could it be: God forsaken by God?' Peter Lombard showed insight when he pointed to the Old Testament ceremony of the scapegoat being run off into the wilderness as a prophecy of Christ going into hell for our sins, so as to bear them all away. Like many others in the Christian theological tradition, he discussed the mysterious separation between the Father and the Son after the Son's cry of dereliction, but Lombard did so in terms of the scapegoat:

So let us profess that God abandoned that man at death in some way, because for a time he exposed him to the power of his persecutors; God did not defend him by displaying his power so that he would not die. The Godhead severed itself because it took away its protection, but did not dissolve the union; it separated itself outwardly so that it was not there to defend him, but was not absent inwardly in regard to the union. If at that time the Godhead had not held back its power, but had displayed it, Christ would not have died. Christ died because the Godhead receded, that is, did not manifest the effect of its power in his defense. – This is the scapegoat, which after the other goat had been sacrificed, was sent *into the wilderness*, as we read in Leviticus [Lev. 16:22].[19]

Some five hundred years after Lombard (of twelfth-century Italy), Thomas Goodwin (of seventeenth-century England) looked at this unfathomable mystery in similar fashion:

For it was not a forsaking in respect of the essence of the Godhead, but of his presence, and so in a way of sense. The Godhead was not separated, though the operation of comfort from the Godhead were sequestered. The union hypostatical continued still with his soul, now filled with the sorrows of death, as well as it did with his body when it lay in the grave. And so as although his body was united to the fountain of life, yet it might die in respect of a natural life: so his soul, although the hypostatical union continued, might yet want comfort, which is life.[20]

---

18. Goodwin, op. cit., 281.

19. Peter Lombard, op. cit., 89.

20. Thomas Goodwin, op. cit., 279.

Was the Holy Trinity split apart?

We may attempt to state this mysterious truth another way, although we will still be far from even beginning to enter into the depths of it: Christ's cry of dereliction does not indicate that the Holy Trinity was ever split apart; for that to happen, everything would collapse into nonbeing, for God would have denied who he is, and his character is the stability of the universe. To split up the Trinity would be to destroy the life of God, and that cannot be done to the ever-living One, to the all-sufficient One, to the 'I AM THAT I AM.' According to John chapter 1, when the Son leaves the Father to come down to earth to be made flesh, still he abides in the bosom of the Father (John 1:18; cf. John 17:21).

Or it could be said this way: since the very being of God consists in the Triune relationships, so that for God to be is to be in relationship within himself, then to break up the inner-trinitarian relationships would be to destroy who God is, and that is impossible, for it would take a power greater than God (and none such exists), and it would require God to be inconsistent with himself (and he cannot deny himself – II Tim. 2:13). Therefore, for the Son to have experienced the abandonment of his Father must mean something other than that.

The turning away of the favor of God

As best we can discern, since the Father is 'of purer eyes than to behold evil' (Hab. 1:13), and since the Son has willingly submitted to be identified with the evil of human sin and its guilt (cf. II Cor. 5:21), then the Father for a time turns away his favorable gaze, with all of its infinite comfort and joy, from the face of his beloved Son. That is what Goodwin means when he says immediately above, 'The Godhead was not separated, though the operation of comfort from the Godhead were sequestered.' As the Psalm says: 'in his favour is life' (Psalm 30:5), and the turning away of the sensible experience of God's favour is a kind of death (2 Thess. 1:9); an absence of God; an experience of hell, that would be far worse for an infinitely holy person than it would for us sinful persons, who cannot even begin to imagine what it would have been like. As the hymn of C. F. Alexander, 'There is a Green Hill Far Away,' says:

> We may not know; we cannot tell,
> What pains he had to bear,
> But we believe it was for us
> He hung and suffered there.

C. H. Spurgeon, the great English preacher, conveyed something of what this divine abandonment must have been like for Christ, in a sermon preached in London, January 24, 1858 (opening the text: 'Yet it pleased the Lord to bruise him; he hath put him to grief: when thou shalt make his soul an offering for sin, he shall see his seed, he shall prolong his days, and the pleasure of the Lord shall prosper in his hand' – Isaiah 53:10):

Beloved, it is not only true that God did design and did permit with willingness the death of Christ; it is, moreover, true that the unutterable agonies that clothed the death of the Saviour with superhuman terror, were the effect of the Father's bruising of Christ in the very act and deed. There is a martyr in prison: the chains are on his wrists, and yet he sings. It has been announced to him that to-morrow is his burning day. He claps his hands right merrily, and smiles while he says, 'It will be sharp work to-morrow, I shall breakfast below on fiery tribulations, but afterward I will sup with Christ. Tomorrow is my wedding-day, the day for which I have long panted, when I shall sign the testimony of my life by a glorious death.' The time is come; the men with halberts precede him through the streets. Mark the serenity of the martyr's countenance. He turns to some who look upon him, and exclaims, 'I value these iron chains far more than if they had been of gold; it is a sweet thing to die for Christ'…One would think he were going to a bridal, rather than to be burned…He sings whilst the fagots are crackling and the smoke is blowing upward. He sings, and when his nether parts are burned, he still goes on chanting sweetly some psalm of old. 'God is our refuge and strength, a very present help in trouble; therefore will not we fear, though the earth be removed and the mountains be carried into the midst of the sea.'

Picture another scene. There is the Saviour going to his cross, all weak and wan with suffering; his soul is sick and sad within him. There is no divine composure there. So sad is his heart, that he faints in the streets. The Son of God faints beneath a cross that many a criminal might have carried. They nail him to the tree. There is no song of praise. He is lifted up in the air, and there he hangs preparatory to his death. You hear no shout of exultation. There is a stern compression of his face, as if unutterable agony were tearing his heart – as if over again Gethsemane were being acted on the cross…Hark! he speaks. Will he not sing sweeter songs than ever came from martyr's lips? Ah! no; it is an awful wail of woe that can never be imitated. 'My God, my God, why hast thou forsaken me?' The martyrs said not that: God was with them. Confessors of old cried not so, when they came to die. They shouted in their fires, and praised God on their racks. Why this? Why doth the Saviour suffer so? Why, beloved, it was because the Father bruised him. That sunshine of God's countenance that has cheered many a dying saint, was withdrawn from Christ; the consciousness of acceptance with God, which has made many a holy man espouse the cross with joy, was not afforded to our Redeemer, and therefore he suffered in thick darkness of mental agony. Read the 22nd Psalm, and learn how Jesus suffered. Pause over the solemn words in the 1st, 2nd, 6th, and following verses. Underneath the church are the everlasting arms; but underneath Christ there were no arms at all, but his Father's hand pressed heavily against him; the upper and the nether mill-stones of divine wrath pressed and bruised him; and not one drop of joy or consolation was afforded to him. 'It pleased Jehovah to bruise him; *he* hath put him to grief.' This, my brethren, was the climax of the Saviour's woe, that his Father turned away from him, and put him to grief.[21]

---

21. Charles H. Spurgeon, 'A Sermon' (No. 173), Delivered on Sabbath Morning, January 24, 1858, by the Rev. C. H. Spurgeon at the Music Hall, Royal Surrey Gardens (from http://www.spurgeon.org/sermons/0173.htm) .

What was the involvement of the Father in the Death of Christ?

Here again we must raise a question that the truest biblical piety can never really answer: what did it mean for the Father that his well-loved Son was going through all this? T. F. Torrance (reflecting on Jurgen Moltmann's *The Crucified God*) rightly said: 'The whole Trinity is involved in the sacrifice of Christ on the cross. In an Easter Oration Gregory Nazianzen once spoke of this awesome fact, "God crucified," as a downright "miracle." "We needed an incarnate God, a God put to death, that we might live…"'[22] Torrance continues:

> God is certainly impassible in the sense that he is not subject to the passions that characterize our human and creaturely existence, and it is certainly true that God is opposed to all suffering and pain. He is, moreover, intrinsically impassible for in its own divine Nature he is not moved or swayed by anything other than himself or outside of himself…
>
> That is the significance of the message of the Cross. God does not obliterate evil by absolute irresistible power, but in his boundless mercy lays hold of it in the incarnate birth, life, and death of his beloved Son, and makes it serve the supreme purpose of his love for the world… in the darkness of dereliction which he endured on the Cross, in which spiritual and physical pain interpenetrated each other, all that unveils for us something of the infinite depth of the active suffering of God… What Christ felt, did and suffered in himself in his body and soul for our forgiveness was felt, done and suffered by God in his innermost Being for our sake.[23]

John R. W. Stott's comments on this point are similar:

> Our substitute, then, who took our place and died our death on the cross was neither Christ alone (since that would make him a third party thrust in between God and us), nor God alone (since that would undermine the historical incarnation), but *God in Christ*, who was truly and fully both God and man, and who on that account was uniquely qualified to represent both God and man and to mediate between them… The New Testament authors never attribute the atonement either to Christ in such a way as to disassociate him from the Father, or to God in such a way as to dispense with Christ, but rather to God and Christ, or to God acting in and through Christ with his whole-hearted concurrence.[24]

That is why nothing need ever be added to the vicarious sufferings of Christ for our salvation. They are significant to, backed up, and ratified in the very heart of God the Father Almighty, and they were offered in 'the eternal Spirit' (Heb. 9:14). That is why the writer of the Epistle to the Hebrews both invites us to come freely to the Lord for full forgiveness, and at the same time warns us of the inexpressible consequences of refusing to come: 'How shall we escape, if we neglect so great salvation; which at the first began to be spoken by the Lord, and was confirmed unto us by them that heard him…?' (Heb. 2:3).

---

22. T. F. Torrance, *The Christian Doctrine of God*, 245, quoting Gregory Nazianzus, *Orationes*, 45. 28f.

23. T. F. Torrance, *The Christian Doctrine of God*, 247-249.

24. John Stott, *The Cross of Christ*, 156.

Did God Die?

As we contemplate Christ, the God/man, dying on the cross, with the whole Godhead somehow involved in his horrendous experience, the question comes: did God die? As T. F. Torrance once stated in a class (where I was a student in the late 1960s): 'Christ died the death of man, but not the death of God. God cannot die, for he is life; but man does die, and Christ vicariously chooses to die his death (cf. Heb. 2:14-15). In doing so, the Prince of Life conquers death.'

I would add: in dying our death, Christ dies the second death first, exhausting the fires of hell against all of the guilty who will ever be identified with him; then he dies the first death secondly, so that it too is rendered powerless. This gloriously good news means that no person need ever fear either physical or spiritual death – either separation of soul and body when the body gives out (the first death), or separation of rejoined soul and body from God in hell at the Last Judgment (the second death), *if* they cast themselves upon the mercy of Christ while there is still time!

(5) 'I thirst' (John 19:28-29)

'After this, Jesus knowing that all things were now accomplished, that the scripture might be fulfilled, said, I thirst. Now there was set a vessel full of vinegar; and they filled a sponge with vinegar, and put it upon hyssop, and put it to his mouth.'

Why did Christ refuse the first drink, and then call for the other?

Matthew relates that earlier in the process of crucifixion Jesus had been offered 'vinegar to drink mingled with gall: and when he had tasted thereof, he would not drink' (Matt. 27:34). So why would he have refused the sour wine that had a certain medicinal value at the beginning of the crucifixion, but near the end, call for a drink? I believe that K. Schilder's explanation is on the right lines:

> The Saviour asked for a drink. Thus He had returned to the world. You wonder whether this thirst had not caused Him to suffer before. Naturally, but the hellish suffering gone through just now had sunk to a plane so far below that of human suffering, that during the course of those three hours not a single word came from His lips. Then too He thirsted; then not for water, but for the living water, which, when men drink it, they live eternally. That thirst had been sub-human; it conducted Him into the next world. There a cup of water is nothing, is far beyond sight. And Christ's asking sustenance for His body now is in a certain sense evidence to show that Christ has come up out of the deepest abysses. He is among us again in this peopled world. He feels His flesh again. He can pay attention to the material of the sacrifice again: praise be to God... He becomes aware of His body by means of the spirit. Both of these are necessary for the sacrifice that is to come now...
>
> ...the fourth utterance from the cross was the turning point of Christ's dying. In making that statement He arrives at the bottomless abysses, and arrives there as Conqueror. That which must follow now is lighter than that

which has gone by. First He suffered the pain of hell, and died the eternal, and the spiritual death. But that has gone by now. All that is left for Him to do now is to surrender the body, to give up the instrument... In this instrument and by means of it He also as a spiritual man accomplished His hardest work: namely, the descent into the affliction of hell. The body too suffered in that descent; it did even if we cannot say anything about the manner in which it suffered. And now that the work assigned to Him has been completely finished in the body, it is the most natural thing in the world that He Himself should give up this body to the God who gave it.[25]

The refusal of one drink, and the acceptance of the other is in order to provide clarity of consciousness for mediatorial work. Schilder noted: 'At first He did not drink, for He did not wish a sedative. Now He does drink, because He does not wish to be dulled.'[26] He has come back from his triumphant work in taking on the second death, and having achieved that, 'now He can die in the body; His death in the body is already being regarded as a conquest of eternal life.'[27]

As our High Priest, it now remains for him to offer up his body, and drinking the vinegar and gall helps him to do so *consciously*. 'Death does not come upon Him unawares. The suffering does not strike Him unconscious...'[28] Hence the statement in John that Christ said 'I thirst' in order to fulfill Scripture means that:

> The Messiah of the promise may not accept His death as His fate but must perform it as a deed. His death must be a gift, a priestly donation...He must act with a free will...He demands for that service what is necessary to Him in order to fulfill the last act at the altar in righteousness...He is His own priest, and must therefore be alert when the time for the last sacrifice comes.[29]

This is to say that early in the crucifixion, the vinegar/wine would have to some degree *deadened* his sensitivity to the pain he was to endure, whereas at the end, the vinegar/wine actually *increased* his consciousness of the death of the body, which he must soon offer up. Although suffering immense torture and cruelty at the hands of men, the Great High Priest is in charge of the details of the once-for-all sacrifice. Part of his attention to detail was his intention to fulfill Scripture as he said 'I thirst,' according to John 19:28.

'I thirst' fulfills Scriptural prophecy

We could consider this fulfillment of Scripture mentioned in this fifth word from the cross *generally*, as Christ preparing himself for the final high-priestly offering up of his body (Heb. 10:5, employing a variant

---

25. Schilder, *Christ Crucified*, 429-31.

26. Ibid., 438.

27. Ibid., 432.

28. Ibid., 436.

29. Ibid., 437-38.

form of Ps. 40:6).[30] But more *specifically*, his announcement of his thirst is a fulfillment of such Old Testament texts as Psalm 22:15: 'My strength is dried up like a potsherd; and my tongue cleaveth to my jaws; And thou hast brought me into the dust of death'; and Psalm 69:21: 'They gave me also gall for my meat; And in my thirst they gave me vinegar to drink.' In doing so, Christ in fulfilling every prophecy of Holy Scripture is thereby 'offering himself without spot to God' (Heb. 9:14).

Melito reminds us who it is who is thirsting

As we think of the voluntary self-offering of our High Priest as he prepares for the moment of physical death, we must not forget *who he is* in this bleeding sacrifice of his body. One of the best contrasts between the person of the High Priest in his deity and in his humanity as he makes this supreme sacrifice on the basis of the hypostatic union is one of the earliest: 'The Homily on the Passion' by Melito, Bishop of Sardis, probably preached around the year A. D. 169:

> Thou didst put [a scarlet robe upon his] body and thorns upon his head. Thou didst bind the beautiful hands with which he [shaped] thee from the earth; and his beautiful mouth, the mouth that fed thee with life, thou hast fed with gall, and thou hast slain thy Lord in the great feast...*this is* he who was begotten before the morning star, who made the light to rise, who made the day bright, who parted the darkness, who fixed the first mark *for the creation*, who hung the earth *in its place*, who dried up the abyss, who spread out the firmament, who brought order to the world.
>
> He who fixed the stars in heaven, who made bright the heavenly bodies, who made the firmament, who fixed the [luminaries] there...
>
> And so he is raised upon a high cross, and a title is set *upon it* making known him who was slain. Who was he?...He who hung the earth *in its place* is hanged, he who fixed the heavens is fixed *upon the cross*, he who made all things fast is made fast upon the tree, the Master has been insulted, God has been murdered, the King of Israel has been slain... For this reason the lights *of heaven* turned away, and the day darkened, that it might hide him who was stripped upon the cross, shrouding not the body of the Lord, but the eyes of men. For though the people trembled not, the earth trembled; though the people feared not, the heavens were afraid; though the people rent not their garments, the angel rent his; though the people did not lament, the Lord thundered from heaven, and the Most High uttered *his* voice.[31]

The following hymn was written hundreds of years after Melito preached his great sermon, but it conveys some of the truth that he was expressing:

> His are the thousand sparkling rills,
> That from a thousand fountains burst,
> And fill with music all the hills,
> And yet he saith, 'I thirst.'[32]

30. The main Masoretic tradition of Psalm 40:6 says: '...mine ears hast thou opened...,' whereas the variant text (taken over by Hebrews) reads: 'A body hast thou prepared me.'

31. Melito of Sardis, *The Homily of the Passion with Some Fragments of the Apocryphal Ezekiel*, edited by Campbell Bonner (London: Christophers, 1940), 177, 179, 180.

32. Cecil F. Alexander in *Scottish Psalter and Church Hymnary*, (Oxford University Press; London, 1929), no. 101.

The thirst of the incarnate Son of God can be entirely explained by the purely natural factors of the horrible process of crucifixion: the utter drying out of the normal, life-sustaining fluids in the body, as the profuse sweat is poured out and the blood is shed from the large wounds made by the nails in his hands, his feet, his thorn-pierced brow, and from his back, mangled by severe flogging the previous day. Yet there may be more than meets the eye, given that he has just come back from the equivalent of the fires of hell. According to what Jesus said of the rich man in Luke 16, the place of lost souls is a parched realm, where there is no water to quench the thirst (v. 24).[33] But instead of our having to go to that terrible realm of torment, because he went there in our stead and took upon himself all the torment we deserve, and in doing so overcame its thirst, pain and desolation, we are invited to join him in his resurrection life 'in green pastures, beside the still waters' (cf. Ps. 23:2); we are invited to 'a pure river of water of life, clear as crystal, proceeding out of the throne of God and of the Lamb' (Rev. 22:1).

(6) 'It is finished' (John 19:30a)

The sixth utterance from the cross is only one word in Greek, τετελεσται, meaning 'It is finished.' Earlier in John, Jesus had announced to his disciples the goal of his life and ministry: 'My meat is to do the will of him that sent me, and to finish his work' (John 4:34). Near the conclusion of his public ministry, he said to the Father in his high priestly prayer: 'I have glorified thee on the earth. I have finished the work which thou gavest me to do' (John 17:4).

Schilder summarizes Christ's achievements: 'All that had definitely been given Him to do had been accomplished. In other words, He had in His historical life achieved everything that the Scripture had indicated as His messianic task. The eternal and the temporal, the counsel of God and the deed of Christ are combined in this utterance of our Victor.'[34]

The consummate fullness of the finished work of Christ can only be approached by means of several biblical concepts that have to be held together in order to grasp what Christ meant when he said 'It is finished.' These terms and events enter into the successful completion of the Mediator's (a) *active* obedience and (b) *passive* obedience.

Under (a) his *active obedience*, we find such concepts as: [i] Last Adam; [ii] fulfilling the Law; and [iii] fulfilling the messianic prophecies of Scripture. Under (b) his *passive obedience*, we note: [i] payment of debt (or satisfaction); [ii] turning away of divine wrath by means of propitiation; [iii] penal substitution; [iv] ransom price; [v] reconciliation; [vi] victorious achievement (that must be understood of both active and passive obedience, which, of course, are never separated); and [vii] justification. Of all these mediatorial actions, Christ could say on the cross, 'It is finished.'

---

33. His taking upon himself spiritual death during his sufferings on the cross does not mean that there were no physical consequences of this spiritual abasement, although we do not know what they were.

34. Schilder, *Christ Crucified*, 450.

(a) Christ's active obedience: 'It is finished'

Chapter eight of this volume was devoted to Christ's active obedience, especially in light of his incarnate existence as the Last Adam, in which he lived out the life of devout sonship that the Father had always desired.

[i] Last Adam: Devout Son

As we saw in that chapter, whereas the First Adam failed to be a loving and obedient son by willfully disobeying God and seeking to be 'like God,' the Last Adam, in the entirety of body, soul, and spirit, poured himself out to be the Father's true Son, always saying, 'Not my will, but thine be done' (Luke 22:42), and 'I do always those things that please him' (John 8:29). The Gospel of Luke shows the twelve-year-old Christ putting the business of his Father's house first (Luke 2:49), and unveils the constancy of his seeking the Father's face in prayer (e.g. 5:16; 6:12, etc.). As our Mediator, the Son of God in our flesh, through his obedient and holy life turned our humanity back around, face to face with God. In the same way, where Abraham and Israel failed to live as God's loving son, Christ did so in their place.[35] And the heavenly Father, indeed, was well pleased with his Son, as he affirms at his baptism (Matt. 3:17), and also at his transfiguration (Matt. 17:5).

[ii] Fulfilling the Law

God's Son in the flesh fulfilled the will of the Father as expressed in the divine law, both *in spirit* and *in letter*. Christ fulfilled God's will as delivered through Moses *in its spirit*. That was a major issue of contention between Jesus and the Pharisees. He told them that their tendency towards legalism represented an externalization of the law that blinded them to its true intentions (or spirit).

For instance, he attacked their oral tradition, according to which one could avoid giving financial assistance to one's parents by saying that the money was dedicated to God under the name 'Corban' (Mark 7:11). By means of that and other legalistic, externalistic customs from the oral (not written) tradition, Christ's opponents managed to avoid carrying out the true intent of the divine law: 'Howbeit in vain do they worship me, teaching for doctrines the commandments of men. For laying aside the commandment of God, ye hold the tradition of men, as the washing of pots and cups: and many other such like things ye do. And he said unto them, Full well ye reject the commandment of God, that ye may keep your own tradition' (Mark 7:7-9).

Part of that oral tradition was the call to hate one's enemies. But Jesus showed this violated the intent (or spirit) of the written law of God to love one's neighbor: 'Ye have heard that it hath been said, Thou shalt love thy neighbor, and hate thine enemy. But I say unto you, Love your enemies, bless them that curse you, do good to them that hate you, and pray for them that despitefully use you, and persecute you; That ye may be the

---

35. See Chapter 8 for details.

children of your Father which is in heaven... Be ye therefore perfect, even as your Father which is in heaven is perfect' (Matt. 5:43-45a, 48).

In other words, love for God and man is the true intent and spirit of the law: 'And Jesus answered him, The first of all the commandments is, Hear, O Israel; The Lord our God is one Lord: And thou shalt love the Lord thy God with all thy heart, and with all thy soul, and with all thy mind, and with all thy strength: this is the first commandment. And the second is like, namely this, Thou shalt love thy neighbour as thyself. There is none other commandment greater than these' (Mark 12:29-31).

All externalism and legalism pervert this commandment to love,[36] but Jesus fulfilled it whole-heartedly. He did so in our stead. He lived in the *spirit* of the law of God, offering heart and soul to the Father in glad obedience.

Moreover, the incarnate Christ also lived in terms of *the letter* of the law in every way that it pertained to him and to his people: 'Think not that I am come to destroy the law, or the prophets: I am not come to destroy, but to fulfil. For verily I say unto you, Till heaven and earth pass, one jot or tittle shall in no wise pass from the law, till all be fulfilled' (Matt. 5:17,18). Thus he could say to his critics: 'Which of you convinceth me of sin...?' (John 8:46). James said that 'For whosoever shall keep the whole law, and yet offend in one point, he is guilty of all' (James 2:10). Jesus kept the entire law, and never offended in any one point. He was 'holy, harmless, undefiled, separate from sinners' (Heb. 7:26). God's law said: 'My son..., keep my commandments and live...' (Prov. 7:1-2).

Christ did so as our representative, fulfilling every aspect of the Covenant in our name, so that the eternal life he wins in heaven is ours by grace of union to our living head. Church Fathers and Reformers have traditionally believed that the threat to Adam not to eat of the forbidden fruit, 'For in the day that thou eatest thereof thou shalt surely die' (Gen. 2:17), implied a promise of life for obedience. Christ, as the Second Adam, obeys in our place all of God's righteous requirements by refraining from all evil actions and carrying out all good actions, and hence gains eternal life in the presence of the Lord for us.

Paul says that 'Christ is the end of the law for righteousness to every one that believeth' (Rom. 10:4). 'End' (τελος) means completing or fulfillment. Thus, when he cries out 'It is finished,' he means that all that the law required us to be and to do has been fully accomplished in him on our behalf.

[iii] *Fulfilling the Messianic prophecies of Scripture*

When Jesus said, 'It is finished,' he also enunciated the exact completion of all the varied prophecies of the Old Testament concerning the person and work of the coming Messiah. The Gospels frequently state that some

---

36. The externalism and legalism condemned by Christ are illustrated in Matthew 23:23: 'Woe unto you, scribes and Pharisees, hypocrites! For ye pay tithe of mint and anise and cumin, and you have omitted the weightier *matters* of the law, judgment, mercy, and faith: these ought ye to have done, and not to leave the other undone.'

particular detail in Christ's experience was done 'that the Scriptures (or the Prophets) might be fulfilled...' When Jesus opened the scroll (of Isaiah) in the synagogue in Nazareth in order to preach from it, 'he began to say unto them, This day is this scripture fulfilled in your ears...' (Luke 4:21, referring to Isaiah 61:1). Luke 12:50 expresses the driving determination of the soul of Jesus to do all that was necessary to reach the baptism of blood that was his portion as prophesied in the scriptures: 'But I have a baptism to be baptized with, and how am I straitened till it be accomplished!'

Matthew saw the slaughter of the children in Bethlehem by Herod as a fulfillment of the prophecy of Jeremiah concerning the weeping of Rachel (Matt. 2:17, 18, referring to Jer. 31:15). He saw the virgin birth as a fulfillment of Isaiah 7:14 (Matt. 1:22-23), and the coming of Joseph, Mary and the Christ-child out of Egypt as a fulfillment of Hosea 11:1 (Matt. 2:15). Matthew somehow relates Christ's dwelling in Nazareth to his being a Nazarene (cf. Isa. 11:1). The healing of the mother-in-law of Peter, and then of many others, was described as a fulfillment of Isaiah 53:4 – 'Himself took our infirmities, and bare our sicknesses' (Matt. 8:17). His withdrawal from his ministry to great multitudes at the Sea of Tiberias into quietness is a carrying out of Isaiah 42:1-4 (Matt. 12:15-21). Jesus' teaching in parables was seen as a fulfillment of Psalm 78:2 (Matt. 13:34-35).

His entry into Jerusalem on Palm Sunday was a fulfillment of Zechariah 9:9 (Matt. 21:4, 5). His cleansing of the Temple fulfilled Isaiah 56:7 and Jeremiah 7:11. The disciples forsaking Jesus in Gethsemane, after he refused to call in twelve legions of angels, is said to have fulfilled the Scriptures (Matt. 26:53-56; see also Mark 14:49). His statement on the cross 'I thirst' fulfilled the Scriptures (John 19:28). The soldiers casting lots for his garments fulfilled Old Testament prophecy (John 19:24 and Psalm 22:18). His dying on the cross without his bones being broken fulfilled Exodus 12:46 (John 19:36). Their piercing him fulfilled Zechariah 12:10. The purchase of the potter's field by the chief priests with the blood money originally given to Judas Iscariot fulfilled Zechariah 11:12-13, with possible reference to Jeremiah 18:1-4 (the current text of Matthew refers to Jeremiah: cf. Matthew 27:3-10). His being crucified between two thieves fulfilled Isaiah 53:12. And in his second sermon in Acts, Peter also affirmed that Christ's suffering had fulfilled 'those things which God before had shewed by the mouth of all his prophets, that Christ should suffer...' (Acts 3:18).

On the road to Emmaus, the risen Christ (who kept himself from being recognized at first) explained what had happened to him to the bewildered disciples: 'Then said he unto them, O fools, and slow of heart to believe all that the prophets have spoken: Ought not Christ to have suffered these things, and to enter into his glory? And beginning at Moses and all the prophets, he expounded unto them in all the scriptures the things concerning himself' (Luke 24:25-27).

Paul presents the Gospel of Christ as the fulfillment of the Scriptures. He states in his great resurrection chapter: 'For I delivered unto you first of all that which I also received, how that Christ died for our sins according to the scriptures; and that he was buried, and that he rose again the third day according to the scriptures' (I Cor. 15:3, 4). Paul preaches on this same basis in his sermon in the synagogue at Thessalonica, where he shows that since what happened to Christ fulfilled the Scriptures, he is therefore the Messiah: 'And Paul, as his manner was, sent in unto them, and three Sabbath days reasoned with them out of the scriptures, opening and alleging that Christ must needs have suffered, and risen again from the dead; and that this Jesus, whom I preach unto you, is Christ' (Acts 17:2, 3). Similarly, he told the synagogue in Pisidian Antioch that the details of the death of Christ 'fulfilled all that was written of him' (Acts 13:29).

Years after the crucifixion and resurrection, the eyewitness Peter takes us behind the scenes of what was happening as Christ, particularly in his sufferings, sought to fulfill to the letter all that the prophets had predicted Messiah would do. Peter shows us the amazing fact that what Christ was carrying out was not an imposition upon himself from the outside; on the contrary, it was he himself, through his Holy Spirit, who had inspired the prophets to write the very things he must carry out:

> Of which salvation the prophets have inquired and searched diligently, who prophesied of the grace that should come unto you: Searching what, or what manner of time the Spirit of Christ which was in them did signify, when it testified beforehand the sufferings of Christ, and the glory that should follow (I Peter 1:10-11).

On the cross, he who knew so well the Scriptures knew exactly what he was saying when he uttered, just before his death, 'It is finished.' Messiah left nothing undone that needed to be done for lost humanity to be saved, and that was the basis of the preaching both of Paul and of the early church.

(b) Christ's passive obedience: 'It is finished'

Jesus' sixth word on the cross testified to the finishing not only of all necessary active obedience, but also of his passive obedience, in voluntarily taking upon himself all that was entailed by the just penalty upon sinful guilt against an infinitely holy God, and suffering it through to its final exhaustion. The victorious accomplishments of his suffering can be looked at in terms of various biblical pictures, all of which need to be held together to grasp the greatness of what he finished. The cross of Calvary is too full of power and mystery to be encompassed in any one term, or to be neatly dissected by human logic and then somehow re-organized into a clear logical framework, such as might (or might not) be possible with merely temporal and created realities.

The best we can do is to meditate on models and analogies presented to us in the Holy Scriptures, and to open our minds, as best we can, to the rich and varied testimony of the inspired writers to that 'Love divine, all loves excelling' seen at Calvary. While there is a considerable amount of conceptual overlap among these Old and New Testament 'word pictures', we must keep all of them in mind, even to begin to grasp what Christ did on the cross for us. While they cannot ever be analyzed, explained and fitted neatly together in terms of a series of fully comprehensible legal and political concepts, nonetheless the pictures and events given us in Scripture to represent the atonement *are coherent*, and make life-changing sense when surveyed as a whole and received in faith and prayer. These pictures from the divine revelation include: [i] Payment of debt (or satisfaction); [ii] turning away of divine wrath by means of propitiation; [iii] penal substitution; [iv] ransom price; [v] victorious battle; [vi] supreme moral example of devout suffering; [vii] justification; and [viii] reconciliation.

[i] Payment of debt (or satisfaction)

The Western Christian tradition has laid much thoughtful emphasis upon the payment of debt to God in terms of the satisfaction God sent Christ to render to himself. In Appendix I to this Chapter, we survey leading exponents of this teaching, especially Saint Anselm, and also consider objections to it.

But let us note here that sometimes a very important concept comes from the Scriptures, without a precise Scriptural word for the concept (such as 'Trinity'), and such a concept makes much sense of a plethora of passages in the Bible. So it is with the term 'satisfaction.' Paul Wells has brought out this point:

> Although it has often been criticized on the grounds that it is not a biblical term, satisfaction lies close to the meaning expressed by several words in Scripture.[37] It joins in one global description the religious cultic features of sacrifice (expiation, curse, propitiation, purification, blood) and the legal language of condemnation (guilt, penalty, judgment, remission).[38]

Wells also refers to H. Blocher, who argues that 'the satisfaction of justice lies near the heart of sacrificial atonement'.[39]

For the present, we will briefly follow the definition of 'satisfaction' supplied by John Owen: '*Satisfaction* is a term borrowed from the law, applied properly to things, thence translated and accommodated unto persons; and it is *a full compensation of the creditor from the debtor*.'[40] Owen specifies both debtor and creditor:

> …First, the *debtor* is *man*; he oweth the ten thousand talents, Matt. xviii. 24. Secondly, The *debt is sin*: 'Forgive us our debts,' Matt. vi. 12. Thirdly, That which is required in lieu thereof to make satisfaction for it, is *death*: 'In the day that thou eatest thereof, thou shalt surely die,' Rom. vi. 23. Fourthly, The

---

37. He states in note 2 (p. 231): 'It is used in the AV to translate *kapar* in Numbers 35:31-32; later translations, such as NIV or the NKJV use "ransom".' Cf. F. Turretin, *Institutes of Elenctic Theology* II, 243f.

38. Paul Wells, *Cross Words: The Biblical Doctrine of the Atonement* (Fearn, Ross-shire: Christian Focus, 2006), 219.

39. Note 3 (ibid.): 'H. Blocher, 'The Atonement in John Calvin's Theology,' in *The Glory of the Atonement*, C. E. Hill, F. A. James, eds., 283ff.

40. John Owen, *The Death of Death in the Death of Christ*, with an introductory essay by J. I. Packer (London: Banner of Truth Trust, 1969), 153.

obligation whereby the debtor is tied and bound is the *law*, 'Cursed is every one,' etc., Gal. iii. 10; Deut. xxvii. 26; the justice of God, Rom. i. 32; and the truth of God, Gen. iii. 3. Fifthly, The *creditor* that requireth this of us is *God*, considered as the party offended, severe Judge, and supreme Lord of all things. Sixthly, That which interveneth to the destruction of the obligation is the *ransom* paid by Christ: Rom. iii. 25, 'God set him forth to be a propitiation through faith in his blood.'[41]

Owen is saying that *satisfaction* is a proper term for the transaction of the cross, in which the biblical themes of indebtedness and justice are held together. Man owes to God a debt; he sinned, and the payment he owes for his sin is death. God, the creditor, who gives man life, is also the one who paid the penalty owed to himself, and that penalty for our sin was death.

T. F. Torrance wrote: 'In this inconceivable union of God and humanity, then, God in Christ took our place and accomplished what we could not do. The infliction and judgement which we could not bear he bore for us. In our place he made "satisfaction" (to use the language of Anselm) for our sins and for the sins of the whole world.'[42]

And as we see in the appendix to this chapter concerning the teaching of Anselm, the 'satisfaction' that Christ rendered for us was of infinite value. That has been the general position in the Western Church, and it was typically expressed in the sermons of the seventeenth-century Scottish theologian Samuel Rutherford. In line with Anselm, Rutherford states that since sin against an infinite God makes us infinitely guilty, the ransom price for that since must be infinite: '...he gave himself an infinite ransome' and 'endured infinite wrath for us.'[43] 'By his death he not only exhausted the infinite punishment due to us...but purchased to us an infinite and eternal weight of glory, by the worth of his merit.'[44]

When Christ said 'It is finished,' he well knew that he had paid the debt we owed and could never have paid ourselves. In so doing, he bore the righteous wrath of God against that sin which is contrary to the divine character, without any intermission of infinite love between Father and Son; indeed, because of that love, he went through these fires of grief in our place. He takes away the wrath that we deserved and replaces it with the peace and favor that he deserved: 'Blotting out the handwriting of ordinances that was against us, which was contrary to us, and took it out of the way, nailing it to his cross...' (Col. 2:14). Isaiah says: 'But he was wounded for our transgressions, he was bruised for our iniquities: the chastisement of our peace was upon him; and with his stripes we are healed' (Isa. 53:5).

[ii] The turning away of divine wrath by means of propitiation
We have already mentioned the concept of propitiation (in ch. 9). In an appendix to the present chapter, we look more closely at the biblical

---

41. Ibid., 154.

42. T. F. Torrance, *Atonement*, 123.

43. Samuel Rutherford, *The Covenant of Life*, 127, 136.

44. Ibid., 126.

evidence and at theological opposition to this concept of propitiation. It will be sufficient to note here that various biblical terms which indicate 'propitiation', or the turning away of wrath, are not lacking in the New Testament, where they are specifically applied to the substitutionary death of 'the Lamb of God that taketh away the sin of the world'. In sum, the death and hell that are the consequences of the infinite guilt of humankind are abundantly dealt with and utterly removed by the infinitely worthy sufferings of the Holy One of Israel, whose cry of 'It is finished' assures the believer's hope of the favor of the Holy God rather than experiencing the wrath for his sins against that God.

[iii] Penal Substitution

One can speak of penal substitution in brief compass, for most of the issues raised by it are dealt with in the appendix to this chapter, under [ii] **propitiation**. The whole sacrificial system of the Old Testament (which forms the conceptual basis of the New Testament doctrine of sacrifice) is based on the principle of substitution: one dies in the place of another; the blood of one victim is shed to cover the sins of another. The ritual of the Levitical priest laying his hands on the head of the two scapegoats was a picture of the symbolical transfer of the people's sins to a substitute. And so it was when the unclean worshiper laid his or her hands on the lamb, or other animal, to be slain on the altar: it was slain in place of the guilty worshiper.

The New Testament builds upon this principle of substitution, and, in a sense, raises it to an infinite degree when it presents Christ offering himself in the place of sinners as their divinely provided, infinitely worthy substitute. So at the beginning of Christ's public ministry, John the Baptist declares of him at the Jordan River: 'Behold the Lamb of God, which taketh away the sin of the world' (John 1:29). And years after Christ's crucifixion and resurrection Peter wrote, with the same substitution in mind: 'Who his own self bare our sins in his own body on the tree...' (I Peter 2:24). Even in the eternal glory of the highest heavens the substitution will always be remembered and celebrated, for the last book of the New Testament sings the praises of the Lamb who 'was slain, and hast redeemed us to God by [his] blood' (Rev. 5:9), and it also pictures 'a pure river of water of life, clear as crystal, proceeding out of the throne of God and of the Lamb' (Rev. 22:1).

The supreme substitution – that of Christ for sinners – is traditionally qualified by the adjective 'penal'. Paul Wells aptly defines this kind of substitution:

> Penal substitution means that divine justice punishes sin in the substitute, which is the object of the judgment. It means that Christ acted for others in the sense of their liability to judgment, punishment, and retribution. Penal substitution wipes away sin, removes God's reason for anger against it, and lays the basis for a new relationship beyond condemnation and death.[45]

---

45. P. Wells, op. cit., 139.

God does not wipe away sin merely from some benevolent desire to do so; that would be unjust, because the debt of death must be paid. God can forgive sins because he has already punished them when he punished the substitute, Christ, for man's sins on the cross. God poured out his wrath on our sins when he poured out his wrath on his Son. Thus we can say that Christ's substitution was penal – it was his taking mankind's punishment in his own body and soul, so that there is now no more condemnation for those who are in him.

The biblical teaching of penal substitution, and objections to it, are discussed more fully in appendix [iii] to this chapter. Here we can simply note that in terms of I Peter 2:24, when Christ said, 'It is finished,' he was expressing his awareness as the God/man that he had completed the bearing of the divine penalty against human guilt and sin.

[iv] Ransom Price

Jesus himself speaks of his death as 'a ransom for many' (Mark 10:45). To modern readers, the term 'ransom' may not hold much meaning. However, in the ancient culture this term was common. Ransom is 'the securing of a release by the payment of a price'.[46] Wells states: 'Ransom was part of everyday experience with slavery and payment for the release of prisoners.'[47] Scripture, therefore, frequently refers to the death of Christ as the paying of a ransom price so that we sinners could be released from slavery to sin and death, and in doing so, uses the language of the market-place.

While a very few early Christian writers (such as Origen and Gregory of Nyssa) suggested that the ransom was paid to Satan, the church tradition in both East and West did not follow them.[48] Leading exponents of the doctrine of the atonement in the Middle Ages, such as Anselm and Thomas Aquinas, both denied it.[49] Aquinas answered this unbiblical theory as follows:

> Because, with regard to God, redemption was necessary for man's deliverance, but not with regard to the devil, the price had to be paid not to the devil, but to God. And therefore Christ is said to have paid the price of our redemption – His own precious blood – not to the devil, but to God.[50]

In other words, the devil has no legitimate authority over the human race, fallen or unfallen. God alone possesses total authority over all humanity and therefore the ransom is paid by God to himself, not to the usurper, Satan. As Bancroft writes so wonderfully:

> When Satan tempts me to despair
> And tells me of the guilt within,

---

46. John Murray, *Redemption Accomplished and Applied*, 42.

47. Paul Wells, op. cit., 109.

48. See ibid.

49. See Anselm, *Cur deus homo*, Book I, chapter 7; Aquinas, *Summa Theologica*, Part III, Question 48, Article 4.

50. Thomas Aquinas, S. T., III, Q. 48, Art. 4, Reply to Objection 3 (p. 319).

Upward I look and see Him there
Who made an end of all my sin.
Because the sinless Savior died
 My sinful soul is counted free.
For God the just is satisfied
To look on Him and pardon me.[51]

Roger Nicole relates the idea of ransom to a payment to liberate prisoners and also to the emancipation of slaves. He states:

There seems to be a close parallelism in the usage of Scripture. Christ redeemed us from the curse of the law (Gal. 3:13; 4:5), from the guilt of sin (Rom. 3:24; Eph. 1:7; Col. 1:14; Heb. 9:12, 15), and from the power of evil manifest in the corruption of man's nature and in his vain manner of life (Titus 2:14; I Pet. 1:18; cf. passages where man's natural condition is compared to slavery [John 8:34; Rom. 6:17; 7:14]). Sin, original and actual, produces a twofold baneful effect upon man's life and nature: guilt and pollution. To this, in the marvelous purpose of God, corresponds a twofold blessing of redeeming grace: deliverance from guilt or justification; and renewal of nature, or regeneration, carried out in sanctification and glorification.[52]

In other words, the use of commercially based terms such as 'ransom' is in no sense unworthy of Scripture or of theological accounts of the atonement, based upon Scripture. The Bible constantly uses concepts taken from the everyday world that we can understand, as we see in the parables of such as Amos, Isaiah, Jeremiah and above all, Christ. Ransom is one of these worldly terms that we can make some sense of, and so the Holy Spirit guided the writers of the Scriptures to use it, in order to open more clearly for us limited humans the nature of Christ's atonement.

More details on the biblical texts relating to ransom are provided in the appendix to this chapter. We simply note here that Christ must have seen his death on the cross as having paid the ransom price he came to provide, as he said in Mark 10:45. His cry 'It is finished' meant that the ransom had been paid.

[v] Victorious Battle

The apostle John gives a major reason for the coming of the Son of God into the flesh in terms of his entering into *victorious battle against evil powers*: 'For this purpose the Son of God was manifested, that he might destroy the works of the devil' (I John 3:8). This dominical defeating of Satan worked by stages in the ministry of the incarnate Lord.

Christ overcame the devil in the wilderness temptations at the beginning of his public ministry, and soon thereafter was recognized and 'confessed' by the demons he cast out of the sick and afflicted (as we especially see in the Gospel of Mark). After the seventy returned from their successful mission in his name and power, Jesus exclaimed: 'I saw

---

51. Charitie Less Bancroft, *Before the Throne of God Above*, 1863.

52. Roger Nicole, *Standing Forth: Collected Writings of Roger Nicole* (Fearn, Ross-shire: Christian Focus Publications, 2002), 'The Nature of Redemption,' 256-57.

Satan fall like lightning' (Luke 10:18). That is to say, Satan's defeat at the hands of Christ (as we see in the early chapters of Mark when Christ casts out demons and they know who he is), is now expanded into the mission of the seventy disciples. Satan is now shown to be on the losing side, both to Christ and to his church. Satan entered into Judas Iscariot in his final battle against the incarnate Christ after the Last Supper, and then did his worst to defeat the Kingdom of God by crucifying its King.

But Jesus knew that the death he chose to die for the Father's honor and the church's salvation would very soon administer a substantial defeat to the evil one and his malign kingdom. That principal destruction of 'the works of the devil' would be wide-ranging, including (1) in heaven, (2) on earth, and (3) in the realm of departed spirits ('hell' or 'sheol').

(1) The victorious death of Christ on Calvary removed Satan from the once-privileged position he held to 'accuse the brethren' before God (as he had been able to do in the experience of Job – cf. Job 1:6-12). Possibly this is reflected in Luke 10:18 (immediately above). But the exegetical evidence for this is not very strong; it is something we 'overhear', rather than being directly taught. It is not a part of the doctrinal centralities of the faith, although there seems definitely something to it, as may be suggested by such a verse as 'And having made peace through the blood of his cross, by him to reconcile all things unto himself; by him, I say, whether they be things in earth, or things in heaven' (Col. 1:20). The previous verse (19) states that 'in all things he might have the preeminence,' and this would include the subjugation of Satan.

What is exegetically more definite is that Christ's victorious death also severely weakened Satan's power to hold the pagan nations in slavery. That is reflected in symbolic form in Revelation 20:1-3, where Satan is bound 'a thousand years', and shut up 'that he should deceive the nations no more till the thousand years should be fulfilled'. Only in this chapter of Revelation is the word 'millennium' used in Scripture. 'In terms of biblical numbers, ten is the image for fullness and a thousand is ten times ten times ten, so fullness times fullness times fullness equals a vast number of years, without being a precise chronology of human history.'[53] It seems that we are in accordance with the rest of the scriptural teaching on the future to hold that 'millennium' really refers to the time between the first and the second comings of Christ, the time when the Church reaches the world with the gospel mission given her by the risen Lord. During this long and indefinite period, the devil is no longer able to blind the nations.

> Satan no longer possesses the same amount of power over the nations after Jesus' historic victory. That is why even in Jesus' lifetime when he sent out the seventy, he did not send them to the Gentiles or 'the nations.' Why not? Why…only to the lost sheep of the house of Israel? Because Satan had not yet been bound in his authority to deceive the Gentile nations. But after Jesus was crucified the outpoured, infinite Spirit has limited Satan, so that he can no longer keep the heathen nations from being able to receive the truth.[54]

---

53. Douglas F. Kelly, *Revelation: A Sermon Commentary: The Angels Are Already Singing* (Mentor: Christian Focus Publications: Fearn, Ross-shire, 2011), 380.

54. Ibid., 381.

Thus in Matthew 12:28-29, Jesus says: 'But if I cast out devils by the Spirit of God, then the kingdom of God is come unto you. Or else how can one enter into a strong man's house, and spoil his goods, except he first bind the strong man? and then he will spoil his house.'

'One of the great effects of Christ's coming is to bind the strong man... He defeats him in principle, until that final day when he will defeat him not only in principle, but totally in every way.'[55] The victorious defeat of the nation-blinder, Satan, by Christ on the cross is what has made the missionary expansion of Christianity possible for the last two thousand years.

(2) Christ's death won the victory over proud and hateful Satan, who somehow or other took pleasure in every human death since he lied to our first parents about the reality of death (Gen. 3:4). But now, according to Hebrews 2, the tables are turned on the murderous hater of the image of God: 'Forasmuch then as the children are partakers of flesh and blood, he also himself likewise took part of the same; that through death he might destroy him that had the power of death, that is the devil; And deliver them who through fear of death were all their lifetime subject to bondage' (Heb. 2:14-15).

In the death (and resurrection) of Christ, Satan was dealt such a blow that his power was so severely reduced that he is no longer able to terrify God's people with the prospects of death, as he had done formerly. Hence Paul could write: 'For all things are yours; whether Paul, or Apollos, or Cephas, or the world, or life, or death, or things present or things to come; all are yours, and ye are Christ's and Christ is God's' (I Cor. 3:21-22). Paul is saying that because of what Christ has done, even 'death is ours': that is, by the cross and empty tomb, death has been transmuted from a frightful enemy awaiting us on the other side of our deathbed, to a subdued 'door-keeper', who has to bow his head as we pass through into our Father's house of light.

Paul gives us the same truth from a slightly different perspective in Romans 8: 'For I am persuaded that neither death, nor life...nor any other creature shall be able to separate us from the love of God, which is in Christ Jesus our Lord' (vv. 38, 39). Death does not drag us down into darkness, away from God; it is now only a door through which we pass into the fuller light and love of Christ: 'having a desire to depart, and to be with Christ; which is far better'(Phil. 1:23). The death of Christ on Calvary triumphantly accomplished this change in the nature of death for every believer.

John Calvin comments on Christ's deliverance of those 'who through fear of death were subject to lifelong bondage' (Heb. 2:15):

> He had, therefore, to conquer that fear which by nature continually torments and oppresses all mortals. This he could do only by fighting it. Now it will soon be more apparent that his was no common sorrow or one engendered by a light cause. Therefore, by his wrestling hand to hand with the devil's power, with the dread of death, with the pain of hell, he was victorious and triumphed over them, that in death we may not now fear those things which our Prince has swallowed up [cf. I Peter 3:22, Vg.].[56]

---

55. Ibid.

56. John Calvin, *Institutes* II. xvi. 11 (Battles translation).

Not only does Christ's death change our death, and break our fear of it, it also cleanses our consciences during the whole of this earthly life, so that we may with confidence and joy serve the living God: 'How much more shall the blood of Christ, who through the eternal Spirit offered himself without spot to God, purge your conscience from dead works to serve the living God?' (Heb. 9:14). It means that we may 'present our bodies a living sacrifice, holy, acceptable unto God,' and that we live in light of a higher world, so that 'we are transformed by the renewing of our mind, that we may prove what is that good, and acceptable, and perfect will of God' (Rom. 12:1-2).

(3) Christ's sacrifice on Calvary involved his crashing through the gates of hell, and breaking down its dread power, presumably sometime after his cry of dereliction, when he takes on the second death. Most of this victorious battle is hidden from our eyes, but it is alluded to in Colossians 2:14-15: 'Blotting out the handwriting of ordinances that was against us, which was contrary to us, and took it out of the way, nailing it to his cross; and having spoiled principalities and powers, he made a show of them openly, triumphing over them in it.'

K. Schilder describes, as well as any, what is ultimately indescribable:

> And when Christ in that darkness felt Himself called upon to begin the last arduous struggle, He entered into the battlefield and He sought out death and the devil in their own home. The result of that? Well, if the advent of the darkness for Christ spells that moment in which God according to justice sends Him into the worst of devastation, then the moment in which light breaks through again and the darkness recedes, must be an objective testimony to Him that God regards the struggle as having been satisfactorily finished...God Himself draws Him up out of it [i.e. hell] when He again sends light down upon Golgotha...[T]his new advent of the light is evidence to Him that God acknowledges Him as the Worker and Second Adam justified in reference to His last arduous struggle, the passion of the pain of hell.[57]

D. Staniloae of Romania expands these thoughts on what some (in the West) have called the Lord's 'harrowing of hell':

> That Christ was not raised as an object from a death that would have reduced him to complete powerlessness is explained by the Holy Fathers in the fact that he had manifested his power even before the Resurrection of the body in tearing down the gates of hell and in the liberation from there of those who had hope before his coming. He conquers hell with his human soul united with the Godhead. Because of this, he is the first soul that cannot be held in hell, but escapes it. By the irradiation of his divine power, he liberates from hell the souls of those who had believed beforehand in the promises of his coming, of those who had contemplated in the Logos foretold in the Old Testament the intention of his coming into the body. Leontius of Byzantium says, 'Therefore we said that the soul, not because of its nature (for this was the same as that of all the other souls), but because of the Word's Godhead with which he descended into hell, was – in addition to not being held in there – able to break the ties of those held there and who believed in

---

57. K. Schilder, *Christ Crucified*, 431-432.

him.'[58] The Person of the Word who entered through his soul into a direct relationship with those souls has kept them in this relationship, thus in the paradise he has established for them and for all those who will die in him.[59]

This typically Eastern (and Western) Catholic view of Christ's triumphal descent into hell differs from the one we have been offering (in the train of Calvin), in that Calvin, following the order of the seven words on the cross, holds that Christ descended into hell while still on the cross (after the cry of dereliction), and that he came back just before he released his spirit to the Father. But Staniloae and much of both Eastern and Western Catholic churches hold that he did so only after the actual death of his body. This will be discussed near the end of this chapter under 'He descended into hell.' Either way – in terms of whether it occurred while he was still hanging on the cross (and I argue for the way pointed out by Calvin), or whether it occurred after his physical death – the actual results are not finally dissimilar: hell was torn open by the God/man, and 'the strong man' was forcibly bound; hell was not the same after Christ entered it. The evil one suffered a massive defeat on his own territory.

Dr. Thomas Goodwin may be reading back into what happened too much of legal procedure, and yet his essential point seems to be valid:

> And here comes now to be inquired into the just ground upon which it came to pass, that through or by Christ's death Satan should be bereft of that power which he had...And to be sure he lost it upon Christ's death upon a far more fair and legal right than at first or than ever it was given to him: Isa. xlix. 23, 25 it is thus written, 'Shall the prey be taken from the mighty, or the lawful captive delivered? But thus said the Lord, Even the captives of the mighty shall be taken away, and the prey of the terrible shall be delivered: for I will contend with him that contendeth with thee,' etc. Be it literally spoken of Babylon's captivity and redemption, or whatever else, yet this is certain, that that and other were shadows of this of ours by Christ, and therefore applicable in the general thereunto. Now, how far we were lawful captives unto Satan you heard, and God (though the devil be his enemy) will overcome him fairly: *non vi sed justitia*, not by force only, but in justice. 'The lawful captives' (as it is in Isa.) shall be delivered, and that lawfully. It is also a rule fetched from the law of arms, and concertations in games or the like, that 'if a man strive for masteries, he is not crowned' (and so is not reckoned to overcome) 'unless he strive lawfully,' 2 Tim. ii.5.
>
> The truth is, first, that Satan ran into a *praemunire*, or a forfeiture of all his power, by his assailing of Christ (and if there were no other ground, it were sufficient for the loss of all); he in assailing of Christ, and plotting and contriving his death, went beyond his commission, and God on purpose permitted him to do it, to catch him in his snare. Satan's power over sinful man was not a natural, but an accidental, judicial power, and so perfectly limited by commission, which, if he exceeded, especially if so transcendentally (as it fell out in this), he instantly made a forfeiture of it. Know this, then, that Satan's power was over sinful man only; he was not so much as to touch or come near the man Jesus, who was 'holy and harmless, and separate from

58. Leontius of Byzantium, *Contra Nest. et Eutych.* [PG 86b: 1341c].

59. D. Staniloae, op. cit., vol. 3, 250, 251.

sinners.' Now, he coming into the world 'in the likeness of sinful flesh,' Rom. viii., this lion, that 'seeks whom he may devour,' boldly ventures on him, and persecutes him to death; for it was Satan that contrived Christ's death: 'This is the hour,' saith Christ, 'and the power of darkness,' Luke xxii. 53... But more expressly, John viii. 40, 41, 'You seek to kill me;' 'you do the deeds of your father therein, who was a murderer from the beginning,' ver. 44. And Christ seems to give a hint of this very reason: John xiv. 30, 'The prince of this world comes, and hath nothing in me,' as matter for him, by virtue of which he should have authority to have anything to do with me. The devil thus foolishly and sillily lost all, and God took the wise in his own craftiness; and Christ suffered him to go on and to have his whole will upon him, but then took him thereby captive at his will. So God in his righteous judgment ordered that Satan should lose the power that he had, because he exercised that upon Christ which he had not.[60]

Goodwin here asserts that Christ conquered Satan justly, and that Satan was not denied any right, because Satan had no right over the sinless Christ.

Although we are dealing here with a profound mystery, it seems likely that the saints whose graves were opened at the very time Christ was crucified, and were seen in Jerusalem three days after Christ's resurrection, according to Matthew 27:51-53, were the first-fruits of this 'harrowing of hell'. Schilder renders a reasonable opinion on what their resurrection in conjunction with the crucifixion and resurrection means, as evidence of the life-giving power of Christ's death:

They who are here, however, arise from the dead when Christ dies, and may remain here until after His glad Passover day. Thus they establish a relationship between Christ's death and resurrection, preaching the unity which exists between His state of humiliation and His state of glorification... But this great Dead calls other dead *out* of the grave. In Him the area belonging to death grows smaller, ever smaller....Presently they departed from the earthly life again. How? Only God knows. So much is certain: when they re-entered heaven everything there had changed. It was far more glorious than it had ever been. Up to this time the greatest glory of being there had been to lie in Abraham's bosom. Now the greatest honor is to lie in Jesus' bosom as a beloved disciple and to sit at His holy supper as a trusted guest.[61]

Although the general idea of Schilder is correct, a careful reading of Matthew 27:52-53 does not indicate that the saints, who were buried in Jerusalem, were raised immediately from the dead when Jesus died, and the earthquake occurred. The text states that their graves were split open by that quake, but these resurrected saints do not appear until *after Christ himself* was raised, for he is 'the firstfruits of them that slept' (I Cor. 15:20). It was *after* Christ's resurrection that these saints came out of their graves and were seen in Jerusalem. J. W. Wenham plausibly suggests that a period (or full stop) should be placed, not after 'the rocks rent' (in v. 51), but after

60. Thomas Goodwin, *op. cit.*, vol. 5, 303, 304.

61. K. Schilder, op. cit., 525, 526, 527.

'the graves were opened' (in v. 52). Then it is clear that they came out 'after his resurrection' (in v. 53).[62]

In the appendix to this chapter, we look at the rather uneven work of Gustaf Aulen on *Christus Victor* – useful, but needing supplementation. There we also consider the significant connection that N. T. Wright draws between Israel's hope of the victory of the LORD, and what Christ 'in the fullness of the time' provided in his victory on the cross.

[vi] Supreme Moral Example of Devout Suffering

When the Lord Jesus says, 'It is finished,' among other accomplishments, he has provided the supreme illustration of utterly selfless obedience to the honor of God and the salvation of fallen humankind. Surely, he knowingly left us an example to follow, as the Apostle Peter indicates: 'Who his own self bare our sins in his own body on the tree, that we, being dead to sins, should live unto righteousness: by whose stripes ye were healed' (I Peter 2:24). He must have had this in mind in his frequent calls to his disciples to 'take up your cross and follow me' (e.g. Matt. 10:38; 16:24; Mark 8:34; Luke 9:23; 14:27, etc.).

This victory through holy suffering, so strange to the categories of proud human thought, is the Lord's appointed way, not only for his own victory on Calvary, but also for that of his servants in all years to come: they too shall triumph through sharing, in their own way, in his devout willingness to suffer for righteousness' sake. That is indicated as being one of the underlying factors of the holy martyrs, who overcame 'the accuser of the brethren' in the Apocalypse: 'And they overcame him by the blood of the Lamb, and by the word of their testimony, and they loved not their lives unto the death' (Rev. 12:11). It fulfills what Christ taught all his people in the Beatitudes: 'Blessed are they which are persecuted for righteousness' sake; for theirs is the kingdom of heaven' (Matt. 5:10).

But these calls to follow Christ as our example of supreme obedience and highest love are in the context of our union with Christ as the mainspring of the Christian life, rather than being the appointed way to receive salvation, as R. A. Peterson has pointed out.[63] These aspects of the Christian life are profoundly and inextricably interconnected, but one (Christ's atoning death) is *the root* of our salvation, while our sharing his holy example is *the fruit* of it.

Nonetheless, it is both valid and necessary to consider Christ's self-offering to the Father on the cross as one aspect of the atonement he made for his people. But it cannot be taken as primary, for in terms of sheer number of passages in both Old and New Testaments, some kind of sacrificial and substitutionary model is predominant. And also it cannot be taken alone as the sole explanation of the atonement, for as Paul Wells says, commenting on theories that the primary purpose of Christ's death is the melting influence it has on mankind:

---

62. J. W. Wenham, 'When were the Saints Raised?' in JTS 32 [1981]: 150-152.

63. R. A. Peterson, *Calvin and the Atonement* (Fearn, Ross-shire: Christian Focus, 1999), chapter 9.

The problem with these propositions does not lie in their exemplary emphasis. The cross *is* God's supreme demonstration of love. It lies in their reduction of the meaning of the cross to one of its aspects and in the distance they take from the biblical teaching about sacrifice as a whole.[64]

The exemplary-love model, valid and powerful as it is when held in combination with other biblical aspects, cannot – without the help of the others – even begin to plumb either the depths of the massive gulf between sinners and a holy God that was wrought by sin, *nor* the massive love that bridged it through the love of God in Christ. J. I. Packer shows why not:

> It is assumed that our basic need is lack of motivation Godward and of openness to the inflow of divine life; all that is needed to set us in a right relationship with God is a change in us at these two points, and this Christ's life brings about. The forgiveness of our sins is not a separate problem; as soon as we are changed we become forgivable, and are then forgiven at once. This view has little or no room for any thought of substitution, since it goes so far in equating what Christ did *for* us with what he does *to* us.[65]

Packer is saying here that an understanding of the Christian life as one of imitating Christ's loving example is deficient in the way that it deals with our sins. Where the life of Christ only changes what is within us, we still have to deal with what is external to us – an offended God, a broken relationship, and a debt that we owe. However, an understanding of the Christian life as one in which we are justified because of the substitutionary sacrifice of Christ on the cross answers to man's deepest need by restoring us into a right relationship with God, the relationship that we had broken by our sin. Christ was not merely exemplifying how to love; he was changing our relationship with God by substituting himself in our place so that we would be *able* to love.

In the appendix to this chapter, we look very briefly at the most famous exponent of the cross as the exemplification of love, Abelard (1079-1142). Here it is sufficient to state that no small part of the victory that sounded through the voice of the crucified Christ lay in knowing that 'he had finished' setting the absolutely ultimate example of obedience to God and victory over the world.

[vii] Justification

Christ's cry 'It is finished' indicated that by his infinite sufferings to the point of death he was justifying his people from their sins. T. F. Torrance points out that in chapter 3 of Romans, Saint Paul 'expounds the doctrine of the atonement first in terms of *justification* and then a little later in the epistle... in terms of *reconciliation*.'[66]

---

64. P. Wells, op. cit., 124.

65. James I. Packer, 'What did the Cross Achieve? The Logic of Penal Substitution' in *Tyndale Bulletin* 25/1974, 19-20.

66. T. F. Torrance, *Atonement*, 99.

In Jesus Christ, God has intervened decisively in the moral impasse of humanity, doing a deed that humanity could not do itself... The result was, as Paul put it bluntly, the 'justification of the ungodly,' an act in which man, in spite of sin, is put fully in the right with God, and it is such a total and final act that men and women are no longer required to achieve justification by themselves to save themselves before God. They enter into justification through Christ's death, and accept it as a sheer gift of God's grace which is actualised in them as reality and truth.[67]

Torrance answers the question of questions: 'How can God be just and the justifier of the ungodly?' 'The answer is to be found in the death of Christ where God has wrought a double deed in which he has at last meted out upon sin its complete condemnation, and yet one in which in his grace he justifies man, and so in both God justifies himself.'[68]

The main Old and New Testament words lying behind 'justification' are discussed in the Appendix to this chapter. And there we will see how they are fulfilled in Christ's finished work on the cross.

A nineteenth century English evangelical once said it this way:

When Christ was crucified,
the Law was magnified,
sinners were justified,
and God was glorified![69]

[viii] Reconciliation

Both Romans 5:9-11 and II Corinthians 5:14-21 speak of Christ's finished work on the cross as 'reconciliation'. In Romans 5:9-10, Paul explains 'justified by Christ's blood' as being 'reconciled to God through the death of his Son.' As John Murray writes: 'Reconciliation presupposes disrupted relations between God and men. It implies enmity and alienation.'[70]

But does God need 'reconciling', or is it only sinful mankind who needs it? It is true that nowhere does Paul say that God needs to be reconciled; he uses that word for fallen humankind. It is certainly the case that in no sense does God ever need to be conditioned into loving us and bestowing grace upon us, for 'God is love' (I John 4:8), and it was because of this love that he sent his Son (John 3:16).

Samuel Rutherford stated this point clearly:

If God should begin at any point in time to love sinners, his love would have had a beginning. Christ himself would have had a beginning, because love with him is one with his essence and nature...and therefore we are said in Scripture 'to be reconciled to God', and not God to be reconciled unto us. His love is everlasting.[71]

---

67. Ibid., 107.

68. Ibid., 109.

69. The appropriation of justification by the believer will be discussed in volume 3 of this series.

70. John Murray, op. cit., 33.

71. Samuel Rutherford, *Fourteen Communion Sermons*, ed. A. A. Bonar, 2nd ed. (Glasgow, 1877),

So while scripture does not speak of God needing to be reconciled, it does speak of his enmity against sin. Leon Morris rightly notes: 'We conclude then that the biblical teaching on ἐχθρος and ἐχθρα taken in conjunction with the wider biblical teaching on the wrath of God indicates that there is a very real hostility on the part of God to all that is evil, and that this hostility is not incompatible with a deep love of God for sinners.'[72]

Later, Morris provides, in my view, a balanced answer as to the connection of God with reconciliation:

> ...reconciliation in the case of man comes about from outside. God was reconciling the world to Himself. But we cannot say that God was reconciled by any third party; rather He must be thought of as reconciling Himself. Even to say that Christ reconciled God does not give us the true picture; for it suggests a dichotomy in the Godhead and also raises a doubt as to the constancy of God's love. But we must insist that God's love for us remained unchanged throughout the process of reconciliation...God's love never varied. But the atonement wrought by Christ means that men are no longer treated as enemies (as their sin deserves), but as friends. God has reconciled Himself.[73]

Or, as we saw under 'propitiation', God cannot deny his holy character. If he declared sinners to be righteous while they remained in their fallen state, it would be a denial of his integrity. Therefore he finds a way to maintain that holy integrity which is the stability of the universe, and at the same time to extend his pardoning grace to sinners, which is precisely what was accomplished when he reconciled the world to himself in the substitutionary death of his Son.

The wonder of it all is that God the Father already loved us before he sent his Son to reconcile us to himself. The great Puritan Thomas Goodwin captures this reality in the unusual phrase 'he secretly bore good will to us':

> Therefore, in Eph. i. 9, we are said to be 'graciously accepted in him, as the beloved one of his Father,' as it is there. And though he secretly bore good will to us before, yet in that his beloved, he hath *made* us graciously accepted, made way for owning us, and shining graciously upon us, in and through him, whereas without him, he would never have afforded us one good look.[74]

(7) 'Father, into thy hands I commend my spirit' (Luke 23:46)

Christ's last word from the cross takes up Psalm 31:5, 7, 8: 'Into thine hand I commit my spirit: thou hast redeemed me, O LORD God of truth...I will be glad and rejoice in thy mercy; for thou hast considered my trouble; thou hast known my soul in adversities; And hast not shut me up into the hand of the enemy: thou hast set my feet in a large room.'

236.

72. Leon Morris, op. cit., 197-198.

73. Ibid., 220.

74. Thomas Goodwin, op. cit., vol. V, 510.

This inspired quotation is not, as K. Schilder has pointed out, a 'typical *dying utterance*.'[75] On the contrary, 'The person who is speaking here, is a man standing in the midst of life, who is rejoicing in the day of His deliverance. He is not a man standing in the narrow gate of death, in the cleft of the rock of His dying, for – He has just been set in a large place.'[76]

Verse 15 of this 31st Psalm opens a window into what is happening in the seventh utterance from the cross: 'My times are in thy hand.' Schilder states: 'This translated into the language of fulfillment means: 'My Passover seasons are in Thy hand.' Just as the poet of Psalm 31 at bottom wishes to say that he is going to continue on his way with his eyes fastened on God, so Christ calls from the cross: I shall simply go on, my eyes fixed upon God.'[77]

His feet are now, indeed, in 'a large room' (Ps. 31:8), for he has come back out of the narrow, restricting horrors of hell, having suffered there all he needed to suffer to redeem his people, and having changed hell, as it 'took on too much, in taking on Jesus of Nazareth' (to paraphrase a line I once heard from Dr. James S. Stewart). Similarly, K. Schilder writes:

> A great significance lies in the fact that Christ utters a word of life in His dying hour, for He confesses by that means that He is already in the ascendancy. He professes in this way that He is already emerging from the lowest shafts of humiliation, and that He, having arisen from 'the second death,' now is already ascending to heaven. On His way from hell to heaven, He must do what every pilgrim does: He strengthens Himself in His God, confesses His God, and performs the act of the moment.[78]

In other words, Christ has gone through the second death after his cry of dereliction; he has overcome it, and now is prepared to release his spirit so as to die the first death. The second death is the ultimate consequence of guilt: eternal separation from God. Having gone through it, and as an infinite person, having conquered it, he returns in order to experience the first death, which is temporary separation of body and personality, or spirit. Thus, he completes the payment of the full wages of sin upon all mankind: first and second deaths.

It is time, therefore, for him to release his spirit from his body back up to the heavenly Father. It would appear that his last statement, dismissing his spirit, would have come near the end of the period of three hours of darkness that lasted from noon till 3:00 p.m. Spirit 'means not only natural life, but everything in Him that is conscious, that has a will, that motivates Him…consequently…He commends Himself to the Father with His whole conscious life, with His whole mind, and with all His motive powers and drives.'[79] Schilder adds:

75. K. Schilder, op. cit., vol. 3, 471.

76. Ibid.

77. Ibid., 474.

78. Ibid., 481.

79. Ibid., 476.

> He gave Himself up completely. In the book of Ecclesiastes dying is called the returning of the spirit to God who gave it. This is also the thing of primary importance in the death of Christ. However, there is this difference now: His returning was His own deed. He did His returning in the spirit. His spirit moved Him to return.[80]

> Therefore Christ now surrenders His spirit. He does not give it away indiscriminately, but gives it to the Father. He addresses Himself to Paradise... The Saviour enters into the other world, is instantaneously withdrawn from the bourne of time and space, enters into captivity, for all this is implied in dying. Nevertheless He moved about freely in God's universe. He is the man who has fought His way to freedom. The binding which accrues to Him in this instant of time really represents an unbinding.[81]

Although we cannot see into that other world to which the Lord dismissed his spirit, we know that he did not go there alone. Luke 23:43 tells us that he took with him the penitent criminal into the presence of the Father. And in due season, he will take the rest of us sinners there, if we trust in him.

Earthquake and rending of the veil of the Temple

Matthew 27:51 indicates that immediately after Jesus released his spirit, there was an earthquake, of which the violence both split rocks and – most significantly – 'rent the veil of the temple in twain from the top to the bottom' (cf. Mark 15:38; Luke 23:45). The temple (and tabernacle before it) was divided into three parts: the outer court, the holy place, and the holy of holies. This thick veil separated the holy place from the holy of holies, into which only the high priest might enter once a year on the day of atonement (cf. Exod. 26:31; Lev. 16:1-30), from the holy place.

Before the Babylonian captivity, the Ark of the Covenant, with its mercy seat on to which the blood of atonement was sprinkled each year, had rested, unobserved to any but the high priest, in this holy place. In the Ark was the holy Law, and upon the mercy seat which covered it, the blood of sacrifice was offered to cover the sins of the people for yet another year. This place was so holy that the carved cherubim at each end of that mercy seat had to veil their faces with their wings.

In Hebrews 10:20 the body of Christ is made symbolically equivalent to the rent veil, which opens to us 'a new and living way' into the holiest place in heaven 'by the blood of Jesus' (Heb. 10:19). All other offerings before his were preliminary, and thus had to be constantly repeated, but this one is final: 'once for all'(Heb. 10:10-12). Upon releasing his spirit, once his holy and all-sufficient sacrifice had been completed, Christ went into the holy places in heaven, for it was these upon which the earthly holy places were modeled (Heb. 9:23-28).

Because of his appearance in heaven for us, which confirms our eternal redemption (Heb. 9:12), the same eternal Spirit, through whom he offered

---

80. Ibid., 486.

81. Ibid., 499.

himself without spot to God, purges our consciences that we may serve the living God with lively works (Heb. 9:14), engendered by our vital union with him (cf. Rom. 6:3-10). Hence we may offer all the faculties of our beings 'as instruments of righteousness unto God' (Rom. 6:13). Thus, Christ's one final offering, sealed as he releases his spirit to the Father, constantly begets the unending response of countless offerings of his people down to the end of time, so that for them 'to live is Christ' (cf. Phil 1:21).

Therefore, for security of the knowledge that we are always accepted by God, and for the cordial acceptance of our otherwise imperfect works, we may continually resort to the one who in dismissing his spirit, betook himself to the Father, there always to intercede for us:

> Seeing then that we have a great high priest, that is passed into the heavens, Jesus the Son of God, let us hold fast our profession. For we have not an high priest which cannot be touched with the feeling of our infirmities; but was in all points tempted like as we are, yet without sin. Let us therefore come boldly unto the throne of grace, that we may obtain mercy, and find grace to help in time of need (Heb. 4:14-16).

The Confession of the Roman Centurion at the Cross

'Now when the centurion saw what was done, he glorified God, saying, Certainly this was a righteous man...' (Luke 23:47). According to Mark 15:39, he said: 'Truly this man was the Son of God.' We do not know exactly what he meant. Schilder is correct as to the Greek grammar:

> In the original both the word god (the Greek language of the manuscripts has not capital letters) and the word son is used without the definite article. A son of a god, that is what is written. This is a very different statement from the one Simon Peter makes to Jesus. Thou art the Son of the (our) God, the living One (Matthew 16). There the definite article is included before the word 'Son' as well as before the word 'God.' Hence, if we read the text carefully, and do not assume more about this pagan man than what we actually know, we can say nothing about him except that he said: Truly, this was a son of a god. Even the paganism of that day had not completely lost the faith of former days which acknowledged the possibility of supernatural beings, children of the gods, special bearers of special qualifications...The great calm, the mastery, the absence of all that was bitter and ugly, the triumphant trust in God, all this had caused him to reflect...We might say that he had studied Jesus and that he could not rid himself of the impression that Jesus had not lost His life, but that He had surrendered it by an act of His will.[82]

We cannot definitely affirm, therefore, that the Roman centurion at the cross had understood enough to be converted, though we certainly need not deny the possibility. It probably does not take very much understanding, or very many words, in the presence of the dying Christ to be grasped by his saving power. The penitent thief presumably did not know a great deal about the Lord beside whom he was dying, nor was

---

82. Ibid., 532-534.

his request eloquent; yet Christ took him along with himself into heaven. The outcry of the Roman soldier at the cross may well indicate at least a mustard-seed faith.

But what this Roman soldier said does appear to be an instance of Satan's losing his power totally to blind the pagan nations as to who Christ is. It may well be an early illustration of 'the seed of the woman' bruising the head of the evil one, even in the moment of the bruising of his own heel (cf. Gen. 3:15). It is, as far as it goes, a picture of what Jesus had predicted of his passion: 'Now is the judgment of this world: now shall the prince of this world be cast out. And I, if I be lifted up from the earth, will draw all men unto me. This he said, signifying what death he should die' (John 12:31-33).

I believe that his somewhat inchoate confession is already an instance of what will happen in thorough fashion and endless quantity among countless millions between Christ's first and second comings: the binding of Satan over the long-closed minds of the heathen.

> And I saw an angel come down from heaven, having the key of the bottomless pit and a great chain in his hand. And he laid hold on the dragon, that old serpent, which is the Devil, and Satan, and bound him a thousand years, And cast him into the bottomless pit, and shut him up, and set a seal upon him, that he should deceive the nations no more, till the thousand years should be fulfilled: and after that he must be loosed a little season (Rev. 20:1-3).

His Burial

The burial of the abused body of Jesus shows that he was truly dead. The Jewish authorities did not wish the bodies of any of the crucified malefactors to be left hanging on their crosses, since the next day was a Sabbath: 'And if a man have committed a sin worthy of death, and he be put to death, thou shalt hang him on a tree: his body shall not remain all night upon the tree, but thou shalt in any wise bury him that day; (for he that is hanged is accursed of God;) that thy land be not defiled, which the Lord thy God giveth thee for an inheritance' (Deut. 21:22-23).

Water and Blood

If the Romans needed to finish the work of crucifixion within a few hours, then in some cases they used the *crurifragium*; that is, they used heavy instruments to break the bones in order to dispatch the onset of death. They did so with the two criminals on either side of Jesus, but this was not necessary in the instance of Jesus, for they saw that he had already died (John 19:32-33). But in order to have official proof of his death, one of the soldiers thrust a spear into Jesus' side, and immediately blood and water flowed out of the wound (John 19:34). Apparently this separation of blood from the thin, watery serum (or 'water') was evidence of massive clotting of the blood, and the beginning of its breakdown into its constituent elements: hence, proof of the forces of physical death already at work.

No Bones Broken

John states that the preservation of the bones of the Lamb of God from being broken by the soldiers was not a mere coincidence of history; it was another fulfillment of Old Testament prophecy, as was their piercing of him: 'For these things were done that the scriptures should be fulfilled, A bone of him shall not be broken. And again, another scripture saith, They shall look on him whom they pierced' (John 19:36-37).

Preservation from the breaking of the bones of the supreme sacrifice is predicted in Exodus 12:46, where in the Passover instructions for the sacrificial lamb, Israel is instructed: '...neither shall ye break a bone thereof.' And in Numbers 9:12, concerning the Passover: 'They shall leave none of it unto the morning, nor break any bone of it...' There is also a reference to it in Psalm 34:19-20: 'Many are the afflictions of the righteous: but the LORD delivereth him out of them all. He keepeth all their bones: not one of them is broken.'

> According to his body, also, Jesus walked under the protection of special providence. After His resurrection, too, that body...should by a special act of God's power have to retain the stigmata of His wounds...a special providence of God is anxiously watchful of the body of Christ. And hence God prevented the bones of His Righteous One from being broken. His body had a future; it had a purpose, even in its wounds, in its stigmata, for the church of the Passover. God spared the holy lamb of the sacrifice arbitrariness and accident, all meaningless suffering, all alogical humiliation...In the fact that Christ after His resurrection still bears the tokens of the wounds in His body (think of Thomas) we cannot see the natural result of Jesus' being wounded (for the body of the resurrection has its own law of existence), but an effect of Jesus' will. God wanted this preservation of the stigmata – of the wounds – in Christ's body.[83]

The executioner's gaze upon the Christ whom he had pierced with his spear, proving that he was dead, which had been long before predicted in Zechariah 12:10, is found in the context of the many in future Israel who will move from unbelief in the Messiah, to profound sorrow and grief over what the nation did to him, as they see who he is and put all their trust in him. Massive mourning will characterize the once unbelieving nation (Zech. 12:11-14), and it will be followed by 'a fountain opened to the house of David and to the inhabitants of Jerusalem for sin and for uncleanness' (Zech. 13:1). The plunging of many formerly unbelieving Jews into that fountain would occur soon after Calvary and the empty tomb, on the day of Pentecost.

The good offices of Joseph of Arimathaea and Nicodemus

Two of the great leaders of the Jewish nation, Joseph of Arimathaea and Nicodemus, with Pilate's permission, took charge of Christ's body and saw to its burial (John 19:38-39). As Schilder notes:

---

83. Ibid., 550-52.

The grave is an amen which the human being knows he must utter when death comes. The grave is a concealment; it takes away the unclean, the filthy; it is a public confession of the repulsiveness of what once in the creation was an adornment to us... Never had Christ been so concealed as now, never had divinity receded so far as now, never had He become so completely unknown to the sons of His mother as now. The discrepancy between the majesty of God and the body of the man Jesus was never as great as now.[84]

The important counselor Joseph of Arimathaea requested the body and provided his new tomb for its burial (John 19:38), and Nicodemus, another counselor as member of the same Sanhedrin, brought an expensive mixture in generous proportion of myrrh and aloes for the anointing of the deceased (John 19:39). No doubt, Schilder is correct to state that their burial of Christ was an act of confession, '[b]ut it was a confession of love rather than of faith.'[85] Nicodemus and Joseph were presumably no further along in expecting the soon bodily resurrection than were any other of the apostles and disciples.

Yet John's Gospel seems to laud the true love to Jesus that is shown in their willingness to come forward publicly to make arrangements for his decent burial. In the circumstances they did the best they could, and surely, what they did was in the worthy category of the woman who anointed him in the house of Simon the Leper. After she was criticized for the expensive ointment she poured on him, Jesus replied, 'Why trouble ye the woman? for she hath wrought a good work upon me...For in that she hath poured this ointment on my body, she did it for my burial' (Matt. 26:10-12). How highly Jesus thought of this action is seen in the prediction he makes about it: 'Verily I say unto you, Wheresoever this gospel shall be preached in the whole world, there shall also this, that this woman hath done, be told for a memorial of her' (Matt. 26:13).

Christ's burial constituted a low point in his humiliation (since his 'descent into hell' can be considered both as humiliation and exaltation, depending on one's point of view). The Scottish theologian John Dick wrote:

Our Redeemer stooped low indeed when he assumed our nature, but lower still when he submitted to be laid in the grave. This is the last degree of humiliation. All the glory of man is extinguished in the tomb...Who is this that occupies the sepulcher of Joseph? Is it a prophet or a king? No; it is greater than all prophets and kings, the Son of the living God, the Lord of heaven and earth; but there is nothing now to distinguish him from the meanest of the human race; the tongue which charmed thousands with its eloquence is mute, and the hand which controlled the powers of the visible and invisible world is unnerved. The shades of death have enveloped him, and silence reigns in his lonely abode.[86]

---

84. Ibid., 554-555.

85. Ibid., 557.

86. John Dick, *Lectures on Theology*, vol. III, second edition (Edinburgh: Oliver & Boyd, 1838), 175.

As Louis Berkhof noted, the burial of Christ both (1) provides proof of his physical death, and (2) 'removes the terrors of the grave for the redeemed and sanctifies the grave for them.'[87] No Christian goes to an unsanctified grave, for his or her Lord was there first, and rendered it a fit and safe place for their body. Therefore, our grave need never be dreaded.

The Puritan preacher John Flavel saw this with clear insight:

> … But the great end and reason of his internment was the *conquering of death* in its own dominion and territories; which victory over the grave furnished the saints with that triumphant ἐπινίκιον song of deliverance, I Cor. xv. 55. 'O death! where is thy sting? O grave! where is thy destruction?' Our graves would not be so sweet and comfortable to us, when we come to lie down in them, if Jesus had not lain there before us and for us. Death is a dragon, the grave its den; a place of dread and terror; but Christ goes into its den, there grapples with it, and for ever overcomes it; disarms it of all its terror; and not only makes it to cease to be *inimical*, but to become exceeding *beneficial* to the saints; a bed of rest, a perfumed bed; they do but go into Christ's bed, where he lay before them…
>
> Whenever you come to your graves, you shall find the enmity of the grave slain by Christ…Therefore, it is said, I Cor. iii. 21-22. 'Death is yours;'…there you shall find sweet rest in Jesus; be hurried, pained, troubled no more.[88]

No corruption in the grave

While he was in the tomb, his body did not experience the corruption that normally sets in upon physical death. The Westminster Confession of Faith (ch. VIII, 'Of the Mediator') affirms his lack of corruption: '…was crucified, and died; was buried, and remained under the power of death; yet saw no corruption' (par. 4).

The Apostle Peter in his Pentecostal sermon speaks of Christ's lack of subjection to corruption by quoting Psalm 16:10: 'Because thou wilt not leave my soul in hell, neither wilt thou suffer thine Holy One to see corruption' (Acts 2:27), and Paul refers to it in like manner in his sermon at Antioch in Pisidia, also quoting Psalm 16:10: 'But he whom God raised again, saw no corruption' (Acts 13:37).

John Calvin, in his *Commentary of Psalm 16* deals with this question:

> The question, however, may be asked, as Christ descended into the grave, was he not also subject to corruption? The answer is easy. The etymology or derivation of the two words here used to express the grace should be carefully attended to. The grave is called שאול, *sheol*, being as it were an insatiable gulf, which devours and consumes all things, and the pit is called שחת, *shachath*, which signifies *corruption*. These words, therefore, here denote not so much the place as the quality and condition of the place, as if it had been said, The life of Christ will be exempted from the dominion of the grave, inasmuch as his body, even when dead, will not be subject to corruption. Besides, we know that the grave of Christ was filled, and as it were embalmed with the life-giving perfume of the Spirit, that it might be to him the gate to immortal glory.[89]

---

87. Louis Berkhof, *Systematic Theology*, 340.

88. John Flavel, *The Works of John Flavel*, vol. 1, 'The Fountain of Life,' 457, 466.

89. John Calvin, *Commentary upon the Book of Psalms* (Edinburgh: Calvin Translation Society, 1844), verse 16, p. 232.

In his *Commentary upon The Acts of the Apostles*, John Calvin makes the point that Christ is the head of the new resurrection humanity: 'Therefore Christ was far from corruption, that he may be the first-fruits of those which rise from death, (I Cor. xv. 23)...'[90] And he offers other related reasons in comments on Acts 13: 'If the grace be eternal which God saith he will give in his Son, the life of his Son must be eternal, and not subject to corruption' (verse 34).

Calvin is right in stating that Psalm 16:10 does not refer merely to his resurrection, but also to the non-corruption of his body *before* the resurrection: 'Paul affirmeth that that belongeth to Christ alone, that he was free and saved from corruption; for though his body was laid in the grave, corruption had, notwithstanding, no title to it, seeing that it lay there whole, as in a bed, until the day of the resurrection' (Acts 13:35).[91]

The incorruptibility of Christ's body seems to be related to the fact of his utter personal holiness, for he said of Satan: '...for the prince of this world cometh, and hath nothing in me' (John 14:30). Although Christ 'was made sin' (II Cor. 5:21), he was never a sinner, and so the devil could not extract the wages of personal sinfulness from the Lord's body. Rather than death getting the best of him, 'the Prince of Life' (Acts 3:15) was in the process of getting the best of death in all the wideness of its range, upon both soul and body. As Saint Thomas Aquinas says: 'Christ's body was a subject of corruption according to the condition of its passible nature, but not as to the deserving cause of putrefaction, which is sin: but the Divine power preserved Christ's body from putrefying, just as it raised it up from death.'[92]

T. F. Torrance states the reason for the incorruptibility of Christ's body this way:

> That is why death could not hold him even when he entered into and submitted to it, for there was no sin in him which allowed it to subject him to corruption. Death had nothing in him, for he had already passed through its clutches by the perfection of his holiness. Thus by entering into our death as the Holy One of God he robbed it of its sting, and stripped away its power as he accepted the divine judgment in the expiatory sacrifice of his own life, and thus triumphed over the forces of guilt and evil which had made death the last stronghold of their grip over man. He triumphed over the grave through his sheer sinlessness, 'according to the spirit of holiness' (Rom. 1:4). Thereby Jesus also denied to death any natural right over man – rather is death 'the wages of sin' (Rom. 6:23). Death is no more proper to human nature than sin is. Man is made for God, and God is life; therefore death is unnatural.[93]

---

90. John Calvin, *Commentary upon the Acts of the Apostles* (Edinburgh: Calvin Translation Society, 1844), 2:28, 107.

91. Ibid., 537.

92. Thomas Aquinas, *Summa Theologica*, Part III, Second Number (QQ. XXVII-LIX), Q. 51, Third Article, 356.

93. T. F. Torrance, *Space, Time and Resurrection*, 53-54.

(4) His descent into hell

Over the ages, true theologians of the Church have rendered very different accounts of the creedal phrase 'he descended into hell.' Part of the issue is that, as Bavinck pointed out, the word 'Hades' changed its meaning:

> ...the word 'Hades' gradually changed its meaning. The statement that Christ had descended into Hades could only emerge at a time when this word still denoted the 'world after death' in general and had not yet acquired the meaning of 'hell.' For the idea that Christ descended to the place of torment, the actual hell, is nowhere to be found in Scripture, nor does it occur in the most ancient Christian writers. This change of meaning that the word 'Hades' underwent, however, and that had been prepared here and there in the Old and the New Testament (e.g., in Isa. 14:11; Luke 10:15; 16:23), continued in the later church literature and increasingly led to the identification of Hades with Gehenna (hell, place of torment). This, in turn, prompted the rise of the conception that believers at the time of their death went to paradise, not to Hades; that though the idea of Christ's descent into Hades was retained, it was understood in the sense that he went to a specific division of Hades, the later so-called limbo of the fathers, and had moved the devout of the Old Testament from there to paradise or heaven...[94]

The phrase 'he descended into hell' seems to have been added to the Apostles Creed in the fourth century. '[T]hese words already occurred in the confession of the synods of Sirmium (359), Nice (359), and Constantinople (360) and gradually passed from there into all the readings of the Apostle's Creed.'[95]

The Westminster Confession of Faith takes 'Hades' in its original sense: 'the world of departed spirits,' when it states that he 'was buried and remained under the power of death, yet saw no corruption' (Ch. VIII, par. 4). Certainly that affirmation is in line with the clear teaching of Scripture.

Yet at the same time, this is not to deny that in his infinite sufferings for us, he endured the pains of hell (in its second sense). As we have seen, John Calvin understood it to mean the pains of God-forsakenness that Christ endured on the cross, especially after his cry of derelictation. Certainly Calvin is aware that the order of the Creed places Christ's descent into hell *after* his physical death, but considers it inconsequential, since it is a way to look at the invisible reality from the human viewpoint:

> The point is that the Creed sets forth what Christ suffered in the sight of men, and then appositely speaks of that invisible and incomprehensible judgment which he underwent in the sight of God in order that we might know not only that Christ's body was given as the price of our redemption, but that he paid a greater and more excellent price in suffering in his soul the terrible torments of a condemned and forsaken man.[96]

---

94. H. Bavinck, *Reformed Dogmatics: Sin and Salvation in Christ*, vol. 3, 413.
95. Ibid.
96. John Calvin, *Institutes* II. 16. 10.

In general, the Eastern Orthodox Church has held that it was only *after* his death that Christ triumphantly entered into Hades, to despoil it of the Old Testament saints, as D. Staniloae teaches.[97] The traditional Roman Catholic understanding is more or less the same, though with some variations.[98]

However, Scripture itself does not clearly seem to teach that the souls of the Old Testament saints were enclosed in a compartment of hades known extrabiblically as *limbus patrum*. Although we have very little information, it would appear that the Old Testament patriarch Enoch went straight into the presence of God (Gen. 5:22-24), and Elijah appears to have been taken straight into heaven (cf. II Kings 2:1-11). The fact that, at the Mount of Transfiguration, Moses and Elijah 'appeared in glory' (Luke 9:31) would seem to indicate that they had temporarily been sent down from the place of highest glory, which is heaven, the dwelling place of God.

I Peter 3:18-22

I Peter 3:18-22 would seem to suggest that Christ's preaching 'unto the spirits in prison' occurred on his way up to the Father, immediately after his dismissal of his spirit at the end of the crucifixion: 'For Christ also hath once suffered for sins, the just for the unjust, that he might bring us to God, being put to death in the flesh, but quickened by the Spirit: By which also he went, and preached unto the spirits in prison; Which sometime were disobedient, when once the longsuffering of God waited in the days of Noah, while the ark was a preparing, wherein few, that is, eight souls were saved by water. The like figure whereunto even baptism doth also now save us (not the putting away of the filth of the flesh, but the answer of a good conscience toward God,) by the resurrection of Jesus Christ; Who is gone into heaven, and is on the right hand of God; angels and authorities and powers being made subject unto him.'

This unusual and difficult passage is framed by the same verb in verse 19 and 22 (which is not clear in the English translation): πορευθεις, which is an aorist passive participle, meaning 'having been taken up' or 'having gone.' Hence, verse 19 places this 'preaching' in the context of Christ's 'having been taken up,' and verse 22 concludes it by stating of Christ 'having been taken up' into heaven. What happens in between these two verbs must have occurred on his way back to the Father, after the completing of his redeeming work on the cross. Hence, it is part of his exaltation, rather than a continuation of his humiliation.

His preaching in that invisible realm must have been the announcement of his victorious work to lost souls who had drowned with the whole world in the flood of Noah. Long before, they had rejected the preaching of Noah, but now they see the one to whom, in some sense, Noah had been pointing. This passage says nothing about their reaction, other than verse 22, which speaks of, 'angels and authorities and powers being made subject unto him.' The passage shows the cosmic ramifications of the

---

97. D. Staniloae, op. cit., vol. 3, 249-256.

98. Cf. M. Scheeben, *Dogmatik*, III. 298ff., and for a general survey, see *A Catholic Dictionary of Theology*, (London: Thomas Nelson and Sons Ltd, 1967), vol. 2, 161-164.

death of the incarnate Son of God, unbounded by space and time. But it does not indicate that Christ took the lost souls with him up into heaven. At very least, that would be reading into the text something that is not stated or suggested.

I tend to think that it is not suggested because of 'the analogy of faith,' by which we interpret difficult passages in light of plainer passages. As far as I know, no other Scriptural texts indicate that a second chance is offered to those who rejected God during the opportunities of this earthly life. Nonetheless, the death and victory of Christ were so infinitely great that even the lost were made aware of it. It is a fitting conclusion to his work of redeeming the old creation, in order to make ready for the new. As Torrance writes:

> [B]y his cross Jesus Christ *has made a past* – once for all he has put something completely behind him. On one side of the cross there is set the old Adam, the old aeon and all that belongs to them, and they will never be resurrected. 'Old things are passed away,' as St. Paul put it, but on the other side of the cross, 'all things are become new' [II Cor. 5:17]. The cross created a past, but only because it creates a new future, or a 'better hope' as the epistle to the Hebrews puts it [Heb. 7:19]. That is what Christ has done by his redemption: opened up an eschatological vista for faith in which we are already planted in Christ, and with Christ already enter through the veil into God's presence. It is because Christ ever lives as our redeemer, our surety, our atonement, that our life is set on a wholly and eternally new basis. As such Christ is the head of all things, the head of the new age, the messianic king, to whom the whole of the world to come belongs [Eph. 1:10, 19-23; Col. 1:15-20, 2:10; Acts 2:33f.; cf. Rev. 1:5, 17-19, 11:15f., 17:14, 19:16, 22:13].[99]

---

99. T. F. Torrance, *Atonement*, 95-96.

APPENDIX 10.1

METAPHORS FOR THE ATONEMENT

Colin Gunton demonstrated the necessity of a variety of biblical metaphors to understand the atonement: 'But, against Aulen, it must also be emphasised that we do not find the basis for a *theory* of the atonement, particularly if such a theory is opposed to other supposed alternatives.'[1] In this appendix, we consider a variety, not of 'alternatives', but of divinely given 'siblings' to enable us to begin to grasp the atonement of Christ.

[i] Payment of debt (or Satisfaction)

Jaroslav Pelikan has pointed out that the origin of the concept of 'satisfaction' 'would appear to be the penitential system of the church, which was developing just at this time (i.e. eleventh century). The earliest of Latin theologians had already spoken of penance as a way of "making satisfaction to the Lord," and the term "satisfaction" had become standard.'[2]

Anselm
In the eleventh century, Saint Anselm rendered what became a classical account of the substitutionary death of Christ as a fully sufficient satisfaction of the integrity (or honor) of God, which had been attacked by human sin. 'Satisfaction' here means fully acceptable 'sacrifice'.[3]

According to this account, Christ on the cross *made satisfaction to God* for the guilt of our sins, and therefore could say, 'It is finished.' Anselm

---

1. Colin Gunton, *The Actuality of Atonement: A Study of Metaphor, Rationality and the Christian Tradition* (Edinburgh: T & T Clark, 1988), 61.

2. Jaroslav Pelikan, *The Christian Tradition: A History of the Development of Doctrine, 3: The Growth of Medieval Theology (600-1300)* (Chicago and London: The University of Chicago Press, 1978), 143.

3. David Bentley Hart shows that the general thrust of Anselm's teaching on the atonement did not start with him as a sort of Western innovation (supposedly based on certain concepts of Roman Law), but goes back into some of the most substantial Fathers of the Church from the fourth century and onwards, such as Athanasius, Gregory of Nyssa, and John of Damascus, in *The Beauty of the Infinite*, 366ff.

bases his *Cur Deus Homo* to a large degree on the biblically implicit concept of 'rightness' (*rectitude*), which is something like 'the moral order of the universe, founded in the character of God.' 'Rightness' or 'the moral order of the universe' had been profoundly disturbed first by the fall of Satan, and then by the fall of man. Satisfaction has to be rendered to divine justice for the 'rectitudo' of the universe to be restored.

Some have criticized Anselm for supposedly teaching a 'rightness' of the universe that sees God as harshly requiring an infinite restitution to vindicate his offended honor.[4] But David Bentley Hart shows this to be a misreading of Anselm, and answers such charges against *Cur deus homo*:

> For Anselm, God's honor is inseparable from his goodness, which imparts life and harmonious order ['rightness'] to creation, the rejection of which is necessarily death; as the source of all creation's beauty and order. It is the righteousness that cannot contradict itself or will anything amiss; it is justice, not wrath, and its manifestation is the *rectitudo* of God's universal government, its rightness and moral beauty.[5]

Anselm writes: 'Therefore, hold thou most firmly, that without satisfaction – that is, without the spontaneous payment of the debt – neither can God release the sinner unpunished, nor the sinner attain to such bliss as he enjoyed before his sin; not in that way could man be restored to what he was before sinning.'[6]

The seriousness of sin, which disturbs this 'rightness of the universe' by dishonoring God, is determined by the greatness of the person against whom the sin is committed. God is of infinite greatness, and therefore, sin against God is infinite, causing offenders to be infinitely guilty. Anselm's interlocutor speaks of God's proper demands remaining the same, even if worlds were 'multiplied to infinity' (I. XX – p. 51), and Anselm replies that 'You do not therefore make amends unless you repay something greater than is that for which you ought not to have committed the sin' (ibid.). But this price of satisfaction of an infinite person would itself have to be infinite in worth to avail.[7]

For satisfaction for infinite sin to take place, it would require a person of infinite worth to make that offering.[8] Humans, being both limited (finite) and also sinful, could not do so. It thus would take God to accomplish an

---

4. David Bentley Hart in *The Beauty of the Infinite* quotes Lossky's critique of Anselm in these terms (p. 369).

5. Ibid.

6. Anselm, *Cur Deus Homo* (London: Griffith, Farran, Browne & Co., Ltd., 1889), I. XIX (p. 46).

7. 'Now, I pray you to teach me how the death of this one could avail for the many and great sins of all, whereas you can show that one single sin (which we think a very small one) is so infinite that were there displayed an infinite number of worlds as full of creatures as this world, not to be preserved from annihilation unless some one gave one glance contrary to God's will, yet that glance should not be given' (Anselm, *C.D.H.*, II. XIV – pp. 82, 83).

8. 'If his existence be as great a good as his destruction is an evil, incomparably greater a good it is than is the evil of those sins which are exceeded beyond all comparison by his murder... If therefore to yield up the life be the same as to accept death, then as the yielding up of the life outweighs all the sins of men, so also doth the acceptance of death' (Anselm, *C.D.H.*, II. XIV – p. 84).

infinitely valuable offering,[9] but the offering would need to be made by a man, for it was in human nature that the sin occurred, and if humanity is to be redeemed, the offering must take place in that humanity.[10] And this offering would have to be in a sinless man, which is only possible through the miracle of the Virgin Birth.[11] In this sinless humanity, Christ 'is made sin' (II Cor. 5:21), and as such stands in for us sinners as 'he who knew no sin' (II Cor. 5:21). What he does here goes beyond all that is required in atoning for the infinite guilt of the fallen world.[12] The statement of Thomas Aquinas agrees: '[*Reply. Obj. 3*]. "The very least one of Christ's sufferings was sufficient of itself to redeem the human race from all sins..."'[13]

His death was free; it was not necessitated,[14] for God is not compelled by anything outside himself.[15] Commenting on John 10:18, Anselm says: '*But no necessity preceded his will*...So then no one took His soul from Him, but He laid it down of Himself, and took it again; because He had the power to lay down His life, and to take it again, as He Himself said.'[16] As D. B. Hart says: 'Consequently, the only "necessity" Anselm demonstrates in the drama of salvation is a kind of inward intelligibility to the mind grasped by faith.'[17]

Anselm glories in the rich mercy of God:

> For what can be understood as being more merciful than that God the Father should say to the sinner who was condemned to eternal torments, and who had nothing wherewith to redeem himself: 'Take my Only-Begotten Son, and offer Him for thyself'; and the Son Himself: 'Take me, and redeem Thyself'?... And what can be more just than that he, to whom is given a payment greater than all that is owing to him, should, if this be given in payment of what is owing, remit the whole debt?[18]

This text of Anselm shows his Trinitarian understanding of the atonement. It is the life of the Trinity, rather than an extraneous theory of debt and repayment that informs Anselm's teaching. Hart comments:

---

9. '...unless man should repay what for sin he owed unto God; which was so heavy a debt that as no one unless he were man, ought, so unless he were God, he could not pay it, and therefore that some one must be man who also is God' (Ibid., II. XVII – 99, 100).

10. '...You already see how a rational necessity shows that the heavenly kingdom is to be completed from among men, and that this cannot be but by the remission of sins, which no man can have except through a man who shall be God also, and by his death shall reconcile sinners to God. Then we discovered clearly that Christ, whom we confess to be God and man, died for us...' (Anselm, *C.D.H.* II. XV – p. 85).

11. Ibid., II. XVI.

12. 'Do you not think that so great, so lovable good can suffice to atone for the sins of the whole world? Nay, rather can it do infinitely more' (Ibid., 84).

13. Saint Thomas Aquinas, *Summa Theologica*, Part III, Second Number (QQ. XXVII – LIX), Q. 46, Art. 5, Reply Obj. 3 (p. 274).

14. Anselm, *C.D.H.*, II. XVII.

15. Ibid., II. XVIII.

16. Ibid., II. XVIII – p. 98.

17. Hart, op. cit., 371.

18. Anselm, op cit., II. XX – 107.

...Christ's sacrifice belongs not to an economy of credit and exchange but to the trinitarian motion of love, it is given entirely as a gift – given when it should not have needed to be given again, by God, at a price that we imposed upon *him*...the donation that Christ makes of himself draw creation into God's eternal 'offering' of himself in the life of the Trinity.[19]

Thomas Aquinas

Saint Thomas Aquinas (thirteenth century), without replicating the exact approach of Anselm, still teaches rather similar concepts of Christ's having more than paid the debt we owed by 'his infinite worth':[20]

> ...It is written (Ps. lxviii. 5) in Christ's person: *Then did I pay that which I took not away*. But he has not paid who has not fully atoned. Therefore it appears that Christ by His suffering has fully atoned for our sins. *I answer that*, He properly atones for an offense who offers something which the offended one loves equally, or even more than he detested the offense. But by suffering out of love and obedience, Christ gave more to God than was required to compensate for the offense of the whole human race...Christ's Passion was not only a sufficient but a superabundant atonement for the sins of the human race; according to I John ii. 2: *He is the propitiation for our sins; and not for ours only, but for those of the whole world.*[21]

Turretin

Francis Turretin (seventeenth-century) in a similar fashion summarized the debt we owe to God:

> VI. First, sin, which renders us guilty and hated of God and binds us over as debtors to punishment, may be viewed under a threefold relation (*schesei*) either as a debt, which we are bound to pay to divine justice, in which sense the law is called 'a handwriting' (Col. 2:14); or as an enmity, whereby not only are we haters of God (*theostygeis*), but God himself looks upon us with hatred and indignation; or as a crime by which, before God, the supreme Ruler and Judge of the world, we become worthy of everlasting death and malediction. Hence, sinners are sometimes called 'debtors' (Mt. 6:12), then 'enemies' [*echthroi*] of God' (both actively and passively, Col. 1:21), and again 'guilty before God' (*hypodikoi to theo*, Rom. 3:19). Hence we infer that three things were required for our redemption – the payment of the debt contracted by sin, the appeasing of divine hatred and wrath and the expiation of guilt.[22]

[ii] The turning away of divine wrath by means of propitiation

Probably as the long-term result of the European Enlightenment, much theological thought in the West has opposed the very concept of the

---

19. Hart, op. cit., 371-372.

20. Thomas Aquinas, *Summa Theologica* Part III, Second Number (QQ. XXVII. – LIX.), Q. 48, Art. 2, *Reply Obj. 3* (p. 314).

21. Ibid., p. 313, 314.

22. Francis Turretin, *Institutes of Elenctic Theology*, Volume Two: Eleventh Through Seventeenth Topics, 418.

wrath of God, as one sees in the Unitarian *Racovian Catechism*[23] and the Socinianism lying behind it.[24] Herman Bavinck correctly analyzes the position of the Socinians:

> Socinians and their spiritual kin...have fiercely opposed the necessity of satisfaction (atonement). All their arguments come down to saying that justice and grace, satisfaction and forgiveness, and hence also law and gospel, Old and New Testaments, creation and re-creation, are inconsistent with each other, are in fact mutually exclusive... God is not to be conceived as a judge but as a father. Punitive justice, holiness, hatred, wrath against sin are not perfections of God; only love describes his being.[25]

But many, who are not Unitarians and do not go so far as they in denying God's perfections, have also opposed satisfaction. They have held it to be inconsistent with their understanding of the love of God. This viewpoint has been increasingly prevalent since the eighteenth-century Enlightenment.

One has to agree with the assessment of Paul Wells:

> Since the time of the Enlightenment, various solutions have been proposed to make the meaning of the cross more palatable. Today even these compromises with humanism seem irrelevant. The question is: if such a thing as sin exists, and if there is a God, surely he would not have to go to these lengths to deal with a human problem? Voltaire must have hit the spot when he said God is bound to forgive, because that's the business he's in. God is a God of love, if he's a God at all, isn't he?[26]

The answer must be to go back to whether the Holy Scriptures are the revelation of God or not. If they are, and that is the constant assumption of this volume, then we must turn to them to know whether the God of love is also the God of wrath, and if so, how his love and wrath combine in his gracious dealing with those who have deserved being put away from him forever.

We have discussed previously why it is the strength of a holy God to be consistent with his character, and thus to punish sin, which is a contradiction to his character.[27] Paul Wells writes:

> In his holiness, God must reject sin to be consistent with himself. God's judgment is his statement as to what is unacceptable because he is a righteous and a holy God. Judgment occurs when the holiness of God and sin meet up. Even human governments seek to eliminate forms of behavior opposed

---

23. See *Racovian Catechism*, translated by Thomas Rees (London, 1818), questions 380, 383, where it explains Christ's death as primarily an edifying example and not as an atonement.

24. See Faustus Socinus, *De Jesu Christo Salvatore* (Rakow [i.e. modern Crakow]: Rodecius, 1594), II. 121-252. In reply, Thomas Goodwin, for instance, rejected the position of Socinus, who reduced the incarnation and death of Christ to coming to earth to set a good example (with the allied denial that God's wrath against sin must be satisfied): cf. Thomas Goodwin, 'Of Christ the Mediator' in *Works*, vol. V, p. 47. John Owen constantly rebuts the Socinians (and their Catechism) throughout his multi-volumed *Commentary on the Epistle to the Hebrews*. See H. Bavinck, *Reformed Dogmatics*, vol. 3, 347-53; 374-77.

25. Herman Bavinck, *Reformed Dogmatics: Sin and Salvation in Christ*, vol. 3, 374.

26. Paul Wells, *Cross Words*, 14.

27. See Chapter Nine, 298-299.

to the laws of the state. Sin being what sin is, God could not do otherwise than seek its elimination. This is not something imposed on God. It is the free and spontaneous expression of his righteousness, holiness and purity. With regard to sin, God must act in a way that expresses his freedom of decision and action.[28]

Because of his total goodness, God must oppose all that is evil. After discussing the New Testament word ὀργη ['wrath'], Leon Morris notes: 'The point of all this is that the biblical writers habitually use for the divine wrath a word which denotes not so much a sudden flaring up of passion which is soon over, as a strong and settled opposition to all that is evil arising out of God's very nature.'[29]

Torrance also expresses the same point: 'Punishment and wrath are terms speaking of the wholly godly resistance of God to sin, the fact that the holy love of God excludes all that is not holy love. Sin must be judged, guilt must be expiated by its judgment and complete condemnation, else God is not God, and God is not love.'[30]

Although the concept of the wrath of God was denied by the 'radical reformers' of the sixteenth century called the Socinians, and was particularly offensive to the eighteenth-century secular Enlightenment, which denied man's sinfulness and lost interest in God's transcendent holiness, its denial went 'main-stream' in the academic theology and biblical studies of the twentieth century.

This is particularly seen in the career of a leading New Testament scholar of the twentieth century, C. H. Dodd of Cambridge University, who sought to re-interpret 'propitiation' so as to eliminate the reality of the wrath of God. He was on the committee which produced the Revised Standard Version (1946) and later the New English Bible (1961), and, partly owing to his influence, those translations replaced 'propitiation' with 'expiation', or 'the remedy for the defilement of our sins' (which could, depending on one's starting point, be reduced to 'cleansing', rather than 'turning away of wrath').[31] In other words, 'expiation' is considered to deal with cleansing from sin and defilement, whereas 'propitiation', which is certainly based on expiatory sacrifice, goes a step further, and conveys the objective turning away of the wrath of God.

Leon Morris, with great care, answered Dodd's denial of both propitiation and the divine wrath lying behind it. In doing so, Morris emphasizes the profound difference between pagan views of divine anger and 'appeasement' of God[s], and the biblical teaching: 'The Bible writers have nothing to do with pagan conceptions of a capricious and vindictive deity, inflicting arbitrary punishments on offending worshippers, who must then bribe him back to a good mood by the appropriate offerings. Dodd's important work makes this abundantly clear.'[32]

---

28. Wells, op. cit., 70.

29. Leon Morris, *The Apostolic Preaching of the Cross*, 162-63.

30. T. F. Torrance, *Atonement*, 154.

31. e.g. See C. H. Dodd, *The Bible and the Greeks* (London: Hodder & Stoughton, 1935).

32. L. Morris, op. cit., 129.

Yet Morris critiques the length to which Dodd went:

>...Dodd seems to say that all ideas of wrath and propitiation are absent from it. We have already noted his rejection of the idea of propitiation; but in his commentary on Romans he seems to go further and says that the wrath of God is 'an archaic phrase' suiting 'a thoroughly archaic idea.'[33]

Morris, on the contrary, replies: 'To many the wrath of God seems too well rooted in both Old and New Testaments to be relegated to the status of an archaism.'[34]

Morris carefully traces divine wrath in both the Old Testament[35] and the New Testament.[36] He denies Dodd's claims about the absence of true divine wrath in the teaching of both Jesus and Paul:

>...C. H. Dodd says that, in the teaching of Jesus, 'anger as an attitude of God to men disappears, and His love and mercy become all embracing.'[37] St. Paul, he thinks, agrees with this in substance and retains the concept of the wrath of God 'not to describe the attitude of God to man, but to describe an inevitable process of cause and effect in a moral universe.'[38]

Morris answers Dodd's attempts to avoid the concepts of divine wrath and the propitiating of it, especially in his evaluation of Dodd's explanation of 'The ἱλασκομαι WORD GROUP IN THE SEPTUAGINT[39] and similarly with the same WORD GROUP IN THE NEW TESTAMENT.[40] Morris states: 'Dodd totally ignores the fact that in many passages [in the ἱλασκομαι group] there is explicit mention of the putting away of God's anger, and accordingly his conclusions cannot be accepted without serious modification.'[41] The serious reader is referred to the passages mentioned in Morris for details.

>To the men of the Old Testament the wrath of God is both very real and very serious. God is not thought of as capriciously angry (like the deities of the heathen), but, because He is a moral Being, His anger is directed towards wrongdoing in any shape or form. Once roused, this anger is not easily assuaged, and dire consequences may follow. But it is only fair to add that the Old Testament consistently regards God as a God of mercy, so that, though men may and do sin and thus draw down upon themselves the consequences of His wrath, yet God delights not in the death of the sinner, and He provides ways in which the consequences of sin may be averted.[42]

---

33. Ibid., 129-30, referring to Dodd, *Romans*, MNTC, 20f.

34. Ibid., 130.

35. Ibid., 129-36.

36. Ibid., 161-66.

37. Quoting Dodd's *Romans*, 23.

38. Quoting Dodd, ibid., in Morris, op. cit., 161.

39. Morris, op. cit., 136-38.

40. Ibid., 166-88.

41. Ibid., 138.

42. Ibid., 131.

T. F. Torrance indicates the only way that the divine wrath may be removed: 'The wrath of God can be removed only through the righteous infliction of the divine judgment against our sin. Or to use more juridical terms, the wrath of God is removed only when his righteous will has punished sin and judged it.'[43]

Hence, to remove his own wrath in a way fully consistent with his own holy character, God instituted, from the earliest strands of the Old Testament, sacrifices. Many have considered the animal skins that were divinely given to Adam and Eve to cover their nakedness to have resulted from the first sacrifice (although the Genesis text does not specifically say so). Noah offered sacrifices, as did the Patriarchs, long before the sacrificial system was regulated in such massive detail in the Mosaic economy.

James Denney brings out that these sacrifices were made to God, to cover sin: 'It is sacrifice for sin, and not a sacrifice in a vaguer sense. Its value is that somehow or other it neutralizes sin as a power estranging man from God, and that in virtue of it God and man are reconciled... All sacrifice was sacrifice offered *to God*, and, whatever its value, it had that value *for him*.'[44]

Paul Wells states: 'The Old Testament sacrifices, which God had instituted, served to restore fellowship between God and man by the shedding of blood. They were a divinely appointed way of demonstrating that only God could provide man with a way out. Moreover, sacrifices showed that God intervenes through a victim and in doing so restores the relationships.'[45]

There are many types of sacrificial offerings in the Old Testament, as for instance, in the book of Leviticus we are presented with five main kinds of offerings: (1) the burnt-offering (of the herd and flock) – cf. Leviticus 1; (2) meal (or cereal) offering with oil poured upon it – cf. Leviticus 2; (3) peace offering (from the herd) – cf. Leviticus 3; (4) the sin offering (sprinkling of the blood of an animal, with other rituals) – cf. Leviticus 4 and 6; (5) the guilt offering – cf. Leviticus 7.

Of these five offerings, four were blood sacrifices. The worshiper who sought forgiveness laid his hands on the head of the animal, symbolically transferring his or her sins to the substitute (cf. Lev. 1:4), and the priest slew the animal and sprinkled the blood, as a sign of divine cleansing (cf. Lev. 1:11). Then the fire, a sign of God's all-consuming holiness, burnt up the animal remains, as a picture of an offering of the life to God, and a 'sweet savour' of devotion to him (cf. Lev. 1:17; 2:2, etc.).

The shedding of blood was all-important to these sacrifices. The reason is clarified in Leviticus 17:11: 'For the life of the flesh is in the blood: and I have given it to you upon the altar to make an atonement for your souls: for it is the blood that maketh atonement for the soul.' This indicates that life must be given for life: when the blood is shed, the life pours out (cf.

---

43. Torrance, *Atonement*, 153-154.

44. James Denney, *The Christian Doctrine of Reconciliation* (Carlisle: Paternoster, 1998 reprint), 29.

45. Wells, op. cit., 86.

Deut. 12:23 and Rom. 6:23). It carries out the principle of substitution: the life of the animal substitute is rendered to God on the altar in place of the sinful person making the sacrifice. Thus, God covers sin and guilt, for he is the one who provides this mode of forgiveness.

This theme is expounded in the Epistle to the Hebrews, where 9:22 says: 'without the shedding of blood there is no remission.' Hebrews shows the superiority of the final sacrifice of Christ to all the earlier animal sacrifices, 'For it is not possible that the blood of bulls and of goats should take away sins' (Heb. 10:4). No doubt, their blood covered sins, until what (rather, who) they were given to point towards came.

One could ask why animal sacrificial blood only covered sins, without finally removing it. The reasons seem to be threefold: (1) the blood must be offered from within humanity, where the sin was originally committed, that is, from human personality, and (2) the person and his blood must be of infinite worth. (3) Scripture also teaches that animals are not created in the image of God as is humankind. Hence the incarnation of Christ is fully fitting in that he becomes a man who, being in the image of God, is the crown of the created order.

Therefore, Christ alone, God in human nature, would be able to offer such a finally availing sacrifice. Hebrews 10:5-12 makes this difference between the Levitical sacrifices and the sacrifice of Christ crystal clear. It interprets Psalm 40:6 as referring to 'the body' God prepared for his Son (Heb. 10:5), and contrasts that to the 'burnt offerings' in which God had no pleasure (Heb. 10:6), as well as 'sacrifice' (v. 8). It further contrasts the necessary daily repetitions of the Levitical sacrifices with the once-for-all sacrifice of Christ, after which, unlike the High Priest in the Tabernacle/Temple (which had no chair in the holy of holies), he could sit down in completion of his finished work (cf. Heb. 10:12 and 1:3). This work was consummately perfect: 'For by one offering he hath perfected for ever them that are sanctified' (Heb. 10:14).

Hebrews goes on to show that Christ's completed work is the inauguration of the new and final phase of the one overarching covenant of grace: 'the New Covenant' (Hebrews 10:15-18, quoting Jeremiah 31:31-34; see also Hebrews 8:7-13). Here (as elsewhere) we see that sacrifice with its blood-shedding is in the context of the covenant established by God, ratified by sacrifice, and received through faith, as we see with its archetypal administration in Abraham (cf. Genesis 15:1-21). As Paul Wells has noted: 'If the cause of alienation between God and man is that the covenant has been broken, then restoration must be made according to the law of the covenant. The cause of guilt has to be dealt with...'[46]

T. F. Torrance shows that sacrifice can only be understood within the context of covenant:

A breach in the covenant, therefore is not only a breach with God but a breach in the actual existence of Israel...Thus the wrath of God is God's holiness and faithfulness directed against breaches in the covenant, and it

---

46. Paul Wells, op. cit., 79.

is wrath precisely because God in his love affirms Israel to be his child and gives himself in covenant mercy to be Israel's God...Hence it cannot be denied that in the Old Testament cult and covenant the expiating of guilt before the wrath of God is the chief element leading to the restoration of true communion with God.[47]

As we have seen in the first volume of this systematic theology, the 'faultiness' or 'imperfection' of the 'first covenant' (the Mosaic) is traced to the difference in priesthood: that is, the imperfect (or temporary, which could only 'cover' sins) – or the Aaronic, with its constant need of repetition, is contrasted to the perfect (or final, which actually takes away sins) – or that of Christ our Great High Priest, who once he said 'It is finished' and 'dismissed his spirit' was then able to take his seat on high in retrospect of his completed work of atonement and reconciliation (cf. the contrasts offered in Hebrews 9).[48]

This shedding of the blood of the Great High Priest is a 'propitiation' for all the sins of his people for all eternity. One of the major Old Testament Hebrew verbs lying behind the concept is *kaphar* (meaning to cover), and in the *piel* form of the verb (*kipper*) signifies 'covering sin'. Synonyms used along with it include verbs 'such as *kasha*, to cover, and *machah*, to blot out.'[49] Torrance adds: 'The verb *kipper* is very rarely used literally, but is generally used in an extended sense meaning to cover sin or nullify through the offering of a propitiatory gift...or the act of appeasing the wrath of a king by a propitiatory action.'[50]

The Old Testament use of words in the *kaphar* group demonstrate that 'God is primarily the subject, for it is ultimately God himself who atones, who blots out sin... Even when the priest carries out the liturgical act of atonement, he does what is appointed by God...to cover the sin with the blood of sacrifice...by way of witness to the fact that it is always ultimately God himself and only God who can atone sin and put it away.'[51]

After many grammatical and exegetical details, Leon Morris argues that one of the main Greek verbs used in the LXX to render *kipper*, ἐξιλάσκομαι, is in line with propitiation: 'The thought of the offering of a ransom which turns away the divine wrath from the sinner still seems to be the basic meaning of the verb.'[52]

In the New Testament, three Greek words in particular (all linguistically related to ἐξιλάσκομαι above) indicate the act of covering sin and turning away the wrath of God: *hilaskomai* (Heb. 2:17), *hilasmos* (I John 2:2; 4:10), and *hilasterion* (Rom. 3:25):

---

47. Torrance, *Atonement*, 38.

48. See my *Systematic Theology*, vol. I, chapter 6, especially pp. 409-11.

49. T. F. Torrance, op. cit., 34, where he lists Psalms 32:1; 85:2(3) for *kasha*; Jeremiah 18:23 for *machah* (and *kipper*); Nehemiah 4:5 (Hebrew text 3:37) for the use of both.

50. Ibid., where for propitiatory gift he mentions Jacob's gift to Esau (Gen. 32:20-21), and for the wrath of a king, Prov. 16:14.

51. Ibid.

52. L. Morris, op. cit., 133.

'Wherefore in all things it behoved him to be made like unto his brethren, that he might be a merciful and faithful high priest in things pertaining to God, to make reconciliation for the sins of the people' (Heb. 2:17).

'And he is the propitiation for our sins; and not for ours only, but also for the sins of the whole world' (I John 2:2).

'Herein is love, not that we loved God, but that he loved us, and sent his Son to be the propitiation for our sins' (I John 4:10).

'Whom God hath set forth to be a propitiation through faith in his blood, to declare his righteousness for the remission of sins that are past, through the forbearance of God' (Rom. 3:25).

C. H. Dodd, for example, argued that Romans 3:25 was not about propitiation, but about expiation of sin.[53] Paul Wells shows the underlying man-centered assumption of this position:

> The removing of sin is something that concerns man. This implies that sin does not affect God in a direct way... In Scripture, however, sin is not just a question of impurity or uncleanness in man that needs removing... If man's sin is not cleaned up and he dies with it, what happens to him? Biblically the answer must be that he undergoes the judgment of God because of his sin. Why? – because God is bound to judge sin according to retributive justice.[54]

Morris summarizes: 'In view of the wide range of the usage, and the absence of any factor in the context of Rom. iii. 25 which indicates a specific limiting of the term, it seems best to understand it as signifying "means of propitiation," the means being indicated by the following "in his blood."'[55]

Not a few theologians and biblical scholars have resisted the concept of 'propitiation', as we have seen, but many of them also have been no less opposed to 'the blood'. Yet, if one accepts the New Testament as a divine revelation, it is impossible to get away from its very frequent references to the blood of Jesus. As B. B. Warfield said: 'Nothing can be more certain, for example, than that all the references to the "blood" of Jesus are one and all ascriptions of a sacrificial character and effect to His death.'[56] Warfield divides these references into four groups: (1) certain general passages,[57] (2) certain Eucharistic passages,[58] (3) the formula, διὰ τοῦ αἵματος [through the blood] (or its equivalent),[59] and (4) the formula ἐν τῷ αἵματι [in the

---

53. In Dodd's *The Epistle to the Romans* and *The Bible and the Greeks*. See discussion by Leon Morris in *The Cross in the New Testament*, 347-50 (reference from Paul Wells, op. cit., 197).

54. Paul Wells, op. cit., 193-94.

55. L. Morris, op. cit.., 172.

56. B. B. Warfield, 'Christ Our Sacrifice' in *The Person and Work of Christ* (Phillipsburg, NJ: Presbyterian & Reformed, 1950), 421.

57. 'certain general passages': Heb. ix. 14, 20; x. 29; xii. 24; I Pet. i. 19; I John i. 7.

58. 'certain eucharistic passages': Mt. xxvi. 28; Mk. xiv. 24; Luke xxii. 20; I Cor. xi. 25; John vi. 53, 54, 55, 56; I Cor. x. 16.

59. διὰ τοῦ αἵματος: Acts xx. 28; Eph. i. 7; Col. i. 20; Heb. ix. 12; xiii. 12 (I John v. 6), Rev. xii. 11.

blood] (or its equivalent).[60] These numerous mentions of the blood are not mere footnotes, easily explained away; they are central to the significance of the work of Jesus Christ, according to several different authors of the New Testament.

Yet, presumably in order to avoid the clear implication of such passages on the blood of Christ as a propitiatory (or even expiatory) sacrifice, various scholars have argued that the shedding of the blood does not refer so much to a substitutionary laying down of the life in penal consequences for sin, as to the pouring out of the blood in a sort of 'renewal of life', outside a punitive context. Leon Morris interacts with several of these scholars, who 'have urged the opinion that by "the blood" life is meant rather than death, so that the essential thing in sacrifice is the offering up of the life.'[61] And he refers to others who hold the more traditional view, that the blood means substitutionary sacrifice, with the primary reference to death.[62]

He notes that in the Old Testament the Hebrew word for blood (*dam*) is used 362 times. He lists five different ranges of meaning, and concludes:

> From these figures it is clear that the commonest use of *dam* is to denote death by violence, and, in particular, that this use is found about twice as often as that to denote the blood of sacrifice... As far as it goes, then, the statistical evidence seems to indicate that the association most likely to be conjured up when the Hebrews hear the word 'blood' used was that of violent death.[63]

He adds:

> We conclude, then, that the evidence afforded by the use of the term *dam* in the Old Testament indicates that it signifies life violently taken rather than the continued presence of life available for some new function, in short, death rather than life, and that this is supported by the references to atonement.[64]

In the New Testament, Morris lists ninety-eight references to blood (αἷμα), and some of these are 'without any implication of life or death or the like'.[65] But '[t]wenty-five times the word indicates violent death, this being the largest group, as we have already seen to be the case in the Old Testament.'[66] Many of these refer to animal sacrifices, and some do not. Several passages clearly point to covenant blood, which is sacrificial.[67] Of these and other references, Morris draws this conclusion:

---

60. ἐν τῷ αἷματι: Rom. iii. 25; v. 9; I Cor. xi. 25 (27); Eph. ii. 13; Heb. x. 19 (xiii. 25); I John v. 6; Rev. i. 5; v. 9; vii. 14.

61. Morris lists: Milligan, Westcott, Hick, and Vincent Taylor (Morris, op. cit., 108).

62. Morris lists: J. Denney, Moffatt, Armitage Robinson, Behm (in TWNT), and F. J. Taylor (TWBB), (Morris, ibid.).

63. Ibid. 109-10.

64. Ibid., 117.

65. Ibid.

66. Ibid., 118.

67. Rom. iii. 25; Heb. xii. 24; xiii. 12; I Pet. i. 2; i. 19; Rev. vii. 14; xii. 11; I Jn. i. 7.

When we were dealing with sacrifice in the Old Testament we saw reason for thinking that the infliction of death rather than the release of life was the dominant thought, and there is nothing in these passages concerning the death of Christ viewed as a sacrifice to disturb that conclusion... Thus it seems tolerably certain that in both the Old and New Testaments the blood signifies essentially the death. It is freely admitted that there are some passages in which it is possible to interpret the blood as signifying life, but even these yield a better sense (and one which is consistent with the wider biblical usage) if understood to mean 'life given up in death.' In particular, there seems no reason for disputing the dictum of J. Behm: 'Blood of Christ' is like 'cross,' only another, clearer expression for the death of Christ in its salvation meaning.[68]

A straightforward reading of the multitude of New Testament texts that deal with Christ's death and its purposes and accomplishments, therefore, cannot fail to emphasize the centrality of propitiation of God's just wrath, and of the infinite value of the precious blood of Christ in doing so. But God is the one who both offers and receives the propitiation. The Father (John 3:16), the Son (Matt. 20:28), and the Spirit (Heb. 9:14) are the subjects of it, both as to its coming from within the eternal counsel of the Godhead (cf. Rev. 13:8) and as to its victorious execution in history (cf. Phil. 2:13; John 17:2; Isa. 53:10-12).

[iii] Penal Substitution

Isaiah 53:4-5, so frequently applied in the New Testament to the work of Christ, teaches penal substitution: 'Surely he hath borne our griefs, and carried our sorrows: yet we did esteem him stricken, smitten of God, and afflicted. But he was wounded for our transgressions, he was bruised for our iniquities: the chastisement of our peace was upon him; and with his stripes we are healed.' Paul Wells notes six points about this text of Isaiah:

- the bearing of sin indicates figuratively that sins are taken away and pardoned;
- the way sins were borne was by the servant being bruised, smitten, and afflicted;
- the nature of sin bearing was a punishment;
- the punishment was of divine origin;
- it was accomplished for others;
- the suffering of the victim resulted in healing.[69]

He adds that 'The penal nature of the substitution can be considered from two angles – either that of the penalty laid on the redeemer or of the acquittal that secures the prisoner's release.'[70] Further: 'The mediator removes liability to penal judgment and guilt in the sense of condemnation leading to death. That Christ "bore our sins" means that

---

68. Ibid., 121-122.

69. Paul Wells, op. cit., 145.

70. Ibid.

he took on himself their fatal consequences and died the death that we ought to have died.'[71]

New Testament descriptions of the Gospel, found in both John and Paul, seem to fit naturally with the concept of penal substitution (without employing that exact term). Luther is said to have called John 3:16 'the Gospel in a nutshell': 'For God so loved the world that he gave his only begotten Son, that whosoever believeth in him should not perish, but have everlasting life.' John 3:36 speaks of the wrath of God abiding on those who do not believe in the Son. Hence, divine wrath is not absent from the announcement of the good news of forgiveness in Christ. Indeed, what Christ did in his coming is the divinely chosen way to set aside the divine wrath.

Speaking to Nicodemus, the teacher in Israel, Jesus prophetically refers to his own future 'lifting up' in terms of Moses having 'lifted up' the brass serpent on the pole in the wilderness so that those who looked to it could be healed from deadly snake-bites (John 3:14-15). 'Lifting up of the serpent' was a foreshadowing of Christ being lifted up on the cross, as he is made a curse for us (cf. Gal. 3:13; Deut. 21:23). The curse comes on those who 'continue not in all things which are written in the book of the law to do them' (Gal. 3:10; Deut. 27:26). Or, as Romans 6:23 states it: 'The wages of sin is death…' The divine curse against sin, resulting in the death of the sinner was voluntarily endured by Christ for the sake of us sinners. Because he died in our place, having taken all our sins and the penalty they deserved upon himself, we are given pardon and eternal life. That is precisely what is meant by penal substitution.

I Corinthians 15:3 tells us what the gospel is which Paul preached (cf. I Cor. 15:1): 'For I delivered unto you first of all that which I also received, how that Christ died for our sins according to the Scriptures…' This great resurrection chapter then goes on to trace the 'corruption' of our physical body in death (cf. v. 42) to our connection with the first Adam in his sin (cf. vv. 21, 22). It shows that Christ is the 'last Adam' (v. 45) or 'the second man' (v. 47). By dying for our sins (v. 3), he replaces our death and corruption with life and incorruption (v. 42). That is to say, he substitutes himself for his sinful people. He takes on their guilt, corruption, and death, and gives them in exchange his purity, incorruption, and life. That is the basic meaning of penal substitution.

So far as I know, a majority of the objections to penal substitution seem to be related to the idea that if God is love, then he could not require infinite punishment for sin. For God to require a penalty for sin is thought to give a harsh view of his character. On this viewpoint, biblical texts that imply something like penal substitution should be explained in a non-penal way. But is that not to take liberties with the plain teaching of Scripture? In particular, is it not to imagine a God who is different from who he has revealed himself to be? Is it not to take in a certain direction some of his attributes (such as mercy and love), and to ignore other ones (such as consistency of character and holiness)?

---

71. Ibid., 148.

Of course, those who oppose penal substitution (or even substitution itself) would not deny God's attribute of holiness. Rather, it is a matter of emphasis. By some of them, God's love tends to be interpreted outside its biblical context of being an expression of the character of God, which means that it is holy love, always accompanied by God's righteous integrity in the way it is exercised. As we saw under 'propitiation,' for God not to punish sin would be to deny who he is; it would be a denial of the eternal consistency of his character, which lies at the basis of who he is, and of the moral structure of the universe. To use the attribute of love to render irrelevant the attribute of justice is to present a false doctrine of God. Taken far enough, it can become a functional replacement of the God of Israel and the Church, as set forth in Holy Scripture, with a deity acceptable to the humanistic Enlightenment. That is the price of de-emphasizing or even denying one divine attribute at the expense of another.

As Thomas Crawford wrote: '[God] acts in conformity with [all of his attributes] at all times... As for the divine justice and the divine mercy in particular, the end of his work was not to bring them into harmony, as if they had been at variance with one another, but jointly to manifest and glorify them in the redemption of sinners. It is a case of *combined action*, and not of *counteraction*, on the part of these attributes, that is exhibited on the cross.'[72]

But at the same time, the sheer wonder of the Gospel is that it is the true God, the one who presents himself to us in Holy Scripture both as holy love and as he who can never deny his own character; it is precisely he, who, without denying who he is, comes down to us 'to be wounded for our transgressions' in such a thoroughly just, as well as infinitely loving way, that all our transgressions are forever taken away from us as we look to him as our sin-bearer. Karl Barth shows that God does not deny his Godness to do so:

> ... God shows Himself to be the great and true God in the fact that He can and will let His grace bear this cost, that He is capable and willing and ready for this condescension, this act of extravagance, this far journey...God is not proud. In His high majesty He is humble. It is in this high humility that He speaks and acts as the God who reconciles the world to Himself.[73]

Commenting on John 10:17-18, James Henley Thornwell takes us very close to the heart of God as he describes what the incarnate Son of God went through for the honor of his Father's character in the salvation of the church:

> His satisfaction is not merely the ground upon which others are at liberty to approach and adore the Divine perfections; it is itself a stupendous act of prayer and an amazing tribute of praise. We dare not entertain the thought,

---

72. Thomas J. Crawford, *The Doctrine of Holy Scripture Respecting the Atonement* (Wm. Blackwood, 1881), 453-454.

73. K. Barth, *Church Dogmatics* IV/1, 159.

even for an instant, that the Father is harsh or vindictive, or that a cloud obscures the benevolence of his nature, when the very circumstances which are most revolting in the tragedy of Calvary are elements of a worship which the Son delighted to render, and felt that the Father was glorious in accepting. Considered as an act of worship, there is a majestic awe, a moral sublimity thrown around the death of Jesus, which fails to be impressed when attention is exclusively confined to the legal principles which made it indispensable to the pardon of the guilty. It is invested with a sacredness which makes us pause and adore. Never was there such a doxology as when Jesus died, and the whole work of redemption is a grand litany which has no parallel in the history of the universe. There can be no wonder that the Father should love the Son…never, never will there be displayed again, such piety as that which burned in the bosom of Jesus when He laid down His life of Himself.[74]

Therefore, through the penal substitutionary atonement, the Triune God has through his infinite love fully satisfied his own undeniable righteousness at his own expense for those who could never pay such a price. That atoning transaction is backed up to the full and for all eternity in the very character of the God who made it. Therefore, no sinner who claims it need ever fear rejection. All that remains for sinners to do is 'to receive the atonement' (cf. Rom. 5:11). Or, in the words of the beloved apostle: '…And let him that is athirst come. And whosoever will, let him take the water of life freely' (Rev. 22:17).

[iv] Ransom Price

Roger Nicole has listed the major references to the ransom made by Christ under '*Language of the Market-place*':

- 'The Son of man came … to give his life a ransom for many' (Matt. 20:28; Mark 10:45).
- 'who gave himself a ransom for all' (I Tim. 2:6).
- 'being justified freely by his grace through the redemption that is in Christ Jesus' (Rom. 3:24).
- 'Christ Jesus who was made unto us … redemption' (I Cor. 1:30).
- 'in whom we have redemption through his blood, the forgiveness of our trespasses' (Eph. 1:7; cf. Col. 1:14).
- 'who gave himself for us that he might redeem us from all iniquity' (Titus 2:14).
- 'having obtained eternal redemption… Death having taken place for the redemption of the transgressions' (Heb. 9:12, 15).
- 'Ye were redeemed, not with corruptible things, with silver or gold, from your vain manner of life… but with the precious blood of Christ' (I Pet. 1:18, 19).
- 'Ye were bought with a price' (I Cor. 6:20; 7:23).
- 'Christ redeemed us from the curse of the law' (Gal. 3:13; cf. 4:5).
- 'thou wast slain and didst purchase unto God with thy blood men of every tribe' (Rev. 5:9; cf. 14:3, 4).

---

74. James Henley Thornwell, *Collected Writings: Volume 2: Theological and Ethical* (The Banner of Truth Trust: Edinburgh, 1986 reprint), 419.

- 'the church of the Lord which he purchased with his own blood' (Acts 20:28).
- 'The redemption of God's own possession' (Eph. 1:14; cf. I Thess. 5:9; Heb. 10:39; I Pet. 2:9).
- 'Forgive us our debts' (Matt. 6:12; cf. Matt. 18:21-35; Luke 7:41-43, 47).

Cf. also passages in which God is represented as the redeemer of his people in the Old Testament, and additional texts in which the terms 'remit,' 'remission' are used with respect to sin.[75]

[v] Victorious Battle

Since the 1930s, the most famous discussion of the death of Christ as victorious battle has been offered by Gustav Aulen. We must briefly survey it, both with appreciation and with necessary criticism, from a Biblical viewpoint. Although its influence is largely past, various approaches to the atonement have a way of resurfacing across the centuries, and in due time, this one is also likely to do so.

Gustav Aulen's *Christus Victor*

Aulen's re-emphasis of the theme of Christ's atonement as victorious battle was translated into English in 1931.[76] It brought back to the fore a theme that had been neglected by both liberal and conservative Protestantism for generations: Christ's battle with and defeat of the devil and his evil powers. Probably, as a result of the rationalism of the Enlightenment, both liberal and conservative ends of the theological spectrum had been long uneasy with the subject of the devil and his evil kingdom, and both preferred to deal with more 'rational' aspects of the atonement; the liberals with the exemplary approach to Christ's death as the supreme illustration of love, and the conservatives with penal substitution.[77]

Aulen did a service to twentieth-century theology in bringing back Christ's victory over the devil to front-stage. He calls it the 'dramatic' view of the atonement, and one would not wish to quarrel with that term.[78] Yet there are serious weaknesses in his presentation of 'the drama of victory over evil', not least in his calling it 'the dominant idea' in the New Testament doctrine of atonement.[79] Equally problematic is his use of the cosmic battle concept to exclude other important biblical metaphors of the atonement. He lays such exclusive emphasis upon this 'dramatic' approach that he essentially negates the others, and, in particular, writes off penal substitution as having been dragged into Western theology a

---

75. Roger Nicole, op. cit., 254-55.

76. G. Aulen, *Christus Victor. An Historical Study of the Three Main Types of the Idea of the Atonement* (London: SPCK, 1931).

77. Aulen, op. cit., 25-29 discusses the lack of sympathy found in both conservatives and liberals for the reality of the demonic.

78. Ibid., 21.

79. Ibid., 22.

thousand years after the New Testament times.[80] According to him, only what he calls 'the classic' view truly goes back to the New Testament and to the Church Fathers.[81]

But, for instance, he mentions Romans 3:24 without rendering an account of what it meant in the larger argument of Saint Paul. He says that it 'cannot rightly be taken to support the Latin doctrine of the Atonement...'[82] But why not? In order to remove it as a witness to satisfaction, he gives only one side of the traditional teaching of, let us say, Anselm or Calvin. He writes: 'According to that doctrine the offering is made to God from man's side, from below; in Paul it is the Divine love itself that makes the redemption.'[83]

On the contrary, Anselm, Aquinas and Calvin (representatives of the 'Latin view') do not deny, so far as I can tell, that when Christ makes the divine offering in his humanity on behalf of his people, it is at the same time motivated and empowered by nothing less than the divine love. Thus, Aulen's removal of Romans 3:24 from the ranks of testimonies to the substitutionary sacrifice (or 'satisfaction') offered by Christ rests on a misunderstanding of what the 'Western' satisfaction theory actually taught. And it does not show any serious exegetical engagement with that crucial text.

Aulen appears largely to write off the highly significant Old Testament background of sacrifice, and, in an exaggerated Lutheran fashion, puts it into the category of mere obedience to the Law.[84] Without needing to subscribe to the whole range of the 'New Perspective on Paul',[85] at least some of the work of N. T. Wright, for instance, would be salutary here.[86] It is surprising that Aulen, who discusses the Epistle to the Hebrews, does not see how profoundly rooted it is in the grace of the Old Testament sacrificial system.[87]

His reading of many of the leading Church Fathers is also marked by a failure to grasp the wholeness of their thought on the atonement. By way of illustration, let us only mention one of them: Irenaeus of Lyon. Most of what Aulen affirms about his teaching is correct. He properly describes Irenaeus' development of the Pauline doctrine of the two Adams, with particular reference to 'recapitulation'.[88] Yet again, he so emphasizes Irenaeus' teaching on the accomplishments of the Incarnation that he

---

80. He claims that the 'dramatic' theory 'was, in fact, the ruling idea of the Atonement for the first thousand years of Christian history' (ibid., 22-23). And 'the Latin type of Christian doctrine [he means 'satisfaction' and penal substitution] turns out to be really a side-track in the history of Christian dogma...' (p. 31).

81. He assumes, without serious exegetical evidence, that his view of the atonement was that of the New Testament, although he does candidly admit that it is an *a priori* assumption with which he approaches the New Testament (p. 77).

82. Ibid., 88.

83. Ibid., 89.

84. Ibid., 95-96.

85. See pp. 412-17 of Volume One.

86. e.g. cf. N. T. Wright, *What Saint Paul Really Said* (Eerdmans: Grand Rapids, MI, 1997).

87. Aulen, op. cit., 90-93.

88. Ibid., chapter II – Irenaeus, pp. 32-51.

loses sight of his affirmation on blood atonement as the payment of a debt owed to God.[89]

This limitation of view in Aulen places him in the category of those interpreters criticized by J.N.D. Kelly who have accused Irenaeus of teaching a 'physical' atonement, as though his mere incarnation automatically in and of itself saved the race, which he assumed.[90] It is true that Irenaeus does not explore in any systematic way the connection of the death of Christ with the redemption of those whom he represents as the Last Adam. But he says enough to indicate that he believed that Jesus' death was a redeeming sacrifice.

Irenaeus states that Christ redeemed us by blood 'from the apostasy' (*Adversus Haereses* 3.5.3); that he 'purified the Gentiles by his blood' (3.12.6); that he 'died and was buried for the human race' (3.9.2). After quoting Matthew 23:35, Irenaeus states: '[Christ] thus points out the recapitulation that should take place in his own person of the effusion of blood from the beginning, of all the righteous men and of the prophets, and that by means of himself there should be a requisition of their blood' (5.14.1).

In other places, Irenaeus points out the results of Christ's death: it removed our condemnation (4.8.2); it redeemed the fallen race from captivity and brought it to communion with God and to immortality (5.1.1): 'Our Lord also by his passion destroyed death and dispersed error, and put an end to corruption, and destroyed ignorance, while he manifested life and revealed truth, and bestowed the gift of incorruption.'

In sum, Aulen is right to state that the major emphasis of Irenaeus is on turning around our human nature, and in so doing to win the battle over Satan and all his powers of corruption. But a careful reading of *Adversus Haereses* will demonstrate the interconnected theme of the sacrificial shedding of Christ's blood in a manner that certainly fits with the later development in the Church of substitution and satisfaction to God, and indeed with the previous New Testament inculcation.

And the same failure to look at more than one side of an issue characterizes much of Aulen's presentation of Christ's atonement as victorious battle. The core of what he affirms about the death of the Lord winning glorious victory over sin, death, and hell is generally well said, and certainly has been neglected. But he fails to consider other biblical images that must be held together at the same time in order to convey the richness of the atonement of Christ, such as satisfaction and penal substitution. If an interpreter of the atonement chooses only one to the exclusion of the others (all of which are affirmed by Scripture), then his doctrine lacks wholeness, and cannot convey the fullness of biblical truth on the death of Christ.

---

89. He does mention some of Irenaeus' references to the blood of Christ (e.g. pp. 43, 47), but is unable to follow the logic of Irenaeus' thought, in his insistence that it is not a 'juridical' doctrine of the atonement (p. 43). His explanation as to why it is not, is far from satisfactory in the terms of the plain meaning of the words of Irenaeus.

90. J. N. D. Kelly, *Early Christian Doctrines* (San Francisco, CA: Harper & Row, 1978), 173.

N. T. Wright on the Old Testament Background of the Victory of Christ

Wright notes that 'The earliest Christians regarded Jesus' achievement on the cross as the decisive victory over evil.'[91] He expands:

> This, then, was how Jesus envisaged the messianic victory over the real enemy. The satan had taken up residence in Jerusalem, not merely in Rome, and was seeking to pervert the chosen nation and the holy place into becoming a parody of themselves, a pseudo-nation intent on defeating the world with the world's methods...discovering the nation as a whole deaf and blind to his plea, he determined to go, himself, to the holy place, and there to do what the chosen people ought to do...we can be confident of what he thought he was thereby going to achieve. He would bring Israel's history to its climax. Through his work, YHWH would defeat evil, bringing the kingdom to birth, and enable Israel to become, after all, the light of the world. Through his work, YHWH would reveal that he was not just a god, but God.[92]

Wright significantly adds: 'Jesus therefore took up his own cross... It was to become the symbol of victory, but not of the victory of Caesar, not of those who would oppose Caesar with Caesar's methods. It was to become the symbol, because it would be the means, of the victory of God.'[93]

Wright lists a large number of scriptural texts that predict the coming victory of the LORD on Zion as a new exodus, to finish for his people what the first exodus began. That greater exodus was accomplished in principle in the victorious death of Christ on Calvary. I merely list (following N. T. Wright), without quoting them, these passages that foreshadow the victory of Christ's atonement.[94]

[vi] The Supreme Example of the Suffering of Selfless Devotion to God

Peter Abelard taught that the primary significance of the cross was its power to inspire love in us: 'by the faith we have concerning Christ love is increased in us, through the conviction that God in Christ has united our nature to himself and that by suffering in that nature he has demonstrated to us the supreme love of which he speaks; through this love "we cling to him and to our neighbor in an indissoluble bond of love for his sake."'[95]

In yet another passage he quoted these words [i.e. John 15:13] to prove that Christ had 'instructed and taught us perfectly' by his death and resurrection, 'proposing an example' through the manner of his dying, 'exhibiting a life of immortality' by his rising from the dead... And on the

---

91. N. T. Wright, *Jesus and the Victory of God*, 607.

92. Ibid., 608-09.

93. Ibid., 610.

94. Isa. 4:2-6; Isa. 24:23; Isa. 25:9-10; Isa. 35:3-6, 10; Isa. 40:3-5; 9-11; Isa. 52:7-10; Isa. 59:15-17, 19-21; Isa. 60:1-3; Isa. 62:10-11; 63:1, 3, 5, 9; 64:1; Isa. 66:12, 14-16, 18-19; Ezek. 43:1-7; Hag. 2:7, 9; Zech. 2:4-5, 10-12; Zech. 8:2-3; Zech. 14:1-5, 9, 16; Mal. 3:1-4; Ps. 50:3–4; Ps. 96:12–13; Ps. 98:8–9.

95. Peter Abelard, *Rom. 2* (CCCM 11: 111-12), quoted in J. Pelikan, op. cit., vol. 3, 128.

basis of these words of Christ he could even define redemption itself as 'that supreme love in us through the passion of Christ,' replacing the fear of God with love for him.[96]

Pelikan shows that, although in certain places Abelard does mention the blood of Christ as a ransom price,[97] still 'all of this language was put into the service of an interpretation of the cross as a means for God "to reveal his love to us or to convince us how much we ought to love him 'who spared not even his own Son' for us."'[98]

His contemporaries pointed out the inadequacy of such a viewpoint. Anselm stated that it would 'be useless for men to be imitators of him [i.e. of Christ] if they were not participants in his merit.'[99] Bernard of Clairvaux said that Abelard, in denying God's attributes beyond that of love, was following the Pelagian heresy rather than Christianity.[100]

In refutation of Abelard, Bernard listed 'the three chief parts of our salvation: the form of humility, in which God "emptied himself"; the measure of love, which extends to death…and the mystery of redemption, for which he sustained the death that he bore…'[101] As Pelikan summarizes: 'Humility and love were absolutely necessary, and the example of Christ was essential; but none of this "has a foundation nor even any reality if redemption is missing."'[102]

Some five hundred years later, Abelard's desire to replace the idea of Christ's death as the payment of sacrifice owed to God's righteousness with an exemplification of love was taken in a far more radical direction by the Unitarian Faustus Socinus in the turmoil of the radical fringe of the Reformation. In 1578 he wrote an intense attack against substitutionary atonement in *De Jesu Christo Servatore*. J.I. Packer describes its main polemic against the traditional biblical doctrine of satisfaction and propitiation:

> What Socinus did was to arraign this idea as irrational, incoherent, immoral and impossible. Giving pardon, he argued, does not square with taking satisfaction, nor does the transferring of punishment from the guilty to the innocent square with justice; nor is the temporary death of one a true substitute for the eternal death of many; and a perfect substitutionary satisfaction, could such a thing be, would necessarily confer an unlimited permission to continue in sin. Socinus' alternative account of New Testament soteriology, based on the axiom that God forgives sin without requiring any satisfaction save the repentance which makes us forgivable, was evasive and unconvincing, and had little influence.[103]

---

96. J.Pelikan, op. cit., 128.

97. Abelard, *Sermon 12* (PL 178:484).

98. Pelikan, op. cit., 129.

99. Anselm, *Cur deus homo* 2. 19.

100. Bernard of Clairvaux, *Epistle* 100. 9. 23.

101. Bernard of Clairvaux, as quoted in Pelikan, op. cit., 129.

102. Ibid.

103. James I. Packer, 'What did the Cross Achieve?,' 4.

Answers to these strong attacks on the traditional Christian doctrine of the atonement are to be found through the various parts of this appendix. Nevertheless, it is important to affirm that true Christianity has always proclaimed the necessity and privilege of following Jesus very closely, in the power of his Spirit and in accordance with his Word, and thereby of imitating him. Charles H. Spurgeon is representative of many, as he expresses this point in his daily devotional for 17 May (morning) on I John 2:6 ('So to walk even as He walked'):

> Why should Christians imitate Christ? They should do it for *their own sakes*. If they desire to be in a healthy state of soul – if they would escape the sickness of sin, and enjoy the vigour of growing grace, let Jesus be their model. For their own happiness' sake, if they would drink wine on the lees, well refined; if they would enjoy holy and happy communion with Jesus; if they would be lifted above the cares and troubles of this world, let them walk even as he walked. There is nothing which can so assist you to walk towards heaven with good speed, as wearing the image of Jesus on your heart to rule all its motions. It is when, by the power of the Holy Spirit, you are enabled to talk with Jesus in His very footsteps, that you are most happy, and most known to be the sons of God. Peter afar off, is both unsafe and uneasy.
>
> Next, *for religion's sake*, strive to be like Jesus. Ah! poor religion, thou hast been sorely shot at by cruel foes, but thou hast not been wounded one-half so dangerously by thy foes as by thy friends. Who made these wounds in the fair hand of Godliness? The professor who used the dagger of hypocrisy. The man who with pretenses, enters the fold, being nought but a wolf in sheep's clothing, worries the flock more than the lion outside. There is no weapon half so deadly as a Judas-kiss. Inconsistent professors injure the gospel more than the sneering critic or the infidel.
>
> But, especially, for *Christ's own sake*, imitate His example. Christian, lovest thou thy Saviour? Is His name precious to thee? Is His cause dear to thee? Wouldst thou see the kingdoms of the world become His? Is it thy desire that He should be glorified? Art thou longing that souls should be won to Him? If so, *imitate* Jesus; be an 'epistle of Christ, known and read of all men.'[104]

[vii] Justification

In the Old Testament the Hebrew word *tsedeq* or *tsedaqah* refers to the righteousness of God and to the righteousness required of man in relation to the character and will of God. The adjective *tsadiq* 'means primarily "to be in the right with God"... The verb *tsadaq* in its hiphil or causative form *hitsdiq* means to "put in the right with God" and so to make righteous...'[105]

In the LXX *tsedeq* and *tsedaqah* are generally translated by *dikaiosune*, 'but often by *eleos* or *eleemosune* (mercy, pity, compassion). But *hesed* (steadfast love) is also translated by *eleos* as well as by *dikaiosune*, and *emeth* (truth) is also translated by *eleemosune* and *dikaiosune*.'[106]

---

104. Charles Haddon Spurgeon, *Morning and Evening: Daily Readings* (Zondervan Publishing House: Grand Rapids, Michigan, 1965), 276.

105. Torrance, *Atonement*, 99, 100.

106. Ibid., 101.

In the New Testament, *dikaiosune* (righteousness) goes back mainly to the Old Testament *tsedeq* and *tsedaqah*. In the Septuagint, *tsedeq* is rendered by *dikaiosune* 81 times, and *tsedaqah* by *dikaiosune* 134 times, but *tsedaqah* is the word for the positive act of righteous mercy…This means that we must take the meaning of *dikaiosune* to be a positive act of divine deliverance in mercy and truth, as in the Old Testament expressions.[107]

Torrance notes:

> [D]*ikaioun* [to justify] in Greek has a double meaning, to do justice to someone, to judge, condemn, that is to judge in order to put right (justify as rectify), but also to deem right (justify as declare right). In the New Testament *dikaioun* goes back to the Hebrew *hitsdiq*, put in the right with God, a positive act of grace…[108]

While we must postpone a fuller discussion of the exegetical and theological details involved in justification, and especially the appropriation of it, until the third volume, we will by way of anticipation simply note here its central idea as conveyed through a few major texts. The wonder of Christ's work on the cross is that God justifies the ungodly!

Romans 4:5 speaks of believing on him 'that justifieth the ungodly'. Romans 3:26 indicates that when God justifies those who believe in Jesus (all of whom are by nature ungodly), he remains righteous (or just). Several passages of the New Testament show how it is possible for God to justify sinners and to remain just.

Romans 5:17 contrasts the death that reigns over sinners through their connection with Adam with 'the gift of righteousness' by Jesus Christ, in which they 'reign in life'. The contrast between Adam and Christ is continued in verse 19: 'For as by one man's disobedience many were made sinners, so by the obedience of one shall many be made righteous.'

In order to emphasize the truth of all humankind being counted in the category of ungodly, Romans 3:20 states that no one can keep the law so as to achieve justification for themselves. That fact, says Paul, was already witnessed to in the Old Testament ('the law and the prophets') – Romans 3:21. What they were looking forward to was to be 'justified freely by his grace through the redemption that is in Christ Jesus' (Rom. 3:24).

Romans 3:25 shows us how God can both remain just and justify the ungodly (who believe): 'Whom God hath set forth to be a propitiation through faith in his blood, to declare his righteousness, for the remission of sins that are past…' We have previously discussed 'propitiation' in this appendix. In brief, here (and in Hebrews 9:5) it means 'mercy seat': the covering of the Ark of the Covenant in the most holy place. It is to be understood as 'propitiatory offering' of blood, turning away the just wrath of God against sin, in analogy with I John 2:2; 4:10 and Hebrews 2:17. This means that God has demonstrated his righteousness as he offers a substitutionary sacrifice for sin, which answers to all the just claims of his

---

107. Ibid.
108. Ibid., 101-02.

holy wrath against all ungodliness. The blood of Christ makes that infinite propitiation. His precious blood not only covers all our sins against the law within the Ark but even goes further than the ritual of the mercy seat was able to do: it totally removes our guilt, not just covers it.

Yet it is God himself who provides this propitiatory offering. We do not propitiate him; God is the subject, not the object of this infinitely availing work. God the Father sends God the Son to reconcile a fallen race to himself; in doing so, he offers a fully sufficient propitiation to the necessarily unchanging integrity of his own character, so that he may at the same time 'be just, and the justifier' of the ungodly who believe in Jesus.

The concept of God's imputation of this finished work to the account of sinners who believe will be considered in volume 3 of this series. In sum, this justification of the ungodly by the one who bore their iniquities (cf. Isa. 53:11) was like the sounding of the silver trumpet of redemption as Christ cried out on Calvary: 'It is finished.'

PART THREE

THE EXALTATION OF CHRIST

The Exaltation of Christ is the most glorious event that ever happened; it makes an old and dying world fresh and new; full of never-ending life. Christ's exaltation is the basis of the continuing existence of the Church, and – along with the saving events of the humiliation which preceded it – is the content of the gladsome message that the Church seeks to communicate to all humankind in its universal mission, to the ends of the earth and to the end of the age. It follows immediately upon The Humiliation of Christ (discussed in chapters 7 to 10), and is the reward the Father gladly paid for all that his Son had willingly accomplished. As has been appropriately said, the resurrection is the Father's 'Amen' to the cross. But the exaltation of Christ includes even more than the resurrection:

Holy Scripture indicates four stages, or saving events, in Christ's Exaltation: (1) Resurrection, (2) Ascension, (3) Session, and (4) Return. These are summarized in the ancient Apostles Creed, recited in millions of churches across the world every week, for almost nineteen hundred years. The Creed states: '...the third day he arose again from the dead; he ascended into heaven, and sitteth on the right hand of God the Father Almighty, from thence he shall come to judge the quick and the dead.'

We shall, for convenience sake, divide the Exaltation of Christ into two sections: Chapter XI – The Resurrection of Christ, and Chapter XII – The Ascension, Session, and Return of Christ (with details of the return postponed until a later volume).

CHAPTER 11

THE RESURRECTION OF CHRIST

Never did the power of the Triune God shine forth more beautifully with such glory and power than in the bodily resurrection of Jesus Christ. Thomas Boston expresses this power most graphically. After speaking of *God's power over natural elements*, he speaks of an even more stupendous power exercised in the resurrection:

> ...in the resurrection of Christ, God exercised a power..., and quenched the flames of his own wrath, that was hotter than millions of Nebuchanezzar's furnaces: he unlocked the prison doors wherein the curses of the law had lodged our Saviour, stronger than the belly and ribs of a leviathan... In this the power of God was gloriously manifested. Hence he is said to be raised from the dead 'by the glory of the Father,' i.e. by his glorious power; and 'declared to be the Son of God with power, by the resurrection from the dead,' Rom. i. 4.[1]

In order to enter into the event that determines our own eternity, we consider here: (a) The event of the resurrection of Christ, and the order of his appearances; (b) The nature of his resurrection; (c) The physical reality of his resurrection; (d) The significance of his resurrection; and (e) The agents of the resurrection.

(a) The Event of the Resurrection of Christ

All four Gospels relate the glorious event of the Lord's rising from the dead, and what they say about it agrees in substance, yet it has not been easy to determine all details of the exact order of his resurrection appearances, although the visit on 'Easter Sunday morning' of certain women to the now empty tomb definitely comes first in all four Gospels.[2] It is clear

---

1. Thomas Boston, op. cit., 85-86.

2. James S. Stewart in *The Life and Teaching of Jesus Christ* (New York: Abingdon Press, 1957), 174-75, comments on these slight differences in details: 'Divergences of detail may certainly be found in

that the tomb was empty, his body was gone, a holy angel (or, according to Luke and John, two angels) at the empty tomb told his disciples that Christ was risen (cf. Mark 16:5-7; Luke 24:2-7; John 20:12), and afterwards he was seen by many different people on several different occasions.

The probable order of resurrection appearances

A close reading of the four Gospels will demonstrate different presentations of resurrection events on Easter Sunday, and in the following days. Matthew, Mark, Luke, and John do not list Christ's appearances in exactly the same order. But these rather different listings of who saw the risen Lord, and of when they occurred, are not necessarily contradictory. Dr. John Wenham of Latimer House, Oxford, has, I believe, done the finest single monograph on how to reconcile these resurrection testimonies, which are otherwise somewhat confusing as to the order in which they occurred.[3]

In order to accomplish this purpose of harmonization, Wenham closely studies the Gospel texts, and at times engages in a certain amount of responsible speculation (e.g. as to who stayed where on the night of the crucifixion, and who was related to whom among the disciples). None of his speculations run contrary to the teachings of the New Testament, or is contrary to reasonable historical expectations.

Out of his remarkable reconstruction of the movements of the disciples of Jesus during the crucifixion and resurrection events, we may concentrate on only one of his major concerns that will help us gain a coherent view of what took place in what order: Where did the disciples of Jesus lodge the night after his crucifixion? What Wenham suggests is not definitive, but is in no sense against Scripture, and does seem to give a greater coherence to these momentous occurrences.

Where did the disciples of Jesus lodge the nights after his crucifixion?

This question helps make sense of what persons first saw the empty tomb, and of who met the risen Jesus in various locations later in the day. If Wenham is right, the disciples lodged in two different places after the crucifixion: (a) in the house of the Apostle John inside Jerusalem and (b) at Bethany, some two miles from Jerusalem.

---

the various Gospel accounts of this supreme event. But these, so far from shaking and destroying the credibility of the narratives, actually enhance it... Here were the other eyewitnesses of the event – Mary Magdalene and others – living through a time of supreme emotion and excitement. Is it to be wondered at that, when at a later day the evangelists came to gather the memories of these crowded, glorious hours and to set them down in their Gospels, some differences of detail should have appeared? Does that detract in the smallest degree from the value of their evidence? On the contrary, we should have had far more reason to be uneasy if such differences had not been there. For then it would have been hard to resist the conclusion that the various accounts had been deliberately harmonized. A good illustration of the way in which such surface variations as we find here are bound to come into reports of stirring and exciting events is provided by the experience of World War I; eyewitnesses of one particular event would describe in each in his own way... It is the witness of men who were themselves utterly convinced, and from first to last it carries conviction.'

3. John Wenham, *Easter Enigma* (Eugene, Oregon: Wipf and Stock, reprint of 1992 edition).

(a) The house of John inside Jerusalem

It would appear that John, the beloved disciple, had a home within Jerusalem. His ownership of a house in Jerusalem seems very likely: he was known to the High Priest (John 18:15), and some ancient sources indicate that while the Zebedee family's main residence and fishing business was in Capernaum, they possessed a house in the capital, since they supplied fish to the Temple, and frequently needed to be there when the fish were delivered.[4]

John took the mother of Jesus to his house on Friday afternoon (John 19:27), and from there, along with Peter, went to the tomb on Easter Sunday morning (John 20:3). According to Wenham: '*In John's house* were Peter and John and Jesus' mother, Zebedee and Salome, the last named expecting the arrival of the two Marys [i.e. Mary Magdalene, and Mary the mother of James] shortly after dawn. *In the Hasmonean palace* were Joanna and "Susanna."'[5]

(b) The house of Mary, Martha, and Lazarus at Bethany

Wenham writes: 'So as Saturday drew to its close, there were (on our best reckoning) *at Bethany* nine apostles, now joined by the two Marys and Clopas. These three doubtless slept uneasily listening for cock crow, anxious to set out for the city at the first streaks of daylight.'[6]

After the arrest of Jesus in Gethsemane, the disciples fled: 'When the arresting party arrived from the city their obvious line of retreat was to Bethany. So we may assume that they all set off in that direction. Evidently Peter and John thought better of it and decided to mingle with the crowd returning to the city, but Matthew and the others presumably lay low in or near that village on Good Friday and over the Sabbath.'[7] As we shall see, in the nature of the case, the group who stayed in Bethany would find out about the resurrection somewhat later than those who had stayed in the house of John.

The following order seems probable:

1. Appearance to Mary Magdalene very early on Resurrection Day – Mark 16:9-10; John 20:1-18.
2. Appearance to other women early that 'Sunday' – Matthew 28:9-10.
3. Appearance to Cleophas and another depressed disciple on the road to Emmaus in the afternoon of Resurrection Day – Mark 16:12-13; Luke 24:13-32.
5. Appearance to Peter on the same day – Luke 24:34.
6. Appearance to the eleven disciples on the evening of the same day – Mark 16:14; Luke 24:36; John 20:19.
7. Another appearance to the eleven, a week later, with Thomas present – John 20:26-31.

---

4. Wenham, op. cit., 146, refers to Nonnus, a fifth century author, whose paraphrase of John's Gospel said that the High Priest knew John through his fishing business (See J. H. Bernard, International Critical Commentary, *The Gospel According to St. John* Vol. 2 [T & T Clark, Edinburgh, 1928] 593 n. 3).

5. Wenham, op. cit., 75.

6. Ibid.

7. Ibid., 45.

8.   Appearance to seven of the disciples, beside the Sea of Galilee – John 21.
9.   Appearance to five hundred brethren at one time – I Corinthians 15:5-8, and most likely Matthew 28:16-20.
10.   Appearance to James, at an unknown time and place – I Corinthians 15:7.
11.   His final appearance on the occasion of his ascension – Mark 16:15-20; Luke 24:50-51; Acts 1:1-13.

It is entirely possible that the risen Christ appeared on more occasions than the ones listed above, for as Acts 1:3 says: 'To whom also he showed himself alive after his passion by many infallible proofs, being seen of them forty days, and speaking of the things pertaining to the kingdom of God...' Similarly, Acts 13:31 may point in this direction: 'And he was seen many days of them which came up with him from Galilee to Jerusalem, who are his witnesses unto the people.'

We shall make some further remarks on several of these post-resurrection appearances.

1. Appearance to Mary Magdalene very early on resurrection day (Mark 16:9-10; John 20:1-18).

Wenham devotes an entire chapter to arguing that Mary Magdalene was, in fact, Mary of Bethany, sister of Martha and Lazarus.[8] Church Fathers disagreed on this identification, and the interested reader is referred to Wenham. Whether Mary the sinner and Mary of Bethany were the same does not affect the order of resurrection appearances followed by Wenham.

It is definite that Mary Magdalene (who, Wenham argues, may have been Mary of Bethany) was the first to see the risen Jesus (Mark 16:9-10; John 20:1-2). She then rushed off to Peter and John (who were also staying in John's house where she was lodging), and shortly afterwards returned to the tomb, and stood there weeping. She had first thought that he was the gardener, but when she heard Jesus utter her name, she cried out 'Rabboni' and fell to his feet, holding on to them (John 20:11-18).

It is at least possible that some other women had already been to the tomb, and found it empty. This could be implied by the words of Mary *'we* do not know where they have laid him' (John 20:2). Yet Wenham seems right: 'This seems improbable as Mary is always mentioned first. Furthermore, the thought of resurrection (which the angel's message would have given her) does not appear to have been in her mind, only the thought that no one would have removed the stone unless it was to take away the body. John's account strongly suggests that she came and went before anyone had entered the tomb.'[9]

Peter and John at the empty tomb

After Mary Magdalene's returns to John's house and relates her stupendous news, Peter and John ran to the now empty tomb (John 20:3). Luke 24:12 mentions only Peter's going into the sepulcher and seeing

---

8. Ibid., Chapter Two, pp. 22-33.
9. Ibid., 91.

the abandoned grave clothes, but what Luke quotes from the report of the Emmaus disciples indicates his awareness of more than one disciple having gone into the empty tomb: 'some of those who were with us went to the tomb' (Luke 24:24). Yet they saw only the empty tomb and grave clothes, whereas Mary Magdalene saw the risen Lord himself.

Peter, the more impetuous one, went into the tomb first, whereas John was more hesitant, but when John finally did go in and saw the grave clothes, 'he saw and believed' (John 20:8). The empty burial wrappings (to be described later) convinced him that the Lord had broken the bonds of death.

2. Appearance to other women early on Easter Sunday (Matt. 28:9-10; Luke 24:22-23).

Luke 24:22-23 says that 'certain women also of our company made us astonished, which were early at the sepulcher; And when they found not his body, they came, saying, that they had also seen a vision of angels, which said that he was alive.' Matthew 28 gives us more information on these chosen women.

It would appear that Mary Magdalene (who had seen the Lord first) shortly after telling the apostles in John's house, returned to the sepulcher with 'the other Mary' (Matt. 28:1). The risen Jesus appears to the two Marys, and tells them to spread the message of his resurrection quickly to his disciples (Matt. 28:7).

There are definite differences between the appearance of the Lord to Mary Magdalene when she was alone, and his appearance to her and the other woman a bit later. As Wenham writes: 'The first is individual, the second is collective; in the first Jesus comes up quietly from behind, in the second Jesus meets them and hails them; the discourse in the two cases is also quite different.'[10]

I believe that Wenham is correct in deducing that other women were involved in meeting the risen Lord, and in being commissioned to tell the disciples whom they had seen. Although not certain, it is possible that there was yet another meeting with the risen One on the road after some of these women had left the Garden Tomb.

According to Wenham, 'The women's commission was less than half fulfilled with nine disciples in Bethany still uninformed, so presumably two or more of them agreed forthwith to tell them the news. The likeliest volunteers would seem to be Salome, mother of James the elder, and Mary, mother of James the younger… One must picture this meeting somewhere on the tract between Jerusalem and Bethany, that is to say, on some part of the Mount of Olives. The women saw him, came up to him, fell on their knees and held his feet. Jesus told them not to fear, but to go and deliver a message to his "brethren".'[11]

Matthew briefly reports this meeting: 'And as they went to tell his disciples, behold, Jesus met them, saying, All hail. And they came and held him by the feet, and worshipped him. Then said Jesus unto them, Be not afraid: go tell my brethren that they go into Galilee, and there shall they see me' (Matt. 28:9-10).

---

10. Ibid., 95.

11. Ibid., 95-97.

3. Appearance to Cleopas and another depressed disciple on the road to Emmaus in the afternoon of Resurrection Day (Mark 16:12-13; Luke 24:13-32).

Wenham gives us reason to think that James the son of Clopas is the same person as James the son of Alphaeus (that is, James the younger), and that Clopas is probably the same as Cleopas. Thus he was father to one of the apostles.[12] If Hegesippus (whom the great Church Historian, Eusebius, quoted) was right, then Clopas/Cleopas was the brother of Joseph, husband of the Virgin Mary, and thus foster-uncle to Jesus Himself.[13]

With this probable family connection, it is likely that Clopas and his wife Mary (who had been at the cross and empty tomb), and the family of Zebedee and Salome were staying in the home of John in Jerusalem, which would have been crowded at Passover time.[14] According to Luke 24, Cleopas tells the as yet unknown stranger (i.e. the risen Lord) that 'certain women of our company...had...seen a vision of angels, which said that he was alive' (v. 22). Then, as they walked along the road and talked, the stranger opened their minds to understand the teaching of the Old Testament that the Messiah (Christ) 'must first have suffered, and then enter into his glory' (Luke 24:28).

We do not know who the other disciple was, but when the three travelers reached the village of Emmaus (some seven miles from Jerusalem), the two bewildered disciples courteously invited the mysterious stranger into the house for an evening (or perhaps late afternoon) meal. They asked him to bless the food, and 'he was known of them in breaking of bread' (Luke 24:35). Probably as he stretched out his hands to bless the bread, they saw the nail prints in the body of the risen One, who was now presiding at their table.

The disciples quickly left to return to Jerusalem in order to tell the other disciples what amazing things had just happened. They were able to enter Jerusalem before the closing of the city gates, and joined the other disciples at their evening meal (Luke 24:33).

4. Appearance to Peter on the same day (Luke 24:34).

Wenham reasonably suggests that this meal to which Cleophas and the other disciple came to join the other apostles was taking place in the large house of John Mark's parents (which he thinks was the same as 'the upper room' where the last supper was held. And he argues that the Garden of Gethsemane was part of the property of this wealthy family).[15]

By the time the Emmaus disciples arrived, they were told that the Lord had already appeared to Simon Peter (Luke 24:34). We are not told in the Gospels where this meeting took place, but Peter (by his Aramaic name, Cephas) is listed first in the Apostle Paul's list in I Corinthians 15:5:

---

12. Ibid., 37-38.

13. Ibid., 38.

14. Ibid.

15. Ibid., 47-49; 104.

'And that he was seen of Cephas [i.e. Peter], then of the twelve.' 'This appearance comes first in Paul's list, though he is careful not to say that it was the first time that Jesus was seen by anyone.'[16]

5. Appearance to the eleven disciples on the evening of the same day (Mark 16:14; Luke 24:36; John 20:19).

In his list of resurrection appearances, Paul first mentions Peter, and says that he appeared 'Then to the twelve' (I Cor. 15:5). 'The twelve' is a summary number, for in John's account two of the original twelve were not present (cf. John 20), and in Luke's account others were also there. As Wenham says: 'It is evident that Paul's use of "the twelve" and Luke's use of "the eleven" are ways of referring to the apostolic body collectively, rather than exact numerical computations.'[17]

Luke and John describe this appearance 'to the twelve' in somewhat different detail. Luke writes: 'And as they thus spake, Jesus himself stood in the midst of them, and saith unto them, Peace be unto you. But they were terrified and affrighted, and supposed that they had seen a spirit. And he said unto them, Why are ye troubled? and why do thoughts arise in your hearts? Behold my hands and my feet, that it is I myself; handle me, and see; for a spirit hath not flesh and bones, as ye see me have. And when he had thus spoken, he shewed them his hands and his feet. And while they yet believed not for joy, and wondered, he said unto them, Have ye here any meat?' (Luke 24:36-41).

John writes: 'Then the same day at evening, being the first day of the week, when the doors were shut where the disciples were assembled for fear of the Jews, came Jesus and stood in the midst, and saith unto them, Peace be unto you. And when he had so said, he shewed them his hands and his side. Then were the disciples glad, when they saw the Lord. Then said Jesus to them again, Peace be unto you; as my Father hath sent me, even so send I you. And when he had said this, he breathed on them, and saith unto them, Receive ye the Holy Ghost; Whose soever sins ye remit, they are remitted unto them; and whose soever sins ye retain, they are retained' (John 20:19-23).

It would appear that by the time Clopas was telling the others behind closed doors in Jerusalem what had happened at Emmaus, Jesus suddenly came and stood in the midst of them. They were frightened, and wondered if it were a ghost, but the risen Lord spoke peace unto them. He invited them to examine his resurrection body, which still had the prints of the nails and of the spear. To show them the substantial reality of his continuing human nature, he asked if they had any food available.

Thus, his resurrection body was transformed: it could become invisible, and pass through stone walls and closed doors. But at the same time it was also substantial and still human; it could be touched; the signs of the wounds were still there, and he could eat, if he wished.

---

16. Ibid., 104.

17. Ibid., 106.

6. Another appearance to the eleven, a week later, with Thomas present (John 20:24-31).

Thomas, one of the original twelve disciples, had not been present on 'Easter Sunday evening' when Jesus appeared to the group in Jerusalem. When they told him the good news, Thomas replied that he would not believe unless he could place his finger in the nail prints in his hands, and his hand in the hole in his side (John 20:25). Eight days later, while the disciples were still in Jerusalem (before their return to Galilee), the risen Jesus appeared to the group, which included Thomas, and called on him to put his finger in the nail prints and his hand in the wound in his side. Thomas cried out: 'My Lord and my God!'

7. Appearance to seven disciples, beside the Sea of Galilee (John 21).

Several of the disciples had followed Simon Peter into a boat to fish all night. They caught nothing, but in the early morning, Jesus was standing on the shore (though they did not at first recognize him). He asked if they had any fish, and when they answered no, he told them to cast the net on the right side of the boat. When they did this, the net filled with so many fish that it was difficult to drag it in.

John seems to have been the first that recognized that it was Jesus, and when he said so, Simon Peter jumped into the sea and swam to shore to greet the Lord. When everyone came to shore, they found that Jesus had built a charcoal fire, and invited them to put some of the fish on it for breakfast, which he gave to the astonished disciples, along with some bread. They realized that a mere ghost does not cook breakfast! The risen Jesus is still a real man, able to take part in the blessings of the common life, though not limited in the way he was formerly.

'When John declares this to be the third revelation of Jesus to the disciples after he was raised from the dead, it is not to be taken as implying ignorance of his individual appearance to Peter or of his appearance to Cleopas and his friend, but it refers to collective appearances to the apostles.'[18]

8. Appearance to five hundred brethren at one time (I Corinthians 15:6, and most likely, Matthew 28:16-20).

Paul does not tell us where this meeting with five hundred brethren at one time took place, but there are good reasons for thinking that this large meeting is the one described in Matthew 28, where 'the Great Commission' was given to the Church. Matthew writes that the eleven went to a mountain in Galilee to which Jesus had directed them (Matt. 28:16). This meeting in Galilee, was not a small one, and while Mark does not describe it, he seems to indicate it, when he relates the earlier word of the angel to the women at the empty tomb: '…he goeth before you into Galilee: there shall ye see him, as he said unto you' (Mark 16:7).

Such a large gathering must have been, as Wenham says, 'a *convened meeting*'.[19] His suggestion seems reasonable, that Jesus had commanded

---

18. Ibid., 112.

19. Ibid., 113.

seven of his apostles to convene this large meeting (during his appearance reported by John in chapter 21).[20] He sent them to a particular mountain in Galilee, to give them 'the Great Commission'. 'It must have been an absorbing undertaking to list the villages of Galilee and to recall the committed believers in each place, and then to arrange for them all to be informed without arousing the suspicions of neighbours or of Herod's government.'[21]

The fact that so many attended (at least five hundred) would explain Matthew's words about this crowd that 'some doubted' (Matt. 28:17). Wenham's words make good sense about the nature of this doubt among some who saw him:

> As in the case of the appearance to the women, Jesus seems to have approached them from a distance. The eleven evidently recognized him at once and prostrated themselves in worship. Some of the others, though fully aware that Jesus had risen, were slower to let themselves believe that the approaching figure was really he… As on previous occasions his appearance was unhurried, so that all the five hundred who were present might have no temptation to think of it later as a hallucination…[22]

It does not mean that any of the apostles doubted, but rather some others of those who were present.[23]

9. Appearance to James (I Cor. 15:7).

The James to whom the risen Lord appeared was most likely the half-brother of Jesus himself, who became the leader of the church in Jerusalem after Peter was imprisoned, and is mentioned as a church leader in Acts (12:17; 15:13; 21:18) and Galatians (1:19; 2:9, 12). The resurrection chapter in I Corinthians (ch. 15) does not tell us the time or place of this private meeting between the risen Lord and his brother James. 'John tells us that the brothers [of Jesus] did not believe…at the time of the crucifixion… But by the time of the Ascension six weeks later we find the Lord's brothers praying with the apostles [as Acts 1:14 shows].'[24] As to the timing, all we know is that the Lord met with James before the ascension.

10. His final appearance at the Ascension (I Cor. 15:7; Mark 16:15-20; Luke 24:50-51; Acts 1:1-13).

After the Great Commission given to the apostles and the five hundred brethren in Galilee, there was a final appearance, probably to the remaining apostles, just before the ascension. The long ending of Mark seems to be referring to it, immediately after speaking of the supernatural signs (in 16:17), and adds: 'So after the Lord had spoken unto them, he was

---

20. Ibid., 115.

21. Ibid.

22. Ibid., 115-116.

23. See ibid., 114.

24. Ibid., 117.

received up into heaven, and sat on the right hand of God. And they went forth, and preached every where, the Lord working with them; and confirming the word with signs following. Amen.' (Mark 16:19-20).

Luke speaks of this final appearance before the ascension: 'And he led them out as far as to Bethany, and he lifted up his hands, and blessed them. And it came to pass, while he blessed them, he was parted from them, and carried up into heaven...' (Luke 24:50-51).

This final appearance is described in Acts 1. Acts 1:2 states that it was to the apostles. This chapter quotes the words of the risen Lord concerning the coming of Pentecost, and their world-wide witness (Acts 1:4-8). Then we are told: 'And when he had spoken these things, while they beheld, he was taken up; and a cloud received him out of their sight. And while they looked stedfastly toward heaven as he went up, behold, two men stood by them in white apparel; Which also said, Ye men of Galilee, why stand ye gazing up into heaven? this same Jesus, which is taken up from you into heaven shall so come in like manner as ye have seen him go into heaven' (Acts 1:9-11).

Some good commentators have thought that these passages are actually referring to the Great Commission to the five hundred on the mountain in Galilee. While possible, it is far more likely that this is a separate and final appearance. Wenham gives several reasons for thinking so.

He gives three reasons why Mark's account is not the same as the Great Commission in Galilee: (1) Mark's account does not seem to move outside the Jerusalem area; (2) the Great Commission and the words of Jesus in Mark 16 'in spite of their common thrust have remarkably little in common verbally – little more than the word "Go" and the two closely related words translated "all".'[25] (3) 'the emphasis in Matthew is on the authority of the risen Christ, while the emphasis in Mark is on the miraculous powers which are to be granted to those who believe...'[26]

Wenham notes that Luke makes no mention of orders to return to Galilee, nor does he promise any further appearances, but says that they are to remain in Jerusalem until they are clothed with power from on high (Luke 24:49).[27] This final appearance was near Jerusalem (not in Galilee). According to Luke 24:50, he led them out 'as far as Bethany'. Wenham believes that this means 'the Mount of Olives at the summit where the descent to Bethany comes into view'. The ascension did not take place at Bethany itself, which is nearly two miles from the city, but as Acts says, at 'Olivet, which is near Jerusalem, a Sabbath day's journey away...'[28]

Post-Ascension Appearances

It is not our purpose here to expound in any detail the post-ascension appearances of the Lord, although we will mention them. (1) The first

25. Ibid., 120.

26. Ibid., 121.

27. Ibid., 123.

28. Referring to E.F.F. Bishop, *Jesus of Palestine* (Lutterworth, London, 1955), 269. Quoted by Wenham in Ibid., 121.

Christian martyr, the deacon Stephen, saw the risen Lord in heaven as he was being stoned (Acts 7:55-56). (2) The risen Lord came down and appeared to Saul of Tarsus on the way to Damascus (Acts 9:1-9; 22:5-12; 26:12-18). Also Saul (Paul the Apostle) reports that the risen Lord appeared to him when at a later time he was in a trance in the temple of Jerusalem (Acts 22:17-21). The risen Christ also appeared to the beloved apostle John, as related in the Apocalypse (e.g. Rev. 1:9-20; 4:1-11, and also chapters 5–8, 20–22).

Complexity of the Order of Appearances is no ground for Scepticism

Borg and Crossan, for instance, leading members of the Jesus Seminar, were not alone in arguing that differences in the resurrection narratives seemed to indicate that they were not to be taken as reports of historical events.[29] But that is a very poor historical argument in light of the fact, as demonstrated above, that no one has as yet shown any clear contradiction among these several accounts of the resurrected Jesus. The real problem that causes these scholars to discount the reality of the resurrection is not the complexity of the order of appearances, but rather their underlying presuppositions: either the non-existence of the God of the Bible, and/or the truthfulness of what his written Word reveals. Their commitment to the naturalism of the European Enlightenment (which excludes God and his supernatural intervention into history), rather than a careful reading of historical texts, makes them exclude unwelcome events of history that run contrary to their philosophy. As W. Pannenberg once noted: 'Unfortunately, however, what passes as the authority of historical competence in the Jesus Seminar is often claimed for judgments that are not unprejudiced.'[30]

A clear illustration of how their naturalist assumptions automatically exclude historical evidence is seen in the way members of the Jesus Seminar, in order to avoid taking seriously the teaching of Scripture on the reality of the resurrection of the body of Jesus, have sought to replace physical evidence with less threatening psychological claims. At a very long distance, they offer a psychological evaluation of what the apostles thought they saw. Crossan is not the only one to resort to psychological claims to discount a physical resurrection, for E. Renan in his *Life of Jesus* had done so much earlier. Both of them, and others over the years, have engaged in desperate attempts to explain away the certainty of the apostles that they had seen the risen Lord, by arguing that it could all be traced to a trance.[31] But a mere assertion that what the apostles saw was only some kind of psychological disturbance does not constitute valid historical research. Rather, it is an effort to rule out of court embarrassing

---

29. M. J. Borg and J. D. Crossan, *The Last Week: What the Gospels Really Teach About Jesus' Final Days in Jerusalem* (San Francisco: HarperSanFrancisco, 2006), 218-219. Bart Ehrman does so as well (see pp. 468-476 of this chapter).

30. W. Pannenberg, 'The Historical Jesus as a Challenge to Christology,' in *Dialog 37* (1998), 22.

31. J. D. Crossan and J. L. Reed , *In Search of Paul: How Jesus's Apostle Opposed Rome's Empire with God's Kingdom* (San Francisco: HarperSan Francisco, 2004), 88.

evidence. Crossan and Reed have no possible way to go back over two millennia in order to disprove a physical resurrection, so as to replace it with psychological phenomena. Again, such a claim is an attempt to keep from considering widely attested facts that do not harmonize with their philosophy of naturalism.

Another effort of some in the Jesus Seminar to evacuate the historicity of the resurrection is in line with the Post-Modernism that explains literary texts as attempts of various political or religious communities to establish power over rivals. Hence, they have claimed that the various accounts of the resurrection appearances in different orders demonstrate 'a rivalry among leaders in the early Jesus movement.'[32] But such a superficial reading back of Post-Marxist political theories onto the early Church utterly fails as a rival explanation of the resurrection of Christ. Once pointed out, it deserves no further comment, other than to say that God has shown great mercy to those who have repented of wrong views of his Son, as we see in the experience of the Apostle Paul.

(b) The nature of his resurrection

As to the qualities of the Lord's resurrection body, the accounts of his appearances that we have just studied indicate at the same time both (i) a continuity with his crucified body, and (ii) a discontinuity between the crucified and the risen body.

(i) A continuity between the crucified (or physical) body and the risen (or spiritual) body

His resurrected body is clearly the same body in which he was crucified, because the tomb was empty when he appeared, and the grave clothes laid aside. Jesus' voice could still be recognized, as by Mary Magdalene (John 20:16, though at first she did not realize whose voice it was – John 20:13-18). Although he could make himself unrecognizable (as on the road to Emmaus in Luke 24:15-16), yet he could also make himself known as the very Jesus with whom they had walked.

It seems likely that when the risen Lord revealed himself to the two Emmaus road disciples in the breaking of bread, in the act of stretching out his hands to bless the evening mercies they would have seen the nail prints in the palms of his hands! This is certainly consonant with Revelation 5:6 that speaks of him in the midst of the throne of God, as 'a lamb that had been slain' (figurative though part of the verse is). But the continuing presence of the wounds in his hands, feet and side are without question shown in the response of the risen Jesus to doubting Thomas: 'Reach hither thy finger, and behold my hands; and reach hither thy hand, and thrust it into my side; and be not faithless, but believing. And Thomas answered and said unto him, My Lord and my God' (John 20:27-28).

---

32. R. W. Funk and the Jesus Seminar, *The Acts of Jesus: What Did Jesus Really Do?* (San Francisco: HarperSanFrancisco, 1998), 454.

The body of the risen Jesus was definitely substantial in terms of physical existence: he could be heard, seen, and touched. Indeed, he was able to cook breakfast on a coal fire by the seaside (John 21:1-14), which he then gave to Peter and other disciples, and he ate along with them (John 21:12). He also had, in an earlier appearance, eaten 'a piece of a broiled fish and of a honeycomb' (Luke 24:42-43).

His continuing physicality is brought out in his sudden appearance to ten of the disciples in Jerusalem, after the meal at Emmaus on the evening of resurrection day. The risen Lord saw that 'they were terrified… supposing that they had seen a spirit' (Luke 24:37). He answers: 'Behold my hands and my feet, that it is I myself; handle me, and see; for a spirit hath not flesh and bones, as ye see me have. And when he had thus spoken, he showed them his hands and his feet' (Luke 24:37-40).

The Puritan preacher, John Flavel, emphasized the substantiality and same personal identity of the risen body of our Lord:

> Christ's body was raised substantially the same body that it was before; and so will ours. Not another, but the same body. Upon this very reason the apostle uses that identical expression, I Cor. xv. 53. 'This corruptible must put on incorruption, and this mortal, immortality.' Pointing, as it were, to his own body when he spake it; the same body, I say, and that not only *specifically* the same, (For indeed no other species of flesh is so privileged) but the same *numerically*, that very body, not a new or another body in its stead. So that it shall be both the *what* it was, and the *who* it was.[33]

(ii) A discontinuity between Christ's crucified (physical) body and his risen (spiritual) body

It was the same Lord; it was the same body. But there was a profound difference, a discontinuity. After his resurrection, he could make himself unrecognizable. Apparently he could go through stone walls or fast-closed doors, as he seems to have done in order to get into the inner room where the somewhat frightened disciples were cowering in Jerusalem the evening of resurrection day (cf. Mark 16:14; Luke 24:36; John 20:19). He could be in Emmaus and then suddenly appear in Jerusalem.

A spiritual body

It would appear that his resurrection body was able directly to pass through the grave clothes in which his crucified body had been wound. Joseph of Arimathaea had seen to it that Christ's body was wrapped in linen. The burial custom of the Jews at that time seems to have involved wrapping the body round with strips of linen cloth, and then sprinkling spices between the folds of the strips, so that the body prepared for burial would have looked somewhat like an Egyptian mummy (cf. Matt. 27:59; Mark 15:46; Luke 23:53). John 19:39, 40 gives us more details, especially as to the usage of fine spices within the folds of the linen shroud: 'And there came also Nicodemus, which at the first came to Jesus by night, and

---

33. John Flavel, 'The Fountain of Life,' op. cit., I. 493.

brought a mixture of myrrh and aloes, about an hundred pounds weight. Then took they the body of Jesus, and wound it in linen clothes with the spices, as the manner of the Jews is to bury.'

When John and Simon Peter went into the empty tomb on resurrection morning, they saw 'the linen clothes lie. And the napkin that was about his head, not lying with the linen clothes, but wrapped together in a place by itself' (John 20:6, 7). As best we can tell, this seems to indicate that the resurrection body of Jesus had, as it were, 'spiritualized,' and passed through the grave clothes, so that the heavy weight of the spices would have made the former shell of the 'mummy' go flat in the absence of the body which had held it up.

Although the collapse of the linen bindings about the body of Jesus seems the most plausible explanation of the testimony of John, the assumption that his grave clothes consisted largely of linen strips wound about him is not the only way of looking at what happened. John mentions the napkin that had been on his head as lying, not with the linen cloths, but wrapped in a place by itself (John 20:7). Wenham summarizes the different details on this matter in John as compared with the synoptic Gospels: 'Of interest is the mention by Luke in 23:53 of a linen shroud (*sindon* – in the singular) and here of *the linen cloths* (*othonia* – in the plural). The former is the word used by Matthew and Mark and the latter by John.'[34] He goes on to state the difficulty of knowing exactly what these two terms mean:

> *Sindon* would certainly be a suitable word for a large sheet or shroud, and it is commonly so translated, but in itself it means no more than a piece of linen. *Othonia* is either a diminutive word which would be suitable to describe small pieces of linen, or it could be an adjective of quality used as a noun, in which case it would refer to pieces of any size, including a large sheet. In other words, the *othonia* might be the bandages which bound wrists and ankles or they might include the shroud as well. One thing seems clear: John is not describing burial cloths which collapsed in situ with the removal of the body, he is showing that the *soudarion* at least had been folded up by supernatural hands and moved to a separate place.[35]

The Shroud of Turin?
It is beyond my competence to go into the issue of whether the Shroud of Turin may be the true burial cloth of Christ. Many serious scholars hold that it is, especially since the discovery in 1898 of a photographic likeness of a deceased figure on the ancient cloth, that was found to be a photographic negative. No one has yet explained how a photographic negative came to be upon a cloth long before photography was invented. Painting would not have done it.[36]

34. Wenham, op. cit., 92.

35. Ibid., 93.

36. See Ian Wilson, *The Shroud of Turin: The Burial Cloth of Jesus Christ?* (Doubleday & Company: Garden City, New York, 1978), chapter II. See also John H. Heller, *Report on the Shroud of Turin* (Houghton Mifflin Company: Boston, 1983), especially chapter 5.

But Thomas de Wesselow, who denies the physical resurrection of Christ, but is intrigued by the Shroud of Turin, has sought to explain how it may have become a photographic negative (in terms of a chemical process known as 'Maillard reaction').[37] In 1988 scientists at three laboratories in Britain, Switzerland and the United States carbon-dated it to between 1260 and 1390, suggesting it was a medieval fake.[38] But on the contrary, a Swiss archeologist, Maria Grazia Siliato, claimed that she had proven the authencity of the Shroud, in answer to the Carbon-14 datings. (She claimed that they were flawed since they were taken from the corner of the cloth, which has been repaired several times since 1400).[39] In the absence of further information, one is inclined to agree with what John Heller says at the end of his detailed study of evidences for and against the Shroud: 'The Shroud remains, as it has over the centuries, a mystery.'[40]

The energy that created and sustains the universe

The resurrection cannot be accurately compared to a butterfly coming out of a chrysalis, for the chrysalis has been worked open at one end, and it is a purely physical thing coming out of a purely physical thing. Jesus' resurrection was different. We cannot know exactly what happened. It would seem that the sheer essence of him who is 'the resurrection and the life' was, as it were, distilled into pure spiritual energy (which is, after all, the basis of the entire created universe), and re-emerged outside the windings of the grave clothes, leaving them as they were.

It appears, then, that the stone was rolled away from the door of the tomb, not to let the Lord out, but to let the disciples in, so that they could see that he was risen, and alive forevermore! In this sense, the resurrection of Jesus was profoundly different from that of his friend, Lazarus of Bethany. When Jesus raised Lazarus, he had to command the bystanders to loose him from his grave clothes, for his was a resuscitated physical body, not a transformed spiritual body (cf. John 11:44). Lazarus' grave clothes still bound him, but Jesus had left his behind.

The Apostle Paul speaks of it as 'a spiritual body': 'It is sown a natural body; it is raised a spiritual body...And so it is written, The first man Adam was made a living soul; the last Adam was made a quickening spirit' (I Cor. 15:44-45). His resurrection body is a glorified body, and as such, surpasses all our presently limited understandings. It does not seem to be subject to the same laws of physics that we are under in this present physical world, but rather is perfectly fitted to the environment of the new heavens and the new earth, wherein righteousness dwells (cf. II Peter 3:13).

Yet this does **not** mean that the body has been replaced by a totally spiritual subsistence, which has swallowed up, and thereby negated its

---

37. Thomas de Wesselow, *The Sign: The Shroud of Turin and the Secret of the Resurrection* (Dutton: New York, 2012).

38. Quoted from *Skeptic News*, August 15, 2012 (http://web.ebscohost.com/ehost'delivery?sid=ee).

39. Ibid.

40. Heller, op. cit., 218.

substantiality and true humanity. T. F. Torrance has addressed this difficult concept with judiciousness:

> The resurrection of the body to be a 'spiritual body' no more means that the body is resolved away into spirit than the fact that we are made 'spiritual men' in Christ means that our humanity is dissolved away in him. To be a spiritual man is not to be less than man but more fully and truly man. To be a spiritual body is not to be less body but more truly and completely body, for by the Spirit physical existence is redeemed from all that corrupts and undermines it, and from all or any privation of being. Hence we must take the *empty tomb* in the Gospel reports quite seriously – the body of Jesus Christ was raised, certainly a spiritual body, but it was no less body because it was a body healed and quickened by the Spirit in which all corruption had been overcome.[41]

Yet 'spiritual body' is nonetheless profoundly different from 'physical body'. William Milligan seems accurately to capture the meaning of 'spiritual body' as described by Paul in I Corinthians 15:

> …by this ['a spiritual body'] he means neither that their bodies shall wholly evaporate into spirit, nor that they shall lose the marks by which upon earth they were distinguished from one another. He means rather that, when raised from their graves or changed, their bodies shall be what they are not now, a full and appropriate expression and organ of their spiritual life, still indeed retaining their individuality, but independent of the limitations by which in our terrestrial state matter is confined… Such a body, being the framework in and by which the Spirit works, must be conformed to the Spirit which rules in all its members. It must interpose no obstacle to the accomplishment of the Spirit's aim. It must rather obey its every impulse, and must accompany it in its every flight.[42]

The Incoherence of the Jesus Seminar's Account of the Spiritual Body

As anyone who has interacted with the writings of the Jesus Seminar would expect, they do not accept the reality of the transformation of Jesus' physical body into a spiritual one. To do so would go against their presupposition that the resurrection appearances 'did not involve the resuscitation of a corpse'.[43] They state that Paul's conversion experience and the vision of Stephen during his stoning are psychological visions, rather than objects of physical sight.[44]

But again, one has to ask: how could they know this? The reality of Christ's burial clothing left in the empty tomb does not comport with a mere psychological state of affairs among the witnesses, nor does Jesus' showing the disciples that he has 'flesh and bones' fit such a claim. Acts 2:30-32 says that the body of Jesus was unlike the body of David in that it did not decay, for it was raised up.

---

41. T. F. Torrance, *Space, Time and Resurrection*, 140-141.

42. William Milligan, *The Ascension of our Lord* (London: Macmillan and Co., 1894), 19.

43. Funk and the Jesus Seminar, op. cit., 461.

44. Ibid.

Instead of continuing to list other details that show the incoherence of their 'psychologizing away' all evidence for the bodily resurrection, it will be sufficient to look at their underlying methodology. To do so, one has only to point out the glaring inconsistency of the Jesus Seminar in setting forward their claims of presenting a non-resurrected Jesus. They are clearly forced to employ various texts of the New Testament in order to get enough information to write their books (so as to disprove his resurrection), but at the same time, they exclude those parts of it that do not fit their naturalistic starting-point. Such intellectual inconsistency does not commend the integrity of their project, and therefore it cannot be considered a serious alternative to a believing exposition of the entire text of the New Testament.

Here we do best to stand within the community of faith: Israel and the Church, to whom the Holy Scriptures were given.[45] Only upon the ground where God has made himself known, can we grasp the parts in light of the whole, and the whole in light of the parts in all aspects of the Christ Event. From within the Holy Scriptures we may join David, as he says: 'In thy light shall we see light' (Psalm 36:9). To make sense of the Scriptures, faith is required, and for faith to be in exercise within our personalities, the Holy Spirit is required. Jesus gives us the right to call upon God in the Saviour's name for the downcoming upon us of the Holy Spirit (Luke 11:13). It is sincerely hoped that some who follow the Jesus Seminar may do so. Far stranger things have happened!

(c) The physical reality of his resurrection

T. F. Torrance has argued that denials of the resurrection, supposedly on the basis of science, are based, not on true science, but on an outdated dualistic 'scientism':

> Whether the dualism concerned is epistemological or cosmological or both (which is usually the case), there results a conception of reality and a frame of mind which automatically and indeed dogmatically excludes any idea of miracle or of resurrection or of any such objective act of God within the concrete structures of the world, as 'an interference in the laws of nature,' and therefore as 'scientifically inconceivable'...
>
> In actual fact this reduced itself to a conception of a rigid uniformity of all natural processes which by definition excluded as 'real' any event which did not conform to its 'system.' Such a view, however, began to shatter itself against the actual 'fact' of the electromagnetic field which could not be explained in such a mechanistic way, and since the emergence of relativity theory has had to give way to a profounder and more differential view of reality in which energy and matter, intelligible structure and material content, exist in mutual interaction and interdetermination. This is a dynamic view of the world as a continuous integrated manifold of fields of force in which relations between bodies are just as ontologically real as the bodies

---

45. See Kelly, *Systematic Theology*, *vol. I*, 'We know God and His Truth only in the Covenant Community Appointed by Him' (419-444).

themselves, for it is in their interrelations and transformations that things are found to be what and as and when they are.[46]

While most of science has moved on past the post-Newtonian dualism,[47] which saw the world as a collection of discrete particles, moving about in a closed causal, mechanistic framework, which excluded openness to higher levels of reality to make sense of the lower (to refer to Godel's famous theorem), much of theology is still operating in the older theory, and therefore automatically excludes any miracle, and especially the supreme miracle of the resurrection of Christ. But they do not do so because of the facts of operational science; they do so on the basis of an outmoded mechanistic theory, with which they still feel comfortable, even though it removes all hope. What Paul said must be said of such thinkers: 'If in this life only we have hope in Christ, we are of all men most miserable' (I Cor. 15:19).

In other words, this mechanistic theory is no longer the main assumption of scientists and philosophers in the way it was before Einstein's Relativity Theory. For instance, Richard Swinburne, well-known professor of philosophy at Oxford, although positing contradictions and errors in Holy Scripture, and not generally accepting the traditional theology of the Reformation, nonetheless has written extensively against the secularist, mechanistic thesis that 'science' or 'natural law' precludes the existence of God, the incarnation of Christ, or the resurrection of Christ.[48] In an Appendix to his recent book on the resurrection, Swinburne works out a formal logical argument to demonstrate the high probability that Jesus Christ, the incarnate Son of God, rose from the dead.[49] He works in terms of the probability calculus, developed in the seventeenth century. In it 'The maximum probability for an event is 1, the minimum 0, and if something is as probable as not it has a probability of ½.'[50] I am not well enough trained in formal logic to grasp all of the steps in his argument, but merely note that the results of his demonstration amounts to .97 percent (out of the highest 1.00).[51]

I do not suggest that this kind of logical reasoning (even though as best I can tell, it is probably correct) will necessarily convince people to believe in the resurrection of Christ, if they do not want to, nor do those who already believe need this sort of possible assistance. But I mention it here only to show that some major intellectual leaders do not subscribe to the inherent impossibility of such divine miracles as incarnation and resurrection, and that in itself may be of encouragement to some who are otherwise wavering.

---

46. T. F. Torrance, *Space, Time and Resurrection* (Edinburgh: The Handsel Press, 1976), 181, 184, 185.

47. e.g. See T. F. Torrance's *Theological Science* (op. cit.), passim.

48. See especially his trilogy: *The Coherence of Theism* (1977, revised 1993); *The Existence of God* (1979, revised 1991), and *Faith and Reason* (1981).

49. Richard Swinburne, *The Resurrection of God Incarnate* (Clarendon Press: Oxford, 2003), 204-216.

50. Ibid., 204.

51. Ibid., 214.

The canons of secular historiography not applicable here

Whether they are committed to outmoded mechanism or not, the inability of some to come to terms with the reality of Christ's bodily resurrection can be looked at in another way. What the Almighty God did in the original creation of all things out of nothing, and what he does in the new creation when he triumphantly raised his Son as 'the first-fruits of them that slept' (I Cor. 15:20), cannot be perceived by means of the canons of secular historiography.

Torrance is helpful again on this matter:

> The methods and canons of credibility with which the secular historian works are strictly appropriate only to the kind of historical happening in a world still schematized to the conditions and determinations of sin and guilt, and therefore are not properly or adequately applicable to the resurrection event that triumphs over them in the redemption of time and history.
>
> The kind of time we have in this passing world is the time of an existence that crumbles away into the dust, time that runs backwards into nothingness. Hence the kind of historical happening we have in this world is happening that decays and to that extent is illusory, running away into the darkness and forgetfulness of the past. As happening within this kind of time, and as event within this kind of history, the resurrection, by being what it is, resists and overcomes corruption and decay, and is therefore *a new kind of historical happening* which instead of tumbling down into the grave and oblivion rises out of the death of what is past into continuing being and reality. This is temporal happening that runs not backwards but forwards, and overcomes all illusion and privation or loss of being... Hence while the resurrection is an event that happened once for all, it remains *continuous live happening* within history, and must therefore be interpreted as running against the patterned stream of history, or the secular framework of our space and time.[52]

Valid evidence depends on historical persons

D. Staniloae also addresses in a way not dissimilar to T. F. Torrance the historical character of the resurrection. He writes, with some reference to W. Pannenberg:

> *If the persons to whom the risen Christ appeared are historical persons, through them it was possible to verify,* according to all the rules of historical method, if not the manner of Christ's Resurrection and the characteristics of his risen body, in any case *the fact of the Resurrection.* It does not have verisimilitude in the analogy with other historical phenomena, but it responds otherwise to the demands of verifying methods for a historical fact. Considering that verisimilitude is a 'premise' or a 'prejudgment' that a researcher has before any research is done, he does not have the right to repudiate, on the basis of this 'subjective' apriority, a fact that is proven through research to be real...
>
> W. Pannenberg bases his position on this issue on a different conception of history, in which he gives serious attention to its contingence by not deriving the events from a rigid, natural causality, but underlying their

---

52. T. F. Torrance, *Atonement*, 245, 246.

uniqueness against the affirmation of the essential uniformity of everything that is occurring in it.[53]

Through this Pannenberg offers an objective basis for the fact that the principle of verisimilitude, or of analogy, is met in the case of the Lord's Resurrection by a fact that discounts them. This basis cannot be other than the opening of history to an order beyond strictly immanent causality, closed in a rigorous repetition of similar phenomena. No one can prove that history does not have such an opening. Not only do evident, unique, and inexplicable forces from the strictly historical plane prove its contingency, but no one can prove incontestably that in the generality of the historical plane's usual facts, factors above the human, immanent ones do not participate in the generating of historical facts. Who can show, in fact, where the boundary of humanity is? Is not humanity open to a superhuman domain whose inspirations and forces influence, help, or hinder it? Without a doubt.[54]

An Orthodox Jewish look at the witnesses to the resurrection

An Orthodox Jewish rabbi, Dr. Pinchas Lapide, has written in favor of the authenticity of Christ's bodily resurrection, with emphasis upon the validity of the witnesses:

> (1) According to all four Gospels, women are the first ones to find the tomb of Jesus open and empty. In a purely fictional narrative one would have avoided making women the crown witnesses of the resurrection since they were considered in rabbinic Judaism as incapable of giving valid testimony (compare Luke 24:11)...

> (2) In addition there is the fact that the women at the empty tomb were in the greatest excitement, 'for trembling and astonishment had come upon them.' They even fled at first from the tomb 'and they said nothing to anyone, for they were afraid' (Mark 16:8)...

> According to all New Testament reports, no human eye saw the resurrection itself, no human being was present, and none of the disciples asserted to have apprehended, let alone understood, its manner and nature. How easy it would have been for them or their immediate successors to supplement this scandalous hole in the concatenation of events by fanciful embellishments! But precisely because none of the evangelists dared to 'improve upon' or embellish this unseen resurrection, the total picture of the Gospels also gains in trustworthiness.[55]

---

53. W. Pannenberg, 'Dogmatische Thesen zur Lehre von der Offenbarung,' in *Offenbarung als Geschichte*, Pannenberg, ed. (Gottingen, Germany: Vanderhoeck & Ruprecht, 1965), 98ff, quoted in Staniloae, op. cit., vol. 3, 241.

54. D. Staniloae, op. cit., 241-242.

55. Pinchas Lapide, *The Resurrection of Jesus* (London: SPCK, 1983), 95-97.

Significant Differences Between General (or 'Secular') Historiography and that of New Testament Scholars.

All of this is to say that how we determine what constitutes valid historical evidence will depend upon our underlying historiography, which in turn depends upon our view of ultimate reality. Michael R. Licona has published a major study of the significant differences between the historiography used by most general (i.e.,'secular,' though not necessarily 'secularist') historians, and that used by most modern New Testament scholars.[56]

As we noted in the first volume of this series, Torrance and others have pointed out how much of modern physics decades ago moved past the post-Newtonian dualism between the physical world and the human mind, so that there has been a return to realism, which is based on the understanding that the external world is real, and that our minds are constituted to know it to a considerable degree. But large numbers of New Testament scholars seem still stuck in the assumption that we must be skeptical about knowing anything accurately in nature and in history; not least in what the Biblical texts tell us about the life of Jesus.

Concerning the contemporary work of the general historical academy, Licona argues that '...post-modernism has lost the battle of ideologies among professional historians, and realism remains on the throne, although chastened.'[57] Craig Blomberg (as quoted by Licona) states that the skeptical methodology used by many New Testament scholars to this day, if applied to ancient history 'would find the corroborative data so insufficient that the vast majority of accepted history would have to be jettisoned.'[58]

The reason for the rejection of a realist (or at least, 'critical realist')[59] reading of the New Testament text by scholars (such as those in the Jesus Seminar) is based on their metaphysical naturalism, 'which is no less a philosophical construct than supernaturalism and theism.'[60] This kind of anti-supernatural bias excludes a serious reading of the New Testament text on the resurrection.[61]

Who, for instance, could accept as serious historiography, or even as logically coherent, John Dominic Crossan's statement: 'Emmaus never happened. Emmaus always happens?'[62] Standing, as they have to, on the

---

56. Michael R. Licona, *The Resurrection of Jesus: A New Historiographical Approach* (IVP Academic, 2010).

57. Michael R. Licona, op. cit., 86.

58. Craig Blomberg, *The Historical Reliability of John's Gospel: Issues and Commentary* (InterVarsity Press: Downers Grove Ill., 2007), 304, quoted in Licona, op. cit., 96.

59. See discussion of 'critical realism' by Licona in op. cit., 89-90, 107, 156, note.

60. Ibid., 604.

61. Licona says it well: 'This is dangerous and it thwarts a proper practice of history. For when bias is left unchecked and method is followed haphazardly, the results are a practice of history that is a sort of fantasy world where undisciplined imagination reigns, responsible method is consigned to lower-class housing and largely ignored, and exegesis serves as a torture chamber where the historian stretches biblical texts and the meaning of words until they tell him what he wants to hear' (op. cit., 130).

62. J. D. Crossan, *The Historical Jesus*, op. cit. xiii.

grounds of unproved assumptions, modern naturalists are no less credulous than the believers whom they reproach for it.[63]

As a simple believer, one could wish that the left-wing of New Testament scholarship would follow their brethren in the general, secular arm of the historical academy in moving from methodological skepticism to some kind of critical realism, which is open to the real world, and to the plain teaching of ancient (or modern) texts. Licona's interaction with the skeptical biblical scholar Bart Ehrman on this point is illuminating, and the interested reader is referred to it.[64]

The Nominalistic New Testament Theology of Bart Ehrman and His approach to the Resurrection

Although Bart Ehrman is Professor of New Testament at the University of North Carolina at Chapel Hill, which is an undergraduate and a postgraduate institution, it is to be noted here that the significance of his writing is more on the popular level rather than academic research in New Testament scholarship (although he would be well able to achieve the most serious research). But of course, there is always an important place for popularization, and he is very effective in spreading his ideas of the lack of veracity of the New Testament writings in general, and of the unreliability of its presentation of Jesus Christ. Perhaps for his ability to communicate concepts that are becoming more acceptable to the increasingly secularized public, he is widely listened to by much of the American popular culture, and has had significant influence among the younger generations, who are not so well churched as previous generations.

But to understand what Ehrman is really doing, one must look beneath the details of his articles and books on various issues in New Testament theology. If one does so, one will discern a pattern, or a methodological program in major sections of his writings, by which he pursues his research. It is worth examining this procedure before discussing his teaching on the resurrection, for it serves as its context. The methodology of a large part of Ehrman's writings seems to be based on what one might call a sort of philosophical *Nominalism* in which he mainly looks at bits and pieces of New Testament material as movable parts of a puzzle, and does not see any overarching pattern of objective truth.

Since the late fourteenth century (with the powerful Nominalist theologian, William of Ockham), on down to the present, by way of the deconstructionists, these kinds of intellectuals have worked with a damaged relation between existence and language, and have assumed a split between idea and image, which makes it impossible to express an overarching reality to which the language should refer.[65] (This does *not* mean that

---

63. '...credulity is not unique to believers and can be present in the historical work of skeptical scholars who uncritically accept poorly supported natural hypotheses that are terribly ad hoc' in Licona, op. cit., 491.

64. Ibid, 171-182, 588-599.

65. T. F Torrance has analyzed the underlying problem with nominalism as follows: 'Nominalism so focuses on the form of the words themselves (which are held to represent only individual phenomena, not universal realities or classes) that their reference to the reality above

any particular modern scholar necessarily studies the fourteenth century Nominalist theologians and then sets out to follow them. Rather, when scholars wish to evade the clear meaning of a text, it is a tendency of the human mind to seek to avoid its teaching by so focusing on discrete pieces, broken off from the whole, that what Athanasius termed 'the scope' of the text is eclipsed, and the mind of man is no longer under the direct mastery of the objective truth).[66] Thus, Nominalism is opposed to Realism, for among other concerns, Realism assumes a true relationship between the written text and the external reality to which it leads you.[67]

The long history of Realism (going back to Plato) is far more complex than I can discuss here, and there are variations within the Realist tradition.[68] For instance, in company with the general Church Tradition, I write, not from the position of 'extreme realism' (that – with Plato – assumes 'forms' existing in a separate realm from what we perceive about nature), but rather 'moderate realism' (that –with Aristotle and Aquinas – sees 'forms' [or 'universal concepts'] as existing in the mind that has perceived these realities through sense perception, although they are not free creations of the mind, but truly reflect objective realities outside the mind). Or, to be more precise, when it comes to the usage of words and the interpretation of written texts, we may call the epistemology of the classical Christian tradition: 'critical realism':[69] that is to say, a true text can accurately convey objective truth from outside itself, but that text does not totally include the fullness of that reality, and is under the reality, not above it; aspects of this are discussed by Alvin Plantinga.[70]

In precise contradiction to Realism, I am suggesting that Ehrman, in his theological writings, is following a sort of Nominalist procedure (though he may or may not be consciously aware of the details of the philosophical and epistemological bearings of Nominalism and Realism). Before going further into Ehrman's methodology, we must look more closely at how Nominalism works. In his classic study of Nominalism, Paul Vignaux notes with reference to Ockham's 'Second Distinction in the First Book of his *Commentaries on the Four Books of (Lombard's) Sentences* (Question VI, E), that:

---

them can only be indirect. But with realism, signs or words fulfill their semantic function properly when we attend away from them to the realities they signify or intend...[they] serve as transparent media through which those realities show themselves' (from his Chapter (2) on 'Theological Realism' in *The Philosophical Frontiers of Christian Theology*, B. Hebblethwaite and S. Sutherland, eds. (Cambridge University Press, 1982), 96).

66. See T. F. Torrance's discussion of 'the scope' of the texts of Scripture in *Divine Meaning: Studies in Patristic Hermeneutics* (T & T Clark: Edinburgh, 1995), 236-244.

67. For a fuller account of nominalism and realism as they relate to theological issues, see Douglas Kelly, Volume 1, op. cit., 36-46, 90, 116-117, 226, 301.

68. Many of the issues that arose in the history of Realist philosophy are found in the articles referenced in these footnotes from Vignaux and Gorce in *Le Dictionnaire de Théologie Catholique*. More recent reflections are in John Peterson, *Introduction to Scholastic Realism* (Peter Lang, 1999); J. P. Moreland, *Universals* (McGill-Queen's University Press: Toronto, 2001), and in Edward Feser, *The Last Superstition: A Refutation of the New Atheism* (St. Augustine's Press: South Bend, Indiana, 2008), especially chapters 2 and 3.

69. See discussion on p. 467 of this volume.

70. Alvin Plantinga, *Warrant and Proper Function* (Oxford University Press: New York, 1993), particularly chapter 6. See also p. 467, footnote 59, in this chapter on 'critical realism.'

> It is not the [actual or objective] things that we know, but propositions about things…The content of thought matters little; we are presented here with a purely formal point of view…The sort of logic which is the starting point of nominalism makes [from one's mental concept] a mere word; the knowing process does not result in a grasp of eternal content by the mind, but merely gives a word about a thing, which remains exterior to it, and thus thought plays the role of a kind of algebra.[71]

T. F. Torrance has shown in detail how this sort of nominalistic split between existence and language, between image and idea, worked in the demythologization program of Rudolph Bultmann.[72] And Ehrman seems to be following some aspects of Bultmann's theology at a more popular level.[73]

Before coming to Ehrman's peculiar account of the resurrection, we may look first at the broader context in which he employs nominalistic methodology in many of his popular books to deal with textual variants of the New Testament. Certainly he is an expert in the textual history of the New Testament documents, and also of the early centuries of Church History. But he uses his expertise in a direction that goes quite contrary to almost two thousand years of the Christian tradition (which always assumed that the scriptural texts, for all their variations, accurately conveyed objective truth from above them, which gave rise to them).

In order to avoid the truths to which the inspired texts are pointing, some sort of 'Nominalism' is perhaps one of the most effective tools (though, as we shall see, it is not the only one that Ehrman employs). But in major areas of his work, some kind of nominalism is the direction that Dr. Ehrman takes. And the way this scholar handles the text of the New Testament will later help us understand the approach he takes to the resurrection. But before we come to the subject of this chapter – the resurrection of Christ – we need to glance at Ehrman's nominalistic approach as he uses variant readings of the New Testament text (or at least the competing sects to which he imaginatively ascribes them) as though they were competing soldiers against one another, rather than seeing them as the rich, diverse yet finally unified testimony they are to an extremely well-established, ancient, textual tradition.

He spends the larger part of one of his books doing so, in which he marshals different textual readings, sometimes magnifying the significance of the differences between them, and nearly always failing to consider very well known and reasonable possibilities of resolution, which a person as well read as he would be fully aware of. In *The Orthodox Corruption of Scripture: The Effect of Early Christological Controversies on the Text of the New Testament*, he notably fails to look at substantial counter evidence in claiming that "'orthodoxy", in the sense of a unified group

---

71. Paul Vignaux, 'Nominalisme', an article in *Dictionnaire de Théologie Catholique*, Tome 13, Premiere Partie, A. Vacant et al., eds. (Librarie Letourzey et Ane: Paris, 1936), 743 (my translation).

72. See T. F. Torrance, *Incarnation: The Person and Life of Christ*, 274-96.

73. Some of Ehrman's books have no references to Bultmann (such as his *Jesus Interrupted*). But Ehrman's *The Orthodox Corruption of Scripture* does include several references to Bultmann.

advocating an apostolic doctrine accepted by the majority of Christians everywhere, did not exist in the second and third centuries.'[74] He attempts to lift up to the same level as orthodox Christianity (or maybe above it) heretical sects that were consistently rejected by the historic Christian Church.[75]

Consistent with his nominalistic concentration on different pieces of the puzzle (some of which were either never considered by the main Church tradition, or were summarily rejected) in order to avoid the overall portrait it paints, he (by reusing Walter Bauer's 1934 speculation on the many competing groups in early Christianity) posits a large number of contenders for the faith, as though they were more or less equal in validity, but not in continuing influence (which the supposedly aggressive and politically influential 'orthodox' finally won).[76] Hereby, he manages to avoid the message of the widely attested major texts of the Church. Indeed, to achieve his goal, he goes so far as to label traditional orthodoxy as only one among many competitors for ecclesiastical power, or (in somewhat later terms) 'heresies'.

Michael Kruger and Andreas Köstenberger,for example, address with depth Ehrman's approach in *The Heresy of Orthodoxy*, where they point out Ehrman's strange interpretation of many New Testament variants as a way to disprove an extremely well-accredited ancient text. They note:

> For [Ehrman], the quest for the original text is somewhat of an 'all or nothing' endeavor. Either we know the wording of the original text with absolute certainty (meaning we have the autographs, or perfect copies of the autographs), or we can have no confidence at all in the wording of the original text. Unfortunately, this requirement of absolute certainty sets up a false dichotomy that is foreign to the study of history. As historians, we are not forced to choose between knowing *everything* or knowing *nothing* – there are degrees of assurance that can be attained even though some things are still unknown. This false dichotomy allows Ehrman to draw conclusions that are vastly out of proportion with the actual historical evidence. Although his overall historical claim is relatively indisputable (that the New Testament manuscripts are not perfect, but contain a variety of scribal variations), his sweeping conclusions simply do not follow (that the text of the New Testament is unreliable and unknowable). We can have *reliable* manuscripts without having *perfect* manuscripts. But it is precisely this distinction that Ehrman's 'all or nothing' methodology does not allow him to make.[77]

But, interestingly, when an ancient textual tradition that supports a central orthodox doctrine does *not* have very many variants (as is the case with a number of texts that confirm the divinity of Christ), then he

---

74. Bart D. Ehrman, *The Orthodox Corruption of Scripture* (Oxford University Press: New York, 1993), 7.

75. As in Ehrman, *Lost Christianities: The Battles for Scripture and the Faiths We Never Knew* (Oxford University Press: New York, 2003).

76. Ehrman, *The Orthodox Corruption of Scripture*, 7-9.

77. Andreas Köstenberger and Michael Kruger, *The Heresy of Orthodoxy* (Crossway: Wheaton, IL, 2010), 228-229.

meets this embarrassment by inventing the qualification that 'Because it was the victorious party of later centuries that by and large produced the manuscripts that have survived antiquity, we should not expect to find in them a large number of textual modifications that support an adoptionistic Christology.'[78] Would this kind of tampering with inconvenient evidence by bringing in a gratuitous hypothesis hold up in a court of law? Would it not be deemed to be a way of begging the question?[79]

What I have called Ehrman's methodological 'nominalism' (i.e. a manipulation and focusing upon many supposedly disparate pieces in the apparent interests of avoiding sight of the whole) functions within his underlying commitment to 'deconstructionism', which is itself a certain kind of nominalism that degrades any overall truth by reducing different claims to truth to self-serving assertions of competing communities of power (as in deconstructionism).[80] Of course, much that he writes is true, and nearly always interesting, but the way Ehrman's uses a certain variety of nominalism is like (as a good friend of mine once remarked) 'shattering a mirror into small shards in order to see better' (i.e., actually, to keep from having to face an unwelcome truth). Functionally, with the traditional Biblical assumption of *realism*, we assume that the text accurately points above us to objective realities, where we find universal truths (and not just disconnected individual pieces), so that the text itself is master of what we seek to understand. But with *nominalism*, there is such an impassible space between text and reality, that the interpreter places himself into that space, and becomes master of the text.

This is the precise opposite of what Saint Paul declared in Romans 10:17: 'So then faith cometh by hearing, and hearing by the word of God.'

This brief overview of Ehrman's nominalistic denial of realism in his handling of early Christianity and the New Testament text is manifestly exhibited in his account of the resurrection of Christ. On the one hand, it is typical of his nominalistic breaking into separate shards the New Testament witness through calling on 'multiple Christianities' and variant

---

78. Ehrman, op. cit., 97. But in fairness to him, he openly states what his overall objective is: namely, that while, 'By far the vast majority [of textual variations] are purely 'accidental,' ...My interest in the present study, however, is not with accidental changes but with those that appear to have been made intentionally' (27).

79. I do not wish to suggest that all of his dealings with variant textual readings are this slight. Frequently he brings up issues that do require serious discussion, and in so doing, makes reference to such widely respected scholars as Bruce Metzger, who taught him at Princeton, and actually dedicates a book to Dr. Metzger. However, even in a number of these cases, his methodology is still what I have termed 'nominalistic', as for instance with his discussion of variants in I John 4, where he imagines a whole history to explain differences. He posits the varying texts as having come from controversies over 'Separationist Christologies' of the Gnostics, in chapter 3 of *The Orthodox Corruption of Scripture*. I call his imagined history 'nominalistic' in the sense that he multiples competing witnesses (without serious evidence of their historical existence – at least in the instance of the textual variations before him) in order to keep from considering the clear message of the written text.

80. A typical illustration of deconstructionist employment of a Marxist-derived competition between power groups (as a way to avoid considering the truth to which the text points) is found in Aviezer Tucker, where he states: 'these stories should be read as metaphors or as fabrications in the service of the political or other interests of their authors' (Tucker, 'Miracles, Historical Testimonies, and Probabilities,' in *History and Theory* 44 [2005], 385).

ancient texts. In the case of the resurrection, as usual, he brings in the 'broken' (from the larger discourse and reference of the text) and separate 'shards' of varying witnesses to the resurrection of Christ, in order to pit them one against another (as, for instance, with supposed 'contradictions' in who went to the empty tomb[81]).

But here, in dealing with the resurrection of Christ, Ehrman shows us the heart of what must have driven him to make use of a certain form of nominalism, which is the refusal to accept some great, unwelcome reality, presumably because of one's underlying presuppositions. Those presuppositions can usefully be summarized in his denial of the functional impossibility of miracles (because these would indicate the unwonted intervention of *a transcendent God*).[82] Indeed, in one of the standard articles on Realism, M. Gorce states that many people reject realism because they do not want to face squarely the dilemma: 'God or nothing.'[83]

> Why was the tomb supposedly empty? I say supposedly because, frankly, I don't know that it was. Our very first reference to Jesus' tomb being empty is in the Gospel of Mark, written forty years later by someone living in a different country who had heard it was empty. How would he know?... Suppose...that Jesus was buried by Joseph of Arimathea...and then a couple of Jesus' followers, not among the twelve, decided that night to move the body somewhere more appropriate...But a couple of Roman legionnaires are passing by, and catch these followers carrying the shrouded corpse through the streets. They suspect foul play and confront the followers, who pull their swords as the disciples did in Gethsemane. The soldiers, expert in swordplay, kill them on the spot. They now have three bodies, and no idea where the first one came from. Not knowing what to do with them, they commandeer a cart and take the corpses out to Gehenna, outside town, and dump them. Within three or four days the bodies have deteriorated beyond recognition. Jesus' original tomb is empty, and no one seems to know why.
>
> Is this scenario likely? Not at all. Am I proposing this is what really happened? Absolutely not. Is it more probable that something like this happened than that a miracle happened and Jesus left the tomb to ascend to heaven? Absolutely! From a purely historical point of view, a highly unlikely event is far more probable than a virtually impossible one...[84]

We have seen how Ehrman avoids a 'realist' acceptance of the New Testament witness to the resurrection of Jesus (in typical nominalist fashion) by attempting to show a multitude of irresolvable contradictions as the sole manner of accounting for the considerable number of accounts of Christ's resurrection appearances. But he also has another ploy: he

---

81. Ehrman, *Jesus Interrupted*, 48.

82. One assumes that Ehrman is following to a magnified degree the positon of Rudolph Bultmann, who says in his *Kerygma and Myth* that the apostolic kergyma (which teaches the supernatural world-view involved in Christ's true incarnation, miracles, atoning death, resurrection and ascension) cannot be accepted by modern man, because it contains major elements that do not fit with the contemporary Enlightenment viewpoint, See *Kerygma and Myth: A Theological Defense*, Trans. Reginald H. Fuller (Harper & Row: New York, 1961), 3.

83. M. Gorce, 'Réalisme,' an article in *Dictionnaire de Théologie Catholique*, Tome 13e, le partie, A. Vacant et al., eds. (Librarie Letouzey et Ane: Paris, 1936), p. 1875 (my translation).

84. Bart Ehrman, *Jesus, Interrupted* (Harper Collins: NY, 2009), 177.

frequently attacks the reliability of the reported events by the writers of the texts about the resurrection. For example, he claims to have provided evidence that 'the stories about [the risen Jesus] were changed (or invented).'[85] But contrary to this assertion by Bart Ehrman, Christian scholars have offered very convincing evidence for the historical authenticity of these accounts for hundreds of years (I mention some of them earlier in this chapter). Yet whether it is a nominalist concentration on variations in textual tradition (so as to avoid having to look at what they say), or whether it is a denial of the honesty of those who wrote the texts, this popular writer seems deeply driven to deny the miracles that only the Sovereign God can perform.

And in addition to the nominalistic breaking apart of the overarching truth of the given texts, and then using them to contradict one another, and as well as denying the honesty of those who wrote these texts, Ehrman employs still another tool: he unashamedly denies the possibility of the miraculous being and working of the Incarnate Son of God, as clearly set forth in the New Testament. He literally makes fun of the Gospel accounts of Jesus having walked on water by following the nineteenth-century German sceptic, David Friedrich Strauss's 1835-36 *The Life of Jesus Critically Examined*.[86]

Able scholars have answered Dr. Ehrman's denial of the functional possibility of miracles, and I will not repeat their clear-headed responses here.[87] They will repay careful study for those who may find distressing Ehrman's assumption that miracles are so unlikely as to be all but impossible. [88] However, it is appropriate to provide one representative and succinct answer, taken from a review of Ehrman's *Jesus Interrupted* by Dr. Michael Kruger:

> ...Ehrman makes statements that are overtly circular and often presupposes his own naturalistic worldview. For example, he declares, '[The resurrection] is the least likely [explanation] because people do not come back to life, never to die again, after they are well and truly dead' (176). But, isn't the question of whether people can 'come back to life' the very issue being debated? If so, then how can Ehrman simply assume they cannot as the basis for his argument? He may as well argue, 'People can't rise from the dead because people can't rise from the dead.' As the reader completes chapter 5, a growing irony begins to emerge--Ehrman has built his entire book on the premise that his ideas reflect the consensus of modern scholarship but it is becoming more and more clear that he stands very much in the minority.[89]

---

85. *Jesus: apocalyptic prophet of the new millennium* (Oxford University Press: New York, 1999), 52.

86. Ibid., 27-29.

87. For instance, see Licona, op. cit., 171-182, and a debate between William Lane Craig and Bart Ehrman, 'Is There Historical Evidence for the Resurrection of Jesus?' (Held at College of the Holy Cross, Worcester, Massachusetts on March 28, 2006, 34 pages), downloaded http://www.philvaz.com/apologetics/p.96.htm

88. Unlike Ehrman, Swinburne of Oxford, for instance, does not hold that some kind of 'natural law' precludes miracles in general, or the resurrection in particular. See the discussion of Swinburne earlier in this chapter.

89. Book review by Dr. Michael Kruger of Bart Ehrman's *Jesus, Interrupted*, in Westminster

Sadly, Ehrman's essential unbelief in the resurrection of Christ (even though he never totally denies the resurrection, as far as I can tell) may not be too hard to account for. Although a highly educated and very intelligent scholar, what Dr. Ehrman has done is knowingly to put himself outside the divinely chosen community of faith.[90] But as we have seen in the first volume of this series, from the beginning, God has chosen a covenant community in which to reveal his saving truth to the entire world: Israel in the Old Testament, and the Church in the New.[91] The Church is 'the pillar and ground of the truth' (I Tim. 3:15), and outside spiritual union with its Head, and communion with the saints and with their historic, authoritative teaching, one cannot make sense of what the covenant book of Scripture teaches the people of God.

Hence, two things are required to understand the truth of the resurrection of Christ (and they are, by grace, available to all who will ask God for them): first, the illumining presence within one's life of the same Holy Spirit who inspired the Holy Text (cf. John 3:3 and I Cor. 2:14). He causes us to hear the Shepherd's voice in these Scriptures (cf. John 10:3).

Second, we who are brought into union with the risen Christ through faith are thereby in communion with the rest of his chosen people throughout all the ages of Israelite and Christian history. In that communion of the saints, there is found a willing submission to the apostolic doctrine (such as the acceptance of the early Church of the decrees of the First Council of Jerusalem - cf. Acts 15). This unity of the Church in receiving the apostolic truth conveyed through the Holy Scriptures continued through the centuries.[92] (Of course, this

See the appendix of this chapter for a discussion of how the Truth of God is always known in the Church.

historical unity of the people of God in the revealed truth, supernaturally maintained by the Hoy Spirit, is exactly contrary to the case that Dr. Ehrman has long argued against Christian Orthodoxy.[93])

But bowing the knee to the risen Lord opens our eyes to the world around us, and enables us to hear the truth and to speak the truth about the Creator and Redeemer, about life and its meaning, without being distracted from the objective truth by nominalistic skepticism. It is significant to note that when people meet the risen Christ in a saving way, it helps them, in principle, to make sense of the world around them, and of the language they use, more clearly than ever before. In particular, they can distinguish between their own mind and the realities it knows from the outside, so that they will not be bogged down in thinking that their minds determine what is real, or that there is no overarching connection

---

Theological Journal 71, no.2, Fall 2009, 507.

90. I felt sorry to read his account of his loss of Christian faith in some of his books, such as *Forged: Writing in the Name of God – Why the Bible's Authors Are Not Who We Think They Are* (HarperOne: New York, 2011), 1-5, and *Jesus, Interrupted*, Preface ix-xii.

91. Douglas Kelly, *Systematic Theology*, vol. 1, 24-35.

92. For the fact that we must be part of the Church in order to understand the Truth of God, see Appendix 1 to this chapter.

93. As in his *The Orthodox Corruption of Scripture.*

between individual aspects of the world and of thought. Thus, 'realism' is restored, and the obfuscation of 'nominalism' is left forever behind.[94]

From this renewed frame of mind, one can then – with realism – make sense of the teachings of Holy Scripture on such matters as the resurrection of Christ, so that it opens up a new world for them. This 'new world' is the same one that the Church has long seen by God's transforming grace, and increasingly understood and appreciated by believing and studying God's Covenant Word to his chosen people.

Any scholar who purposely places himself outside the witness of the Holy Spirit continually given to the communion of the saints, who willing submit to the truth of Scripture as delivered to and through the historic Church, thereby can expect darkness of understanding of the basic realities of God, including the resurrection of Christ.

One would wish to respond to such chosen blindness with a divinely offfered invitation of grace: 'Seek ye the LORD while he may be found, call ye upon him while he is near: Let the wicked forsake his way, and the unrighteous man his thoughts: and let him return unto the LORD, and he will have mercy upon him; and to our God, for he will abundantly pardon' (Isa. 55:6,7).

Belief in the resurrection is demanding, even for non-skeptics

Even if we are not methodological nominalists and skeptics, it is still a great matter to believe in the bodily resurrection of the Lord Jesus Christ. Both Saint Irenaeus and John Calvin can help us here. Irenaeus writes:

> Those men, therefore, set aside the power of God, and do not consider what the word declares, when they dwell upon the infirmity of the flesh, but do not take into consideration the power of Him who raises it up from the dead. For if He does not vivify what is mortal, and does not bring back the corruptible to incorruption, He is not a God of power. But that He is powerful in all these respects, we ought to perceive from our origin, inasmuch as God, taking dust from the earth, formed man. And surely it is much more difficult and incredible, from non-existent bones, and nerves, and veins, and the rest of man's organization, to bring it about that all this should be, and ought to make man an animated and rational creature, than to re-integrate again that which had been created and then afterwards decomposed into earth…For He who in the beginning caused him to have being who as yet was not, just when He pleased, shall much more reinstate again those who had a former existence, when it is His will [that they should inherit] the life granted by Him.[95]

Two helps for believing in the resurrection

John Calvin realistically accepts the difficulty of the human mind in accepting the bodily resurrection. Then he mentions two considerations to help us believe:

---

94. Richard Weaver wrote a famous book arguing that the adoption of nominalism by Western intellectuals in place of realism lies behind the percipitous intellectual, spiritual and moral decline of Western Society, which is only excellerating in the 21st century. See his *Ideas Have Consequences* (University of Chicago Press: Chicago, 1948).

95. Irenaeus, *Adversus Haereses*, V.3.2.

It is difficult to believe that bodies when consumed with rottenness, will at length be raised up in their season. Therefore, although many of the philosophers declared souls immortal, few approved the resurrection of the flesh. Even though there was no excuse for this point of view, we are nevertheless reminded by it that it is something hard for men's minds to apprehend. Scripture provides two helps by which faith may overcome this great obstacle: one in the parallel of Christ's resurrection; the other in the omnipotence of God.[96]

(d) The significance of his resurrection

Glorious victory – over the Fall of Adam and all its tragic consequences: that is the far-reaching significance of the bodily resurrection of Jesus Christ! The 16th century Scottish Reformer, John Knox, considered the resurrection of Christ to be 'the chief article of our faith.'[97] John Calvin writes:

> Nevertheless [after having discussed the marvelous achievements of his death], we are said to 'have been born anew to a living hope' not through his death but 'through his resurrection' [I Peter 1:3p.]. For as he, in rising again, came forth victor over death, so the victory of our faith over death lies in his resurrection alone. Paul's words better express its nature: 'He was put to death for our sins, and raised for our justification' [Rom. 4:25]. This is as if he had said: 'Sin was taken away by his death; righteousness was revived and restored by his resurrection'...
>
> But because by rising again he obtained the victor's prize – that there might be resurrection and life – Paul rightly contends that 'faith is annulled and the gospel empty and deceiving if Christ's resurrection is not fixed in our hearts' [I Cor. 15:17p.].[98]

These two realities, Christ's death and his resurrection, must always be held together in order to comprehend the significance of either, and in sum, the significance of the whole Christ event. Calvin notes this interconnection: 'So then, let us remember that whenever mention is made of his death alone, we are to understand at the same time what belongs to his resurrection. Also, the same synecdoche applies to the word "resurrection"; we are to understand it as including what has to do especially with his death.'[99]

Hence, the victorious resurrection of the Lord, following his atoning death, exercises never-ceasing, life-giving influence in many different directions: it is the firm foundation of Christianity – our forgiveness for the past, our strength for the present, and our hope for the future. Its wide, reviving and restoring range can be considered under four points: (i) sins are eternally paid for in full: believers are justified; (ii) it is the power of our regeneration, and sanctification; (iii) it is the power and model of our glorification; and (iv) it is the overcoming of the decay of time.

---

96. John Calvin, *Institutes*, III. XXV. 3. (Battles' translation).

97. See the 1560 *Scots Confession* (of which Knox was a chief author), section 10.

98. Calvin, op.cit., II. XVI. 13.

99. Ibid.

(i) Sins are eternally paid for in full (Justification)

When God raised Jesus from the dead, three days after his death by crucifixion, he was giving fullest approval to and acceptance of the price he paid for all our sins in his suffering and death on the cross. Paul conveys this point plainly in various places: 'Who was delivered for our offences, and was raised again for our justification' (Rom. 4:25). The Greek preposition διά rendered 'for' in the two clauses of this sentence, takes the accusative case following the verb 'was delivered up' (παρεδόθη), thereby indicating 'on account of.' If it had been followed by the genitive case, it would have meant 'through,' not 'on account of.' Hence, Christ was 'delivered up' to the cross on account of our offences, and raised up from the dead on account of our justification. That is, nothing more could ever be required by God for a sinner to be justified, other than 'receiving the atonement' (which God affirmed by the Lord's resurrection) – Romans 5:11.

In the great resurrection chapter, Paul makes the same point: 'And if Christ be not raised, your faith is vain; ye are yet in your sins' (I Cor. 15:17). In other words, if Jesus were still physically dead, it would mean that God the Father had not accepted his holy life and atoning death as satisfactory for the cleansing of the sins of the world.

Donald M. Mackinnon spoke of the resurrection as 'the Father's Amen to the work of Christ...By the Resurrection the very stuff of Christ's self-oblation perfected in death is given a universal contemporaneity. More, it becomes the ultimate context of our lives.'[100]

The victory of Christ over death was because sin and the evil one had nothing in him to cause him to be corrupted. As Torrance writes:

> Death had nothing in him, for he had already passed through its clutches by the perfection of his holiness. Thus by entering into our death as the holy one of God he robbed it of its sting [I Cor. 15:54f.], he took away its power as he accepted the divine judgment in the expiatory sacrifice of his own life, and thus triumphed over the forces of guilt and evil which had made death the last stronghold of their grip over man. He triumphed over the grave through his sheer sinlessness.[101]

(ii) It is the power of our regeneration and sanctification

John Calvin speaks of Christ's death (which he always holds together with his resurrection) as bringing his people 'a twofold blessing': liberation from death and mortification of our flesh.[102]

He sees us as co-participants in both blessings brought by the Head of the Church, and thereby teaches that our participation in union with the risen One provides the power of sanctification, that is to mortify sin. Calvin's emphasis in the following passage is on our share in the cross, but, as we shall see, it is not disconnected from the resurrection that followed it:

100. Donald M. Mackinnon, with G. W, H. Lampe, *The Resurrection*, 9, quoted in T. F. Torrance, *Space, Time and Resurrection*, 68, note 9.

101. T. F. Torrance, *Atonement*, 216.

102. John Calvin, *Institutes*, II. XVI. 7 (Battles translation).

The second effect of Christ's death upon us is this: by our participation in it, his death mortifies our earthly members so that they may no longer perform their functions; and it kills the old man in us that he may not flourish and bear fruit. Christ's burial has the same effect: we ourselves as partakers in it are buried with him to sin. The apostle teaches that we have been united with Christ in the 'likeness of his death' [Rom. 6:5], and 'buried with him … into the death' of sin [Rom. 6:4]; that 'by his cross the world has been crucified to us, and we to the world' [Gal. 2:19; 6:14 p.]; that we have died together with him [Col. 3:3]. By these statements Paul not only exhorts us to exhibit an example of Christ's death but declares that there inheres in it an efficacy which ought to be manifest in all Christians, unless they intend to render his death useless and unfruitful.[103]

Calvin is able to ascribe such transforming, sanctifying power to Christ's death, because it issued in his resurrection: 'Therefore, by his wrestling hand to hand with the devil's power, with the dread of death, with the pains of hell, he was victorious and triumphed over them, that in death we may not now fear those things which our Prince has swallowed up [cf. I Pet. 3:22, Vg.].'[104]

Calvin typically holds together Christ's death and resurrection as the power for the Christian life, as we see, for instance, in a section on the importance of baptism:

…Have not we then been buried in baptism with Christ, made partakers in his death, that we may also be sharers in his resurrection [Rom. 6:4-5]? Moreover, this fellowship with Christ's death and life Paul explains to be the mortifying of our flesh and the quickening of the Spirit, because 'our old man has been crucified' [Rom. 6:6, Vg.] in order that 'we may walk in newness of life' [Rom. 6:5, Vg.]. What is it to be equipped for battle, but this?[105]

And in his comments on 'the wondrous exchange' (*mirifica commutatio*) – already quoted – Calvin showed that it means an ascent with Christ to heaven for us:

H. Bavinck succinctly lists '*the ethical*' benefits of Christ's exaltation (among many others), '… the *ethical*, that is, regeneration (John 1:12-13), being made alive (Eph. 2:1, 5), sanctification (I Cor. 1:30; 6:11), being washed (I Cor. 6:11), cleansed (I John 1:9), and sprinkled (I Pet. 1:2) in body, soul, and spirit (2 Cor. 5:17; I Thess. 5:23).'[106]

Specifically, Ephesians 2:1-3 represents the fallen human race as 'dead in trespasses and sins,' but verse 4 shows that through the rich mercy and love of God towards us, 'God hath quickened us together with Christ… and hath raised us up together…' (vv. 5-6). Thus, our regeneration is presented by Saint Paul as an effect of the resurrection of Christ.

Scottish theologian John Dick expands this concept of regeneration as a sort of resurrection:

---

103. Ibid.

104. Ibid., II. XVI. 11.

105. Ibid., IV. XIX. 8.

106. H. Bavinck, *Reformed Dogmatics*, vol. 3, 451.

...the sinner is passive; for, till divine grace is exerted upon him, he is incapable of moral activity, and in the language of inspiration, is 'dead in trespasses and sins.' He is in the same situation with a man who is literally dead, and who, when lying in the grave, cannot contribute in any degree to the restoration of his life. He is like Lazarus, who had no concern in his own resurrection, knew not the voice which called upon him to come forth, if the power which accompanied it had not brought back his spirit from the invisible world, and reunited it to his body. Regeneration is the effect of preventing grace, or of grace which precedes our endeavours, and operates alone.[107]

The Spirit through whom Christ offered himself to God (Heb. 9:14), and in whom Christ was raised from the dead (Rom. 8:11), baptizes the elect into the one body of Christ (I Cor. 12:13). The Spirit of Christ baptizes them into union with Christ in his death and resurrection (Rom. 6:3-6), which provides the continuing power for their dying to sin and rising to new, Christ-based life (Rom. 6:6-13). Hence, the Christian life is the experience of co-resurrection with Christ in the Holy Spirit, who produces through the personality of those in union with the risen Lord, 'the fruit of the Spirit': 'But the fruit of the Spirit is love, joy, peace, longsuffering, gentleness, goodness, faith, meekness, temperance...' (Gal. 5:22-23).

He [Christ] said to his disciples, 'Because I live, ye shall live also' [John 14:19], and he fulfils his word by the inhabitation of the Holy Ghost. By nature they 'are dead in sin,' but they are 'quickened together with him' [Eph. 2:5], that is, in connexion with him, and after the manner of his resurrection. As in the natural body the head is the seat of sensation, and feeling and motion are communicated to all the members by means of the nerves, which have their origin in the brain; so from him flow those influences by which believers are endowed with moral sensibility, and perform the various functions of the Christian life. 'I live,' says Paul, 'and yet not I, but Christ liveth in me; and the life which I now live in the flesh, is by the faith of the Son of God, who loved me, and gave himself for me' [Gal. 2:20].[108]

This union with the crucified, risen One impels us in the holy direction of seeking to be like him. Bavinck summarizes relevant texts on our imitation of the risen Lord as 'the *moral* benefits, consisting in the imitation of Christ, who has left us an example (Matt.10:38; 16:24; Luke 9:23; John 8:12; 12:26; 2 Cor. 8:9; Phil. 2:5; Eph. 2:10; I Pet. 2:21; 4:1).'[109]

Peter Abelard and others over the centuries have not been wrong to emphasize the crucial importance of following Jesus, as long as they do not exclude the other aspects of his death.[110] Much of the most influential devotional writings of the church across the ages has focused on following the crucified and risen Christ, as Bernard of Clairvaux's *Sermons on the Song of Songs*, Thomas a Kempis' *The Imitation of Christ*, John Calvin's section in his *Institutes* on the Christian life (often known as 'The Golden Booklet

---

107. John Dick, *Lectures on Theology*, vol. III, 282.

108. Ibid., 305-306.

109. Bavinck, op. cit., 3, 451.

110. See chapter ten of this work, p. 405-6

of the Christian Life')[111], Brother Lawrence's *The Practice of the Presence of God*, and Samuel Rutherford's *Spiritual Letters*. Many important aspects of the theology of these writers profoundly differ, but there remains a commonality of devotion to what Jesus has done for us.

The death and resurrection of Christ, and our following of him, are wonderfully tied together in an old Scottish Gaelic prayer from the Highlands:

"Thoughts"	"Smaointean"
God's will would I do, My own will bridle;	Toil Dhé dhianam Mo thoil féin srianam;
God's due would I give, My own due yield.	Dlighe Dhé thugaim, Mo dhlighe féin thoiream;
God's path would I travel, My own path refuse;	Slighe Dhé siubhlam, Mo shilghe féin diùltam;
Christ's death would I ponder, My own death remember;	Bàs Chrìosda smaoineam, Mo bhàs féin cuimhneam;
Christ's agony would I meditate, My love to God make warmer;	Cràdh Chrìosda meobhram, Mo gràdh Dhé teódham;
Christ's cross would I carry, My own cross forget;	Crois Chrìosda giùlnam, Mo chrois féin timheam;
Repentance of sin would I make, Early repentance choose;	Aithreachas pheacaidh gabham, Aithreachas trathail tagham;
A bridle to my tongue I would put, A bridle on my thoughts I would keep;	Strian ri m' theangaidh cuiream, Strian ri m' aigne cumam;
God's judgment would I judge, My own judgment guard;	Breitheanas Dhé breithneam, Mo bhreitheanas féin faiream;
Christ's redemption would I seize, My own ransom work;	Saorsa Chrìosda greimeam, Mo shaorsa féin oibream;
The love of Christ would I feel, My own love know.[112]	Gaol Chrìosda faiream, Mo ghaol féin aithneam.

(iii) It is the power and model of our glorification

The risen Christ, who is the head of all his people, is the model and power of their ultimate goal and end. He makes this clear in the Gospel of John. He said in John 14:19, in the context of the indwelling Holy Spirit, whom the risen One sends to his people: '…because I live, ye shall live also.' At the tomb of her brother, Lazarus, Jesus said to Martha: '…I am the resurrection and the life; he that believeth in me, though he were dead, yet

---

111. Taken from Calvin's *Institutes*, III. chapters 6-11.

112. Alexander Carmichael, *Carmina Gadelica: Hymns & Incantations Collected in the Highlands of Scotland in the Last Century* [i.e. 19th century], (Floris Books: Edinburgh, 1997), Number 230, p. 204.

shall he live: And whosoever liveth and believeth in me shall never die. Believest thou this?' (John 11:25-26).

But if believers are forgiven, why do they still die?

This interesting question has been addressed by some great theological preachers, although not, to any significant degree, in the standard textbooks of theology over the centuries. However, The Heidelberg Catechism (1563) gives a brief answer in Question 42: 'But since Christ died for us, why must we also die? A. Our death is not a satisfaction for sin, but the abolishing of sin, and our passage into everlasting life.'[113]

But at more length, two famous preachers of the Reformed Tradition, Theodore Beza of sixteenth-century Geneva, and Benjamin M. Palmer of nineteenth-century New Orleans, have both raised and answered the question of why do persons who are justified by grace through faith, and thus in vital union with the risen Christ, still have to pass through physical death?

Beza answers as follows in his fifteenth Sermon on the Resurrection (1592):

> But if God thus pardons sinners from their guilt, and is fully reconciled to them, then why is it that nevertheless they are subject to the first death, just as much as every other sinner? Here is the answer: the origin, in fact, of both the first and the second death must be traced to the first man, from whom thereafter then proceeded in all of mankind every sort of actual sin; the least of which deserves both the first and second deaths, and all of those [actual sins] have been effaced. as well as the guilt [of original sin] by the satisfaction of Jesus Christ.
>
> The first death still remains, yet its nature has totally changed, by means of this reconciliation, for it no longer is accompanied by the wrath and anger of God; rather he withdraws them from the miseries of this life, in order to bring them into the enjoyment of eternal life, with joy unspeakable to their soul.
>
> And as far as the body is concerned, far from this separation from the soul being detrimental, on the contrary, by this means, it is also no longer an instrument of sin, and its putrefaction becomes for it a preparation for the spiritual life, as the Apostle explains at length in I Corinthians 15. The first death, therefore, is by its very nature one of the great penalties of sin, yet it has been turned into a gift of God for believers, by which their natural misery is changed into an immensely better estate, and this is what they hope for with the Apostle in II Cor. 5:2 and Philippians 1:23...[114]

B. M. Palmer says much the same in two sermons he preached on Romans 8:10-11: 'And if Christ be in you, the body is dead because of sin;

---

113. H. Witsius comments as follows: 'XLV. But say you believers are still to die; and therefore Christ did not satisfy for them by his death. I answer, the Catechumens have been taught to answer this objection from question 42 of the Heidelberg catechism. By the death of Christ, death hath ceased to be what it was before, the punishment inflicted by an offended judge, and the entrance into the second death, and is become the extermination of sin, and the way to eternal life; and at the last day it shall be altogether abolished...', in op. cit., 231, 232.

114. Theodore Beza, Sermon 15 *Sur L' Histoire de la Résurrection*, op. cit., 453 (my translation).

but the Spirit is life because of righteousness. But if the Spirit of him that raised up Jesus from the dead dwell in you, he that raised up Christ from the dead shall also quicken your mortal bodies by his Spirit that dwelleth in you.' The two sermons are entitled 'The Death of Believers No Evidence Against Their Justification' (Part I and Part II).[115] After carefully placing these verses in their broader and narrower context, the great preacher outlines his first message as follows:

1. The body is the instrument with which we sin, and through which that sin is made patent to the observation of others.
2. It is not the design of grace to take evil out of the world, as to its being; but only to destroy its penal character, and to convert it into an instrument of spiritual discipline.
3. The body of the Christian must die in order to its sanctification, that it may be fitted for the world of glory.
4. The sudden translation of believers without death, would subvert the principle of grace, which is the ground principle of the whole Gospel scheme.
5. The successive translation of believers, without dying, would anticipate the decisions of the judgment day, and rob the resurrection morn of its glory.[116]

We might summarize the points raised by Beza and Palmer in answer to the question of why believers, who are already justified in Christ, must pass through physical death with the rest of fallen humanity, in a verse from the great resurrection chapter: 'Now this I say, brethren, that flesh and blood cannot inherit the kingdom of God: neither doth corruption inherit incorruption' (I Cor. 15:50). That is to say, 'flesh and blood' *as presently constituted* cannot go directly into the Kingdom; our bodies are still part of a fallen, dying, disintegrating world, and as such they cannot pass immediately into the glories of heaven *without a great change*. Of course, consequent to this transformation, we shall be possessed of incorruptible, immortal bodies – substantial and real human bodies – but not marked by the wages of sin. But they have to be transformed in order to go into the kingdom of purity and bliss: either by means of physical death before the Lord comes, or on the day of his coming, they shall be transformed and caught up together with him into the clouds (I Thess. 4:16-17). Either way, the great change is necessary.

Hence, in their own ways, Beza and Palmer remind us that once we become Christians, we are baptized into his death and resurrection (cf. Rom. 6:3-10). By grace, we are made alive together with him, and are somehow already 'seated with him in heavenly places' (cf. Eph. 2:4-6). Jesus is the first-fruits of the resurrection harvest, and we are the later

---

115. Benjamin Morgan Palmer, *Sermons*, Vol. II (Clark & Hofeline: New Orleans, 1876), Nos. XVI and XVII. The two volumes of Palmer's Sermons (originally printed, week by week iin the New Orleans newspaper) have been reprinted into one volume by Sprinkle Publications: Harrisonburg, Virginia, 2002. In that edition, what is termed in the original publication as No. XVI is now numbered as pp. 171-182, and No. XVII is found in pp. 183-195.

116. Palmer, op. cit., No. XVI.

fruit (I Cor. 15:20-24). His resurrection guarantees our own resurrection, in due season. First, we are raised spiritually with him as the Holy Spirit regenerates us, and at the end of the age, we shall be raised physically with him (cf. I Thess. 4:13-18).

The Holy Spirit, who comes down from the risen One to indwell believers, will at the right time raise up their physical body in union with the Lord, as we saw immediately above in Romans 8:11. Then, on that glad, final day, we shall be made like the risen Lord: 'Beloved, now are we the sons of God, and it doth not yet appear what we shall be; but we know that, when he shall appear, we shall be like him; for we shall see him as he is' (I John 3:2).

Palmer's Second Sermon on Romans 8, 10,11.

Palmer goes on in his preaching on this passage, in his own words '...to enlarge upon the two grounds upon which [the resurrection of believers] is based in the text, to-wit: *connexion between the believer and Christ, and the indwelling of the Holy Ghost.*'[117] His outline is:

> I. The body of the saint will be raised because equally redeemed by Christ and equally, with the soul, united to Him.
> II. The body of the saint will be raised because of the indwelling of the Holy Ghost.

He then concludes with two applications:

> (1) These moral grounds of the resurrection satisfy us as to its certainty, and bear us over all the difficulties with which it is invested.
> (2) The comfort is precious which flows from this truth, in view of death both to ourselves and to those whom we love.

Centuries before these two preachers, much the same truth was conveyed through the writing of Saint Irenaeus,[118] T. F. Torrance refers to him (and other Fathers who followed Irenaeus in this image) as follows:

> As the early Fathers used to express it, when a baby is born it is usually born head first, but when the head is born the whole body follows naturally, for it is the birth of the head that is the most difficult part. Now Christ the Head of the Body is already resurrected, the First-born of the New Creation, and as such he is the pledge and guarantee that we who are incorporated with him as his Body will rise with him and be born into the new creation in our physical as well as our spiritual existence.[119]

D. Staniloae summarizes the Greek Patristic teaching on this point:

> This content can be summed up as follows: the body of the risen Christ is a body raised to the full spiritual transparence, and in this nature it was

---

117. Ibid., No. XVII.

118. Irenaeus, *Adversus Haereses* III. 20. 3.

119. T. F. Torrance, *Space, Time and Resurrection*, 142.

filled with holiness, with deification, being like this before the Father. But this holiness, transparence, and deification are also communicated to us by parting of his body and, therefore, Christ's Resurrection means not only his communion with the Father, but also his entrance into full communion with us. This communion is first latent for us, having to become actualized through Christ's dwelling in our being through his Spirit.[120]

Wipe Away Your Tears in the Grave Clothes of the Risen Christ

What an immense difference this fact makes as we face our own death and that of our loved ones! C. H. Spurgeon has beautifully described it, in his own inimitable way, in terms of the disused grave clothes and spices left by the risen Christ in his empty tomb:

First, He has left in the grave the spices. When He rose He did not bring away the costly aromatics in which His body had been wrapped, but He left them there. Joseph brought about one hundred pounds of myrrh and aloes, and the odor remained. In the sweetest spiritual sense, our Lord Jesus filled the grave with fragrance. It no longer smells of corruption and foul decay...

Yonder lowly bed in the earth is now perfumed with costly spices and decked with sweet flowers, for on its pillow the truest Friend we have once laid His holy head! We will not start back with horror from the chambers of the dead, for the Lord, Himself, has traversed them – and where He goes no terror abides. The Master also left His grave clothes behind Him. He did not come from the tomb wrapped about with a winding sheet. He did not wear the burial clothes of the tomb as the garments of life, but when Peter went into the sepulcher he saw the grave clothes lying carefully folded by themselves. What if I say He left them to be the hangings of the royal bed-chamber wherein His saints fall asleep?

See how He has curtained our last bed! Our dormitory is no longer bare and drear, like a prison cell, but hung around with fair linen and comely tapestry – a chamber fit for the repose of princes of the blood! We will go to our last bedchamber in peace because Christ has furnished it for us! Or if we change the metaphor, I may say that our Lord has left those grave clothes for us to look upon as pledges of His fellowship with us in our low estate and reminders that as *He* has cast aside the death garments, even so shall *we*. He has risen from His couch and left His sleeping robes behind Him in token that at our waking there are other vestures ready for us, also.

What if I again change the figure and say that as we have seen old tattered flags hung up in cathedrals and other national buildings as the memorials of defeated enemies and victories won, so in the crypt where Jesus vanquished death His grave clothes are hung up as the trophies of His victory over death, and as assurances to us that all His people shall be more than conquerors through Him that loved them? 'O death, where is your sting? O grave, where is your victory?' Then, carefully folded up and laid by itself, our Lord left the napkin that was about His head. Yonder lies that napkin now. The Lord needed it not when He came forth to live.

You who mourn may use it as a handkerchief with which to dry your eyes. You widows and fatherless children – you mourning brothers and you weeping sisters – and you, you Rachels, who will not be comforted because your children are not here, take this which wrapped your Saviour's face and

---

120. D. Staniloae, op. cit., vol. 3, 258-259.

wipe away your tears forever! The Lord is risen, indeed, and therefore thus says the Lord, 'Refrain your voice from weeping and your eyes from tears, for they shall come again from the land of the enemy…'[121]

(iv) It is the overcoming of the decay of time

Ever since the fall of Adam, the entire cosmos has been marked by decay and disintegration as time passes and natural and historical events unfold within that context of fallen time. According to Romans 8, the creation itself has labored under the 'vanity' that involves corruption and pain (cf. Rom. 8:19-22).

The book of Ecclesiastes paints a grim but realistic picture of the decay that is built into the processes of the cycles of nature, human life, and historical events. Everything, even human life itself, wonderful works of architecture, agriculture, and art, is marked by 'vanity' or emptiness (cf. Eccl. 1 and 2). Rich and poor, wise and foolish, all 'turn to dust again' (Eccl. 3:20, and 12:7). 'All that cometh is vanity' (Eccl. 11:8). Yet because God the Creator exists, and exercises mercy upon those otherwise condemned to emptiness and decay, there is meaning and hope in the passage of decaying time (cf. Eccl. 12). This is to say that Ecclesiastes leaves us with only one hope: one that must come to us from outside this created order that has been subjected to 'vanity' or 'futility.' Thus, in the fullness of time (Gal. 4:4), the eternal Son of God, who passed 'through the heavens,' coming from outside of creation into creation, and 'born of a woman,' became a man to represent mankind, hence single-handedly restoring to beauty and holiness a created order that had been subjected to vanity (cf. Rev. 5:1-10).

Only one thing was never subject to the decay of time after the Fall, and that was the human nature of the incarnate Christ. He lived his life on earth without any corruption whatsoever, and thus, time could exercise no downward pull upon him into its decay. Then, as our sin-bearer, he took on all the forces of death, decay and vanity, and overcame them from within, as manifested in his bodily resurrection. In so doing, Christ *healed our time.*

T. F. Torrance writes:

> …space and time are not abrogated or transcended. Rather are they healed and restored, just as our being is healed and restored through the resurrection…The healing and restoring of our being carries with it the healing, the restoring, the reorganizing and transforming of the space and time in which we now live our lives in relation to one another and to God.[122]

> The deed of atonement on the cross has *retroactive effect*, going back to the very beginning. And so Christ in the *Apocalypse* claims to be the first and the last, the alpha and the omega [Rev. 1:17; 22:13]…He alone has power to open the seals of destiny, to cancel the power of guilt, and to liberate humanity from the determination of a guilty past. Guilt and the irreversibility of time, as we know it in a sinful world, are bound up inseparably…But in the cross, Jesus Christ descended into that awful *sheol* of human existence, into hell

---

121. Charles H. Spurgeon, 'The Lord is Risen, Indeed,' Metropolitan Tabernacle Pulpit, No. 1106 (April 13, 1873), vol. 19, pp. 1-2, quoted from www.spurgeongems.org.

122. Torrance, *Atonement*, 247-248.

itself…By his atonement, he broke into it and broke it open, leading captivity captive [Eph. 4:8], and now he holds the keys of death and hell in his power [Rev. 1:18; cf. I Cor. 15:54-57].[123]

Because of this transformation of our decaying time through the death and resurrection of Christ, human life, relationships, and work become full of significance and lasting fruitfulness. That is the message of Saint Paul at the end of the great resurrection chapter: 'But thanks be to God, which giveth us the victory through our Lord Jesus Christ. Therefore, my beloved brethren, be ye stedfast, unmoveable, always abounding in the work of the Lord, forasmuch as ye know that your labour is not in vain in the Lord' (I Cor. 15:57-58).

(e) The Agents of his resurrection

The whole Triune Godhead participated in the resurrection of Jesus. This is an illustration of the doctrine of *perichoresis*: where one person of the Godhead is present and active, the others are also present and active, for the persons of the Trinity are not separated as are created persons. For the eternal persons of the Trinity to exist is to indwell one another, so that each one coinheres in the activity of the others.

The Father raised up Jesus
Many texts of the New Testament speak of the Father raising up the Son: Acts 2:24: 'Whom God hath raised up…'; Acts 2:32: 'This Jesus hath God raised up…'; Acts 3:15: 'And killed the Prince of life, whom God hath raised up from the dead…'; (also in Acts, see: 5:30; 13:37; 17:31); Romans 4:24: '… if we believe on him that raised up Jesus our Lord from the dead'; 10:9: '… and shalt believe in thine heart that God hath raised him from the dead, thou shalt be saved'; I Corinthians 6:14: 'And God hath both raised up the Lord, and will also raise up us by his own power'; I Corinthians 15:15: '…because we have testified of God that he raised up Christ…'; 2 Corinthians 4:14: 'Knowing that he which raised up the Lord Jesus shall raise up us also by Jesus…'; Galatians 1:1: '…and God the Father, who raised him from the dead'; Colossians 2:12: '…God, who hath raised him from the dead'; I Thessalonians 1:10: 'And to wait for his Son from heaven, whom he raised from the dead…'

Jesus raised up himself
But also in the New Testament, 'Jesus is presented as the subject of the act of Resurrection.'[124] As he predicts his coming passion in Matt. 20:19, Jesus speaks of himself as 'rising' (rather than 'being raised'): 'And shall deliver him to the Gentiles to mock, and to scourge, and to crucify him: and the third day he shall rise again.' He speaks of his 'rising' similarly in Mark 9:31 and Luke 18:33, using the active voice of the verb, rather

---

123. Ibid., 130-131.
124. D. Staniloae, op. cit., vol. 3, 247.

than the passive. I Thessalonians 4:14 also uses the active voice. In the following texts, the passive voice is used concerning the Lord having been raised: Luke 24:34, John 2:22, I Corinthians 15:4, 12 and II Corinthians 5:15.

In John 10:18, Jesus speaks of himself both as laying down his life, and as taking it up again: 'No man taketh it from me, but I lay it down of myself. I have power to lay it down, and I have power to take it again…'

The Holy Spirit raised up Jesus

Hebrews 9:14 speaks of Christ offering himself to God through the Holy Spirit on the cross, and Romans 8:11 speaks of the Holy Spirit's activity, along with the Father, in the resurrection of Jesus: 'But if the Spirit of him that raised up Jesus from the dead dwell in you, he that raised up Christ from the dead shall also quicken your mortal bodies by his Spirit that dwelleth in you.' Romans 1:4 connects the Holy Spirit to the resurrection of Christ: 'And declared to be the Son of God with power, according to the spirit of holiness, by the resurrection from the dead,' as does I Peter 3:18: 'For Christ also hath once suffered for sins, the just for the unjust, that he might bring us to God, being put to death in the flesh, but quickened by the Spirit.'

The Resurrection was a Triune action

Staniloae has summarized the scriptural testimony to the threefold activity in the resurrection of the Lord:

> By alternately attributing the act of Resurrection to the Father and to the Son one shows their cooperation, which includes an intense cooperation of the Holy Spirit. The Father from whom the Spirit proceeds and in whom the Son also is, spiritualizes the Lord's body through the Spirit. But where the Spirit is active, Christ cannot be an object; he, too, is active. In this common act of supreme pneumatization of the body, the supreme communion between the Father, the Son, and the Holy Spirit is achieved. Only because of this full pneumatization will the Spirit irradiate into the world from the Son's body, the Spirit who proceeds from the Father and will be sent into the world through Christ as man. For Christ is not passive in this irradiation of the Spirit from his body…
>
> If Christ did not undergo the Resurrection as an object but was its co-subject together with the Father, it follows that he himself conquered or participated in conquering death, exercising in this act, his power as King, which is not only as God but also as man. In fact, only by recognizing this do we maintain the hypostatic union in all its reality with its resulting implications upon the human nature…
>
> *…Thus, Christ's Resurrection was not only the result of the Father's decree, but it was prepared also by this union of his humanity with the Godhead through his divine Hypostasis, which also bore the human nature.*[125]

In sum, as we see the entire Holy Trinity active in Christ's incarnation and in his atoning death, so we also see the Triune activity in his victorious

---

125. Ibid., 247-249.

resurrection. Hence, all that Christ was and continues to be for us as the one Mediator between God and man is backed up to the fullest extent in the innermost life of the Triune God. Thereby the salvation of all who believe in Christ is as certain, lasting, and secure as God is God: 'I AM THAT I AM.'

Meeting the Risen Christ

Theodore Beza has an encouraging word for those who would like to meet the risen Christ, but do not know how. He contrasts the relative futility of going on pilgrimage to the empty tomb in Jerusalem with actually meeting the Lord today:

> [Why seek out the site of the Jerusalem tomb] instead of seeking Jesus Christ who is living in heaven, who is to be met in the preaching of the Word and the administration of the sacraments? For the true Jerusalem is celestial, which is the Lord's Church...And if one must search for him on earth, he is spiritually present in his Word and sacraments, and he may be found everywhere that he is served in spirit and in truth, without having to run here and there, as in the time of the Law and of the Temple in Jerusalem. For as the Lord himself expressly said in John 4:20-24 [to the woman at the well who asked where to worship – 'Woman, believe me, the hour cometh, when ye shall neither in this mountain, nor yet at Jerusalem, worship the Father...true worshippers shall worship the Father in spirit and in truth...'], and as the Apostle follows Moses in Romans 10:8, we do not have to mount up to heaven, nor pass over the sea...we shall find Christ with the eyes and feet of faith, thereby mounting even to the high places, where he is seated at the right hand of God, according to the exhortation of the Apostle in Colossians 3:1 ['If ye then be risen with Christ, seek those things which are above, where Christ sitteth on the right hand of God...'].[126]

The beloved Easter hymn of Edmund Budry continues to prove literally true for millions:

> Lo! Jesus meets us, risen from the tomb;
>> Lovingly he greets us, scatters fear and gloom;
> Let his church with gladness, hymns of triumph sing,
>> For her Lord now liveth, death hath lost its sting.
>
> Thine be the glory, risen, conquering Son;
>> Endless is the victory, thou o'er death hast won.[127]

---

126. Theodore Beze, op.cit., 94,95 (my translation).

127. Edmund Budry, 'Thine be the Glory', (the French original composed in 1884, and the English translation by Richard B. Hoyle in 1923), stanza 2.

APPENDIX 11.1

THE TRUTH OF GOD IS KNOWN IN THE CHURCH

God makes himself known in creation and in human conscience (cf. Romans 1 and 2)[1], and supremely in the God-breathed Scriptures of the Old and New Testaments (cf. II Tim. 3:16 – 'All Scripture is God-breathed' *Theopneustos*), which sets forth above all else, the eternal Son of God in his pre-existence, his incarnation, holy life, atonement, resurrection, ascension, and promised return, and government of all until he comes. God in Christ, in and through the Holy Spirit, established a community of faith; Israel, (out of which came the Old Testament), which was continued and largely fulfilled in the New Testament Church, (through which he gave us the apostolic Scriptures), always illuminated by the Spirit of God, and into which he calls those who are to be saved. Thus, God himself has determined the grounds on which he makes himself known, and those grounds (as concerns salvation and holy life and service) are found in a divinely established community of faith: first, Israel and then the Christian Church, through whose life he provided the world with the Holy Scriptures.

It is necessary to abide in that community of faith in order to understand the Scriptures which he provided as the way of salvation, life, and transformation of all things. We cannot make sense of God and the Holy Scriptures as disconnected individuals. We need to be part of the historic (and continuing) Christian Church, with its authoritative summations of saving truth through its various councils, if we are to make sense of God and the verities of his Word. We see something of how this necessity of understanding within the fellowship of the community of faith worked, both in the New Testament itself, and then in the centuries that followed.

The decrees of the first apostolic council in Jerusalem itself worked on the basis of fidelity to the clear teaching of the revelation of God given to the Covenant Community. As they sought to address the divisive issue of whether new converts to Christ from Gentile paganism should first

---

1. See Douglas Kelly, *Systematic Theology* vol. 1, 129-180.

have to go through Jewish rites such as circumcision, and then adhere to Mosaic laws, the leading apostles who spoke, Peter and James, both referred the entire matter to God and his revealed will. Unlike the claims of post-modernist deconstructionism, they did not pit one power group with its truth claims over against another, but turned directly to God for his guidance. Peter stated that Gentile converts need not first become observant Jews because of divine election of them to salvation through the preaching of the Gospel (Acts 15:7-9). They showed that they had been chosen by their believing reception of the Christ Peter offered, and thus the cleansing of their hearts by faith (Acts 15:9).

Then James referred the matter to the prophecy of Amos (9:11-12), which predicted that the true 'restoration of the ruined tabernacle of David' would be accompanied by the residue of the Gentiles seeking the Lord. James, therefore, on the basis of Holy Scripture (in Amos) agrees with Peter that God himself planned to receive the Gentiles who believed 'through the grace of the Lord Jesus Christ', without adding other rituals to it. Hence, this issue was decided by the Jerusalem Council by seeking the will of God in the Scriptures of what we now call the Old Testament.

The writing of the New Testament is a prime illustration of the necessity of standing within the community of faith ordained from eternity by God in order to know God and his will. The Lord gave the books of the Old Testament to the community of faith he elected in Israel. Christ recognized and his apostles affirmed the authority (or canonicity) of these books, as we see them mentioned in various ways in such contemporary Jewish writers as Philo and Josephus. Michael Kruger has published a careful study on the development of the canon, to which the interested reader is referred.[2]

The procedure of the Jerusalem Council in Acts 15 exemplifies how the New Testament was composed by meditation on the significance of the Person and work of Christ as the fulfillment of the Old Testament prophecies, types, and ceremonies. The apostolic writers (and those in their company) stood within the believing community of Israel to grasp and express who the Messiah was. Christ had told his disciples that 'I have many things to say unto you, but ye cannot receive them now...' (John 16:12). He goes on to promise that when the Holy Spirit comes (after Christ's death, resurrection, and ascension) '...He will guide you into all truth: for he shall not speak of himself; but whatsoever he shall hear, that shall he speak: and he will show you things to come' (John 16:13). By this means, the Lord equipped the apostles (and their chosen co-workers) to understand who he was in the light of the Old Testament Scripture, and to express it in accurate writing, so that what the apostles wrote was dominical; it had the Lord's authority. Thus it was seen by the New Testament community of faith to be on the same high level of divine inspiration as the Old Testament. That is seen in how Peter assesses Paul's writing to be 'Scriptures' (II Peter 3:16). Paul wrote his letters to particular churches (as Corinth and Galatia), and to particular individuals (as to Timothy and Philemon), and the communities of believers were given

---

2. See Michael J. Kruger, *Canon Revisited* (Crossway: Wheaton, Ill, 2012).

perception by the same Holy Spirit who had inspired those Pauline texts to recognize that they were from God, and thus were authoritative and hence canonical (cf. II Tim. 3:16).

As has often been said, the canon is not an inspired list of books, but a list of inspired books! And to the Church was given the spiritual perception and dominical authority to recognize what was inspired and what was not. The Christian Church did not create the canon, but it was put in place by God to recognize it, and to vouchsafe it to the world.

This means that the Bible came from within Israel (the Old Testament), and from within the Christian Church (the New Testament), but ultimately from the Lord himself. That is, it was inspired by God, but written by chosen witnesses within the community of faith, who were in communion with the Lord and with other believers. The principle here is that of Paul's command to 'work out your own salvation with fear and trembling. For it is God which worketh in you to will and to do of his good pleasure' (Phil. 2:12-13).

The Bible was given to and through Israel and the Church. It did not come from ancient schools of rhetoric, or from the philosophical academies of Athens, Rome and Alexandria; it did not come from the heretics (for its truth often condemned them, so that they denied all or much of it – as Marcion rejected most of the New Testament, and all of the Old). It came from within the community of faith which was called into being by God, sustained and guided by him, and thus is always the only ground on which God has given himself to be known. Modern scholars who reject humble and believing fellowship within the Church, thereby preclude themselves from truly understanding both the contents of the Bible that has come through it, and to a large degree as well, much of the significance of the ordered cosmos in which the revelation was given to us by God.

We see this principle at work all across the ages: God is truly known only upon the ground where he has chosen to make himself known, and that is Israel and the Church. Probably within a century after the Jerusalem Council, the Apostles' Creed arose, and was based on the Trinitarian baptismal formula. It was a working out by the second-century saints of the Great Commission of Christ in Matthew 28. This joint submission to the Trinitarian truth and its implications was carried on in the Nicene Council and the others. In these councils, it was found that Christ had continued to be with his Church as the Holy Spirit kept guiding it into all truth (cf. John 16:13). The truths to which true Christians submitted were not new truths, but an opening up and application of the truths found in the inspired Word of God.

Irenaeus in the second century A.D. showed the essential oneness of this faith taught by the true Church, and always received by the community of the saints:

> The Church, though dispersed throughout the whole world, even unto the ends of the earth, has received from the apostles and their disciples this faith: in one God, the Father Almighty, Maker of heaven and earth, and the sea

and all things that are in them; and in one Christ Jesus, the Son of God, who became incarnate for our salvation, and in the Holy Spirit, who proclaimed through the prophets the dispensations of God, and the advents, and the birth from a Virgin; and the passion and the resurrection from the dead, and the ascension into heaven in the flesh of the beloved Christ Jesus our Lord and God and Saviour and King, according to the will of the invisible Father, 'every knee should bow, of things in heaven and things in earth, and things under the earth, and that every tongue should confess to him'...the church, having received this preaching and this faith, although scattered throughout the whole world, yet as if occupying but one house, carefully preserves it. She also believes these points as if she had but one soul, and one and the same heart; and she proclaims them and teaches them, and hands them down with perfect harmony, as if she possessed but one mouth. For although the languages of the world are dissimilar, yet the import of the tradition is one and the same. For the churches which have been planted in Germany do not believe or hand down anything different, nor do those in Spain... (from *Adversus Haereses* I.X.1,2).

Irenaeus had been typical of many others among the early Fathers who based doctrinal orthodoxy and church unity upon 'the rule of truth' (*regula veritatis*), which we have discussed in some detail in vol. 1 of this series (pp. 429-435). The 'rule of truth' (by which people could readily discern true Christian doctrine from false, heretical parodies of it), usually involved these three elements: (1) a brief historical exposition of the self-revelation of the Persons and activity of the Triune God; (2) the apostolic, scriptural basis of this tradition; (3) the ecclesiastical unity produced and maintained by this articulated belief.

Irenaeus was carrying on the widespread procedure of the Christian communities in the apostolic period itself, as Philippe Rolland, an expert in the documents of the New Testament, has demonstrated in his 1997 *La Succession Apostolique Dans Le Nouveau Testament* [*The Apostolic Succession in the New Testament*]. In order to ascertain the authentic New Testament teaching on the doctrinal authority of the apostles and their disciples through the continuing ordination of church leaders (e.g. elders and bishops) in the early churches, the author takes the dating of various New Testament epistles 'back to the drawing board', in contrast to the *a priori* ideas of the Higher Criticism, which have been prevalent for the last century and a half.

He pursues the most careful research *within these documents*, and in particular, provides massive evidence for the suggested dates and inter-dependencies, through lists and tables of the Greek vocabulary employed by the New Testament writers. One might say that his research is, in the best sense, *a posteriori* (based on hard evidence) rather than *a priori* (the imposition of a predetermined theory onto the text).This linguistic research, with its implications for dating the epistles, provides the historical context for an understanding of what the New Testament writers taught and practiced about the necessity of handing down accurately the content of apostolic doctrine within the true church for all time to come.

He shows that although the actual expression (or a variation of it) *'apostolic succession'* occurs first in the Letter of Clement of Rome to the

Corinthians (written between the years A.D. 90 to 100), the notion of it is found much earlier in the Letters of Paul addressed to Timothy (I Tim. 4:14; II Tim 1:6, as well as II Tim. 2:2).[3] Rolland gives reasons why there is no credible evidence to date the Pastoral and Catholic Epistles some decades after the deaths of Peter and Paul, by which unsupported supposition (i.e. *a priori*) these letters are considered by the Higher Criticism ' to have been written by other hands, and thus are said to be 'pseudonymous.'[4] On the contrary, he states:

> I maintain that the organization of the Church which is attested within the New Testament was already in place by the year AD 60, before the deaths of Peter and Paul. I have brought forward a new method to situate the apostolic letters

3. Philippe Rolland, *La Succession Apostolique dans le Nouveau Testament* (Editions de Paris: Paris 1997), 9.

4. I would respectfully dissent from his attribution of the underlying motivation for what gave rise to the Higher Criticism to the determination of Martin Luther and 'the separated brethren' to hold on strongly to 'salvation by faith alone.' (Rolland asserts this connection on p. 83, although he does admit that Luther held to 'the fundamental conviction of the truth of the Scriptures', on p. 13). Although Luther was wrong-headed on his view of the Epistle of James, the other 16th century Protestant luminaries of exegesis and theology, such as Calvin, Bullinger, Viret and Beza, as well as the succeeding generation of leading Protestant scholars, such as John Owen, Thomas Goodwin in England, and Voetius, Gomarus and Witsius on the continent, did not follow Luther on this point. I am not aware that any of them attributed a late date (or pseudonymity) to the writing, for instance, of the Pastoral Epistles or of James. Certainly this late dating became a point of controversy in the 19th century debates over the validity of Anglican orders, but that was not *the origin* of the matter. The origin of late dates (under supposedly false names) of the Letters of Timothy, Peter, James, etc. can be traced to the philosophy of the 18th century Enlightenment, which necessarily wished to weaken the authority of the Holy Scriptures. It was part of a larger movement in Higher Criticism, such as the JEDP strand theory of the Pentateuch, etc. As Paul Hazard showed it was essential to the program of the Enlightenment to negate the authority of Holy Scripture, in order to replace it with the ideals of a secularist paradise, free from Biblical constraints. He wrote: 'How could the Holy Scripture have been spared? Since it represented the supreme authority, it was logical that when one came to examine it, one would criticize it. When they could show that it contradicted itself, the libertines rejoiced' (in Paul Hazard, *Le Crise de la Conscience Européene*, Paris: Librarie Anttheme Fayard, 1981, p. 171). More specifically, Jean Zumstein in his *Dictionnaire du Protestantisme* , showed that 'From an epistemological point of view, the historico-critical method is a fruit of the humanist and rationalist tradition, which crystalized in the 18th century…The polemical dimension of the project is evident: the interpretation of the Scripture is wrenched away from the power of the Church. It thereby becomes subsidiary to a reading of the text which sees itself as autonomous, rational and critical.' (See Jean Zumstein, in *Dictionnaire du Protestantisme*, Pierre Gisel, (Ed.): Geneva: Labor et Fides, 1995, pp. 124-128.) Zumstein and others have shown that in order to keep abreast of 'the latest scholarship', first the Protestants, and then the Roman Catholics played into the hands of Enlightenment views of the Bible, leading to the massive decline of Christianity in the West. But there seems to be a re-thinking of these matters among several scholars, such as Rolland of France, and also Eta Linnemann of Germany (e.g. see her *Historical Criticism of the Bible: Methodology or Ideology?* Grand Rapids: Baker, 1990), and several years earlier, the great Jewish Old Testament scholar, Umberto Cassuto of the University of Jerusalem (see his *The Documentary Hypothesis and Composition of the Pentateuch*, English Translation, Jerusalem, 1961), demonstrated the non-viability of the JEPD strand theory, from an Hebraic textual and historical point of view. The eminent 20th century French expert in Hebrew (especially knowledgeable in the Dead Sea Scrolls in the years following 1963), l' Abbé Jean Carmignac, was led by his research to conclude that the Synoptic Gospels (Matthew, Mark, and Luke) had been first written in Hebrew, within a very few years of the life of Christ, and later translated into Greek (see his *La Naissance des Évangiles*, Guibert: Paris, 1984). This indicated that they were all written within the lifetime of those who had known Jesus. Two outstanding articles on reverses in Higher Criticism are: Jean-Marc Berthoud, 'Quelle critique biblique?', originally published in a periodical from Lausanne: *Résister et Construire* in December 1998, and Bertrand Rickenbacher, 'Remarques sur la méthod historic-critique' in *Résister et Construire*, January 1999. Since this journal is no longer being published, these articles can be accessed on-line: http://calvinisme.ch/index.php/R%C3%A9sister_et_construire.

in relation to one another, by which one can establish their relative chronology, and then their absolute chronology, by means of those epistles whose date is more or less certain (such as I Thessalonians in 50 or 51), I Corinthians in the spring of 56, Romans during the winter 57-58, Hebrews before the Jewish Revolt of 66. The Letters which current exegetical science declares inauthentic (notably the Epistle of James, the Epistles of Paul to Titus and Timothy, the first Epistle of Peter and the Epistle to the Ephesians) appear in fact to be after the Epistle to the Hebrews. These epistles therefore are shown [by my research] to have been written before the death of Peter and Paul, between 64 and 67.[5]

The reader is referred to Rolland's volume for what, at least to me, is convincing evidence of the early dating of these epistles (before the Fall of Jerusalem in AD 70). Rolland is not alone. John A. T. Robinson in later life changed his mind, and argued that all of the New Testament was composed before AD 70.[6] If that re-dating be granted, then the teaching of these epistles on the central task of the leaders of the early Church to safeguard the apostolic doctrine entire and unchanged at the heart of its life, demonstrates the New Testament origin of a solid *apostolic succession of divinely revealed doctrine*, which has continued to the present within the various branches of the true and universal church.

Rolland concludes:

> One of the theological consequences of these arguments is that one should attribute to the apostles themselves, and not to anonymous writers of the next generation, the setting in place of an apostolic succession, in the person of Titus and Timothy and the 'presbyter-bishops' whom they were charged to institute, and whose presence in the paulinian communities is equally well attested in the First Epistle of Peter. As Ephesians underlines it, the ministeries are a gift that God gave to his Church, in order to keep us from being 'tossed to and fro, and carried about by every wind of doctrine' (Eph. 4:14). The edifice [of the Church] is solidly built on the foundation of the apostles.[7]

This view of apostolic authority grounded in the inspired Scriptures, and safeguarded and passed down in the Church, was the rule in Christianity, both East and West, through the Patristic and most of the Medieval ages. Over a thousand years after Irenaeus, and other Fathers who required conformity to 'the rule of truth,' Saint Thomas Aquinas, the greatest theologian of the Medieval West (13th century), believed that the unity of the Church in submission to its fuller understand of the apostolic truth, was always based on foundation of belief in the Holy Scriptures. Church tradition was authoritative insofar as it reposed upon these divinely given Scriptures, but did not constitute a separate source of truth, as is carefully argued by Florent Gaboriau, against the general interpretations of twentieth-century Thomism.[8]

---

5. Ibid., 12.

6. See J. A. T. Robinson, *Redating the New Testament* (1976).

7. Ibid., 123.

8. *Thomas D' Aquin A La Croisée du Siecle* (Messages: L'Age D' Homme: Lausanne, Switzerland, 2013).

The magisterial Protestant Reformers of the sixteenth century continued to show great respect for the authority of the Church Councils of the first five centuries, and considered themselves in line with them, though always reserving the right of critiquing them in light of God speaking in Scripture. That is, they believed in the absolute authority of the Holy Scriptures, and the relative authority of many of the Church Councils. The Lutheran Augsburg Confession (xiv), as well as Luther's earlier Large Catechism (art. iii) taught this very thing, and they were followed by John Calvin in his Institutes of the Christian Religion, Book IV.

Calvin writes that 'The power of the church, therefore, is not infinite but subject to the Lord's Word and, as it were, enclosed within it' (IV. 8.1). He adds that 'Not even the apostles were free to go beyond the Word; much less their successors' (IV. 8.9). Yet Calvin does not take this to mean that Church Councils have no binding authority on Christians: 'If one seeks in Scripture what the authority of councils is, there exists no clearer promise than in this statement of Christ's: "Where two or three are gathered together in my name, there I am in the midst of them"' (Matt. 18:20)... (IV. 9.2). Calvin adds: 'Thus councils would come to have the majesty that is their due; yet in the meantime Scripture would stand out in the higher place with everything subject to its standard in this way' (IV. 10.8).

Calvin then specifies the ancient church councils that are particularly binding on all true Christians: 'In this way, we willingly embrace and reverence as holy the early councils, such as those of Nicea, Constantinople, Ephesus I, Chalcedon, and the like, which were concerned with refuting errors – insofar as they relate to the teachings of faith. For they contain nothing but the pure and genuine exposition of Scripture, which the holy fathers applied with spiritual prudence to crush the enemies of religion who had then arisen' (IV.9.8).

Calvin makes it clear that our respect is always owed to the decrees of Church Councils, as we find them faithfully passing down the truths of Holy Scripture: '...we shall determine from Scripture which one's decree is not orthodox. For this is the only sure principle on which to distinguish.' (IV.9.9).[9]

Pierre Viret, Swiss ministerial colleague of Calvin, said much the same in his 'Third Dialogue on the Authority of Councils'. Along with the Churches of the Reformation, he recognized the authority of the first four councils: Nicea (325), Constantinople I (381), Ephesus (431), and Chalcedon (451). Yet at the same time, like Calvin and the other Reformers, he recognized that even good and ancient councils could err, and thus, always had to be judged in light of Scripture.[10]

Not only the continental Lutheran and Reformed Churches, but also the early leaders of the great Anglican Church held to the authority of Church Councils, but always under Scripture. According to Ford Lewis Battles:

---

9. Calvin then gives an illustration of the truth of Chalcedon, as opposed to the incorrect theology of Ephesus II, which in fact contradicted Chalcedon, in his Institutes IV.9.9.

10. Pierre Viret, Instruction Chriétiénne Tome premier, Édition établie, présentée et annotée par Arthur-Louis Hofer (L'Age D' Homme: Lausanne, 2003), 505,533.

Calvin names with full approval (as faithful to Scripture) the four general councils commonly held of special authority, e.g., by Anglican writers such as Jewel and Hooker. This passage is of 1543, earlier than Bullinger's *Decades* (1550). The latter work is introduced by a statement on the four general synods, giving their essential definitions, with supporting patristic documents. The *Decades* became highly influential in England, especially after its authorization as required reading for the clergy by a convocation under Archbishop Whitgift, 1586. Jewel was a disciple of Bullinger.[11]

In Scotland, the sixteenth-century Reformers sought to be 'the Catholic Church Reformed' or 'The Universal Kirk', as Wotherspoon and Kirkpatrick bring out in *A Manual of Church Doctrine according to the Church of Scotland*.[12]

> The Scottish Reformers in 1558 had this definition in view[13] when they required that 'the Church be reformed in accordance with the precepts of the New Testament, the writings of the Ancient Fathers, and the Godly and approved laws of the Emperor Justinian (in whose code the Theodosian Edict had been incorporated).' In the same sense the Second Helvetic Confession cites the Edict, and continues: 'Since we are then every one of us of this Faith and Religion, we trust that we shall be held by all not for heretics but for Catholics and Christians.'[14]

Within two years, the 1560 Scots Confession taught the same in section 20: General Councils, their Power, Authority, and the Cause of their Summoning:

> As we do not rashly condemn what good men, assembled together in General Councils lawfully gathered, have set before us; so we do not receive uncritically whatever has been declared to men under the name of the General Councils, for it is plain that, being human, some of them have manifestly erred, and that in matters of great weight and importance. So far then as the Council confirms its decrees by the plain Word of God, so far do we reverence and embrace them.

Nearly a century later, the Westminster Assembly did so as well in its *Confession of Faith*, where it taught that Church synods and councils are 'to be received with reverence and submission, not only for their agreement with the word, but also for the power whereby they are made, as being an ordinance of God, appointed thereunto in his word' (ch. XXXI. 'Of Synods and Councils', par. 3). Yet they also state clearly in the following paragraph (4): 'All synods or councils since the apostles' times, whether

---

11. Footnote of Ford Lewis Battles to his translation of John Calvin's *Institutes of the Christian Religion* IV.9.8 (note 8 on p. 1171).

12. *A Manual of Church Doctrine according to the Church of Scotland*, by H. J. Wotherspoon and J. M. Kirkpatrick, Second Edition: Revised and Enlarged by T. F. Torrance and Ronald Selby Wright (Oxford University Press: London, 1960), 9.

13. 'The word 'Catholic' has also a canonical and juristic sense which is decided by the Edict of Gratian, Valentinian, and Theodosius (A.D. 380): that those are to be called Catholics who believe 'the one Godhead and equal majesty and holy tri-unity of the Father, the Son, and the Holy Ghost.'

14. Wotherspoon and Kirkpatrick, op. cit., 10.

general or particular, may err, and many have erred; therefore they are not to be made the rule of faith or practice, but to be used as a help in both.'

In our modern individualistic West (which we, in company with Richard Weaver, have already spoken of as being in crucial respects 'nominalistic' – although very few would recognize this word), many true believers think of themselves only as separate and lone Christians, no doubt with their Bible in hand, and some kind of fellowship in a local congregation. However, they are at the same time deprived of the strengthening sense of fellowship in 'the holy catholic church', including its broad and deep doctrinal heritage, as, for instance its first four Councils have been passed down, officially expounded, and lived out for over a millennium and a half.[15]

This makes them ready prey for submitting to the spirit of the age and the blind spots, errors, and passing fads of their ever-changing culture. But there is a far better way than the myopia of time-bound provincialism ('old is bad; new is good') that cuts people's roots and leaves them blowing from one place to another like autumn leaves in the wind. A keen awareness that God still gives himself to be known in the Church, as he always has, is essential for sound doctrinal understanding of the Word of God written, and for pastoral strength, and missionary power. Calvin has summarized this necessity well (referring to Cyprian's *Letters* iv.4):

> ... let us learn from the simple title 'mother' how useful, indeed how necessary, it is that we should know her. For there is no other way to enter into life unless this mother conceive us in her womb, give us birth, nourish us at her breast, and lastly, unless she keep us under her care and guidance until, putting off mortal flesh, we become like the angels [Matt. 22:30]. Our weakness does not allow us to be dismissed from her school until we have been pupils all our lives. Furthermore, away from her bosom one cannot hope for any forgiveness of sins or any salvation, as Isaiah [Isa. 37:32] and Joel [Joel 2:32] testify... By these words [i.e. Ps.106:4-5] God's fatherly favor and the especial witness of spiritual life are limited to his flock, so that it is always disastrous to leave the church' (IV.1.4).

---

15. Those who do not see themselves as rooted in the larger fellowship of the Christian Church often also seem to have a problem understanding that they belong to a divinely created order that can – to some real degree - be understood with the human mind, and realistically expressed in normal language. Sometimes the failure to submit one's understanding to the larger human and creational realities (as well as to Scriptural ones) can involve thinkers in a sort of 'solipsism,' in which they are so turned in on themselves and their own feelings and fears, that they cannot see the larger reality, which alone can give them significance and peace.

CHAPTER 12

THE ASCENSION, SESSION,
AND RETURN OF CHRIST

The Risen Christ in his glorified body ascended back up to the glorious realm where his Father is seated. This is the second aspect of his Exaltation that is mentioned in the Apostles Creed, and Holy Scripture shows us that it is a continuing part of his redemptive work.

The Second Stage of Christ's Exaltation: His Ascension

The risen Christ ascended back up to the Father; that is the second stage of his Exaltation. We note (a) the event of his ascension, (b) its time and place, (c) its significance, and (d) our attitude towards it.

(a) The event of his ascension

Holy Scripture indicates that forty days after his resurrection, the risen Lord ascended up on high, in view of his disciples, and that the disciples went forth preaching the Word, which the risen Lord confirmed with signs following. The ancient addition to the sixteenth chapter of the Gospel of Mark (vv. 9-20) states: 'So then after the Lord had spoken unto them, he was received up into heaven, and sat on the right hand of God. And they went forth, and preached every where, the Lord working with them, and confirming the word with signs following. Amen' (Mark 16:19-20).

Luke 24 relates that after Jesus had shown how the Old Testament pointed to him, he commissioned his disciples to preach the Gospel, and led them out of the city. He instructed them to remain in Jerusalem until the promise of the Father would come upon them to endue them with power from on high. Then he blessed them with uplifted hands, was parted from them and ascended into heaven: 'And he led them out as far as to Bethany, and he lifted up his hands, and blessed them. And it came to pass, while he blessed them, he was parted from them, and carried into heaven. And they worshipped him, and returned to Jerusalem with great joy; And were continually in the temple, praising and blessing God. Amen' (Luke 24:50-53).

The Shekinah Cloud

Acts 1 similarly places the ascension after the risen Lord's instructions to his disciples to await the gift of the Spirit and to be his witnesses to the world. It adds that he was taken up in a cloud. It appears to have been the same cloud that expressed the glory of God – the Shekinah: a bright, shining presence, imbued with the divine presence – which rested upon the Tabernacle in the wilderness (Ex. 13:21; 40:34), and came down after Solomon's prayer in the new Temple (I Kings 8:10-11). It exhibited the glorious presence of God in Tabernacle and Temple, not least in the holy of holies, and thus was appropriate to his entrance into the supreme holy place above.

> And when he had spoken these things, while they beheld, he was taken up; and a cloud received him out of their sight. And while they looked stedfastly toward heaven as he went up, behold, two men stood by them in white apparel: Which also said, Ye men of Galilee, why stand ye gazing up into heaven? this same Jesus, which is taken up from you into heaven, shall so come in like manner as ye have seen him go into heaven (Acts 1:9-11).

Active and passive verbs used of the ascension

Two Greek verbs are generally used in these and other New Testament texts to express the ascension: (1) ἀναβαινω, which indicates going up by one's own power (thus, in the active voice), and (2) ἀναλαμβανω, meaning to be taken up (thus, in the passive voice, ἀναλαμβανομαι).

(1) ἀναβαινω, according to T. F. Torrance, is the Greek rendering of the Hebrew *alah*, and has cultic significance:

> It is used regularly in the Pentateuch of Moses' ascent of Mount Sinai, with the sense of going up to or ascending to the Lord. It came to be a regular term for going up to the Temple, while within the Temple it was used for ascension into the Holy of Holies. At the same time the word was used for the offering of sacrifice, while the noun, *olah*, may be used as a technical terms for the whole burnt offering.[1]

> It is in this way, apparently, that the term ἀναβαινω is applied to the ascension of Jesus Christ with distinct theological import – cf. Acts 2:34; John 3:13; 6:62; 20:17; Eph. 4:8-10...Used in these ways the term *ascension* is essentially concerned with the Royal Priesthood of the crucified, risen and ascended Christ, exercised from the right hand of divine power.[2]

(2) ἀναλαμβανομαι usually bears the sense of 'to be lifted up.' It is used in Mark 16:19; Acts 1:2; 1:22; I Tim. 3:16.

---

1. T. F. Torrance, *Space, Time and Resurrection*, 107.

2. Ibid., 108.

References to the ascension outside Mark and Luke

In addition to these main ascension texts, there are certain references to Christ's ascension in Matthew and John, although they do not describe it specifically as do Mark and Luke. Matthew reports the words of Jesus to the high priest: 'Hereafter shall ye see the Son of man sitting on the right hand of power, and coming in the clouds of heaven' (Matt. 26:64). This may be more a reference to Christ's coming in judgment than to the ascension, but there is certainly a connection between them in that in each case, he had to go up first, before he would come down.

There are various references in John's Gospel that express aspects of what happened in the ascension. These references may include both his lifting up on the cross and his ascension: 'And no man hath ascended up to heaven, but he that came down from heaven, even the Son of man which is in heaven. And as Moses lifted up the serpent in the wilderness, even so must the Son of man be lifted up...' (John 3:13-14). Jesus says in John 6:62: 'What and if ye shall see the Son of man ascend up where he was before?' (using the Greek verb ἀναβαινω). In John he often speaks of his 'going to the Father' (cf. John 14:28; 16:5, 10, 17, 28).

Soon after his resurrection, Christ said to Mary Magdalene near the empty tomb: 'Touch me not (or, more accurately, 'do not hold on to me'); for I am not yet ascended to my Father; but go to my brethren, and say unto them, I ascend unto my Father, and your Father; and to my God, and your God' (John 20:17) – also using ἀναβαινω.

I Timothy 3:16 mentions the ascension in what is generally considered an early hymn of praise: 'And without controversy great is the mystery of godliness: God was manifest in the flesh, justified in the Spirit, seen of angels, preached unto the Gentiles, believed on in the world, received up into glory.'

Peter, in explaining the meaning of Christian baptism, relates one's good conscience toward God to Christ's resurrection and ascension: 'The like figure whereunto even baptism doth also now save us (not the putting away of the filth of the flesh, but the answer of a good conscience toward God,) by the resurrection of Jesus Christ: Who is gone into heaven, and is on the right hand of God, angels and authorities and powers being made subject unto him' (I Peter 3:21-22).

The Apostle Paul in Ephesians 4:8-12 speaks of the ascension as a fulfillment of Psalm 68:18: 'Wherefore he saith, When he ascended up on high, he led captivity captive, and gave gifts unto men. (Now that he ascended, what is it but that he also descended first into the lower parts of the earth? He that descended is the same also that ascended up far above all heavens, that he might fill all things.) And he gave some, apostles; and some, prophets; and some, evangelists; and some, pastors and teachers; For the perfecting of the saints, for the work of the ministry, for the edifying of the body of Christ...'

Christ's descent into the lower parts of the earth probably refers to his suffering the pains of hell on the cross and/or his announcing his victorious work on the cross to those in infernal regions, as he passes through on his way to the Father, as is mentioned in I Peter 3:18-22. The results of his ascension are his 'filling of all things,' which seems to imply his ultimate exaltation in and over the entire cosmos, eventually resulting in its total restoration from corruption into the glorious liberty of the children of God (Rom. 8:21), and his providing officers for his church for the edification of the body of Christ (Eph. 4:10, 12-13).

Milligan rightly notes that '[i]n several of his apocalyptic visions also, Saint John beholds the exalted "Son of man" encompassed by the splendour of His heavenly abode.'[3]

Peter Toon suggests that the vision in Revelation 12:1-6 of a woman giving birth to a child, whom a dragon tried to devour, is a description of the Lord's ascension and exaltation:

> After the child, Jesus the Messiah, is born, he is snatched up to heaven…The description in Revelation 12 moves from birth to ascension, with no mention of the ministry and passion. The main point in the vision is that Jesus, once delivered from the hostile powers which sought to attack and conquer him, is placed upon the throne in heaven…[4]

We will discuss aspects of the Epistle to the Hebrews later, under the heading 'the significance of the ascension', but here simply note that the argument of Hebrews, which turns largely on the superiority of the priesthood of Christ, constantly assumes the reality of Christ's ascension. Hebrews 7:26 speaks of him as '…made higher than the heavens'. Hebrews 8:5 contrasts what Christ did in the heavenly tabernacle with what Moses did in the earthly one, and 9:23 and 24 speak of his purifying the heavenly sanctuary, where he has appeared in the presence of God for us. Hebrews 12:2 describes him after his endurance of the cross as having 'sat down at the right hand of God.' Though strictly speaking this verse refers to his session, it no doubt includes his prior ascension.

Psalms and Daniel refer to the ascension

From early centuries Church Fathers and ancient liturgies have seen the Psalms and other Old Testament texts as predictive descriptions of Christ's ascension. The New Testament itself does so, as we have seen the way Ephesians 4:8 employs Psalm 68:18. This Psalm may have historically referred to David taking the ark from the house of Obed-Edom to Jerusalem (2 Sam. 6:12), with a celebratory procession to Mount Zion. Paul saw it as prefiguring the exaltation of the Son and Lord of King David, who would give gifts to his people.

Psalm 110 is more frequently quoted in the New Testament than any other Old Testament passage. Originally it described God's blessing upon the line of King David. It both guaranteed his authority as from God (vv. 1-3), and affirmed his priesthood 'after the order of Melchizedek' (v. 4). This messianic Psalm is applied to the exaltation of Christ, with special

---

3. Milligan refers to Rev. 1:13; 5:11-13; 6:9-17; 14:1-5, in op. cit., 8.

4. Peter Toon, *The Ascension of Our Lord* (Thomas Nelson Publishers: Nashville, TN, 1984), 9.

reference to his 'sitting down' at God's right hand, the place of supreme power and honor. Following his completed work on Calvary and his resurrection, Jesus was taken up to heaven to sit on the Throne (Heb. 1:3).

There he must reign until he has put all his enemies under his feet (I Cor. 15:25, referring to Ps. 110:1, 2, 5, 6). Matthew 22:44 and Luke 20:42 show Jesus repeating Psalm 110:1 to the Pharisees (and scribes and elders), so as to show his supremacy over David. In Acts 2:34 and 35, Peter quotes Psalm 110:1 as referring to Christ's victorious ascension. Hebrews 5:6, 6:20, and 7:17, 21 quote Psalm 110:4 as speaking of Christ's priesthood after the order of Melchizedek. Hebrews 10:12, 13 quotes Psalm 110:1, 2, and 4 as describing the finality of Christ's offering, and its inevitable results of victory over his enemies.

Another messianic and royal psalm, Psalm 2, is also frequently quoted in the New Testament. It is used by the divine voice with reference to Christ's Sonship at his baptism and transfiguration (cf. Matt. 3:17; 17:5; 2 Pet. 1:17). Paul uses it to set forth the resurrection (Acts 13:33), and Revelation 12:5 and 19:15 use it to describe both Christ's incarnation and exaltation. Though written by David, it was taken to be predictive of the fuller work of his exalted Son and his eternal Lord.

When Jesus spoke to the Jewish chief priest at his trial (Matt. 26:64) he referred to Daniel 7:13-14: 'I saw in the night visions, and behold, one like the Son of man came with the clouds of heaven, and came to the Ancient of days, and they brought him near before him. And there was given him dominion, and glory, and a kingdom, that all people, nations, and languages, should serve him: his dominion is an everlasting dominion, which shall not pass away, and his kingdom that which shall not be destroyed.' This can be understood to be related to his ascension, his session, and his coming in judgment.

(b) The time and place of the ascension

(i) Its time

Luke tells us that Jesus ascended to the Father forty days after his resurrection (Acts 1:3). Certainly this going up in the Shekinah cloud in his resurrection body in view of his disciples was the definitive lifting up to glory, and when we speak of Christ's ascension, it is of this event, forty days following the resurrection, that we speak.

Yet it is possible that there had been earlier 'ascensions' or passings of the risen Christ in his glorified body between heaven and earth. Gerrit Dawson, following Peter Toon, draws attention to an earlier ascension (on Easter Day):

> In John 20:17, Jesus tells Mary Magdalene not to touch him because he has not yet gone up, or ascended, to his Father. But then he instructs her in 20:17 to go to his brothers and tell them 'I go to my Father and to your Father.' The verb there is *anabaino*, in the present active indicative, which denotes an action that is occurring or will occur imminently. Then, when Jesus next appears, he breathes on the disciples, saying 'Receive the Holy Spirit'

(John 20:22)…Since Jesus had said that the Spirit could not come until he had gone away (John 16:7), this breathing out of the Spirit assumes a going up to the Father on Easter Day.[5]

During those forty days between his resurrection and final ascension, the risen Lord from time to time met with his disciples, and instructed them. But it would seem that for most of that time he was not visible to them. Hence, given the nature of his glorified body as suited for the upper world, but also able to manifest itself in the lower world, it would be no surprise if more than once he was back and forth between the Father's presence above and the disciples' presence below.

(ii) Its place, and questions of spatiality

It is much easier for us to discern the time of Christ's ascension than how his risen body moved from one place, or realm, to another place, or realm. However, this does not seem to be a problem for the New Testament, which straightforwardly says that he 'descended into the lower parts of the earth' (cf. Eph. 4:9), and that he was taken up on a cloud 'out of their sight' (Acts 1:9). It is a safe assumption that at least part of the function of space, location, clouds, stars, and directions that appear to the human observer 'up and down,' were established by God in the created order to say something about who he is, and what our relationship to him is.

Smoke from the sacrificial altars of the Old Testament rose upwards towards God; worshipers in the Tabernacle and Temple lifted their hands and their hearts upwards; Elijah was taken upwards, out of human sight, in a fiery chariot to God; 'Psalms of ascent' (Psalms 120-134) were sung by the Hebrew pilgrims on their way upwards to Jerusalem for the holy festivals. Such Psalms directed the eyes of the believers upwards to God (cf. Ps. 121:1), and called the tribes to go up to his city (cf. Ps. 122).

According to Hebrews 11:10, Abraham was looking for 'a city that hath foundations, whose builder and maker is God,' and his descendants saw themselves also as pilgrims on earth, who 'seek a country; that is, an heavenly…' (cf. Heb. 11:13, 14, 16). A major function of Jerusalem was to point God's people upwards to that heavenly city. Saint Paul understands it to point to 'Jerusalem which is above…the mother of us all' (Gal. 4:26).

Hence, in the various strands of the Old Testament, it was instinctively understood that 'upwards' speaks of divine transcendence, and is a constant reminder to faith of his presence and help coming down from above to assist his people on earth. Ecclesiastes 5:2 uses this sense of transcendence to warn worshipers not to talk too much: '…for God is in heaven, and thou upon earth: therefore let thy words be few.'

C. S. Lewis saw this creational function of 'up and down' as an inbuilt pointer to God:

> They [writers of Scripture] never thought merely of the blue sky or merely of a 'spiritual' heaven. When they looked up at the blue sky they never doubted

5. Gerrit Dawson, *Jesus Ascended: The Meaning of Christ's Continuing Incarnation* (P&R Publishing: Phillipsburg, NJ, 2004), 36-37. He refers to Peter Toon, op. cit., 9-12.

that there, whence light and heat and the precious rain descended, was the home of God: but on the other hand, when they thought of one ascending to that Heaven they never doubted He was 'ascending' in what we should call a 'spiritual' sense.

It is a fact, not a fiction, that light and life-giving heat do come down from the sky to Earth. The analogy of the sky's role to begetting and of the Earth's role to bearing is sound as far as it goes. The huge dome of the sky is of all things sensuously perceived the most like infinity. And when God made space and worlds that move in space, and clothed our world with air, and gave us such eyes and such imaginations as those we have, He knew what the sky would mean to us. And since nothing in His work is accidental, if He knew, He intended. We cannot be certain that this was not indeed one of the chief purposes for which Nature was created; still less that it was not one of the chief reasons why the withdrawal was allowed to affect human senses as a movement upwards. (A disappearance into the earth would beget a wholly different symbolism).[6]

But how does the risen Christ going up on a cloud to God's presence fit with what we seem to know about cosmology, especially with our heliocentric understanding of the relation of the spinning planets with the sun, and the vast system of galaxies beyond? There have been various approaches to make some sense of what Holy Scripture never explains.

In the late nineteenth century, Scottish theologian William Milligan suggested that the ascension indicated not a change of *place* but a change of *realms*.[7] But what is the final difference between *place* and *realm*? Change of *realm* raises as many questions as change of *place*, and in and of itself cannot really say any more about how and where the body of Christ went up than can *place*.

However, where Milligan is especially helpful is in his emphasis upon the ascension of Christ's spiritual body in terms of *relationship* within the Holy Trinity:

> When we say 'Our Father which art in heaven' we cannot mean that the Father to whom we pray dwells only in some distant region of the universe. He must be also by our side, in this world as well as beyond it; and the thought of his nearness to us in one of the conditions of effectual prayer… The words 'which is in heaven' point to no locality, but to the state or condition of being to which our Lord belonged… 'heaven is a state rather than a place.' The thought of locality may, no doubt, be involved in it, but it is not the main thought.[8]

In the later twentieth century, T. F. Torrance did significant research, indicating that a biblical view of space and time would have us look at God's relationship to space, not in terms of locality itself, but rather in terms of his creative, redemptive, and providential omnipotence over it.

> The concept of an infinite differential in the rationality of God allows us to say that God is free from any necessity, spatio-temporal, causal or logical,

---

6. C. S. Lewis, *Miracles: A Preliminary Study* (Glasgow: Fontana Books, 1960), 161-162.

7. See William Milligan, *The Ascension of Our Lord*, Lecture I (pp. 1-60).

8. Ibid., 21, 23, 25.

in His relationship with the creation...we must not think of the Incarnation as an intrusion of the Son of God into the determinations and conditions of space and time, or of His miraculous acts within them as in any way an abrogation of the space-time structures of this world that we call natural laws. Rather is the Incarnation to be understood as the chosen path of God's rationality in which He interacts with the world and establishes such a relation between creaturely being and Himself that He will not allow it to slip away from Him into futility or nothingness, but upholds and confirms it as that which He has made and come to redeem...This means, for example, that space must be defined in terms of bodies or agents conceived as active principles, making room or creating space for themselves in the universe...[9]

In his *Space, Time and Resurrection*, Torrance shows that as concerns both incarnation and ascension, we are to think of space, not as a *receptacle*, but in terms of relationships.[10]

Time and space must both be conceived in relational terms, and in accordance with the active principles or forces that move and make room for themselves in such a way that space and time arise in and with them and their movements – they are not receptacles apart from bodies or forces, but are functions of events in the universe and forms of their orderly sequence and structure...'place' for God can only be defined by the communion of the Persons in the Divine life – that is why doctrinally we speak of the *'perichoresis'* (from *chora* meaning space or room) or mutual indwelling of the Father, Son and Holy Spirit in the Triunity of God...In the nature of the case, statements regarding that ascension are *closed at man's end* (because bounded within the space-time limits of man's existence on earth) but are *infinitely open at God's end*, open to God's own eternal Being and the infinite room of his divine life.[11]

All of this indicates that space and time, aspects of that order which God created by his power out of nothing, are his servants, not his masters. They are there to serve the Trinitarian persons and the relationships they establish with their image-bearers. We need know no more than that.

(c) Its significance

The ascension signifies (i) the completion of Christ's offering to the Father, (ii) the entrance into the continuing phase of his high-priestly intercession for his church, and (iii) the security of the final goal involved in God's creation of humankind.

(i) The completion of Christ's offering to the Father

Christ's once-for-all sacrifice for all the sins of his people had been accepted and affirmed in his bodily resurrection (e.g. Rom. 1:4; 4:25). By his ascension into the Father's presence, he completes his already

9. T. F. Torrance, *Space, Time and Incarnation* (London: Oxford University Press, 1969), 67, 69.

10. Torrance, *Space, Time and Resurrection*, 123-142.

11. Ibid., 130-132.

accepted offering in that place upon which the earthly Tabernacle had been modeled (cf. Heb. 8, 9, and 10). Torrance describes the main point:

> The resurrection and ascension, however, do not mean that Christ's priestly sacrifice and oblation of himself are over and done with, but rather that in their once and for all completion they are taken up eternally into the life of God, and remain prevalent, efficacious, valid, or abidingly real. Christ is spoken of in the Epistle to the Hebrews, as the *Prodromos* or the *Archegos*, the One who has gone ahead and broken a way through into the immediate presence of God, and is *our* Prince and Leader, so that all who are united with him may through the living way which he has prepared in himself enter into the heavenly sanctuary.[12]

Bavinck rightly points out that upon Christ's ascension into the holy places above, there does not need to be a renewed offering of his blood, for that was fully and sufficiently completed on earth:

> One should note, however, that the author of this letter [Hebrews] nowhere says that Christ entered heaven *with* his blood, the way the Old Testament high priest on the great Day of Atonement entered the holy of holies with blood to sprinkle it on and before the mercy seat. He only says that Christ once for all entered the sanctuary through his blood (Heb. 9:12). He did not take with him the blood that was shed on the cross to sprinkle it in the heavenly sanctuary…But by means of his blood, on the basis of the sacrifice made on the cross, he secured for himself the right to enter heaven to appear in God's presence on our behalf.[13]

In other words, as Bavinck writes: 'It [Christ's sacrifice] is both historical and transhistorical: because it was the sacrifice of the Son by the power of the Holy Spirit, it is an act of and at the same time the enablement for his eternal, royal priesthood in heaven.'[14]

(ii) The entrance into the continuing phase of his high priestly intercession for his Church

To say that the ascension *completes* Christ's offering to the Father means that in the supreme sanctuary above, he *continues applying* all the beneficial results of that once-for-all sacrifice for the final glorification of his Church for whom he made the sacrifice. John Calvin wrote: 'The high priest used to enter the Holy of Holies not only in his own name, but in that of the people, as one who in a way carried all the twelve tribes on his breast and on his shoulders…so that they all went into the sanctuary together in the person of the one man.'[15]

---

12. Torrance, *Space,Time and Resurrection*, 114-115.

13. H. Bavinck, *Reformed Dogmatics*, vol. three, 477.

14. Ibid., 478.

15. John Calvin, *The Epistle of Paul the Apostle to the Hebrews*, trans. T. H. L. Parker, ed. David W. Torrance and Thomas F. Torrance, *Calvin's New Testament Commentaries*, vol. 8 (Grand Rapids: William B. Eerdmans Publishing Company, 1965), 87.

As William Milligan wrote: '...He now pleads the cause of His people with all-prevailing intercession on their behalf. He applies to them the work which He accomplished upon earth; and, as One whom the Father heareth always, He obtains for them the measure of grace which they require, until at last they are perfected in glory.'[16]

Hebrews 7 speaks of this continuing intercession as 'an unchangeable priesthood' (i.e. 'after the order of Melchizedek'), contrasting it with the Aaronic priests, who, because death finished their priesthoods, 'were not suffered to continue' (v. 23): 'But this man, because he continueth ever, hath an unchangeable priesthood. Wherefore he is able also to save them to the uttermost that come unto God by him, seeing he ever liveth to make intercession for them' (vv. 24, 25).

The eighth chapter of Revelation shows, in symbolical fashion, something of this continuing intercession of Christ for his imperfect saints on earth. It states that after the prayers of the saints are taken up into heaven, those prayers (imperfect, because those who offer them are imperfect), are sprinkled with incense upon the golden altar before the Throne (v. 3). Then those perfume-sprinkled prayers 'ascend up before God' and as a result, 'fire is cast into the earth' (v. 4). What could the incense be but the continuing perfections of him who was crucified, risen, and ascended for us?

The eighth chapter of Romans indicates that the Spirit (called in verse 9 'the Spirit of Christ') helps us pray, even when we do not know how to articulate the holy longings he puts within us, so that we are interceding in accordance with the will of God (vv. 26, 27). Thus, our great high priest continually both perfumes the prayers of his people, and puts pressure within them to 'groan for' the right things.

Christ's continuing priesthood includes much in addition to what we think of as intercession with the Father. As Milligan points out: 'I know thy works' is the language in which the exalted Redeemer addresses each of the seven churches of Asia...and He 'knows' them in order that He may furnish them with the supplies of strength and guidance which their ever-varying circumstances require.'[17] Milligan continues his meditation on 'a constant activity of the glorified Lord on behalf of the members of His body...'[18]:

> Thus it is that He watches over every manifestation of love, however trifling, made by the believer in His name. No gift of meat to the hungry, or water to the thirsty...is unnoticed by Him. Each is marked in His book of remembrance, and it shall not be forgotten in the Judgment...Rightly conceived, the work of Intercession on the part of our heavenly High-priest seems to be that, having restored the broken covenant and brought His Israel into the most intimate union and communion with God, He would now amidst all their remaining weaknesses, and the innumerable temptations that surround them, preserve them in it.[19]

---

16. W. Milligan, op. cit., 149.

17. Milligan, op. cit., 156-157.

18. Ibid., 157.

19. Ibid., 157-158.

Immediately after the account of Jesus' ascension, Mark displays the continuing work of the risen One with his witnessing Church. 'And they went forth, and preached every where, the Lord working with them, and confirming the word with signs following. Amen' (Mark 16:20). The solicitude of the ascended High Priest is the basis of the Church's expansion to the end of time. And the intercession of the ascended One keeps his people safely in the exact place where they should be. Saint Paul indicates that Christ's continuing intercession for his people is the bond of their temporal and eternal security: 'Who is he that condemneth? It is Christ that died, yea rather, that is risen again, who is even at the right hand of God, who also maketh intercession for us' (Rom. 8:34).

(iii) The security of the final goal of God's creation of humankind

The ascension of Christ is the guarantee that God's plans for the redeemed human race will be brought to fruition. As the Westminster Shorter Catechism succinctly states: 'The only Redeemer of God's elect is the Lord Jesus Christ, who, being the eternal Son of God, became man, and so was, and continueth to be, God and man in two distinct natures, and one person, for ever' (Question 21). That is, Christ takes our humanity into the eternal realm, or as Dr. John Duncan of nineteenth-century New College in Edinburgh is often quoted: 'The dust of the earth now sits on the throne of the universe.'

Milligan expands on the accomplishment of the ascension:

> In the Ascended Lord all weakness passes away; all that limits the universal diffusion of His Spirit is removed; and human nature glorified with the glory of the Divine may become the portion of every child of Adam. In that nature the Lord Jesus Christ has ascended to His Father. We who are partakers of it are His 'brethren' [John 20:17]. And as He ascends before our eyes, we behold the pledge of perfect and everlasting communion established between God and man.[20]

In other words, Christ does not discard his humanity; he lifts it up with him into the eternal presence of the Father, and thereby guarantees that we too, in our own created humanity, shall be lifted up to that blessed place when our own time comes. The book of Revelation speaks of the consummation of all history as a wedding between the enthroned Lamb and the people of God 'prepared as a bride adorned for her husband' (Rev. 21:2). We are invited: 'Come hither, I will shew thee the bride, the Lamb's wife' (Rev. 21:9).

In going above in his glorified body, 'our risen Head' is the guarantee that all the members of his body will in due season be raised to be with him, where he is 'that they may behold his glory' (John 17:24). He has gone to his Father's house to prepare a place for them all, and will at the right moment come to take them home (cf. John 14:2-3). He will do for all of his people what he did for the first Christian martyr, Stephen. He will watch over their deaths with tender care, and then receive their spirits (Acts 7:59-60).

---

20. Ibid., 35.

John Flavel tells us:

> 'For he went to prepare a place for you' (John 14:2). He was…the first that
> entered into heaven directly, and in his own name; and had he not done
> so, we would not have entered when we die, in his name. The Fore-runner
> made way for all that are coming on, in their several generations, after him.
> Nor could your bodies have ascended after their resurrection, but in the
> virtue of Christ's ascension. For he ascended…in the capacity of our head
> and representative; to his Father, and our Father: For us, and himself too.[21]

(d) Our attitude towards the ascension

Saint Thomas Aquinas indicates the frame of mind Christ's ascension calls
for among his disciples of all time:

> …in order to direct the fervour of our charity to heavenly things. Hence
> the Apostle says (Col. iii, 1, 2): *Seek the things that are above, where Christ is
> sitting at the right hand of God. Mind the things that are above, not the things that
> are upon the earth*: for as is said (Matt. vi. 21): *Where thy treasure is, there is
> thy heart also*. And since the Holy Ghost is love drawing us up to heavenly
> things, therefore our Lord said to His disciples (John xvi. 7): *It is expedient
> to you that I go; for if I go not, the Paraclete will not come to you; but if I go, I will
> send Him to you*. On which words Augustine says (*Tract*. xciv. *super Joan.*): *Ye
> cannot receive the Spirit, so long as ye persist in knowing Christ according to the
> flesh. But when Christ withdrew in body, not only the Holy Ghost, but both Father
> and Son were present with them spiritually*.[22]

Our time on earth, though of intense and lasting significance, is very short.
Our experience above will be of endless duration. One is a preparation
for the other. To which of the two should we give the most attention?
This present world, though a wonderful gift of creation in and of itself,
is fallen and filled with struggle and difficulties. The ascension calls us
not to define our attitudes by the challenging, and at times discouraging,
circumstances here below, but 'to lift up our eyes to the hills,' where our
ascended Lord is orchestrating all that happens in the earthly experience
of his people for his glory and for our not-yet-seen benefit.

John Calvin in his fourth ascension sermon calls us to define our
thoughts about earthly life with an eye upon the ascended Lord, and in so
doing, we will appreciate our sojourn in this world even more:

> Thus, since He has gone up there, and is in heaven for us, let us note that
> we need not fear to be in this world. It is true that we are subject to so much
> misery that our condition is pitiable, but at that we need neither be astonished
> nor confine our attention to ourselves. Thus, we look to our Head Who is
> already in heaven, and say, 'Although I am weak, there is Jesus Christ Who
> is powerful enough to make me stand upright…Yes, the devil is called the
> prince of this world. But what of it? Jesus Christ holds him in check; for He

---

21. John Flavel, *Works*, vol. I, 508.

22. Thomas Aquinas, *The Summa Theologica*, Part III, Second Number, (QQ. XXVII-LIX), 428.

is King of heaven and earth. There are devils above us in the air who make war against us. But what of it? Jesus Christ rules above, having entire control of the battle. Thus, we need not doubt that He gives us the victory. I am here subject to many changes, which may cause me to lose courage. But what of it? The Son of God is my Head, Who is exempt from all change. I must, then, take confidence in Him.' This is how we must look at His Ascension, applying the benefit to ourselves.[23]

The Third Stage of Christ's Exaltation: His Session (or 'Enthronement')

The Apostles Creed is in accordance with the witness of the New Testament when it mentions the Session of Christ as the third stage of Christ's Exaltation. While relatively little has been written on it by the theologians of the Church, it has always been affirmed in the major Creeds and Conciliar Documents of the Church, and has high significance in spite of the brevity of its treatment in the general theological consensus of the Christian Tradition.

It, in particular, supplies the richest pastoral encouragement to those who suffer, or otherwise walk through dark valleys. The Good Shepherd is on the Throne, and he is also guiding his people in hard and narrow places with his rod and staff (cf. Psalm 23 and John 10). Psalm 32:8 promises his people: 'I will guide thee with mine eye,' and another Psalm says, 'The eyes of the Lord are upon the righteous, and his ears are open unto their cry' (Psalm 34:15).

He alone, who is both Creator and Redeemer in one, and now enthroned as our royal Priest above, is competent for such delicate and mighty pastoral care of all his people. Andrew Murray reminds us to keep the eyes of our faith upon Christ's session above, for it enables him to order our difficult circumstances below to work out in exactly the right way:

> If we but believed that our Redeemer is our Creator! He knows us; He appoints and orders our lot; nothing that comes to us but what He has in His hands. He has the power to make our circumstances, however difficult, a heavenly discipline, a gain and a blessing. He has taken them all up into the life-plan He has for us as our Redeemer. Did we but believe this, how we should gladly meet every event with the worship of an adoring faith. My Creator, who orders all, is my Redeemer, who blesses all.[24]

His Session is of greatest moment to those who, in obedience to Christ's Great Commission, take the Gospel into cultures which are either ignorant of the Lord, or are actively hostile to him. The one whom the messianic Psalm (2) prophetically sets forth, is daily answering what he instructed his missionary servants to ask him: 'Ask of me, and I shall give thee the

---

23. John Calvin, *The Deity of Christ and Other Sermons*. Trans. Leroy Nixon (Audubon, NJ: Old Paths Publications, 1997), 238-239.

24. Andrew Murray, *The Holiest of All*, 61.

heathen for thine inheritance, and the uttermost parts of the earth for thy possession' (v. 8). From his place of enthroned glory and limitless power, he is watching with tender eye and mighty arm over those who in his Name are seeking to plant new churches, cleanse corrupt ones, and to reform oppressive and sinful structures of humanistic states. He is the power of the powerless, and delights to use 'the weak things of the world to confound the wise...and hath chosen the weak things of the world to confound the things whch are mighty...to bring to nought things that are...' (I Cor. 1:27-28). Because he rules from the Sovereign Throne, it becomes surprisingly true, against all human expectations, that 'them that honour me I will honour...' (I Sam. 2:30).

The New Testament states that the ascended Christ *sat down* on the right hand of God. This is a culminating aspect of his exaltation. To grasp its greatness, we look at (a) various New Testament texts which refer to it, and also (b) at some Old Testament texts that help us understand its meaning. Then we consider (c) its significance for his continuing dignity and ministry until his return.

(a) New Testament texts on the Session

In Matthew 19:28, Jesus speaks (with reference to Psalm 110) of his return when the cosmos shall be restored: 'In the regeneration when the Son of man shall sit on the throne of his glory.' In Matthew 26:64 and Luke 22:69 (with reference to Daniel 7), he told the high priest: '...nevertheless I say unto you, Hereafter shall ye see the Son of man sitting on the right hand of power, and coming in the clouds of heaven.'

In the longer version of Mark 16, we are told: 'So then the Lord Jesus after he had spoken unto them was received up into heaven, and sat down at the right hand of God' (v. 19). Peter's sermon in Acts 2, quoting Psalm 110:1, speaks of Christ's session at God's right hand, from which place comes down the Holy Spirit, so that victory over all his enemies is assured (Acts 2:33-36).

Ephesians 1:20 and 21 speak of his session: 'Which he wrought in Christ, when he raised him from the dead, and set him at his own right hand in the heavenly places. Far above all principality, and power, and might, and dominion, and every name that is named, not only in this world, but also in that which is to come.' Ephesians 2:6 speaks of the church's sharing in the session of Christ: 'And hath raised us up together, and made us sit together in heavenly places in Christ.'

In the interests of holy living through heavenly mindedness, Colossians 3:1 exhorts believers: 'If then ye were raised together with Christ, seek the things that are above where Christ is seated on the right hand of God. Set your minds on the things that are above, not on the things that are upon the earth. For ye died, and your life is hid with Christ in God.' Hebrews 1:3 explains the session of Christ as the result of his completed work of propitiation: '...when he had by himself purged our sins, sat down on the right hand of the majesty on high...'

The theme of his session is continued in Hebrews 8, where the superiority and finality of his priesthood 'after the order of Melchizedek' is contrasted with the preliminary and repetitive priesthood after the order of Aaron: 'We have such an high priest, who is set on the right hand of the throne of the Majesty in the heavens…' How this relates to Christ, the Melchizedek high priest, *sitting*, is contrasted to the *standing* of the Aaronic order in Hebrews 10:11-12 (referring to Psalm 110:1): 'And every priest standeth daily ministering and offering oftentimes the same sacrifices, which can never take away sins; But this man, after he had offered one sacrifice for sins for ever, sat down on the right hand of God…'

Revelation 3:21 refers to his sitting with the Father: 'He that overcometh, I will give to him to sit down with me in my throne, as I also overcame and sat down with my Father in his throne.' His sitting down there is, as elsewhere, a significant sign of his victorious work on earth for his people, and guarantees that they will be given the grace 'to sit with him'.

(b) Old Testament texts that illumine the session

Arthur J. Tait helpfully listed 'the Old Testament foreshadowing' of Christ's session, as 'found in the application of the idea of session to the conception of Jehovah, and still more in the description which is given in Ps. cx of the Messianic King.'[25] I follow him here.

1) There is the idea of rest and cessation from labor, as when Abraham 'sat in the tent door in the heat of the day' (Gen. 18:1), or Moses after his flight from Egypt 'sat down by a well' (Exod. 2:15).

2) There is a sense of honor and dignity, as when the first-born of Pharaoh was said to sit on his throne (Exod. 11:5), or Solomon providing a throne beside his own for his mother (I Kings 2:19).

3) Session is also connected with the administration of justice, as when Moses was seated to hear the cases of the people who were standing around him (Exod. 18:13; Num. 35:12; Josh. 20:6). The King sat on the throne of judgment in Proverbs 20:8. Psalm 9 refers to God's maintaining the cause of his people as he sits on the throne, judging righteously (vv. 4 and 7). Joel foresees God's sitting 'to judge all the nations round about' in reference to his coming to the valley of Jehoshaphat (Joel 3:12).

4) Session can be connected with sovereignty or kingship, as the king was the one who sat on the throne of power (I Kings 1:13; 22:10). Micaiah the prophet, as he announced judgment on wicked King Ahab, said: 'I saw the Lord sitting on his throne, and all the host of heaven standing by him on his right hand and on his left' (I Kings 22:19; 2 Chron. 18:18). Psalm 2 describes the Lord's sovereignty over earthly kings as 'he that sitteth in the heavens' (v. 4). Psalm 29:3 shows God's power over nature as his sitting as 'king at the flood.' Psalm 47 similarly speaks of his power over the nations in terms of session: 'God reigneth over the nations: God sitteth upon his holy throne' (v. 10). Psalm 110:1 (already frequently quoted) speaks of his total sovereignty over his enemies.

---

25. Arthur James Tait, *The Heavenly Session of Our Lord: An Introduction to the History of the Doctrine* (London: Robert Scott, MCMXII), 3.

Isaiah, in the vision by which God called him, saw the Lord seated on his throne above, with his train filling the temple below (Isa. 6:4). The Ark of the Covenant, with its two cherubim on either side of the mercy seat, represented the throne of God (cf. I Sam. 4:4; Ps. 80:1). Zechariah's messianic predictions of 'the Branch' include his sitting and ruling (Zech. 6:12f.).

(c) The significance of Christ's Session

Christ's session is closely linked to his ascension, and is a further aspect of it, though not reducible to it. Bavinck writes:

> It [his session] is closely related to, but not identical with, the resurrection and ascension and is clearly distinguished from them (Acts 2:32-43; I Pet. 3:21-22; Rom. 8:34). This seat at the right hand of God had already been predicted by Christ (Matt. 19:28; 22:44; 25:31; 26:64), and after the resurrection and ascension had taken place, the disciples immediately knew that he was seated at the right hand of God (Acts 2:34; 7:54). They regularly make mention of it in their letters (Rom. 8:34; Eph. 1:20; Col. 3:1; Heb. 1:3; 8:1; 10:12; 12:2; I Pet. 3:22; Rev. 3:21). Sometimes the terminology is slightly varied. Sometimes it is said that the Father made him sit down at his right hand (Acts 2:30; Eph. 1:20) and then that he himself sat down there (Mark 16:19; Heb. 1:3; 8:1; 10:12) and is now seated there (Matt. 26:64; Luke 22:69; Col. 3:1; Heb. 1:13). Being seated there is rendered in Hebrews 12:2 in the perfect tense and hence viewed as an ongoing state...[26]

We may summarize the significance of Christ's session under the classical rubrics of Christ as (i) Prophet, (ii) Priest, and (iii) King.

(i) Christ Seated as Prophet

> It is from the Father's throne, where the risen, ascended Son is now sitting, that the Holy Spirit is sent down upon the waiting Church at Pentecost. Before He (Christ) parted with His disciples He promised them the Holy Spirit, to aid their memories, teach them new truths, guide them into all the truth, and enrich them out of the fullness of Christ, John 14:26; 16:7-15... From that day on Christ through the Spirit was active as our great Prophet in various ways: in the inspiration of Scripture; in and through the preaching of the apostles and of the ministers of the Word; in the guidance of the Church, making it the foundation and pillar of the truth; and in making the truth effective in the hearts and lives of believers.[27]

From the point of view of the composition and inspiration of the New Testament, both the session of Christ and the sending down of his Spirit from the occupied throne are of essential significance. When Christ 'sat down at the right hand of the majesty on high,' there was not a shred of the New Testament yet written. But from the heart of the Holy Trinity, the Holy Spirit came forth 'to guide them into all truth,' to 'bring all things

---

26. Bavinck, op. cit., 446.

27. Berkhof, op. cit., 353.

to their remembrance' that Christ had taught them (John 14:26), and to 'receive of the things of Christ and show it unto them' (John 16:14, 15). Previously, before Christ's death, resurrection, ascension and session, they had not been able to make sense of such things (John 16:12). But now, the result of the Holy Spirit's coming from the throne of Father and Son is the writing of the New Testament.

(ii) Christ Seated as Priest

Christ successfully completed in all its fullness his propitiatory work on earth, and so could cry out: 'It is finished!' John Owen properly brings out in his *Commentary on Hebrews* that Christ's session was not a continuation of the purging of our sins, but rather a consequence of this completed work.[28] Owen noted that what remained for our great High Priest to do was to apply the benefits of his propitiation, as he intercedes for them.[29]

This completion of the atoning work is underlined by Christ's sitting down, especially as we contrast it to how the Levitical high priests had to stand up in Tabernacle and Temple. In the Holy of Holies, there was the Ark of the Covenant, but no chair, for the priest must continue to stand as he sprinkled the blood on the mercy seat. The next year he would have to return, still standing, in order to repeat the ceremony, for it was not yet finished. It would take better than animal blood fully to remove sins (cf. Heb. 9:11-15)! But once the precious blood of Christ was poured out, and the offering accepted for all eternity by God, then our High Priest could sit down!

On the basis of that fully accepted propitiatory atonement for sinners, Christ – still as our High Priest – who ever lives to make intercession for us (Heb. 7:25), continues his priesthood through prayer on our behalf unto the end of time. Henry B. Swete explains it:

> Heaven is not a place for sacrifice, and our Lord is no longer a sacrificing Priest: He has offered one sacrifice for sins for ever. But His Presence in the Holiest is a perpetual and effective presentation before God of the sacrifice once offered which is no less needful for our acceptance than the actual death upon the cross. He has indeed somewhat to offer in His heavenly priesthood, for He offers Himself as representing to God man reconciled, and as claiming for man the right of access to the Divine presence...[30]

Swete's point here is important: although we (rightly) think of Christ as interceding on our behalf with the Father, in accordance with 4:15-16, and 7:25, still it is not so much his words of request, as the very presence of his glorified body, still bearing its wounds (cf. Revelation 5:6 – 'a Lamb standing in the throne as it had been slain') in unbreakable union with his Godhood that successfully 'pleads the case' of his people in any and every situation. That is, he continually, by his presence on the divine throne,

---

28. John Owen, *Commentary on the Epistle to the Hebrews*, at 1:3, vol. 3, 128.

29. Ibid., vol. 6, 24.

30. Henry B. Swete, *The Ascended Christ: A Study in the Earliest Christian Teaching* (London: Macmillan and Co., Ltd., 1910), 43.

offers himself to God for his needy people as their all-prevailing High Priest. His presence as the worthy Lamb still perfumes the prayers of his people and makes them acceptable to God (cf. Rev. 8:2-6).

Thomas Boston grasped the significance of our High Priest above perfuming our prayers while we imperfectly sanctified believers still must live in this fallen world:

> [Christ's intercession consists] In his presenting his people's prayers and petitions unto God, and pleading that they may be accepted and granted for his sake. Their prayers and religious performances are both impure and imperfect; but his precious merit, applied by his powerful intercession, purifies and perfects them...Hence he is represented, Rev. viii. 3 as an angel standing at the golden altar which was before the throne, with a golden censer in his hand, offering up the prayers of all saints, perfuming them with the incense that was given him...and renders them acceptable to God.[31]

(iii) Christ seated as King

As Bavinck states: 'As it is, we do not yet see that all things are subject to him, but he has nevertheless been crowned with glory and honor and must reign as king "until he has put all his enemies under his feet" (I Cor. 15:25).'[32]

His session on the throne of God indicates his supreme authority as king, to work all things to the benefit of his people, and to the glory of the Triune God. Saint Thomas Aquinas describes the exercise of the now-seated king of all:

> ...Christ is said to sit at the right hand of the Father, inasmuch as He reigns together with the Father, and has judiciary power from Him; just as he who sits at the king's right hand helps him in ruling and judging. Hence Augustine says (*De Symb.* ii): *By this expression 'right hand,' understand the power which this Man, chosen of God, received that He might come to judge, Who before had come to be judged.*[33]

Augustine and most theologians and commentators over the centuries have pointed out that 'right hand' is not necessarily literal, but refers to relationship within the persons of the Holy Trinity. In a certain sense, it may be literal, but the issue is the relational reality to which the expression metaphorically points. Tait notes a number of Old Testament texts that demonstrate what 'right hand' actually means in a biblical context:

> *The Right Hand of God*, when used in the Old Testament to indicate position occupied, is a metaphorical expression signifying (1) Honour. Comp. I Kings ii. 19; Ps. xlv. 9; Matt. xxv. 33. (2) Bliss. Comp. Ps. xvi. 11. (3) Authority. Comp. Deut. xxxiii. 2; Pss. xlviii. 10; lxxvii. 10. (4) Power. Comp. Pss. xvii. 7; xviii. 35; xx. 6; xxi. 8; lx. 5; lxxiv. 11; xcviii. 1; cxviii. 15 f.; Is. xlviii. 13; lxii. 8.
>
> In the one hundred and tenth Psalm it should be noted that the king is at the right hand of the LORD for the purpose of participating in His power,

---

31. Boston, op. cit., 216-217.

32. Bavinck, op. cit., 447.

33. Thomas Aquinas, op. cit., 411.

and the LORD is at the right hand of the king for the purpose of imparting power…[34]

An indication that 'sitting at God's right hand', while certainly true, is not the only account we have of what the ascended Christ is presently doing. At his martyrdom, Stephen, the first Christian martyr, saw the Lord standing (Acts 7:55). The beloved apostle John in his vision in Revelation also saw the Lord standing in the midst of the throne (Rev. 5:6). In the last chapter of the New Testament, at the end of the Apocalypse, we see the Lamb standing in the midst of the throne, which he shares with God (Rev 22:1). He is therefore King over the entire cosmos, whether presented as sitting or standing.

Epiphanius shows that the one who rules us as king always does so as our priest:

> Our Lord Jesus Christ…was thus 'priest for ever after the order of Melchizedek' (Heb. 5:6 and Ps. 110:4), and at the same time king according to the original succession, so that he held in his hands the priesthood at the same time as the legislative power. For the seed of David by Mary was installed upon the throne for eternity, 'and his kingdom shall have no end.' Yet in fact, his kingdom is not of this world, as he told Pontius Pilate in the Gospel: 'My kingdom is not of this world.'[35]

Our sovereign King still bears priestly nailprints in his hands, so that everything that comes into his people's lives must pass through the almighty hands that were scarred with those nails for our salvation, which includes our temporal and eternal well-being. That is why the Apostle Paul can tell us, 'And we know that all things work together for good to them that love God, to them who are the called according to his purpose… He that spared not his own Son, but delivered him up for us all, how shall he not with him also freely give us all things?' (Rom. 8:28, 32).

Or to put it another way, our Sovereign Master, from his Throne above, that without diminution has always ruled over all, sees to it from moment to moment that, as the Psalmist stated, 'Surely the wrath of man shall praise thee: the remainder of wrath shalt thou restrain' (Psalm 76:10). The enthroned Christ so powerfully and tenderly cares for his church, that he lets nothing whatsoever come into the lives of any of his people – whether motivated by human or demonic wrath – unless it will bring praise to God (which is also the deepest spiritual motivation of his Spirit-anointed people). Anything – including the hottest and most hateful wrath from God-hating Satan – that would not advance the divine glory (which is the eternal joy and well-being of God's saints) will not ever be allowed to happen even to the weakest and least of them.

Martin Luther's *Large Catechism* summarizes the practical benefits for God's people that derive from Christ's dominion, as he is seated on the Throne:

---

34. Tait, op. cit., p. 9, note 2.

35. Epiphanius, *Panarion* 29. 4, 5-6 (GCS 25, pp. 324-25).

Afterward he rose again from the dead, swallowed up and devoured death, and finally ascended into heaven an assumed dominion at the right hand of the Father. The devil and all powers, therefore, must be subject to him and lie beneath his feet until finally at the last day, he will completely divide and separate us from the wicked world, the devil, death, sin, etc.[36]

He keeps them from that well-filled Throne as 'the apple of his eye' (Psalm 17:8 and Zechariah 2:8). His eye is upon us, and therefore, we keep an eye upon this Christ 'who is even at the right hand of God, who also maketh intercession for us' (Rom. 8:34). In that context, the Apostle Paul affirms the ultimately victorious results of such solicitious watch-care and unfailing intercession of our enthroned High Priest, and he affirms it with great joy. Immediately after mentioning 'tribulation, distress, persecution, famine, nakedness, peril, sword' (Rom.8:35), and even being 'killed all the day long for the sake of Christ, and accounted as sheep for the slaughter' (v. 36), he includes it all when he says that '...in all these things we are more than conquerors through him that loved us' (v. 37). Paul then draws out the victorious confidence that he wants every Christian to take hold of - even in situations of persecution and loss of every earthly good – because of who is on the Throne, exercising an infinitude of power, joined with the most tender care and exquisite wisdom unceasingly exercised over his people: 'For I am persuaded, that neither death, nor life, nor angels, nor principalities, nor powers, nor things present, nor things to come, nor height, nor depth, nor any other creature, shall be able to separate us from the love of God, which is in Christ Jesus our Lord' (vv. 38-39).

The supernatural benefits of his Session extend not only to his over-ruling our bad circumstances, and his protection of his church in evil times and places, but perhaps even more basically, to what he is now doing for his church from that sovereign throne of grace. From that honored seat of mediatorial victory, he is continually pouring his resurrection life into the souls and bodies of his people on earth, thus enabling them to live as Christians in union with him. Few have expressed it better than Andrew Murray, as he comments on the boldness with which we are exhorted 'to enter into the holy place,' where Christ is now sitting (Heb. 10:19-22):

Oh the blessedness of a life in the Holiest! Here the Father's face is seen and His love tasted. Here His holiness is revealed and the soul made partaker of it. Here the sacrifice of love and worship and adoration, the incense of prayer and supplication, is offered in power. Here the outpouring of the Spirit is known as an ever-streaming, overflowing river, from under the throne of God and the Lamb. Here the soul, in God's presence, grows into more complete oneness with Christ, and more entire conformity to His likeness. Here, in union with Christ, in His unceasing intercession, we are emboldened to take our place as intercessors, who can have power with God and prevail. Here the soul mounts up as on eagle's wings, the strength is renewed, and the blessing and power and the love are imparted with

36. *The Large Catechism of Martin Luther*, Translated by Robert H. Fisher (Fortress Press: Philadelphia, 1959), 58.

which God's priests can go out to bless a dying world...O Jesus! our great High Priest, let this be our life![37]

The hymnwriter teaches us to sing aloud with joy, and with liberation of spirit, of the consequences of the Session of Christ:

My times are in Thy hand:
    My God, I wish them there;
My life, my friends, my soul I leave
    Entirely to Thy care.

My times are in Thy hand,
    Jesus, the Crucified:
Those hands my cruel sins had pierced
    Are now my guard and guide.

My times are in Thy hand:
    I'll always trust in Thee;
And after death, at Thy right hand
    I shall forever be.[38]

Hence, the Lord Jesus Christ, 'the fellow of Jehovah,' still sharing our humanity as our Shepherd, who was once smitten for our sakes (cf. Zech. 13:7), but is now triumphantly seated 'at the right hand of the Majesty of high' (Heb. 1:3), brings the members of his Church to the new birth, generation upon generation, and in so doing, sends his Holy Spirit to awaken them to faith and repentance, and thus justifies them; continues to sanctify them throughout their pilgrimage; protects them through all of his watchful providences upon them; makes them fruitful in union with him (cf. John 15); reaches the nations through them (cf. Matt. 28:18-20); gets glory through them that he reflects back to his Father (cf. John 17), and at length receives them into his kingdom of bliss above, where they shall forever share in the beauty of the peace of the thrice-blessed God.

The fourth stage of the Exaltation of Christ: His Return

At the end of the age, at the appointed hour, Christ will return in power and glory to conclude all of history, to raise the quick and the dead, to sit in judgment, and to restore all things to a more than primeval beauty, thus ushering in for all who have trusted in him an eternity of bliss. But the exposition of this major doctrine must be postponed to our last volume.

Nevertheless, in anticipation, we will simply say that he who came the first time as sacrificial lamb (cf. Isaiah 53), will come the second time as conquering Lion of the Tribe of Judah (Gen. 49:9-10). He who once came 'to bear the sins of many... shall appear the second time without sin unto salvation' (Heb. 9:28). What a beautiful sight must this bearer

---

37. Andrew Murray, op. cit., 355-56.

38. By William Freeman Lloyd (1791-1853).

of salvation be; he who beautifies his bride must indeed be resplendent with transformative glory! What a fulfillment of Isaiah's prophecy that 'the people that walked in darkness have seen a great light!' (Isa. 9:2). The uncreated light that once shone for fleeting moments through the Saviour on the Mount of Transfiguration is now so constantly and fully radiant from this God/man in the glory, that his beautiful shining renders sun and moon quite unnecessary in the bliss of the new heavens and new earth, for 'the glory of God lightens it, and the Lamb is the light thereof' (Rev. 21:23).

F. W. Faber has caught the focus of every eye on that glad day, when faith is turned into sight, when 'the vision glorious' is at last fulfilled, and yet will somehow continue to wax greater and lovelier, and ever more alluring, across the endless reaches of an eternity of bliss:

> How beautiful, how beautful
>   The sight of Thee must be,
> Thine endless wisdom, boundless power,
>   And awful purity![39]

As we continue to contemplate the beauty of Christ throughout all our earthly days, and look forward to its ever greater fulness above, we would do well to take to heart a devotional call of Andrew Murray, especially as we turn our hearts to our Lord's certain return:

> 'The blessed hope and the appearing of the glory of our great God and Saviour Jesus Christ' ... 'He shall come to be glorified in His saints, and to be marvelled at in all them that believe.' Then we shall all meet, and the unity of the body of Christ be seen in its divine glory. It will be the meeting place and the triumph of divine love. Jesus receiving His own and presenting them to the Father. His own meeting Him and worshipping in speechless love that blessed face. His own meeting each other in the ecstasy of God's own love. Let us wait, long for, and love the appearing of our Lord and Heavenly Bridegroom. Tender love to Him and tender love to each other is the true and only bridal spirit.[40]

This volume on the Beauty of Christ could well be concluded by the singing of a widely-loved hymn from Silesia, probably composed by the seventeenth century:

> Fairest Lord Jesus! Ruler of all nature!
> O Thou of God and man the Son!
> Thee will I cherish, Thee will I honour,
> Thou my soul's glory, joy, and crown!
>
> Beautiful Saviour! Lord of the nations!
> Son of God and Son of Man!
> Glory and honour, Praise, adoration
> Now and forevermore be Thine!

---

39.   Frederick W. Faber (1814-1863), 'My God, how wonderful Thou art,' sixth stanza.

40.   Andrew Murray, *Waiting on God* (Nisbet & Co. Ltd.: London, 1896), 'Twenty-Eighth Day: Waiting on God for the Coming of His Son,' 132.

BIBLIOGRAPHY

A

Primary Sources

1. Bible

Unless otherwise stated, English Bible quotes are from the Authorized Version.

Biblia Sacra Utriusque Testamenti Editio Hebraica et Graeca. Stuttgart: Germany, 1994.

2. Other Jewish, Patristic, and Related Texts

Athanasius. *Contra Arianos*. *Nicene and Post-Nicene Fathers*, vol. iv. Edinburgh: T & T Clark, 1891.

Athanasius, *Contra Gentes*. *Ibid*.

Athanasius, *Ad Epictetum [Letter to Epictetus]*. *Ibid*.

Athanasius, *Ad Serapionem [Letter to Serapion]*. *Ibid*.

Athanasisus, *De Incarnatione*. *Ibid*.

Augustine. *On the Trinity*. *Nicene and Post-Nicene Fathers*. Grand Rapids, MI: Eerdmans, 1956.

Augustine. *Quaestiones in Exodium 2.73*; Migne, *Patrologia Latina*, 34.

Basil. *Against Eunomius*. *Nicene and Post-Nicene Fathers*, vol. viii. Edinburgh: T & T Clark, 1894.

Basil. *De Spiritu Sancto*. *Nicene and Post-Nicene Fathers*, vol. viii. Edinburgh: T & T Clark, 1894.

Basil. *The Hexameron*. *Nicene and Post-Nicene Fathers*, vol. viii. Edinburgh: T & T Clark, 1894.

Cyril of Alexandria. *Against Nestorius. A Library of the Fathers of the Holy Catholic Church.* Oxford: James Parker, n.d.

Cyril of Jerusalem. *Catechetical Lectures.* Nicene and Post-Nicene Fathers, vol. vii. T & T Clark: Edinburgh, 1893.

Cyril of Alexandria. *Commentary on the Incarnation of the only Son* 3; Migne, *Patrologia Graece* 75.

Cyril of Alexandria. *Commentary on John.* Translated by E. B. Pusey. Library of the Fathers. Online Edition: 1874/1885.

Cyril of Alexandria. *Concerning the Incarnation of the Saviour*; Migne, *Patrologia Graece*, 75.

Cyril of Alexandria. *Concerning the True Faith for Queens*; *Patrologia Graece*, 76.

Cyril of Alexandria. *Contra Theodoretum*; Migne, *Patrologia Graece*, 76.

Cyril of Alexandria. *De incarnatione Unigeniti*; *Patrologia Graece*, 75.

Cyril of Alexandria. *Dialogues.* French translation by Georges de Durand: *Dialogues sur la Trinite Tome II.* Paris: Les Éditions du Cerf, 1977.

Cyril of Alexandria. *Glaphyra*; *Patrologia Graece*, 69.

Cyril of Alexandria. *In Iohannis Evangelium*; Migne, *Patrologia Graece*, 73.

Cyril of Alexandria. *In Iohannis Evangelium*; Migne, *Patrologia Graece*, 74.

Cyril of Alexandria. *That Christ is One*; Migne, *Patrologia Graece*,75.

Epiphanius, *Panarion. Die Grieschischen christlichen Schriftsteller der ersten drei Jahrhunderte.* Edited by K. Holl. Leipzig, 1922.

Epiphanius. *The Panarion of Epiphanius of Salamis.* Translated by Frank Williams. Leiden: Brill, 1997.

Gregory of Nazianzus. *Epistle 101. Nicene and Post-Nicene Fathers*, vol. vii. Edinburgh: T & T Clark, 1893.

Gregory of Nazianzus. *The Fourth Theological Oration. Nicene and Post-Nicene Fathers*, vol. vii. Edinburgh: T & T Clark, 1893.

Gregory Nazianzus. *Oration XXIX*; Migne, *Patrologia Graece*, 46.

Gregory of Nyssa, *Against Apollinarius*; Migne, *Patrologia Graece*, 45.

Gregory of Nyssa. *On the Making of Man. Nicene and Post-Nicene Fathers*, Volume V. Nicene and Post-Nicene Fathers. Grand Rapids, MI: Eerdmans, 1956.

Gregory of Nyssa. *On the Soul and the Resurrection. Ibid.*

Gregory of Nyssa. *The Great Catechism. A Select Library of the Nicene and Post-Nicene Fathers, Volume V.* Grand Rapids, MI: Eerdmans, 1994.

Hilary. *De Synodis. Nicene and Post-Nicene Fathers*, vol. ix. Edinburgh: T & T Clark: 1898.

Hilary. *De Trinitate. Nicene and Post-Nicene Fathers*, vol. ix. Edinburgh: T & T Clark: 1898.

Hippolytus of Rome. *Philosophumena* or *Refutation of All Heresies. Ante-Nicene Fathers*, vol. v, T & T Clark: Edinburgh, 1867.

Irenaeus. *Adversus Haereses*. Ante-Nicene Fathers, vol. i, T & T Clark: Edinburgh, 1884.

Irenaeus. *Démonstration de la Prédication Apostolique*. Paris: Éditions du Cerf, 1959.

John Chrysostom. *Homily on Matthew V. 2;* Migne, *Patrologia Graece*, 57

John Chrysostom. *Sermons on Hebrews, Hom. IV.3;* Migne, *Patrologia Graece*, 63.

John of Damascus. *De Fide Orthodoxa. Nicene and Post-Nicene Fathers*, vol. ix. T & T Clark: Edinburgh, 1898.

John of Damascus. *Dialectica* 30; Migne, *Patrologia Graece*, 94.

Justin Martyr. *Dialogue with the Jew Trypho. Ante-Nicene Fathers*, vol i. Edinburgh: T&T Clark, 1884.

Leontius of Byzantium. *Adversus Nestorium;* Migne, *Patrologia Graece*, 86a.

Leontius of Byzantium. *Libri tres contra Nestorianos et Eutychianos*, sources Chrétiennes, Les Éditions du Cerf, Paris 1998.

Maximus the Confessor. *Opuscules theologiques et polemiques* Migne, *Patrologia Graece*, 91.

Maximus the Confessor. *Questions (and Responses) to Thalassius*.

Maximus the Confessor. *Selected Writings*. Translated by G C. Berthold and Introduction by Jaroslav Pelikan. Classics of Western Spirituality. New York: Paulist Press, 1985.

Melito of Sardis. *The Homily of the Passion with Some Fragments of the Apocryphal Ezekiel*. Edited by Campbell Bonner. London: Christophers, 1940.

Origen. *Contra Celsum*. Translated with Notes by Henry Chadwick. Cambridge: Cambridge University Press, 1980.

Origen. *De Principiis. Ante-Nicene Fathers*, vol. iv. Edinburgh: T & T Clark, 1867.

Symeon the New Theologian. *The Discourses*. Translated by C.J. de Catanzaro. New York: Paulist, 1980.

Symeon Neotheologus, *Orationes Ethicae*, ed. J. Darrouzes, Symeon le Nouveau Theologien, *Traites theologiques et ethiques*. Sources chretiennes 122, 129. Paris: Cerf, 1966, 1967.

Tertullian, *De Anima. Ante-Nicene Fathers*, vol iii. Edinburgh: T&T Clark, 1867.

Tertullian, *De Prescriptionibus Haereticorum. Ante-Nicene Fathers*, vol. iii. T & T Clark: Edinburgh, 1867.

Tertullian. *De Carne Christi. Ante-Nicene Fathers*, vol. iii. T & T Clark: Edinburgh, 1867.

Migne, J. P. *Patrologia Graece*. Paris: Imprimerie Catholique, 1857-1866. 161 vols.

Migne, J. P. *Patrologia Latina*. Paris: Imprimerie Catholique, 1844-1855. 217 vols.

Corpus Scriptorum Ecclesiasticorum Latinorum. Vienna: Committee of Austrian Academy of Sciences, 1866 to the present.

The Ante-Nicene Fathers. Edited by Alexander Roberts and James Donaldson. 1885-1887. 10 vols. Repr. Peabody, Mass.: Hendrickson, 1994.

The Nicene and Post-Nicene Fathers. Edited by Alexander Roberts and James Donaldson. 1885-1887. 14 vols. Repr. Peabody, Mass.: Hendrickson, 1994.

3. Gnostic Material and Related Studies

Apocalypse of Peter. The Nag Hammadi Library in English. Translated by James Robinson. New York: Harper and Row, 1977.

Jonas, Hans. *The Message of the Alien God & The Beginnings of Christianity: The Gnostic Religion*, Third Edition. Boston, MA: Beacon Press, 2001.

Robinson, James, Translator. *The Nag Hammadi Library in English*. New York: Harper and Row, 1977.

The Apocalypse of Paul. The Nag Hammadi Library in English. Translated by James Robinson. New York: Harper and Row, 1977.

The Apocryphon of John. The Nag Hammadi Library in English. Translated by James Robinson. New York: Harper and Row, 1977.

The Dialogue of the Savior. The Nag Hammadi Library in English. Translated by James Robinson. New York: Harper and Row, 1977.

The Tripartite Tractate. The Nag Hammadi Library in English. Translated by James Robinson. New York: Harper and Row, 1977.

Zostrianos. The Nag Hammadi Library in English. Translated by James Robinson. New York: Harper and Row, 1977.

B

Medieval to Modern Literature

à Brakel, Wilhelmul. *The Christian's Reasonable Service*. Translated by Bartel Elshout. Edited by Joel R. Beeke. Grand Rapids, MI: Reformation Heritage Books, 1999.

A Catholic Dictionary of Theology, Volume 2. London: Thomas Nelson and Sons Ltd, 1967.

Abbott, Walter M., ed. *The Documents of Vatican II*. London/Dublin: Geoffrey Chapman, 1966.

Aker, Ben, et.al. "The Necessity for Retaining Father and Son Terminology in Scripture Translations for Muslims." General Assembly of the Assemblies of God. Accessed online February 24, 2013 at: http://www.fatherson.ag.org/download/paper.pdf.

Alexander, Cecil F. "All things bright and beautiful." *Scottish Psalter and*

Church Hymnary. London: Oxford University Press, 1929.

Alexander, Cecil F. "No. 101." *Scottish Psalter and Church Hymnary*. London: Oxford University Press, 1929.

Alexander, W.M. *Johann Georg Hamann: Philosophy and Faith*. The Hague: Martinus Nijhoff, 1966.

Anatolios, Khaled. *Retrieving Nicaea: The Meaning and Development of Trinitarian Doctrine*. Grand Rapids, MI: Baker Academic, 2011.

Anselm. *Cur Deus Homo*. London: Griffith, Farran, Browne & Co., Ltd., 1889.

Aquinas, Thomas. *Summa Contra Gentiles*. Translated with Notes by Charles J. O'Neil. Notre Dame: University of Notre Dame Press, 1957.

Aquinas, Thomas. *Summa Theologica*. Translated by the Fathers of the Dominican Province. London: R. & T. Washbourne, Ltd., 1914.

Atkinson, B.F.C. *The Theology of Prepositions*. London: Tyndale Press, n.d.

Aulen, G. *Christus Victor: An Historical Study of the Three Main Types of the Idea of the Atonement*. London: SPCK, 1931.

Baillie, Donald. *God Was in Christ*. New York: Charles Scribner's Sons, 1955.

Balthasar, Hans Urs Von. *The Glory of the Lord: A Theological Aesthetics, Volume 1: Seeing the Form*. Translated by Erasmo Leiva-Merikakis. San Francisco: Ignatius Press, 1982.

Bancroft, Charitie Less. "Before the Throne of God Above." *Church Hymnary*, 4th Edition. Norwich, UK: Canterbury Press, 2005.

Barr, James. "Abba isn't Daddy." *Journal of Theological Studies* 39, No.1 (1988).

Barth, Karl. *Church Dogmatics I.1 The Doctrine of the Word of God*. Edited and Translated by G. W. Bromiley. Edinburgh: T & T Clark, 1975.

Barth, Karl. *Church Dogmatics I.2 The Doctrine of the Word of God*. Edited by G. W. Bromiley and T. F. Torrance. Translated by G. T. Thomson and Herold Knight. Edinburgh: T & T Clark, 1998.

Barth, Karl. *Church Dogmatics II.1 The Doctrine of God*. Edited by G. W. Bromiley and T. F. Torrance. Translated by T. H. L. Parker, et al. Edinburgh: T & T Clark, 1964.

Barth, Karl. *Church Dogmatics II.2 The Doctrine of God*. Edited by G. W. Bromiley and T. F. Torrance. Translated by G. W. Bromiley, et al. Edinburgh: T & T Clark, 1978.

Barth, Karl. *Church Dogmatics III.1 The Doctrine of Creation*. Edited by G. W. Bromiley and T. F. Torrance. Translated by J. W. Edwards, et al. Edinburgh: T & T Clark, 1998.

Barth, Karl. *Church Dogmatics IV.1 The Doctrine of Reconciliation*. Edited by G. W. Bromiley and T. F. Torrance. Translated by G. W. Bromiley. Edinburgh: T & T Clark, 1997.

Barth, Karl. *The Knowledge of God and the Service of God According to the Teaching of the Reformation*. Translated by J.L.M. Haire and Ian Henderson. London: Hodder and Stoughton, 1938.

Bauckham, Richard. *Jesus and the Eyewitnesses: The Gospels as Eyewitness Testimony*. Grand Rapids, MI: William B. Eerdmans, 2006.

Bavinck, Herman. *The Doctrine of God*. Translated and Edited by William Hendriksen. Edinburgh: Banner of Truth Trust, 1977.

Bavinck, Herman. *Reformed Dogmatics, Volume 3: Sin and Salvation in Christ*. Translated by John Vriend and Edited by John Bolt. Grand Rapids, MI: Baker Academic, 2008.

Belz, Emily. "Inside Out." *World Magazine* 7 May 2011.

Belz, Emily. "Holding Translators Accountable." *World Magazine* 9 September 26 2011.

Belz, Emily. "The battle for accurate Bible translation in Asia." *World Magazine* 25 February 2012.

Berkhof, Louis. *Systematic Theology*. Grand Rapids: Eerdmans, 1996.

Berkouwer, G.C. *The Conflict with Rome*. Translated by H. de Jongste under supervision of David H. Freeman. Philadephia, PA: The Presbyterian and Reformed Publishing Co., 1958.

Bernard, J.H. *The Gospel According to St. John, Volume 2*. The International Critical Commentary Series. Edinburgh: T&T Clark, 1928.

Berthoud, Jean-Marc. *L'alliance de Dieu à travers l'Écriture sainte: Une théologie biblique*. Lausanne: L'Age D'Homme, 2012.

Berthoud, Jean-Marc. *Le règne terrestre de Dieu*. Lausanne: L'Age D'Homme, 2011.

Berthoud, Jean-Marc. *Pierre Viret: A Forgotten Giant of the Reformation: The Apologetics, Ethics, and Economics of the Bible*. Tallahassee, FL: Zurich Publishing, 2010.

Berthoud, Jean-Marc. "Quelle critique biblique?" *Resister et Construire* December 1998. Accessible online at: http://calvinisme.ch/index. php/R%C3%A9sister_et_construire

Betz, John R. *After Enlightenment: Hamann as Post-Secular Visionary*. West Sussex: Wiley-Blackwell, 2009.

Beza, Theodore. *Sur L' Histoire de la Résurrection*. Geneva: Jean le Preux, 1593.

Bindley, T.H. *The Ecumenical Documents of the Faith*. Westport, Conn.: Greenwood Press, 1950.

Black, Matthew. "The Maranatha Invocation and Jude 14–15 (I Enoch 1:9)." *Christ and Spirit in the New Testament: Essays in Honour of Francis Digby Moule*. Edited by Barnabas Lindars and Stephen S. Smalley. Cambridge: Cambridge University Press, 1974.

Black, Matthew. *The Scrolls and Christian Origins*. London: Thomas Nelson, 1961.

Blocher, Henri. "The Atonement in John Calvin's Theology." *The Glory of the Atonement: Biblical, Historical & Practical Perspectives: Essays in Honor of Roger Nicole*. Edited by C. E. Hill and F. A. James. Downers Grove, Ill.: InterVarsity Press, 2004.

Blomberg, Craig. *The Historical Reliability of John's Gospel*. Downers Grove, Ill.: InterVarsity Press, 2001.

Blomberg, Craig. *The Historical Reliability of John's Gospel: Issues and Commentary*. Downers Grove Ill.: InterVarsity Press, 2007.

Bonhoeffer, Dietrich. *Christology*. London: Collins Fontana Library, 1966.

Borg, M.J. and J. D. Crossan. *The Last Week: What the Gospels Really Teach About Jesus' Final Days in Jerusalem*. San Francisco: HarperSanFrancisco, 2006.

Boston, Thomas. *The Beauties of Boston: A selection of his writings*. Edited by Samuel McMillan. Inverness: Christian Focus Publications, 1979.

Bousset, William. *Kyrios Christos: A History of the Belief in Christ from the Beginnings of Christianity to Irenaeus*. Translated by J. Seely. Nashville: Abingdon, 1970.

Brown, Colin. *Jesus in European Protestant Thought 1778-1860*. Grand Rapids, MI: Baker Book House, 1985.

Brown, Colin, ed. *New International Dictionary of New Testament Theology*. Exeter: The Paternoster Press, 1975.

Brown, Gray. "A Brief Analysis of Filial and Paternal Terms in the Bible." *The International Journal of Frontier Missiology* 28:3 (2011).

Brown, Gary. "A New Look at Translating Familial Language." *The International Journal of Frontier Missiology* 28:3 (2011).

Brown, Raymond E. *The Gospel according to John (1-X11)*. New York: Doubleday, 1966.

Brown, Rick. et. al. "Muslim-idiom Bible translations: Claims and facts." *St Francis Magazine* Vol. 5, No. 6 (December 2009).

Brown, Rick. "Presenting the deity of Christ from the Bible." *International Journal of Frontier Missions* Vol. 19, No.1 (2001).

Brown, Rick. "The 'Son of God': Understanding the Messianic Titles of Jesus." *International Journal of Frontier Missions* Vol. 17, No. 1, 41–52 (2000).

Brown, Rick. "Why Muslims are repelled by the term 'Son of God'." *Evangelical Missions Quarterly* Vol 43, No.4 (2007).

Brown, Rick, Leith Gray, and Andrea Gray. "Translating Familial Biblical Terms: An Overview of the Issue." *Mission Frontiers* 20 October 2011.

Bruce, F.F. *Commentary on the Epistle to the Hebrews*. London: Marshall, Morgan & Scott, 1964.

Bruce, A.B. *The Humiliation of Christ: In Its Physical, Ethical and Official Aspects*. Edinburgh: T. & T. Clark, 1876.

Bultmann, Rudolf. *Jesus and the Word*. Translated by L.P. Smith and E. H. Lanterno. New York: Scribner's, 1958.

Bultmann, Rudolf. "The History of Religious Background of the Prologue to the Gospel of John." Translated by John Ashton. *The Interpretation of John*. Edited by John Ashton. Issues in Religion and Theology, No. 9. Philadelphia: Fortress, 1986.

Bultmann, Rudolf. *Kerygma and Myth: A Theological Defense*. Translated by Reginald H. Fuller. New York: Harper & Row, 1961.

Bultmann, Rudolf. *The Theology of the New Testament*. New York: Scribner, 1951.

Budry, Edmund. "Thine be the Glory." Translated by Richard B. Hoyle. *Trinity Hymnal*. Philadelphia: Great Commission Publications, 1990.

Calvin, John. *Commentary upon the Acts of the Apostles*. Edinburgh: Calvin Translation Society, 1844.

Calvin, John. *Commentary upon the Book of Psalms*. Edinburgh: Calvin Translation Society, 1844.

Calvin, John. Commentaries *on the Epistles of Paul to the Galatians and Ephesians*. Translated by William J. Pringle. Edinburgh: Calvin Translation Society, 1854.

Calvin, John. *Commentary on a Harmony of the Evangelists, Volume I*. Calvin's Commentaries. Translated by William Pringle. Grand Rapids, MI: Baker Books, 2005.

Calvin, John. *Commentary on a Harmony of the Evangelists, Volume III*. Calvin's Commentaries. Translated by William Pringle. Grand Rapids, MI: Baker Books, 2005.

Calvin, John. *Commentary on Romans*. Calvin's Commentaries. Translated by William Pringle. Grand Rapids: Baker Books, 2005.

Calvin, John. *Institutes of the Christian Religion*, 2 vols. Edited by John T. McNeill. Translated by Ford Lewis Battles. Louisville: Westminster John Knox Press, 2006.

Calvin, John. *Sermon XXXVII on the Ninth Chapter of Job*. Edinburgh: The Banner of Truth Trust, 1993.

Calvin, John. *Sermon XXVIII, 1 Samuel 8*. Translated by Douglas F. Kelly. Calvin Studies Colloquium. Edited by Charles Raynal and John Leith. Davidson, NC: Davidson College Presbyterian Church, 1982.

Calvin, John. *The Deity of Christ and Other Sermons*. Translated by Leroy Nixon. Audubon, NJ: Old Paths Publications, 1997.

Calvin, John. *The Epistle of Paul the Apostle to the Hebrews*. Translated by T. H. L. Parker. Edited by David W. Torrance and Thomas F. Torrance. Calvin's New Testament Commentaries, Volume 8. Grand Rapids, MI: William B. Eerdmans Publishing Company, 1965.

Caponi, Francis J. "Beauty, Justice, and Damnation in Thomas Aquinas." *Pro Ecclesia*. Vol. XIX, No. 4.

Carmichael, Alexander. *Carmina Gadelica: Hymns & Incantations Collected in the Highlands of Scotland in the Last Century*. Edinburgh: Floris Books, 1997.

Carmignac, Jean. *La Naissance des Évangiles*. Paris: Guibert, 1984.

Carson, D.A. *Exegetical Fallacies*. Grand Rapids, MI: Baker Book House, 1990.

Carson, D.A. *Jesus the Son of God: A Christological Title Often Overlooked, Sometimes Misunderstood, and Currently Disputed*. Wheaton, Ill: Crossway, 2012.

Carson, D.A. *The Gospel According to John*. Leicester, England: Inter-Varsity Press, 1991.

Carson, D.A. *Commentary on John*. Grand Rapids, MI: Eerdmans, 1991.

Carson, D.A. "Matthew." *The Expositor's Bible Commentary*. Grand Rapids, MI: Zondervan, 1984.

Cassuto, Umberto. *The Documentary Hypothesis and Composition of the Pentateuch*. Jerusalem, 1961.

Charles, R.A. *A Critical and Exegetical Commentary on The Revelation of St. John*. International Critical Commentary. Edinburgh: T & T Clark, 1920.

Chemnitz, Martin. *The Two Natures in Christ*. Translated by J. A. O. Preus. St. Louis, MO: Concordia Publishing House, 1971.

Clements, Don C. "At the PCA General Assembly: Ad Interim Study Committee on Insider Movements Overwhelmingly Approved." *The Aquila Report*, 24 June 2012. Accessed Feb 24, 2013 at: http://theaquilareport.com/at-the-pca-general-assembly-ad-interim-study-committee-on-insider-movements-overwhelmingly-approved/

Colwell, E.C. "A Definite Rule for the Use of the Article in the Greek New Testament." *Journal of Biblical Literature* 52 (1933).

Copleston, F.C. *A History of Philosophy: Volume 6, Modern Philosophy*. New York: Image Books, 1960.

Courthial, Pierre. "Actualité de Chalcédoine." *Ichthus* No. 116 (1983).

Courthial, Pierre. *Le Jour des Petits Recommencements: Essai sur l' Actualité de la Parole (Evangile-Loi) de Dieu*. Lausanne: L'Age D'Homme, 1996.

Craig, William Lane, and Bart Ehrman, "Is There Historical Evidence for the Resurrection of Jesus?" Transcript of Debate Held at College of the Holy Cross, Worcester, Massachusetts on March 28, 2006. Accessed online at: http://www.philvaz.com/apologetics/p96.htm

Crawford, Thomas J. *The Doctrine of Holy Scripture Respecting the Atonement*. Wm. Blackwood, 1881.

Crossan, John Dominic. *The Historical Jesus: The Life of a Mediterranean Jewish Peasant*. San Francisco: Harper/SanFrancisco, 1991.

Crossan, J.D. and J. L. Reed. *In Search of Paul: How Jesus's Apostle Opposed Rome's Empire with God's Kingdom*. San Francisco: HarperSan Francisco, 2004.

Cullman, Oscar. *The Christology of the New Testament*. London: SCM, 1963.

Cullmann, Oscar. *The Early Church: Studies in Early Church History and Theology*. Edited by A. Higgins. Philadelphia: Westminster, 1956.

Daniélou, Jean. *Message évangelique et culture héllénistique*. Paris, 1961.

Dawson, Gerit. *Jesus Ascended: The Meaning of Christ's Continuing Incarnation*. Phillipsburg, NJ: P&R Publishing, 2004.

De Haan, M.R. *The Chemistry of the Blood*. Grand Rapids: MI: Zondervan Publishing House, 1943.

De Wesselow, Thomas. *The Sign: The Shroud of Turin and the Secret of the Resurrection*. Dutton: New York, 2012.

Delattre, Roland A. *Beauty and Sensibility in the Thought of Jonathan Edwards: An Essay in Aesthetics and Theological Ethics*. Eugene, OR: Wipf & Stock Publishers, 2006.

Dempster, Stephen A. *Dominion and Dynasty*. Downers Grove, Ill.: Inter-Varsity, 2003.

Denney, James. *Studies in Theology*. London: Hodder and Stoughton: 1895.

Denney, James. *The Christian Doctrine of Reconciliation*. Carlisle: Paternoster, 1998.

Denzinger, Henricus. *Enchiridion Symbolorum*. Barcinone: Herder, 1965.

Dick, John. *Lectures on Theology, Volume III*. 2nd Edition. Edinburgh: Oliver & Boyd, 1838.

"Divine Familial Terms: Answers to Commonly Asked Questions." *Wycliffe.org*, 30 March 2012. Accessed April 2012 at: http://www.wycliffe.org/SonofGod/QA.aspx.

Dodd, C.H. *The Bible and the Greeks*. London: Hodder & Stoughton, 1935.

Dragas, George. *Saint Athanasius of Alexandria: Original Research and New Perspectives*. Rollinsford, NH: Orthodox Research Institute, 2005.

Dragas, George. "The Eternal Son: An Essay on Christology in the Early Church with Particular Reference to Saint Athanasius the Great." *The Incarnation: Ecumenical Studies in the Nicene-Constantinopolitan Creed A.D. 1981*. Edited by Thomas F. Torrance. Edinburgh: The Hansel Press, 1981.

Dunn, James D.G. *Christology in the Making: A New Testament Inquiry into the Origins of the Doctrine of the Incarnation*. Grand Rapids: William B. Eerdmans, 1996.

Dunn, James D.G. *Jesus, Paul and the Law: Studies in Mark and Galatians*. Louisville, KY; Westminster/John Knox, 1990.

Dunn, James D.G. *The Evidence for Jesus*. Philadelphia: Westminster Press, 1985.

Dupont, J. *Les Tentations de Jésus au Desert. Studia Neotestamentica 4*. Bruges: Desclée de Brouwer, 1968.

Edwards, Jonathan. "A Treatise on Grace." *Selections from the Unpublished Writings of Jonathan Edwards of America*. Edited by A. B. Grosart. Edinburgh: N.P., 1865.

Edwards, Jonathan. *Charity and Its Fruits*. London: Banner of Truth, 1969.

Edwards, Jonathan. *Miscellanies*. Yale University Collection of Edwards Manuscripts: Yale University Library, n.d.

Edwards, Jonathan. "Notes on the Mind." *The Philosophy of Jonathan Edwards From His Private Notebooks*, Edited by Harvey G. Townsend. Eugene, OR: University of Oregon Press, 1955.

Edwards, Jonathan. *The Nature of True Virtue*. Ann Arbor, MI: University of Michigan Press, 1960.

Edwards, Jonathan. *Religious Affections*. Edited by John E. Smith. New Haven, Yale University Press, 1959.

Edwards, Jonathan. *Works, Volume 1*. Edinburgh: Banner of Truth, 1974.

Edwards, William D., et. al. "On the Physical Death of Jesus Christ." *Journal of the American Medical Association*. Vol. 255, No. 11 (March 21, 1986).

Ehrman, Bart D. *Forged: Writing in the Name of God – Why the Bible's Authors Are Not Who We Think They Are*. HarperOne: New York, 2011.

Ehrman, Bart D. *Jesus: apocalyptic prophet of the new millennium*. New York, Oxford University Press, 1999.

Ehrman, Bart D. *Jesus, Interrupted*. Harper Collins: NY, 2009.

Ehrman, Bart D. *Lost Christianities: The Battles for Scripture and the Faiths We Never Knew*. New York: Oxford University Press, 2003.

Ehrman, Bart D. *The Orthodox Corruption of Scripture*. New York: Oxford University Press, 1993.

Einstein, Albert. *Ideas and Opinions*. New York: Modern Library, 1994.

Einstein, Albert. *Out of My Later Years*. Westport, CT: Greenwood Press, 1970.

Einstein, Albert. *The World as I See It*. New York: Covici-Frede, 1934

Evans, Eifion. *Bread of Heaven: The Life and Work of William Williams*. Pantycelyn. Bridgend, Wales: Bryntirion Press, 2010.

Evans, Stephen C. *Exploring Kenotic Christology: The Self-Emptying of God* (Regent College Publishing: Vancouver, British Columbia, 2006).

Faber, Frederick W. "My God, how wonderful Thou art." *Trinity Hymnal*. Philadelphia: Great Commission Publications, 1990.

Ferguson, Sinclair. *The Holy Spirit*. Downers Grove, Ill.: IVP, 1996.

Feser, Edward. *The Last Superstition: A Refutation of the New Atheism*. South Bend, IN: St. Augustine's Press, 2008.

Flavel, John. *The Works of John Flavel, Volume 1*. London: The Banner of Truth Trust, 1968.

Florovsky, Georges. "A review of *The Philosophy of the Church Fathers, vol. 1: Faith, Trinity, Incarnation*." *Religion and Life*. Vol. 26, No. 3 (Summer), 451-53.

Florovsky, Georges. *The Collected Works, Volume 7: The Eastern Fathers of the Fourth Century*. Vaduz, Europa: Buchervertriebsanstalt, 1987.

Forsyth, P.T. *The Person and Place of Jesus Christ*, 2nd Edition. London: Hodder and Stoughton, 1910.

Frame, John. *Apologetics to the Glory of God: An Introduction*. Phillipsburg, NJ: P&R Publishing, 1994.

Freke, Timothy, and Peter Gandy. *The Jesus Mysteries: Was the 'Original Jesus' a Pagan God?* Random House Digital, 2001.

Freeman, David N., ed. *Anchor Bible Dictionary, Volume 3*. New York: Doubleday, 1992.

Funk, R.W., and the Jesus Seminar. *The Acts of Jesus: What Did Jesus Really Do?* San Francisco: HarperSanFrancisco, 1998.

Gaboriau, Florent. *Thomas D' Aquin A La Croisée du Siècle*. Lausanne, Switzerland: L'Age D' Homme, 2013.

Gardiner, John Eliot. Bach: *Music in the Castle of Heaven* (Alfred A. Knopf: New York, 2013)

Garner, David B. "A world of riches." *Reformation 21* (April 2011). Accessed on 7 November 2013 at http://www.reformation21.org/articles/a-world-of-riches.php

Gerhardsson, Birger. *The Testing of God's Son: (Matthew 4:1-11 & PAR): An Analysis of an Early Christian Midrash*. Eugene, OR: Wipf and Stock, 2009.

Gilson, Étienne. *Études sur le role de la pensée médiévale dans la formation du système cartésien*. Paris: Verin, 1930.

Girardeau, John L. *Discussions of Theological Questions*. Harrisonburg, VA: Sprinkle Publications: 1986.

Goodwin, Thomas. "Exposition of Ephesians." *The Works of Thomas Goodwin, Volume 1*. Eureka, CA: Tanski, 1996.

Goodwin, Thomas. "The Heart of Christ in Heaven unto Sinners on Earth." *The Works of Thomas Goodwin, Volume IV*. Edinburgh: James Nichol, 1862.

Goodwin, Thomas. "The Mediator." *The Works of Thomas Goodwin, Volume 5*. Eureka, CA: Tanski, 1996.

Gorce, M. "Réalisme." *Dictionaire de Théologie Catholique*. Edited by A. Vacant et al. Paris: Librarie Letouzey et Ane, 1936.

Gray, James M. "O Listen to Our Wondrous Story" (1904). *Hymns and Sacred Songs*. Edited by E.O. Excell, G.H. Shorney, and F.G. Kingsbury. Chicago: Hope Publishing Company, 1918.

Griffith-Dickson, Gwen. "Johann Georg Hamann." *Stanford Encyclopedia of Philososphy*. Accessed online at: http://plato.stanford.edu/archives/sum2013/entries/hamann/

Gros, J., et.al. Eds. *Growth in Agreement: Reports and Agreed Statements of Ecumenical Conversations on a World Level, 1982-1998*. Grand Rapids, MI: William B. Eerdmans, 2000.

Grunder, Karlfried. *Figur une Geschichte: Johann Georg Hamann's 'Biblische Betrachtungen' als Ansatz einer Geschichtsphilosophie*. Freiburg/Munich: Verlag Karl Alber, 1958.

Gunton, Colin. *The Actuality of Atonement: A Study of Metaphor, Rationality and the Christian Tradition*. Edinburgh: T & T Clark, 1988.

Hamann, Johann Georg. *Samtliche Werke, historisch-kritische Ausgabe*. Edited by Josef Nadler. Vienna: Herder, 1949-1957.

Hansen, Colin. "The Son and The Crescent." *Christianity Today*, February 2011.

Harnack, Adolf von. *History of Dogma*. London: Williams & Norgate, 1897.

Harnack, Adolf von. *The Date of the Acts and of the Synoptic Gospels*. Translated by J. R. Wilkinson. London: Williams & Norgate, 1911.

Harris, Charles. *Trust Your Eye: An Illustrated History of Painting* (Cambria Printers Ltd.: Ceredigion, Wales, 2013).

Hart, David Bentley. *The Beauty of the Infinite: The Aesthetics of Christian Truth*. Grand Rapids, MI: William B. Eerdmans, 2003.

Hays, Richard B. *The Faith of Jesus Christ: An Investigation of the Narrative Substructure of Galatians 3:1 – 4:11*. Chico, CA: Scholars Press, 1983.

Hazard, Paul. *Le Crise de la Conscience Européene*. Paris: Librarie Anttheme Fayard, 1981.

Heidl, György. *Origen's Influence on the Young Augustine: A Chapter of the history of Origenism*. Piscataway, NJ: Gorgias Press, 2003.

Heldenbrand, Richard L. *Christianity and New Evangelical Philosophies*. Warsaw, IN: Words of Life, 2003.

Heller, John H. *Report on the Shroud of Turin*. Boston: Houghton Mifflin Company, 1983.

Hengel, Martin. *The Johannine Question*. Translated by John Bowden. London: SCM, 1989.

Hengel, Martin. *The Son of God: The Origin of Christianity and the History of Jewish-Hellenistic Religion*. Translated by John Bowden. Philadelphia: Fortress, 1976.

Heppe, H. *Reformed Dogmatics*. Heppe, Heinrich. *Reformed Dogmatics*. Revised by Ernst Bizer. Translated by G. T. Thomson. Grand Rapids: Baker, 1978.

Herbert, George. "Dulness." *George Herbert and the Seventeenth Century Religious Poets*. Selected and Edited by Mario A. Di Cesare. New York: W.W. Norton and Company, 1978.

Herbert, George. *Love Bade Me Welcome: Daily Readings with George Herbert*. Edited by Gerrit Scott Dawson. Lenoir, NC: Glen Lorien Books 1997.

Higgins, A.J.B. *Jesus and the Son of Man*. London: Lutterworth, 1964.

Holland, Tom. *Contours of Pauline Theology: A Radical New Survey of the Influences on Paul's Biblical Writings*. Fearn, Ross-shire: Christian Focus Publications, 2004.

Hooker, M.D. "Is the Son of Man really insoluble?" *Text and Interpretation: Studies in the New Testament Presented to Matthew Black*. Edited by E. Best & R. McL. Wilson. Cambridge: Cambridge University Press, 1979.

Hooker, M.D. *The Son of Man in Mark*. London: SCM, 1967.

Hoskyns, Edward C. *The Fourth Gospel. Revised 2nd Edition*. London: Faber & Faber, 1947.

Houghton, S.M. *A Faith to Confess: The Baptist Confession of 1689, rewritten in Modern English*. Haywards Heath, Sussex: Carey Publications, 1982.

Hurtado, Larry W. *Lord Jesus Christ: Devotion to Jesus in Earliest Christianity*. Grand Rapids: Eerdmans, 2003.

Irving, Edward. *The Collected Writings of Edward Irving, Volume V*. London, 1865.

Jaki, Stanley L. *The Road of Science and the Ways to God: The Gifford Lectures, Edinburgh, 1974-1975 and 1975-76*. Port Huron, MI: Real View Books, 2005.

Jay, Pierre. *L'Exégèse de Saint Jerome d'Àpres son 'Commentaire sur Isaie.'* Paris: Etudes Augustiniennes, 1985.

Jenkins, Philip. *The Next Christendom: The Coming of Global Christianity*. Oxford University Press: 2011.

Jeremias, Joachim. *The Eucharistic Words of Jesus*. London: SCM, 1966.

Jeremias, Joachim. *The Prayers of Jesus*. London: SCM, 1967.

Jones, Mark. *Why Heaven Kissed Earth: The Christology of the Puritan Reformed Theologian, Thomas Goodwin (1600-1680)*. Gottingen: Vandenhoeck & Ruprecht, 2010.

Kant, Immanuel. *Critique of Judgment*. Translated by J. H. Bernard. London, 1932.

Kant, Immanuel. *Critique of Pure Reason*. Translated by Norman Kemp Smith. London: Macmillan and Co., 1934.

Kant, Immanuel. *Groundwork of the Metaphysics of Morals*. Translated by T. K. Abbott. London, 1909.

Kant, Immanuel. *Prolegomena to Any Future Metaphysics*. Translated with Introduction and Notes by P. G. Lucas. Manchester, 1953.

Kant, Immanuel. *Religion within the Limits of Reason Alone*. Translated by T. M. Greene and H. H. Hudson. Glasgow, 1934.

Kant, Immanuel. "What is Enlightenment." *What is Enlightenment: Eighteenth Century Answers and Twentieth Century Questions*. Edited by James Schmidt. Berkeley: University of California Press, 1996.

Kasemann, Ernest. "A Critical Analysis of Philippians 2:5-11." *God and Christ. Existence and Province*. Journal for Theology and Church 5. New York, 1968

Kelly, Douglas F. *Revelation: A Sermon Commentary: The Angels Are Already Singing*. Fearn, Ross-shire: Mentor Christian Focus Publications, 2011.

Kelly, Douglas F. *Systematic Theology, Volume 1: Grounded in Holy Scripture and Understood Light of the Church*. Fearn, Ross-shire: Mentor, 2008.

Kelly, J.N.D. *Early Christian Doctrines*. San Francisco: Harper, 1978.

Kerrigan, A. *St. Cyril of Alexandria's Interpretation of the Old Testament*. Rome, 1952.

Kittel, Gerhard, and Gerhard Friedrich, eds. *Theological Dictionary of the New Testament*. Translated by Geoffrey W. Bromiley. 10 Vols. Grand Rapids: Eerdmans, 1964-1976.

Klossowski, Pierre. *Les Méditations bibliques de Hamann*. Éditions de Minuit: Paris, 1948.

Knight, George A.F. "A Biblical Approach to the Doctrine of the Trinity." *Scottish Journal of Theology Occasional Papers*, No. 1. Edinburgh: Oliver & Boyd, 1953.

Köstenberger, Andreas, and Michael Kruger. *The Heresy of Orthodoxy*. Wheaton, IL: Crossway, 2010.

Koyré, Alexandre. *Essai sur l'idée de Dieu et les preuves de son existence chez Descartes*. Leroux: Paris, 1922.

Kruger, Michael J. *Canon Revisited*. Crossway: Wheaton, Ill, 2012.

Kruger, Michael. "Bart Ehrman, *Jesus, Interrupted*." Book Review. *Westminster Theological Journal* 71, No.2 (Fall 2009).

Laats, Alar, and Kadri Lääs. "The Concept of the Communication of the Majesty in the Theology of Martin Chemnitz." Trames 2002, 6 (56/51). *Journal of the Humanities and Social Sciences* # 1, 2002.

Ladd, George Eldon. *New Testament Theology*. Grand Rapids, MI: Eerdmans, 1993.

Lampe, G.H.W. *A Patristic Greek Lexicon*. Oxford: Clarendon Press, 1978.

Lampe, G.W.H, ed. *The Cambridge History of the Bible: The West From the Fathers to the Reformation*. Cambridge: Cambridge University Press, 1969.

Lane, William L. *Hebrews 1-8*. Word Biblical Commentary, Vol. 47A. Dallas, TX: Word Books, 1991.

Lapide, Pinchas. *The Resurrection of Jesus*. London: SPCK, 1983.

Lee, J.A.L. *A History of New Testament Lexicography*. New York: Lang, 2003.

Leith, John H. *Creeds of the Churches*. Garden City, NY: Doubleday & Company, 1963.

Lemann, Augstin. *Histoire complète de l'idée messianique chez le peuple d'Israël*. Cadillac: Éditions Saint-Rémi, 1909.

Lewis, C.S. *Miracles: A Preliminary Study*. Glasgow: Fontana Books, 1960.

Lewis, C.S. *The Weight of Glory and Other Addresses*. HarperOne: New York, 1980.

Licona, Michael R. *The Resurrection of Jesus: A New Historiographical Approach*. Downers Grove, Ill.: IVP Academic, 2010.

Lightfoot, J.B. *Saint Paul's Epistle to the Philippians*. London, 1888.

Linnemann, Eta. *Historical Criticism of the Bible: Methodology or Ideology?* Grand Rapids: Baker, 1990.

Lloyd, William Freeman. "My times are in Thy hand." *The Hymns and Hymn Writers of the Church*. Edited by Charles Nutter and Wilbur F. Tillett. New York: Eaton & Mains, 1911.

Loofs, Friedrich A. *Leontius von Byzanz und die gleichnamigen Schriftsteller der grieschen Kirche*. Leipzig: J. C. Hinrichs, 1887.

Luther, Martin. *Luther's Works, Volume 37: Word and Sacrament III*. Edited by Robert H. Fischer. Philadelphia: Fortress Press, 1961.

Luther, Martin. *The Large Catechism of Martin Luther*. Translated by Robert H. Fisher. Philadelphia: Fortress Press, 1959.

Luther, Martin. *Treatise on Christian Liberty*. Luthers Werke, Weimarer Ausgabe VII. Weimar, 1883-.

Machen, J. Gresham. *The Virgin Birth of Christ*. Grand Rapids, MI: Baker Book House, 1971.

Mackintosh, H.R. *The Doctrine of the Person of Jesus Christ*. Edinburgh: T & T Clark, 1913.

Mackintosh, H.R. *Types of Modern Theology*. London: Charles Scribner's Sons, 1937.

Maclean, Malcolm. *The Lord's Supper*. Fearn, Scotland: Christian Focus Publications, 2009.

MacQuarrie, John. *Principles of Christian Theology*. New York: Scribner, 1966.

Maimonides. *The Laws of Prayer and Priestly Blessings*. Accessed online at: http://www.chabad.org/dailystudy/rambam.asp?tDate=3/28/2012&rambamChapters=3

Maimonides. *The Guide to the Perplexed*. Translated by Shlomo Pines. Chicago: University of Chicago Press, 1974.

Marshall, Bruce. *Christology in Conflict: The Identity of a Saviour in Rahner and Barth*. Oxford: Basil Blackwell, 1987.

Marshall, I. Howard. *The Origins of New Testament Christology*. Downers Grove, Ill: Inter-Varsity Press, 1976.

Martin, R.P. *Carmen Christi: Philippians 2:5-11 in recent interpretation and in the Setting of Early Christian Worship*. Cambridge: Cambridge University Press, 1967.

Mascall, E.L. *Existence and Analogy*. Norwich: Darton, Longman & Todd Ltd., 1966.

Masson, Jacques. *Jésus Fils de David Dans les Généalogies de Saint Mathieu et de Saint Luc*. Dissertatio ad Lauream in Facultate S. Theologiae apud Pontificiam Universitatem S. Thomae in Urbe. Paris: Tequi, 1981.

Mayer, G. "Logos." *Index Philoneus*. Berlin/New York: 1974.

McLeod, Frederick J, S.J. *The Roles of Christ's Humanity in Salvation: Insights from Theodore of Mopsuestia*. The Catholic University of America Press: Washington, DC, 2005.

Michaels, J. Ramsey. *The Gospel of John*. The New International Commentary on the New Testament. Grand Rapids, MI: William B. Eerdmans, 2010.

Miller, Patrick D. *The Ten Commandments*. Louisville, KY: Westminster/John Knox Press, 2009.

Milligan, William. *The Ascension of our Lord*. London: Macmillan and Co., 1894.

Morris, Leon. *The Gospel According to John*. Grand Rapids, MI: William B. Eerdmans, 1995.

Moore, Patrick. "Notable and Quotable." *The Wall Street Journal*, 18 January 2011.

Moreland, J.P. *Universals*. Toronto: McGill-Queen's University Press, 2001.

Morris, Leon. *The Apostolic Preaching of the Cross*. Grand Rapids, MI: Eerdmans, 1955.

Moule, C.F.D. "Further Reflections on Philippians 2:5-11." *Apostolic History and the Gospel*. Edited by W. W. Gasque and R. P. Martin. Exeter: Paternoster, 1970.

Moule, C.F.D. *The Origins of Christology*. Cambridge: Cambridge University Press, 1977.

Mueller, M.M. *Saint Caesarius of Arles: Sermons, Volume 1*. Washington, DC: The Catholic University of America Press: 1956.

Mueller, M.M. *Saint Caesarius of Arles: Sermons, Volume 2*. Washington, DC: The Catholic University of America Press: 1963.

Mueller, M.M. *Saint Caesarius of Arles: Sermons, Volume 3*. Washington, DC: The Catholic University of America Press: 1972.

Muller, James. *Commentary on Philippians*. Grand Rapids: Eerdmans, 1955.

Murray, Andrew. *The Holiest of All: An Exposition of the Epistle to the Hebrews*. Oliphants Ltd.: London, 1965.

Murray, Andrew. *Waiting on God*. London: Nisbet & Co. Ltd., 1896.

Murray, Francesca Aran. *Christ the Form of Beauty: A Study in Theology and Literature*. T & T Clark: Edinburgh, 1995.

Murray, John. *Redemption Accomplished and Applied*. Wm. B. Eerdmans Publishing Co.: Grand Rapids, MI, 1955.

Murray, John. "The Imputation of Adam's Sin." *Justified in Christ: God's Plan for us in Justification*. Edited by K. Scott Oliphant. Fearn, Scotland: Christian Focus, 2007.

Neill, Stephen C. and N.T. Wright. *The Interpretation of the New Testament: 1861-1986*, 2nd Edition. Oxford: Oxford University Press, 1988.

Nicole, Roger. *Standing Forth: Collected Writings of Roger Nicole*. Fearn, Ross-shire: Christian Focus Publications, 2002.

Oberman, Heiko A. *The Harvest of Medieval Theology*. Durham, NC: The Labyrinth Press, 1983.

Oliphant, K. Scott, Ed. *Justified in Christ: God's Plan for us in Justification*. Fearn, Ross-shire: Christian Focus, 2007.

Osborne, Grant R. *Revelation*. Baker Exegetical Commentary on the New Testament. Grand Rapids, MI: Baker Academic, 2008.

Ottley, R.L. *The Doctrine of the Incarnation*. London: Methuen, 1911.

Owen, John. *Commentary on the Epistle to the Hebrews*. Edinburgh: The Banner of Truth Trust, 2010.

Owen, John. *Works, Volume 1*. Edinburgh: The Banner of Truth Trust, 1965.

Owen, John. *Works, Volume 2: Communion with God*. Edinburgh: The Banner of Truth, 2010.

Owen, John. *Works, Volume 3: The Holy Spirit*. Edinburgh: The Banner of Truth Trust, 2009.

Owen, John. *Volume 6: Exposition of Hebrews*. Edinburgh: The Banner of Truth Trust, 1965.

Owen, John. *The Death of Death in the Death of Christ*. With an introductory essay by J. I. Packer. London: Banner of Truth Trust, 1969.

Packer, James I. "What did the Cross Achieve? The Logic of Penal Substitution." *Tyndale Bulletin* 25/1974.

Palmer, Benjamin Morgan. *Sermons, Volume II*. New Orleans: Clark & Hofeline, 1876.

Pannenberg, Wolfhart. *Jesus – God and Man*. London: SCM Press, 1968.

Pannenberg, Wolfhart. *Systematic Theology*. Translated by G. W. Bromiley. Grand Rapids: William B. Eerdmans, 1991.

Pannenberg, Wolfhart. "The Historical Jesus as a Challenge to Christology." *Dialog* 37 (1998).

Pannenberg, Wolfhart. "Dogmatische Thesen zur Lehre von der Offenbarung." *Offenbarung als Geschichte*. Edited by Wolfhart Pannenberg. Gottingen, Germany: Vanderhoeck & Ruprecht, 1965.

Park, Abraham. *God's Profound and Mysterious Providence as Revealed in the Genealogy of Jesus Christ from the Time of David to the Exile in Babylon*. Singapore: Periplus Editions: 2011.

Park, Abraham. *The Unquenchable Lamp of the Covenant: The First Fourteen Generations in the Genealogy of Jesus Christ*. Singapore: Periplus Editions: 2010.

PCA Ad Interim Study Committee on Insider Movements. "A Call to Faithful Witness – Part One – Like Father, Like Son: Divine Familial Language in Bible Translation – a Partial Report (Part One of Two Parts) of the Ad Interim Committee on Insider Movements to the Fortieth General Assembly of the Presbyterian Church in America." 14 May 2012. Office of the Stated Clerk of the General Assembly of the Presbyterian Church in America.

Pelikan, Jaroslav. *The Christian Tradition: A History of the Development of Doctrine, Volume 3: The Growth of Medieval Theology (600-1300)*. Chicago and London: The University of Chicago Press, 1978.

Pelikan, Jaroslav. *The Preaching of Chrysostom*. Fortress Press: Philadelphia, PA, 1967.

Pergolesi, Giovanni Batista. "Stabat Mater." Translation 2010 Naxos Rights International, Ltd. Translation Accessed at: http://www.naxos.com/cataloque/item.asp?=8.572121

Peter Lombard. *The Sentences, Book 3: On the Incarnation of the Word*. Translated by Giulio Silano. Toronto: Pontifical Institute of Medieval Studies, 2008.

Peterson, John. *Introduction to Scholastic Realism*. Peter Lang, 1999.

Peterson, R.A. *Calvin and the Atonement*. Fearn, Ross-shire: Christian Focus, 1999.

Plantinga, Alvin. *Warrant and Proper Function*. Oxford University Press: New York, 1993.

Popovitch, Justin. *Philosophie Orthodoxe de la Vérité: Dogmatique de l'Eglise Orthodoxe, Volume II*. Translated by Jean-Louis Palierne. Lausanne: L'Age D'Homme, 1993.

Principe, Walter H. *The Theology of the Hypostatic Union in the Early Thirteenth Century. Volume 1: William of Auxerre's Theology of the Hypostatic Union*. Toronto: Pontifical Institute of Mediaeval Studies, 1963.

Principe, Walter H. *The Theology of the Hypostatic Union in the Early Thirteenth Century. Volume 2: Alexander of Hales' Theology of the Hypostatic Union*. Toronto: Pontifical Institute of Mediaeval Studies, 1967.

Principe, Walter H. *The Theology of the Hypostatic Union in the Early Thirteenth Century. Volume 3: Hugh of Saint-Cher's Theology of the Hypostatic Union*. Toronto: Pontifical Institute of Mediaeval Studies, 1970.

Principe, Walter H. *The Theology of the Hypostatic Union in the Early Thirteenth Century. Volume 4: Philip the Chancellor's Theology of the Hypostatic Union*. Toronto: Pontifical Institute of Mediaeval Studies, 1975.

Radbertius, Paschius. *Concerning the Birth of the Virgin*. Migne, *Patrologia Latina* 120.

Rahner, Karl. *The Trinity*. New York: Continuum, 2001.

Raitt, Jill. *The Eucharistic Theology of Theodore Beza. Development of the Reformed Doctrine*. Chambersburg: American Academy of Religion, 1972.

Rankin, W. Duncan. *Carnal Union With Christ in the Theology of T. F. Torrance*. Unpublished Ph.D. dissertation, Edinburgh University, 1996.

Renan, Ernest. *La Vie de Jésus*. Paris: Michel Levy Frères, 1863.

Rees, Thomas, Translator. *The Racovian Catechism*. London, 1818.

Richmond, James. *Faith and Philosophy*. London: Hodder and Stoughton, 1966.

Rickenbacher, Bertrand. "Remarques sur la méthod historic-critique." *Résister et Construire*, January 1999. Accessible online at: http://calvinisme.ch/index.php/R%C3%A9sister_et_construire

Ridderbos, Herman. *Paul: An Outline of his Theology*. Translated by John R. deWitt. Grand Rapids, MI: William B. Eerdmans, 1978.

Ridderbos, Herman. *The Coming Kingdom*. Presbyterian and Reformed Publishing Company: Phillipsburg, New Jersey, 1962.

Robertson, A.T. *A Grammar of the Greek New Testament in Light of Historical Research*. London: Hodder and Stoughton, 1919.

Robertson, Archibald T. *Word Pictures in the New Testament, Vol V*. Nashville: Broadman Press, 1932.

Robinson, John A.T. *Redating the New Testament*. Philadelphia: Westminster Press, 1976.

Robinson, John A.T. *Twelve More New Testament Studies*. London: SCM, 1985.

Rolland, Phillippe. *La Succession Apostolique dans le Nouveau Testament*. Paris: Editions de Paris, 1997.

Romanides, John S. "H. A. Wolfson's Philosophy of the Church Fathers." *Greek Orthodox Theological Review* 5, 55-82 (1989).

Romanides, John S., et.al, Eds. "Unofficial Consultation Between Theologians of Eastern Orthodox and Oriental Churches." *Greek Orthodox Theological Review*. Vol. 10, No. 2 (Winter 1964-1965).

Rutherford, Samuel. *Fourteen Communion Sermons*. Edited by A. A. Bonar. Glasgow, 1877.

Rutherford, Samuel. *The Covenant of Life Opened: Or A Treatise of the Covenant of Grace*. Edinburgh: n.p., 1655.

Schaff, Philip. *The Creeds of the Greek and Latin Churches*. London: Hodder and Stoughton, 1877.

Scheeben, M. *Handbuch der katholischen Dogmatik*. London/St. Louis: Herder, 1946-47.

Schilder, Klaas. *Christ in His Suffering*. Translated by Henry Zylstra. Grand Rapids, MI: Wm. B. Eerdmans, 1945.

Schweitzer, Albert. *The Quest of the Historical Jesus: A Study of its Progress from Reimarus to Wrede*. London: A. & C. Black, 1954.

Schilpp, P.A. *Albert Einstein: Philosopher-Scientist*. New York, 1949.

Schmid, H. *Die Dogmatik*. English translation. The Doctrinal Theology of the Evangelical Lutheran Church, 2nd Eng. edition, Revised according to the 6th German edition. Philadelphia: Lutheran Publication Society, 1889.

Schnetzler, C. et al. *Pierre Viret d'Àpres Lui-Meme*. Lausanne: Georges Bridel & Cie, 1911.

Silva, Moises. *Philippians*. Baker Exegetical Commentary on the New Testament, 2nd Edition. Grand Rapids, MI: Baker Academic, 2007.

Simnowitz, Adam. "How Insider Movements Affect Ministry: Personal Reflections." *Chrislam: How Missionaries Are Promoting an Islamized Gospel*. Edited by Joshua Lingel, Jeff Morton and Bill Nikides. Garden Grove, CA: i2 Ministries, 2011.

Skeptic News. 15 August 2012. Accessed through http://web.ebscohost.com/ehost'delivery?sid=ee.

Slotemaker, John T. "Pulchritudo Christi: The Sources of Thomas Aquinas's Understanding of the Beauty of Christ." *Archa Verbi: Yearbook for the Study of Medieval Theology*, Vol. 8/2011. Munster: Aschendoff Verlag, 2011.

Socinus, Faustus. *De Jesu Christo Salvatore*. Rakow: Rodecius, 1594.

Spurgeon, Charles H. "A Sermon (No. 173). Delivered on Sabbath

Morning, January 24, 1858 at the Music Hall, Royal Surrey Gardens." Accessed at: http://www.spurgeon.org/sermons/0173.htm.

Spurgeon, Charles Haddon. *Morning and Evening: Daily Readings.* Zondervan Publishing House: Grand Rapids, Michigan, 1965.

Spurgeon, Charles H. "The Lord is Risen, Indeed." Metropolitan Tabernacle Pulpit, No. 1106 (April 13, 1873), vol. 19, pp. 1-2. Accessed from www.spurgeongems.org.

Staniloae, Dumitru. *The Experience of God: Orthodox Dogmatic Theology, Volume 3: The Person of Jesus Christ as God and Savior.* Translated and Edited by Ioan Ionita. Brookline, Massachusetts: Holy Cross Orthodox Press, 2011.

Stewart, James S. *The Life and Teaching of Jesus Christ.* New York: Abingdon Press, 1957.

Still, William. *Towards Spiritual Maturity: Overcoming all evil in the Christian Life,* Revised Edition. Fearn, Ross-shire, Scotland; Christian Focus, 2010.

Stott, John R. *The Cross of Christ.* Leicester: InterVarsity, 1989.

Swete, Henry B. *The Ascended Christ: A Study in the Earliest Christian Teaching.* London: Macmillan and Co., Ltd., 1910.

Swinburne, Richard. *The Resurrection of God Incarnate.* Clarendon Press: Oxford, 2003.

Tait, Arthur James. *The Heavenly Session of Our Lord: An Introduction to the History of the Doctrine.* London: Robert Scott, MCMXII.

Tanner, Norman P., Ed. *Decrees of the Ecumenical Councils I: Nicea I to Lateran V.* Washington, DC: Georgetown University Press, 1990.

Temple, William. *Christus Veritas.* London: Macmillan, 1926.

Temple, William. *Christus Veritas.* London: Macmillan Co., 1934.

"The Formula of Concord." *The Creeds of the Evangelical Protestant Churches.* Edited by Philip Schaff. London: Hodder and Stoughton, 1877.

The Scots Confession. Book of Confessions. Louisville: Geneva Press, 1996.

The Westminster Confession of Faith. The Confession of Faith: Together with the Larger Catechism and the Shorter Catechism with the Scripture Proofs. Atlanta, GA: The Committee for Education & Publications, PCA Bookstore, 1990.

Thomasius, Gottfried. *Christi Person und Werk, Volume 1.* Erlangen, 1886.

Thornwell, James Henley. *Collected Writings: Volume 2: Theological and Ethical.* Edinburgh: The Banner of Truth Trust: 1986.

Toon, Peter. *The Ascension of Our Lord.* Nashville: Thomas Nelson Publishers, 1984.

Torrance, Iain R. *Christology After Chalcedon: Severus of Antioch and Sergius the Monophysite.* Eugene, OR: Wipf and Stock, 1998.

Torrance, J.B., and Roland C. Walls. *John Duns Scotus in a Nutshell.* Edinburgh: Handsel Press, 1992.

Torrance, T.F. *Atonement: The Person and Work of Christ*. Edited by Robert J. Walker. Downers Grove, Ill.: IVP Academic, 2009.

Torrance, T.F. *Christian Theology & Scientific Culture*. New York: Oxford University Press, 1981.

Torrance, T.F. *Divine Meaning: Studies in Patristic Hermeneutics*. Edinburgh: T&T Clark, 1995.

Torrance, T.F. *Incarnation: The Person and Life of Christ*. Edited by Robert J. Walker. Downers Grove, Ill.: IVP Academic, 2008.

Torrance, T.F. *Reality and Scientific Theology*. Edinburgh: Scottish Academic Press, 1985.

Torrance, T.F. *Space, Time and Incarnation*. New York: Oxford University Press, 1969.

Torrance, T.F. *Space, Time and Resurrection*. Edinburgh: The Hansel Press, 1976.

Torrance, T.F. *The Christian Doctrine of God, One Being Three Persons*. Edinburgh: T&T Clark, 1996.

Torrance, T.F. *The Doctrine of Grace in the Apostolic Fathers*. Edinburgh: Oliver and Boyd, 1948.

Torrance, T.F. *The Mediation of Christ*, Revised Edition. Edinburgh: T & T Clark, 1992.

Torrance, T.F. *The Philosophical Frontiers of Christian Theology*. Edited by B. Hebblethwaite and S. Sutherland. Cambridge: Cambridge University Press, 1982.

Torrance, T.F. *The Trinitarian Faith*. London: T&T Clark, 1992.

Torrance, T.F. *Theological Science*. London: Oxford University Press, 1969.

Torrance, T.F. *Theology in Reconciliation*. Eugene, OR: Wipf & Stock, 1996.

Torrance, T.F. *Theology in Reconstruction*. London: SCM Press, 1965.

Torrance, T.F. *Transformation and Convergence in the Frame of Knowledge*. Eugene, OR: Wipf and Stock, 1998.

Towner, Philip H. *The Letters to Timothy and Titus*. The New International Commentary on the New Testament. Grand Rapids, MI: William B. Eerdmans, 2006.

Trakatellis, Demetrios. *The Transcendent God of Eugnostos: An Exegetical Contribution to the Study of the Gnostic Texts of Nag Hammadi With a Retroversion of the Lost Original Greek Text of Eugnostos the Blessed*. Translated by Charles Sarelis. Brookline, MA: Holy Cross Orthodox Press, 1991.

Tucker, Aviezer Tucker. "Miracles, Historical Testimonies, and Probabilities." *History and Theory* 44 [2005].

Turretin, Francis. *Institutes of Elenctic Theology, Volume Two: Eleventh Through Seventeenth Topics*. Translated by G. M. Giger and Edited by J. T. Dennison. Phillipsburg, NJ: P & R Publishing, 1994.

Van Bruggen, Jacob. *The Future of the Bible*. Nashville: Thomas Nelson, 1978.

Van Dixhoorn, Chad. *Reforming the Reformation: Theological Debate at the Westminster Assembly 1643-1652*. 7 Vol PhD diss. Cambridge University, 2004.

Vignaux, Paul. "Nominalisme." *Dictionnaire de Théologie Catholique*, Tome 13, Premiere Partie, A. Vacant et al., eds. Paris: Librarie Letourzey et Ane, 1936.

Viret, Pierre. *Instruction Chriétiénne Tome premier, Édition établie, présentée et annotée par Arthur-Louis Hofer*. Lausanne: L'Age D' Homme, 2003.

Vos, Geerhardus. *Biblical Theology: Old and New Testaments*. Grand Rapids: William B. Eerdmans, 1980.

Vos, Geerhardus. *The Self Disclosure of Jesus*. Grand Rapids, MI: Eerdmans, 1954.

Warfield, B.B. *Biblical Foundations*. London: The Tyndale Press, 1958.

Warfield, B.B. *The Person and Work of Christ*. Phillipsburg, NJ: Presbyterian & Reformed, 1950.

Washburn, Christian David. *St. Roberto Bellarmino's Defense of Catholic Christology against the Lutheran Doctrine of Ubiquity*. Amazon.com: UMI electronic books, 2004.

WEA Global Review Panel. "Report to World Evangelical Alliance for Conveyance to Wycliffe Global Alliance and SIL International." 4/26/13. Accessed on 11/7/13 at: http://www.worldea.org/images/wimg/files/2013_0429-Final%20Report%20of%20the%20WEA%20Independent%20Bible%20Translation%20Review%20Panel.pdf

Weaver, Richard. *Ideas Have Consequences*. University of Chicago Press: Chicago, 1948.

Webb, Clement C.J. *Kant's Philosophy of Religion*. Oxford: Clarendon Press, 1926.

Wells, Paul. *Cross Words: The Biblical Doctrine of the Atonement*. Fearn, Ross-shire: Christian Focus, 2006.

Wenham, John. *Easter Enigma*. Eugene, Oregon: Wipf and Stock, reprint of 1992 edition.

Wenham, J.W. "When Were the Saints Raised?" *Journal of Theological Studies*. 32 [1981]: 150-152.

Wescott, B.F. *Commentary on John's Gospel*. London: John Murray, 1894.

Wilson, Ian. *The Shroud of Turin: The Burial Cloth of Jesus Christ?* Garden City, New York: Doubleday & Company, 1978.

Witherington, Ben. *The Jesus Quest: The Third Search for the Jew of Nazrareth*. 2nd Edition. Downers Grove, Ill.: Inter-Varsity, 1997.

Witsius, Herman. *The Economy of the Covenants Between God and Man: Comprehending A Complete Body of Divinity*. Translated by William Crookshank. London: Printed for M. Baynes et al., 1822.

Wolfson, Harry A. *The Philosophy of the Church Fathers: Faith, Trinity, Incarnation*. Third Revised Edition. Cambridge, MA: Harvard University Press, 1976.

Wotherspoon, H.J. and J.M. Kirkpatrick. *A Manual of Church Doctrine according to the Church of Scotland*, Second Edition. Revised and Enlarged by T. F. Torrance and Ronald Selby Wright. London: Oxford University Press, 1960.

Wright, N. T. *Jesus and the Victory of God*. London: SPCK, 2004.

Wright, N.T. *The New Testament and the People of God*. Fortress Press: Minneapolis, 1992.

Wright, N.T. What *Saint Paul Really Said*. Eerdmans: Grand Rapids, MI, 1997.

Zumstein, Jean. *Dictionnaire du Protestantisme*. Edited by Pierre Gisel. Geneva: Labor et Fides, 1995.

SCRIPTURE INDEX

PERSONS INDEX

SUBJECT INDEX

Christian Focus Publications

Our mission statement –

STAYING FAITHFUL
In dependence upon God we seek to impact the world through literature faithful to His infallible Word, the Bible. Our aim is to ensure that the Lord Jesus Christ is presented as the only hope to obtain forgiveness of sin, live a useful life and look forward to heaven with Him.

Our Books are published in four imprints:

CHRISTIAN
FOCUS
Popular works including biographies, commentaries, basic doctrine and Christian living.

CHRISTIAN
HERITAGE
Books representing some of the best material from the rich heritage of the church.

MENTOR
Books written at a level suitable for Bible College and seminary students, pastors, and other serious readers. The imprint includes commentaries, doctrinal studies, examination of current issues and church history.

CF4•K
Children's books for quality Bible teaching and for all age groups: Sunday school curriculum, puzzle and activity books; personal and family devotional titles, biographies and inspirational stories – Because you are never too young to know Jesus!

Christian Focus Publications Ltd,
Geanies House, Fearn, Ross-shire,
IV20 1TW, Scotland, United Kingdom.
www.christianfocus.com